please turn the page for more rave reviews . . .

"ILLUMINATE[S] A FASCINATING DECADE."
—*The San Diego Union-Tribune*

"FASCINATING . . . Readers searching for the legendary 'Happy Days' in David Halberstam's wonderful romp through *The Fifties* will find them in his depictions of genial Ike, the classic '55 Chevy, and the origins of McDonald's and Holiday Inns. But they will also discover a darker period that included the sleazy Joe McCarthy, quiz-show cheat Charles Van Doren, the murder of Emmett Till, and the CIA's covert destruction of popular governments in Guatemala and Iran. . . . Sensitive, intelligent and always interesting popular history."

— *Detroit Free Press*

"Always engaging . . . Excellent popular history . . . Halberstam shows us the ugliness and uplift, the loud events and quiet discontents. A confusing age of affluence and anxiety gets its due."

— *The Miami Herald*

"David Halberstam's big, luminous book on America during the 1950s makes the decade seem like only yesterday. . . . He's a grand storyteller."

— *The Baltimore Sun*

"The fifties were more than just a midpoint decade in a century; they were to be the crucible in which the rest of the 20th century was forged. Halberstam here touches every thread in the warp and woof of the national fabric. This is the true drama of history . . . A superb book."

— *Library Journal*

THE
FIFTIES

David Halberstam

FAWCETT COLUMBINE · NEW YORK

A Fawcett Columbine Book
Published by Ballantine Books

Copyright © 1993 by The Amateurs Limited

This edition published by arrangement with Villard Books, a division of Random House, Inc. Villard Books is a registered trademark of Random House,
Inc.

Library of Congress Catalog Card Number: 93-91045

ISBN: 0-449-90933-6

Cover design by Brad Foltz

Manufactured in the United States of America

First Ballantine Books Edition: June 1994

10 9 8 7 6 5 4 3 2

For Julia Sandness Halberstam

PREFACE

T he fifties were captured in black and white, most often by still photographers; by contrast, the decade that followed was, more often than not, caught in living color on tape or film. Not surprisingly, in retrospect the pace of the fifties seemed slower, almost languid. Social ferment, however, was beginning just beneath this placid surface. It was during the fifties, for example, that the basic research in the development of the birth-control pill took place; but it was not until a decade later that this technological advance had a profound effect upon society. Then, apparently overnight, rather conservative—indeed cautious—sexual practices were giving way to what commentators would speak of as the sexual revolution. It was in the fifties that the nation became wired for television, a new medium experimented with by various politicians and social groups. Ten years later television had begun to alter the

political and social fabric of the country, with stunning consequences.

Three decades later, the fifties appear to be an orderly era, one
with a minimum of social dissent. Photographs from the period tend
to show people who dressed carefully: men in suits, ties, and—when
outdoors—hats; the women with their hair in modified page-boys,
pert and upbeat. Young people seemed, more than anything else,
"square" and largely accepting of the given social covenants. At the
beginning of the decade their music was still slow and saccharine,
mirroring the generally bland popular taste. In the years following
the traumatic experiences of the Depression and World War II, the
American Dream was to exercise personal freedom not in social and
political terms, but rather in economic ones. Eager to be part of the
burgeoning middle class, young men and women opted for material
well-being, particularly if it came with some form of guaranteed
employment. For the young, eager veteran just out of college (which
he had attended courtesy of the G.I. Bill), security meant finding a
good white-collar job with a large, benevolent company, getting
married, having children, and buying a house in the suburbs.

In that era of general good will and expanding affluence, few
Americans doubted the essential goodness of their society. After all,
it was reflected back at them not only by contemporary books and
magazines, but even more powerfully and with even greater influence
in the new family sitcoms on television. These—in conjunction with
their sponsors' commercial goals—sought to shape their audience's
aspirations. However, most Americans needed little coaching in how
they wanted to live. They were optimistic about the future. Young
men who had spent three or four years fighting overseas were eager
to get on with their lives; so, too, were the young women who had
waited for them at home. The post–World War II rush to have
children would later be described as the "baby boom." (Everything
else in the United States seemed to be booming, so why not the
production of children as well?) It was a good time to be young and
get on with family and career: Prices and inflation remained relatively low; and nearly everyone with a decent job could afford to own
a home. Even if the specter of Communism lurked on the horizon—
particularly as both superpowers developed nuclear weapons—
Americans trusted their leaders to tell them the truth, to make sound
decisions, and to keep them out of war.

For a while, the traditional system of authority held. The men
(and not men *and* women) who presided in politics, business, and
media had generally been born in the previous century. The advent

of so strong a society, in which the nation's wealth was shared by so many, represented a prosperity beyond their wildest dreams. During the course of the fifties, as younger people and segments of society who did not believe they had a fair share became empowered, pressure inevitably began to build against the entrenched political and social hierarchy. But one did not lightly challenge a system that seemed, on the whole, to be working so well. Some social critics, irritated by the generally quiescent attitude and the boundless appetite for consumerism, described a "silent" generation. Others were made uneasy by the degree of conformity around them, as if the middle-class living standard had been delivered in an obvious trade-off for blind acceptance of the status quo. Nonetheless, the era was a much more interesting one than it appeared on the surface. Exciting new technologies were being developed that would soon enable a vast and surprisingly broad degree of dissidence, and many people were already beginning to question the purpose of their lives and whether that purpose had indeed become, almost involuntarily, too much about material things.

ONE

ONE

In the beginning, that era was dominated by the shadow of a man no longer there—Franklin D. Roosevelt. He had died in 1945, but his impact on American politics was so profound that even the most powerful Republican leaders believed privately that their party might be permanently in the minority. Roosevelt had been cast forth in the midst of two transcending events—the Great Depression and World War Two. The first was responsible for a massive reordering of the American economy and society, thereby creating a huge, new base for the Democrats; the second permitted Roosevelt to emerge as an international leader in a time of great crisis and to prolong his presidency for two additional terms. During that time, the infrastructure of the Democratic party became ever more powerful and Roosevelt was able to extend his reach into the courts.

Roosevelt was the ultimate modern politician, the first great master of modern mass communications in a democracy. For millions of poorer Americans and for the new immigrants and their children, his ability to exploit radio and make it seem his personal vehicle had a particular resonance. To them, Roosevelt was not only President-for-life, he was their guide to the rites of American politics.

The effect of this on the Republican party, mired as it was in political attitudes that predated the Depression, World War Two, and the coming of radio, was devastating. In July 1949, some nine months after his own shocking defeat by Harry Truman (which seemed to promise the Roosevelt coalition would go on ad infinitum), Thomas E. Dewey met with Dwight Eisenhower, then the president of Columbia University, to begin the process of coercing Ike to run for the presidency in 1952 as a Republican. Eisenhower's notes of that meeting are unusually revealing of the Republican dilemma: "All middle-class citizens of education have a common belief that the tendencies towards centralization and paternalism must be halted and reversed. No one who voices these opinions can be elected. He [Dewey] quotes efforts of Hoover, Landon, Willkie, Himself. Consequently we must look around for someone of great popularity and who has not frittered away his political assets by taking positive stands against national planning, etc, etc. Elect such a man to Presidency, *after which* [N.B.: italics Ike's] he must lead us back to safe channels and paths." In effect Dewey was saying that the solid citizens who could make the right decisions for the future of the country had, because of the New Deal, become a minority and that the nation had fallen into the clutches of dark and alien forces.

Not surprisingly, the Republican party was traumatized and bitterly divided. Certainly, the Democratic party was divided as well, between the liberal Northern urban coalition and the Southern conservative Jim Crow wing. But for all their differences, the Democrats had a certain glue: They won, and in victory there was patronage and power, a combination that transcended ideology. For the Republicans there was only the taste of ashes. They had been out of office since 1932. The shadow of the Depression still hung over them, and the Democrats were still running against Herbert Hoover, portraying the Republicans as the party of cold, uncaring bankers. Were the Republicans forever to be trapped by those events then twenty years in the past?

Of the divisions within the Republican party, the most obvious was a historic, regional one. On one side were the lawyers and bankers of Wall Street and State Street, their colleagues through the great Eastern industrial cities, and those in the powerful national media, based in New York. They were internationalist by tradition and by instinct: They had fought against the New Deal in states where the power of labor was considerable but had eventually come to accept certain premises of the New Deal. By contrast, the Republicans of the heartland were essentially unchanged by the great events that had overtaken them; they were resentful of World War Two and suspicious of how Roosevelt had gotten them into it. This was particularly true of the many German-Americans in the region. Instinctively Anglophobic, they were wary of our growing involvement in Western Europe and our close alliance with the British. If they had a bible other than the Bible, it was the conservative, isolationist *Chicago Tribune* of Colonel Robert R. McCormick. They were anxious to go back to the simple, comfortable world of the twenties, before the New Deal had empowered labor unions, before air travel had shrunk the Atlantic Ocean into a pond, and before scientists had ever thought about developing intercontinental ballistic missiles to catapult atomic warheads into their midst.

They lived in God's country, a land far from oceans and far from foreigners, and they were all-powerful in their own small towns. Many had gone to college and returned home to succeed their fathers in family businesses. They had always controlled their political and economic destinies locally, and they presumed that by acting in concert with others like themselves in other small towns, they could control the national destiny. Earlier in the century they had regarded Taft, Harding, Coolidge, and Hoover as the guardians of their values in Washington; they had considered the nation's capital an extension of their own small towns. Now they looked at Washington and saw the enemy. Even in their own towns, their mastery had been limited by the rise of arrogant, impertinent labor unions. Even worse, they seemed to have lost control of their own party. That was the final insult. Confident that they represented Republicanism and true patriotism, they were at war with the Eastern Republicans, who, in their eyes, were traitors, tainted by cooperation with the New Deal. Robert Taft, the conservative wing's great leader, believed Easterners had fallen victim to the liberal press and *labor unions*. As Taft wrote in a letter to a friend about Tom Dewey: "Tom Dewey has no real courage to stand up against the crowd that wants to smear any Republican who takes a forthright position against the New Deal."

The conservatives had lost in 1940, when the Easterners had blitzed them at the last minute with Wendell Willkie at the convention. A Hoosier by birth, Willkie had to their minds lost touch with his roots and become a captive of the East. "The barefoot boy from Wall Street," he was called. Willkie had, said Alice Roosevelt Longworth, "grass roots in every country club in America." Then in 1944, with Willkie virtually supporting Roosevelt against his own party (which, of course, did not surprise the conservatives—they had known that about him before he knew it himself), the same Eastern forces coalesced behind Thomas E. Dewey, the modern, reformminded governor of New York. The Easterners knew, after all, what it took to be elected governor of New York in this day and age—the kind of deals necessary with labor and ethnic groups. The first time around, Dewey was easily defeated by an aging, sickly Roosevelt, who won his fourth term. But in 1948, the Republicans were finally free from Roosevelt's personal charm. The Easterners nominated Dewey a second time.

The 1948 campaign proved to be a watershed for the Republicans. They were absolutely confident that Thomas E. Dewey would beat Truman, whom they saw as a small-town haberdasher, devoid of Roosevelt's charm and as uncomfortable with an open radio microphone as the average Republican. But there was the problem of Dewey's stiffness. Alice Longworth described Dewey as looking like "the little man on the wedding cake." "The chocolate soldier," the *Chicago Tribune* called him. He had come to prominence as a crime-busting D.A. and then had proved a capable governor of New York. During the 1940s he had become a serious internationalist, thus becoming the singular target of the Republican isolationists. To Colonel Robert McCormick, of the *Chicago Tribune,* and his followers, Dewey was virtually a New Deal Democrat. "If you read the *Chicago Tribune* you'd know I am a direct lineal descendant of FDR," Dewey once noted.

For all his bureaucratic skills, Dewey was a cold piece of work. He was, said one longtime associate, "cold—cold as a February icicle." "The little man," Roosevelt had called him privately, referring not merely to his lack of height. Even those who worked closely with him and who admired him thought he was unbending and self-righteous. "He struts sitting down," said Lillian Dykstra, a close friend of Martha Taft, and thus not an entirely unbiased source. Dewey was uncomfortable with political bonhomie; he would spend as little time as possible with working politicians (and when he did, more often than not he offended them); he could not bear to go to wakes or funerals, a crucial ritual in the Irish-dominated politics of New York City. His disrespect for other politicians extended to both Republicans and Democrats in Congress, whom he referred to privately as "those congressional bums." Campaigning for the presidential nomination on his own train with such supporters as the governor of Connecticut, he would excuse himself from his guests after the morning's stops and lunch alone. "Smile, Governor," a photographer once said to him. "I thought I was," he answered.

His strengths were his sense of purpose, his integrity, and his political cleanliness. "An honest cop with the mind of an honest cop," William Allen White called him. When he signed autographs he would date them, so that no stranger could imply a closer relationship than truly existed. In 1948 he refused—and this was a point of honor—to use the Communist-in-government issue as a political weapon, and he refused, despite mounting pressure from the Republican right, to do any red-baiting, even as that was becoming ever more fashionable in postwar American politics. He had forbidden one of his New York colleagues to mail a letter critical of George Marshall and his policies in China to the editor of a local paper. During the 1948 campaign, when Harold Stassen had presented something of a surprise challenge to Dewey's renomination, he and Dewey had debated during the Oregon primary on the question of whether or not the Communist party should be outlawed or not. Dewey argued that it should not. He was against outlawing it, he said, because "you can't shoot an idea with a gun." Some of his advisers suggested that he soft-pedal his advocacy of civil liberties, that this was not the right time for it. He refused, telling them, "If I'm going to lose, I'm going to lose on something I believe in." The debate had been the forerunner of the televised presidential campaign debates to come twelve years later, and some 40 to 60 million people were said to have listened. Dewey carried Oregon, and won the nomination. During the regular campaign, the right-wing New Hampshire publisher William Loeb and his favorite senator, Styles Bridges, pleaded with Dewey to start hitting the Communist-in-government issue. He listened to them and then, in the words of Hugh Scott, one of his campaign aides and later a senator, he said he would "fleck it lightly." The right-wingers were furious. As far as they were concerned, he was throwing away their best issue. Yet Dewey remained adamant. He thought it degrading to accuse the President of the United States of being soft on Communism. He was not, he told Styles Bridges, the Republican national campaign manager, "going around looking under beds." His aides got nowhere, Herbert Brownell, his top political adviser, decided, because his wife hated the idea of partisan attacks. She wanted him to be, in her words, more presidential. This was not the first time she had blocked the requests of the political men around him. For years Brownell and others had thought his trademark mustache—which perhaps gave him a crisp no-nonsense look as a district attorney—was a detriment for him as a national politician, because it made him look cold and unfeeling. In photographs and in newsreels, it was the only thing that people seemed to remember about him. "His face was so small, and the mustache was so large," Brownell later lamented. Again and again his political people suggested the removal of the mustache, but every time the idea was vetoed by Mrs. Dewey.

He was a heavy favorite to win, and he took the high road. Thus there was not a great deal dividing Truman and Dewey on foreign policy, and on domestic issues Dewey had no great desire to emphasize whatever differences existed. Dewey was also wary of attacking too hard; he did not want to appear as the prosecutor he had been. He would be above pettiness, above partisanship. His platform, said Samuel Rosenman, the Roosevelt-Truman speechwriter, was fit for any good New Dealer to run on.

In truth he campaigned not as the challenger but as the incumbent, as a man who had already been elected President by endless polls and surveys. He would be the good administrator who cleaned out the mess in Washington after sixteen years of Democratic rule. The idea of a Truman victory seemed impossible to nearly everyone. George Gallup even told the Republican high command that it was a waste of their money to continue polling, since the results were a foregone conclusion. But Harry Truman had not spent all those years in the Pendergast machine for nothing. That summer he ambushed Dewey; he called the Congress back into session and fed it legislation that underlined the vast differences between Dewey the modern Republican as presidential candidate and the Republican party as embodied by those conservatives still powerful in the Congress and still fighting the New Deal. It was the defining moment of the campaign. It resurrected Truman and gave him something to run against. Even so, no one really believed he could win. Dewey's chief campaign tactic was to make no mistakes, to offend no one. His major speeches, wrote the *Louisville Courier Journal,* could be boiled down "to these historic four sentences: Agriculture is important. Our rivers are full of fish. You cannot have freedom without liberty. The future lies ahead . . ." In the final few weeks a few Republicans sensed that the tide had turned against Dewey. Among them was Bob Taft. He knew Dewey was going to lose, he told *The New York Times* writer Bill White, when his wife Martha stopped listening to his speeches on the radio and watching his occasional appearances on television.

On election eve, the *Chicago Tribune* had its famous headline proclaiming Dewey's victory, and Alistair Cooke had already sent in his piece for the *Manchester Guardian* entitled, "Harry S Truman, A Study in Failure." But even with Roosevelt gone, the Republicans blew the election. But Truman won and the Republicans now faced four more years out of office. The bitterness within the party grew. So much for the high road in American politics. The Communist issue would be fair game in the near future. It was the only way they knew how to fight back.

It was a mean time. The nation was ready for witch-hunts. We had come out of World War Two stronger and more powerful and more affluent than ever before, but the rest of the world, alien and unsettling, seemed to press closer now than many Americans wanted it to. An unwanted war had not brought a true peace, and there would be many accusations that the Democrats had won the war but lost the peace. As David Caute wrote in *The Great Fear,* the true isolationists thought that Roosevelt had dragged us "into the wrong war: wrong allies, wrong enemies, wrong outcome." A peace that permitted Soviet hegemony over Eastern Europe was unacceptable to many Americans. There had to be an answer; there had to be a scapegoat: These things could not merely have happened, not in a fair and just world. Nor would anyone in the United States Congress score points with the folks back home by pointing out that the Soviets held Eastern Europe because they, more than anyone, had borne the brunt of the Wehrmacht, and at a terrible price—the loss of some 20 million people. We knew of the war what we chose to know; to most Americans it had begun only on December 7, 1941, and as for the action in Europe, it had begun only *after* the American forces landed on the continent in June 1944.

The domestic coalition to fight the war, which Franklin Roosevelt had put together, had been more fragile than anyone realized. Republican politicians had been out of power for too long, and their postwar political rhetoric had a basic purpose and tone: It was about getting even. There were, in those days following the war, a great many speeches given in civic clubs and chambers of commerce in towns throughout America about the need to get back to Americanism, returning to the American way, and the domestic dangers of Communism and Socialism. Included under the label of Socialism, in the minds of those giving the speeches (and among many of those hearing them), was almost any part of the New Deal. In 1946 B. Carroll Reece, the Tennessee congressman and chairman of the Republican National Committee, said the coming election would be a choice between "Communism and Republicanism." George Murphy, an actor, singer, and dancer turned politician, told one Republican fund-raiser, "Party labels don't mean anything anymore. You can draw a line right down the middle. On one side are the Americans, on the other are the Communists and Socialists." No matter that in the dramatic wartime and postwar expansion of the American economy many of these heads of industry had become substantially wealthier. It was time to get even for the New Deal. Whittaker Chambers, who would be the key witness against Alger Hiss, wrote in his book *Witness,* "When I took up my little sling and aimed at communism I also hit something else. What I hit was the forces of that great socialist revolution, which in the name of liberalism, spasmodically, incompletely and somewhat formlessly, but always in the same direction, has been inching its ice cap over the nation for the last two decades."

In the early years of his administration Truman was hardly an ideal target for the angry conservatives; he was so solidly Midwestern, small-town, and unpretentious that he was perilously close to being one of their own. If there was an enemy, someone who represented a target for all the accumulated resentment of the past and all the tensions of class, region, and education, it was Dean Acheson—he of Groton, Harvard, Wall Street, and State, the very embodiment of the Eastern establishment. His timing, as he ascended to the position of secretary of state, was not exactly ideal. On January 21, 1949, the day on which Acheson was sworn in, Chiang Kai-shek turned over what remained of his command on the mainland to one of his generals and left for Formosa. The civil war in China was over, and the Communists had won. It was a bad omen.

In the face of what may well have been some of the most relentless domestic criticism aimed at a public official in this century, Acheson showed one fatal flaw: He never failed to show his contempt for his critics and their ideas. Once, when Senator Taft called for a reexamination of American foreign policy, Acheson retorted that the idea reminded him of a farmer "who goes out every morning and pulls up his crops to see how they have done during the night." He had many qualities, but the capacity to resist his innate snobbery was not one of them. Even his clothes and personal manner, British in style, were viewed by the right-wingers as one more snobbish affectation on his part. It meant that American styles of clothes and haircuts were not good enough. ". . . I watch his smart-aleck manner, and his British clothes and that New Dealism . . . and I want to shout,

Get out, Get out. You stand for everything that has been wrong with the United States for years," said Senator Hugh Butler of Nebraska. Even his mustache seemed to offend. Averell Harriman once told Acheson: "Shave it off. You owe it to Truman."

Acheson came honestly by his Anglophilic tendencies. His father had been born in Ulster and, at the age of fourteen, immigrated to Canada, where he eventually married a handsome young woman from a wealthy Canadian family. They moved to Connecticut when Dean was a year old. Of his mother's love of things English, he wrote, "My mother's enthusiasm for the Empire and the Monarch was not diluted by any corrupting contact with Canadian nationalism." Fearless and intellectually superior, he possessed a highly developed sense of integrity and honor. In a world in which the old order had collapsed and a new and dangerous adversary risen up, he retained a clear view of the challenges America faced: to prop up an exhausted and shattered Europe and, at the same time, to make this policy acceptable to his own countrymen. Acheson was far more successful at the former than the latter. His internationalism was instinctive, although he was far less interested in such exotic places as Asia and Africa than he was in Europe. He was not alarmed by the collapse of China, and he urged Congress not to exaggerate the consequences. China, he told them, "was not a modern, centralized state, and the Communists would almost certainly face as much difficulty in governing it as had the previous regimes."

In his first year as secretary of state he was dogged by the turn of events in China and by the growing anger among the Republicans. However, it was when the Alger Hiss case broke that he became the perfect target for the right-wing. The case symbolized (or seemed to symbolize) the divisions of an entire era. A man named Whittaker Chambers, his own background quite shady, charged that Hiss had been a fellow member of the Communist Party while serving in the government. At first it seemed an accusation unlikely to stick. Chambers—aka David Breen, Lloyd Cantwell, Charles Adams, Arthur Dwyer, Harold Phillips, Carl Carlson, and perhaps George Crosley—was a confessed former underground member of the Communist party, an admitted homosexual ("a pervert," as the director of the FBI, J. Edgar Hoover, often referred to him and other homosexuals in private memos), and unusually sloppy in dress and personal hygiene. His political past was so filled with dramatic changes of direction and ideology that it made even his closest friends uneasy. The man he accused of being a Communist was strikingly patrician and handsome. His aristocratic bearing seemed to confirm his political legitimacy and sum up his perfect pedigree: Johns Hopkins, Harvard Law School, and *Harvard Law Review*. Felix Frankfurter arranged a clerkship for him with the famed Oliver Wendell Holmes, the preeminent jurist of his generation. At the time of the accusations, Alger Hiss was head of the Carnegie Endowment, the chairman of whose board was none other than John Foster Dulles.

Even members of the House Un-American Activities Committee, or HUAC, who were inclined to believe any accusations about anyone, looked down on Chambers. The House Committee was made nervous, even intimidated, by Hiss's immediate and complete denial of ever having known Chambers, and seemed on the verge of withdrawing from the case. Only a very junior member, Richard Nixon (Rep. of Calif.), persisted—among other reasons, because he was being fed secret FBI documents—and kept the Committee from backing off completely.

The setting was this: August 3, 1948, the House Committee, which included a large number of the most unattractive men in American public life—bigots, racists, reactionaries, and sheer buffoons—held hearings in which Whittaker Chambers not only said that he himself was a Communist but that there was a Communist group in the government in the late thirties and that Alger Hiss was a member of it. Hiss denied the accusation and denied under oath that he had ever even known Chambers. His friends rallied round. Dean Acheson, then a law partner of Hiss's brother, Donald, helped with the early legal planning; William Marbury, a prominent Baltimore attorney and a very old and close personal friend, sent a note to Donald Hiss, who had been similarly accused: "If you and Alger are party members, then you can send me an application." Hiss himself seemed to play down the seriousness of the charges, and told his wife, Priscilla, "Don't worry, little one. This will all blow over. I will handle it."

On August 5, that is precisely what he did. Before the Committee, Hiss seemed imposing, almost imperious, a paragon of the establishment. His appearance caused the British journalist Alistair Cooke to call him "an American gentleman, one of the incomparable human products, all the rarer for the heavy parodies that crowd it out, the glossy tailored caricatures of metropolitan society . . . Here was a subject for Henry James; a product of New World courtesy, with a gentle certitude of behavior, a ready warmth, a brighter, naiver grace than the more trenchant, fatigued, confident, or worldlier English prototype."

"I am not and never have been a member of the Communist party," he said under oath. When asked by the chairman, Karl

Mundt, if he recognized photos of Chambers, he answered, "I might mistake him for the [acting] chairman of the Committee." This line received considerable laughter. It was the high-water mark for him in the case. All day he was relaxed and confident. By the end of the day, Mundt congratulated Hiss for his forthright testimony. John Rankin, the virulent racist from Mississippi, came over to shake his hand. "Let's wash our hands of the whole mess," said F. Edward Hebert, the Louisiana Democrat. Only Richard Nixon wanted to push on. There was something about Hiss that he did not like and did not trust. Nixon, rejected after his graduation from Duke Law School by all the top New York law firms, was always conscious of social distinctions and East Coast snobbery, and he was irritated rather than impressed by Hiss's imperiousness. Someone was clearly lying. Why not have the two men confront each other? Nixon suggested. Robert Stripling, the Committee's chief investigator, later said in an interview that "Nixon had his hat set for Hiss. It was a personal thing. He was no more concerned about whether or not Hiss was [a Communist] than a billygoat." The confrontation was set for August 17.

Even those who knew and liked Chambers marveled at his paranoia and his need to dramatize almost everything he did. When he went out for a simple lunch with friends, he would have to come up with an elaborate method of exiting the building in case anyone was following him. A Coolidge Republican at the start of his undergraduate years, then a didactic Communist, he eventually became the most unforgiving anti-Communist intellectual in the country.

Anyone who later read his personal memoir, *Witness,* could understand why he was so tortured. His had been a childhood of unrelieved misery. His father was an alcoholic who eventually left home for a homosexual lover. As a boy, Chambers used to say to himself: "I am an outcast. My family is outcast. We have no friends, no social ties, no church, no organization that we claim and that claims us, no community." In his post-Communist years, as a senior writer at *Time,* it became clear he was a man of considerable talent and one of the most accomplished writers on the Luce publications of that era. He was, the journalist Murray Kempton noted, the perfect writer for a somewhat gloomy news magazine given in those days to portentous warnings about the future of the West and its relationship with the East. "There was no one who could do the drumroll of alarm, of Western civilization come to the brink, like Chambers," Kempton said.

On August 16, Hiss wavered for the first time: Perhaps he had known the person testifying against him under another name. The picture of Chambers, he said, "is not completely unfamiliar." Then, rather late in the session, he said that he had written down the name of someone it might be. The name he wrote down was George Crosley. The next day, unbeknownst to Hiss, a confrontation was arranged at Room 1400 of the Commodore Hotel. With Hiss already in the room, Chambers was brought in. "Are you George Crosley?" Hiss asked. "Not to my knowledge," answered Chambers. Then Chambers added: "You are Alger Hiss, I believe." "I certainly am," Hiss said. Hiss asked Chambers to speak, then asked him to speak more loudly, then asked him to open his mouth wider. Have you had any dental work done on your teeth? he asked. Finally, Hiss said that he did not need to ask any more questions, that he had known this man as George Crosley. He thereupon demanded that Chambers make his accusations in a public arena, without the protection from libel offered by the Committee. "I challenge you to do so, and I hope you will do it damn quickly," he said. Chambers did so on national radio.

Eight days later, their public confrontation took place, and the Hiss case exploded into America's collective consciousness. At first even the general public thought that Hiss, so eminently respectable, might be wearing the white hat and Chambers, so unattractive, the black, but slowly, as evidence mounted, the tide of public opinion shifted. From the beginning, Nixon was impressed by how steadfast, unflappable, and unbending Chambers was. He did not use a lawyer as Hiss did, he did not study the transcript before each session as Hiss did, and he did not qualify his statements ("to the best of my recollection") as Hiss often did. He was willing to take a lie-detector test, as Hiss was not.

By August 25, Karl Mundt was saying to Hiss, "You knew this man [Chambers]; you knew him very well. You knew him so well that you trusted him with your apartment; you let him use your furniture; you let him use, or gave him, your automobile. You think you probably took him to New York. You bought him lunches in the Senate Restaurant. You had him staying in your home . . . and made him a series of small loans. There seems to be no question about that." It was a damning moment. At the end of the hearing, Parnell Thomas announced that one of the two men would be tried for perjury. For the liberals, and thoughtful people of any stripe, a dilemma arose: Could it be that this committee—so scabrous, indeed almost farcical, so insensitive to the rights of individuals and which had so often and so carelessly thrown around charges of Communism—was actually on to something? And if so, was there a larger truth to this? Was the New Deal itself on trial, as Hiss himself was quick to claim? Look who spoke well of Hiss: Dean Acheson; Adlai Stevenson; even John Foster Dulles (at least early on, anyway, until warned privately by Nixon to keep some distance). Two members of the Supreme Court, Felix Frankfurter and Stanley Reed, appeared as character references at his first trial.

The case began to assume dimensions far greater than anyone had ever imagined. "As 1949 went on," Eric Goldman wrote in *The Crucial Decade,* "Whittaker Chambers receded into the background; the specific testimony was less and less discussed. Even the figure of Alger Hiss, the individual, blurred. Everything was turning into Alger Hiss the symbol." "There was," Alistair Cooke once noted, "a strong desire in both those who believed Hiss guilty and those who believed him innocent to make him out to be a more representative Rooseveltian figure than he was." In fact, Hiss had hardly been a key player in the State Department: He was not a Kennan or a John Paton Davies or a Paul Nitze. He was a high-level clerk. Both sides in the Hiss case, Kempton wrote, overplayed the importance of Hiss as a figure in the government.

The Hiss case broke just as the lines in the Cold War were becoming more sharply drawn. In March 1948, when Jan Masaryk, the Czech foreign minister and an admired symbol of democratic hopes in that country, committed suicide. Then, in the summer of 1948 the West used the Berlin airlift to bypass the Berlin blockade created by the Soviets. As much as anything else, those two events signaled that the wartime alliance between the Soviets and the West was over. A new, edgier, political era had begun.

In response to Hiss's denials, Chambers began to escalate his charges, now accusing Hiss of partaking of espionage. This was buttressed with dramatic documentary evidence that Chambers said he had squirreled away for just such an occasion some ten years earlier, when he had left the Party. The evidence—State Department documents copied either in Hiss's handwriting or some documents typed on what was claimed to be Hiss's typewriter—was particularly incriminating. Whether Hiss actually participated in espionage was never proven and the evidence was, at best, flawed. The government briefly pondered going after him on espionage, decided its case was insufficiently strong, and went instead for a lesser perjury charge.

In the two ensuing trials, even those who were unbiased and who tried to separate the record from their own political biases always had a feeling that there were missing pieces and that each of the principals was holding back something, whether it was Hiss shielding his wife, as some, including his own lawyers, thought, or a homosexual infatuation on the part of Chambers for Hiss, as others thought. More than forty years later, the pieces still did not entirely add up. If there was a romance, thought Murray Kempton, the *New York Post* columnist who later wrote exceptionally well about the two men, it was platonic, the attraction of what he called "The Other": Hiss, coming from his airless, aristocratic, tightly controlled background, with the constant need to live up to family expectations; Chambers, and his quasi-adventurous underground life, filled with mystery and intrigue. But, as Kempton said, "each got the other wrong—Hiss was not really an aristocrat, and Chambers was not that much of an adventurer." The first trial ended in a hung jury; the vote was 8–4 for a perjury conviction against Hiss. That, according to one of Hiss's friends and lawyers, Helen Buttenweiser, was the only time she had ever seen Alger shocked—stunned by the fact that eight of his fellow citizens did not believe him. In the second trial the jury found Hiss guilty of perjury, and he was sentenced to five years in a federal prison.

Beginning on March 21, 1951, Hiss served forty-four months of his five-year term. Hiss continued to protest his innocence. Forty years later the old divisions caused by the case were very much alive. A coterie of loyalists still believed Hiss innocent. They took heart in 1992 when a top Soviet intelligence officer seemed to exonerate Hiss. But a few weeks later the Russian qualified his statement, saying he had been pushed by friends of Hiss, who asked him to comfort an old man. Chambers's memoir, *Witness,* was published in 1952, and became a national best-seller. Chambers still brooded about the future and not just Communism, but liberalism, as the enemy. Sidney Hook, reviewing *Witness,* noted of Chambers, "He recklessly lumps Socialists, progressives, liberals, and men of good will together with the Communists. All are bound according to him by the same faith; but only the Communists have the gumption and the guts to live by it and pay the price . . . The logic by which he now classifies liberals and humanists with the Communists is not unlike the logic by which, when a Communist, he classified them as Fascists."

Hiss's conviction darkened an already bleak period, exacerbating the growing political division over the issue of domestic subversion. Even before the Hiss case Yalta was an issue, a magic word for the Republicans, uttered recklessly in the 1946 congressional campaigns, a free and easy chance to attack Roosevelt and the New Deal. Republicans claimed the agreement was the work of a tough and treacherous Stalin, who duped an exhausted and desperately ill Roosevelt, and that it was filled with secret accords and that we had sold out a free Poland. The reality had been quite different; if anyone had been for the Yalta agreements, it had been the American military, whose top brass was in no way convinced that the atomic bomb would work. Fearing that more than a million Americans might be lost in the invasion of the Japanese mainland, the Joint Chiefs had supposedly pressured Roosevelt to get the Russians to come into the war against Japan.

But now Yalta was an even more powerful and divisive word, a synonym in the new political lexicon for "betrayal." For *Alger Hiss* had been at Yalta, albeit, as diplomat Chip Bohlen noted, in a rather minor capacity. That didn't matter. Hiss was soon elevated to a position as a principal architect of the Yalta accords. "The Alger Hiss group," in the words of Senator William Jenner, one of the more rabid of the right-wing Republicans, "engineered the Yalta sell-out." To Joseph McCarthy, Yalta and Hiss were something that he could readily seize on: "We know that at Yalta we were betrayed. We know that since Yalta, the leaders of this Government, by design or ignorance, have continued to betray us. . . . We also know that the same men who betrayed America are still leading America. The traitors must no longer lead the betrayed."

At Dean Acheson's confirmation hearings for secretary of state in January 1949, many of the questions seemed to be about Acheson's relationship with Hiss and Hiss's role at Yalta. Finally, Senator Tom Connally, one of Acheson's supporters, said, "It seems that the only argument some persons can present is to holler about Alger Hiss, and then refer to Yalta. They seem to have to dig up something about the dead President of the United States, and then go back to Yalta."

Their main target was now Acheson. When Hiss was convicted of perjury, Acheson knew he would be asked about his onetime associate. Feeling that his own beliefs concerning loyalty and obligation were at stake, Acheson thought of what he would say long before the question was asked. He was the son of an Episcopal bishop, and he believed honor had to be placed above political expediency. There were times when a man had to be counted. He chose his words carefully. "I do not intend to turn my back on Alger Hiss," he told a reporter from the *Herald Tribune*. Pressed further, Acheson said to look in their Bible for Matthew 25:36, a passage in which Christ called upon His followers to understand that anyone who turns his back on someone in trouble turns his back on Him:

"Naked, and ye clothed me; I was sick and ye visited me; I was in prison and ye came unto me." Later he explained that he was following "Christ's words setting forth compassion as the highest of Christian duties." His words were those of a very brave man, but they were also political dynamite. Had he, mused Scotty Reston of *The New York Times* years later, phrased his thoughts in terms ordinary men could understand, had he simply said he would not kick a man when he was down, a great deal less damage might have been done. Acheson's words were, historian Eric Goldman wrote, "a tremendous and unnecessary gift to those who were insisting that the foreign policy of the Truman Administration was being shaped by men who were soft on Communism." As Goldman noted, Richard Nixon almost immediately responded: "Traitors in the high councils of our own government have made sure that the deck is stacked on the Soviet side of the diplomatic tables."

A month later Acheson did something very un-Achesonian; realizing that he had not only damaged himself but, far more important, wounded his President, he tried to explain himself. "One must be true to things by which one lives," he said, changing few if any opinions. That someone as innately suspicious of Russian intentions as Dean Acheson was to become the primary target for the right-wing isolationists was in itself a reflection of the Alice-in-Wonderland quality of that time. Years later he would loom as the quintessential Cold Warrior, the architect of a hard, edgy, anxious peace with the Soviets.

Carving out a policy that drew a line and limited Soviet expansion, creating a consensus for that policy and at the same time contending with but not overreacting to Soviet moves, demanded skill and resolve and vision. Americans might have dreamed of a Europe which much resembled that of the pre–World War Two map, but the Russians were already in place in the East. In 1946 George Kennan was asked about denying Soviet ambitions in Eastern Europe. "Sorry," he answered, "but the fact of the matter is that we do not have the power in Eastern Europe really to do anything but talk." For many Americans, that reality was almost impossible to accept. Acheson himself despaired of America's difficult new role of international leadership. "We have got to understand that all our lives the danger, the uncertainty, the need for alertness, for effort, for discipline, will be with us. This is new for us. It will be hard for us."

All of this profoundly affected Truman. He had come to the presidency unprepared in foreign affairs, barely briefed on major foreign policy issues by the Roosevelt people. He had, he came to realize, arrived at a historic moment. To him and to his closest foreign policy advisers, it was like a replay of the days right before World War Two. In March 1948, after what seemed to him a series of catastrophic foreign-policy events, he wrote to his daughter, Margaret, "We are faced with exactly the same situation with which Britain and France were faced in 1938–39 with Hitler. Things look black. A decision will have to be made. I am going to make it."

TWO

To the complete surprise of the nation's political establishment and journalists, Harry Truman's fellow citizens elected him to the presidency, and yet it was only after he was out of office that people truly came to appreciate the full measure of the man and his virtues. History tended to vindicate many of his decisions—some of them, such as the intervention in Korea, made under the most difficult circumstances—and as the passions of the era subsided he came to be seen as the common man as uncommon man.

In the beginning, his lack of pretense and blunt manner worked against him, standing in stark contrast to Roosevelt's consummate elegance; later those same qualities were seen as refreshing proof of the rugged character of this fearless small-town man, and, by implication, of all ordinary Americans. As President he was accused of demeaning the Oval Office by turning it over to Missouri roughnecks and poker-playing back-room operators who drank bourbon and told off-color jokes—his "cronies," as *Time* magazine, then the semi-official voice of the Republican party, called them. To some extent that charge was true, although Truman was old-fashioned enough not to permit off-color jokes. He liked to call the White House "the great white jail." Even that came to be viewed with tolerance and a certain amount of amusement; after he spent every day grappling with the difficult issues of government, who could begrudge him the pleasure of seeking out old friends in order to relax? To the degree that he could, he continued as he had before, above all to be true to himself in all friendships.

He neither flattered nor responded to flattery. On the rare occasions he showed his anger, it was not over issues of state but rather because he had personally taken offense. Once he wrote a letter threatening to kick a music critic in the genitalia because the critic had panned a concert by his daughter. Even here he was sure that ordinary people would be on his side. "Now, you wait and see," he told his angry wife and daughter after they found out about the letter. "Every man in the United States that's got a daughter will be on my side." And they were, he added later in an interview with Merle Miller. He did not like people who put on airs—"stuffed shirts" and "fuddy-duddys," as he called them. He used simple words in his speeches, never "two-dollar words" or "weasel words." His experiences in the military as an artillery officer made him wary of many generals; he liked his generals modest and thought of such men as MacArthur and Patton as big-brass fancy hats. Much to the annoyance of Dean Acheson, he referred to the State Department people as "striped-pants boys."

He had virtually no personal income, and he and his family always lived modestly. He knew the value of a dollar and would complain loudly if he thought he had been overcharged, as on the occasion of a breakfast at the famed Peabody Hotel in November 1941: "Had breakfast in the coffee shop downstairs and they charged me fifty-five centers for tomato juice, a little dab of oatmeal and milk and toast. I don't mind losing one hundred dollars on a hoss race or a poker game with friends, but I do hate to pay fifty-five centers for a quarter breakfast . . ." The straightforward simplicity of his style would come to seem marvelously human compared to that of the subsequent inhabitants of the White House, ever more image-conscious and isolated from the public by a growing number of handlers, public relations men, and pollsters.

He was the last American President who had not been to college and yet he was quite possibly the best-read President of modern times. His unusually bad eyesight (he was as "blind as a mole," in his own words) had precluded his participation in sports, so as a boy, he had read prodigiously. His broad knowledge of history often surprised his White House aides, a good number of whom had been to elite boarding schools and colleges and were at first inclined to think of themselves as better educated than he.

He was a late bloomer. His early life had been filled with failure, and it was only as a National Guard captain in World War One that he distinguished himself. His entry into the political arena came late in life—he won his first race for a local office at age thirty-eight, and with the help of the Pendergast machine, he narrowly won a Senate seat when he was fifty. As he wrote Bess in 1942, upon the occasion of their twenty-third wedding anniversary, "Thanks to the right life partner for me we've come out pretty well. A failure as a farmer, miner, an oil promoter, and a merchant, but finally hit the groove as a public servant—and that due mostly to you and Lady Luck."

Within the world of Kansas City politics he had a sterling record for honesty. "Three things ruin a man," he liked to say: "power, money, and women. I never wanted power, I never had any money, and the only woman in my life is up at the house right now." He certainly never wanted to be President, but thanks to the considerable muscle of the machine, he slipped into Washington as a senator and soon thereafter, somewhat to his own surprise, was given the 1944 vice-presidential nomination. Then a few months after his inauguration, Roosevelt died and he became the accidental President. Unprepared he may have been, but he turned out to have the right qualities: the ability to take considerable pressure, and, if need be, to wave aside momentary political advantage to do what he thought was right in the long run. In a way his early failures helped him later to empathize with his fellow Americans and allowed him to arrive in the White House without the overweening ambition and distorted values that often distinguish those who devote themselves to the singular pursuit of success.

From the start, he realized that he would be competing not so much with his Republican opponents but with the ghost of his predecessor. Roosevelt had revolutionized the presidency with his use of radio; his seductive Fireside Chats had made it seem like he was visiting with ordinary Americans in their own homes. Roosevelt's voice—warm, friendly, filled with confidence—suited the medium perfectly. Truman, on the other hand, had no skill with radio. His voice—twangy and simple—was disappointing. Not surprisingly, his most effective venue for communicating with his constituents was the whistle-stop—speaking from the rear platform of a train stopping in small towns. There he could attack the opposition in simple but cutting language, and his audience, knowing he was one of their own, would yell back, "Give 'em hell, Harry."

His essential color was gray, wrote the famed journalist John Gunther: "bright grayness. Both the clothes and hair were neat and gray. The gray-framed spectacles magnified the gray hazel eyes, but there was no grayness in the mind . . ." If his language when he was young was that of a rural Missouri boy, filled with crude references to African-Americans as "niggers," he went far beyond his predecessor in terms of activism for civil rights; if his letters had once been filled with unkind references to Jews and to New York as a "kike town," he, more than any other politician in the world, was responsible for the creation of Israel.

Even Churchill was impressed with him, and the manner with which he set out to inform himself and the ease with which he accepted responsibility. "A man of immense determination," said Churchill upon first meeting him at Potsdam, adding the next day, quite shrewdly, "He has direct methods of speech and a great deal of self-confidence and resolution." "Straightforward, decisive, simple, entirely honest," Dean Acheson wrote his son soon after meeting him. There was a certain jauntiness to his walk and his attitude toward life. He was not afflicted by inner doubts. He made his decisions quickly and cleanly by listening to the evidence and the best advice of those around him, and he did not look back. He was not particularly introspective. Politics was the art of the possible: At the poker table, you took the hand you were dealt and you played it as best you could. Then you slept well.

The backlash against his presidency and the vestiges of the New Deal grew more bitter after his election. On his desk he kept a sign that read THE BUCK STOPS HERE. In the midst of that difficult period, Truman once reminisced with Arneson Gordon, a State Department expert on disarmament, about how he had handled various crises. Arneson later set down Truman's thoughts: "He mused about how many 'bucks' he had stopped: the abrupt termination of Lend Lease after the war: bad advice, a blooper; the Truman Doctrine, re. Greece and Turkey: good; the Berlin airlift, right again; and the Marshall Plan, a 'ten strike.' Over-all, the batting average was pretty good, he thought." At that point, Arneson noted, the conversation took an interesting turn. "He wondered though whether the decision to reduce drastically the defense budget might have been unwise.

True it had been enthusiastically welcomed by the public and the Congress. But considering the unsettled state of world affairs and especially the uncooperativeness of the Russians, was it prudent? He sighed." It was a remarkably astute assessment from Truman the amateur historian judging Truman the professional politician.

One thing he understood and demanded was loyalty. He gave it unconditionally to those who served him, and he expected nothing less in return. He admired Dean Acheson from the start for his uncommon abilities, intelligence, and courage. Their unlikely and exceptionally close friendship was forged one night in November 1946, when Truman had returned to Washington during one of the lowest moments in his political career, after the midterm sweep by the Republicans of both houses of Congress. There, alone at the train station, to meet him was Acheson. Shortly after Truman's inauguration as Vice-President, Tom Pendergast died. By that time, Pendergast was a disgraced, bankrupt man recently let out of prison for income-tax evasion, his once considerable fortune squandered on the horses, his physical strength eroded by illnesses. The one thing that had held back Truman's career when he had first arrived in Washington—the one taint on him—was the Pendergast connection. But Truman opted to go to the funeral, a clear sign of his determination to put obligation, as he defined it, over popularity. Some five years later when Acheson made his I-shall-not-turn-my-back-on-Alger-Hiss statement, he rushed to apologize to the president. Truman told him about the Pendergast funeral and not to worry. "Dean," the President said. "Always be shot in front, never [from] behind."

By the summer of 1949 America had enjoyed a four-year monopoly of the atom bomb. It had been finished too late to use against Germany. Nonetheless, it arrived in time to be a trump card in the growing tensions between the United States and the Soviet Union. A few hours before the first test, Truman said to his aides, apropos of his imminent meeting with Stalin at Potsdam in July 1945: "If it explodes—as I think it will—I will certainly have a hammer on these boys." And midway through the conference, Winston Churchill did indeed notice a change in Truman's behavior. Subsequently, after Churchill learned of the successful test at Alamogordo, he confided to Harry Stimson, the American secretary of war: "Now I know what happened to Truman yesterday. When he got to the meeting after having read the report, he was a changed man. He told the Russians just where they got off and generally bossed the meeting."

That monopoly had given America an edge in the immediate postwar era. Our defense plans, such as they were, were largely based on our exclusive control of the bomb. The initial assumption on the part of America's top scientists and intelligence analysts was that the Soviets were some five years behind us in developing nuclear weapons. That forecast did not change: As the new decade approached, we assumed that they were *still* five years behind us. If anything our military-intelligence people were even more confident: The Army thought the Soviets would not have the bomb until 1960, the Navy, not until 1965; the Air Force, though, estimated 1952. In general we were skeptical of Soviet expertise, especially with regard to Soviet science. There was a joke at the time, the scientist Herbert York noted, "that the Russians could not surreptitiously introduce nuclear bombs in suitcases into the United States because they had not yet been able to perfect a suitcase." Among those who held firmly to the idea of Soviet ineptitude was Truman himself. When he first met the head of Los Alamos, J. Robert Oppenheimer, in 1946, Truman asked Oppenheimer when the Russians would be able to build a bomb. Oppenheimer answered that he did not know. "I know," Truman said. "When?" Oppenheimer asked. "Never," the President said.

The American monopoly on nuclear weapons ended on September 3, 1949. On that day a long-range reconnaissance plane, which the United States used to sample the stratosphere, showed an unusually high level of radioactivity—a filter on the plane read 85 counts a minute—anything above 50 triggered an alert. A second filter showed 153 counts a minute. The overpowering evidence was that the Soviets had exploded some kind of atomic device.

Two days later another plane, flying from Guam to Japan, showed a count of more than 1,000. Scientists in Washington discovered fission isotopes of barium and cerium in the samples, and shortly thereafter an additional fission isotope, molybdenum, was found. The only question remaining was whether this was the result of a device intentionally exploded by the Russians or a nuclear accident. A panel of nuclear specialists in Washington decided that the Russians had indeed set off an atomic bomb, much like the one at Alamogordo, and that the explosion had taken place sometime between August 26 and 29. They even figured out the general location—on the Asian part of the Soviet landmass. The American code name for the explosion, in honor of Joseph Stalin, the Soviet dictator, was known as Joe One.

By September 19 the five members of the Atomic Energy Commission went to tell the president that there was no doubt about what had happened. Truman, still dubious, kept asking, "Are you *sure?*" He then speculated that captured German scientists must have been responsible. (Truman never completely accepted the fact that the Russians had the bomb; in 1953, when his presidency was over, he told a group of reporters, "I'm not convinced that Russia has the bomb. I'm not convinced that the Russians have achieved the know-how to put the complicated mechanism together to make an A-bomb work.") The commissioners pushed for Truman to make an immediate announcement, lest the news leak from the government or, even worse, from the Russians themselves. David Lilienthal, head of the Atomic Energy Commission, argued that the news would be less jarring if it came from Truman himself. But the British pound had been devalued the day before and the world's financial centers were already panicked; it was decided that the President should wait a few days.

On September 23, 1949, Harry Truman announced that the Soviets had exploded an atomic device. He did not use the word *bomb,* and his statement was carefully worded to minimize alarm: "Ever since atomic energy was first released by man, the eventual development of this new force by other nations was to be expected. This probability has always been taken into account by us," the President's statement said. Nonetheless, the American atomic monopoly had ended. It was, Lilienthal noted in his diary the night before, "what we'd feared ever since January, 1946." Both American foreign and domestic politics were instantly and dramatically altered. This, noted Senator Arthur Vandenberg, the leading Republican internationalist, "is now a different world." At a congressional meeting right after Truman's announcement, Senator Tom Connally, arguing for support of the president's programs said, "Russia has shown her teeth."

There were no contingency plans. J. Robert Oppenheimer testified before Congress and a troubled Senator Vandenberg asked him, almost pleadingly, "Doctor, what shall we do now?" "Stay strong and hold on to our friends," Oppenheimer answered. In the words of SAC commander Curtis LeMay—who had a penchant for saying aloud what some other military men were merely thinking—Joe One ended "the era when we might have destroyed Russia completely and not even skinned our elbows in doing it." In the postwar years, the President had once confided to David Lilienthal that had it not been for our atomic monopoly, "the Russians would probably have taken over Europe a long time ago." Whether that was true or not, there was no doubt that in the years after World War Two, the Soviets had kept a vast part of the powerful and victorious Red Army in uniform, a significant part of it stationed in the very heart of Central Europe; the Americans, while still posting what was the beginning of a multinational force in Western Europe, had disarmed at what most top military men considered an alarming rate. Indeed America's demobilization, Truman had noted acidly at a cabinet meeting in October 1945, was going so fast that it was not so much a demobilization as a disintegration of the armed forces.

At one point in 1946, Truman, depressed by the lack of congressional support for any degree of military readiness, had confided to Henry Wallace, his secretary of agriculture, that America could not get tough with the Soviet Union because it was down to one fully equipped division. By early 1947 America's armed forces had been cut from their wartime strength of 12 million to 1.5 million; by 1947 the annual military budget had been cut to $10.3 billion, from a wartime high of $90.9 billion.

On this issue the nation was at crosscurrents with itself. The foreign-policy establishment (both Democratic and Republican), located primarily in the East, saw its role ever more clearly as taking the baton as leader of the world's democracies from Britain, whose power continued to ebb after World War Two. If there was a mandate, it was for anti-Communism rather than genuine internationalism. That the postwar peace was both uneasy and expensive was difficult for many Americans to accept. Once allies, the Soviet Union and China were about to become adversaries: archadversaries Japan, Germany, and Italy were becoming allies.

For a time the atomic monopoly had offered us something of a bargain-basement defense policy. Often in this period those whose rhetoric was most jingoistic—in particular the Republican far right—were the most recalcitrant about spending for defense and for foreign aid, and the most reluctant to deal with the realities of the complicated postwar era. One vignette will do: J. Parnell Thomas, who was later to make a significant name for himself as the head of the House Un-American Activities Committee, fancied himself as a man who was going to save America from its Communist enemies while at the same time making sure that we did not pay very much to do it. J. Lawton Collins, a distinguished corps commander in World War Two, remembered going up to the Hill in 1946 with General Dwight Eisenhower to meet with Thomas. The issue was what could be done to speed demobilization—in the then current phrase to "bring the boys home." As Ike and Collins entered the room, they found that Thomas had rigged the setting. Around a table was a group of young women, clearly wives of soldiers, and on the table was a huge pile of baby shoes. The instant the two generals entered the room, news photographers, alerted earlier by Thomas, snapped away: The resulting photos record for posterity the women, the shoes, a grinning Thomas, and a furious Ike.

Neither political party had covered itself with glory during the rush to demobilize. Few politicians dared to speak of an enduring, complicated, and *expensive* peace. Truman, to his credit, tried to pass an act calling for a large trained reserve and national guard. He called it Universal Military Training, or UMT. It had been his dream since he served in World War One, and he envisioned it as a critical part of a permanent "citizens' army." Every young man between the ages of eighteen and twenty would give his country one year and then stand by in a reserve or national-guard unit; they could be conscripted only by an act of Congress. He had broad support from such men as Marshall, Eisenhower, and Stimson, but the Congress was not interested.

Thus America had been cheating as a military power, and, for Truman, the Soviet explosion was terrible news: Already besieged for being soft on Communism, he now faced the terrible decision of whether or not to pursue the development of a hydrogen bomb, a weapon far more powerful than the atomic bomb. The Soviet test left him little room in which to maneuver. For unknown to Truman at the time was the fact that he was about to inherit a major debate that had been raging in scientific circles: whether or not to go ahead with the hydrogen bomb.

The fear of a German victory had quashed any doubts on the part of the scientists who had worked on the Manhattan Project. It was only at the very end of the war, with Germany defeated and Japan near defeat, that questions arose over its use. There were those who thought that a demonstration of the bomb might be as effective as actually using it. But J. Robert Oppenheimer, later pilloried for being soft during the Cold War, took it upon himself to kill a petition of his fellow scientists holding that view. Right after the successful use of the atomic bomb, reporters questioned Oppenheimer about the morality of what the Los Alamos team had achieved and he answered, in words that were to haunt him later, "a scientist cannot hold back progress because of fears of what the world will do with his discoveries."

Most scientific breakthroughs bring satisfaction to those involved. Not this one. From the moment the explosion took place, there was an awareness that an instrument of darkness had been discovered. George Kistiakowsky, who had done so much to fashion the bomb, thought that the Trinity explosion was a glimpse of the apocalypse—"in the last milli-second of the earth's existence—the last men will see what we saw." Kenneth Bainbridge, the director of the test, turned to Oppenheimer and said, "Now we're all sons of bitches." Oppenheimer himself went back to his base and found a normally cool-headed young researcher vomiting outside the office. The reaction, Oppenheimer thought, had begun. When James Conant returned to Washington from Los Alamos, his colleague George Harrison greeted him and said: "Congratulations, it worked." "It worked," Conant answered. "As to congratulations I am far from sure—that remains for history to decide." Nor was Oppenheimer himself immune from the same doubts. A few weeks later he wrote to his high school teacher Herbert Smith, "You will believe that this undertaking has not been without its misgivings; they are heavy on us today, when the future, which has so many elements of high promise, is yet only a stone's throw from despair . . ." Still, there was a consensus in high-level political circles that the atomic bomb had probably saved millions of lives, given the way the Japanese had resisted American forces, island by island.

The debate over the hydrogen bomb was different in every way. It was being made in a time of peace, albeit a shaky one, and unlike the atomic bomb, the very fact of its development was not a closely held secret. Its nickname in defense and scientific circles said it all—the super bomb or, simply, the Super. Lilienthal referred to it in his diary as Campbell's—as in soup. Here, with one terrible strike, was the capacity to unleash 1 million tons of TNT. Given the fact that in all World War Two only 3 million tons of TNT had been used, the imagination could scarcely comprehend this new destructive power. It was far more than a more powerful alternative to the atomic bomb; it threatened the very existence of humanity.

The possibility of creating this terrible weapon had been there for some time. While still engaged in research on the atomic bomb in 1942, Edward Teller and Emil Konopinski had formulated a series of calculations that they believed would show the impossibility of using an atomic bomb to ignite a thermonuclear reaction in deuterium. But as Teller wrote: "The more we worked on our report, the more obvious it became that the roadblocks which I had erected for [Enrico] Fermi's idea were not so high after all. We hurdled them one by one and concluded that heavy hydrogen could be ignited by an atomic bomb to produce an explosion of tremendous magnitude. By the time we were on our way to California . . . we even thought we knew precisely how to do it." Initially, Teller suggested that the explosion might even ignite the nitrogen in the air and the hydrogen in the oceans. The suggestion so upset Oppenheimer that he boarded a train—he was forbidden to use the telephone on matters this grave, and he was also forbidden to fly—to go and talk with Nobel Prize–winning physicist Arthur Compton, who was vacationing in Michigan. Compton's immediate reaction was: "Better be a slave under the Nazi heel than to draw down the final curtain on humanity."

When the atomic, or fission, bomb was dropped in August 1945, abruptly ending the war, the question of the fusion bomb, or the Super, was temporarily set aside. A fission bomb came from splitting the atom, turning matter into energy; a fusion bomb used the intense heat generated by an atomic bomb—equal to or greater than that at the earth's core—to release neutrons that bombarded the compound lithium deuteride inside the weapon. The key to it was heavy water, or heavy hydrogen, water in which deuterium replaced hydrogen. It had to be distilled from tons of ordinary water in an elaborate process. Each kilo of heavy hydrogen equaled about 85,000 tons of traditional TNT. Thus, as Richard Rhodes has noted, twelve kilos of heavy hydrogen was twenty-six pounds, and could be ignited by one atomic bomb. A comparable fission explosion would demand some *five hundred* atomic bombs.

No wonder most of the scientists involved were terrified of what they had wrought. There was, Winston Churchill wrote in 1955, "an immense gulf between the atomic and hydrogen bomb. The atomic bomb, with all its terrors, did not carry us outside the scope of human control or manageable events in thought or action in peace or war."

Oppenheimer himself epitomized the evolution that many of the Los Alamos scientists underwent. He was the leader of the scientific community in those years, and after the successful development of the atomic bomb, he was at the pinnacle of his prestige, achieving something of a mythic status in popular culture. In 1948 he was on the cover of *Time* magazine, and that May, when a new professional journal called *Physics Today* was launched, the first issue had on its cover a photo of Oppenheimer's rumpled porkpie hat. There was no credit line, no title—just the hat. "The bomb, whose glare illuminated a new world also gave the once-obscure brotherhood of physicists a strange new standing," wrote Joseph and Stewart Alsop. "They acquired something of the position in our society of the

Mathematician-Astronomer-Priests of the ancient Mayas who were at once feared and revered as the knowers of the mystery of the seasons, and the helpers of the sun and the stars in their life-giving courses." Oppenheimer, they added, was the unofficial high priest in that new order. When he spoke at Berkeley, his audience was so large that his lectures had to be piped into adjacent rooms. With his gaunt, hauntingly poetic features and literary sensibility, he seemed the embodiment of the modern physicist as Renaissance man. Besides, among his scientific peers he was the rarest thing—a native son, a brilliant scientist who spoke without an accent.

If there was a committee on science, on atomic energy, on government and science, Oppie was certain to be on it, and often would be the head of it. If the politicians wanted to know what the scientists thought or could do, they turned to Oppenheimer; if the scientists wanted an answer about the politicians, they turned to Oppie. He was never a Nobel laureate; it was argued by some he never fulfilled the promise of his exceptional scientific talent. One could speculate that at the very prime of his career he had sacrificed his own work for the good of his nation by becoming the manager of the Los Alamos lab instead of its chief scientist.

His stewardship of Los Alamos was considered a sterling model for all future scientific ventures. He had worked hard to bring in the best scientists in the world and to create an esprit de corps. Although they were isolated in the desert of New Mexico and the tight security measures were daunting, Oppenheimer managed to foster an atmosphere of unusual freedom. I. I. Rabi, the Nobel laureate, once said there was a special quality about Los Alamos—a romance, a palpable sense of magic. There, Johnny von Neumann, quite possibly the world's greatest mathematician and the author of the *Theory of Games,* almost always lost in poker; there, to cut a ski trail, George Kistiakowsky simply detonated trees with Composition C explosive plastique instead of chopping them down. James Tuck remembered the miraculous openness in which young physicists met with the greatest names in their profession. Tuck spoke of Los Alamos as having "a spirit of Athens, of Plato."

Oppie himself listened to everyone. As a leader of men who were brilliant, egocentric, and difficult, he behaved with exquisite grace and sensitivity. He summoned managerial and political skills that no one, including himself, previously knew he possessed. "When anyone mentions laboratory directors," Enrico Fermi, the great Italian physicist, once said, "I think of directors and directors and of Oppenheimer, who is unique."

Before Los Alamos, Oppenheimer was seen as privileged and spoiled. As a graduate student and then as a young instructor, he had been unbearably arrogant. He was so much smarter and quicker than anyone else that when a colleague would start to say something, Oppie would finish the sentence for him. He was intolerant of anyone he thought second-rate, and he did little to hide his disdain. Even those who liked him found him rude. One of his colleagues, Victor Weisskopf, mentioned to Oppie that he planned to write a paper on a particular subject. Oppie replied, "You don't understand enough about it to write a paper." To Weisskopf it was like a slap in the face.

Born in 1904, Oppenheimer was the son of a wealthy Jewish merchant family in New York. His was a home with servants, maids, cooks, chauffeurs. Van Goghs hung on the walls. He was so sheltered that he had few friends his own age. At age nine he told an older cousin, "Ask me a question in Latin and I will answer you in Greek." At twelve he gave a lecture to the New York Mineralogical Society (the officers of the society had thought he was an adult, based on an earlier paper he had written). "I was," he later noted, "an unctuous repulsively good little boy. My childhood did not prepare me for the fact that the world is full of cruel bitter things. It gave me no normal, healthy way to be a bastard." His apprehension of anti-Semitism was partly responsible for his social awkwardness, thought his friend Herbert Smith, a high school teacher. Because of that he was always wary of where he was welcomed and where he was not. (The year before he entered college at Harvard, President A. Lawrence Lowell had called for a quota for Jews. Years later, despite his immense fame that came from heading the Manhattan Project, there was a serious question of whether he could go back to Caltech since Robert Millikan, the president there, felt there were already enough Jews on the faculty.)

He was graduated from Harvard in three years, earning a summa, while making a minimal impression on his classmates. In his yearbook he summed up his experience in Cambridge: "In college three years as an undergraduate." He spoke seven languages, one of them Sanskrit, which he learned in order to read the *Bhagavad-Gita* in its original form. Victor Weisskopf thought there was a terrible sadness to Oppie, a certain inability to love and be loved, which lasted his entire life. Nothing in his personal life was ever easy; if anything saved him from himself it was the sheer power of his intellect and, for a brief time at least, his nation's need to employ it. As a graduate student, he went off to Europe. Edward Condon, a young American physicist also studying overseas, noted his intellectual arrogance at the time: "Trouble is that Oppie is so quick on the trigger intellectually he puts the other guy at a disadvantage. And damnit he is always right, or at least right enough." He got his Ph.D. from the University of Göttingen. A colleague asked James Franck, one of the examiners at his orals, how it had gone. Franck answered, "I got out of there just in time. He was beginning to ask me questions."

He returned to teach at Harvard and then went to Berkeley. He was beloved by some students, who formed an Oppie coterie, imitating his style of dress and speech patterns. As his reputation and that of his colleague Ernest Lawrence grew, it became apparent that American physics was coming into its own. One contemporary decided, "There's a huge difference between a genius and a bright person. The reason Oppenheimer knows so much is that it's easy when you learn ten times as fast as other physicists and remember everything."

He was remarkably sheltered from the world around him. Because of his family's wealth, he had an income of ten thousand dollars a year from investments during the worst of the Depression—a great deal of money at the time. He had no radio or telephone. He read no newspapers or magazines. He found out about the Depression only when friends told him of it. In fact, he knew almost nothing of politics; but living in the hothouse world of Berkeley during the Depression and the Spanish Civil War, he soon began to join fellow-traveling groups. In that sense he was not that different from a good many academics of that period: his brother, Frank, and Frank's wife were both Communist party members, as was Oppie's first fiancée and his eventual wife, Kitty.

But Oppie's fellow-traveling days were short-lived. Colleagues George Placzek and Victor Weisskopf spent time in the Soviet Union during the worst of Stalin's terror. Afterward they visited with Oppie, telling him that yes, it was all true what critics said about Stalin—indeed if anything, it was worse. Hearing it from trusted liberal friends profoundly affected Oppie. Weisskopf felt, though, Kitty Oppenheimer still resisted his reports of Stalin's Russia.

To some he seemed the divided man—part creator of the most dangerous weapon in history—part the romantic innocent searching for some inner spiritual truth. At Los Alamos, he would escape to the mountains, camping by himself, writing poetry. The name given to the first test of the atomic weapon was Trinity. When Leslie Groves, the military overseer of the group, asked why he had chosen that name, Oppenheimer answered: ". . . Why I chose that name is not clear; but I know what thoughts were in my mind. There is a poem of John Donne, written just before his death, which I know and love. From it a quotation:

> . . . As West and East
> In all flatt Maps—and I am one—are one,
> So death doth touch the Resurrection.

"That," he told Groves, "still does not make Trinity; but in another, better known devotional poem, Donne opens, 'Batter my heart three person'd God.' Beyond that I have no clues whatsoever." At the very instant of the Trinity explosion, Oppenheimer quoted a passage from the *Bhagavad-Gita:* "If the radiance of a thousand suns were to burst into the sky, that would be like the splendor of the Mighty One. . . . I am become Death, destroyer of worlds."

The day after the Nagasaki bombing, Ernest Lawrence, the inventor of the cyclotron, found Oppenheimer exhausted, depressed, and wondering aloud whether the dead at Hiroshima and Nagasaki were not luckier than the living. "There was not much left in me at the moment," he later said. The job, as far as he was concerned, was done. As he withdrew from Los Alamos, so did others. He had wielded power there through sheer force of genius, and he seemed to reflect what the others would think before they had time to think it themselves; thus one could predict the changing mood of the scientific community by tracking Oppenheimer. On October 16, 1945, his last official day as head of the Manhattan Project, Oppenheimer told a reporter, "If you ask, 'Can we make them [atomic weapons] more terrible?' the answer is yes. If you ask, 'Can we make a lot of them?' the answer is yes. If you ask, 'Can we make them terribly more terrible?' the answer is probably." "Let the second team take over," Groves later quoted him as saying, a phrase that was wounding to those who stayed behind. David Lilienthal, spending an evening with him in July 1946, noted, "He is really a tragic figure; with all of his great attractiveness, brilliance of mind. As I left him he looked so sad: 'I am ready to go anywhere and do anything, but I am bankrupt of further ideas. And I find that physics and the teaching of physics, which is my life, now seems irrelevant.' "

If Oppenheimer was morally exhausted, then Edward Teller was furious. The departure of the best scientists from Los Alamos meant that full resources would not be devoted to the development of the Super. To Teller, for whom the Super was *the* project, this was a bitter disappointment, both professionally and personally. He could not understand, he said later, the moral difference between the fission bomb and the fusion bomb. Thus began a rift in the scientific world that would become a chasm over the next few years.

The scientists were beginning to find out the limits of their power. They might have become, as C. P. Snow had noted, the "most important military resource a nation state could call upon," but in the end they had little control over the consequences of their work; they pursued the unknown, like great explorers, because it was there. But more and more, they ventured into a world filled with moral ambiguities, if not pure terror. Yet no one exercising political power in the United States or the Soviet Union was very interested in the piety or guilt of the scientists. This was a hard lesson. In the beginning they had been the professors and the politicians, the students— Acheson remembered that right after World War Two, when Oppenheimer tried to brief him and John McCloy about atomic fission, he had used a borrowed blackboard, "on which he drew little figures representing electrons, neutrons, and protons, bombarding one another, chasing one another about, dividing, and generally carrying on in unpredictable ways. Our bewildered questions seemed to distress him. At last he put down the chalk in gentle despair, saying, 'It's hopeless! I really think you two believe neutrons and electrons *are* little men.' We admitted nothing."

They had all been on the same team then. But the new tensions between politicians and scientists were to become apparent at President Truman's very first meeting with Oppenheimer. Truman had been looking forward to it, but the meeting had not gone well. "Mr. President, I have blood on my hands," Oppenheimer told Truman. "Never mind," Truman was supposed to have answered. "It will all come out in the wash." But at that moment Truman decided Oppenheimer was "a crybaby." "Don't you bring that fellow around again," the President told Acheson later. "After all, all he did was make the bomb. I'm the guy who fired it off."

A sure sign that the science of nuclear weapons would come to be dominated by the pressures of politics came in the summer of 1949. The Republican right tried to block administration policy on sharing nuclear information with the British. This merely foreshadowed the true split that came in debate over the Super: James Conant, the eminent chemist and president of Harvard, argued that the Super was an unusable weapon and that the atomic bomb was sufficient to deter aggression. The Super did not necessarily offer greater security, but might only create an endless race for ever more powerful weapons. In its own way, he argued, it might be oddly paralyzing to the possessor. A balanced weapons program might offer greater security.

Even as the members of the AEC were trying to decide what to do about the Super, some of the nation's top military men already thought war with the Soviet Union inevitable. Nor was it just military men and politicians on the fringe. The members of the AEC met with Senator Brien McMahon, a Democrat on the Joint Committee on Atomic Energy, who had written the Atomic Energy Act and was generally considered a moderate. McMahon might have been by the standards of the day a domestic liberal, but he was a devout Catholic, with a heavily Catholic constituency, and thus a hard-liner on the subject of Communism. He had become the single most important congressional figure on the issue of atomic weapons, and unlike the scientists, he had no doubts about using them. The bombing of Hiroshima, he had said on the Senate floor, was "the greatest event in world history since the birth of Jesus Christ." If the Russians got ahead of us in nuclear weaponry, that would, in his words, place "total power in the hands of total evil [which] will equal total destruction." When David Lilienthal met with McMahon he found it extremely dispiriting. "What he [McMahon] is talking about is the inevitability of war with the Russians and what he says adds up to one thing: blow them off the face of the earth quick, before they do the same to us—and we haven't much time."

The political pressure building around Truman to go ahead with the Super was relentless. How could his administration, already accused of being soft on Communism, fail to pursue what seemed to be the supreme weapon—especially one that might eventually end up in the hands of the Soviets. Failure to do so, Acheson noted, "would push the Administration into a political buzzsaw." In addition, a powerful new force was pushing for the Super in the scientific community—Edward Teller. As a refugee, much of whose family still lived in Budapest, under Communist control, he was terrified by the news of Joe One, and at the time he had immediately called Oppenheimer. "What shall we do? What shall we do?" Teller kept asking over the phone. Oppenheimer became so irritated with Teller's emotional outburst that he finally told him, "Keep your shirt on."

Still, Teller had no doubts about which course to pursue, and he distrusted those who were more cautious. Soon after the Soviet explosion, he spent an afternoon with Kenneth Nichols, a top Army official on nuclear policy. Teller's vehemence surprised Nichols, who asked him why he was worrying so much about the situation. "I'm not worrying about the situation," Teller answered. "I'm worrying about the people who should be worrying about it."

Teller began to scour America's universities to recruit young scientists for Los Alamos, but his success was marginal; his was not a project to stir the imagination of America's best young minds. He had wanted Oppenheimer to come back, but Oppenheimer had no taste for it. Failing to get Oppenheimer, he tried for Hans Bethe, whose prestige was almost equal to Oppenheimer's. He visited Bethe at Cornell in October 1949. Bethe was deeply torn by events. He felt that no decent society should pursue a weapon as destructive as the Super. But he was also worried that the Russians might build one, giving them the capacity to blackmail the United States.

Bethe seemed to be the scientist in the center. He talked it over with his wife, who pointed out that he had worked on one terrible bomb already and that he had done this because America was at war with Nazi Germany. She then pointed to the room where their two young children were sleeping. Did he want them to grow up in a world with a hydrogen bomb? she asked. Still unsure of his decision, Bethe decided to talk with Oppenheimer and he went to Princeton the next day. Oppenheimer listened and handed him a letter from James Conant with a particularly devastating critique of the Super. By chance Victor Weisskopf was visiting Princeton that weekend, and the next day he and Bethe drove to New York together. Weisskopf, even more than Oppenheimer, was morally opposed to the Super. "Hiroshima was a blunder and Nagasaki a crime," he had said after the explosion of the atomic bomb, and he had vowed never to work on nuclear weapons again. Weisskopf argued against Bethe's fears of Soviet military and political hegemony. Even if the United States did not build the Super and the Soviets did, the Russians could not dominate the world, for the American stockpile of atomic weapons (two hundred at the time) remained a healthy deterrent. At the time, Weisskopf painted for Bethe a vivid picture of war with the hydrogen bomb, of "what it would mean to destroy a city like New York with one bomb, and how hydrogen bombs would change the military balance by making the attack still more powerful and the defense still less powerful," Bethe later recalled. That night Bethe called Teller and said, "Edward, I've been thinking it over. I can't come." Teller was devastated. He gradually began to believe that there was a conspiracy against him and his bomb, and Oppenheimer was leading it. ("I have explained this to Teller many times," Bethe said years later, "but he and others still blamed Oppenheimer for my not returning to Los Alamos.")

Yet even as resistance among scientists to the Super increased, the American military was beginning to stir, particularly the Air Force, which from the start saw itself as the service charged with nuclear-weapon delivery, and which had no intention of letting the Soviets have a monopoly on this terrifying new weapon.

The political cast of characters, even within the Truman administration, was beginning to change as well. Lilienthal, a product of New Deal liberalism, was politically in decline. He was not merely sympathetic to Oppenheimer with regard to nuclear issues, he was dependent on him—so much so that Leslie Groves liked to joke that Lilienthal would consult Oppenheimer on which tie to wear in the morning. Others, less sympathetic, were on the rise—the most notable among them was Lewis Strauss, who would emerge in the coming decade as the most important political adviser on atomic-energy matters. Truman told Lilienthal that Strauss was coming to the AEC and mentioned only that he was a businessman who had saved $20 million and put it all in government bonds.

Strauss seemed the prototype of a Wall Street tycoon but was, in fact, a man of rather simple origins. He had never been to college. His father was a shoe salesman in Richmond, Virginia, and Lewis Strauss's early days were spent in the same profession. He was nothing if not industrious, and by the time he was twenty he had saved $20,000, a considerable amount in those days. He had intended to go on to college. But in 1917, when he was twenty-one, his mother, who had been deeply affected by the suffering of ordinary people in Europe during World War One, heard that Herbert Hoover was going to head the relief effort to provide people with food. She suggested to her son that he go to Washington to help Mr. Hoover, and shortly thereafter Lewis Strauss did just that. "When do you want to start?" Hoover asked him upon hearing of his mission. "Right now," Strauss answered. "Take off your coat," Hoover said, and Strauss went to work, in pure Horatio Alger style. Within two years he became Hoover's personal secretary. Later, he went off to work for Kuhn, Loeb, married the daughter of a partner, and in time made his fortune on Wall Street. He was an Orthodox Jew who prayed twice a day. As a young salesman he had been on the road in towns too small for a synagogue, but he took the Sabbath off and read the Bible in his hotel room. Once, with his young son, he wrote a child's version of the Old Testament.

During World War Two Strauss served with the Navy in a desk job, and he rose to the rank of rear admiral. It was a title he quite liked, and he preferred thereafter to be known as the Admiral. He had long been interested in nuclear physics, and he hoped that eventually it might provide a cure for cancer, which had caused the death of both his parents. By dint of his years with Hoover, he was a skillful and forceful bureaucratic infighter. "He has more elbows than an octopus," said one critic describing Strauss in internal bureaucratic battles. He brooked no dissent from those underneath him, yet with those above him, like Eisenhower and James Forrestal, he was, as Joseph and Stewart Alsop noted, "all pliability." In his own words, he was a Herbert Hoover black Republican, and he was well connected with conservatives. He was a hard-liner on relations with the Soviet Union, and he was absolutely convinced that the Russians were further ahead on their atomic program than we believed. It had been his idea to create the aerial-surveillance program that found the radioactive fallout from the first Soviet test.

Strauss already had a reputation among the scientists. When Teller first heard he was coming on the AEC, he asked Oppenheimer what he knew of him. "Very smart and very vain," Oppie answered—a phrase, ironically, that some of Oppenheimer's critics would have used to describe him.

Strauss was, for his part, wary of scientists. When he first met Edward Teller, who was Jewish, and by Strauss's lights politically on the side of the angels, he was disturbed that Teller seemed to lack serious religious commitment. He disliked those he believed to be soft on Communism, and developed particular animosity toward Oppenheimer. Earlier, during the testimony on whether or not to share atomic information with the British, Oppenheimer was asked about the overall military value of research isotopes, which Strauss thought were extremely important. "Far less important than electronic devices," Oppenheimer answered. Then he had paused for a moment. "But far more important than, let us say, vitamins. Somewhere in between." That had been the answer of Oppenheimer, the snobbish Berkeley professor at his worst. It had, of course, generated a good deal of laughter in the hearing room, and Strauss had flushed. At the end of his testimony, Oppenheimer turned to Joseph Volpe, an AEC aide, and asked if he had done well. Volpe, remembering the look of anger on Strauss's face, answered, "*Too* well, Robert, much too well."

From the moment the announcement was made about Joe One, Strauss went on red alert; on October 5 he wrote his fellow commissioners a letter reflecting the rapid polarization of political positions at that moment: "It seems to me that the time has come for a quantum jump in our planning (to borrow a metaphor from our scientist friends)—that is to say that we should make an intensive effort to get ahead with the Super. By intensive effort I am thinking of a commitment in talent and money comparable if necessary to that which produced the first atomic weapon. That is the way to stay ahead."

Strauss now became the leader of the more conservative scientists and politicians who were steadily gaining in power. By contrast, the General Advisory Committee (GAC) of the AEC, made up of scientific experts, became the last stronghold of the old guard, men still wary of the H bomb on both moral and technical grounds.

Onetime colleagues were now poised to become sworn enemies. On October 21, 1949, Oppenheimer (who had been surprised by the Russian explosion) wrote James Conant, a fellow member of the General Advisory Committee, of the force gathering against them in favor of the Super. Nothing, he noted, had really changed about the Super since 1942; as far as he was concerned it was still a weapon of the unknown. But there had been "a very great change in the climate of opinion." Pressure was beginning to mount from those scientists with whom he disagreed and who favored the Super: "On the other hand two experienced promoters have been at work, i.e., Ernest Lawrence and Edward Teller. The project has long been dear to Teller's heart and Ernest has convinced himself that we must learn from Operation Joe that the Russians will soon do the Super, and that we had better beat them to it." The congressional attitude, Oppenheimer added, seemed to be, "we must have a Super, and we must have it fast."

The person who would have to make the decision, of course, was Truman, and his room to maneuver was steadily shrinking. Beginning in September 1949, a scenario was being played out in England that would further force Truman's hand. In a time when there were endless accusations about who was a member of the Communist party, who was a fellow traveler, and who was an actual honest-to-God spy, the case of Klaus Fuchs was special. It received far less attention than other, more celebrated, cases in which the actual amount of damage from spying remained in doubt. Because the British were embarrassed by the Fuchs case and wanted to rush it through their legal system, the trial lasted only an hour and a half. Because Fuchs was a talented physicist, with every high-level clearance imaginable, it was appallingly clear that *all* work at Los Alamos through 1946 had been completely compromised. There were even fears that Fuchs might have seriously hindered America's progress on the H bomb.

Fuchs was a German émigré, living in England. An enemy alien at the time the war broke out, he was briefly interned in Britain as such. Under enemy-alien status, as his biographer Robert Chadwell Williams has pointed out, he could not own a car or join a British Civil Defense team, but he could in time work on the most secret aspects of atomic physics.

Fuchs came from a long line of Quaker ministers in Germany. Once merely socialist and pacifist, his family was deeply affected by the terrible outcome of World War One and the rise of Hitler. For them and others like them, the Communists seemed to represent the only answer to the Nazis. Fuchs's mother committed suicide in 1931, and later so did a sister, Elisabeth. Fuchs was wanted by the Gestapo as a member of the Communist party, and he left the country—on orders from the German Communist party—to continue his studies elsewhere. He arrived in England in the winter of 1933–34, one of thousands already fleeing Hitler. A good deal was known in England about his earlier political radicalism, but no one moved on it or checked out the preliminary reports very thoroughly, and he was repeatedly cleared for high-level work by British intelligence. Events, after all, were surging ahead, and soon the Soviet Union was to be England's ally. In May 1941, Fuchs began to work on British aspects of the atomic bomb; within weeks he had volunteered to pass on top-secret information to the Russians. No one from the Party had pressured him to do this—he saw it as his duty. In June 1942 he became a British citizen; in mid-1944, he came over to America with a number of British scientists.

He was the quiet man of Los Alamos. Elfriede Segre would watch him go by, a pallid bachelor, slightly hunched, so sad, so alone, caught in a world of his own, and thought of him as "Poverino—the Pitiful One." Stanislaw Ulam, the brilliant mathematician, noted later that Fuchs never liked to talk about his past or why he had left Germany. Some thought him a man overwhelmed by his own sorrow. He was considered a good physicist, not of the very top rank, but unusually hardworking. By late 1944 he was working in the most sensitive part of the institute, the bomb design and assembly section.

Periodically, he would slip off in a broken-down car to nearby Santa Fe. There, unbeknownst to the others, he would contact his courier, a man named Harry Gold. He gave Gold detailed reports—for example, in June 1945, a month before the Alamogordo test, he supplied a description of the plutonium bomb. He believed that he was working for humanity and peace. When Gold once offered him $1,500 for expenses (of which there were none), Fuchs brusquely

turned him down. He spied purely for political reasons. In the fall of
1945, when most of the top people left Los Alamos, Fuchs stayed on
for an additional year. In 1946 he returned to England and headed
the British nuclear lab at Harwell. There the British authorities,
unbeknownst to the British press and Parliament and their American
colleagues, were trying to build their own bomb. In 1949 Fuchs's
name was advanced for membership in the prestigious Royal Society—no small honor, particularly for someone who had the misfortune not to be born in England. There was talk that the next chair
to open up at Cambridge or Oxford might go to him.

But that summer, American cryptographers cracked the code
used by the Soviets in wartime, and among other things they found
a complete report on the Manhattan Project written by Klaus Fuchs
and transmitted by the Soviet mission in New York to Moscow in
1944. While that did not necessarily mean that Fuchs was an agent,
subsequent discoveries showed that there *was* a Communist agent at
Los Alamos, he *was* a scientist, and his sister had attended an American university, as Fuchs's had. That put him under very close scrutiny. On September 22, the FBI opened a special case on Fuchs; the
code name was Foocase. The authorities had to move cautiously, for
they did not want to tip off the Russians that their code had been
broken. So it was important that Fuchs be made to volunteer a
confession. For William Skardon, the British counterintelligence
agent who worked the case, it was like playing a huge fish on a light
tackle.

Strangely enough, the first step in getting Fuchs to come forward came from Fuchs himself. On October 12, he spoke to Henry
Arnold, chief of security at Harwell. Fuchs said that his father was
moving from West Germany to East Germany to teach, which, he
suggested, might place him in a compromising position and make
him a security risk. What drove Fuchs to take that first step is
unclear—whether disillusionment with postwar Soviet policy in
Europe, exhaustion at leading a double life, or perhaps the vain hope
of heading off an investigation by volunteering such news. He asked
Arnold if he should resign. Arnold told Skardon of the odd conversation.

Harry Truman had no knowledge that British authorities, aided
by the FBI, were closing in on Fuchs. Events in America nonetheless
were assuming a fearful dynamic of their own. In late October,
Oppenheimer wrote of the Super: "What concerns me is really not
the technical problem. I am not sure the miserable thing will work,
nor that it can be gotten to a target except by oxcart. It seems likely

to me even further to worsen the unbalance of our warplans. What does worry me is that this thing appears to have caught the imagination, both of the congressional and military people as the answer to the problem posed by the Russian advance. It would be folly to oppose the exploitation of this weapon. We have always known it had to be done; and it does have to be done, though it is singular proof against any form of experimental approach. But that we become committed to it as the way to save the country and the peace appears to me full of danger."

As the deadline for a recommendation to the AEC on the Super pressed closer, the scientists in the GAC convened a series of meetings. This formidable group included not merely Oppenheimer, its chair, but also I. I. Rabi; Fermi; Conant, of Harvard; and Lee DuBridge, of Caltech; among others. Conant, hardly a radical figure, was a particularly powerful voice within the GAC against proceeding with the Super. He had earlier written Oppenheimer that work would go ahead on the H bomb "over my dead body." When GAC member Oliver Buckley, the head of Bell Lab, mentioned at one meeting that he did not see any moral difference between the atomic bomb and the hydrogen bomb, Conant strongly disagreed: "There are grades of morality." The entire discussion, Conant said, "makes me feel I was seeing the same film, and a punk one, for the second time." As Conant and most of the others saw it, they were already committed to producing a giant fission bomb with a force of 500,000 tons of TNT. How much more power did you need?

Various witnesses were called before the GAC, including the nation's top generals. General Omar Bradley testified that there was no longer any recourse but to go ahead. At that point Oppenheimer asked Bradley about the increasing power of the fission bombs, for half-megaton bombs were now in design. Given that kind of force, he asked, what was the military advantage of the Super? "Only psychological," Bradley answered. Clearly, the issue had moved outside considerations of mere science or even logic. Conant wrote the majority decision, with Oppenheimer, DuBridge, and several others concurring; they called it potentially a weapon of genocide. The minority report, written by Fermi and Rabi, said that the U.S. should not be the first to build the bomb, but that we should reserve the right in case the Soviets proceeded. It suggested we seek some kind of agreement with the Soviets and others and mutually renounce the development of the bomb.

Teller, of course, was furious with both GAC reports. What the GAC was saying, he noted, was, "as long as you people work very hard and diligently to make a better bomb you are doing a fine job, but if you succeed in making progress toward another kind of nuclear explosion, you are doing something immoral. To this the scientists at Los Alamos reacted psychologically. They got mad and their attention was turned towards the thermonuclear bomb, not away from it."

What the scientists felt no longer mattered. In the opinion of the State Department's Gordon Arneson, they seemed so spiritually depleted by the consequences of Hiroshima that the politicians were now reluctant to trust their judgment. Acheson later summed up the mood among the creators of the atomic bomb: "Enough evil had been brought into human life, it was argued by men of the highest standing in science, education and government . . . . If the United States with its vast resources proved that such an explosion was possible, others would be bound to press on to find the way for themselves. If no one knew that a way existed, research would be less stimulated. Those who shared this view were, I believed, not so much moved by the power of its logic (which I had never been able to perceive—neither the maintenance of ignorance, nor the reliance upon perpetual goodwill seemed to me a tenable policy) as an immense distaste for what one of them, the purity of whose motives could not be doubted, described as 'the whole rotten business.' "

Acheson understood the politics of the situation. He believed that it was important to keep the decision on the Super and the secret debate out of the newspapers, and he believed that if the issue went to the Congress, the President would be caught, in his words, in a buzz saw. Referring to an idea suggested by the GAC minority—that America could set an example by disarming—he asked, "How can you persuade a paranoid adversary to disarm by example?"

In November and December of 1949 the pressure on Truman increased. Sensing the power shifting to the conservative side, Lilienthal warned the president to watch out for a blitz on the part of the Congress and others on the Super. "I don't blitz easily," Truman answered. Nonetheless there was a need, Truman's closest aides thought, to make a decision as quickly as possible, before the issue became public. If anything, the need to keep the decision secret signaled that the decision was a fait accompli. Fearing the inevitable, Lilienthal noted in his diary: "We keep saying 'We have no other course'; what we should say is 'We are not bright enough to see any other course.' "

In late November the Joint Chiefs, led by Omar Bradley, an officer Truman greatly admired, weighed in. It would be "intolerable" for us to let the Russians get the weapon first. Nor would American restraint stop them, the Chiefs said. Meanwhile in London, Skardon was beginning to close in on Klaus Fuchs. On December 21, 1949, the two men met for the first time. Skardon asked Fuchs to review his personal history, and over a long session, Fuchs complied. When he was finished, Skardon told Fuchs he was suspected of having passed secret information to the Russians. "I don't think so," Fuchs said. They continued to talk at length and Fuchs maintained his innocence, but his belief in his invulnerability was shaken. Skardon continued to press, lightly at first.

On December 30, Skardon visited Fuchs again and told him that in all likelihood he would lose his position at Harwell because of his father's move to East Germany. Since Fuchs had no life other than his work, Skardon was making the case that he might as well confess, since his professional life was over, to all intents and purposes. Clearly, he would feel better having unburdened himself, Skardon was suggesting. On January 10, 1950, John Cockcroft, who was the director at Harwell, told Fuchs that it would be better if he resigned. Three days later, on January 13, Fuchs finally admitted that he had passed atomic secrets to the Soviets. At this point Skardon backed off and let Fuchs stew for a time. Nine days later, Fuchs called up Arnold, the Harwell security officer, and said he was willing to talk. They had lunch the next day, and Fuchs spoke of his unhappiness with current Soviet policies in Eastern Europe, which had turned out to be far more brutal than Fuchs had expected. He also said he wanted to see Skardon again. On January 24, Fuchs admitted to Skardon that for eight years he had spied for the Soviet Union. Gradually, in subsequent meetings, it all came out: how many times he had passed information, what the technical nature of it was. On January 27, Fuchs walked with Skardon to the War Office and dictated a long confession. On February 2, he was arrested and charged.

On January 27, 1950, an atomic expert in the British embassy informed Robert Murphy, the undersecretary of state, of Fuchs's confession. The members of the GAC learned of it on January 30. On January 31, a National Security subcommittee heard rumors of it. Truman apparently heard of it on February 1.

Even before the President learned of Fuchs's arrest, there were signs that the President had made up his mind to go forward with the Super and that Omar Bradley's recommendation had removed any lingering doubts. Truman had formed a special three-man committee, of Acheson, Lilienthal, and Louis Johnson, secretary of defense, to make a final recommendation. January 31 had been set as the date for their report. Truman asked that their recommendations be unanimous, which was, in a way, a signal to Lilienthal to keep his personal doubts within the confines of the group and not to make a dissent. Lilienthal spoke of his fears of an arms race. Acheson countered by pointing out the growing public and political pressures on Truman. Lilienthal again spoke of his own "grave reservations." Truman cut him short. He did not, the President said, believe that an H bomb would ever be used, but because of the way the Russians were behaving, he had no other course. The meeting lasted only seven minutes. "Can the Russians do it?" Truman asked. All three men nodded yes. "In that case," Truman said, "we have no choice. We'll go ahead." It was Truman's first major decision of the decade.

At almost the same time the news broke about Klaus Fuchs. To those who had opposed the Super, it was devastating. On February 2 Lilienthal noted in his diary, "the roof fell in today." Years later someone asked Edward Teller who had been powerful enough to overrule men as influential as the GAC majority. Three men, Teller answered, "Senator Brien McMahon, Lewis Strauss, and Klaus Fuchs." Strauss had understood immediately that the Fuchs case was a lever to be used domestically, and he seized on it to bring the more dovish scientists in on the Super. In particular he tried to bring Hans Bethe back into the fold by showing him some of the memos that the British had sent back about the extent of Fuchs's spying.

Fuchs pleaded guilty at a trial that lasted only an hour and a half. Whereas American authorities in comparable cases tended to magnify the importance of the proceedings, the British minimized publicity, not only because Fuchs's earlier security clearance was an embarrassment, as Robert Williams has noted, but because the very fact that the British were building a bomb might have raised questions publicly.

Fuchs, the most important spy of the atomic era, seemed without remorse or contrition, although he was concerned that his arrest (not his betrayal) might damage the future of the Harwell lab. His arrogance was remarkable. He was unwilling to give a complete confession to Skardon because, he claimed, Skardon did not have a high enough security clearance. His naïveté was equally astonishing. At one point after his arrest, he told Rudolph Peierls, a onetime superior, that "it was always my intention, when I had helped the Russians to take over everything, to get up and tell them what is wrong with their own system."

He was sentenced to fourteen years in prison. He seemed surprised that virtually no one visited him in prison. His name was withdrawn from the Royal Society. He spent nine years sewing mailbags with his fellow prisoners, after which he was released for good behavior. He was smuggled out of England in 1959 and flown to East Berlin. There, he told reporters that he bore no resentment toward England.

In the Soviet Union, as well, the race was on for the thermonuclear bomb. If Fuchs had not been able to supply the Soviets with the exact details for the Super, as he had for the fission bomb, he had nonetheless given them a general road map. The great Soviet physicist Andrei Sakharov had turned down two earlier opportunities to work on the Soviet nuclear project. In 1948 he and his colleague Igor Tamm were summoned to the office of Boris Vannikov, the top apparatchik in the nuclear department. At first Tamm argued against their transferral. Then, as Sakharov recounts in his memoirs, the direct-line telephone from the Kremlin rang. Vannikov picked it up and told the caller that yes, Tamm and Sakharov were in his office at that very moment, arguing against going to the Installation, the secret city in Russia where nuclear research was taking place. There was a pause while Vannikov listened to someone at the other end. "Yes, sir, I'll tell them," he answered, and hung up. "I have just been talking with Lavrenti Pavlovich [Beria, the head of the KGB]. He is *asking* you to accept our request."

Sakharov would later wonder whether it was possible to have greater reservations than he himself had had as he worked on the Soviet project. Among the American scientists, his sympathies, he later noted, were with *both* Teller and Oppenheimer. In the end he, like Oppenheimer, was punished by his own government for political doubts. Yet he could sympathize with Teller on two counts: First, Sakharov felt that when Teller had initially pushed for the Super, his had been a lonely cause, and he was therefore a scientist following his own conscience at the expense of peer approval; second, he believed that Teller's suspicions of Soviet nuclear intentions were absolutely justified: "The Soviet Government (or more properly those in power: Stalin, Beria and company) already understood the potential of the new weapon and nothing could have dissuaded them from going ahead with its development. Any U.S. move towards abandoning or suspending work on a thermonuclear weapon would have been perceived either as a cunning, deceitful maneuver, or as evidence of weakness and stupidity. In any case the Soviet reaction would have been the same: to avoid a possible trap and to exploit the adversary's folly at the earliest opportunity."

As development of the hydrogen bomb proceeded, someone asked Albert Einstein, whose original equations had paved the way to the atomic age, how the Third World War would be fought. Einstein answered glumly that he had no idea what kind of weapons would be used in the Third World War, but he could assure the questioner that the war after that would be fought with stones.

THREE

The McCarthy era was about to begin. Joseph R. McCarthy, Republican senator from Wisconsin, stepped forward on Thursday, February 9, 1950, to lend his name to a phenomenon that, in fact, already existed. He was the accidental demagogue. On that day he gave a speech in Wheeling, West Virginia, as part of a Lincoln Day weekend celebration. Almost casually, he claimed that there were Communists in the State Department and that they controlled American foreign policy. As one of the reporters who knew him well noted later, McCarthy himself had no idea that his speech would prove so explosive. Otherwise, speculated reporter Willard Edwards of the *Chicago Tribune,* he would have taken along at least one of a handful of right-wing reporters who tutored him and helped him write his speeches. Also, he would have picked a bigger town than Wheeling and a more prominent group than the Ohio County Women's Republican Club. His line about Communists in the State Department was a throwaway. In the middle of a speech, he said, "While I cannot take the time to name all the men in the State Department who have been named as members of the Communist Party and members of a spy ring I have here in my hand a list of 205 that were known to the Secretary of State as being members of the Communist Party and who nevertheless are still working and shaping the policy of the State Department." That began it. Frank Desmond, a reporter for *The Wheeling Intelligencer,* put the statement in his story. Later that night, Norman Yost, his managing editor, who worked as a stringer for the Associated Press, read Desmond's story and phoned in a few paragraphs to the AP office in Charlestown. The AP man in Charlestown called Yost back a little later. Was it really *205* Communists? Yost said he would check with Desmond. Yes, Desmond said, 205 was the right figure. The story moved over the AP wire on Thursday night and made the Friday papers. The circus had begun.

From Wheeling, McCarthy flew west to Denver, where he held an airport press conference and said that he would be glad to show them his list of Communists but that it was in his suit which was on the plane (*The Denver Post* ran a photo of McCarthy on page one that day with a cutline that said "Left Commie List In Other Bag"). Then he went to Salt Lake City, where he made new charges. On Saturday morning, he arrived in Reno, where he was to give a speech that night under the auspices of his colleague Nevada republican George (Molly) Malone. Working as a political reporter for the *Reno Gazette* at that time was a young man named Frank McCulloch (later a distinguished reporter and editor for *Time*) and his colleague Edward Olsen of the A.P. They had read the wire stories from Wheeling and Salt Lake and knew something was up. There was a certain vagueness to McCarthy's accusations, and they set out to pin him down. They went to the airport, and McCarthy, whom they had never met before, wrapped his arms around Olsen's and McCulloch's shoulders as if they were old pals he'd played poker with the night before. Senators were supposed to be distant and aloof. McCarthy was not. Everything about his manner implied that the two reporters had passed some kind of men's-club muster. McCarthy and McCulloch, it turned out, were both ex-Marines. That helped them to bond. That afternoon they found McCarthy in Molly Malone's office in the Sierra Pacific Power Building. He was on the phone to his staff. Any other member of the Senate, McCulloch thought, would have thrown them out immediately, but McCarthy seemed pleased to have them there, as if they were part of what was happening. He was very excited, because he was getting names: "That's great, great," he was saying as he wrote down a name. "You gotta give me more names." McCulloch slid around behind the desk, the better to see what McCarthy was writing down. McCarthy made no attempt to block his view. "Howard Shipley," McCarthy wrote, and then, alongside it, the notation "HARVARD ASTR." "I want more names," McCarthy said. "You have to give me more names." He wrote down a few more names. Soon he was off the phone. "What the hell does HARVARD ASTR mean?" McCulloch asked. "A Harvard astrologer," McCarthy answered. Were these men Communists? both reporters asked. "You come to the meeting tonight and you'll find out," McCarthy answered. He gave them a copy of a telegram he was sending to Truman listing fifty-seven people, he claimed, who were either card-carrying Communists or loyal to the Communist party. They stayed there with him for about an hour, questioning him about how many names were on his list and whether they were actually Communists. His answers were less than precise. But it seemed to McCulloch that McCarthy planned to name four Communists that night, and McCulloch wrote a story along that line. Finally, the meeting broke up. McCulloch went to a phone, and though it was a Saturday, he managed to find an official at Harvard. "What do you know about a Professor Howard Shipley?" he asked. "He's a scientist of some kind there." There was a long pause, and the official said that there was no Howard Shipley at Harvard. You've got to have a Howard Shipley, McCulloch insisted. Well, said the official, perhaps there was some confusion over the name because there was a *Harlow Shapley on the Harvard faculty, an astronomer.* Oh, thought McCulloch. I think we have a problem here.

That night they found McCarthy's speech a disturbing performance. The hall was filled and McCarthy knew how to play the crowd, almost, thought McCulloch, how to orchestrate it. He named four people, including Shapley, but neither Olsen nor McCulloch could tell what he was accusing them of. Were they Communists? Were they Communist sympathizers? Were they, in the rather broad phrase he was to use later that night, people who had furthered the purpose of Communism? His words were deliberately vague. (They were only the first among many to find out how hard it was to pin him down. "Talking to Joe was like putting your hands in a bowl of mush," said George Reedy, who covered him for the United Press.) The number, McCulloch noticed, had gone from 205 to 57 to 4. Or had it? The senator's skill, McCulloch sensed, was the ability to imply a great deal more than he was actually saying.

So that night they grabbed him again and went out to the Mapes Hotel, which was then Reno's finest. At the top-floor bar, the three of them drank and argued and drank some more. McCulloch, who as a journalist had seen many men and women who drank heavily, never before or after saw anyone drink so much so quickly. A round of drinks would arrive. A quick argument ensued about whether the number of Communists was 4 or 57. Five minutes later, another set of drinks arrived, followed by more arguments. Were they Communists or men who served the purposes of Communists? Then another round of drinks, all bourbon and water. Well, goddamn, McCarthy was saying. They had heard him—it was simple. Those people out there in the audience hadn't had any trouble understanding him. No, it wasn't that simple, the two journalists argued. They weren't sure what he had actually said. Then they had more drinks. This all took place in the space of perhaps a half hour. "I'm not saying they're Communists," McCarthy said. They were getting noisier now, but noisy in some strange way, filled with good-fellowship. They must, McCulloch later thought, have seemed like three college roommates at a reunion. There was no antagonism on McCarthy's part, even as Olsen kept badgering him. McCarthy had promised earlier in the day to produce the evidence. Where was it? McCarthy dug into his pockets looking for his lists. He could find no list. Suddenly, McCarthy accused them of stealing his lists. More arguing followed, as did more drinks. Charley Mapes, owner of the Mapes, materialized and told them if they did not hold it down, they were going to have to leave. Getting thrown out of the best hotel in Reno was not easy, McCulloch thought. A few more drinks followed. No names were produced. McCulloch left that night sure that it was a con, that McCarthy did not care at all about Communists. It was all a show, but one thing was real—the desire to be a pal. McCarthy loved the good-fellowship that being a celebrity produced, and he was, McCulloch decided, brilliant at creating an aura of instant friendship.

McCarthy's carnival-like four-year spree of accusations, charges, and threats touched something deep in the American body politic, something that lasted long after his own recklessness, carelessness, and boozing ended his career in shame. McCarthyism crystallized and politicized the anxieties of a nation living in a dangerous new era. He took people who were at the worst guilty of political naïveté and accused them of treason. He set out to do the unthinkable, and it turned out to be surprisingly thinkable.

The problem with America, he was saying, was domestic subversion, as tolerated and encouraged by the Democratic party. China had fallen, not because the forces of history were against the old feudal regime, which was collapsing of its own weight. Rather, it was because of Soviet military and political hegemony. If events in the world were not as we wanted them, then something conspiratorial had happened. No matter that most of his closest colleagues, isolationists all, had voted against varying foreign-aid bills, had rushed to cut back American standing-troop levels, and under no circumstance wanted to send troops to fight in Asia. It was a rare free shot in politics. His message was simple: The Democrats were soft on Communism. With that, he changed the nature of American politics. Our control of events was limited because sinister forces were at work against us.

Democrats would spend the next thirty years proving that they were not soft on Communism, and that they would not lose a country to the Communists. Eleven years after McCarthy's censure by the Senate, Lyndon Johnson would talk to his closest political aides about the McCarthy days, of how Truman lost China and then the Congress and the White House, and how, by God, Johnson was not going to be the President who lost Vietnam and then the Congress and the White House.

McCarthy was, in Richard Rovere's phrase, the political speculator who found his gusher. He was perfectly positioned by dint of his own roots and his constituency: He was an Irish Catholic, who had been urged to take up the issue by an official at Georgetown University, and he had a large German-American population in his home state of Wisconsin, where much of the population accepted the world as defined by the oracle of the region—Colonel Robert McCormick, publisher of the *Chicago Tribune.* When some criticism of McCarthy's attacks began to grow, naturally enough in the East, John Riedl, the managing editor of the *Appleton* (Wisconsin) *Post Crescent,* said, "We don't want a group of New Yorkers and Easterners to tell us whom we are going to send to the Senate. That is our business and it is none of theirs."

McCarthy was shrewd, insecure, and defensive—the poor Irish kid from the wrong side of the tracks in Appleton, Wisconsin, who fought his way out and made it to the Senate. He liked to boast of himself as a back-alley fighter. Others touched the same raw nerve at the same time, but it was McCarthy who had the instincts, the intuition, and perfect pitch to know how to exploit the issue best. He had a wonderful sense of the resentments that existed just beneath the surface in ordinary people, for he himself burned with those same resentments. Class distinctions were critical; he hated the social snobbery, implied or real, in men like Acheson and Hiss. They often seemed more important to him than the issue of Communism. In one of his first speeches after Wheeling, he hammered away at those "bright young men with silver spoons in their mouths." In fact, anti-Communism was peripheral. He had few names of his own: Essentially, he was being fed covertly by Hoover and the FBI. The names, by and large, tended to be fellow travelers from the thirties.

McCarthy was a serious drinker who soon turned into a full-fledged alcoholic. He would gulp down a water glass filled with Scotch in one swallow and then chase it with bicarbonate of soda. As his drinking escalated he would eat a quarter-pound stick of butter, which he claimed helped him hold his liquor. He was, said his old friend from Appleton, Ed Hart, "the town drunk in businessman's clothes."

The alcohol masked massive insecurities. He was almost pathetically eager to please. He loved nothing more than being one of the boys. After berating vulnerable witnesses during the day, he could not wait to go out and be the reporters' pal as they all went out to dinner. It was as if this were all a game and they were in it together. "If you want to be against McCarthy, boys," he told two reporters at an impromptu press conference, "you've got to be a Communist or a cocksucker." Then he roared with laughter. He seemed bothered when reporters kept him at a distance, not participating in the good-fellowship of the tour. He loved to call up his old friends in Wisconsin and, using the operator as a go-between, ask if they would accept a collect call from Dean Acheson in Washington. "He was," said Senator Paul Douglas, who, like many others, was attacked by him viciously and then immediately befriended as if nothing had happened, "like a mongrel dog, fawning over you one moment and the next moment trying to bite your leg off."

He had a talent for imagining conspiracy and subversion. Others, like Bill Jenner of Indiana, had tried it in the past but failed. McCarthy understood the theater of it all, and he was for a brief time a marvelous actor. He knew instinctively how to brush aside the protests of his witnesses, how to humiliate vulnerable, scared people. In the end, he produced little beyond fear and headlines. After a thousand speeches and a thousand charges, the last thing in the world he could probably have recognized was a real Communist or a real spy ring. Perhaps the best epitaph for him came during the Eisenhower years, when he made his fateful and fatal attack on the United States Army, coming up in the end with one left-wing dentist who had been promoted by mistake. The Republican senator Ralph Flanders said contemptuously, "He dons his war paint. He goes into his war dance. He emits war whoops. He goes forth to battle and proudly returns with the scalp of a pink dentist."

The real scandal in all this was the behavior of the members of the Washington press corps, who, more often than not, knew better. They were delighted to be a part of his traveling road show, chronicling each charge and then moving on to the next town, instead of bothering to stay behind to follow up. They had little interest in reporting how careless he was or how little it all meant to him. It was news and he was news; that was all that mattered. "McCarthy was a dream story," said Willard Edwards, of the *Chicago Tribune.* "I wasn't off page one for four years." Edwards, with his paper's permission, helped supply names, did research for speeches, and even wrote drafts of some speeches. Rarely did reporters make McCarthy produce evidence. Rarely, in the beginning, did they challenge him. Once at a press conference in Madison, Miles McMillin, a columnist and an editorial writer on the *Journal,* a paper that had taken on McCarthy, rose to ask him to name names. "You've charged that there are Communists at the *Journal,*" McMillin said. "Name one." McCarthy remained silent. The silence continued. At the press table Art Bystrom, an AP reporter and a friend of McCarthy, said, "Come on, let's get on with it." "Shut up!" Bob Fleming, another *Journal* reporter, told Bystrom. "I'm not going to answer that question if we sit here all day," McCarthy said. So the reporters sat there for fifteen minutes of silence, until McCarthy got up and left the room.

He was particularly skillful at making charges in smaller towns, where the local AP representative would pick it up and use it and it would become news even if it was not the truth. After all, a senator had said it. He knew how to use the mechanics of the journalists' profession against them; he knew their deadlines, when they were hungriest and needed to be fed, and when they had the least time to check out his charges. George Reedy, who had to cover him for the United Press and thus had to match many an AP story, found the experience so odious that he decided to get out of journalism. "Joe couldn't find a Communist in Red Square—he didn't know Karl Marx from Groucho—but he was a United States Senator," Reedy said. He was nothing if not obliging: He had signals for the regulars to let them know there was a reception/press conference, with whiskey, in his room later, or that he wanted to go out with them for dinner. If they needed a story, he was always willing to give them a charge or two. If they wanted to know what the Republican leadership was thinking on other issues, he was perfectly willing to call Bob Taft from his office and ask him a few questions while reporters listened in on an open receiver.

There was no coherent plan to his work. At one point, a New

York publisher called Murrey Marder of *The Washington Post* to ask him to write a book about McCarthy's secret plan to become President. "Joe," Marder answered, "doesn't have a plan about who he's going to have lunch with tomorrow. He never has any plans." It was a relentless search for headlines; every day there had to be a new charge, a new accusation.

Nor was McCarthy alone. The Republican reactionaries had been arriving in Washington for some time; some, like McCarthy, had come to the Senate in the class of '46, and others in 1948. But because of McCarthy's success with red-baiting, the 1950 election was particularly ugly. Senator Millard Tydings of Maryland, a Democratic patrician, had dared to go after McCarthy. Tydings, using a subcommittee of the Senate Foreign Relations Committee, investigated McCarthy's charges and called them a "hoax and a fraud . . . an attempt to inflame the American people with a wave of hysteria and fear on an unbelievable scale." Tydings paid with his Senate seat; McCarthy went after him with money from Texas oilmen, and he was successful.

In Florida, George Smathers beat his mentor, Senator Claude Pepper, in an unbelievably ugly primary: "Joe [Stalin] likes him and he likes Joe," said Smathers. In California, Richard Nixon, who studied Smathers's race against Pepper, defeated Congresswoman Helen Gahagan Douglas in a campaign that was virtually a case study in red-baiting. Even in New York in an unsuccessful Senate race against Herbert Lehman, John Foster Dulles said of his opponent: "I know he is no Communist, but I also know that the Communists are in his corner and that he and not I will get the 500,000 Communist votes that last year went to Henry Wallace in this state." In Illinois, Everett Dirksen defeated Senator Scott Lucas, promising to clean house on Communists and fellow travelers. The Republicans had found their issue and the Democrats were clearly on the defensive.

"The primitives," Dean Acheson called them. Truman was blunter: "The animals," he branded them. They were the Midwestern and Far Western isolationists who were eager to exploit the issue of domestic Communism. With the fall of Chiang they had their red meat. They included: Knowland of California, who would later so exasperate Eisenhower that the President claimed he confounded the age-old question "How stupid can you get?"; Mundt of Indiana, who, after a friend of Hiss's apparently committed suicide by jumping out a window, answered a reporter's request for more names of Communists by answering, "We'll name them as they jump out of windows"; Hugh Butler of Nebraska, who told his supporters in 1946, "If the New Deal is still in control of Congress after the election it will owe that control to the Communist Party"; Bill Jenner of Indiana, who called George Marshall a traitor and charged when Truman fired MacArthur that "this country is in the hands of a secret inner coterie which is directed by Agents of the Soviet Union"; Bricker of Ohio, voted the worst senator in the same poll; Wherry of Nebraska, famous for such bloopers as referring to Vietnam as "Indigo China"; and Welke of Idaho, who fancied himself a professional-baseball scout and maintained that he had never met a ball player who was a Communist. That such men rallied to McCarthy was not surprising. What *was* surprising was that perhaps the most elegant and principled Republican in the Senate, Robert Taft, bent during the early months of McCarthyism.

It sometimes seemed during that period that there were two Tafts—one the thoughtful conservative who was uneasy with the coming of America the superpower and its growing obsession with anti-Communism. That Taft had voted against NATO and other programs that were part of the effort to check the Soviets in Europe. In his speeches, he systematically downplayed the Soviet military threat, and he often scolded the administration for inflated rhetoric about the Communist danger, which he said was provocative to the Russians. He feared the dynamic of the Cold War would turn America into the policeman of the world, transforming it from a democracy to an imperial power, a role, he believed, for which we were ill suited.

Then there was the other Taft, who could exploit the fall of China and attack the administration for being soft on Communism. He spoke of sending the Navy to help Chiang and of giving military aid in China as he would not in Europe. Slowly, he came to use the issue of domestic subversion. He referred to people in the State Department who were "liquidating" the Chinese Nationalists, and he said that State "was guided by a left-wing group who have obviously wanted to get rid of Chiang and were willing at least to turn China over to the Communists for that purpose." He voted against confirmation of George Marshall as secretary of defense.

For men like Taft the use of the Communist issue was a way of gaining some revenge after years in which the Democrats had portrayed Republican domestic policies as cold and heartless. Taft himself had been the target of unusually cruel assaults, which portrayed him as a pawn of the rich.

Two pieces of literature used against Taft were particularly nasty. One was a booklet mocking his life. Supposedly, as a small boy in the Philippines, he had been stung by a jellyfish. "This too," went the book, "must have made a deep impression on Taft. It may have been the start of his fear, distrust and dislike of all foreigners, of immigrants, of all things that are not demonstrably third generation American." That set the general tone.

In addition, labor did a comic book entitled, "The Robert Alphonso Taft Story." One and a half million copies were printed. It portrayed Taft as the spoiled child of the rich, a weak, unpopular boy, poor at athletics, who never had to work and ended up serving the rich, particularly a fat, greedy man named J. Phineas Moneybags. It was the crudest kind of propaganda, and characterized the political-economic undercurrents of the time. Even a genuine conservative intellectual was viewed as an evil cartoon figure by the left, while the right saw the New Deal merely as a front for Communism.

Taft was hardly unaware of the pact with the devil he forged when he sided with McCarthy. The liberal columnist Doris Fleeson criticized Taft for that support, and he berated her and other columnists for making too much of McCarthy. She was stunned by his rage: "You smear me and try to destroy me. . . . There are 96 Senators. Why pick on me?" It was a low moment in an otherwise highly principled career.

Economic conservative he might have been, but he had always been a good man on civil liberties. The Wheeling speech had caught Taft by surprise—McCarthy was not a man to clear his speeches with anyone—and he was not entirely pleased by it. Nevertheless he saw its value: Domestic subversion was a hot issue, and it *worked* for the Republicans. If McCarthy had found no Communists, he should not despair, Taft advised. He should "keep talking and if one case doesn't work out, he should proceed with another one," he added. Despite private doubts, which he expressed to a few close friends and his family, his public support gradually became clear. McCarthy, he said, was like "a fighting marine who risked his life to preserve the liberties of the United States. The greatest Kremlin asset in our history has been the pro-Communist group in the State Department who surrendered to every demand of Russia at Yalta and Potsdam, and promoted at every opportunity the Communist cause in China until today Communism threatens to take over all of Asia."

As far as such men as Acheson were concerned, he had joined the "primitives." Acheson later liked to joke about the awkward ballet that Taft would go through in order not to have his photograph taken next to him at Yale Corporation meetings. Old friends were sure that he was uneasy with his new course, that he took no pleasure in it. But, as Rovere later wrote, Taft confronted McCarthy like an alcoholic fighting the bottle: It was bad but irreversible.

America's obsession with the Cold War was so great that it finally convinced Mike Hammer to stop chasing the garden variety of gangsters and corrupt pols and concentrate instead on stopping domestic Communist subversion. Hammer was the toughest guy in pulp fiction, the creation of a writer named Mickey Spillane, whose phenomenal success heralded a vast change in the economics of book publishing. Spillane's virtually instantaneous success at once titillated and terrified the world of genteel hardback-book publishers. When Spillane's first book, *I, the Jury,* was accepted at Dutton, the editor warned his superior, "It isn't in the best of taste but it will sell." Spillane sold reasonably well in hardcover, 15,000 copies at his best (or, as someone once noted, about 3,000 copies a dead body). His real success came in his paperback sales, which averaged between 2.5 and 3 million on his first six books.

The formula was straight out of pulp fiction from the twenties and thirties: a lot of action and, of course, violence, all the dialogue spoken in tough-guy vernacular, and a lot of tantalizing sexual innuendo. Hammer was a straight, honest private eye who had soured on a real world of corrupt cops, cruddy DAs, and judges who had sold out. He was the avenger, the man who took justice into his own hands, a man who, in the words of Kenneth Davis, author of a book on the paperback revolution, *Two-Bit Culture,* "shot first and asked questions later."

Even a beautiful woman couldn't stop Hammer's patented brand of trigger-happy justice. At first Mike is enchanted by Charlotte, the villain of *I, the Jury* ("Okay, minx, will you marry me?" "Oh, Mike, yes. Yes, I love you so much"). Would there be nuptials? Not bloody likely, as Charlotte is revealed as the killer. When Hammer confronts her in the final scene, she is not above using her physical charms to dissuade him from his sworn duty. Hammer does hesitate: "Charlotte. Charlotte the beautiful. Charlotte the lovely, Charlotte who loved dogs and walked people's babies in the park. Charlotte whom you wanted to crush in your arms and feel the wetness of her lips. Charlotte of the body that was fire and life and soft velvet and responsiveness. Charlotte the killer."

Sensing that she's having an effect on Hammer, Charlotte unzips her skirt and lets it drop to the floor to reveal "transparent panties. And she was a real blonde." But he is not a man to be put off even by a beautiful woman. There will be no trial, he tells her, no jury. "No, Charlotte, I'm the jury now, and the judge, and I have a promise to keep. Beautiful as you are, as much as I almost loved you, I sentence you to death."

But Charlotte has one more move. *"Her thumbs hooked in the fragile silk of the panties and pulled them down. She stepped out of them as delicately as one coming from a bathtub. She was completely naked now, a suntanned goddess giving herself to her lover . . ."* She leans forward to kiss Mike. But Mike is not one to let a beautiful woman stand between him and justice. Kaboom. He draws and fires his .45. "Her eyes were a symphony of incredulity, an unbelieving witness to truth. Slowly she looked down at the ugly swelling in her naked belly where the bullet went in. A thin trickle of blood welled out." As Charlotte dies, she asks Mike one last question: " 'How c-could you?' I only had a moment before talking to a corpse, but I got it in. 'It was easy,' I said."

With that, a hungry audience could hardly wait for the next Spillane/Hammer. Out they came, as if mass-produced, sometimes more than one a year: *My Gun Is Quick* and *Vengeance Is Mine* in 1950, *The Big Kill* and *One Lonely Night* (and *The Long Wait*, not a Mike Hammer book, but featuring a detective who was clearly a Hammer doppelganger) in 1951, and *Kiss Me Deadly* in 1952. Spillane was nothing less than a one-man literary industry. Terry Southern noted that in 1956, when Alice Payne Hackett wrote her informative book *Sixty Years of Best Sellers,* of the ten best-selling fiction titles in American publishing, seven were by Spillane—a remarkable feat, and even more remarkable when one considered that at the time Spillane had written only seven books.

There were probably many reasons for Spillane's incredible success. Certainly, the price was seductive—25 cents at first, slipping up to 50 cents by the early fifties—and the covers tended to showcase busty young women either in the process of taking off their clothes or, clearly, from the looks on their faces, about to take them off. Victor Weybright, the chief editor at New American Library, Spillane's publisher, explained his appeal this way: "The Spillane books are a unique form of 'Americana,' a new kind of folklore . . ." And it was no insignificant reflection of the times that Mike Hammer soon starting taking on Communists instead of gangsters: "They were Commies. . . . They were real sons of bitches who should have died long ago. . . . They never thought there were people like me in this country." Kenneth Davis went so far as to call Hammer a reflection of the McCarthyite soul of the country, "the ultimate cold warrior, an Übermensch for frightened Americans who had heard tales of baby-eating Stalinists. Hammer's methods went beyond loyalty oaths, smears, and blacklisting. The evil of the Communists was battled with the only weapons Hammer possessed: a blast from his forty-five, a kick that shattered bone on impact, strangulation by Hammer's meaty hands."

Certainly, the critics hated him. James Sandoe of the *Herald Tribune* called him "an inept vulgarian." Malcolm Cowley in the *New Republic* called him a dangerous paranoid, sadist, and masochist. Even his own editors seemed a little uneasy with him. Victor Weybright liked to tell reporters that too much was made of the Spillane phenomenon. Such critical salvos did not burden Spillane, who liked to say that he did not care about the critics and that the only critics who mattered were his readers. He thought the literary world was made up of second-rate writers who wrote about other second-rate writers. It was a world of the Losers. "The Losers?" Terry Southern asked him. "The guys who didn't make it," he answered, "the guys nobody ever heard of." Why, asked Southern, would others want to write about Losers? "Because they can be condescending about the Losers. You know, they can afford to say something *nice* about them. You see, these articles are usually written *by* Losers—frustrated writers. And these writers resent success. So naturally they never have anything good to say about the Winners." "Is it hard to be a Winner?" Southern asked. "No, anybody can be a Winner—all you have to do is make sure you're not a Loser," he answered.

FOUR

I t was a war that no one wanted, in a desolate, harsh land. The same policymakers who decreed the necessity for fighting there had only months before declared it of little strategic value and outside our defense perimeter. "If the best minds in the world had set out to find us the worst possible location in the world to fight this damnable war, politically and militarily, the unanimous choice would have been Korea," Dean Acheson once told the writer Joseph Goulden. "A sour little war," Averell Harriman once called it. South Korea became important only after the North Korean Communists struck in the night; its value was psychological rather than strategic—the enemy had crossed a border.

At the beginning of the century, Korea was conquered by Japan and forced to live under a brutal occupation. At one point during the war Franklin Roosevelt spoke almost carelessly of a free and independent Korea after the war; at Yalta there was talk of a trusteeship to be administered by the Big Four. At Potsdam in July 1945, American strategists still thought the final battle against Japan would be difficult and pressed Stalin to help. Having stayed outside the Pacific war for four years, Stalin was delighted to be a part of the denouement. Who could have resisted a chance to gain so much for so little? But the successful use of the atomic weapon changed American thinking. Now we had no need of the Russians in the Far East. Within twenty-four hours of Hiroshima, planners in Washington were redefining America's position in Korea. Even as the Soviet troops, poised in Manchuria, were moving into the northern part of that country, word came down from the War Department to create some sort of division in Korea between the Communist and non-Communist forces. Available American troops were scarce, our physical position, compared to that of the Russians, was hardly enviable, and time was of the essence. Perhaps the entire country would be Stalin's for the taking, if not for the asking. On August 10, 1945, late at night, John J. McCloy, the assistant secretary of war, told two young colonels in the War Office to come up with some sort of demarcation line. The two colonels—Dean Rusk and Charles Bonesteel—studied a schoolboy map of Korea. They noticed a line running across the country at the relatively narrow neck near the midpoint. It was the 38th parallel. Through a procedure slightly more sophisticated than throwing darts at a map, Rusk and Bonesteel suggested this as the dividing line. It was, Rusk thought, a rather risky gambit—that is, if the Russians rejected it and their troops continued to push south aggressively, there was little the Americans could do to hold the line. An offer was made to the Russians, and somewhat to our surprise, they accepted. The first American units did not arrive in the South for another month.

Nothing seemed to show how unprepared America was for its new expanded postwar role than the occupation of Korea. We had no area experts to guide us in those early, awkward days. Wary of all the Korean groups suddenly competing for our attention, we used the existing Japanese colonial administration at first, much to the dismay of the Koreans, who hoped to be liberated from the colonials. Unfortunately, when we finally turned to the Koreans, it was often to those who had collaborated with the Japanese. The first American commander, Major General John Hodge, took an immediate dislike to the people. They were, he said, "the same breed of cat as the Japanese."

Hodge's view seemed to reflect that of most Americans. When

Hodge tried to interest his commander, Douglas MacArthur, in visiting Korea, MacArthur preferred to remain in his imperial splendor as governor general of Japan. "Use your best judgment as to what action is to be taken," he cabled Hodge. "I am not sufficiently familiar with the local situation to advise you intelligently but I will support you in whatever decision you take in this matter." Hodge was so irritated that he tried to transfer out, but MacArthur refused to allow it.

When another American general was told that his next assignment was to head the American advisory group training the South Korean army, he retired from active service. In those days Japan was a poor nation just beginning to pull itself up from the total disaster of the war, but duty there was considered a sweet tour by American soldiers: American dollars went far, the Japanese women were friendly, and ordinary enlisted men lived like aristocrats, sometimes employing two servants. By contrast most Americans who served in Korea in the postwar period remember the lack of amenities, the terrible heat in the summer, the unbearable cold in the winter, and above all the ubiquitous foul smell of human fecal matter, which the farmers used for fertilizer. Night soil, it was called.

In December 1949, the British Foreign Office asked the War Office for a military assessment of Korea. Major J. E. Ferguson Innes wrote back that North Korea was far stronger than South Korea. "[r]egarding American policy," he added, "if in fact one exists, towards South Korea, I can only say we know little, and of their future intentions, even less . . ." In late 1947, George Kennan, the most brilliant American strategist of the era, saw Korea as a singularly hopeless place: "Its political life in the coming period is bound to be dominated by political immaturity, intolerance, and violence. Where such conditions prevail, the communists are in their element. Therefore we cannot count on native forces to help hold the line against Soviet expansion. Since the territory is not of decisive strategic importance to us, our main task is to extricate ourselves without too great a loss of prestige." Yet we stayed.

Eventually, we created a government in the South, headed by Syngman Rhee, a volatile, manipulative figure, whose main appeal to us was that he had spent most of his life in exile in America. He spoke good English, had three degrees from American universities, and since he had been out of the country for most of his life, he had not collaborated with the Japanese. He was one of the early postwar, anti-Communist dictators, with an instinctive tendency to arrest almost anyone who did not agree with him. Only by comparison with his counterpart in the North, Kim Il Sung, did he gain: Sung not only arrested his enemies; he frequently had them summarily executed. Though Rhee, by dint of his intense anti-Communism, had something of a political base in the American Congress, no one who dealt with him directly, either in Washington or Seoul, seemed to like him, certainly not the people at State or Defense. He made them particularly nervous by constantly boasting of his desire to roll back the 38th parallel and rule the entire country. As we were desperately cutting back our military forces, the 30,000 American troops assigned to Korea seemed a disproportionate number to many. General Hodge pushed constantly for the removal of combat troops (most significantly, including himself). By the fall of 1948 we struck a deal with the Russians: We would both withdraw our regular troops, in effect leaving behind proxy armies. At Rhee's request, we left one regimental combat team until June 1949. Our role was to be solely advisory and Rhee's troops were to become combat-ready; but because of Rhee's jingoism and his constant threats to strike above the 38th parallel, we deliberately limited his forces, minimizing his air power and tanks.

As such, our ambivalence remained. We seemed to want no part of the country, and yet we had planted the flag. Deigning to come to Seoul to participate in Rhee's inauguration, MacArthur told Rhee with casual but typical grandiosity, "If Korea should ever be attacked by the Communists, I will defend it as I would California." That being said, America was rapidly withdrawing from South Korea, leaving only an advisory mission behind. We were leaving behind something of an unloved and unattractive government with a new, uncertain ragtag army; the Soviets, by contrast, were leaving behind the real thing: a tough, modern dictatorship with a strong, well-trained, well-armed military force. Unlike Rhee, who was the candidate of the upper class in a nation with few aristocrats, Kim Il Sung was the outsider who hated aristocrats and colonialists. His father had been a schoolteacher who moved his family to Manchuria to escape the Japanese. Kim joined the Young Communist League of East Manchuria while barely a teenager and spent most of his life fighting the Japanese with various Communist guerrilla bands. He eventually became a leader of the guerrilla forces in the northern reaches of Korea and also, it was said, commanded a group of one of the two Korean units that fought alongside the Russians at Stalingrad. He held the Order of Lenin, awarded by Stalin himself. When the Russians moved into the North, he was their obvious choice. At first he was a popular figure, for it was widely known that he had devoted his life to fighting the hated Japanese. That popularity would diminish as the harshness and cruelty of his rule became apparent.

With the aid of the Soviets, he created the North Korean People's Army, or In Min Gun. It was composed of ten divisions, some 135,000 men; its commanders were, more often than not, Koreans who had fought along with the Chinese Communists during their historic defeat of Chiang's army. Most importantly, the Russians left behind about 150 T-34 tanks, one of the most effective weapons against the Germans in World War Two.

Rhee was not the only Korean leader who boasted he would conquer the entire peninsula; Kim Il Sung was every bit as audacious. In the fall of 1949, his boasts escalated. A nervous Rhee pushed the Americans for an expanded army and more hardware; but the Americans, suspicious of Rhee's real intentions, refused. In late 1949 and in the early months of 1950 there was an increasing number of border clashes, almost all of them initiated by the North, whose forces seemed to be probing the Republic of Korea's (ROK) positions. Reports of an imminent North Korean invasion began coming back to American intelligence officers in Seoul. Those reports proved true on the night of June 25. Why Kim Il Sung chose to invade the South no one has ever been entirely sure. Certainly, he was contemptuous of the leaders of the South and their army. There is some evidence he was encouraged by both the Soviets and the Chinese (in his memoirs, Khrushchev noted that Kim had promised Stalin a quick victory), and it seems that Mao told Kim the Americans would not intervene. Certainly, a statement made by Dean Acheson at the National Press Club in January 1950 left Korea out of the American defensive perimeter in Asia. "Dean really blew it on that one," Averell Harriman said years later. That particular speech greatly escalated the tension between the Truman administration and the far right, though, ironically, not because of what the secretary said or did not say about Korea. Rather, the problem was the cool disdain with which Acheson dismissed the hero of the right, Chiang Kai-shek. When World War Two ended, Acheson pointed out, Chiang had possessed the greatest military power of any ruler in Chinese history, and he was fighting an ill-equipped, irregular force. Four years later his army had melted away, the secretary continued, and he was a refugee on a small island. To attribute his monumental failure to inadequate foreign support was to miscalculate entirely what had happened. "[The Chinese people] had not overthrown the government. There was nothing to overthrow. They had simply ignored it," he said. This may have been the truth, but it was impolitic, to say the least, and Acheson was not lightly forgiven for saying it.

Even as tensions mounted along the Korean border, our own army continued to deteriorate from its wartime prime. Not only was the army's size diminished, its equipment was outdated and it had lost a high percentage of its elite troops. To Omar Bradley, it could not "fight its way out of a paper bag." By the end of the Berlin crisis in 1948, it was down to 677,000 men, or ten divisions. In January 1949, Dwight Eisenhower came to Washington as the likely head of the new Joint Chiefs of Staff. He had wanted a budget of $14.4 billion. When Truman offered him the chairmanship, though, Ike turned it down, because he did not think he could live with the $12.3 billion budget. The Truman defense budget, Cabell Phillips wrote in *The New York Times,* had cut "bone and sinew along with the fat."

After Ike turned down the job, Truman offered it to Bradley, who reluctantly accepted it. By May 1949 the standing army was down to 630,000 men. Thirteen months later, in June 1950, due to the general desire to bring the boys home, conservative Republican wariness of intervention, and Truman's own fiscal conservatism, the army consisted of only 591,000 men. The American Century was about to begin, but clearly no one wanted to pay for it. A certain schizophrenia was at work here: We wanted to be the policemen of the world, particularly in Asia, but we certainly did not want to get involved in messy, costly foreign wars. As Acheson once noted, the foreign policy of the United States in those years immediately after the war could be summed up in three sentences: "1. Bring the boys home; 2. Don't be Santa Claus; 3. Don't be pushed around."

Curiously, the Republican right represented the last vestige of isolationism in America. Its members were not so much in favor of stronger American involvement in Asia (for no one had wanted to send American boys to save Chiang) as they were against America's traditionally strong ties to Western Europe, now stronger than ever. In general, they preferred the Pacific to the Atlantic, Asia to Europe. They certainly preferred China (a smiling, happy, and, above all, obedient China) to England (supercilious, snobbish, with its fancy airs and ways). The Pacific, Arthur Schlesinger and Richard Rovere wrote, was their favorite ocean, precisely because it was not the Atlantic, which was the internationalist's ocean (and which connected America to England). In this century, they noted, the Pacific "has become the Republican ocean."

Their attitudes toward Asia were rooted not so much in contemporary realities as in missionary daydreams. Serious study of the complexity of a postwar pluralistic world was not their strong point. As Chiang collapsed of his own weight and his own corruption, Senator Styles Bridges of New Hampshire, a leader in what was to be known as the China Lobby, had announced, "China asked for a sword, and we gave her a dull paring knife." Truman was already on the defensive from assaults about his weakness on Communism made by the Republican right wing. To any objective observer, America had emerged from the war rich and more powerful than ever, its industrial base, unlike that of Europe, undamaged. But to the right-wingers, isolated from much of the real pain caused by the war and dissatisfied with the peace that followed, there was a sense of betrayal.

Thus the North Korean thrust across the 38th parallel stunned a nation whose rhetoric and defense policies were in no way in synch: the rhetoric was grandiose, the policies were minimalist. Despite all the warnings no one was prepared for the assault, or for the toughness of the In Min Gun. As the North Korean forces made their first overt border crossing, the panic was on. The assault consisted of ten divisions, moving in four major thrusts. Many of the top commanders had fought with Mao during the Long March. The elite troops leading the advance were highly disciplined and easily smashed through the relatively frail ROK defenses. The real difference, though, was the Russian T-34 tanks. They had a broad tread, heavy armor plating, and a low silhouette, and they carried one 85 mm gun and two 7.62 machine guns. They had first been used in July 1941 against the German forces advancing on Moscow, and General Heinz Guderian, the famed German panzer commander, had credited them with stopping his drive. Now they were at the head of a long, well-armed column moving against soldiers who had no weapons with which to stop them.

The American advisers in South Korea, in their determination to do with public relations what they could not do on the training ground, had earlier called the South Korean Army the best for its size in Asia, but the truth was a great deal less than that. Faced by the awesome force of the elite units of In Min Gun, it broke and ran. Chaos reigned in Seoul. The bridge over the Han River, which cuts through Seoul and constitutes a natural barrier, was blown before the ROK Army had a chance to retreat. More than five hundred people were on the bridge when it was detonated. By June 28 Seoul had fallen. When Douglas MacArthur arrived in Korea on June 29, landing at Suwon, a small airfield twenty miles south of Seoul, he was stunned by the sight of long lines of South Korean troops retreating, most of them without their weapons. "I did not," said MacArthur angrily, "see a wounded man among them."

The news that the North Koreans had struck stunned the Truman administration. In Washington, Communism was seen as a monolith, and therefore it was assumed the invasion was something that Stalin had decided on. The question therefore was what would the Communists do next, not in Korea, but in the world. Truman, reflecting the fears of many, noted in his diary, "It looks like World War III is here—I hope not—but we must meet whatever comes—and we will." When Lt. Gen. Matthew Ridgway saw the first cables about the North Korean attack, he wondered to himself if this might be "the beginning of World War III . . . Armageddon, the last great battle between East and West."

Truman made up his mind from the start: He would contest the Communists in Korea. "We are going to *fight*," he told his daughter, Margaret. "By God I am not going to let them have it," he told another aide. Almost all his top aides felt the same way: This was the first chance to show that they had learned the lessons of Munich. Probably no one reflected the mood of the national security-military complex better than Omar Bradley, a man not given to hasty rhetoric. Bradley termed the invasion a "moral outrage." If we gave in, he said, it would be appeasement. We had to draw the line somewhere, and Korea "offered as good an occasion for drawing the line as anywhere else."

Drawing the line in Korea was to be one of the few things Truman and MacArthur would agree on. Almost immediately, MacArthur, as was his want, exceeded his authority by ordering the bombing of North Korean airfields. He thought of himself as a sovereign power in the Pacific; the President and Joint Chiefs had hegemony in Europe, in his mind, but not in Asia. That was his. Essentially he believed himself above the authority of his commander in chief. But bombing would not stop the North Korean drive. On June 30, after returning from his personal inspection of the South, MacArthur reported that the South Korean Army was retreating in complete chaos. The only way to hold the line against the North was to introduce American troops. He requested two divisions and one regimental combat team for immediate deployment. In Washington Joe Collins, the Army Chief of Staff, received the fateful cable to send American ground troops to the mainland of Asia. He did not even bother to summon the rest of the Joint

Chiefs. He called MacArthur and told him his request needed presidential approval, but in the meantime he had permission to move a regimental combat team to Pusan. MacArthur demanded a clearer mandate, without delay. By then it was 5 A.M., June 30, in Washington. Truman was already up and the secretary of the army, Frank Pace, called to brief him. Truman immediately approved the use of the Reserve Combat Team (RCT), postponing a decision on more troops. But essentially the deed was done and, without congressional approval: Americans would fight in South Korea. Later that morning the Joint Chiefs met to discuss the rest of the commitment. No one dissented over giving MacArthur the two additional divisions. Events were taking over; no one wanted to go ahead, but as Bradley later noted, "in a sense it was unavoidable and inevitable." A little later the Chiefs met with Truman at Blair House. To their surprise, Truman said that America should not limit MacArthur to two divisions but should send whatever was needed. Indeed, at that meeting Truman noted that he already had an offer from Chiang of 33,000 Nationalist troops, which he was inclined to accept. Acheson, wary of both the quality of the troops and the implications of the offer, quickly suggested we decline, as it might lead to an expanded war.

Initially, Truman tried to downplay the commitment. At a meeting with reporters, he said, "We are not at war." A reporter, searching for a way to describe the commitment, asked the President if it was a "police action." The President, in a moment he would later regret, noted that yes, that was an apt description. Of the American troops ordered to Korea from Japan, only the elite 82nd Airborne was combat-ready. The rest were occupation troops, grown soft from easy duty. According to General William Dean, who commanded them in early days in Korea, they had become "fat and happy in occupation billets, complete with Japanese girlfriends, plenty of beer and servants to shine their boots." These were not the same battle-hardened troops who had swept across the Pacific and defeated elite Japanese units in an endless series of bitter struggles in tiny island outposts. Fewer than one in six had seen combat; many had been lured into service after the war by recruiting officers promising an ideal way to get out of small-town America and see the world. "They had enlisted," wrote one company commander, T. R. Fehrenbach, "for every reason known to man except to fight." Suddenly, after the invasion there was a desperate need for manpower. Men, on their way back to America to the stockade, were reprieved and marched, still in handcuffs, to Yokohama. They would be allowed to fight in Korea as a means of clearing their records. Only as they boarded the planes and ships on their way to Korea were their handcuffs removed. When word of the North Korean invasion reached members of the 34th Infantry Regiment in Japan, the first reaction was, "Where's Korea?" The next was, "Let the gooks kill each other off." On the night of June 30, Lt. Col. Charles B. (Brad) Smith, commanding officer of the First Battalion of the 21st Infantry Regiment of the 24th Division, was called by his commanding officer and told to take his battalion to Korea. At the airport, Brigadier General William Dean told Smith his orders were simple: "When you get to Pusan head for Taejon. We want you to stop the North Koreans as far from Pusan as we can. Block the main road as far North as possible. Contact General Church [who had flown from Tokyo to Taejon in the middle of the night]. If you can't locate him, go to Taejon and beyond if you can. Sorry I can't give you more information. That's all I've got. Good luck to you and God bless you and your men."

Of the four American divisions in Japan, the 24th was, by anyone's standards, the least combat-ready. Most of its training had involved jiggling efficiency reports to reflect combat preparedness. Its equipment was old. A good portion of the ammunition for its mortars was faulty. Its .30-caliber machine guns were worn and not very accurate. Somewhere between a quarter and a half of its small arms were not serviceable. It lacked 3.5 antitank bazookas. Instead, it was equipped with the old 2.36-inch bazooka from World War Two, a good weapon in its time but utterly useless against the T-34s. Another regiment that was dispatched was in only slightly better shape. One of its officers wrote later that it was "rather sad, almost criminal that such understrength, ill-equipped and poorly trained units were committed." Because of the budgets cuts, the Air Force was even hard-pressed to find planes to transport them to Pusan. Yet the Americans set off for Korea astonishingly confident of an easy victory. Almost everyone, from top to bottom, seemed to share the view that the moment the North Korean soldiers saw they were fighting *Americans* rather than ROKs, they would cut and run. It was arrogance born of racial prejudice. One colonel in the 34th Infantry, Harold Ayres, told his troops as they were arriving in Korea, "There are supposed to be North Korean soldiers north of us. These men are poorly trained. Only about half of them have weapons and we'll have no difficulty stopping them."

He and the rest of the American units were in for a rude awakening. The North Koreans were a formidable foe. Their troops were rugged peasants who showed exceptional discipline in battle. Their camouflage was excellent: They wore netting over their helmets and their uniforms so they could fix branches and leaves to them. They moved well over the hard terrain and did not necessarily stay on the roads, as the Americans did. Their battlefield tactics, borrowed from Mao's armies, were deft: They tended to make a frontal approach while sliding flanking troops to the side, and then hit the American forces. What made their attacks even more devastating was that they would infiltrate relatively small units behind the American positions so that when the Americans began to retreat, they ran into the NKPA on all sides and thought themselves completely surrounded. It took a long time for the American commanders to learn to punch through the smaller forces behind them. The North Koreans preferred to fight at night because it limited the effectiveness of America's air power and artillery. The North Korean commanders also ordered their men to engage the Americans in closer combat than the Americans were accustomed to—so that when dawn arrived, American air power would be neutralized.

Even the trip over for the first American units was hard. The C-54 transport planes were so heavy they tore up the runway, so the Air Force had to turn instead to the smaller C-47s, which could hold only eighteen soldiers. Col. Smith himself made it over only on the tenth flight, and he had to leave behind much of his heavy firepower, including two recoilless-rifle teams and two mortar teams. The Koreans cheered them as they moved by train to Ansong on their way to battle—although in retrospect, American lieutenant William Wyrick decided that the Koreans were cheering not the Americans but the train, which would take them further south on its return trip.

General Dean, the RCT commander, broke his unit down into three groups to fight at three different places with virtually no communication with each other. Dean still believed that his job would be relatively short and easy; the American uniforms would do it all. The morale in Task Force Smith was high. As the Americans moved up to the front, they passed ROK engineers busy putting explosives on a bridge in case they had to retreat. The Americans upbraided them for their cowardice and threw their explosives into the river. "No thought of retreat or disaster entered our minds," Colonel Smith later wrote.

On the morning of July 5, Brad Smith and about 540 of his men took up their positions two miles north of Osan, on the high ground, with a good view of the main highway ahead. Much of their artillery support was still back at Pusan. At 7 A.M. a sergeant named Loren

Smith spotted eight enemy tanks. "Hey, Lieutenant," he told Lt. Philip Day. "Look over there. Can you believe?!" Day asked what they were. "Those are T-34 tanks, sir, and I don't think they're going to be friendly toward us." Low-slung and menacing, they were T-34s for sure; following them was a column of infantry and then another column of twenty-five tanks. This was merely the vanguard of a vast advancing force that stretched out some six miles along the narrow highway. Col. Smith's people readied their artillery pieces. A little after 8 A.M., when the tanks were about a mile away, Smith gave the order to fire. But 4.2-inch mortars were useless. Smith had a mere six rounds of HEAT (High Explosive AntiTank shells). The Americans were firing away, there were more and more hits, but the tanks kept coming.

Because he had to conserve his ammunition, Smith ordered his 75 mm recoilless rifles to wait until the tanks were only seven hundred yards away. The recoilless rifles scored hits but did no damage to the tanks. Then, as the tanks came upon the infantry positions, some of Smith's bazooka men, completely heedless to their own safety, closed to thirty yards and fired away. But even firing at virtual point-blank range did not help. It was only with the use of the 105 mm howitzer and the HEAT shells that they knocked out two tanks.

The battle lasted less than an hour, twenty of Smith's men were killed or wounded, and twenty-nine tanks rolled right through them. By early afternoon Smith gave the order to retreat, and when he did many of his soldiers ran, throwing away their weapons. Smith himself had to leave behind his dead and wounded. The Korean War had started.

Unlike Vietnam in the next decade, it did not come back to America live and in color on television. The nation was not yet wired, and Korea, so distant, the names of its towns so alien, did not lend itself to radio coverage, as did the great war that had preceded it. The best reporting in Korea was done by daily journalists, who caught its remarkable drama, heroism, and pathos for a nation that largely didn't care and was not at all sure it wanted to pay attention to such grim news. America tolerated the Korean War while it was on but could not wait to forget it once the war was over. In contrast to World War Two and Vietnam, it did not inspire a rich body of novels, plays, or even movies. Fittingly enough, the most recent history of the war was entitled *The Forgotten War,* a phrase used originally by General Matthew Ridgway. Some forty years after it had begun, there was no monument to it in Washington. Its most famous contribution to American mass culture was the movie and television series *M*A*S*H,* and even that was often associated in the public mind with Vietnam rather than Korea.

It took five days for Smith to round up his men. As one American soldier later said, "Instead of a motley horde armed with old muskets, the enemy infantry were well-trained, determined soldiers and many of their weapons were at least as modern as ours. Instead of charging wildly into battle, they employed a base of fire, double envelopment, fire blocks on withdrawal routes, and skilled infiltration." The first few weeks of the war were like that. Our troops were unprepared, and the leadership at the lower levels was often appalling. Colonel John (Mike) Michaelis, a regimental commander with the legendary Wolfhounds and one of the early heroes of the war, thought the American troops did not know their weapons, or even the basics of infantry life and survival. "They'd spent a lot of time listening to lectures on the differences between communism and Americanism and not enough time crawling on their bellies on maneuvers with live ammunition singing over them. They'd been nursed and coddled, told to drive safely, to buy War Bonds, to give to the Red Cross, to avoid VD, to write home to mother—when someone ought to have been telling them how to clear a machine gun when it jams." Michaelis was the first to notice that the American soldiers had become the prisoners of their own hardware or, in his words, "so damn road bound that they'd lost the use of their legs. Send out a patrol on a scouting mission and they load up in a three-quarter-ton truck and start riding down to the highway."

What had started out as something of a game had turned into a military nightmare for the American troops. Here they were, tens of thousands of miles away from home in this godforsaken country, seemingly abandoned by their own country in a war no one was even willing to call a war. The Korean troops, with whom and for whom they were fighting, seemed to be constantly throwing down their weapons and running. The weather was unbearable—the hottest Korean summer in years, with no sign of the heavy rains that generally cooled things off during that season. There was nothing to drink, and often the desperate men scooped up paddy water, neglecting to use their water-purification tablets. At first there were almost as many casualties from the unrelieved heat and intestinal diseases as from the enemy.

The first week ended with the Americans trying to dig in behind the Kum River, a good natural barrier. It had been a week of unrelievedly bad news: two American regiments torn up, as many as three thousand dead, wounded, or missing. It had been a psychological victory of immense proportions for the North Korean People's Army. Washington was still in shock. MacArthur began drawing up an immense list of what he needed: a Marine regimental combat team, the Second Infantry Division; a regimental combat team from the 82nd Airborne; eleven artillery battalions, an armored group of three medium tank battalions. At the Pentagon, Matt Ridgway recommended most of what MacArthur wanted. He also moved to stem the battlefield panic by rushing 3.5 bazookas and ammo to Korea, along with special instruction teams. He made this a personal mission, assigning his own men to guide them from the fatories to the shipping points to Pusan. There would be none of the usual screwups, he had decided. On July 10, just six days after the first clash, some twenty 3.5 bazookas were on their way along with 1,600 rounds of ammo.

In Washington a fat new $11 billion supplemental appropriation bill was rushed through. Ninety-two National Guard units, or the equivalent of four National Guard divisions, and the entire Marine Reserve were called up. Some units, such as the two battalions of the 29th Infantry Regiment, were supposed to get six weeks of training; instead, they were promised they would receive ten days of intensive training upon arrival in Korea. Once in Pusan, however, they were told that the situation was too critical. Instead, they would have three days to draw equipment and zero in their weapons. Then even that order was rescinded: They were, over the bitter protests of their officers, rushed immediately to Chinju. One day after arrival in-country, they found themselves at the most forward position.

The second week of combat was hardly better than the first. The In Min Gun kept pushing the Americans back. The 24th Division was badly mauled. Unit after unit was torn up, and after absorbing terrible losses and falling back, they regrouped, only to be torn up again. After three weeks in battle, the 24th was at half strength; of the almost 16,000 men who had been committed, only half were still able to fight. More than 2,400 men had been lost, either dead or missing. It was one of the worst periods in American military history; but gradually, fresh troops were pouring into the country. The quality of hardware was improving. The real question was whether this small, outmanned handful of American troops could win its fight against time before being driven into the sea. There was fear of an Asian Dunkirk. General Walton Walker, who had become commander of the Eighth Army, got edgier and edgier. There were reliable reports that he had gone after a T-34 tank with a handgun, had led a bazooka team to stop the enemy tanks, and had, in fact, nailed one at point-blank range. "I got me a tank," he was reported to have said. When one battalion commander, Morgan Heasley, arrived, Walker greeted him at the airport and told him, "I'm sending you up to the river to die."

In late July, General Walker gathered his various unit commanders at a command post at Sanju. Help, he said, was on the way. "We are fighting a battle against time. There will be no more retreating, withdrawal, or readjustment of the lines or any other term you choose. There is no line behind us to which we can retreat. Every unit must counterattack to keep the enemy in a state of confusion and off balance. There will be no Dunkirk, there will be no Bataan, a retreat to Pusan would be one of the greatest butcheries in history. We must fight to the end. Capture by these people is worse than death itself. We will fight as a team. If some of us must die, we will die fighting together. Any man who gives ground may be responsible for the deaths of thousands of his comrades. . . . We are going to hold the line. We are going to win."

Many of his commanders thought Walker histrionic. There were other defensive lines to which they could retreat, wearing down the North Koreans, making them pay an increasingly dear price for the real estate. Slowly, the Americans began to rally. The more compact their position, the better their lines of communication and the greater Walker's ability to switch units back and forth.

By the same token, the North Korean army's lines of communication were now far too long and being taxed by constant bombing. The UN forces moved back across the Naktong on August 1; it was their last great defense line. On August 2 they blew the main highway and railroad bridges (in the process killing hundreds of refugees, who refused to obey orders to get off them). This was the Pusan perimeter, a great bend in the river, running some one hundred miles north and south and then roughly another fifty miles east. To the east was the Sea of Japan; to the south, the Strait of Korea, to the north, rugged mountains that limited NKPA movement. It was only on the long front to its west that the Eighth Army faced its formidable foe. Though the American troops were spread somewhat thin, they had exceptional mobility; they could move units back and forth by rail and by road; they could rush supplies up to the front, which had just been off-loaded at the Pusan docks. In addition, they had brilliant intelligence on the North Koreans, who had been careless with their codes; they used simple ones and changed them only once a week. It took the Americans only one day to break them. Thus Walker had advance knowledge of almost everything the North Koreans were going to do and he was able to shuttle his troops around to head off their attacks.

Slowly, the balance of force was changing. By early August the UN forces, including ROK units, actually outnumbered the In Min Gun. And while the Eighth Army had suffered terrible casualties— more than 6,000 men—so had the North Koreans. Rough American military estimates of damage caused to the NKPA were 35,000 casualties; later, based on careful prisoner interrogation, that figure was judged far too cautious and raised to 58,000. The North Koreans had used most of their best men and equipment in that sudden, shocking first strike. Now they were replacing elite troops with green conscripts, including men from the South drafted willingly or unwillingly as the army had driven toward Pusan. They had gone from some 150 tanks to about 40. If the situation was turning around, not everyone realized it: There were still top-secret plans for a massive Dunkirk-like withdrawal from Pusan, if need be. For the summer of 1950 had proved a dark time, when America was reluctantly being drawn into a world it had never made and when what was happening in Korea amplified our worst fears. There was always the danger that this small war would grow larger. Averell Harriman and General Ridgway visited MacArthur in Tokyo to ask, among other things, that he make certain this did not happen. MacArthur was supremely confident; if the Chinese decided to enter the war, he would deal them such a crushing blow that it "would rock Asia and perhaps turn back Communism." Modesty was never his strong point.

FIVE

Douglas MacArthur had not been home in thirteen years. Truman had twice invited him to receive the appreciation of a grateful nation, but MacArthur turned him down, saying that he was too busy in Tokyo. Since a presidential request was in fact an order, both Truman and George Marshall were furious. Truman suspected that MacArthur's reasons were political, that he was biding his time, in order to create a Republican groundswell with a dramatic return just in time for a primary run. MacArthur's explanation was simpler but predictably vainglorious. He could not return, he told an aide, because, "If I returned for only a few weeks, word would spread through the Pacific that the United States is abandoning the Orient."

He was seventy years old in 1950, a towering figure who had worked long and hard to perpetuate his own legend. As Truman suspected, he hungered for the White House, but in the political arena he was surprisingly clumsy. He was the darling of the far right, corresponding regularly and indiscreetly with all sorts of figures on that side, encouraging them to believe he shared their views that the New Deal signaled the end of Western civilization. As early as 1944, a writer named John McCarten wrote in *The American Mercury,* "It may not be his fault but it is surely his misfortune that the worst elements on the political right, including its most blatant lunatic fringe, are whooping it up for MacArthur."

Not everyone thought he was the right leader for this particular war. He was older than the norm for a combat commander, and his reputation exceeded in some ways those civilians to whom he was supposed to report. Far more than most generals, he held to the idea that the commander in the field was *the* decision maker—not merely tactically, but strategically as well. He was known among his peers as one who manipulated the information he passed on to his superiors in order to justify the plans he intended to carry out. From their years together in the Philippines, when Ike was an aide to MacArthur, Eisenhower understood MacArthur's Olympian style of deciding "what information he wants Washington to have and what he will withhold." This was especially relevant in Korea, a new kind of limited war, which demanded all sorts of political decisions and a certain pragmatism that was alien to MacArthur's sense of duty. Eisenhower thought a younger commander would have been far more appropriate than, as he phrased it, "an untouchable." There was also the danger with MacArthur that he had begun to see his mission in Asia in a quasi-religious light, as the leader of a holy crusade against a godless enemy.

Be that as it may, in 1950 Douglas MacArthur was at the summit of one of the most glorious careers in American history. He was the son of Arthur MacArthur, a Civil War hero who won the Congressional Medal of Honor at age eighteen and who later commanded American troops during the Philippine insurrection ("Arthur MacArthur," one of his aides noted, "was the most flamboyantly egotistical man I had ever seen, until I met his son").

His mother, Pinky, felt that the Army had never treated her husband with proper respect and she had constantly intervened with his superiors trying to gain him promotions and better posts. She failed in that particular course, but later in her life she transferred her energies to her young son. On the day of his final exam for West Point he felt nauseated, but she steadied him with a pep talk: "Doug, you'll win if you don't lose your nerve. You must believe in yourself, my son, or no one else will believe in you. Be confident, self-reliant and even if you don't make it, you will know you have done your best. Now go to it." He passed with the highest grades of anyone taking the exam.

She accompanied him to the Point and took up residence in a nearby hotel for four years, the better to keep her eye on him. She blocked most of his attempts to have serious relationships with women. His first marriage, to a socialite, ended soon, thanks to Pinky. "You must grow up to be a great man like your father," she would say, which of course was the same as reminding him of his duty to her. She connived shamelessly to advance his career, using all her connections from her husband's many years of service. Even as the young MacArthur was finding glory as a brigade commander in World War One, Pinky was writing Secretary of War Newton Baker: "I am deeply anxious to have Colonel MacArthur considered for the rank of Brigadier General and it is only through you that he can ever hope to get advancement of any kind." Baker's failure to respond did not deter her. A few weeks later, she wrote again: "Considering the fine work he has done with so much pride and enthusiasm and the prominence he has gained in actual fighting, I believe the entire Army, with few exceptions, would applaud your selecting him as one of your Generals . . ."

In time he was promoted; at age thirty-eight he became the youngest division commander in the Army. Already he was somewhat paranoid about his contemporaries at headquarters, who, he believed, had denied him his due—the Medal of Honor—which would gain him parity with his father. In 1930, he became the Chief of Staff of the Army, not without a good deal of wheeling and dealing both on his part and, of course, Pinky's. She wrote Black Jack Pershing, who was the dominating American general of his era. "You are so powerful in all Army matters that you could give him his promotion by a stroke of your pen! You have never failed me yet!" When her son became Chief of Staff, she gave him the highest accolade of all: "If only your father could see you now! Douglas, you're everything he wanted to be!" Now she lived in his quarters and acted as his hostess, and he went home to lunch with her every day.

MacArthur was a complete narcissist. He was brilliant, talented, petulant, manipulative, highly political, theatrical, and given to re-markable mood swings. His favorite pronoun was the first person. In one of his most famous statements, promising his eventual return to the Philippines, he said *I* shall return, not *We* shall return. He did not share glory with subordinate commanders (he considered that a weakness) and his headquarters always made sure that he was given full credit for every victory. He once told General Robert Eichelberger that he couldn't understand why Eisenhower had allowed his subordinates like Bradley and Patton to gain so much publicity. It was not something that would have happened in the Pacific.

Like most narcissistic personalities, he idealized life and his role in it: He demanded perfection of himself, and when he erred, he was loath to admit it or accept any responsibility. The blame had to be apportioned—more often than not, to rivals who were suspected of seeking his downfall. It was typical that when the Korean War began and the first American troops sent from Tokyo to Korea turned out to be flabby, MacArthur did not assume responsibility, though they had been under his command. Rather, he blamed the Pentagon. It was as if he had been summoned from some distant planet to command troops that other, lesser generals had permitted to go soft.

He was obsessed with his looks and the degree to which they aided his myth. He always cut a dashing figure, even in World War One, when he had worn nonregulation clothes. A distinguished portrait painter who met him at the time thought he could easily have stepped out of the pages of *The Prisoner of Zenda*. Dwight Eisenhower was once asked by a woman if he had ever met MacArthur. "Not only have I met him, Ma'am; I studied dramatics under him for five years in Washington and for four years in the Philippines." During World War Two, Eichelberger wrote coded letters home to his wife. In them the code word for MacArthur was Sarah, as in Sarah Bernhardt. MacArthur was addicted to publicity and fame; he went nowhere without his chosen coterie of journalists and photographers. It was virtually impossible to take a photo of him that was not posed; he was aware every moment of where the light was best, of how his jaw should jut, and how the cap could be displayed at the most rakish angle.

Judging from the photographs of him, even in 1950 he was a slim, attractive man with perfect eyesight. In fact, he wore glasses, but he never permitted photographers to see them. If his public appearances seemed a bit contrived and self-consciously dramatic, it was because of his speech. He spoke, it seemed, for history in a cadence that some thought rather Victorian. At the end of his military career his cables to Washington were so self-conscious and self-justifying, they came to be known as his "posterity papers." At even the simplest luncheon with a visitor he would dwell on the future of the West and the rise of the East.

It was sometimes difficult to separate fact from legend with so gifted an automythologist as MacArthur. He was nonetheless the most brilliant strategist in the American Army, a great warrior, completely fearless—in the cool and unsympathetic eyes of George Marshall, "our most brilliant general." During World War Two, his leadership in the Pacific dazzled colleagues, political leaders, and military historians alike. In that campaign, starting in early 1942, he had taken a severely understrength Allied army, with little air and naval support, and chartered a course of great originality. His strategy was simple: He shepherded his resources, rarely contesting the Japanese where they were strong, but instead striking at them on smaller islands, where they were weak. The day of the crude frontal attack was over, he had told Roosevelt at a meeting in Waikiki; modern weaponry had made it obsolete. Those inhuman battles of World War One, with their endless casualties, had spelled its end. Only mediocre commanders tried frontal attacks anymore. He used his growing number of bombers with great skill, searching for islands that would offer him better, more strategically located airfields. No general in World War Two used air power better.

He was also uncommonly deft in how he used his forces. He seemed to possess a sixth sense for what the Japanese were going to do and where they were vulnerable. His skills, plus the growing technological might of the Allied forces and the declining resources of the enemy, came together in a masterful campaign, in which he minimized his own losses. Ironically, the success of bombers in this particular theater—used, as they were, against fixed Japanese installations and massive Japanese convoys, marvelous targets all—left him with an exaggerated sense of what air power could do strategically. He was to pay the price for this in Korea.

After World War Two was over, for some five years, he served as the viceroy of Japan. His needs and those of the Japanese dovetailed perfectly—the Japanese needed to worship the man who had conquered them, and he needed to be worshiped. He prided himself on his expertise in Asia, yet there is some question as to how great it really was. He had significantly underestimated the military reach of the Japanese just before World War Two (Roosevelt, who had always recognized MacArthur's political ambitions, kept handy an old report of the general's written on the eve of World War Two, wherein MacArthur had spoken confidently of his ability to hold the Philippines because of the limits of Japanese air power).

Unlike Joe Stilwell, he had no bright area experts who could report to him on the vast changes taking place in Asia. His speeches and conversation were filled with simplistic and racist references "to the Asiatic mind" and "the mind of the Oriental," which blurred the vast ethnic, historical, and social differences of the many countries of Asia. His Victorian mind could not see the revolution against colonialism taking place in Asia, most particularly in China. The China he felt he knew so well no longer existed.

In the Pusan perimeter, the tide was beginning to turn. Day by day as August wore on, American positions grew stronger. The North Koreans were literally and figuratively running out of gas, as well as men and ammunition. This was the moment that MacArthur had been waiting for. From the first moment he had visited Korea, right after the invasion, a strategic vision had taken hold of MacArthur: In one brilliant, audacious move we would make an amphibious assault far behind their lines. They would be unprepared, since most of their army was committed to the South. We would then move quickly both north and east across the thin neck of the country to entrap them. MacArthur even had his site picked out—the great natural port of Inchon, on the west coast. MacArthur would explain to doubters, "It will be like an electric fan. You go to the wall and pull the plug out, and the fan will stop. When we get well ashore at Inchon, the North Koreans will have no choice but to pull out or surrender."

Virtually no one agreed with him. The Navy thought the plan impractical, indeed impossible, because there was no natural beach. One sunken ship could block the whole harbor. The tides could be terrible, up to thirty-two feet. Only the Bay of Fundy had higher. There were only three dates in the next two months on which the tides would be high enough to carry the big landing craft far enough in before the whole shoreline became nothing but mud: September 15, September 27, and October 11. "Make up a list of amphibious 'don'ts' and you have an exact description of the Inchon operation," one naval officer noted. In addition there was evidence that the Russians were aiding the North Koreans by sending mines to protect their harbors. Yet MacArthur remained steadfast in his vision. To him the alternative was a meat-grinder war up the Korean peninsula, with the possibility of slow but steady progress and unacceptable casualties. "Beef cattle in the slaughterhouse," he called it.

The critical meeting on Inchon was held in Tokyo on August 23. Two members of the Joint Chiefs, Joe Collins and Admiral Forest Sherman, went to Tokyo to talk MacArthur out of it. If there must be an amphibious landing let it be more modest, to the south of

Inchon. At the August meeting, one naval officer after another got up to explain the reason why Inchon could not work, why the risks involved were too high. Finally, MacArthur took the floor. The Navy, he said, had never failed him before. After dismissing the doubters, he gave a great soliloquy: "I can almost hear the ticking of the second hand of destiny. We must act now or we will die. . . . We shall land at Inchon and I shall crush them." He finished and there was a moment of silence. Then Admiral Sherman spoke: "Thank you. A great voice in a great cause." Rear Admiral James Doyle, whose job it would be to execute the landing, later said, "If MacArthur had gone on the stage you never would have heard of John Barrymore." The next day Sherman was as nervous as ever ("I wish I had that man's optimism"), but MacArthur had won. Inchon was his.

On the morning of September 15, the Marines landed on Wolni, a small island guarding the mouth of Inchon harbor. The North Korean garrison there, composed of young, inexperienced soldiers, quickly collapsed. That afternoon 13,000 Marines poured ashore against marginal resistance. Only twenty-one men were killed. North Korean forces were routed, moving back as best they could to blocking positions between Inchon and Seoul. Now for the UN forces, it was a race for Seoul, and to entrap the In Min Gun, before they retreated north from Pusan. It was MacArthur's finest hour. If before Inchon he had been an "untouchable," now he was a god. One of the worst defeats in American military history had, overnight, been turned into a stunning success. "The Sorcerer of Inchon," Dean Acheson, not one of his great admirers, called him afterward. From then on, Matt Ridgway wrote mordantly, if MacArthur had suggested "that a battalion walk on water to reach the port, there might have been someone ready to give it a try."

Seoul fell on September 26, eleven days after the landing. But even though the Allied forces moved steadily forward, the bulk of the North Korean forces was slipping away. The Americans had hoped, but failed, to capture it en masse, and some forty thousand men had managed to slip through. MacArthur's forces continued to pursue to the 38th parallel. On October 1, ROK forces became the first UN soldiers to go north of the 38th. In the rush of events and the seeming collapse of the enemy, it was not a decision that weighed very heavily on anyone in Washington at the time. A few of the old China hands, and George Kennan and Chip Bohlen, warned that North Korea was a satellite state and that either Peking or Moscow would not tolerate it if we violated the 38th parallel. Truman, already under fire for being soft on Communism, was in no position to slow down so rapid and spectacular an advance—in truth, a rout. "It would have taken a superhuman effort to say no [to crossing the parallel]," Averell Harriman said later. "Psychologically, it was almost impossible not to go ahead and complete the job." And yet no one had spent very much time, in fact, defining what the job was. Worse, at the highest levels, particularly in MacArthur's command, there was almost complete ignorance about Mao's army and how its extraordinary victory over Chiang had molded it into a remarkable, modern fighting machine.

So it was that we blundered ahead toward the most dramatic confrontation of the Cold War to that date. From the moment that the ROK forces crossed the 38th parallel there were rumblings from Peking. Gradually, as we pressed forward toward the Yalu, these warnings became more strident. The British became increasingly wary, but MacArthur dismissed them as appeasers. American troops crossed the parallel on October 7. The next day, Mao ordered his forces to ready themselves to fight and a massive movement of men started toward Manchuria and the Korean border.

Now Truman himself started to become nervous; the noise from Peking was like a distant but steady drumroll. Moreover, his own shrewdness told him that while his forces were doing well, they were doing it at a price, getting further from their own lines of supply, ever deeper into hostile terrain and doing this as the weather got colder. In late October, he arranged a meeting with MacArthur at Wake Island. The two men were not a natural fit. Long before Korea, Truman, the good old-fashioned unvarnished populist, had written a memo on the dilemma of dealing with MacArthur: "And what to do with Mr. Prima Donna, Brass Hat, Five Star MacArthur. He's worse than the Cabots and the Lodges—they at least talked with one another before they told God what to do. Mac tells God right off. It is a very great pity that we have to have stuffed shirts like that in key positions . . . Don't see how a country can produce such men as Robert E. Lee, John J. Pershing, Eisenhower and Bradley, and at the same time produce Custers, Pattons, and MacArthurs." That, of course, was before they even got to know each other.

At the time of the Wake Island meeting, Truman's standing in the polls was abysmally low. Thus, in the last weeks before the midterm elections, he hoped to bask a little in the reflected glory of the hero of Inchon. He forbade MacArthur to bring his press entourage; instead, only the White House press corps would attend. MacArthur arrived at Wake first. So great was Truman's wariness that he doubted until the very last moment whether MacArthur would come out to the plane to greet him or whether, instead, the President would have to walk over to MacArthur. MacArthur did come over to meet Truman's plane, though wearing his usual open shirt and rumpled field cap. ("If he'd been a lieutenant in my outfit going around dressed like that," Truman later noted, "I'd have busted him so fast he wouldn't have known what happened to him.")

Their meeting seemed to go reasonably well, although both men remained wary of each other. Truman was concerned about Chinese intentions, but MacArthur was reassuring: The victory in Korea, he said, had already been won, and North Korean resistance would end by Thanksgiving. The victory in Korea, he said, had already been won. Perhaps he could get the Eighth Army out by Christmas. Truman pushed a little harder on the question of Chinese intervention. Again MacArthur belittled the possibility. At best only 50,000 or 60,000 could get across the Yalu, and if they tried to move down to Pyongyang, "there would be the greatest slaughter." This statement was a remarkable boast for so brilliant a commander: It showed, above all else, that he had spent no time studying the Chinese army or the tactics with which Mao had defeated Chiang.

When he made that promise to Truman he was not thinking of the modern new Chinese army that had unleashed such a powerful force of nationalism in its victory over Chiang. Rather, he was thinking of a weak army from a feudal society.

SIX

The decision to go ahead with the Super brought Edward Teller the scientific and political prominence he had both sought and avoided. It was characteristic of Teller's ambivalence about his scientific role that he wanted credit for the development of the hydrogen bomb but also hated being referred to as the father of it. Teller was four years younger than Oppenheimer. Like Oppenheimer he had always been precocious, and like Oppenheimer he did not hide it very well. As a young boy he was capable of sitting at the family dinner table and announcing: "Please don't talk to me—I have a problem." The problem was, of course, a mathematical formula he was working on in his head. When he was six he would put himself to sleep by calculating the number of seconds in a minute (60), an hour (3,600), a day (86,400) . . .

His early years in a bourgeois family in Budapest were as sheltered and privileged as Oppie's. There were cooks and maids and nannies. Evidently, there was a vast gap between young Edward's astonishing intellectual accomplishments and his maturity in other areas. When he was eight years old, Edward still insisted that his nanny put his socks on for him. When she complained of this, he accused her of preferring his sister to him—a response that would not surprise those who knew him later as an adult. As a Hungarian Jew, Teller inherited a constant sense of vulnerability. Jews comprised 5 percent of Hungary's population, but they represented a quarter of the journalists, half the doctors, and half the lawyers. Béla Kun, a disciple of Lenin, created the first version of a Communist Hungary in 1919, when he nationalized all the commerce and the land. Kun was Jewish, as were most of his advisers. When Kun fell, there was a virulent outbreak of anti-Semitism. Within months, a right-wing fascist government was created under Admiral Miklós Horthy. Max and Ilona Teller—he a lawyer, she the daughter of a banker and cotton manufacturer—were better off economically under Horthy than under Kun, but more culturally isolated than ever, and more vulnerable to prejudice.

Edward was eleven when Kun came to power. He was subjected to considerable anti-Semitism at school, even more so because he lacked social skills. Once, when an algebra teacher worked out a formula, Teller dissented and worked out the correct solution. "So you are a genius, Teller? Well, I don't like geniuses," the teacher said. Another teacher addressed his students as "Gentlemen, Jews, and Pollack," because he wasn't certain whether Pollack was a Jewish name or not. Max Teller encouraged his son to get out of Hungary as soon as he could. Two weeks before his eighteenth birthday, he left for the Institute of Technology at Karlsruhe; at the time, Germany was not just a mecca for the emerging study of the natural sciences but something of an oasis for Jews as well—at least compared to Central Europe.

That refuge did not last long; soon Hitler was on the rise and the Nazi propaganda machinery was attacking Einstein and what it called Jewish physics. In 1933, when Hitler was called on to form a government, Teller was twenty-five. A year later, he came to America. No one doubted his brilliance. Once on a visit to Copenhagen, he was invited along with Otto Frisch, another émigré physicist, to spend the weekend at Niels Bohr's country home. Two days away from work made Teller restless, Frisch later recalled, and on the train ride back to Copenhagen he asked Frisch to create mental games for him. Frisch pondered the request and told him to imagine a chess board with eight queens arranged so that none of them could take another. Teller thought for about twenty minutes and then gave Frisch the answer. Then they began playing chess, albeit without a board, calling out their moves. It was soon clear that Frisch, brilliant though he was, was no match for Teller.

In America, Teller quickly became part of a select group of the world's greatest physicists. He lived and taught in Washington, where many of their professional meetings were held, and the group often ended up at his home. In those days he was gregarious and loved to play music. Mici, his wife, was a gracious, outgoing hostess, and their home was something of a salon for fellow scientists. In the months before the war, these scientists were bonded as men rarely were; not only were they of the same profession, they were mostly exiles in this new land and acutely aware of the darkness falling across Europe—as most Americans were not at the time. They traveled together, shared houses. That closeness made the eventual split between Teller and Oppenheimer unusually painful, tearing apart the center of this tightly bound group. Years later, talking about those divisions and trying to understand how men who had once had so much in common could end up so bitterly divided, Hans Bethe described both Teller and Oppenheimer as different from the others. "We, men like Weisskopf and I and Placzek, were more traditional men of science. If we were not perfect rational men, we were nonetheless men of rationality and that rationality was defined by our work. . . . But both Oppie and Teller were different. They were both much more emotional men, Teller openly so, Oppie equally emotional, I think, but more skillful in controlling it. And because they were more emotional, they were more vulnerable than the others in the group to the exterior world and the immense pressures that it would bring upon them after the Hiroshima bomb, and as the political importance of being a nuclear physicist became evident."

Teller, noted Bethe, was many things but he was never a team player. At first he had seemed almost smitten with Oppenheimer, so brilliant, so attractive, so *American*—the one native son among the great names of physics. On the surface there was no one more unlike Oppenheimer than Teller—his dark countenance made fierce by great, bushy eyebrows—gregarious, volatile, spinning like a top through the world of Los Alamos, often disrupting those around him. There was a sense that Teller was someone special, brilliant but harder to contain. Only Enrico Fermi, who was like a father figure to him, could calm him down, or bring him out of his darker moods, by simply saying, "Edward, Edward!" Fermi alone could tease Teller and get away with it. Stan Ulam later would remember Fermi, saying in his heavy accent, "Edward-a how come-a the Hungarians have not-a invented anything?"

Inevitably, the special relationship between Teller and Oppenheimer could not last. Many date the beginning of the rift to the moment when Oppenheimer made Hans Bethe the head of the theoretical division—Teller had assumed the position would be his. "That I was named to head the division was a severe blow to Teller, who had worked on the bomb project almost from the day of its inception and considered himself, quite rightly, as having seniority over everyone then at Los Alamos, including Oppenheimer," Bethe later recalled. Even worse, Victor Weisskopf was named the deputy director. Teller thought himself the scientific superior to Weisskopf and said as much to Weisskopf, who replied that it might be true, but that he, Weisskopf, got on better with his colleagues.

During the spring of 1942, Teller had lobbied Bethe heavily for permission to go ahead on the hydrogen bomb. "One might say," Bethe coolly noted later, "that scientifically Teller is overfertile. New ideas and new combinations of old ideas simply tumble out of his brain." Bethe pleaded with him to concentrate on the fission bomb, but those requests had little effect. Even during the war Teller remained preoccupied with the fusion bomb. Bethe met with Oppenheimer and his top people over what to do with Teller, and for a time there was even talk of getting rid of him. The compromise solution was to let him work on his fusion bomb in a separate section while everyone else was working on the fission bomb. For a time the subject of Teller's dissent, his tendency to provoke others, and his sensitivity to slights became something of a joke at Los Alamos. But looking back, Victor Weisskopf believed that in reality, a great political-scientific schism had already begun then. As Teller's position on the H bomb began to isolate him professionally, he turned away from the world of science and found his allies in the world of politics. Starting in those years, Bethe and Weisskopf saw Teller change; the outgoing, enthusiastic young man was replaced by someone darker, angrier, and ever more reactionary.

Though there were periods in the years immediately after World War Two when Teller seemed optimistic about the future, they became briefer and briefer. Back in Hungary, his family was being punished by the harsh new puppet regime that had taken power in Budapest, and Teller was among the first to develop a realistic vision of the new totalitarianism being enforced across Eastern Europe. He believed that one adversary was merely being replaced by another, and therefore his politics quickly became far more conservative than his peers'. In the immediate postwar period "he was," said Enrico Fermi, "terribly anti-Communist, terribly anti-Russian."

In addition to his vehement political feelings, there was his scientific obsession: the hydrogen bomb. Years later, in a secret meeting with an FBI agent, Teller said that he believed Oppenheimer had opposed the Super out of vanity, his desire not to see his own work outdone. If anything, mutual colleagues thought, the statement was more revealing about Teller than about Oppenheimer. For Teller's career, his psyche, and the Super were all blended together as one: Those who opposed his bomb opposed him. It was a true obsession, thought his colleague Robert Serber. In the early days at Los Alamos, he would make calculations on the Super, and someone, most likely Hans Bethe, would punch holes in them. The next day Teller would be back pushing them again as if nothing had ever happened. Serber remembered an important conference at Los Alamos in April 1946 to go over the calculations on the Super. Serber and others found Teller's projections on the Super overly optimistic. To Serber, they seemed half done, guesses really. Serber met with Teller and said the final report was not acceptable; the two went over it and toned it down considerably. A few months later, a librarian called Serber back at Berkeley to tell him that a document had come in with his name on it: It was the report on the conference—the *original* version.

Teller's obsession with the H bomb began to isolate him from his colleagues, at first professionally and then politically and socially as well. Increasingly, he became friendly with powerful senators and Air Force generals—and, most important, with Lewis Strauss. Suddenly, it seemed he had turned into a tough and skillful political infighter. The political climate had changed to his advantage, and Teller now had the access that Oppenheimer had enjoyed in the past. In the spring of 1950, Teller pushed Oppenheimer yet again to help him recruit for the H bomb project, but Oppenheimer told him, "You know in this matter I am neutral." Teller was furious. Old slights were remembered, old wounds reopened. He began to believe that Oppenheimer was deliberately blocking him and that Oppenheimer, above everyone else, was his opponent within the scientific community. He was wrong: Other important physicists were far more vocal in their opposition and used their influence more openly with younger colleagues against going ahead. And yet none knew better than Oppenheimer himself the importance of his own prestige, that if he had gone back to Los Alamos, he would have been a great magnet, "even if I had done nothing but twiddle my thumbs."

Nevertheless, under the pressure of the growing tension with the Soviets, Los Alamos began gradually to build up again with a new group of scientists. Many senior people, who had at one time opposed the idea of the Super, returned to help advise. Fermi came around—not because of any personal preference for it, but because he believed that once the President had made the political decision, it was not the job of scientists to stand in the way; after the Korean War broke out, Bethe came around, still ambivalent, half hoping he could show it couldn't be done. But the road to the Super was not easy. The mathematical equations were not yet right, nor was Teller a particularly gifted group leader. There was always a sense among his colleagues that Teller, no matter how brilliant, raced ahead of his own evidence. George Placzek, who never made a statement unless he was entirely certain he could prove it, liked to tease Teller when he would blurt out an idea: "Well yes, Edward, you may be right, and it may be important, but you have not proved it yet." Likewise, Felix Block would say to him, "Edward! You are jumping ahead of yourself again. You must wait and be sure." He did not like it when the chief mathematician, Ulam, dissented at meetings. Ulam, who in no way disagreed with most of Teller's political views, found Teller unusually difficult, obstinate, single-minded, overly ambitious, and comfortable only with acolytes.

The Super required immensely sophisticated mathematical equations. Years later, Andrei Sakharov came to America and met with his American counterparts. Jerome Weisner, the science adviser to both Eisenhower and Kennedy, asked how much help Klaus Fuchs's espionage had been to the Soviets on the hydrogen bomb. Somewhat to his surprise, Sakharov retorted, "We got the same kind of help you did—it was all the wrong information." In fact, the calculations on the Super remained wrong until the last minute. Teams of mathematicians, armed only with slide rules in those days, put in long, grueling hours under Ulam.

What the physicists working on the hydrogen bomb needed was a machine that would help them with the overwhelming amount of high-level computation. By chance, at that very moment a number of mathematicians were trying to transform the old-fashioned electric calculator into a machine for the modern world by equipping it with vacuum tubes in order to do high-speed, high-powered computing. Some people called the new invention a human brain; others called it the computer. The early military computer, ENIAC, arrived too late to be used for the fission bomb (it did its first calculations of the Los Alamos lab in December 1945), but in the critical years of the fusion bomb, 1950–52, work on the early models had progressed far enough to be of considerable help. The leading theoretician of the computer, John von Neumann of Princeton, was a close friend of the leading scientists of Los Alamos. He was far ahead of anyone else in understanding the logic of the computer, what it could do, and how it could do it.

The key to the new technology was the coming of electronics. Radar represented the first important use of electronics during the war, and in the postwar years, there was to be nothing less than a revolution in the field, first with vacuum tubes and then with transistors. It was all about weight and speed. In the traditional electrical circuit there was a small metal switch, which had to be moved electrically. It was tiny and seemed to weigh virtually nothing. But compared to what was going to replace it—an electron—it was absurdly heavy. Because an electron weighed so much less, it could be moved far faster, at a speed, in the words of Tom Watson, Jr., of IBM, "close to the speed of light." In the late forties, even the fastest electrical relay system in an IBM business machine could do only four additions per second, while the primitive new computer produced during the war could do some five thousand. The scientific and industrial implications were profound; in terms of technology, it was like going from the Wright brothers' airplane to a mach-three jet.

Two young engineers, John Mauchly and Pres Eckert, created the first working computer, ENIAC, or Electronic Numerical Integrator and Computer, at the Moore School of the University of Pennsylvania, primarily for the military and for the Aberdeen Proving Grounds, where it would chart ballistic trajectories. It was an awkward machine, taking up some 15,000 square feet. When Tom Watson, Jr., first visited ENIAC in 1945, he asked why it was so hot in the room. "Because we are sharing this space with 18,000 radio tubes," Eckert replied. Eckert, then only thirty-one years old, was immensely confident that this was the machine of the future and that IBM's electrically based machines were soon to be the dinosaurs of the computing world. At the time Watson did not believe him, though he was soon to change his mind.

Yet the true visionary of its potential was von Neumann. He had become interested in computers during the war. Already considered by many the most gifted mathematician of his generation, he turned his attention completely to this new idea in midcareer. He had an obscene interest in this new machine, which would astronomically extend man's mathematical capabilities, he wrote his friend Oswald Veblen in 1943. Because of this obsession, he speculated he would return from England "a better and impurer man." In 1944 Herman Goldstine, who was representing the government on the ENIAC program, ran into von Neumann at Aberdeen and mentioned Mauchly's and Eckert's work. Goldstine was stunned by how much von Neumann already knew and how his mind seemed to race ahead, even in this brief and casual conversation, about what computers might do eventually.

He started to collaborate closely with Mauchly and Eckert on the successor machine—EDVAC (Electronic Discrete Variable Arithmetic Calculator). As part of that work, he sat down one day and wrote out a 101-page paper on the theory of the use of the machine. His paper was so original and convincing that it became in effect the standard primer on the use of the computer. It also enraged Mauchly and Eckert, who believed that he was trying to take credit for their work. (Actually, von Neumann had written the paper rather casually, with no expectation that it would be published.)

Von Neumann was so talented that his colleagues joked that he was a Martian who did an exceptional job of posing as a humanoid with a heavy Hungarian accent. "It all came so easily for him and he was so far ahead of everyone else." mused his friend Herman Goldstine, himself one of the early architects of computing, "that he was like Mozart. Or perhaps because he was so quick and liked to be everywhere, doing everything that was on the frontier of math, Cellini or Michelangelo." At Los Alamos, it was universally recognized that if Johnny von Neumann said it would work, it would work. If Johnny said it wouldn't work, it wouldn't work.

Von Neumann had grown up in Budapest, a contemporary and schoolmate of Edward Teller and Eugene Wigner. Unlike Teller, who came from the same Jewish haute-bourgeois background, von Neumann was ebullient and witty. The anti-Semitism he encountered in his childhood and the eventual need to leave Hungary never darkened his vision as it did Teller's. He had always been the best student, with the best grades; from the time he was ten, his mathematical ability was so obvious his teachers suggested to von Neumann's father that his son be tutored. For the next eight years, he studied with a professor at the University of Budapest; by the time of his high school graduation, he had begun to collaborate with the professor on papers.

Herman Goldstine remembered a story that von Neumann, as a student, had attended a lecture by the legendary Hermann Weyl, who boasted that he could solve a difficult theorem in forty-five minutes. Weyl indeed solved it in forty-five minutes, but when he was finished, von Neumann stepped up and said, "Professor Weyl, may I show you something?" He had solved it in four lines. There might, Goldstine added, have been mathematicians of his generation who were as good, but there were none who were as fast.

His office, said a colleague, was like that of a dentist, with young mathematicians lined up to see von Neumann, hoping to get some help with the equations on which they were working. In one such case, von Neumann sat down and, without use of pencil or paper, solved the equation. A few nights later, von Neumann was at a concert when the same young man walked over; he explained sheepishly that he had been so dazzled by the performance that he had forgotten to write down the answer. Von Neumann reeled off the answer again. The young man thanked him and disappeared. Von Neumann turned to Herman Goldstine, who was with him, and said: "I just want you to know that that SOB is going to publish what I just gave him without a footnote referring to me."

He was restless and quickly got bored. When he had friends over to dinner, he would often excuse himself to go into an adjoining room to work—though he'd still listen in on the conversation and comment when something interested him. His friends weren't offended—they knew it was just Johnny being Johnny.

He was a man of immense charm who brought an old-world zest for life to the ascetic world of American science. He could remember endless jokes and stories, which he loved to trot out on all occasions. He could always summon the right limerick for the right person. He was sometimes rather bawdy, and he liked to play games at all times, particularly when he was in cars, where he would use the plates of oncoming cars to compute all sorts of mathematical possibilities. He liked to say, his closest friend and colleague Stan Ulam pointed out, that a mathematician did his best work at the age of twenty-five and then it was all downhill. When he first made that comment, von Neumann had just passed age twenty-five. Over the years, Ulam noted, von Neumann systematically extended the age limit on brilliance, always keeping it just below his then current age. It was, Ulam thought, part of von Neumann's sense of irony and his ability to be self-effacing.

Like his old schoolmate Teller, he was politically conservative, a hard-liner as the Cold War developed, deeply suspicious of the

Soviets. He believed in the need to escalate the technology of America's arms, first with the Super, and then later as a key figure in the planning of the ballistic-missile program. He disliked Oppenheimer, both personally—thinking him too prissy and self-righteous—and professionally—thinking him too left-wing and wrong on his attitude toward the Super. Yet later he would testify on behalf of Oppenheimer at his security hearings. He thought, in fact, that Oppenheimer was in the end badly treated by his government. Egalitarian societies like America, von Neumann told his colleague Herman Goldstine, are very cruel to truly gifted people: "In England they would have made him an Earl and if he wanted to, he could have gone around among his students with his penis hanging out, and everyone would have been charmed by his eccentricity."

By 1946, Mauchly and Eckert decided to go into private enterprise, where they intended to build the next model to the UNIVAC, or Universal Automatic Computer. Von Neumann went to the Institute for Advanced Study (IAS) at Princeton, taking many of the most talented people who had worked on the earlier computers with him, including Goldstine. This denied Eckert and Mauchly the most brilliant theoretician of their time and many of their ablest people, and put a ceiling on what they might achieve.

At Princeton, von Neumann started trying to raise money to build his own computer. It was not easy. The great marriage between American science and American business was still to come. The obvious company to take the lead was IBM, an electrical business machine company. But Tom Watson, Sr., the dominant figure in the company, believed that the electronic revolution would not touch his business. He was, Tom Watson, Jr., later wrote, "like the king who sees a revolution going on in the country next door to his own, yet is astounded when his own subjects get restless. He didn't realize that a new era had begun. IBM was the classic company with tunnel vision because of its success." It was in danger, the younger Watson noted, of being like the railroad industry missing the air travel revolution and the movie industry missing the television revolution.

Still, von Neumann, absolutely confident of his course, plunged ahead. He scrambled with somewhat limited success to raise the money from the Institute and other sources to fund his project. By 1950 he felt the growing pressure, particularly from Los Alamos, and from other parts of the defense industry, for more computing power. The race to finish the Institute computer paralleled the race to do the Super calculations. The IAS computer was dedicated in June 1952, and it was to become the most important model of its time, the forerunner of not just the IBM 701, that company's first venture into computing, but also the JOHNNIAC, the Rand Corporation's first computer, affectionately named after von Neumann himself. Years later, after his company somewhat belatedly rose to the challenge of the computer age, Tom Watson, Jr., spoke of how the Cold War had made IBM the undisputed king of the computer business; what was equally true was that the Cold War made the computer a mandatory technology.

The computers that were soon to come would have made the calculations for the Super easy. As it was, they remained an immense problem. Mathematician Stan Ulam was not particularly happy about bringing a fusion bomb into the world, but he was fatalistic about it: If it proved doable, he believed, then sooner or later it would be done, which to his mind diminished the moral anguish. By February 1950, Ulam was convinced that Teller's earlier estimates on the amount of tritium needed were off. Ulam tried calculations with more tritium, but again the bomb did not seem to work. He found dealing with Teller increasingly difficult, and he became irritated by Teller's reluctance to accept the fact that his calculations were off.

In April 1950, Ulam went to Princeton to talk with von Neumann and Fermi about the math. Oppenheimer joined them and seemed, Ulam thought, to be somewhat pleased that they were having some serious problems. At one point, when von Neumann pointed out yet another error in the calculations, Oppenheimer winked at Ulam. That helped convince Ulam that some of Oppie's objections to the Super were, subconsciously at least, a matter of ego—those of the man who had started a revolution with the atomic bomb witnessing the arrival of an even more powerful revolution. Their discussions in Princeton seemed to indicate that they had to increase the amount of tritium in the theoretical design.

As difficulties persisted, Teller became more and more difficult. The atmosphere at Los Alamos was tense and hostile: Teller isolated himself, and Norris Bradbury, who had succeeded Oppenheimer as head of the laboratory, became furious as success continued to elude them. Hans Bethe, who still managed to get on with Teller better than most, had always thought his colleague had a tendency toward depression, but he had never seen him this badly off—so forlorn that he couldn't even participate in scientific give-and-take at meetings but instead would leave and go back to his room to be alone. The clock was ticking and the first important test, called Greenhouse, was imminent. All Teller could say when people pressured him was that they had to have lots of tests, lots of tests. Discussions with him were not so likely to be discussions as bitter arguments. Ironically, at the same time, he was complaining to officials in Washington that Conant, Oppenheimer, and others were undermining his efforts by creating an antagonistic attitude in the scientific community. Yet to his scientific peers it was obvious that the project was failing because Teller's numbers did not work.

When Ulam returned from Princeton with the news that they would need different calculations, Teller did not take the news well. "He was pale with fury yesterday literally but I think is calmed down today," Ulam wrote von Neumann. For a time, Teller even challenged Ulam's motives. Earlier GAC skepticism about the project was proving legitimate, "far more justified than the GAC itself had dreamed in October 1949," Bethe later noted. In Bethe's words, Teller was a desperate man. His egocentrism became something of a joke among the other scientists at Los Alamos: At one point Ulam wrote von Neumann that he had thought of a new idea, had communicated it to Teller, but because Teller seemed to like it, "perhaps that meant it would not work either."

Then in February 1951, thanks largely to Ulam's projections, they made the breakthrough. Even Oppenheimer was impressed with the new calculations. They turned him back instantly from the moralist who doubted the practicality of the Super to the physicist with a passion for adventuring into the unknown. "That's it," he said when he saw Ulam's new calculations. "Sweet and lovely and beautiful."

Still, Teller did not relax. He remained, even in victory, a man apart. He was notably ungenerous about sharing credit with Ulam, and although the United States government was willing to issue a joint patent to the two men, Teller refused it. The idea of swearing under oath that he had invented the bomb together with Ulam was completely unacceptable to Teller. Indeed, it would be perjury, he noted, so he never filed for a patent. To Ulam, this was no surprise.

By the time the first thermonuclear test took place, on November 1, 1952, at Eniwetok, Teller was no longer at Los Alamos, and so estranged from most of his colleagues that he did not even attend.

The code name for the first explosion was Mike. Mike was not a bomb; rather, it was a device in a lab building on the small atoll of Elugelab. It weighed some 65 tons, so heavy that it recalled Oppenheimer's joke that if we needed to use the Super in war, we would have to deliver it by oxcart. It yielded some 10.4 million tons of TNT, or a force a thousand times greater than the Hiroshima bomb. Leona Marshall Libby, a witness to the explosion, wrote of it: "The fireball expanded to three miles in diameter. Observers, all evacuated to 40 miles or more away, saw millions of gallons of lagoon water turned to steam, appear as a giant bubble. When the steam had evaporated, they saw that the island of Elugelab where the bomb (or building) had been, had vanished, vaporized also. In its place a crater ½ mile deep and two miles wide had been born in the reef."

Teller watched the event at a seismograph in the Livermore laboratory at Berkeley, where he found the generally more conservative scientific staff congenial company. At the time he used to joke, "I'm leaving the appeasers to join the fascists." As the needle on the seismograph danced back and forth violently, Teller sent a coded message to his estranged colleagues at Los Alamos: "It's a boy."

Soon after the test, Teller lunched with Rabi and Oppenheimer. "Well, Edward, now that you have your H bomb, why don't you use it to end the war in Korea?" Oppenheimer asked him. Teller said that he answered, "The use of weapons is none of my business, and I will have none of it."

The Russians were not far behind. By the summer of 1953, they had completed the planning for their first thermonuclear test. They had, Sakharov discovered in July, made very little in the way of plans for the fallout. At the last minute, the Russians took emergency precautions, guided primarily by American literature on the subject. The Russian test was on August 12, 1953, some four years after their first atomic test. The sight was similar to that viewed by the American scientists: the cloud bigger than that of the fission bombs, turning "a sinister blue-black color." In Washington it was given the name Joe Four. Two years later, on November 22, 1955, the Russians finally tested a thermonuclear bomb. On this day Sakharov did not wear the requisite dark goggles but faced away from the explosion, turning only after he saw the flash reflected on the buildings he was facing. Several minutes later, he saw the shock wave coming at them and yelled at his colleagues to jump. Even the men who had built the bomb were awed by its power. At a meat-packing plant a hundred miles away, the windows shattered. Even further away, in a small town soot blew into people's homes.

Not unlike many of his American colleagues, Sakharov was torn by what he had done. In addition like many of the American scientists, he came to feel a loss of control over his work. At a celebration dinner given by Marshall Mistofan Nedelin, the military director of the test, Sakharov gave toast: "May all our devices explode as successfully as today's, but always over test sites and never over cities." Those at the table, Sakharov noted, fell silent. Then Nedelin said he would like to tell a parable: "An old man wearing only a shirt was praying before an icon. 'Guide me, harden me. Guide me, harden me.' His wife, who was lying on the stove, said: 'Just pray to be hard, old man. I can guide it in myself.' Let's drink to getting hard." Sakharov felt as if he had been lashed by a whip at that moment. The story was not merely crude but blasphemous as well. Its point was to put the scientists in their place. "We, the inventors, scientists, engineers and craftsmen," he later wrote, "had created a terrible weapon, the most terrible weapon in human history; but its use would lie entirely outside our control. The people at the top of the Party and military hierarchy would make the decisions. Of course, I knew this already—I was not *that* naive. But understanding something in an abstract way is different from feeling it with your whole being, like the reality of life and death . . ."

SEVEN

E ven as Douglas MacArthur promised Harry Truman that the Chinese would not enter the Korean War and that if they did, he would slaughter them, the Chinese Fourth Field Army was entering the country. The Fourth Field Army was one of the great infantry forces of the modern era, even though it consisted of peasants and remarkably little hardware. It had fashioned a brilliant victory over Chiang, who had far greater firepower. It moved on foot instead of by wheels and, lacking even the simplest of modern communication systems, coordinated its attacks with bugles—which had the additional advantage of terrifying the adversary. The troops had grown up in a world where the enemy always controlled the skies. Therefore they were trained not to move at all when an airplane passed overhead. To say that they were tough and experienced was a vast understatement. They marched (or trotted)

286 miles to their assembly point at the Yalu in eighteen days, carrying only eight to ten pounds of gear and supplies: a weapon, a grenade, eighty rounds of ammunition, perhaps a week's supply of rice, and a tiny bit of meat and fish. An American soldier, by contrast, carried sixty pounds. Being familiar with the terrible cold of the Korean winter, the Chinese soldiers did have thickly padded, quilted jackets. They were not expert marksmen; rather, they were trained to attack close to their enemy and unleash bursts of automatic fire, a method that demanded that they take extremely heavy casualties.

Some people thought the Fourth Field Army was the best that the Chinese had. It was divided into six groups; each consisted of four 30,000 man armies, and each of these had three divisions of about 8,000 to 10,000 men. They started crossing the Yalu, it was believed, on October 13. They used the regular bridges and built some of their own—invisible underwater fords, by means of sandbags. Their camouflage was so good, and MacArthur's intelligence was so bad, that none of their movements was detected. By the time MacArthur made his reckless pledge to Truman to slaughter them, there were probably at least 130,000 Chinese soldiers already in the country.

Though we did not know much about the Chinese, they knew a great deal about us. They received a pamphlet about the American troops just before the first battle began. The Americans, it said, were not to be underestimated. They were good soldiers, well equipped, and had the advantages of mobility and modern firepower in their attacks, enabling them to make lightning-quick strikes. But their weaknesses were noted as well: They did not fight well when forced to defend, and attacks at night would panic them, forcing them to leave behind their heavy equipment.

As both forces moved inexorably toward a confrontation at the Yalu, MacArthur was no longer merely the commander of the American forces, he was the sole policymaker as well. Washington had permitted him to cross the 38th parallel but had placed a strict ban on his going too far north or doing anything that might seem unduly provocative to the Chinese. His orders were to stay away from the Yalu, but seeking to capture the North Korean army that had escaped after Inchon, he simply disobeyed. At this point, the UN troops, whose misfortune it was to be carrying out MacArthur's last great dream of glory, were undersupplied, underclothed, underfed, and far from their base camp. As those United Nations units moved forward they began to feel a growing sense of isolation. Something ominous was in the air. In late November, a British officer was taking his first bath in weeks when word was brought to him that four men on horseback had been spotted near his brigade headquarters. He dressed and rushed over just in time to see them ride off. He knew instantly that they were Chinese, not North Korean. Later, he came to refer to them as the four horsemen of the Apocalypse.

In Tokyo, MacArthur urged his two main forces on to their appointed meeting place at the Yalu. The optimism at his headquarters was at its height. The war was virtually finished, MacArthur told reporters in briefings. There was talk about bringing the boys home for Christmas. In Washington, the Defense Department started canceling plans for projected troop shipments to Korea. Yet the In Min Gun had fled north in October, and some American field commanders regarded it as disturbing: Almost overnight the enemy seemed to have disappeared.

There had been an agreement between MacArthur and the Joint Chiefs of Staff (JCS) that as he moved nearer to the Yalu, he would clear all movements with them. In mid-October, the JCS readily approved crossing a line across the north at Chongjiu-Yongwon-Hamhung. But fearing that the Chiefs would stop his forward movement, MacArthur became less forthright. On October 17, he sent a directive to Washington that unilaterally set a new forward line of Sonchon-Pyongwon-Songjin, thirty miles further north. That was still arguably within his orders. What he intended to do, though, was use this, not so much as a final position, but as a staging area to go even further north.

On October 24, he ordered his troops forward. He did not clear this with the JCS, but the Chiefs heard of it through the Army backchannel and warned him that these moves were not consistent with their previous instructions. MacArthur snapped back that there were military reasons for doing this and that he had the right to go ahead based on instructions from Marshall and from the Wake Island meeting. That stunned Washington.

The first ROK troops reached the Yalu on October 25 and began taking the first Chinese prisoners. These men were captured all too readily and almost seemed to be offering themselves up as an early warning signal. Some units of the ROK Eleven Corps were hammered by enemy forces that seemed a great deal more fierce than the North Koreans. More Chinese prisoners were taken. Their uniforms were different from those of the North Koreans, and they spoke Chinese with southern accents. General Paek Sun Yup, the temporary ROK commander, spoke fluent Chinese. "Are there many of you here?" he asked. "Many," one answered. General Walton Walker, still not accepting that the Chinese had arrived, noted that a few Chinese prisoners were not necessarily significant. "After all," he said, "a lot of Mexicans live in Texas . . ."

Despite the growing evidence of a Chinese military presence, MacArthur's headquarters remained absolutely adamant that it had not encountered the Chinese. On October 29, John Throckmorton, commander of the Fifth Regiment of the 24th Division, was moving on a northwesterly course toward the Yalu when he ran into unusually stiff resistance at a North Korean blocking position. The intensity of fire was, Throckmorton thought, different and disquieting. He took eighty-nine prisoners, two of whom were Chinese. He was only forty miles from the Yalu. "By that time I could feel the hair raising on the back of my neck," he said. On October 30, Ned Almond, the commander of X Corps, went by chopper to visit an ROK unit that had taken sixteen Chinese prisoners. After looking at the prisoners and talking with their South Korean captors, he sent a message to MacArthur's headquarters that fully organized Chinese units were in the country. But his message had little impact.

Just after dusk on November 1, the Chinese forces hit an American unit with their full fury for the first time. The unit was part of the Eighth Cavalry Regiment, which held positions just north and west of Unsan. At first the Americans had been there in support of ROK troops. Now, suddenly, they were desperately trying to save themselves. They were facing, it was estimated later, nothing less than two, and quite possibly three, full divisions of Chinese troops.

It was a new kind of war. Just when the Americans thought they might have slowed the assault, more Chinese would come—like an endless human wave. A few men in an American defensive position would lay down a perfect field of fire and kill a hundred attacking Chinese. But then the bugles would sound; the attack would begin again. When the relief forces finally reached the site where the Third Battalion of the Eighth Regiment had been hit, they found a ghostlike scene. At one point an artillery battery had been overrun, its 155s and tractors carefully arranged in a defensive ring. There were American bodies everywhere. Not a living soul was anywhere. One NCO thought the site resembled another Little Big Horn. It had been a devastating defeat. Some six hundred men in the regiment had been lost, all told.

Yet MacArthur continued to give orders, pushing his units forward despite their vulnerability and the terrible cold. Sadly, MacArthur remained in Tokyo, refusing to accept the evidence that the war had changed. That did not surprise his peers.

During World War Two, MacArthur once started telling George Marshall a story by saying, "My staff tells me . . ." Marshall had cut him off: "General, you don't have a staff, you have a court." If MacArthur's staff was known as a hard-core center for sycophants, then it was likely that the greatest sycophant of all was General Charles Willoughby, MacArthur's intelligence officer. Now, at this vital juncture, he brushed aside the entreaties of those who were warning him that the war had suddenly changed. His estimates continued to coincide with what his boss *wanted* to happen. The Chinese were not going to come in; the time for that was already past. They would have come in much earlier and helped defend Pyongyang, the North Korean capital. To the growing despair of the field commanders, he could not be moved. Jack Chiles, Almond's G-3, or plans officer, who knew the MacArthur headquarters well, said, "MacArthur did not want the Chinese to enter the war in Korea. Anything MacArthur wanted, Willoughby produced intelligence for. . . . In this case Willoughby falsified the intelligence reports. . . . He should have gone to jail."

The front-line units were told to press on. MacArthur would not be deterred from his drive to link his forces at the Yalu. By November 3, Truman was becoming worried by the recurring reports of Chinese intervention and the hammering of the Eighth Cavalry; the JCS cabled MacArthur asking the extent of Chinese involvement. The next day MacArthur replied that he now saw Chinese intervention as a "distinct possibility," to give covert assistance to the North Koreans. This would let them "salvage something from the wreckage." MacArthur ordered George Stratemeyer to bomb the Korean end of the twelve bridges across the Yalu—a violation of the old JCS order to stay well clear of the Manchurian borders. His decision alarmed Washington, which told him to desist. He drafted a cable in which he threatened to resign immediately. An aide talked him out of sending it. Instead, he cabled, "Every hour that this is postponed will be paid for dearly in American and other United Nations blood. . . . I cannot overemphasize the disastrous effect both physical and psychological that will result from the restrictions which you are imposing . . ." He ended the cable with a barely concealed threat: Failure to do as he said would result in "a calamity of major proportions for which I cannot accept the responsibility without his [Truman's] personal and direct understanding of the situation."

It was a stunning reversal on MacArthur's part: Until then he had been saying with great disdain that the Chinese would not come in; now he seemed to be promising a slaughter of his own men. What he had said would never happen was happening. Characteristically, MacArthur made no apology for what might normally be viewed as a mistake of apocalyptic proportions, the failure to judge accurately both Chinese intentions and his ability to detect and confront them. If anything, his new reading of the Chinese threat seemed to make him more arrogant and more volatile than ever. It was Washington that had dictated policies, he seemed to be saying, for which he would no longer accept responsibility. The buck had been passed. The JCS and the administration, wary of confrontation, backed down and let MacArthur bomb his bridges. It was the gravest provocation imaginable to the Chinese. It was not even tactically intelligent—in a few weeks the Yalu would freeze anyway.

In Washington, the top officials—Truman, Acheson, Marshall—felt events were slipping outside of their control. What were the Chinese up to? They had struck with great success, "and yet they seemed to have vanished from the face of the earth?" wrote Acheson. "And what was MacArthur up to in the amazing military maneuver which was unfolding before our unbelieving eyes?" Acheson wrote in his memoirs. These early days in November represented, Acheson later decided, the last possible moment to avert the tragic confrontation that seemed just over the horizon. The Chinese had given clear warning of their intentions. But, he noted, "We sat around like paralyzed rabbits while MacArthur carried out this nightmare." When MacArthur announced on November 17 that he would make his final drive to the Yalu, Washington warned him only to take the high ground overlooking the Yalu valley and go no further.

It was a fateful moment. By dint of his arrogance, foolishness, and vainglory MacArthur was about to take a smaller war that was already winding down and expand it to include as an adversary a Communist superpower thereby adding more than two years to its life; he was to damage profoundly America's relations with China; and he was to help start a chain of events that was poisonous in terms of domestic politics—feeding political paranoia, giving the paranoics what they needed most: a tangible enemy. His troops pressed on. He interpreted the silence from the Chinese forces after the November 1 assault as a sign of exhaustion. He was sure that his air offensive had curtailed the ability of the Chinese to reinforce any units already in Korea. He told the U.S. ambassador to Korea on November 17 that the Chinese had only 30,000 men in the country (in fact, the figure was at least 300,000 by this time). On November 24, MacArthur flew to the front, to be present for the start of the drive. He toured the front-line ranks and then returned to Tokyo, where he issued a communiqué boasting of how American air power had isolated the battlefield, and describing the operation he was then unleashing. "If successful, this should for all practical purposes end the war," he said. The arrogance of that communiqué was remarkable, even for MacArthur. As Clay Blair noted, it tipped off the Chinese that a major offensive was coming and at the same time let the Chinese know that we were unaware of the size and intentions of their troops. There was no stopping him. "Complete victory seemed now in view," his successor Matt Ridgway, who was generally sympathetic to him, later wrote, "a golden apple that would handsomely symbolize the crowning effort of a brilliant military career. Once in reach of the prize, MacArthur would not allow himself to be delayed or admonished. Instead he plunged northward in pursuit of a vanishing enemy and changed his plans from week to week to accelerate his advance without regard for dark hints of possible disaster."

The drive toward the Yalu began on November 24, the day after Thanksgiving. The weather was terrible. The wind-chill factor made it twenty or thirty degrees below zero. Rifles froze and men had to piss on them to thaw them out. Batteries in vehicles froze and the jeeps and trucks could not be started. For the first day and a half the offensive went reasonably well. There was little resistance. But on the evening of November 25, the Chinese struck again. It was a terrifying moment. The Americans clung to the thin, narrow, icy roads in valleys while above them, on the high ground, well-armed, well-led, and well-clothed Chinese troops rained down murderous fire. The Chinese came at American units in a kind of V, called Hachi-Shiki's. As they got closer, they unfolded the V and began to envelop the American position on its flanks. Like the In Min Gun, they would send a smaller unit to the rear to hammer the Americans as they tried to retreat. Panic resulted, and more often than not, the victims threw down their heavy equipment as they ran.

It was clear from the start that this was a devastating assault. Many of the American units were in desperate trouble. Still, on November 27, Ned Almond launched the second part of the offensive—the X Corps offensive, the other pincer to link up with the Eighth Army. There was a certain madness to it all. MacArthur, Joe Collins wrote years later, was marching forward "like a Greek hero of old to an unkind and inexorable fate." The front-line troops were being hammered by forces that greatly outnumbered them, and some commanders—those of the Marines, for example—were instinctively moving their men back and regrouping them. On the morning of November 28, Almond visited various forward units by helicopter.

He continued to urge them forward. He dismissed the Chinese as nothing but the remnants of a few divisions fleeing north. "We're still attacking and we're going all the way to the Yalu. Don't let a bunch of Chinese laundrymen stop you," he said. So much for the Fourth Field Army. He moved to raise the morale by giving out medals. Don Carlos Faith, a battalion commander, was given a silver star and told to give two more to men of his own choosing. Faith was appalled. As a way of showing his displeasure, Faith singled out the two soldiers nearest him—a wounded sergeant and a headquarters mess sergeant. The moment Almond flew away, Faith tore the medal from his jacket and threw it in the snow.

By November 28 it was clear that this was an epic disaster and that the great MacArthur had been outgeneraled by the Chinese. The question was suddenly how much of the 2nd Infantry Division and how much of the First Marines would get out alive. The heaviest burden fell on the 2nd Infantry Division. Trying to slip out of what seemed like a three-sided trap, the commanders of the 2nd hit what at first seemed like a company-strength blocking force to their south—nothing that they could not handle. In fact, they were moving into one of the most brutal ambushes in military history. The most basic rule of warfare is that it is critical to hold the high ground, and in this case the Chinese held all the high ground and the Americans were in the thin valley road below; as the Chinese fire rained down, it dawned on the Americans that there might be a regiment or two manning this position.

It was a gauntlet, and the military historian S.L.A. Marshall would so describe it in his book *The River and the Gauntlet.* Over six miles, the Chinese had some forty machine guns and about ten mortars. Along the way the Americans fought not just the constant machine gun fire raining down on them from above, but struggled with new roadblocks caused by their own abandoned vehicles. Five miles along the way, there was a terrifying stretch known as the Pass. It was a brief quarter-mile-long cut in a hill. Along it were steep embankments fifty feet high. There was no possibility of slipping out and escaping through the hills. Everywhere, men seemed to be dead and dying. When the division commander, Laurence (Dutch) Keiser reached the Pass in the midafternoon, he found it so clogged with the wreckage of American vehicles as to be virtually impossible. "Who's in command here?" he asked one group of men huddled behind a truck. No one answered him. At one point Keiser stumbled on a corpse. The body came alive. "You damn son of a bitch," it said, cursing its general. "My friend, I'm sorry," was all the division commander could say.

Some three thousand men were killed, wounded, or somehow lost running the Gauntlet that day. That it wasn't worse was a miracle. In the final few days of November alone, the 2nd Division took some five thousand casualties, or roughly one third of its men. December was just as ghastly. In the words of the British military historian Max Hastings, "Most of the Eighth Army fell apart as a fighting force in a fashion resembling the collapse of the French in 1940, the British in Singapore in 1942."

In the weeks following the Chinese attack, MacArthur seemed to be offering the President only the choice between a much larger war in which he claimed he would ultimately triumph or a complete rout. The Truman administration was in many ways fighting if not for its life, at least for its legitimacy. On November 30, at a White House press conference a reporter asked Truman whether, since he had said that America would take any and all steps to meet its military obligations, that might include the atomic bomb. The President answered, "That includes every weapon we have." "Mr. President," a reporter continued. "You said 'every weapon we have.' Does that mean that there has been active consideration of the use of the atomic bomb?" "There has always been active consideration of its use," he answered. It was a time of desperation; MacArthur's arrogance had not only resulted in a devastating defeat in the field but a psychological defeat for us as well.

The meetings at the Pentagon were the bleakest that anyone could remember. The word *Dunkirk* hung constantly in the air. The Joint Chiefs were paralyzed by the constant bad news from the front: They no longer trusted or believed in MacArthur but they were afraid to challenge him. Finally Matt Ridgway, the Army vice chief of staff tried to embolden his colleagues. Though technically not a chief he asked for permission to speak: "My own conscience finally overcam my discretion." He blurted out, "We need to take immediate action. We owe it to the men in the field and to the God to whom we have to answer for these men's lives to stop talking and act." A little later, as the meeting was breaking up, Ridgway grabbed General Hoyt Vandenberg and asked him why the Joint Chiefs didn't send orders to MacArthur *telling* him what to do. Vandenberg just shook his head. "What good would that do? He wouldn't obey the orders. What can we do?" "You can relieve any commander who won't obey orders, can't you?" Ridgway asked. Vandenberg gave him a long look, both puzzled and amazed. "This was," Acheson later noted, "the first time that someone had expressed what everybody thought—that the Emperor had no clothes on." Now a collision course was set.

By early December, the UN forces had retreated from Pyong-yang in a rout and the Chinese had occupied it. Four days later, large elements of Tenth Corps withdrew from Wonsan by sea and two days later it moved out of Hungnam. On December 15, Truman declared a state of national emergency.

What probably saved the American and United Nations forces was a fluke. On December 23, General Walton Walker, who had a reputation for driving recklessly, was killed in a jeep accident. Walker, who had been the commander of the Eighth Army since the American forces first arrived in Korea, was considered tough and feisty, but in far over his head in terms of the larger skills needed for so demanding an assignment. Some of the top American generals had wanted to relieve him much earlier but had been afraid of the consequences as far as public relations were concerned. Now Matt Ridgway would command the Eighth Army. He got the news in Washington on December 23. The next day he left for Tokyo, asking the Army Vice-Chief of Staff Ham Haislip to tell his wife that he would not be spending Christmas with her—he simply could not bear to tell her himself. In Tokyo he talked with Douglas MacArthur, who praised the toughness and skills of the Chinese infantry-men and spoke somewhat mordantly of the limits of air power in isolating a battlefield and stopping infiltration by the enemy. Then MacArthur told him, "The Eighth Army is yours, Matt. Do what you think best."

Matthew Bunker Ridgway was arguably the preeminent Ameri-can soldier of this century. He was an upper-class American; his father had been a judge in Brooklyn, an uncle helped design the New York subway system, and his mother, Julia Starbuck Ridgway, had been a concert pianist. To Matt Ridgway, the military was not just a career, it was a calling. His sense of duty had a touch of the mystical to it. "He was," noted a West Point contemporary, Russell Reeder, "a twelfth-century knight with a twentieth-century brain." Even in the peacetime Army he seemed different—not merely better read and more serious, but more committed than other men. George Catlett Marshall, whose protégé he became, had to warn him repeatedly about pushing himself too hard. When World War Two began, Ridgway found himself in command of the 82nd Division, then the All-American Division. "He was," said Jim Gavin, who replaced him in the 82nd when Ridgway became a corps commander, "a *great* combat commander. Lots of courage. He was right up front every minute. Hard as flint and full of intensity, almost grinding his teeth with intensity; so much so, I thought, that man's going to have a heart attack before it's over. Sometimes it seemed as though it was a personal thing: Ridgway versus the Wehrmacht. He'd stand in the middle of the road and urinate. I'd say, "Matt, get the hell out of there. You'll get shot! No! He was defiant. Even with his penis he was defiant."

Upon arriving in Korea, he spent the first few days visiting every front-line unit, wearing his trademark grenade pinned to one shoulder strap. Many soldiers had the impression that he wore two grenades; actually, the other object was a medical kit. From this came his nickname, Old Iron Tits. He was appalled by MacArthur's distance from the battlefield, by the paucity of division and regimental commanders at the front, and by the lack of daily intelligence on the enemy, a result of not enough patrolling.

This army had completely lost its confidence, he decided. Morale was nonexistent. The men seemed to go about in a daze, "wondering when they would hear the whistle of that homebound transport." They were surprisingly poorly fed and poorly clothed, given the wealth of the nation back at home. Worse, they had become far too dependent upon their wheels to fight an enemy that had no wheels. In truth, he thought the soldiers were dangerously close to going soft. "There was nothing but our own love of comfort that bound us to the road," he later wrote. "We could get off into the hills too." What he wanted to create "was a toughness of soul as well as body." He chewed out the division and regimental commanders right after the start of the New Year. They knew too little about the front, and they were spending too much time in their CPs. If the ordinary soldiers had gotten soft, it was because their commanders had allowed them to do so.

He knew exactly what he wanted to do: take the high ground, employ his artillery effectively, create far stronger defensive positions, and fight better at night by using massive numbers of flares. He was going to grind the Chinese down, erode their vast numbers with his superior artillery. He analyzed the strengths of the Chinese army, how they had compensated for their lack of materiel. He would illuminate the nighttime battlefield with flares from C-47s, and make each Chinese offensive too expensive. His own confidence grew day by day. Within two weeks of arriving, he wrote his old friend Ham Haislip that it could be done. "The power is here," he wrote. "The strength and means we have—short perhaps of Soviet military intervention. My own overriding problem, dominating all others, is to achieve the spiritual awakening of the latent capabilities of this command. If God permits me to do that, we shall achieve more, much more than our people think possible—and perhaps inflict a bloody defeat on the Chinese which even China will long remember, wanton as she is in the sacrifice of lives." That might be, but he was taking no chances that his forces would be driven into the sea, as some had feared. Back at Pusan he prepared a super defensive line back at the Pusan port—a monster trench, protected by barbed wire and powerful artillery positions. Just in case.

At the same time he was pushing subordinates like Mike Michaelis to be even more aggressive. He visited Michaelis's regimental headquarters. "Michaelis," he asked. "What are tanks for?" "To kill," Michaelis had answered. "Take your tanks north," Ridgway had said. "Fine, sir," Michaelis had answered. "It's easy to take them there. It's getting back that's going to be the most difficult. They always cut the road behind you." "Who said anything about coming back?" Ridgway answered. "If you can stay up there 24 hours I'll send the [25th] Division up. If the Division can stay up there 24 hours, I'll send the [1] Corps up."

He was everywhere. No unit, no matter how small, was safe from his visit. "The man who came to dinner," one high official at 1 Corps headquarters called him sardonically. Another high officer said, "Oh God! He came to *every* briefing, *every* morning . . ." But it was working. He was slowly breathing life back into an army that had been not merely defeated but humiliated. His goals were modest. Real estate was important to him only as a means of giving the United Nations some leverage when it came to the final negotiations for peace. Yet even as Ridgway steadied his forces, MacArthur was still issuing apocalyptic cables to Washington, saying that unless we widened the war, we were going to be driven off the Korean peninsula.

In mid-January, Joe Collins and Hoyt Vandenberg visited the Eighth Army and were much impressed. Collins later went back and gave a surprisingly optimistic briefing to Truman, the cabinet, and the Chiefs. It was a different army. "Ridgway alone," said Collins, "was responsible." It was a personal triumph of the rarest sort. As Omar Bradley, not a man who lightly used superlatives, wrote in his autobiography, "It is not often in wartime that a single battlefield commander can make a decisive difference. But in Korea, Ridgway would prove to be the exception. His brilliant, driving, uncompromising leadership would turn the tide of battle like no other general's in our military history." In Washington they stopped talking about being driven out of Korea or using the atomic weapon. Years later, noting that America had considered the use of an atomic weapon, Max Hastings, the British military historian, said of Ridgway and the men under his command: "The men who turned the tide on the battlefield in Korea in the first weeks of 1951 may have also saved the world from the nightmare of a new Hiroshima in Asia."

Not surprisingly, the better Matt Ridgway did, the more difficult Douglas MacArthur became. It was becoming clear that the earlier failure of the Eighth Army was that of its commander. (In 1954 MacArthur told Jim Lucas, one of his more favored journalists, that Ridgway was the worst of his field commanders—this view to be published after MacArthur's death: Such was the bitterness of a man whose reputation had been so badly damaged by the defeat along the Yalu.) MacArthur still made cameo visits to Korea, accompanied by his press coterie, usually on the occasion of a major success. Ridgway finally had to send a message filled with flattery asking him not to come, since it was clear to the Chinese that every MacArthur trip usually coincided with the start of an offensive. At the same time MacArthur's provocations of the administration escalated; there were regular interviews with journalists in Tokyo in which he criticized the idea of a limited victory. True victory, he said, was the unification of Korea. By this time the top British military were convinced that MacArthur personally wanted war with China.

The British were not alone in such suspicions. Omar Bradley wrote that "his legendary pride had been hurt. The Red Chinese had made a fool of the infallible 'military genius' . . . the only possible means left to MacArthur to regain his lost pride and military reputation was now to inflict an overwhelming defeat on those Red Chinese generals who had made a fool of him. In order to do this he was perfectly willing to propel us into all-out war with Red China, and possibly with the Soviet Union, igniting World War III and a nuclear holocaust."

Knowing that the Truman administration planned to announce on March 24 that it would seek a cease-fire as the first step in arranging a settlement with the Chinese, MacArthur cut the ground out from under the President by making his own announcement. He taunted the Chinese, virtually calling them a defeated army, saying that China's "exaggerated and vaunted military power" lacked the industrial base necessary for modern warfare. If only, he continued, the restrictions imposed on him were lifted, he would strike so viciously that they would be doomed to military collapse. It was not just an insult to the Chinese but a slap in the face to the President, who was seeking a means to peace.

Truman was furious. It was then that the President decided to fire his general. "I've come to the conclusion that our Big General in the Far East must be recalled," he wrote in this diary. A few days later, MacArthur, who surely must have known what he was doing, drove the last nail into his own coffin. He wrote a letter to Joe Martin, the Republican House minority leader, supporting Martin's view that Chiang's troops should be called into this war. MacArthur knew the letter would be released by Martin: It was filled with grand statements about the real battleground being Asia. But the final sentence was the killer: "There is no substitute for victory."

Truman talked the problem over with his top advisers, who warned him that firing MacArthur would initiate the biggest political battle of his administration. Truman had hoped to bring some grace to the denouement by sending a personal emissary to break the news to the general, but word leaked out, and MacArthur heard the news over the radio. That seemed to underscore the heartlessness of the decision. Still, the scandal was preferable to dealing with a provocative and disobedient commander in the field.

In Tokyo, when he heard, MacArthur turned to his second wife, and said, "Jeannie, we're going home at last." The next day MacArthur told Ridgway, who had come to replace him, that he had been fired because Truman was mentally unstable. He knew this, he said, because he had close friends who knew Truman's doctor. The President, MacArthur claimed, would not live more than six months. Ridgway found the conversation a fascinating glimpse into the mind of a supreme egotist: In the world according to MacArthur, it was Truman who was irrational.

The firing was as divisive an act as anyone could remember—in terms of class, religion, culture, and geography. It was not just that everyone had an opinion about what had happened, it was that everyone had to voice it. There were fights in bars between strangers and fights on commuter trains between men who knew each other and who had, up to that moment, been friends and had concealed their political differences. Acheson, who always managed to keep his sense of humor about the attacks from the right, got into a cab soon after the anger had erupted. The driver turned around to look at his passenger. "Aren't you Dean Acheson?" he asked. "Yes, I am," Acheson answered. "Would you like me to get out?" It was a story he loved to tell.

It was to that nation, that outpouring of emotion, that MacArthur came home. At first it seemed like one vast parade that would never end. It began in Tokyo, on the morning of April 16, 1951, where nearly 250,000 Japanese lined the streets to bid their postwar ruler farewell, many of them waving small Japanese and American flags. The next stop was Hawaii, and at Hickam Field the crowd was estimated by reporters at 100,000. In San Francisco some 20,000 people came out to the airport; the crowd surged forward, swallowing up Governor Earl Warren in the process. The next morning nearly 500,000 people watched him deliver a brief speech at city hall. There he told not only the audience but also millions watching on television that he did not intend to enter politics. He hoped, he said, that his name would never be used in a political way. "The only politics I have is contained in a single phrase known well to all of you—'God Bless America!' "

The last big stop on MacArthur's return was Washington. He arrived near midnight, and again the crowd at the airport was immense, though it included no member of the Truman cabinet. In Washington MacArthur was to address a joint session of Congress. It was MacArthur at his most formidable, powerful, theatrical, manipulative, and wonderfully selective with the record. Among other things, he claimed in his speech that the Joint Chiefs agreed with his policies in Korea, which was a boldfaced lie. He seemed to back off from a direct confrontation with China ("No man in his right mind would advocate sending our ground forces into continental China"), but at the same time he called for a blockade which was an act of war, the removal of restrictions on Chiang, and logistical support so the Nationalists could invade the mainland.

Then came the peroration, marvelously rich in memories and pure nostalgia: "I am closing my fifty-two years of military service. When I joined the Army even before the turn of the century, it was the fulfillment of all my boyish hopes and dreams. The world has turned over many times since I took the oath on the plain at West Point, and the hopes and dreams have long since vanished. But I still remember the refrain of one of the most popular barracks ballads of that day, which proclaimed most profoundly that—'Old soldiers never die; they just fade away.' And like the old soldier of that ballad, I now close my military career and just fade away—an old soldier who tried to do his duty as God gave him the light to see that duty. Good-bye."

The response seemed to divide along party lines. Representative Dewey Short, a Missouri Republican, said afterward, "We saw a great hunk of God in the flesh, and we heard the voice of God." To former president Herbert Hoover, MacArthur was "the reincarnation of Saint Paul into a great General of the Army who came out of the East." Truman, typically, was blunter: "It was nothing but a bunch of damn bullshit."

EIGHT

T here never was a country more fabulous than America," wrote the British historian Robert Payne after visiting America in the winter of 1948–49. "She sits bestride the world like a Colossus; no other power at any time in the world's history has possessed so varied or so great an influence on other nations . . . Half of the wealth of the world, more than half of the productivity, nearly two-thirds of the world machines are concentrated in American hands; the rest of the world lies in the shadow of American industry . . ." Driven by the revolutionary vision of Henry Ford, the United States had been the leader in mass production before the war; ordinary Americans could afford the Model-T, while in Europe where class lines were sharply drawn, the rather old-fashioned manufacturers preferred building expensive cars for the rich. In addition they fought such heretics as Ferdinand Porsche, who wanted to make the *Volksauto,* or people's car, a German version of the Model T. World War Two only widened the existing gap. It ravaged Europe, but taught those running America's industries to meet brutal schedules and norms that only a few years previously would have been considered impossible. The war had diverted the economy to the military from the consumer, but once the war was over, the consumer was not to be denied.

Henry Luce was the first to speak of the coming of the American Century: Some forty years later Naohiro Amaya, a Japanese intellectual and high-level civil servant, would say that the American Century was the same thing as the Oil Century—an era in which the economy was driven by oil instead of coal and in which, for the first time, the worker became a consumer as well. Daniel Yergin described this liberated worker-consumer as the Hydrocarbon Man. Unlike the worker who toiled in the coal age, the Hydrocarbon Man was the beneficiary of his own labor. He owned a car and a house and enjoyed a generally improved style of living. In the coal age, Amaya pointed out, many workers worked for small wages to produce giant machines like the steam engine; accordingly, the industrial process enriched only the owner of the factory. In the Oil Century people worked at Ford or GM plants, where they mass-produced machines whose price was so low they could be bought by the very people who made them. Karl Marx, Amaya liked to say, was the last great philosopher of the coal age; his workers were locked into a serflike condition. Had Marx witnessed the industrial explosion of the Oil Century and the rising standard of living it produced among ordinary workers, he might have written differently.

The Oil Century, Yergin said, was just beginning in 1949, and America, with its accessible, inexpensive domestic oil sources, was the first nation to enjoy it. During the war, vast new pipelines and great refineries were built to create even easier access to oil. So the price of oil (which was a far more efficient source of energy, anyway) remained low after the war. This was not just some abstract economic concept; it had tremendous impact, driving a surging economy at all levels. There were frequent gas-price wars among filling stations—which would advertise that their price at the pump was a half cent lower than that of the neighboring stations.

In addition most industrialists of the era saw oil as a means of fostering more stable social-political conditions. Digging coal out of the mines was a difficult, dangerous process, which made workers tough and resentful. They responded by organizing such unions as the United Mine Workers, led by John L. Lewis, probably the most combative labor leader of his generation. Lewis feared no one—mine owners, media, or even such liberal Presidents as Franklin Roosevelt and Harry Truman; he was even immune to pleas that his tactics were impeding the war effort. Fear of men like him and their ability to block consistent production was a powerful incentive for industrialists to switch from coal to oil. It was to become an international trend in which America led the way. In the period from 1949 to 1972, American consumption of oil went from 5.8 million barrels per day to 16.4 million barrels per day. In 1949, coal accounted for two thirds of the world's energy; by 1971, oil accounted for two thirds.

In America the years immediately after World War Two saw one of the great sellers' markets of all time. There was a desperate hunger for products after the long drought of some fifteen years, caused first by the Depression and then by World War Two. At first there was actually a premium on buying a car; customers often had to pay something under the table to dealers in order to get on the waiting list for the relatively few new cars available. Like many returning veterans, William Levitt, who was soon to become America's foremost builder of mass housing, found that he had to pay a thousand dollars extra, almost half the list price, to buy a Nash for his mother.

If ever there was a symbol of America's industrial might in those years, it was General Motors, a company so powerful that to call it merely a corporation seemed woefully inadequate. It was the largest, richest corporation in the world and would, in the coming decade, become the first corporation in the history of mankind to gross a billion dollars. Its primary competitor, the Ford Motor Company, hovered near bankruptcy after the war, thanks to the madness and paranoia of its founder. Ford was rescued only after Henry Ford II was permitted to take a top management team from General Motors, a move encouraged privately by Alfred P. Sloan, the chairman of GM's board, because he feared that if Ford went under GM would be vulnerable to antimonopoly charges by the Justice Department. General Motors dominated the market so completely that when one of its top executives, Charlie "Engine" Wilson, left GM to become Eisenhower's defense secretary, he was widely quoted as saying that what was good for General Motors was good for the country. That is what he probably *thought,* but what he actually *said* was: "We at General Motors have always felt that what was good for the country was good for General Motors as well." In good years GM made virtually as many as or more cars than all of its competitors combined.

The only thing standing between the corporation and virtually limitless profits was the possibility of labor unrest. During 1945–46, there was a bitter strike over wages at General Motors that lasted some one hundred days. The issue came down to a one-penny-an-hour difference, which GM could easily have afforded. Management held the line, as much as anything else, to teach the United Auto Workers (UAW) a lesson. At the same time, the strike had significantly reduced the corporation's production and its profits, so it had been a lesson to GM executives as well. Wilson, the head of the corporation, and Walter Reuther, the head of the union, had an unusually good personal relationship, and Wilson, for a General Motors executive, was exceptionally sympathetic to the plight of the working man. Looking to the horizon and seeing nothing standing between him and unlimited sales and profits except labor unrest, Wilson signed a historic agreement with Reuther and the union in 1948, guaranteeing not only traditional wage increases but also raises tied to a cost-of-living index. In effect it made the union a junior partner of the corporation, tying wages not merely to productivity but to such other factors as inflation as well. The agreement reflected the absolute confidence of a bedrock conservative who saw the economic pie as so large that he wanted to forgo his ideological instincts in order to start carving it up as quickly as possible. Some conservatives in the industry were not thrilled with the agreement and its implications for the future, but in the short run, it had the desired effect; it brought GM virtually a generation of peace with its work force. "The treaty of Detroit," *Fortune* called it, and added: "General Motors may have paid a billion for peace, [but] it got a bargain." In those days GM was so mighty it knew it could simply pass on the burden of higher labor costs to the customers (and knew also that by signing such an agreement, it had set, as well, the basic labor rate for Ford and Chrysler, which with their lesser resources and smaller scales of production would find it far more burdensome. Ford and Chrysler would set their prices on their new models once they learned what GM was going to do).

General Motors, in the years after the war, made ever bigger cars. It moved in that direction because it was the nature of the beast. There had been one brief skirmish within the corporate hierarchy when Wilson wanted to do a low-price car at Chevy in the late forties. He had in mind a car that would cost under a thousand dollars. There was even a brand name for the new car—the Cadet— and engineering on it was pursued to a relatively advanced stage. Charles Kettering, the company's most brilliant inventor, was one of the few top executives sympathetic to Wilson's idea, but it was Kettering's invention of the high-compression engine using high octane gas that, as much as anything else, helped tip the balance away from small cars.

Small cars meant smaller profits, while basic production costs stayed the same. Producing a fender for a big car, the GM analysts liked to point out, was not much more expensive than producing a fender for a little car. The financial people reported that they would have to sell three hundred thousand Cadets a year for three years just to pay for its tools and dies. Worse, who was to tell how many Cadet sales might have gone instead to larger cars, where GM made a larger profit? By 1947 the Cadet was shelved. In December 1949 a reporter asked Wilson if there would ever be an inexpensive car priced under a thousand dollars again. No, he answered, that was in the past. "People don't want the kind of car you would have to make in order to price it under a thousand dollars. You would have to take too much out to get the price down and there are too many things you couldn't cut."

General Motors had been waiting a long time for this market of abundance; in fact Alfred P. Sloan, the company's corporate architect, had been planning for it for some twenty-five years, but his dream for a super corporation to exploit an affluent society was delayed first by the Depression and then the war. Sloan was seventy-five before the country's affluence finally caught up with his vision for GM. It had been his belief since the mid-twenties that the American market could be broken down into a few essential niches, defined by economic and social status. Crucial to Sloan's dream was the annual model change, designed to make car owners restless with the cars they owned and eager for newer products. But GM's categories were the core of its success. They made car owners restless by playing off their broader aspirations. The Chevy was for blue-collar people with solid jobs and for young couples just starting out who had to be careful with money; the Pontiac was for more successful people who were confident about their economic futures and wanted a sportier car—one thinks of the young man just out of law school; the Olds was, in the beginning of the decade, a bit more sedate—for the white-collar bureaucrat or old-fashioned manager; the Buick was for the town's doctor, the young lawyer who was about to be made partner, or the elite of the managerial class; the Cadillac was for the top executive or owner of the local factory. Typically, when two brothers, Dick and Mac McDonald, after floundering for most of their lives, finally succeeded in a big way with a small hamburger stand in San Bernardino, the first thing each of them did was buy a new Cadillac. That signaled they had joined the proprietorial class, and like the other town leaders, they dutifully turned in their Caddies each year for the latest model. Caddies cost about five thousand dollars, and the price with the trade-in—for that was one of the advantages of a Caddy: it held its value—was seven hundred dollars annually.

It was hard to think of a more unlikely figure than Alfred Sloan to lead a revolution of consumer affluence. He had no love of cars. His employees could not conceive of him showing up at the company's test track to drive the latest hot model. Cars, he had thought as a young man, were "impractical toys . . . a dangerous nuisance." Mr. Sloan, as he was always called, stayed indoors, behind his desk, suit jacket on, tie knotted, tall and ascetic. His manner was distant, for decisions were never to be influenced by friendship—that would be a weakness. Indeed it was hard to imagine him out of the office; he and his wife did not entertain much, and recreation was essentially an alien word to him. It was in his office that he was happiest, for there he could study his figures and organizational charts, seeking the truth that only they could reveal. The charts gave him pleasure; he could look at them and see the company with its complicated industrial tasks deftly and justly apportioned, not to mention the financial monitoring capabilities skillfully imbedded throughout it. To him these charts represented a beautiful harmony between corporate discipline and industrial dynamism. Product was important at a place like GM, but product was not Alfred Sloan's primary impulse—the corporation would always produce plenty of talented young men who could create product. The system was Sloan's love. He was a man of order, who had come to power at General Motors in the early twenties during a period of terrible chaos. Billy Durant, the founder of General Motors, had been brilliant; he had seen the advantages in binding together several smaller companies and had gone on a colossal buying spree, purchasing auto companies and suppliers alike, including a ball-bearing company headed by a young man named Alfred P. Sloan. Durant had created a potential automobile giant, but it was also a company loaded with debt, with too many of its companies vying for the same share of market. Of the seven car companies in Durant's early United Motors Corporation, the forerunner of GM, only two were profitable— Cadillac and Buick—both with secure market niches. Sloan thought Durant's fatal flaw was that he could create but not administer. When Sloan became president of the company, bankruptcy loomed just over the horizon.

Sloan later wrote, "I believe it is reasonable to say that no greater opportunity for accomplishment was ever given to any individual in industry than was given to me when I became president. . . . I determined right then and there that everything I had was to be given to the cause. No sacrifice of time, effort or my own convenience was to be too great. There were to be no reservations or alibis." He was the prototype of all the managerial men to come later, and his rise at GM symbolized the rise of the new managerial class in America, leading some to bemoan the effect upon American entrepreneurship. Fearing that talented mavericks and tinkerers were being replaced by bookkeepers and bankers, Russell Leffingwell, a partner in J. P. Morgan, warned the Senate Finance Committee in 1935 that "the growth of corporate enterprise in America has been drying up individual independence and initiative. We are becoming a nation of hired men, hired by great aggregates of capital."

Sloan's first task was to challenge the powerful but stagnant Ford Motor Company. The era of mass car production had been inaugurated by the first Henry Ford, with his Model T. Before that, cars were exclusively the property of the wealthy. Ford figured out how to manufacture cars in such volume that the price dropped steadily—for every dollar I bring the price down, I can sell a thousand more cars, he bragged. In so doing, he changed the very nature of the American economy. Under Henry Ford that first era of auto production was, most assuredly, Puritan. The Model T was simple, boxy, functional. A buyer could choose a car in any color he wanted, Ford boasted, as long as it was black. There were no frills.

Starting in the late twenties, Sloan and his colleagues at GM inaugurated the second stage of the automobile era, in which the car was not merely transportation but a reflection of status, a concept to which most Americans responded enthusiastically as they strove to move upward into the middle class, and then the upper middle class. Under Sloan, the buyer was supposed to covet an ever showier, ever more expensive car; as such a car was not a permanent possession, it was an economic benchmark on life's journey to the top. Sloan presented the choices to the buyers that Henry Ford had reserved to himself. He had little sympathy for the rigid, unchanging ways of the old man. "We had no stake in the old ways of the automobile business; change meant opportunity," Sloan later noted.

After World War Two, Sloan pondered what Americans wanted, and he decided they wanted styling first, automatic transmissions second, and high-compression engines third. He gave carte blanche to his top designer, Harley Earl. If, in a poorer time, Henry Ford represented the Calvinist era, Harley Earl was the standard-bearer of the new age of affluence and abundance. It is possible that no one exerted as much influence on American style and taste in the fifties as he, and no one reflected more accurately what the country had become. The cars he produced in the fifties, wrote the critic Stephen Bayley, "were brought about by a deliberate corporate policy of encouraging dreams. Harley Earl invented the dream car at a moment in American history when the future seemed rosy rather than intimidating, and when there was confidence that a better future would be brought about more quickly by ever increasing consumption of ever changing style."

Earl was plucked out of Hollywood by Sloan and Lawrence Fisher in 1927. His father had been a carriage builder there and Harley Earl had started out as one of the early customizers in the new auto business, adapting cars for the least conservative of Detroit's customers: movie stars. Even before he left Hollywood there was a distinctive stamp to Earl cars: They were longer, lower, ever sleeker, ever more rounded, and even when they were standing still, they were to give the impression of power and motion. He cut down the height of the standard frames and added a middle section to the frame. His prewar cars were original, stylish, and a significant break from the boxy look that had become the staple of Detroit in the twenties and thirties.

His mandate came directly from Sloan, and he began a new department, the art and color department, as it was known. Now, models of new cars, which had previously been tiny, were created life-size. "The trouble with small models is that your eyes don't shrink with the model," Earl liked to say. When he had arrived in Detroit, the engineering departments were all-powerful, and the advertisements for cars emphasized such features as generator capacity. But gradually, given Sloan's mandate, power shifted to the styling room. At first he had to fight the division heads, many of whom had come up from engineering and who were contemptuous of his new-fangled ways and attempts to gussy up their cars. Those were battles he would always win; he was, it turned out, a very good corporate infighter. Even Harlow Curtice, the president of the company, learned this, though he usually shared Earl's vision. On one occasion, they were both in the styling room and Curtice did not like a particular car. They argued, but not for long. Earl picked up the phone and dialed it. "Hello, Alfred," he said. There was a quick exchange of pleasantries. Then down to business: "I'm here with

Harlow and we're having something of a disagreement. I wondered if you could set Harlow straight."

A Harley Earl car was easy to spot. He was fascinated by jet airplanes, so long and slim that they appeared to be racing into the future; he admired sharks, long, sleek, and powerful, and his futuristic cars were, in no small way, based on their shape, with a single metal dorsal fin in the rear. "My sense of proportion tells me that oblongs are more attractive than squares," he once wrote, "just as a ranch house is more attractive than a square three-story flat-roofed house or a greyhound is more attractive than a bulldog."

Earl was a great showman. In order to push a particular design before skeptical board members and division heads, he would mount the car four inches above where he really wanted it. The executives would circle the car, murmuring their approval. Then, by prearranged signal, Earl would take out a handkerchief and wipe his brow; the car would be released from its props and lowered to the proper height. The difference was stunning. At the lower height it looked ready to explode out of its blocks. The executives were duly impressed. His chief aim was to give his cars the look of motion, even while they were at rest. With one touch of the eraser he scrubbed the running boards. He hid the rear tire from view.

In a corporate culture in which the individual was *always* subordinated to the corporate good and in which a certain anonymity was increasingly valued, Harley Earl deliberately stood apart. After all, he had seen Cecil B. DeMille create his own mystique by going everywhere with a riding crop and wearing boots. Earl was tall, about six feet six, and it was said that he decided to hire no one over six feet six, so that he could always tower over his staff. "The world," he would say, "stands aside for the man who knows where's he's going." When he entered the room, his manner left no doubt that he expected to be catered to and, of course, listened to. Though Harley Earl needed glasses, he almost never wore them because he believed they detracted from his image and thus diminished his power. Other GM executives drove Cadillacs (or the car of their division after the order came down from Harlow Curtice that it was not becoming for executives of Chevy to drive Caddies), but Harley Earl drove the LeSabre, a highly futuristic car he himself had designed. Typically, it was based on a jet plane, the F-86 Sabre jet; the cost to the company of building this prototype was estimated at roughly $7 million. But at least it was an *American* car. He made sure that he was not one of those stylists who designed for an American company but drove a foreign car. When his son, Jerry, announced he was planning to drive a Ferrari, Earl put his foot down: "No son of mine is going to drive one of those damn Ferraris," he said. He immediately ordered the design shop to produce a special Corvette for his son.

Other executives lived in the General Motors base camp of Bloomfield Hills; Earl lived in Grosse Pointe, where the proprietorial class had built fabled residences; soon the new General Motors design shop was located in Warren, near Grosse Pointe, for Earl's convenience. Earl had hundreds of suits, many of them linen and in offbeat colors. Other executives allowed themselves only three colors for suits: dark blue, light gray, and dark gray. Earl seemed to have a duplicate copy of each suit, which he kept in a massive closet in his office, so that if his clothes became wrinkled during the day, he could change and put on a fresh outfit. Even his shoes looked as if there were shoe trees still in them. When he was meeting with the GM board, his clothes, if anything, were even more eccentric, more flamboyant than usual. His staff would watch him go before the board in a cream-colored linen suit and a dark blue shirt (the reversal of colors normally mandated for GM executives) and *blue suede shoes*. They knew he was making a statement, that he was artistic, that he knew design and taste as they did not and, finally, that he was outside their reach and they were not to fool with him. In retrospect, thought Don Frey, a Ford executive, Harley Earl's cars looked exactly the way he dressed: a little overripe, but one accepted at the time that this was style. If Earl could have put chrome on his clothes, thought Frey, he most surely would have.

He was Mr. Earl—never, ever Harley—to those who worked for him, no matter how long or how successfully. He was tyrannical to his subordinates: He raged at them, pushed them, and always demanded more. His word was law: In the late fifties, GM made a tentative step toward participating in racing, but Earl would not allow the drivers on the Chevy team to practice in the racing car itself because he did not want the paint job damaged. He liked to keep his subordinates on edge. He might, for example, visit the Buick design room in the late morning and look at a sketch. His face would grow grimmer and grimmer, and finally he would ask, "Who did this one?" Some poor assistant designer would finally be forced to admit that the idea was his. "Well, the next time I come in I don't want to see it because it's no damn good." Off he would go for lunch, but beware the poor designer who did not act immediately on such a warning, for Earl was sure to come back in a few hours to check whether the offending sketch had indeed been taken down. If it had not, he would rip it off the wall. Another specialty of his was to peer over a working stylist's shoulder and say rather casually to the claque that arrived with him from the design committee (this sycophantish semicircle was known by the designers in the studio as "the magic crescent"), "Don't you fellas agree if we raise that one thirty-second of an inch from one end to another, it'll look better?" He was suggesting several hours more work for something that no one would notice. It was a no-win situation, thought Robert Cumberford, a young designer: You could pretend to change it and try to get away with it, or you could change it and then find that Earl was in a bad mood and refused to believe that you had actually made the adjustment.

If he was not above abusing an employee in front of his colleagues, then he could also be perfectly friendly later the same day if he met him at a social function. He was particularly charming to the wives of his young assistants, and after meeting him, those wives were likely to say to their husbands, "How can you complain and call him a tyrant—why, he's the most gracious and courteous man I've ever met."

Not everyone admired what Earl was doing. Some critics thought his cars reflected the postwar excesses of American society: They were too large and flashy without being better, they believed. To the doubters, he was the prince of "Gorp" (that is, the combination of fins and chrome that marked the industry's cars in those years). At Ford he was known, part respectfully, part not so respectfully, as the Cellini of Chrome. One of his foremost colleagues, the famed industrial designer Raymond Loewy, took the occasion of a 1955 speech before the Society of Automobile Engineers to criticize the entire philosophy behind Earl's cars, which he said had become like jukeboxes on wheels: "Is it responsible to camouflage one of America's most remarkable machines as a piece of gaudy merchandise?" he asked. Form, Loewy added, "which should be the clean-cut expression of mechanical excellence, has become sensuous and organic." Loewy was warning Detroit that form had overtaken function. Yet if Earl's designs did not always please intellectuals, they were stunningly successful with car buyers. Curiously, he did little sketching himself; rather, he would take an idea—from an advertisement he had seen in a magazine, or a photo of an airplane—and suggest his staff work from it.

Earl steadily eroded the autonomy of the division heads. Design became the critical decision and that decision was Earl's. Engineering became steadily less important. In fact because of Earl and Sloan, all three major auto companies became caught in a vicious syndrome: a worship of the new at the expense of the old, even if on occasion the old was better. The annual model change forced the companies to opt for a less efficient and less attractive car, just for the sake of change. Or as George Walker, the head of styling at Ford, said at the end of the Earl era, the process contained the seeds of its own destruction: "The 1957 Ford was great, but right away we had to bury it and start another. We design a car, and the minute it's done, we hate it—we've got to do another one. We design a car to make a man unhappy with his 1957 Ford 'long about the end of 1958."

Earl himself became quite cynical. Young designers who went to work for the company in the mid-fifties and who had admired his earlier work were stunned by his attitude. Robert Cumberford remembered an early orientation meeting with a class of young stylists. Earl stood in front of the group and looked long and hard at them. "General Motors," he began, "is in business for only one reason. To make money. In order to do that we make cars. But if we could make money making garbage cans, we would make garbage cans."

Cumberford's close friend Stan Mott had a similar experience: "Listen," Earl told a group of designers that included Mott. "I'd put smokestacks right in the middle of the sons of bitches if I thought I could sell more cars." In all of this the process was becoming increasingly sterile: It was not merely change for change's sake, but actually a kind of pseudo-change. The industry's engineers were largely idle, as their skills were ignored. Thus, during a time when the American car industry might have lengthened its technological lead on foreign competitors, it failed to do so. Instead, the industry fiddled with styling details, raising and lowering the skirts, adding and augmenting fins, changing color combinations. Fins, the most famous automotive detail of the era, represented no technological advance; they were solely a design element whose purpose was to make the cars seem sleeker, bigger, and more powerful. "It gave them [the customers] an extra receipt for their money in the form of visible prestige marking for an expensive car," Earl said, summing up the essential thrust of the industry during the decade. That failure would come back to haunt the entire industry in the seventies. Indeed, it was Earl who coined the phrase that came to symbolize that era, "dynamic obsolescence."

In the fifties bigger was better, and Americans, it seemed, wanted bigger cars every year. If General Motors assaulted the new American market with ever bigger cars, it was Charles Kettering who was the technological enabler of that era. Kettering was the chief of research for GM, the resident technological genius. He was the country boy as inventor ("I am a wrench-and-pliers man," he liked to say, with undue modesty). His inventions were critical to the company's, indeed to the industry's, success, beginning with the starter motor, which used a self-starter in the ignition instead of a heavy crank. This device, included for the first time on the 1912 Cadillac, had encouraged women and older people to drive. A long series of other major innovations, all of them wildly practical, followed: heaters for cars; all-purpose Duco paint, which modernized the painting process and changed the time required for paint on cars to dry from seventeen days to three hours; and antiknock fuel. But it was Kettering's work on high-compression engines and higher octane gas that unlocked the era of bigger, heavier cars with more equipment on them.

By 1946, when he began to devote his time to building a high-compression engine, he had been retired from the company for three years, but he still pursued his longtime goal. The combination of a higher-compression engine and a higher-octane gas, he was convinced, would permit a far more powerful engine. The vapor of the gas could be more tightly confined in the cylinders before exploding, thus driving back the pistons with increased force. For years Kettering had been pushing the oil companies to develop a higher-octane gas, but they had been notably unresponsive. Their complacency irritated him greatly: "When Mother Nature formed petroleum in the earth she did not have the automobile in mind any more than the hog intended his bristles for toothbrushes, and it is foolish to expect the best molecules in gasoline to be found in crude oil," he said. Kettering came up with a high-octane gas himself, and in 1947, at the age of seventy-one, he presented a technical paper to his colleagues on his work: a new V-8 engine and a new high-compression ratio from higher-octane gas. The new engine was installed for the first time on the '49 Cadillac. Greater efficiency might have been what Kettering sought, but his colleagues at GM saw only bigger, more powerful cars bearing more and heavier accessories. The way was cleared for power steering, power brakes, and air-conditioning.

All this signaled the changing of the company culture during the fifties. Charlie Wilson, who had come up from engineering, left to serve in government. His successor, Harlow Curtice, was a salesman, who believed passionately in bigger and gaudier cars and who had led the fight against the Cadet. Curtice had grown up in Petrieville, a small town in Michigan, and had gone to a nearby business school, called the Ferris Institute. Founded by Woodbridge Ferris, a United

States senator, the school emphasized hard work: The young men practiced their arithmetic outdoors at six o'clock in the morning by shouting their answers to math questions, with no paper or blackboard to help them. After graduation, Curtice took a job as a bookkeeper at the AC Spark Plug company, a partly owned subsidiary of General Motors. He rose to controller and eventually to president of AC, thereby earning his big chance: the presidency of Buick. Buick, of all the GM divisions, was the most troubled at the time; it had slipped to fewer than 45,000 cars a year after a high of 245,000. Here was the perfect place for an ambitious young man. Curtice was good with figures, but unlike many of the men who came after him, he also loved cars. In the words of his close friend and fellow GM executive Tony De Lorenzo, "he could see beyond the figures—he knew that they were not just dead little numbers on a piece of paper, but he understood what they meant in terms of trends and taste."

When Curtice had taken over at Buick, in 1933, the first call he made was to Harley Earl. "Harley, what do you drive yourself?" he had asked. "A Cadillac," Earl answered. "I'd like you to design a Buick for me that you'd like to drive," Curtice said, setting the tone for a new sexier Buick division. He turned Buick around quickly, and he did it in bad times. He was a devotee of the Sloan/Earl philosophy and he believed in styling as the manifestation of status. Earl was impressed with him. More than any of the other division heads, he liked to say, Curtice was always in the design room, trying to get a sense of which way the stylists were going. By quadrupling Buick's sales, to 200,000 a year, Curtice became the rising star at the company. When Wilson left for Washington in January 1953, it was Curtice's company.

Eisenhower's was the first Republican administration in twenty years, and it promised greater tolerance of big business. For years the biggest limitation at GM in terms of market share had been self-imposed, for fear that if its market share ever went above 50 percent, the Justice Department's antitrust people would come in and break up the company. Now all such restraints were off. Curtice did not believe in such gentlemanly restraint. If the feds wanted to stop GM, it would have to come and get him: "You never stand still in this business. You either go up or down." he said. He intended to dominate GM so completely that John DeLorean noted some twenty years later with a measure of nostalgia, the last person really to run GM was Harlow Curtice. In 1953, when GM had 45 percent of the market, Curtice announced he wanted 48 percent for 1954. By 1956 it was 51 percent and even that was not enough. As Robert Sheehan noted in an article about Curtice in *Fortune* in 1956, the joke around the company went: "You know what the boss says—it means that we're losing almost five out of every ten deals." "Fifty percent, hell," Curtice himself told Semon (Bunkie) Knudsen, the son of the man who had turned Chevrolet around for Sloan and was himself tapped to head Pontiac. "I want *seventy-five percent* of the market."

NINE

The surging size and increased emphasis on style and luxury in American cars were just one sign of the new abundance of the era. After World War Two most Americans had a vision of a better life just ahead. At the core of it was owning one's own house—and as Henry Ford's invention and a rapidly improving network of roads and highways opened up the vast spaces of farmland surrounding American cities, the vision started to become a reality: Suburbia. Indeed, people knew even what they wanted to pay for their first house: $5,000, which was then roughly equal to an average family's wages for two years. Right after the war, auto workers made about $60 a week, or $3,000 a year, while workers in other parts of the manufacturing sector made about $2,400. If a new car was a critical status symbol, a house was something else. More often than not, the people who intended to own one had, in the past, rented apartments, which symbolized not merely a lack of space but also a lack of independence and security. Owning a house came to be the embodiment of the new American dream. As promised by endless Hollywood films, it represented fulfillment, *contentment:* confident dads, perky moms, and glowing children, attending good schools and, later, college. A house brought the American family *together* (at precisely the moment, of course, when cars and television began pulling it apart). If the first great business figure of the American Century was Henry Ford, the second, arguably, was William J. Levitt.

It was Bill Levitt who first brought Ford's techniques of mass production to housing, up to then the most neglected of American industries. Until he arrived on the scene, builders were small-time operators, employing multiple subcontractors ("graduate carpenters and bricklayers," Levitt called them). The typical prewar builder put up fewer than five houses a year (few put up more than two a year since the Depression). Levitt revolutionized the process of home building with remarkable planning and brilliant control procedures. These techniques made it possible to provide inexpensive, attractive single-unit housing for ordinary citizens, people who had never thought of themselves as middle-class before. As much as anyone, William Levitt made the American dream possible. As Paul Goldberger of *The New York Times* noted years later, "Levittown houses were social creations more than architectural ones—they turned the single detached single-family house from a distant dream to a real possibility for thousands of middle-class American families." It was, Levitt liked to boast, capitalism in the most personal sense. "No man who owns his own house and lot can be a Communist. He has too much to do," he once said.

It was the war that taught Levitt the promise of the future and how to reach for it. In 1941 he and his brother, Alfred, won a government contract to build 2,350 war workers' homes in Norfolk, Virginia. At first it was a disaster; everything went wrong. Saddled with union workers who, in their view, asked for too much and produced too little, they were unable to make a profit or meet a tight schedule. The Levitts and their managers knew they had to change the essential philosophy of home building in order to meet their deadlines. They analyzed the construction process and broke it down into basic components. There were, they figured out, twenty-seven separate steps, so they would train twenty-seven separate teams—each team would specialize in one step. This solution enabled them not only to find a way around the acute shortage of skilled carpenters—for it demanded less talented workers—but also to speed up the entire process. They also figured out that the traditional method of paying workers hourly wages and overtime was not a good way to maximize production. They carefully studied each job, how to do it well, and how much time it took. Then they figured base salaries according to average schedules and paid extra to those exceeding the norms—in effect, they were paying for piecework at a high level. This made it possible for the worker to augment his base salary by accomplishing more—instead of merely working longer. As the war ground on, the Levitt team became increasingly expert in mass building.

Eventually, Bill Levitt was transferred to serve with the Seabees in the Pacific, where he was commissioned to build instant airfields for the Navy. Unburdened by union restrictions and the constraints of conventional building limitations, and operating under terrible deadlines—for lives were in the balance if the airfields were not completed—Levitt took on tasks that no one thought could be done and pulled them off. At night, Levitt sat around with other young men in the Seabees, all of whom had backgrounds in building and contracting, and they would brainstorm about their work—what they were doing that day, how to do it faster, and also what they would do after the war. The Navy, Bill Levitt said years later, provided him with a magnificent laboratory in which to experiment with low-cost mass housing and analyze it with his peers—a chance he might never have had in civilian life.

As for the future, Bill Levitt had no doubts: It consisted of men like himself building mass housing for the families of young veterans, who were going to return overnight to civilian life. "Just beg, borrow, or steal the money and then build and build," he kept saying to his friends, about a dozen of whom followed him into his company. When some talked about the risks involved, he would tell them to examine their own desires and needs. What did they want? A car, and then what else? A house, of course. What were their friends all telling them about their own postwar plans? That the first thing they were going to do was get married or, if they were already married, have kids: Most were going to have to live with their parents for a few years because none of them had their own place in which to live.

Even before the war, Bill Levitt had taken out an option on a thousand acres of farmland near Hempstead, Long Island. It was relatively inexpensive, a steal, he thought, and while he was over in the Pacific, he urged his brother, Alfred, to keep up the option. Alfred Levitt, an architect, was the more artistic member of the family. He seemed not to understand his brother's grand design for the postwar years: Alfred looked at the Hempstead land and saw a lot of potato farms being cleared for a few houses; Bill Levitt looked at it and saw a gargantuan, virtually self-contained suburban community.

No industry had suffered more than housing during the Depression and World War Two; housing starts fell from 1 million a year to fewer than 100,000. But during the same period the marriage rate and, not surprisingly, the birthrate increased sharply, the latter reaching 22 per 1,000 in 1943—the highest it had been in two decades. As everyone returned from the war, the housing situation was not merely tight—it was a crisis. Some 50,000 people were reportedly living in Army Quonset huts. In Chicago it was so bad that 250 used trolley cars were sold for use as homes. Estimates placed the number of new houses needed immediately at over 5 million. A federal housing bill was rushed through that contained very little in the way of controls, and a great deal in the way of federal insurance to protect builders by means of federal mortgage guarantees. "The real estate boys read the bill, looked at one another in happy amazement, and the dry rasping noise they made rubbing their hands together could have been heard as far as Tawi Tawi," a writer named John Keats noted of the moment. The stored-up energy of two decades was unleashed. In 1944 there had been only 114,000 new single houses started; by 1946 that figure had jumped to 937,000: to 1,118,000 in 1948; and 1.7 million in 1950.

Bill Levitt was sure that he was riding the wave of the future. "We believe that the market for custom housing, like that for custom tailoring, no longer exists. People who want to buy that kind of thing will always be able to get it, but the real market is for the ordinary, mass-produced suit of clothes. And you can't build thirty thousand-dollar houses by the six thousands," he said even as he started his first development. In 1946 the Levitts pushed ahead with Bill Levitt's dream of creating his own community in Hempstead, by adding more and more acreage to what they already owned. There, some twenty miles from Manhattan, they set out to create the largest housing project in American history. At first it was called Island Trees, but inevitably the name Levittown stuck. ("Well," he said years later, talking about the change in name, "the original name was something of an embarrassment. After all, here was this great new place called Island Trees, a very fancy name, and it was flat as could be as far as the eye could see, with only these two scrawny trees in the front to give it the name . . .")

Levittown was an astonishing success from the very beginning.

The first Levitt house could not have been simpler. It had four and a half rooms and was designed with a young family in mind. The lots were 60 by 100 feet, and Bill Levitt was proud of the fact that the house took up only 12 percent of the lot. The living room was 12 by 16 feet. There were two bedrooms and one bathroom. A family could expand the house by converting the attic or adding on to the outside. The house was soon redesigned with the kitchen in the back so that the mothers could watch their children in the yard. In his book *Crabgrass Frontier,* Kenneth Jackson noted that in their simplicity, durability, and value, the early Levitt houses were not unlike the Model T. The basic Levitt Cape Cod sold for $7,990; later, an expanded ranch-style house sold for $9,500. In the beginning the Levitts threw in a free television set and a Bendix washing machine as incentives. At first only veterans were invited to buy. A small showcase home was erected on a plot near New York City for easy inspection: "This is Levittown!" went the ad in *The New York Times.* "All yours for $58. You're a lucky fellow, Mr. Veteran. Uncle Sam and the world's largest builder have made it possible for you to live in a charming house in a delightful community without having to pay for them with your eye teeth . . ." The ad ran on a Monday. On Tuesday, Bill Levitt went out to check the model home. There was a line of some thirty people. "What are you doing here?" he asked one of the men in line. "I'm out here to look at one of these Levitt houses and buy one," the man answered. "But they're not available until next Monday," Levitt protested. "Doesn't matter," the young man said. Bill Levitt was shaken. It was one thing, he realized, to sit around on a small Pacific island in 1944 and brainstorm about the need for postwar housing; it was another to run smack into the full fury of it. The line grew day by day, and the ex-GIs themselves figured out how to police it, creating a system to let people take a break and eat without losing their place in line. Indeed, a kind of community began to form among those in line. These people, after all, were going to be each other's neighbors. After the office opened in March 1949, 1,400 contracts were drawn on a single day.

Selling mass-produced homes, though, was not the hard part. The hard part was building them, and the Levitts were ready. The most critical lesson they had learned in Norfolk was the necessity of forgoing the basement—the most difficult and complicated part of a house—for a slab foundation. That meant flattening the existing terrain with a bulldozer and then merely laying concrete slabs. If the slab deprived householders of the ancient right to a dank, dark basement, in which they could store all the things they would never use anyway, it also jump-started the process for the builder. Who needed basements, anyway? Bill Levitt wondered. The ancient Romans had not built basements, he would point out when the question arose, and who was he, Bill Levitt, to question the Romans? At first a local Hempstead bureaucrat, obviously a basement lover, denied them a building permit "on general principles." General principles, Levitt raged. What were those? But then a few days later a devastating editorial attacking general principles as manifested in Hempstead ran in the *Herald Tribune,* and the official backed down.

Levitt was quick to admit that he had borrowed Henry Ford's production system at the great Rouge plant in Detroit. But his adaptation of it was sheer genius: A car was small enough to be moved along an assembly line while the workers remained stationary. Obviously, one could not do that with houses, so why not make the teams of workers mobile, moving them from one stationary house to the next? As such he created a new kind of assembly line, of specialized groups of workers who performed their chores and moved on. The site, as Levitt liked to point out, became the factory. The Levitts did not believe in prefabricating their houses; they had learned that it was too rigid a method. Instead, they had their own system of preassembling. Everything, William Levitt said, had to be made simple. As he saw it, America was not a country of skilled workmen—there were few enough of them around under the best of circumstances, and none were likely to go to work for Levitt's company, where the stress was laid not on individual, elegant workmanship but on the maximum number of houses to be built in a given amount of time. Because his workers were less skilled, Levitt had many of the critical parts preassembled elsewhere. That made the on-site assembly easier, so ordinary workers, aided by power tools— just then coming into use—could take it from there. Of the tedium involved in so mechanized a process, Alfred Levitt once said, "The same man does the same thing every day, despite the psychologists. It is boring; it is bad; but the reward of the green stuff seems to alleviate the boredom of the work."

At first the construction trucks kept getting bogged down in the muddy potato fields, so the Levitts figured out they had to go in first and create a sufficiently finished road to avoid the problem. Safe from the mud, the trucks would come in and drop off building materials at exact intervals of sixty feet. The floors were made of asphalt, and the walls of composition Sheetrock. There were floor men and side men and tile men and men who did the white painting and men who did the red painting. By July 1948 they were building

180 houses a week or, in effect, finishing thirty-six houses a day. It was, Bill Levitt noted, like clockwork: "Eighteen houses completed on the shift from 8 to noon, and 18 more houses finished on the shift from 12:20 to 4:30." The system had to be foolproof: Anything that slowed it down—a strike by a subsidiary union, a shortage of nails or lumber—would throw off the entire schedule, and they would lose money. So they made their own nails, buying thirteen nail-making machines and a great supply of scrap iron; they made their own cement; and they even produced their own lumber, buying thousands of acres of timberland in Oregon and building a mill there.

Some 17,000 houses were built in the first Levittown and 82,000 people lived there. One swimming pool was built for every thousand houses. There were five schools, built by the county on public contract, which did not please pre-Levittown residents, who felt they were supporting these new arrivistes. Churches were erected on land furnished by the Levitts. One man had, in effect, created a community all his own, although he provided only the bedrooms, nothing more. It was a strange new world where each day the men got in their cars or boarded trains to go off to jobs in New York City, twenty miles away; it was not unlike an old whaling port where the men periodically went off for several months to hunt their quarry, leaving their wives to tend the community. But here, the men returned home at 6 P.M. each night.

Bill Levitt was thirty-eight when the war was over. He was the son of Abraham Levitt, whose parents were Russian-Jewish immigrants. A self-made success as a real estate man in Long Island, Abraham was in the business for some twenty-five years before he made his first tentative move into building, around 1929. During the 1920s, the Levitt family lived in a lovely brownstone in Brooklyn's Bedford-Stuyvesant section. But when the senior Levitt heard that a local black district attorney was moving into the area, he gathered his own family together and told them, "If this man moves in, the neighborhood will soon be black, and then the only question left for us is whether we'll be able to sell our house and for how much. The longer we wait, the more the price will go down." With that, Abraham Levitt sold his brownstone and moved his family to Long Island, a pioneer of the great migrations that were soon to come—blacks moving from the rural South to Northern inner cities, and whites fleeing them from the inner cities to the suburbs. By 1934, the Levitts had built a two-hundred-unit subdivision on Long Island. It

---

was called Strathmore, and the houses sold for between $9,000 and $18,000.

Bill Levitt was young and confident and intensely ambitious. Eric Larrabee described his appearance as like that of "a retired Marx brother turned master of ceremonies in a run-down night club." He did not lack for ego. He tended to refer to the company in the third person, as "Levitt," as if the company were a person: "Levitt plans to build here . . ." or "Levitt isn't the kind of company you can push around . . ." William Levitt was, of course, the real Levitt of "Levitt." By the time of their third Levittown, Abraham had retired and Alfred, unable to get along with his brother, had sold his shares of stock and gotten out of the company.

Bill Levitt was nothing if not tough. He did not even think of himself as a builder. "My father always taught me when you talk to a builder, keep your hands in your pockets," he once said. He went against the grain in a number of ways. In an age largely sympathetic to unions and which saw a major increase in their economic and political power, Levitt fought them every inch of the way. Benefactor of the common man Levitt might have been. But he liked to say that Thomas Jefferson made the greatest mistake in history by implying that all men were equal. They might be created equal, he would say, but they were not equal: Some were more talented, some compensated for lack of talent by working harder, and some were neither talented nor hardworking and that was where the union came in. The job of the union, he insisted, could be reduced to a simple idea: the protection of the slowest and least efficient worker. Because of that, Bill Levitt hired only nonunion workers. He paid them top dollar and offered all kinds of incentives that allowed them to earn extra money. Levitt workers often made twice as much a week as those who had comparable jobs elsewhere, but they did it on terms set by Bill Levitt.

Levitt bought appliances from wholly owned Levitt subsidiaries, which meant that he had to pay fewer middlemen. The very idea of middlemen enraged Bill Levitt—the idea that people might make a profit on goods they had never seen or touched. If the number of middlemen were reduced, he liked to say, the price could be brought down considerably—"if only in three-cent stamps," because less paperwork would have to be sent through the mails. When Levitt bought appliances, he bought them by the carload. The entire operation was so efficient, Eric Larrabee noted in *Harper's* magazine, that the Levitts could spend about $1,500 less on carpentry and materials than competitors. No one had ever seen anything like it before.

("How do you build forty houses a day—$40 million worth a year—that will please the American government, the American public and the American Institute of Architects? Levitt has the answer," ran a caption in a *Fortune* magazine article in October 1952.) Knowing that many first-time homebuyers feared being fleeced by lawyers and businessmen during the paperwork, the Levitts simplified the buying process as well. There were no down payment, no closing costs, and no secret extras. Veterans who signed up for the first Levitt houses had to put down a one-hundred-dollar deposit, which they eventually got back. It was an unusual and appealing concept: The price was the price.

The homebuyers themselves seemed quite pleased with Levitt homes, which over the years proved unusually sturdy. Those who bought into Levittown were, more often than not, leaping ahead of their parents in terms of their standard of living. Yet the very nature of what Levitt was doing and the scope of his success made him a target for those who disliked and even feared the new mass culture of postwar society. "*For literally nothing down,*" wrote John Keats, "you too can find a box of your own in one of the fresh-air slums we're building around the edges of American cities . . . inhabited by people whose age, income, number of children, problems, habits, conversations, dress, possessions, perhaps even blood types are almost precisely like yours . . . [these houses] actually drive mad myriads of housewives shut up in them."

There was no small amount of snobbery to the attacks on the Levitts; most of it came not from dissatisfied customers but from people who were fortunate enough, because of their backgrounds, to be able to afford more traditional middle-class housing. For those people, housing—like the choice of a profession—was a matter of preference and options. The most relentless critic of the new suburb was Lewis Mumford, one of the most distinguished architectural and social commentators of his time. Mumford claimed that Levitt was using "new-fashioned methods to compound old-fashioned mistakes." "Mechanically it is admirably done," Mumford said, "socially the design is backward." Mumford's attacks struck Levitt as essentially unfair and uninformed. Had Mumford, he asked, even bothered to find out about the housing these young people had vacated for their new Levitt houses?

Mumford did not stop with one or two articles. His attacks were persistent and more than a little cruel. It was as if Levitt and his subdivision came to symbolize all that Mumford hated about the homogenization (and democratization) of American culture then being wrought by the combination of increasing affluence and mass-production technology. Levittown, he implied, represented the worst vision of the American future: bland people in bland houses leading bland lives. The houses were physically similar, theorized Mumford, so the people inside must be equally similar; an entire community was being made from a cookie cutter. In 1961, some ten years after the completion of the first Levittown, Mumford described it as "a multitude of uniform, unidentifiable houses, lined up inflexibly, at uniform distances on uniform roads, in a treeless command waste, inhabited by people of the same class, the same incomes, the same age group, witnessing the same television performances, eating the same tasteless prefabricated foods, from the same freezers, conforming in every outward and inward respect to a common mold manufactured in the same central metropolis. Thus the ultimate effect of the suburban escape in our time is, ironically, a low-grade uniform environment from which escape is impossible." Other critics agreed. The original version of *The Invasion of the Body Snatchers,* noted writer Ron Rosenbaum, was "about the horror of being in the 'burbs. About neighbors whose lives had so lost their individual distinctiveness they could be taken over by alien vegetable pods— *and no one would know the difference.* And those evil pods that housed the aliens and stole the souls of the humans: Were they not metaphors, embodiments of the Cape Cod pods of Levittown and the like, whose growth and multiplication came from sucking the individuality out of the humans housed in them?"

But others thought that Mumford was not quite fair; the young sociologist Herbert Gans, who decided to buy a house in the third Levittown with his young family, was surprised by the rich and diverse quality of life there. Levitt loathed critics like Mumford. When people spoke to him of the texture of a community, he turned cold: He was in the business of putting up good low-cost housing; he was not in charge of human relations after the building was finished. It was the classic confrontation of the doer and the critic, of the older America and the newer, entrepreneurial one. The criticism was, for someone of Bill Levitt's background, like being told that no matter how successful he was, how much money he made, and how many good houses he built for people who wanted them, he was somehow not good enough for acceptance by the privileged, educated classes. When in 1956 the Levitt group decided to offer a greater variety of houses, Levitt said at the meeting, "Now Lewis Mumford can't criticize us anymore." In the press release on his third Levittown, Levitt wrote, "We are ending once and for all the old bugaboo of uniformity. . . . In the new Levittown we build all the different houses . . . right next to each other within the same section." (Almost thirty years later, when Ron Rosenbaum wrote a piece for *Esquire* magazine celebrating the most important men and women of the last half century, he called Levitt, only to discover that the builder was still angry about Lewis Mumford. "I think by now we've shown that critics like Lewis Mumford were wrong," Levitt told Rosenbaum. He thereupon launched upon a bitter diatribe that concluded: "I think that Lewis Mumford has been shown to be a prophet without honor.")

Certain differences were most definitely not welcomed in Levittown, however. Blacks could not buy in—a Levitt policy that lasted for two decades, long after the nation began legally trying to rid itself of lawful segregation. "The Negroes in America are trying to do in 400 years what the Jews in the world have not wholly accomplished in 600 years. As a Jew I have no room in my mind or heart for racial prejudice. But . . . I have come to know that if we sell one house to a Negro family, then 90 or 95 percent of our white customers will not buy into the community. That is their attitude, not ours. . . . As a company our position is simply this: We can solve a housing problem, or we can try to solve a racial problem but we cannot combine the two," Levitt said in the early fifties. At first the Levitts forbade fences, but in time fences appeared. For a time the Levitts supervised lawn cutting and sent families the bills, but soon the owners took that over. Owners were forbidden to dry clothes outside unless it was on a specially designed rack. But despite all the rules and the conformity implied by the identical houses and lots, American ingenuity and individuality could not be suppressed. Slowly, steadily, the owners in Levitt developments and those like them began to adapt their houses, putting their own stamp on them.

Levitt became aware that his reputation as the builder of the cheapest housing available was turning into a liability as the society became increasingly affluent. If he upgraded his house, he thought, he would upgrade his customers, and thus his reputation as well. In Long Island he had built primarily for young veterans; his second development, in Bucks County, was primarily for blue-collar buyers; in the third Levittown he decided to reach for a somewhat more affluent group, thereby increasing his profit margin as well.

In the new subdivision, the schools would be built by Levitt and included in the price of the house. He asked two prominent architects to submit plans for the new houses, but was thoroughly disgusted when they submitted plans for houses costing about $50,000. With that, Levitt quickly returned to his own architects. Instead of only one model of house, there were now three, a "Cape Cod," with four bedrooms, selling for $11,500; a three-bedroom one-story "Rancher" for $13,000; and a two-story "Colonial," with three or four bedrooms, costing $14,000 for three bedrooms and $14,500 for four.

Even if the price was going up, he kept the down payment low, because he did not want to scare away young middle-class families with incomes of $6,000 and $7,000 a year. But a conscious effort was made to find a slightly more affluent buyer. One potential customer showed up wearing shabby clothes and with the beginnings of a beard and was turned down; a few days later, the same buyer returned clean-shaven and wearing a suit and was welcomed. Herbert Gans has pointed out that Levitt deliberately had his salesmen wear dark suits, like bankers, instead of the flashier clothes often associated with salesmen. They were not to pressure the buyer, and some even took lessons from a speech teacher.

There was a sense of adventure and excitement among his neighbors in Levittown, Gans thought. Everyone, he noted, "was looking forward to occupying his new home and this engendered a spirit of optimism and the trust that other purchasers shared this spirit. After all, Levittown would be a new community, and newness is often identified with perfection in American culture."

What was taking place was nothing less than the beginning of a massive migration from the cities, to the farmland that surrounded them. Starting in 1950 and continuing for the next thirty years, eighteen of the nation's twenty-five top cities lost population. At the same time, the suburbs gained 60 million people. Some 83 percent of the nation's growth was to take place in the suburbs. By 1970, for the first time there were more people living in suburbs than in cities. Bill Levitt had helped begin a revolution—that of the new, mass suburban developments; 10 percent of the builders were soon putting up 70 percent of the houses. By 1955 Levitt-type subdivisions represented 75 percent of the new housing starts. All over America, subdivisions were advertising that buyers could come in for no down payment and others were asking, "one dollar down." Row houses became a thing of the past; as Kenneth Jackson pointed out, the new auto-connected suburb was only half as densely populated as the older suburbs, which had been connected to cities by streetcars. It would change the very nature of American society; families often became less connected to their relatives and seldom shared living space with them as they had in the past. The move to the suburbs also temporarily interrupted the progress women had been making before the war in the workplace; for the new suburbs separated women physically from the workplace, leaving them, at least for a while, isolated in a world of other mothers, children, and station wagons.

TEN

As more and more people were moving to the suburbs, a need was created for new places and ways in which to shop—and also for new things to buy to fill these thousands of new houses. This was no small phenomenon in itself—shopping and buying were to become major American pastimes as the ripple effect of the new affluence started to be felt throughout the economy. In the summer of 1953, Eugene Ferkauf was driving through rural Long Island when he passed through an area of pretty farmland. The area—Westbury—was as yet untouched by the vast migration that Bill Levitt had initiated and which was continuing to sweep across Long Island, but Ferkauf knew it was just a matter of time before the heavy equipment of the developers would replace the farmers' tractors. All around, farmers were being bought out by developers. Some developers even called such regions "fertile acres" because of the rush of young families to settle here.

Ferkauf was already the principal owner of five wildly successful discount stores in the greater New York City area. Two of them were in the suburbs—one in White Plains and one in Hempstead, Long Island—but Ferkauf was not satisfied with them. The Hempstead site was fairly typical for him, chosen by the take-whatever-was-available method. This generally resulted in locations and buildings that were less than ideal. Ferkauf personally considered the Hempstead store a dump—it occupied a failed former Grand Union grocery store and faced a cemetery. Despite that, the store had prospered, thanks to Ferkauf's amazing discounts and the seemingly unquenchable desire of his young customers for ever more appliances. In fact, all of Ferkauf's stores had been phenomenal successes. The first had opened in 1948 and its sales had exploded from the very first day. The customers had found the stores not through advertising (for in the beginning there was none) but by word of mouth.

Ferkauf understood his new customers—and how they were different from prewar customers—for in many ways he was just like them. They were young and hungry to buy, because they owned virtually nothing. They were prosperous but not rich. Above all they were confident in themselves and their futures in a way that Ferkauf, growing up in harder times and poorer neighborhoods, found striking. They did not fear debt, as their parents had. Their grandparents—Italian, Irish, Jewish—had been immigrants who lived in tenements on the Lower East Side, and their parents had eventually moved to better apartments in the Bronx, Brooklyn, and Queens. Now they were striking out on their own, going after their share of the American dream by moving to the suburbs. They differed from their parents not just in how much they made and what they owned but in their belief that the future had already arrived. As the first homeowners in their families, they brought a new excitement and pride with them to the store as they bought furniture or appliances—in other times young couples might have exhibited such feelings as they bought clothes for their first baby. It was as if the very accomplishment of owning a home reflected such an immense breakthrough that nothing was too good to buy for it. Ferkauf knew their migratory patterns well: The people from the Bronx went to Westchester and, sometimes, New Jersey; those from Brooklyn and Queens moved out to the Island. Thanks to his early success, Ferkauf himself had left his tiny $75-a-month apartment in Brooklyn and bought a huge house in Jamaica, Queens—a "mansion," in his somewhat ironic words—for $75,000.

Ferkauf was among the first to realize the commercial possibilities of catering to this new middle class. He liked dealing with them: They were smart, they knew what they wanted, they appreciated his bargains, and they rarely argued. They did not waste his time, and he did not waste theirs. Dealing with them was not, as it had been in his father's day, about the art of selling, which involved elaborate rituals: a lengthy give-and-take, and making a shrewd reading of what the customer really wanted. In that process selling was almost an end in itself.

As Ferkauf looked at the potato fields of Westbury, he experienced a great vision of the new suburbia: a sparkling, huge new store with vast parking facilities. It would be 90,000 square feet and contain an endless variety of sub-stores: an appliance store, a supermarket, a toy store, a men's clothing store, and perhaps others as well. There would be no more taking whatever real estate agents gave him and adapting buildings that could never be made to fit his needs. In fact, he had always wanted a store that was not merely successful but also beautiful—like Lord & Taylor, a showplace the customer would also admire. Westbury would be the site for that store; there was plenty of space, easy access to the highways that connected Long Island to New York City, and best of all, it was only ten minutes from Levittown.

Ferkauf pushed everyone—architects, contractors, and painters—to build the new store quickly. He was in a rush, for time was money, and he wanted to catch the 1953 Christmas season. Miraculously, the builders met Ferkauf's deranged schedules and the store was finished in ninety days. Despite his usual confidence, Ferkauf wondered this time whether he was reaching a bit too high and his operation was getting too big for its own good. He was terrified, in fact, that he would open this, his greatest store, and it would fail. If there was one thing Ferkauf hated it was an empty store; he thought it resembled nothing so much as a corpse.

Ferkauf still smarted from the fact that traditional retailers in New York City had initially made fun of him and his discount stores. There was a manic quality to his first stores. Even as his stores grew in size and number, they were run as ma-and-pa operations. There were no amenities and only minimal service. His philosophy was to sell as much merchandise as possible in the shortest period of time possible with a minimal markup. If a manufacturer's representative dared peer inside his store, Ferkauf, never turning from the sale at hand, would scream at him: "One hundred washing machines, and now get lost. . ." or "Two hundred toasters, and get out already and drop dead."

Even the smallest transaction in the first Korvettes, on East 46th Street, was conducted with a certain frenzy: The salesman seemed desperate to get on to the next customer, the customer eager to be gone from this overcrowded, noisy little space. In the beginning no one had a title, including Ferkauf. Eventually, as the company grew, his friends insisted he take one: chairman of the executive committee of E. J. Korvettes. Most assuredly, though, he did not have an office or a secretary. He never wore a jacket and tie, preferring instead sports shirts and sweatshirts. If he *had* to arrange a meeting with a lawyer or an investment banker, he would set it up in the lobby of the Plaza Hotel. There, in a posh armchair, he would conduct his business—one did not have to stay at the Plaza to be a man of the Plaza.

As his business expanded, Ferkauf kept hiring his old buddies from Brooklyn. They were mostly from Samuel Tilden High School and retained their street nicknames: Ferkauf was Euje, and there were Schmaltzy, Kuzzy, Lobster, Leaky, and Gimp. Ferkauf, his friends joked, had emptied all the poolrooms of Brooklyn to staff his store. The atmosphere of the store was not far from that of the open street stalls of the old Jewish peddlers on Orchard Street on New York City's Lower East Side. In fact, one of Ferkauf's salesmen, Willie Shapiro, would sometimes cry out the traditional wail of Orchard Street, "Ladies, ladies, come over, come over, we've got the merchandise, we've got the merchandise."

On occasion there were cultural tensions. Once Ferkauf turned to a well-dressed lady and said, "Can I help you, dear?" That was courtesy where he came from. "I should slap your face for calling me dear," she said. People lined up and took a number as they came into the store. "This is the lowest form of merchandising I've ever seen," Ferkauf once heard a customer say. He felt as if someone had slapped *his* face. The strain on everyone's vocal cords was considerable. Ferkauf popped cough drops all day to protect his throat; at night his mouth would be so sour from their flavor that he could not taste dinner. Eventually, he was operated on several times for the removal of polyps from his vocal cords.

The Tilden men were known as Gene's Boys, or the Boys. "It was like a kibbutz," Ferkauf noted years later. They had known each other forever. Some were related, and those who came aboard in the beginning soon brought their friends and relatives. A bunch of them would drive to work together from Brooklyn every morning. Eventually, quite a few of the Boys became rich. Ferkauf paid everyone—including himself—modest base salaries, but he rewarded exceptional performance generously with bonuses and later, after the company went public, with stock. But there was an unwritten agreement that the stock was never to be sold—Ferkauf regarded it as a breach of faith similar to telling the secret rules of a boys' club to outsiders. Ferkauf always found out if anyone sold the stock; then he would be finished at Korvettes. If one of the Boys had a problem or needed something, he was to come directly to Ferkauf. Once, several of them talked to each other and realized they had a common problem. After several years of working for relatively little, they still had cramped apartments in Brooklyn; they were all married and several had kids or kids on the way. They wanted their own houses out on Long Island, so they went as a group to Ferkauf. He listened to them, then called his banker to ask for $1.5 million, which he distributed among them for the new houses.

Loyalty was placed above all else. Once the New York area was hit by a torrential downpour. Ferkauf called up the White Plains store to talk to one of his buddies. The man was not there. He had been called home by his wife because their basement was flooding. To Ferkauf that was nothing less than desertion. He was furious and withheld the man's annual bonus. Of the boys he had known growing up, Ferkauf denied a job to only one. As a kid, that man had violated the honor code of their neighborhood softball game, erasing Ferkauf's name from the chalkboard list of waiting players, writing his own name in.

The name—E. J. Korvettes—came from the names of (E)ugene, as in Ferkauf, and (J)oe, for his friend and partner Joe Swillenberg. Korvettes was a mutation of the World War Two Canadian subchaser the Corvette (there was already a line of clothes called Corvette). Because the spectacular growth of Ferkauf's chain came right at the end of the Korean war and because all the young men running it were Jewish, it was believed, incorrectly, by many people who worked in the store, and even more by those who shopped there, that the name stood for (E)ight (J)ewish (Kor)ean War (Vet)erans.

Ferkauf had started out by working with his father, who had owned two luggage stores in midtown Manhattan. Harry Ferkauf was a skilled salesman, good at working the customers. He was, however, cautious and conservative—as befit an immigrant who had been hit hard by the Depression. In 1931 he had been forced to close his first venture—a small company that manufactured leather briefcases. The first of his two modest stores that followed was Terminal Luggage, on Lexington Avenue near Grand Central, below street level: TWO STEPS DOWN WILL SAVE YOU TWICE AS MUCH read the sign.

His first years were terribly difficult: The store survived, not so much on sales but because his father's one employee, Frank Tomasini, was a terrific repairman. Things got so bad that Harry Ferkauf could not pay Tomasini; that did not seem to bother the repairman, who came in anyway, worked as hard as ever, and then went out to eat at a soup kitchen. As the Depression eased, business began to pick up and in 1937 Harry opened a second store. It was not long before his young son began to work at the store with him.

One of their best customers was an executive at Texaco, and one day Harry Ferkauf casually asked him about the possibility of a summer job for his son. "Harry, you know how I feel about you and Gene," the man replied, "but Texaco doesn't hire Jews." From that day Gene Ferkauf knew that if he was to be a success, he would have to do it on his own; the world's great companies were not interested in the likes of him.

When Gene Ferkauf graduated from high school, his father gave him the keys to the better of the two stores. There was no discussion of college. But Gene was soon bored. There was, he thought, a certain hopelessness in sitting there every day waiting for customers to come to him. It was too passive a life. Gene knew there were other kinds of luggage stores in that area—discount stores. He was intrigued by the energy of the combative, aggressive men who ran them. They took their fate into their own hands. His father, on the other hand, was from the old school: a gentleman who ironed his tie and pants every day, then brushed his suit carefully before putting it on. Gene hated wearing suits. "Can't you get a second suit?" Harry would say. "How many suits does a person need?" Gene would answer. Harry often came into the store after 11 A.M., and if there was a matinee he wanted to see, he might take the afternoon off. His sense of honor was invested in the store: He took a belt from the belt rack and then went to the cash register and rang up two dollars. "Why did you do that?" his son asked. "It's your store. You can do anything you want here." "If you're good to your store, it'll be good to you," Harry answered.

Harry Ferkauf was good with people. The art of conversation came naturally to him. His son was almost pathologically shy and lacked that skill. Because of that, Gene soon began to think of trying to run a discount house. There was a formula to this: The discounters took the wholesale price, added 10 percent for handling, and doubled this to get the going retail price. Then they took 25 percent off. When he went into the Army for World War Two, he retained this vision of a different, more active store. Waiting in the Philippines for the

coming invasion of Japan, he would talk with his old high school
friend Joe Swillenberg about this idea.

By 1946, he was back in New York and discounting his luggage.
He printed up cards that gave the store's name and address and
promised major discounts, and then he started dropping them off at
office buildings. The other merchants in the area complained to his
father. Harry regarded discounters as the enemy: They were crude,
and he felt they undermined the legitimacy of serious businessmen
like himself.

Daily arguments began to arise between father and son. By no
account, including his own, was Gene Ferkauf very pleasant in these
struggles. "Why are you doing this?" his father would say. "There's
no need for it. The store is profitable enough as it is." The more his
father complained, the more merchandise Gene Ferkauf added to his
discount list. Soon there were pens, watches, gloves, and then small
appliances. The other merchants continued to complain: "Harry,
what's Gene doing? Why is he doing this to us?" The son, of course,
remained adamant: "Pop, I don't care, forget about it, forget what
they say. Just leave me alone."

The arguments became worse: "Who sent for you?" Gene
would say to his father. "Stay in your own store." "Don't have such
a big mouth," Harry would answer. Now Gene not only discounted,
he was determined to give a bigger discount than anyone had ever
given before. It worked. People began to pour into the little store on
their lunch hour. Soon he was doing more than $500 a day in busi-
ness. His father was doing $50. One day in April 1948, Harry came
in the door. It was a beautiful day. "Why don't you take the day off
and see a movie?" Harry said. With that, Gene threw the keys on the
floor and quit.

Years later, he regretted his behavior toward his father. "I was
the bad guy in all of that," he said. Harry died within a year; he had
been sick for some time, but Gene always believed he had expedited
his father's death. Still, he remembered that on the day he quit, he
had done $500 in business *before lunch.*

Going out on his own terrified Gene. He had a wife and a baby
daughter. He had never been to college, and in that period more and
more people his age seemed to have gone there or were going there
under the GI bill. He pondered either opening his own store or
entering Macy's training program. In the back of his mind were his
father's words: Never work for anyone else, but if you do, at least
work on commission. Don't be a salary man. Sitting by the outdoor
skating rink in Rockefeller Center, Gene realized that he was terri-

fied of failure, that he had no prospects and he had better do something. He gave himself a pep talk. Everyone else, he told himself, was back from the war and *doing something*. All the other veterans were getting on with their lives. Sign a lease for a store and show you can do it, he told himself. That afternoon he rented a small store at 6 East 46th Street, one flight up, for $440 a month. It was in the Grand Central Station area, which was the heart of the city in this age before airplanes. Later that day, he learned he had been accepted into Macy's training program.

He spent $1,500 of his $4,000 savings to fix up the store; the rest went to inventory. When he told his father about the new store, Harry was heartbroken. It was a betrayal, in his eyes. "How could you do this to me?" he asked. Harry wouldn't even talk about it (yet, unbeknownst to Gene, his father guaranteed the notes on his first store). His first employee was Murray Beilenson, a friend from the quartermasters' corps in the army. He had accounting skills, which Ferkauf lacked. Ferkauf and his wife blanketed the office buildings in the area with thousands of his new cards, which promised discounts of 33⅓ percent on all major brands. One advantage he had in those early days, he realized later, was that the city was so focused commercially around Grand Central. Gene had a simple philosophy: He was going to take discounting further than it had ever been taken before. If he could make a one-dollar profit selling a refrigerator, he said at the beginning, then he would do it, because he could make a million dollars by selling a million of them.

On opening day he was terrified. But people poured into the store: On the first day, he sold $3,000 worth of goods. Sometimes Ferkauf seemed to be waiting on four people at a time. A few days later, his father looked in and asked what kind of daily volume he was doing. "Three thousand a day," the son said. "You've done it," his father said, pleased in spite of all their differences. In that first Christmas season he averaged $13,000 a day; he could scarcely believe his own success.

If Gene Ferkauf seemed to have broken with his father almost overnight and then surpassed him with his vision and fearlessness, there was nothing unusual about that; it was typical of this postwar generation of Americans, who were more flexible and more ambitious than their parents. They were willing to try different, less traditional careers and go after greater rewards, to marry people from different ethnic and religious backgrounds, to pull up stakes and move across the nation if necessary. America was becoming ever more the land of the new, a nation that revered the young, forgot the past: People routinely changed careers and moved to different parts of the country.

Ferkauf thrived on the madness of those early days. There were never enough clerks. Ferkauf and Beilenson would lug the appliances up the stairs themselves. Sometimes, the customers even helped. "Don't you carry cameras?" one customer asked on a Tuesday, and by Wednesday they carried cameras. The customers would line up in the morning and only a certain number would be let in at the same time. During the holiday season, the line would stretch all the way to Fifth Avenue. Ferkauf and his buddies were working so hard they sometimes could not get home at night; after closing late, they would spend the next three or four hours hauling appliances upstairs to be ready for morning. They grabbed a few hours' sleep at a midtown hotel and then, still groggy, came back to work early in the morning. The pressure was so enormous that Ferkauf found he couldn't eat, so he took to drinking milk all day long. He had to wear gloves to protect his hands while carrying packages and untying the string that bound them.

Within a year he dominated the discount trade. If a large appliance at most stores cost around $300, at Korvettes it was, more often than not, $210—the $200 Ferkauf paid for it, plus the $10 profit he made. It was a cash business—all cash in the register and then money into the bank. Pure instinct carried him. In that first year, he did $1 million worth of business, of which $80,000 was profit, and turned over his inventory thirty times—figures that most storeowners couldn't even dream about at the time. If other discount stores gave a 25 percent markdown, Ferkauf made his a straight 33⅓ percent. It soon became a hard policy that if he couldn't give a third off an item, he wouldn't handle it. He gave this discount even if his profit was only a dollar or two or even nothing at all. It was the volume that mattered, he knew; if he could establish his image as the top discounter in the region, he would get the volume, and with that came the profits. His biggest draw turned out to be large appliances, because with his discount, customers could save $100 or so off the list price. It turned out, though, that the small appliances—toasters, hair dryers, juicers ("small apples," in the lingo of the business)—were what carried the store.

If there were limitations on his business, they were of space and time. He promptly solved this by working out a deal with a distributor. He would buy sixty washing machines from the distributor, provided that the distributor keep them at his warehouse. That way the appliance would never even see Ferkauf's store—it was the distributor's job to make the delivery. The manufacturers were going crazy. Some pleaded with him to raise his prices; some even refused to sell to him. But one day a holdout salesman walked into the store and Ferkauf waved before him a check for $10,000. "Take it, it's yours. Ship me anything you want," he shouted. To a salesman, the commission on a sum like that was irresistible, and he promptly shipped a large order of Zenith radios.

The success of Korvettes was like nothing anyone had ever seen before. Ferkauf expanded quickly, despite the arguments of his buddies, who pleaded with him to be content with what he already had. "Gene, we're already doing so well," one of them said. "Why take a chance?" He refused to listen. The vendors were nervous, too. Ferkauf, to be sure, had done well as a small-time operator, but could a man so volatile, a man who was always shouting run a large store? They doubted it. One vendor told him, "Gene, if you open one more store, we can't ship to you anymore." "So we'll go to Westinghouse," Ferkauf told him.

By 1951 he opened his second store, on Third Avenue between 42nd and 43rd, on the site of a former cafeteria. The third store was in White Plains, the fourth between Fifth and Sixth avenues in Rockefeller Center, and the fifth in Hempstead. Then came the Carle Place store in Westbury and the new age of Korvettes. Here was the prototype for the future. Opening day was set for December 2, 1953.

On that first day over a thousand people showed up, completely overwhelming the salespeople. In those first few weeks, the employees were not even allowed to leave the premises for lunch; if they did, they wouldn't be able to get back inside because the crowds were so large. Instead, Ferkauf sent runners out to bring back hundreds of sandwiches and cups of coffee, which the salespeople would gulp down in the dingy basement. (Years later, Ferkauf marveled at the brilliant success of Toys "R" Us, a chain that had drawn from many of his ideas and yet added an innovative twist of its own: self-service—letting the customer pick up the goods and bring them back to the counters themselves.)

On that first day, they did a staggering $138,000 worth of business. From December 2 to Christmas, they did $2 million in sales. In the next year, the Westbury store grossed $28 million. Ferkauf was one of the big boys now. Each store seemed bigger and handsomer than the last, and the formula still worked. He was expanding into the suburbs almost exclusively now—New Jersey, Connecticut, and Pennsylvania, as well as New York. In the fall of 1956 *Fortune* magazine did a long article on Ferkauf and Korvettes, and it showed a memorable graph: In six years, starting in 1950, the total sales had gone up 2,650 percent.

In December 1955, needing money to fund his continuous expansion, Ferkauf took the company public. The stock opened at 10, and Ferkauf and his family kept 40.4 percent, or 502,420 shares. As the stock soon ascended above 60, he had an odd sense of being rich without being rich. All of this was just some kind of voodoo, he thought. It was not real. Sometimes a small voice in his head would tell him that he was worth $30 or $40 million, but if anything, that aspect of his success—all the money and all the things it could buy—intimidated him. He had little time for the niceties that came with wealth. There were more orders to fill and more stores to open. In 1956, he built three giant stores on the Carle Place model and then in the next few years he undertook the greatest expansion in the history of American retailing. Korvettes erected twenty-five stores in three years. At the same time, he was closing the old, small stores in the city. By decade's end E. J. Korvettes had total annual sales of $157.7 million.

ELEVEN

T wo brothers, who, in the beginning, failed at almost everything they did, were among the first to understand that the fundamental changes taking place in American society concerning where people lived and worked would also affect how they ate. It was then that the luck of Dick and Maurice (Mac) MacDonald took a startling turn for the better. The McDonald brothers moved to California from their native New Hampshire in 1930, driven by the grim economy that had forced textile and shoe factories to close throughout the Northeast. They tried various odd jobs on the periphery of the movie industry, with no notable success: "We were both pushing lights around the Columbia studio and it became very clear to both of us after a few years that no one was going to take the McDonald brothers aside and make us producers," Dick McDonald remembered. They had never liked working for large companies and had often talked of running a place of their own. They had good reason to distrust big companies: their father, Pat McDonald, had worked in a shoe factory in Manchester, New Hampshire, for forty-two years in an age when there were no pensions or vacations. In his last year he was called in by his boss and told, "Pat, I think you've outlived your usefulness to us. We think we've had your best years. I'm afraid we don't need you here anymore."

At the height of the Depression, the brothers opened a small movie theater, but it quickly went bust. As far as they could tell, the only business making money at the time was a nearby hot-dog stand run by a man named Walker Wiley. So in 1937 they opened a stand near the Santa Anita racetrack; they did well from the start, but when the racing season ended, business would dry up.

Finally, Mac McDonald decided they should build a bigger place in San Bernardino, a growing blue-collar city of perhaps 100,-000 people. "We weren't going to sell to the country club set," noted Dick McDonald. The problem was financing: It was going to take $7,500, they estimated. They approached various banks, only to be asked again and again how much collateral they had. Collateral? thought Dick McDonald. All we have is our smiles. Finally, in desperation, they went to the one they were sure would turn them down, because it was so big: the Bank of America. Unlike the others, S. P. Bagley, the manager, listened carefully and asked them to come back in a week so that he could take their proposal to the bank's finance committee. A week later they nervously reappeared. The finance committee, he reported, was far from enthusiastic, "but sometimes I like to play a hunch, and I have a hunch that McDonald's is going to make it and make it big," he said. "I can't give you the full $7,500, but what about a loan of $5,000?" So it was in 1940 they opened a small drive-in restaurant in San Bernardino.

Somewhat to their own surprise, they were an immediate hit and were soon making a profit of $40,000 a year. Their customers came in two varieties, they decided: teenage boys, with their first patched-up used cars, who liked the place as a hangout to flirt with the cute carhops, and young families, in which sometimes both parents worked, who ate there because it was relatively fast and cheap. Obviously, the brothers wanted to encourage the second group and discourage the first.

The McDonalds figured they needed even greater speed. On the average, customers had to wait some twenty minutes for their food. "My God, the carhops were slow," remembered Dick McDonald.

"We'd say to ourselves there had to be a faster way. The cars were jamming up the lot. Customers weren't demanding it, but our intuition told us they would like speed. Everything was moving faster. The supermarkets and dime stores had already converted to self-service, and it was obvious the future of drive-ins was self-service."

The McDonalds had understood an important new trend in American life: Americans were becoming ever more mobile and living farther from their workplaces than ever before. As they commuted considerable distances, they had less time and always seemed to be in a rush. Life in America was surging ahead and one of the main casualties was old-fashioned personal service. Their customers wanted to eat quickly.

Therefore, the brothers began to look for the weaknesses in their operation that caused the delays. Obviously, the carhops would have to go, but to their surprise the McDonalds discovered another impediment to faster service as well: Their menu was surprisingly large, including hamburgers, hot dogs, barbecue, and all manner of sandwiches. However, when the McDonalds checked their receipts, they found that 80 percent of their sales consisted of hamburgers. "The more we hammered away at the barbecue business, the more hamburgers we sold," Dick McDonald said later. So they decided to get rid of the labor-intensive barbecue and sandwiches and narrow the menu to the venerable American hamburger. That would allow them to mechanize the food-preparation process as well.

They did not realize it until much later—during those years they had little time for such reflection—but they had caught the crest of an important new phenomenon: American life was speeding up significantly; the nature of the American family was changing, and so was the family dinner.

Suddenly, the McDonalds found themselves blossoming as brilliant innovators in the one thing they knew: fast food. In the fall of 1948 they closed down for several months, fired all their carhops, and began to reinvent the process. They replaced their small three-foot cast-iron grill with two stainless-steel six-footers; the new grills were custom-designed, and the stainless steel was not only easier to clean, it held the heat better (if they had put too many hamburgers on the cast-iron grill, it lost heat). They replaced the plates and silverware, which had a tendency to disappear anyway, with paper bags, wrappers, and paper cups. That eliminated the need for the dishwasher. They cut the menu from twenty-five items to nine, featuring hamburgers and cheeseburgers, and they made the burgers a little smaller—ten hamburgers from one pound of meat instead of eight.

The McDonalds, rather than their customers, chose the condiments: ketchup, mustard, onions, and two pickles (condiment stations had always been an eyesore, as far as they were concerned—slopped ketchup was everywhere). The McDonalds decided they wanted a machine to make their patties. Dick pondered the question and then figured out that a candy company that made peppermint patties must have just the right device. Posing as a free-lance writer, he visited a number of candy companies, asking how they made their patties so perfect every time, until he finally found a small machine, where a worker, by pushing one lever, could deliver just the right amount of mix. The same machine could make hamburger patties.

Under the new system, if a customer wanted something different on his hamburger, he faced a major delay in service. The McDonalds believed choices meant delays and chaos. After some experimentation—regular heat lamps had failed—they figured out that they could keep the hamburgers hot with infrared lights. "Our whole concept was based on speed, lower prices, and volume," Dick McDonald said. In front of the drive-in they erected a sign with a chef whose name was Speedy. MCDONALD'S FAMOUS HAMBURGERS, said the sign. BUY 'M BY THE BAG. And larger than the letters of the name was the price: 15 CENTS.

To the McDonalds' surprise, business fell off at first. Deprived of their trysting spot, some of the old carhops and teenage boys came back and heckled them. For a time the McDonalds had to tell employees to park their cars in the parking lot so that it would look like they always had a few customers. But as the McDonalds added milkshakes and french fries, they began to be more successful than ever. By 1950, the teenagers had departed to more tolerant hangouts and were replaced by working-class families, who, thanks to the McDonalds' low prices, could afford to feed their families restaurant meals for the first time. The kitchen was enclosed by glass, and children liked watching the burgers cooking on the stainless-steel grills. The children were seen as important from the beginning, and the word was put out that the staff was to be very nice to kids, because kids came equipped with parents.

What the McDonald brothers were doing with food was, as John Love pointed out, what Henry Ford had done to automobile manufacturing (and what Bill Levitt had done with housing): They turned their kitchen into an assembly line. Because they were pioneers, they had to invent much of their own kitchen equipment. In this they were greatly aided by Ed Toman, a local friend who had a small machine-tool shop and no previous experience in the world of

food, save inventing a small device to grind orange peels for marma-
lade. His San Bernardino shop was primitive, with no air-conditioning; the heat seemed to overwhelm all but Toman. He helped design
the lazy Susan (stainless steel, of course) on which to prepare two
dozen hamburger buns with condiments; a larger, stronger stainless-
steel spatula; and the one-squeeze stainless-steel pump that shot just
the right amount of mustard or ketchup onto the burger and which,
John Love noted, Toman failed to patent, thus costing him a chance
to be a millionaire.

Inside the kitchen, everything was mechanized: There were three
grill men, who did nothing but cook patties; two milkshake men; two
french-fries men; two dressers (who wrapped the hamburgers); and
out front were three countermen, who took the orders. Much of the
food was preassembled; the slack time between the rush hours was
used to prepare for the next onslaught.

Here was the perfect restaurant for a new America, and it was
a smashing success. There were long lines at rush hour, and by 1951,
the gross annual receipts were $277,000, some 40 percent higher than
in the old premechanized days. By the mid-fifties, the brothers were
sharing profits of $100,000 a year, a dazzling figure for men selling
items that cost fifteen cents apiece. Soon all kinds of would-be competitors were studying them, trying to figure out how to repeat their
formula for success. In 1952 they were on the cover of *American
Restaurant* magazine. From then on, they were deluged with mail—
as many as three hundred letters a month—asking them how they
had done it. When aspiring entrepreneurs introduced themselves to
the brothers, they were uncommonly generous in sharing expertise.

In 1952 James Collins, later the largest Kentucky Fried Chicken
franchiser and the head of Sizzler restaurants, was a young man just
setting out to start his own coffee shop. But hearing of the success of
the McDonald brothers, he decided to drive out to San Bernardino
to see for himself. He arrived just as the lunch crowd descended. "I
have never seen anything as breathtaking since then," he said later.
"There was a line of people halfway out to the curb and the parking
lot was full. There was nothing else like it. They had two hamburger
lines and they were handling people every ten seconds. I tore up my
coffee shop plans and entered the hamburger business, and except for
the fact that I sold hamburgers for 19 cents, everything else was the
same as McDonald's."

In fact, so many people were making the trek to their little
hamburger stand that the McDonalds knew sooner or later they would
have to franchise the operation. In 1952, they reluctantly sold their

first franchise rights. In truth they were already content with their lives and saw no reason to expand—they were making more money than they had dreamed of, they had lovely houses with tennis courts, new Cadillacs every year. Neither had children and therefore there were no thoughts of leaving a financial empire to their heirs. They thought of McDonald's as a one-shot operation, and they had little interest in a great national network of hamburger stands bearing their name.

The first franchise went for a one-time fee of a thousand dollars. They were surprised when the franchiser, Neil Fox, an independent gas retailer in Phoenix, wanted to keep their name on his stand. "What the hell for?" asked Dick McDonald. "McDonald's means nothing in Phoenix." The Carnation company studied their success and was so impressed it offered to take them national on a major scale: They would start in San Francisco, sweep down the California coast, and then move eastward across the country. That sounded like the fast track, and the brothers wanted no part of it. "We are going to be on the road all the time in motels, looking for locations, finding managers. I can just see one hell of a headache if we go into that kind of chain," Maurice McDonald told his brother.

Years later, after the McDonald brothers had sold out for far less than they might have, someone asked Dick McDonald if he had any regrets. Not at all, he answered: "I would have wound up in some skyscraper somewhere with about four ulcers and eight tax attorneys trying to figure out how to pay all my income tax."

If the McDonald brothers knew their limits, then Ray Kroc was a man who had always seen his future as limitless. He was the classic American boomer, a self-made man, a high school dropout. He was suspicious of college graduates because he thought college tended to separate businessmen from the very people with whom they would have to deal, and, worse, it tended to make them a little lazy. As he turned into the populist as business tycoon, he became convinced that business schools made their students arrogant, and for a long time McDonald's was conspicuous for its lack of MBAs. Kroc believed in himself and his special vision of the American dream: If he only kept trying, surely one day lightning would strike and he would become rich and successful.

As a young man, Kroc held a variety of jobs, selling, among other things, paper cups and Florida real estate, and playing piano for bands when things got really tight. His drive was incredible, and he was always spurred by the fact that his father, a successful Western Union operator, had become rich speculating in land in the twenties and then had lost everything in the Depression. On the day of the senior Kroc's death his desk contained his last paycheck from the telegraph company and a garnishment notice for the amount of his wages. If there ever was a businessman with the instincts of the common man, it was Ray Kroc. He boasted, with good reason, of his ability to anticipate mass taste, and he was rarely wrong (although briefly there was an unfortunate sandwich put out by McDonald's called the Hulaburger, which Ray Kroc loved and which featured two slices of cheese and a piece of grilled pineapple).

One of Kroc's early jobs was as a paper-cup salesman, and he understood not only his own product but what part paper—quick consumption, carry-out food possibilities, and labor-cost savings, through the elimination of dish washing—was beginning to play in American life. He was *always* looking for the idea or invention that would make his fortune. On his route he made the acquaintanceship of a man named Earl Prince, an engineer who also ran a chain of dairy parlors. In the late thirties, Prince, in no small part pushed by Kroc, developed a machine that used a single motor to drive five separate spindles, thus greatly accelerating the milkshake-making process. He called it the Multimixer, and it was a powerful machine, or, as Ray Kroc liked to boast, "You could mix concrete with the damn thing." When Kroc's employer, the Lily-Tulip paper-cup company, turned down the idea of selling it across the country, Kroc decided to handle it himself. In 1939 he started his own business, Malt-A-Mixer.

Kroc set out to sell the entire country these amazing machines, and to make sure he covered all his bases, he even sent out a newsletter to bars extolling the virtues of the sexy new mixed drinks they could make (with a Multimixer), including the Delicado ("After Dinner You'll Love Delacado. Brandy or Your Favorite Liqueur Multimixed With Ice Cream"). The war put his dream on hold because the materials for the Multimixer were no longer available, but when it was over, his business exploded. He and two associates sold 9,000 Multimixers a year, and Kroc was making $25,000 a year. It was not the big strike he had hoped for, but by the standards of the time, he was wealthy. But by the early fifties, the tide was running out on Multimixers: Sales were dramatically down, and there was competition from a rival company. Kroc had the foresight to realize that it was not so much the product that was the problem as its prize customer—the neighborhood drugstore. The great move to the suburbs was the death knell for that small-town institution.

By 1954 Kroc was looking for an alternative source of income, so he and a friend invented something called a Fold-A-Nook, two benches and a small table that folded down from the wall and thereby made a small kitchen seem roomier. He exhibited it at a trade show in Los Angeles and sold not a single one. He was still selling Multimixers at the time and the one thing that puzzled him was the success of a small hamburger spot in San Bernardino, which seemed to buck the national trend: The rest of the nation wanted fewer Multimixers; this place called McDonald's needed ever more; most drugstores needed, at best, two Multimixers, but in early 1954, the McDonald brothers ordered their ninth and tenth machines—that meant they were making something on the order of fifty milkshakes at a time. In addition, Kroc was getting calls from other fast-food operators, who told him they wanted the same kind of mixers the McDonalds were using.

In early 1954, Kroc went to San Bernardino to take a look. He was stunned. He arrived an hour before lunch, but there were already long lines. He immediately liked what he saw: attendants in spiffy white shirts and trousers and white paper hats, and no flies clustered around the back of the place. Kroc got in line and began to talk with the customers. He innocently pointed out that he had never waited on line for a hamburger before. The regulars, as he had hoped, gave him unsolicited testimonials: The place was clean, it was fast, it was cheap, and the hamburgers were good. Besides, they said, you did not have to tip. That alone struck home with him. Orders, he was amazed to discover, were being filled in about fifteen seconds apiece. The hamburgers cost 15 cents each, a slice of cheese cost 4 cents more, a shake was 20 cents, and a coffee was a nickel. One out of three customers wanted a shake, and even here the McDonalds had improved upon Kroc's beloved Multimixer. Ed Toman, their personal inventor, had taken Ray Kroc's machine and cut four inches off the spindles. That meant that the shakes could be made right in the twelve-inch paper cups—there was no need to transfer from the mixer to the cup. Kroc sat all afternoon and watched. The McDonalds were glad to see him—he was, after all, something of a celebrity in the business. Mr. Multimixer, they called him. They assured him that this was a typical day. Kroc asked the McDonalds when the rush stopped. "Sometime late tonight when we close," Dick McDonald said. At first, Ray Kroc began to think how good it would be to expand McDonald's because of what it could mean to his troubled Multimixer business. And the more he thought about it, the more he was convinced he had seen the future and it was hamburgers.

At the moment Ray Kroc entered their world, the McDonald brothers had issued all of nine franchises and were looking for a new manager to handle franchising. Soon after his visit, Kroc called Dick McDonald. "Have you found a franchising agent yet?" he asked. "No, Ray, not yet," McDonald answered. "Well then, what about me?" Kroc said.

He took over the franchise end at the age of fifty-two, a diabetic who had already lost his gallbladder. Starting out all over in a new field when most men were starting to think about retirement, he was unbelievably hardworking and ambitious, and his ability to outwork everyone in his office was soon a legend. He made $12,000 at the start, half of what he had made as a Multimixer man. But he was sure this was the big break he had always been looking for. "It was," he once said, "practically life or death for me."

Years later, he was asked why he went with the McDonald brothers when he could so easily have stolen their system. Part of it was the name itself: McDonald's simply sounded right to him. He did not think that a chain named Kroc's would have the same appeal. In addition, he had been in and out of a thousand kitchens in his years as a paper-cup and mixer salesman, and this was by far the best operation he'd ever seen. He knew that the McDonalds had learned to do things right only after making many mistakes and it was well worth whatever it cost him to avoid repeating those mistakes.

He saw immediately that the prime customers were *families,* young couples, a little unsure of themselves, often with children in tow. They were comfortable at McDonald's as they might not have been at a more traditional restaurant; they came, ordered, and ate in the car, and if their children were misbehaving, it wouldn't annoy the other clients. It was an inexpensive, easy night out for the family. In the early days a family of four could eat at McDonald's for about $2.50. At first, the various franchises did their best business on Saturday night, and next best on Friday night—the customers obviously regarded it as a treat. Then they began to do well on Sunday afternoon, and then, at last, on the weeknights. Soon there were advertising slogans reflecting the thrust of the business: "Give Mom a Night Out," and then "Give Mom a Night Off." These were, as Fred Turner, Kroc's heir to the company later noted, the forerunner of the famous McDonald's slogan "You Deserve a Break Today."

Kroc understood that the McDonalds were taking advantage of a phenomenon—the instant suburbs, where millions of Americans were now living. He liked to boast that when he looked for a new site, he did not so much measure traffic along the highway as determine the size and stability of a community by counting the church steeples and the number of schools. He had no use for downtown areas: He vowed often that there would never be a McDonald's in Chicago's Loop, ostensibly the perfect place for a fast-food emporium. In his view, the commuters would desert during peak dinner hours, and he was not enthusiastic about the remaining clientele: They were not, most assuredly, family people, and he saw McDonald's as predominantly a family restaurant. The people who would eat at a downtown McDonald's might well be bums or, worse, and they might damage the image of his restaurant. He wanted no women working at the stands, because he thought they were there to flirt rather than work—and that would conflict with the image of a family restaurant. Women in short skirts behind the counter would attract young men in black leather jackets—as in the carhop days of old—and he wanted no part of that. "I've made up my mind that all hamburger joints had jukeboxes, telephones, and cigarette machines and that your wife and my wife wouldn't go to a place with leather-jacketed guys and smoke-filled rooms," he once said.

At the center of all of the hoopla was a very small piece of meat, soon to be standardized in the McDonald's handbook at 1.6 ounces. It was made of "commercial-grade" ground chuck and formed into a patty 3⅝ inches in diameter. The fat content was between 17 and 20 percent. It was served with a quarter-ounce of onion, a teaspoon of mustard, a tablespoon of ketchup, and a pickle one inch in diameter. There was, in Kroc's mind, something beautiful about a hamburger as opposed to, say, hot dogs. He wanted no part of hot dogs, whose popularity he felt was regional; confined to such places as New York and Philadelphia. In addition, he perceived them as a snack instead of a full meal. As he found beauty in the hamburger, he thought hot dogs unattractive—both aesthetically and commercially. The hamburger, he liked to say, could be assembled on his terms, but people were determined to have hot dogs their own way. That demanded a condiment station, which the McDonald brothers had eliminated—rightly, in his view—as the messiest place in the whole restaurant.

Above all, he wanted consistency so that a hamburger in California would be an advertisement for one in Chicago or New York. If the McDonald brothers had built the perfect hamburger stand, Ray Kroc envisioned the perfect nationwide chain. The trick was to impose his will upon independent owners, which took an odd combination of pure democratic instinct and totalitarian will. Kroc brooked little in the way of dissent, and he expected everyone to work as hard as he did.

At first, Kroc granted most of his licenses in California, which, because of the dominance of the auto there and the exceptional year-round climate, qualified as the birthplace of the fast-food franchise. But Kroc, who lived in suburban Chicago, soon found that it was hard to impose rules on California operators from such a distance. In fact, they sometimes seemed to be in a virtual conspiracy to break his beloved rules of standardization, serving foods that were not supposed to be on the menu, posting higher prices than those agreed on, and committing other equally egregious sins. These were not evil men and women, though sometimes they might have seemed so to him. Rather, they did not hate dirt as much as he, or they were, on occasion, willing to put the price of the hamburger above the price he had specified. There was a certain contradiction here: Kroc wanted highly individual small-time owners to risk all their savings in classic American entrepreneurial style, but he wanted those same people to obey all the rules emanating from Chicago headquarters. Clearly, the latter came to be the most important qualification. His philosophy had an almost Orwellian quality to it. In 1958 he told the McDonald brothers: "We have found out, as you have, that we cannot trust some people who are nonconformists. We will make conformists out of them in a hurry. Even personal friends who we know have the best of intentions may not conform. They have a difference of opinion as to various processing and certain qualities of product. . . . You cannot give them an inch. The organization cannot trust the individual; the individual must trust the organization [or] he shouldn't go into this kind of business." Fearing for his control, Kroc even stopped giving out California franchises for a time, awarding them instead to apparently more conformist Midwesterners.

He opened his own first hamburger stand in Des Plaines, suburban Chicago, in April 1955; at the time he was so desperately short of cash that he had to borrow the money necessary to put up his showplace McDonald's. He even offered the banks half the stock in his company for a mere $25,000. Fortunately for his own financial future, and probably also for the future of McDonald's, he found no takers.

He was a hands-on owner, the first person there every morning, setting up, checking things out, then going into downtown Chicago, working all day at his headquarters, trying to expand the network, and then stopping back at night to close and clean up. "Every night you'd see him coming down the street, walking close to the gutter, picking up every McDonald's wrapper and cup along the way," said Fred Turner, who started as one of Kroc's first grill men and later became chairman of the company. "He'd come into the store with both hands full of cups and wrappers. He was the store's outside pickup man." Actually, cleanliness and order were fetishes with him. If he went into a colleague's office and there was a picture slightly out of kilter on the wall, he straightened it; if there was a loose thread on the couch, he would pick it up and throw it away. He gave his top people little packets with nail files, combs, and brushes, and for one executive, whose nose hair he judged as too long, he included a tiny pair of scissors. He demanded that all his employees be clean, down to their fingernails, and sometimes he even asked them to brush their teeth more carefully. He wanted no beards or mustaches, no wrinkled clothes, and no gum chewing. Years later an advertising man named Barry Klein came by the headquarters to work out some proposals. Klein, in the style of his profession and the times, wore his hair long. Everyone waited for Kroc to explode, but he merely swallowed his anger and muttered to a colleague, "That SOB better be good." Executives in the main office were to leave their desks clean at the end of the day. Every day, the windows at all McDonald's had to be cleaned, the parking lot had to be hosed down, and the garbage cans scrubbed. Mopping of the floors inside was a continuous process.

He knew he was going to be a great success at McDonald's even before the Des Plaines store opened. He called a man named Waddy Pratt, the regional dealer for Coke, and said, "My name's Ray Kroc and I'm opening a restaurant and I want to sell Coke because it's the best goddamn product there is." Pratt trekked out to the Des Plaines store, and the two of them stood in the parking lot, like two figures from a Sinclair Lewis novel. Kroc repeated: "I believe in Coke. So I'm going to buy it." Then he added: "And orange soda and root beer, too." "I'm sorry, we're not in the rainbow flavors," Pratt said, using the industry's term for the other sodas. "Well, you better get into them because I plan to have a thousand of these stores pretty soon," Kroc said. Pratt looked around him and thought, We are standing over a hole in the ground that this man says will be a restaurant and in addition he is telling me he's going to own 999 more just like it. This man is not playing with a full deck. (Years after, Kroc would remind Pratt of that day: "I guess you wish you'd gotten in on orange soda and root beer right then and there, right, Waddy, you'd have made millions more.") Kroc even knew exactly how he wanted the soda delivered: in tin containers instead of the usual gallon glass jugs. Pratt told him Coke didn't handle it in tin. "Don't lie to me," Kroc said, and with that Pratt realized that he had heard somewhere about military shipments overseas of Coke in tin. "It's not available in retail in America in tin," he said. Kroc was getting edgier, but Pratt came up with a compromise: If Kroc's people would clean out the jugs, Pratt would have them picked up and sold to another merchant in town, and the five-cent-a-jug price would be turned over to Kroc. Kroc loved that idea: "You mean I get to cut my costs five cents a jug?" he asked incredulously.

From the start his restaurant was successful; by the second full year it did a total volume of $200,000, which meant that his pretax profits were around 20 percent, or $40,000. His hard work became legend within the company. He remained wary of talent and education. "Nothing in the world can take the place of persistence," he liked to say. "Genius will not. Unrewarded genius is almost a problem. Talent will not. The world is filled with unsuccessful men of talent. Education alone will not. The world is filled with educated derelicts."

His associates were amused when he was asked, as he often was, the secret of his success, because they knew the answer. He would begin, "I am of Bohemian extraction and I have always believed in hard work . . ." He would then tell his favorite anecdote about Bohemian upward mobility: A Bohemian lived in the basement floor of his own building and ventured upstairs to the first and second floors only to collect the rent. The only ethic he knew was hard work, and he saved every bit of money he made, no matter how small. According to Kroc, family responsibilities were an important part of the Bohemian ethic: Children (not the government) were to take care of their parents and grandparents as they grew older. To the day he died, Ray Kroc harbored a bitter grudge against Franklin D. Roosevelt because of Social Security.

As it became wildly successful, the company retained its distinctly populist culture. Everyone, no matter how important the job, was supposed to answer his or her own phone; there were to be no secretaries standing between the general public and McDonald's executives. Once Kroc called down to his Atlanta operation and a secretary asked who was calling. Kroc went ballistic and demanded that the secretary be fired on the spot; her superiors had to hide her from Kroc for a year until the incident had blown over.

If the most important component of Kroc's Bohemian ethic was hard work, the second most important was thrift. The ketchup came in large cans, and employees were told to open any supposedly empty cans and scrape out every last bit of remaining ketchup. Even if it was only a spoonful, spoonfuls from thousands of cans added up. Even after he had become a millionaire, Kroc would visit various McDonald's to patrol for unused packets of sugar, salt, and pepper, which had been left on the tables, in order to keep them from being thrown out. Ray Kroc was this way not just about his business but about his personal life. In his later years, as one of the wealthiest men in America, he dined at a fancy restaurant in Bel Air, ordered trout amandine, ate only half of it and, as he was finishing, asked the waitress to put the remains in a doggy bag. "Ray, what in God's name are you going to do with half of a trout amandine?" asked Waddy Pratt, who had gone to dinner with him. "I'm going to take it home and have it for breakfast tomorrow," said Kroc.

There were frequent letters to the wives of McDonald's employees imploring them to be thrifty: cigarettes should be bought by the carton; socks, toilet paper, and toothpaste should be bought in quantity and on sale. "When beef, steaks, and chops are extremely high," he added in one letter, "it certainly seems logical to use more fish, fowl, casserole dishes, and things of that sort that really have more flavor and save a lot of money. The same is true of baked goods. I had some pumpkin bread that Virginia Lea baked that was made with canned pumpkin, orange juice, flour, dates, and nuts that was out of this world. At one time you could bake a month's supply. The same might be said for chicken pot pie when stewing chickens are on sale. One day could be spent processing this and putting it in the freezer. So what I am saying is that the smarter you are, the farther your money will go."

In many comparable chains, the franchiser made his money up front, either through expensive equipment sales or through heavy franchise fees; that put a heavy burden on the franchisee and took away much of the incentive on his part to help make the local operation successful. Ray Kroc wanted none of that. He kept the entry price for a McDonald's franchise around $80,000 in the beginning, a figure that was about one third the price of starting up an independent small restaurant. From the beginning he believed that the head of the chain and the smallest franchisee were not merely partners on paper but that they were in this together, that each could bring the other down, and that any weakness in the chain threatened the whole.

The company made its money by taxing sales at the seemingly minuscule rate of 1.9 percent. "Ray, you've got to be crazy," Tony

Weismuller, one of Kroc's country-club friends, who owned a heating company, said. "There's no way you can make money on 1.9 percent." In the beginning, Kroc stumbled on his way to figuring out who were the perfect franchisees; he went first to his pals at his suburban Chicago country club, sure that these were the paradigms of America's business success. Later he realized they lacked the true grit and absolute commitment that Kroc demanded for his new empire. They were, it turned out, men who had already made it, and they either looked down on the hamburger business or thought it something of a lark. Few were willing to work the backbreaking hours that owning one of these restaurants demanded or surrender as much independence as Kroc demanded. One old pal decided to charge 18 cents instead of 15 cents for a hamburger and, even worse, wore a beard—which Kroc hated. At one point Kroc even ordered the offender to take down his arch, but his friend refused. Many of his old friendships turned so sour through business involvements that Kroc found it difficult to mention their names.

The best owners, he learned, were people who had not yet made it but who were ready to bet their entire lives on one break: people like him. They had worked hard all their lives, saved a surprising amount of money, and always dreamt of owning their own business. Often, both husband and wife would be involved, and they did not so much work there as live there. He gave Sandy and Betty Agate an early franchise in Waukegan because he was encouraged by the simplicity of their background and remarkable determination: Sandy was a pressman who went to night school to get a degree in optometry and Betty, who was Jewish, sold Catholic Bibles door to door. Their franchise became one of the early showplaces. When potential franchisees showed up, Kroc often sent them to see the Agates, who would tell their entire success story and even show their tax returns. Kroc gloried in the success of such families, and it did not bother him at all if they were making a great deal more money than he was in those early years. His ego was always invested in the success of the chain, not his own financial gain.

He was a fanatic about quality control, and he became furious if he thought an owner was buying substandard ingredients. The Department of Agriculture permitted up to 33 percent fat in hamburger meat, but Kroc kept it much lower, and he kept beef additives out. He soon developed equipment with which he could test the quality of the meat at his local stands. He pushed owners to use only the best potatoes and worked hard to make sure that the potato wholesalers did not rebag and substitute second-rate potatoes. He treated his suppliers well, and did not try to exploit his relationship with them as many franchisers did. Indeed, when he received price breaks based on the volume of business he was doing, Kroc passed much of the savings back to his franchisees. That was unheard of in this cut-throat business.

He started franchising in 1955, when his own McDonald's was one of only two he had awarded. At first he moved very slowly. In 1956, he awarded twelve more. In 1957, there were forty; by 1958, 79; by 1959, 145; and by 1960, 228. As the new decade began they were planning to open a hundred new restaurants a year. The word was out and the rush was on. Soon the company was becoming more identified with Ray Kroc than with the McDonald brothers. "I put the hamburger on the assembly line," Ray Kroc said in 1959, and in the larger sense, at least, he was right.

His success mounted as the highway became ever more a part of the social fabric of American life. Powerful new competitors entered the field, but by and large, Kroc treated them with scorn; they were out to make money, he said, not to make hamburgers and perform a service. They had no quality-control systems, no love of the product, no desire to make every small part of the chain as good as its whole.

Unlike the McDonald brothers, Kroc was a fierce competitor and remarkably ungenerous with others trying to establish themselves on what he considered his turf. For a long time he even refused to join any groups representing the food industry, for fear of giving away the secrets of his success. It was, he said, "ridiculous to call this an industry. This is not. This is rat eat rat, dog eat dog. I'll kill 'em and I'm going to kill 'em before they kill me. You're talking about the American way of the survival of the fittest." Asked on another occasion how he felt about his competition, he answered with a vintage Krocism: "If they were drowning to death I'd put the hose in their mouth."

His whole life became McDonald's. He would talk about little else and had no interest in those who did not share his obsession. It was said that an earlier marriage foundered because his wife did not love McDonald's enough; a third marriage succeeded because it was to a woman already steeped in the culture of the company. Finally, he had someone to talk to. Everything about the company, he thought, was pure artistry. "Consider, for example, the hamburger bun," he once said. "It requires a certain kind of mind to see the beauty in a hamburger bun. Yet is it any more unusual to find grace in the texture and softly curved silhouette of a bun than to reflect lovingly on the hackles of a favorite fishing fly? Or the arrangements and textures and colors in a butterfly's wings? Not if you're a Mc-Donald's man. Not if you view the bun as an essential material in the art of serving a great many meals fast. Then this plump yeasty mass becomes an object worthy of sober study . . ."

Toward the end of his life, after suffering several partially disabling strokes, he sat in his office in San Diego and watched the traffic at a nearby McDonald's through a telescope, clocking it against a watch and picking up the phone to yell at the manager if he thought the service was too slow.

By 1961, Kroc had started preliminary talks with the McDonalds about buying them out. The brothers were doing well: They made an annual profit of $100,000 on their own stand and in 1960, they took in an additional $189,000 from the franchises—they got one half of one percentage on sales, which by then had reached $37.8 million. The relationship between Kroc and the brothers was becoming ever more strained. Their heart had always been in their own stand. He had come to think of them as careless and lazy, people who thought in small terms, willing to sit on the sidelines and make an easy profit while he did all the heavy lifting. The brothers themselves wanted out, but they wanted out on their terms: $2.7 million to sell the name and the company to Kroc, which meant $1 million after taxes for each brother. It was a great deal of money, and Kroc was already in debt from expanding. Nevertheless, he sensed it was a bargain: The chain was growing at roughly a hundred stands a year, and would hit Kroc's magic goal of one thousand by the end of the decade.

With the help of his financial aides, Kroc put together the loan and bought out the brothers. It was not easy to accomplish: Despite the self-evident success of McDonald's, most banks and Wall Street financiers wanted no part of putting money into fast food. After pulling it off, Kroc's long-simmering resentment toward the brothers finally surfaced: "Art, I'm not normally a vindictive man," he told one friend, Art Bender, a franchisee in Sacramento, "but this time I'm going to get those sons of bitches." Now he had the chance. He forced them to take their own name off their restaurant in San Bernardino (they changed the name to the Big M instead), and he put up a brand-new McDonald's one block away. The real glory years for the chain were just beginning. Kroc's old estimate of 1,000 outlets had been far too modest; some thirty-seven years after he took over the franchising, there were 8,600 McDonald's in America, and 12,000 in the rest of the world. He achieved wealth beyond his wildest dreams—$600 million, by some estimates)—but was completely uninterested in what wealth could bring him (other than buying a baseball team, something he had always wanted). He told one reporter, "I have never worshiped money and I never worked for money. I worked for pride and accomplishment. Money can become a nuisance. It's a hell of a lot more fun chasin' it than gettin' it. The fun is in the race."

TWELVE

The vacation that changed the face of the American road occurred in the summer of 1951. Kemmons Wilson was a successful home builder in Memphis, Tennessee, and he and his wife decided to take their five children to see the nation's monuments in Washington, D.C. In those days, before superhighways, tourism was a far smaller industry than it is today. Air travel was prohibitively expensive, and the railroads were in decline. The family car was becoming the key to the new tourism. The Wilson family was fairly typical; its new Oldsmobile experienced far fewer flat tires and mechanical mishaps than prewar cars, but with all the rest and bathroom stops required for that many children, it was hard to make more than three hundred miles a day. Each afternoon, the Wilsons would have to search for one of the new landmarks of the American road, the motel. Young families generally tried to stay away from downtown hotels, which were either too expensive or, more likely, in various stages of neglect and disrepair, reflecting the early decline of some urban neighborhoods.

But motels in those days were not exactly reliable, either. Usually located right on the main roads, they were convenient and seemed more modern than the old hotels and the alternative of dark, musty roominghouses. But at this moment, the motel business was still in its infancy and there was little in the way of industry standards. There was no way to tell which motels were clean and comfortable and which, despite the flashiness of their signs, were rattraps. At the end of the day, most motorists, tired and irritated, pulled into a motel, got out, and checked the rooms to see if the place passed inspection. Some motels, Wilson later recalled, were godawful; some were very pleasant. The only way you could tell which was which was to see for yourself. The price per night varied in those days between $8 and $10. That was not so bad, but Wilson was enraged to find that every motel charged extra for children. The fee was usually $2 per child, even though his children had brought their own bedrolls. Thus, for a family like his, the final cost tended to be around $20. Even worse, there was rarely a place to eat nearby, and so he and his family would have to pile back into the car and hunt for a decent family restaurant.

Day by day on the trip, Wilson became more irritated until he finally turned to his wife, Dorothy, and announced that he was going to go into the motel business. Everyone in this country, he thought, had a car and a family, and sooner or later everyone had to go somewhere. Dorothy Wilson listened to him with growing trepidation—when Kemmons Wilson said he was going to do something, he did it. "How many of these motels are you going to build?" she asked nervously. He felt she was laughing at him. "Oh, about four hundred," he answered. "That ought to cover the country." "And," he added, "if I never do anything else worth remembering in my life, children are going to stay free at my motels."

The Wilson children finally got to see the Washington Monument and the Lincoln Memorial, but their father had seen something else: a vision of the American family on the road. He was absolutely sure it would be a success. "I like to think that I'm so damn normal that anything I like, everybody else is going to like too. The idea that my instincts are out of line just doesn't occur to me," he once said. That was the beginning of the modern American motel chain, a phenomenon made inevitable by America's growing love and dependence on the road.

Wilson did not waste any time going ahead with his idea. He was thirty-eight at the time, a high school dropout, but possessed of limitless self-confidence. He loved dealing and selling (as a young jukebox salesman, he had taken his wife to a Wurlitzer convention on their honeymoon). At the time of his trip to Washington, he was already a millionaire from his home-building business, but he lived so unpretentiously that no one but his banker knew for sure. "The things that Kemmons does now that he has money," one friend noted later in his life, when he was worth some $200 million from the motel business, "are the exact same things he would be doing if he didn't have money."

On the way home from Washington, Wilson measured the rooms of the different motels his family stayed in, and by the time he got back to Memphis, he knew exactly how big a motel room should be: 12 feet by 30 feet, plus a bathroom. Though he was neither artist nor architect, he had always done the basic sketching for his designs. He called a draftsman friend of his named Eddie Bluestein, gave him the specifications for the rooms, and asked him to draw up the plans. Wilson emphasized that he wanted everything as simple as possible, so that anyone who could build the simplest of houses could also build a motel. A few days later Bluestein delivered the sketches, and at the top of the drawing he had written HOLIDAY INN. Wilson asked him where he had gotten the name. "I saw Bing Crosby's *Holiday Inn* on television last night," Bluestein answered. "It's a great name," Wilson said. "We'll use it."

If anyone embodied the old-fashioned American success story, it was Kemmons Wilson. He was born in 1913 in Osceola, Arkansas; his father was an insurance man who died of what was probably Lou Gehrig's disease when Kemmons was nine months old. But Doll Wilson, who never married again, told her son that he could do anything he wanted, and she proceeded to help him do it—some forty years later, as a woman in her late sixties, she was still working full-time for Holiday Inns. As a boy, Kemmons held many jobs: He sold the *Saturday Evening Post;* he sold popcorn at movie theaters; and he became the pinball king of Memphis. He was surprisingly successful in all these pursuits, and before he was twenty he made good on a long-standing vow: He built a house for his mother. He was nothing if not fearless. Taking $1,000 worth of pinball profits to buy the land, he put up the house himself for $1,700. He was so enthusiastic that he built it on the wrong lot, and eventually had to swap deeds with the real owner. Shortly thereafter, the local Wurlitzer distributorship became available; the price was $6,500, and

Wilson approached a mortgage company to see if he had been able to borrow the money against the house. A banker duly approved the loan. That set Kemmons Wilson to thinking—he had built a house for only $2,700 and yet he could borrow $6,500 against it, even in the worst of times. The future was not in pinball machines or jukeboxes, he decided: It was in building houses.

In the three years before he entered the service at the start of World War Two, Wilson was well on his way to becoming a millionaire. There was a reason for his success: He always built a significantly larger house for the same price as, or for less than, his competitors. The secret to this, which he told no one else at the time, was that space in the middle of a house doesn't cost very much. A house with big rooms had the same number of windows and bathrooms as a smaller one. Everything else was essentially the same—the cost of the plumbing and electrical wiring. In those days, building in Memphis cost about $10 a square foot, but the cost in the center of a home, he was sure, was something more like $2 or $3 a square foot.

In the years after the war, Wilson became very successful, building perhaps two hundred houses a year in the $7,500 to $12,000 range. He owned a lumberyard on the main drag from Memphis to Nashville, a prize location. He decided it was the perfect place for his first motel, which would contain 120 rooms. If he did everything right, Wilson believed, it would cost, restaurant and all, about $325,000. He took out a loan for that amount, but brought the entire project in for $280,000, thereby keeping some money for his next one. He built it in ninety days; it opened in August 1952, exactly a year after Wilson had taken his fateful trip to Washington. Most men would have been pleased with that kind of schedule, but Wilson was irritated that he had missed most of the summer tourist season. The first Holiday Inn had a restaurant, a gift shop, a swimming pool, and in each room there was an air conditioner and a free television set (at other motels it cost $1 extra to rent a television set). Wilson charged his customer $4 a night for a single room, and $6 for a double. Children, as he had vowed, stayed free. Within two years he had built three more motels, covering the three other main approaches to Memphis.

There was also the sign. From his childhood job working in movie theaters, he remembered how vital signs and marquees were. In the case of motels, the sign had to serve as a landmark, a powerful visual magnet, visible from far down the road. It had to be striking from both directions, and so it was—at a height of fifty feet.

Dorothy Wilson was pleased by her husband's early success but amused by the fact that it was not yet exactly nationwide—he was 396 motels short of his original boast, to be exact. At this point Wilson turned to the people he knew best and felt most comfortable with—home builders. Getting into the motel business was a lark, he told those friends, nothing but sticks and bricks. They would be asked to do nothing but what they already did so well. He told his friend Wallace Johnson, the vice-president of the National Home-builders' Association, that they had the basis for the biggest motel chain in America right at their fingertips. Wilson's idea was simple enough: Each home builder wanting to be a part of his group would pay $500 for the right to own a Holiday Inn in his own city; he would also pay a user's fee, plus five cents a night per room.

They called a meeting and some seventy home builders showed up. Wilson was excited—there he was, surrounded by his pals, build-ers all, men without illusions, who were doers, and he was sure that within a year there would be Holiday Inns in every major city and at every key highway junction in America. He was wrong. By the end of the year only three builders had followed through. In retrospect it was one of the great bargain-basement offers of all time, and Wilson was lucky that his colleagues did not take him up on it. Why so few had signed on always puzzled Wilson; his idea was so simple, he was sure.

Gradually, it dawned on Wilson that they did not see the world around them changing—the numbers of highways growing and au-tomobile travel increasing. "They just weren't interested—they had one business already going and they had no interest in trying an-other. They were not men who wanted to explore life," he said later. So he came up with a new idea: He would become the head of Holiday Inns, franchise them to others. (In his mind—there is no proof of this—he became the first man to franchise ownerships of this kind in the country.) Wilson now turned instead to the men in Memphis who he knew had disposable cash and good credit—doc-tors, dentists, lawyers. The word spread, and soon a group of Nash-ville doctors called Kemmons Wilson to get in on the deal. Wilson started building his motels at $3,000 a room and selling the fran-chises at $3,500 a room. "We were," noted Wilson, "already making a clean profit of $500 a room on just the building."

The motels were a success from the start. The rooms always seemed to be filled. In 1954 eleven more Holiday Inns opened, and there was growing confidence among Wilson, his employees, and his investors they were all on the right track. That year saw the first franchised Holiday Inn built. In 1956 the country passed a giant $76 billion federal-highway program; America was finding its way to Kemmons Wilson's doorsteps. Not only would there be more and better highways, but with the coming of the cloverleaf and the bypass, travelers could avoid going through cities altogether if they wished. This was another benchmark in the decline of inner-city hotels. The growth of his company spiraled beyond his control, and in 1957 he decided to take it public; Wilson and his handful of partners sold 120,000 shares of stock at $9.75 a share in the first day.

For a long time Wilson had the field all to himself. One of his singular skills, it turned out, was that he had a great eye. He could come into any city and instinctively pick out the single best site for a Holiday Inn. "Looking for land," he once said, "is like going on an Easter egg hunt and sometimes you find the golden egg." He always knew the kind of location he wanted—highly visible, on the right side of the road heading into a city, with a lot of additional acreage in case he wanted to expand.

He became ever more professional at it. Once, a friend in Meridian, Mississippi, asked him to come down and check out a potential site for a Holiday Inn. Wilson flew down, checked out the land, thought it awful, flew around some more, and saw another spot that he decided was perfect. His friend protested that he already owned the first tract of land. "That's the worst reason in the world I've ever heard for building on a piece of land—just because you own it. Now, you listen to me, because I'm going to give you one bit of advice and it will mean the difference between success and failure: You sell that first piece, and you buy this other and you'll be just fine." Which the man did, becoming the owner in time of four successful Holiday Inns.

That, Wilson later realized, was the real fun of it—picking the sites, choosing the franchises. He would select the best areas and the best applicants and then chart a trip, going, say, west from Memphis, through Arkansas and Texas and New Mexico. He would then fly off in his single-engine Bonanza. He would eat his meals while he was up, flying, checking out these towns and small cities in the early morning and early evening—the best times, he thought, because you could see the traffic patterns.

His eye became legend in the business. Years later, when the world of chain motels had become much more competitive, Wilson attended a conference in New Jersey along with executives from Howard Johnson, Sheraton, and Ramada. At one point a young man got up and asked Marion Isbell of Ramada, "Mr. Isbell, what criteria do you use for picking a location?" "It's really simple," Isbell answered. "All I do is go into a city and find out where Kemmons Wilson has a good Holiday Inn and I put a Ramada Inn right next door—it's a good system and it really works."

Kemmons Wilson's chain quickly grew to fifteen hundred motels. At one point it was building a new inn every two and a half days and a new room every fifteen minutes. By the early seventies, Holiday Inns had more than three times as many rooms—208,939—as either of its main competitors, Ramada and Sheraton, and Wilson was getting as many as ten thousand requests a year for franchises. Wilson knew the people requesting franchises were people just like himself—people who had probably not been to college but who believed in themselves and saw this as their chance, he liked to say, to own a piece of the American dream.

THIRTEEN

As the booming postwar economy changed the face of American business, a technological breakthrough transformed the communications industry, sending powerful shock waves through all levels of the society.

By 1949, radio was on the verge of being overtaken by television as a commercial vehicle. For more than two decades, radio had virtually been minting money; now it was struggling, changing, and trying to find a new role. The signs of decline and flux were everywhere; one of the most startling took place in June 1949, when *The Fred Allen Show,* perhaps the best and most sophisticated radio show of its era, died after an eighteen-year run. The moment Fred Allen learned of television, he hated it. He called it "a device that permits people who haven't anything to do to watch people who can't do anything." Allen had realized earlier that the handwriting was on the

wall. "Television," he wrote, "was already conducting itself provoca-
tively, trying to get radio to pucker up for the kiss of death. Young
men with crew cuts were dragging TV cameras into the studios and
crowding old radio actors out into the halls."

For more than a decade, Allen owned his time slot. He had been
the foremost of radio's comics, living proof of continuity in that
world. He was the rare entertainer who commanded both a mass
audience and the affection of the intelligentsia. His jokes were not
about mothers-in-law or women drivers; rather, they were dry, with
a certain melancholy bite. There was nothing smooth about his
delivery. Indeed, his voice, O. O. McIntyre, a Broadway columnist,
wrote, "sounded like a man with false teeth chewing on slate pencils." He was irreverent and, on more than one occasion, churlish.
He feuded regularly with network executives, who, he was convinced, were always trying to censor him. It was said that he always
slipped two or three outrageous jokes into his scripts in order to
trade them off to network censors for the dicey jokes he wanted to
save. Of one network executive who always seemed to be looking
down, he asked, "Why don't you look up?" he asked. "Is it because
you're ashamed, or did you play quarterback for Yale?"

Even on the air he often made fun of the people who ran the
network. "I'm Tinken, Vice-President in Charge of No Smoking in
the Halls. You sent for a Vice-President?" he would say in character.
At one point, one of those vice-presidents threatened to take him off
the air, so Allen had him picketed by midgets carrying signs saying
THIS NETWORK IS UNFAIR TO LITTLE PEOPLE.

Much of his humor was topical. Of a movie star who went to
church in dark glasses, Allen said, "He's afraid God might recognize
him and ask for his autograph." It was an age when it was still
permissible to poke fun at ethnic foibles. No one did this better than
Fred Allen, through his cast of characters on "Allen's Alley." In that
skit Allen, as the master of ceremonies, would venture down the alley
and knock on the door of its residents: Senator Claghorn was a
blowhard Southern politician; Mrs. Nussbaum was a tart Jewish
skeptic with a heavy Yiddish accent; Titus Moody was a New England Yankee skinflint; and Ajax Cassidy was a professional Irish-
man. The entire tour lasted five minutes, one minute per character.
Much of the show's skilled writing was done by Allen himself,
though later a young Columbia graduate named Herman Wouk
helped out. The critical element, though, was Allen's timing.

In Allen's glory years, the entire nation huddled around their
radios anticipating his gags and laughing almost before they were

out of his mouth. Did the newsreels do the March of Time? Allen did the "March of Trivia." Did Major Bowes of *The Major Bowes' Original Amateur Hour* make a big thing out of visiting small towns and blathering about their wondrous qualities? Then Allen lampooned him with "Admiral Crow's Amateur Hour": "Tonight we salute that quaint old city nestling back in those peaceful hills. The city we all love and venerate: two hundred miles of hail-fellow-well-met. Here the first eyedropper was made. Here it was that John Brundle jumped out of a window, landed on his rubber heels, and got the idea for the first pogo stick . . . the first hot-dog stand not to charge for its mustard was opened here. Situated on the shores of the second largest lake in America, the home of the biggest dental floss factory in the world . . . we love you . . . Tonight we salute . . . Tonight . . . Tonight our honor city is . . . (pause) Who took that slip of paper? Boy! . . . Don't stand there gaping! Get me a vice-president or an aspirin."

Perhaps his most celebrated stunt was his bogus feud with Jack Benny, then the country's top-rated radio comedian. It started casually enough. Allen had made a humorous remark about Benny. Benny, sensing the possibility of fresh material, picked up on it. Soon it escalated. They would appear on each other's shows to trade insults. "You wouldn't dare talk to me like that if my writers were here," Benny once said. The two of them even scheduled a fight. Joe Louis, heavyweight champion of the world, appeared on Allen's show to help him train for the bout with the dreaded Benny. A group of schoolchildren gathered outside Allen's childhood home yelling for him to beat Benny for the good of Dorchester, Massachusetts. Eventually, the two met on Benny's show for the big event. There was, of course, no fight, but only one program in history had been higher rated, a Roosevelt Fireside Chat.

But once television came on the scene, the end came quickly for Allen's popularity. Perhaps, as his biographer, Robert Taylor, noted, it was the changing era. Allen's mordant, dark humor had worked when America was on hard times; as he mocked the successful and pompous, he had touched the right nerve in the society. But as the country began to undergo unparalleled prosperity, people no longer wanted to make fun of success—they wanted to share in it. Another reason, as Allen himself noted, was that it had simply run too long. "Even without the coming of television," he wrote, "the survey figures showed a gradual shrinking in the mass audience. The audience and the medium were both getting tired. The same programs, the same comedians, the same commercials—even the sameness was starting to look the same."

Toward the end, he was feeling burned-out. For eighteen years he had written, produced, and acted in his own show. During the thirty-nine-week season he rarely took a day off. "A medium that demands entertainment eighteen hours a day, seven days every week has to exhaust the conscientious craftsman and performer," he wrote. "Radio was the only profession in which the unfit could survive."

Yet in 1948 he was at the height of his popularity. Then ABC, with nothing to lose, put a dinky show called *Stop the Music!* against him. It was an early incarnation of the game show, and it was wonderfully hokey. Bert Parks, the master of ceremonies, would play a current hit song. After a few bars of music, Parks would shout, "Stop the music!" and would call a listener at home. If the listener could identify the tune—and the musicians were not, after all, playing Mozart piano sonatas—Parks would scream again and gush forth with all the goodies the listener had just won. The nation was transfixed. Allen was appalled: "Reduced to essentials a quiz show required one master of ceremonies, preferably with prominent teeth, two underpaid girls to do research and supply the quiz questions, and a small herd of morons stampeded into the studio audience and rounded up at the microphone to compete for prizes . . ." Be that as it may, it worked. *Stop the Music!* went from nothing to a 20.0 share by January 1949; Allen fell from his 1948 28.7 high to 11.2 in the same period. He tried to fight back. He arranged with an insurance company to award five thousand dollars to any potential listener of *Stop the Music!* who missed out on the phone call and the fabled prizes because he was listening to Allen. He did a skit called "Cease the Melody," in which he handed out many prizes, and because most television sets were still in bars, the first prize was a television set, complete with a saloon and bartender to accompany it. But it was too late. The Ford Motor Company pulled its sponsorship of his show, and in a few months he was gone. James Thurber, the great American humorist, described Allen's flight as "for me more interesting than Lindbergh's." His show might have lasted a little longer, Allen said afterward, but he knew it was time to quit when his blood pressure was higher than his ratings. "When television belatedly found its way into the home after stopping off too long at the tavern, the advertisers knew they had a more potent force available for their selling purposes. Radio was abandoned like the bones at a barbecue," he wrote.

Some of the radio comedians made the transition to television; Allen did not. His humor was too dry: He had loved radio precisely because it depended on the listeners' imagination to create a whole world out of words. In television, he noted, that world was determined by budgets, scenic designers, and carpenters. Nor was he in good odor at NBC after more than a decade of making fun of its executives. Allen proposed a television version of "Allen's Alley," using the format of Thornton Wilder's *Our Town*. It might have worked, but the executives saw it as too expensive, so they never tried it. Instead, Allen became one of several hosts for a new variety show to air against Ed Sullivan ("Sullivan," Allen had said sardonically but prophetically, "will stay on television as long as other people have talent"). He was uncomfortable on television from the start; the technicians would hear his jokes in rehearsal and therefore not laugh when the show was live. Allen premiered in the fall of 1950; by December of that year he was gone. After he gave up his radio program, he wrote his old friend Herman Wouk, saying that he had spoken at several dinners and had written the introduction to a cookbook. "But don't think for a minute I'm doing all this to be popular. I'm just trying to keep from being unpopular. I'm fending off oblivion." He also described his book, *Treadmill to Oblivion,* to Wouk. It was virtually his own epitaph: "It is the story of a radio show. A radio program is not unlike a man. It is conceived. It is born. It lives through the experience that fate allots to it. Finally the program dies and like a man is forgotten except for a few people who depended upon it for sustenance or others whose lives had been made brighter because the program existed." When he was stricken dead with a heart attack in March 1956, a certain kind of humor went with him.

There was a genteel quality to radio success. Erik Barnouw has pointed out that in 1950 there were 108 different series that had been on the radio for a decade or more, and twelve had been on for two decades or more. On television, the stakes were bigger and more volatile. In this more intimate medium, success could come (and depart) far more quickly.

As the decade started, the television map of America was a spotty affair, not improved when the Truman administration put a four-year freeze on awarding new stations. In 1953, when Dwight Eisenhower took office and ended the freeze, there were 108 stations, but only twenty-four cities had two or more. In those days the networks were patched together for a particular big event—a heavyweight fight or the World Series. Not until the fall of 1951 did the coaxial cable stretch across the country. But Americans had already begun to adapt their habits to accommodate their favorite programs. Studies showed that when a popular program was on, toilets flushed all over certain cities, as if on cue, during commercials or the moment the program was over. Radio listenership was significantly down. People went to restaurants earlier. Products advertised on television soared in public acceptance. Book sales were said to be down. Libraries complained of diminished activity. Above all, television threatened the movie business. By 1951, cities with only one television station reported drops in movie attendance of 20 to 40 percent, and wherever television appeared, movie theaters began to close; in New York City, Erik Barnouw noted, fifty-five theaters closed by 1951 and in Southern California, 134.

The first example of the unprecedented power of television was the meteoric rise of Milton Berle. Berle was the quintessential vaudeville slapstick comic. For better or for worse, no one ever accused him of being droll. His humor was manic and often vulgar. It depended heavily on sight gags. (When Fred Allen finally bought a television set in 1950 and saw Berle, he was appalled by what he thought the crudeness of the show.)

Berle arrived on television in 1948, almost by chance. He had heard that the Texaco people were looking for a master of ceremonies for a television version of *Texaco Star Theatre*. Berle knew instinctively that television was right for him. Texaco tried out several hosts, but it was obvious that Berle was the most successful. At the time he started, there were only 500,000 television sets in America. Almost from the start, his Tuesday night show on NBC was an *event*. The early history of television and the story of Berle's show were close to being one and the same thing. Those who didn't have television sets visited those who did. The very success of Berle's show accelerated the sale of television sets; those Americans who did not yet own sets would return home after watching him at their neighbors' houses and decide that, yes, it was finally time to take the plunge.

A year into the show, his fame was so great that his face was on the cover of both *Time* and *Newsweek* in the same week. He was television's first superstar. He was forty-two in 1950, but his entire life had been spent in the theater. At the age of six he won a Charlie Chaplin lookalike contest wearing his father's clothes and shoes and a mustache cut from his mother's furs. At the time his mother was a department-store detective, but she soon found her real calling: a stage mother. Alternately guarding her son and ruthlessly pushing him forward, she would roar with laughter if the audience seemed a bit slow. Before he was ten he was on the vaudeville circuit; at twelve he was in a hit show called *Floradora* and was paid forty-five dollars a week. From then on, he always seemed to find work. He would do anything to make people laugh; it was his means of winning approval. Years later he would note with some sadness that his mother's method was not necessarily the best for rearing a child: "You take a kid at the age of five, and make him the star of the family, and then take the same kid out into the world and make him a star with everyone catering to him as if he were more than another perishable human being, and it's a miracle if that kid doesn't grow up to be a man who believes he's Casanova and Einstein and Jesus Christ all rolled into one."

While still in his teens, he was opening the Palace, the best of the vaudeville houses, and by the time he was twenty-three, he was serving as master of ceremonies, a job he held for two years. As a star, he headlined at theaters around the country. He brought an almost demented energy to the job. He never allowed the pace to slacken. He would do anything for a laugh—don a wig, a dress, or false teeth, fall on his face or take a pie in it. There was never a pause in the action for the audience to catch its breath. He could not duplicate his success on the stage for radio. He tried several radio shows of his own, but they all flopped. He needed the audience right there with him. Whereas Allen's humor was cerebral, satirizing the world around him, Berle's work was about himself. He needed the audience to see him—what you saw was what you got.

In the late fall of 1948, his television show enjoyed a 94.7 rating, which meant that of all the sets in the country being used, 94.7 percent were tuned to his show. In the beginning NBC had lost money on its television shows, but by 1950 the tide turned: Sales for broadcast time tripled. In 1952 the industry made a profit of $41 million.

At this earliest stage of its history, television was primarily an urban phenomenon. According to *Variety,* of the 1,082,100 television sets operating in American homes in 1949, some 450,000 were in New York City and most of the remaining ones were in Philadelphia, Washington, Boston, Chicago, Detroit, and Los Angeles. Berle was a classic Borscht Belt comedian. His live audience was primarily Jewish and urban; therefore, he was playing to what might be considered a home crowd. Five million people watched him every night and 35 percent of them lived in New York.

It was a marvelous time for him. He was being paid five thousand dollars a week to do what he knew best and what he probably would have done for nothing. (People who called him at home would have to listen to five or six jokes before they could get a word in.) In 1951, fearing that he would go to a rival network, NBC signed him to a thirty-year contract for $200,000 a year. It was at precisely that moment that he started to slip. In part he was done in by the coaxial cable. Its coming meant television was reaching into smaller towns and rural areas. People there were not native Berle fans, and his flip references to New York neighborhoods and stores fell on alien ears. As his ratings began to decline, he became more manic than ever, rushing across the stage feverishly interrupting other acts. For his fifth season, 1952–53, the format of the show was changed. Goodman Ace, a talented comedy writer, was hired. There was to be more form, less freewheeling by Berle himself, the very thing that in the beginning had seemed to make the show so popular. It ended up fifth in the ratings for that year, and Texaco dropped its sponsorship. By 1954–55 he had fallen to thirteenth, and the next year he was in charge of a show that went on every third week. In 1955 he was dropped from the show. Eventually, NBC worked out a new contract in which his annual salary was cut to $120,000 a year and he was allowed to work on other networks. Berle became the first figure to experience both the power and the volatility of television. The highs were higher than anything in the past, and it generated an astonishing intimacy between performer and audience. But because of that intimacy, the audience could be fickle and a star could descend just as quickly as he rose. It was a lesson that various entertainers, actors, and even politicians were going to learn the hard way.

FOURTEEN

Television would change more than just the face of comedy and entertainment. Politics was soon to follow, and from then on politics became, in no small part, entertainment. The first political star of television was a freshman senator from Tennessee, intelligent, shrewd, but also awkward and bumbling. No one would have accused Estes Kefauver of being, in the phrase that came to haunt many a television figure in the coming years, just another pretty face. His face was, to be kind, plain. Nor was Kefauver particularly eloquent. Speaking in front of groups, both large and small, he often stumbled. Words escaped him; awkward pauses punctuated his sentences. Part of his success with ordinary people, thought his senatorial colleague Albert Gore, came from the fact that he was so awkward and uncomfortable as a speaker that listeners felt a responsibility to help poor old Estes out.

If at first he appeared something of a caricature—the hillbilly who came to Washington—in reality he came from an extremely privileged old Tennessee family. He was well educated, a graduate not only of the University of Tennessee but of Yale Law School. "I've met millions of self-made highbrows in my life," his friend Max Ascoli, the editor of *The Reporter* magazine, once said of him, "but Estes is the first self-made lowbrow." He was also extremely ambitious. When Kefauver was first elected to Congress in 1939, Lee Allen, the head of Kefauver's local Democratic committee, turned to him and said, "Well, Estes, you're a congressman." Kefauver pondered the idea for a minute and then answered, "Lee, they're a dime a dozen."

From the start, it was clear that he was different from other Southern senators in that racial prejudice offended him and he would not accept the traditional conservative position on civil rights. It was true that he came from a border state where racial attitudes were not as harsh, and it was true also that he saw civil rights as a matter of conscience. In large part, though, his more liberal stance came from his own soaring ambition and desire to hold national office. As early as 1942, as a junior congressman, he broke with the Southern Democrats in Congress by voting against the poll tax. That had provoked the bile of the virulent racist from Mississippi, John Rankin, who stood on the House floor, pointed his finger at Kefauver, and said, "Shame on you, Estes Kefauver."

Backed by a coalition of the state's more liberal newspapers, he decided to run against Senator Tom Steward in 1948 and, in the process, to challenge the powerful machine of boss Ed Crump in Memphis. The Crump machine responded by red-baiting Kefauver, inevitably comparing his record, as was the fashion in those days, with the radical congressman Vito Marcantonio (Will Gerber, Crump's hatchet man at the time—who was better at political intrigue than at spelling—wrote his friend Senator Kenneth McKellar, "We are anxious to get everything we possibly can to show that Kefauver has been voting right along with Marc Antonio . . .). At this point Crump made a fatal mistake and claimed that Kefauver was a fellow traveler and a "pet coon for the Soviets." Kefauver seized on the remark. The coon, he noted, was a uniquely American animal: "You wouldn't find a coon in Russia." In addition, he added, a coon was tough and could lick a dog four times its size. When Crump persisted with the charge, Kefauver said, "I may be a pet coon, but I ain't Mr. Crump's pet coon." Soon the coon became his trademark. For a time Kefauver traveled with a live racoon, but afraid that it might die on the campaign trail, he switched to a coonskin cap, a powerful symbol in a state that had given the nation Davy Crockett and Sam Houston. He won the election handily, dealing a severe blow to the Crump machine. A surprisingly well connected liberal senator from a border state, he was in a perfect position to be launched toward even higher office—the vice-presidency, at the very least.

On January 5, 1950, he took a first step in that direction by introducing a bill to investigate organized crime in the United States. He had become interested in it as a member of the House Judiciary Committee, after talks with a number of mayors who believed that racketeering was extremely well organized, operated on a national basis, and therefore was too powerful for local law enforcement officers to deal with. This was an explosive issue, because the kind of crime Kefauver was going after had deep roots in every big city, and those cities were controlled by Democratic political machines. Thus he risked alienating the most powerful kingmakers in his own party. Kefauver was being pushed on the issue by, among others, Phil Graham, the publisher of *The Washington Post,* and a major political gadfly and power broker in Washington. Graham was afraid that if someone like Kefauver did not take up the investigation, sooner or later a Republican would and it would be a huge political embarrassment to the Democrats. Kefauver at first seemed reluctant, but Graham uttered the magic words: "Don't you want to be Vice-President?"

So, aware of the political pitfalls ahead but thinking he had received the go-ahead from top Democratic urban officials in the country, Kefauver took his crime investigation on the road. The committee scheduled hearings in fourteen cities and its investigation lasted ninety-two days. The hearings uncovered important new material, and there was a pattern to it: Everywhere he went there was something called organized crime, or the Mob, and it was invariably intertwined, either voluntarily or involuntarily, with some local Democratic administration. The longer the hearings went on, the less amused his fellow Democrats were, and among those least amused was that old Democratic loyalist (and product of a big-city machine himself) Harry S Truman.

On March 12, 1951, Kefauver finally arrived in New York City. No one had expected the New York hearings to be particularly important, but in fact they turned out to be a landmark, not so much in the history of crime or crime fighting as in the history of television and the coming of a national political theater. On a handful of previous occasions television had covered hearings (for example, three years earlier, when the Senate Armed Forces Committee had considered Universal Military Training, and also the HUAC hearings on Alger Hiss), but the Kefauver hearings were broadcast nationally, a first for this kind of television.

Actually, Kefauver, who was hardly averse to publicity, had not sought to have his hearings covered by television and had no idea until the last minute that they were going to be. On March 12, 1951, they went live on a relatively primitive hookup, but it was national. It went to twenty cities in the East and the Midwest. Because television was so new, all programming was still quite limited, and that was particularly true in the daytime. The networks had barely gotten around to filling their evening slots, let alone morning and afternoon. By some estimates only 1.5 percent of American homes had television sets in use during the morning hours. That meant that any company could buy commercial time at that hour on the cheap. By chance, *Time* magazine was planning a subscription drive and decided to sponsor the telecast of the hearings, first in New York City and then in Washington, for fifteen days.

In a way, Kefauver's timing could not have been better. A year or two earlier and there would have been no audience; a few years later, there might have been less excitement—for people might have been more blasé. In the New York area alone in the previous twelve months the number of homes with television sets had gone from about 29 percent to 51 percent. That meant that for the first time in any metropolitan area in any city in the world, there were more homes with television sets than those without. All over the city, and then in other cities, as his hearings continued, housewives called their friends up to tell them of this exciting new show.

For the Kefauver hearings contained innately explosive drama. There, live and in black and white, were the bad guys on one side, looking very much like hoods, showing by the way they spoke and in other ways they never quite realized that they were part of the underworld; on the other side were Kefauver and his chief counsel, Rudolph Halley, the good guys, asking the questions any good citizen would about crime. Estes Kefauver came off as a sort of Southern Jimmy Stewart, the lone citizen-politician who gets tired of the abuse of government and goes off on his own to do something about it.

On March 13, Frank Costello, alias Francisco Castaglia, reputedly the leader of organized crime in New York, testified. Costello had little in the way of an actual criminal record, but step by step he had moved from apprentice to bootlegger to slot-machine operator to gambling-house owner. He had been Lucky Luciano's top lieutenant, and when Luciano had been deported, Costello had taken over as America's top racketeering figure. By 1950 his influence at Tammany Hall was pervasive. As he became more successful, he diversified his business interests, moving into more legitimate fields. By this time he seemed, or at least wanted to seem, perfectly respectable. As such, Costello objected to the cameras showing his face. "Mr. Costello doesn't care to submit himself as a spectacle," his lawyer noted. After some consultation the committee agreed; his face would not be shown. A television technician suggested showing Costello's hands. That proved truly devastating. Those hands relentlessly reflected Costello's tension and guilt: hands drumming on the table; hands gripping a water glass, fingers tightly clenched; hands tearing paper into little shreds; hands sweating—all the while accompanied by the words of the committee's relentless pursuit. Costello's attempts to represent himself as merely a businessman who had made a success in the new world were not convincing. The television lights were hard on his eyes, he claimed. It was time to go home. He walked out, to be followed by a contempt subpoena.

Some 70 percent of New York City television sets were on, which gave the hearings twice the ratings achieved by the World Series during the previous fall. People in the other cities hooked up were also mesmerized. The newspapers wrote stories about husbands coming back to find the housework unfinished, their wives glued to the television set and wanting to talk only about the inner workings of the mob. In New York, Con Ed had to add an extra generator to supply the power for all the television sets. The editors of *Life* magazine understood immediately that American politics had changed. "The week of March 12, 1951, will occupy a special place in history," *Life* wrote. "The U.S. and the world had never experienced anything like it. . . . All along the television cable . . . [people] had suddenly gone indoors . . . into living rooms, taverns and club rooms, auditoriums, and back offices. There in eerie half-light, looking at millions of small frosty screens, people sat as if charmed. For days on end and into the nights they watched with complete absorption . . . the first big television broadcast of an affair of their government, the broadcast from which all future uses of television in public affairs must date. . . . Never before had the attention of the nation been so completely riveted on a single matter. The Senate investigation into interstate crime was almost the sole subject of national conversation."

Estes Kefauver became America's first politician to benefit from the glare of television—even though the hearings had been devastating to his own party. They had shown that it was almost impossible to tell where the power and influence of the mob ended and that of the city officials began; former mayor Bill O'Dwyer, newly minted as Truman's ambassador to Mexico, admitted that he had knowingly appointed men with connections to organized crime to high office. (Some of Truman's aides thought that O'Dwyer should resign immediately, but Truman, a man of old-fashioned loyalties, would have none of it.) Kefauver immediately went on the lecture circuit and made a handsome additional income. Magazines competed to put him on their covers. He appeared as a mystery guest on the television show *What's My Line?* and gave the fifty-dollar fee to charity. Hollywood wanted him for a bit part in a Humphrey Bogart movie called *The Enforcer.* He put his name to a ghostwritten four-part series for the *Saturday Evening Post,* "What I Found in the Underworld." His book, written jointly with Sidney Shalett, *Crime in America* was on *The New York Times* best-seller list for twelve weeks. Something of an erratic husband and a womanizer (Capitol Hill's nickname for him was the Claw, for his habit of groping women in Senate elevators), he was chosen father of the year. A poll of 128 Washington correspondents placed him second only to Paul Douglas in ability.

Television had catapulted him to the very head of the line in the Democratic party, which was at that moment in dire trouble, among other reasons because of the hearings he had just held. When his young counsel Halley, a novice in elective politics, ran for president of the New York City Council in the fall of 1951 as a reform candidate on the Liberal line, he won, beating all the major-party candidates. Kefauver understood immediately that he was in an ideal position to run for the presidency without seeming to run. He could travel from city to city, reporters would attend his press conferences, and he would push aside questions of his own ambition and talk instead on the grave question of crime in the nation's cities. Kefauver claimed he was not interested in running for office. He was the outsider taking on the corrupt politicians from the corrupt machines. Without even knowing it, he had become the prototype for a new kind of politician, who ran not against his opponents but against the political system itself.

Eventually, Estes Kefauver did announce his candidacy for the presidency and filed for the New Hampshire primary. By chance, at almost the same time *Time* magazine polled the television industry for its annual awards and the Kefauver hearings won two; he also won an Emmy from the American Academy of Television Arts and Sciences for special achievement in "bringing the workings of our government into the homes of the American people." He could not attend the awards banquet but accepted the Emmy by phone from New Hampshire, where he was busy campaigning.

FIFTEEN

B y 1952 television was seeping ever more deeply into the nation's bloodstream. By the end of the year there were 19 million sets in the country, and a thousand new stores selling television sets opened each month.

Politics, for the first time, was being brought to the nation by means of television. People now expected to *see* events, not merely read about or hear them. At the same time, the line between what happened in real life and what people saw on television began to merge; many Americans were now living far from their families, in brand-new suburbs where they barely knew their neighbors. Sometimes they felt closer to the people they watched on television than they did to their neighbors and distant families. In 1954 Gardner Murphy, research director of the famed Menninger Foundation in Kansas, arranged a demonstration for some advertising firms in

Chicago. He rented a suite at the Drake Hotel in Chicago, set up eight television sets in it, and then directed a team of social scientists to study advertisers and the programs they sponsored. The team's conclusions about *The Arthur Godfrey Show,* then the top-rated morning program, were intriguing: "Psychologically, Mr. Godfrey's morning program creates the illusion of the family structure. All the conflicts and complex situations of family life are taken out and what is left is an amiable, comfortable family scene—with one important omission: there is no mother in the Godfrey family. That gives the housewife-viewer the opportunity to fill that role. In her fantasy Godfrey comes into her home as an extra member of her family; and she fancies herself as a specially invited member of his family . . ."

Nothing showed the power of this new medium to soften the edge between real life and fantasy better than the coming of Lucille Ball. In 1951 she was forty years old, in the middle of a less than dazzling show-business career. In films she was seen more as a comedienne than as an actress, and she tended to draw what one executive termed "second-banana roles"—generally low-budget that did not go to the top stars. "The Queen of the B movies," she was sometimes called. Often, it seemed, she was hired because someone else did not want the role. In the opinion of casting agents and directors, she was a little rough, a little obvious for the more sophisticated roles that might go to Katharine Hepburn. She had enjoyed some measure of success in radio, and in 1948, hoping to save her shaky eight-year marriage to Cuban band leader Desi Arnaz, she opted to do a radio comedy show called *My Favorite Husband* so that she would not have to travel away from home so much. Her radio husband was a pleasant Midwestern banker from Minneapolis, as Lucy herself later said, "certainly not—great heavens—Desi Arnaz from Cuba." In 1950, when CBS executives asked her to do a weekly situation comedy on television, no one was unduly excited. That was their mistake, for Lucille Ball was destined for television, where her slapstick talents could be properly appreciated. Lucy had a marvelous comic voice but, like Berle, she was primarily a *visual* comedienne. She had a perfect sense of timing, a wonderfully expressive face, and was just wacky and naive enough to generate sympathy rather than irritation. In this early sitcom she would encounter weekly dilemmas of her own creation, but she always managed to stay just this side of the brink of disaster, remaining lovable to her husband and her friends, Fred and Ethel Mertz.

Lucy and Desi Arnaz were an unlikely couple, not merely on television but in real life as well. If Lucy was to be a dizzy housewife, she deserved at the very least, in the minds of the CBS executives, a straight-arrow husband to put up patiently with her foibles, but no, she insisted that Arnaz be cast as her husband. The people at CBS, from Bill Paley on down, were appalled. So were the advertising people, who had a big say in the casting. Desi Arnaz was not exactly a household name; his English was poor. No one, a CBS executive told her, would believe a show in which she was married to a Cuban bandleader. "What do you mean nobody'll believe it?" she answered. "We *are* married." She remained adamant, and finally a reluctant Paley gave in. After the pilot was shot and shown to a high-level group of entertainment people in New York, they voted resoundingly against Arnaz. "Keep the redhead but ditch the Cuban," said the lyricist Oscar Hammerstein. He was told it was a package deal. "Well, for God's sake, don't let him sing. No one will understand him," Hammerstein said.

But Lucy understood something that the producers initially did not: Viewers certainly knew that Desi was her real husband, and that made the show itself all the more believable. Since Desi played a Cuban bandleader on the show, his profession in real life, who could tell where reality ended and the show began?

At first Lucy, the producer, and the writers grappled with the story line. There was talk that Lucy should be a Hollywood star, but she vetoed that—she knew that the heroine should not be a star, because ordinary Americans believed that movie stars had no problems. Who would identify with an actress? But an ordinary housewife who longs to be a star, she suggested—that was another thing entirely. "Everybody wants to be in show business like Lucy did and they could relate to that," she later said of the program's main theme. Slowly, the concept evolved: They were Ricky and Lucy Ricardo; he was a musician who longed for an ordinary life and an ordinary marriage. "I want a wife who's just a wife," he said in the pilot. She was the housewife who wants nothing more than to be a star. Gradually, against great odds, the show was put together, and after a series of rejections, the producers found a sponsor, the Philip Morris company. It premiered on Monday, October 15, 1951. The first episode was called "The Girls Want to Go to a Nightclub." An announcer named John Stevenson introduced the show by speaking from the Ricardos' living room. "Good evening and welcome. In a moment we'll look in on Lucille Ball and Desi Arnaz. But before we do, may I ask you a very personal question? The question is simply this—do you inhale? Well, I do. And chances are you do too. And because you inhale you're better off—much better off—smoking

Philip Morris and for good reason. You see, Philip Morris is the one cigarette proved definitely less irritating, definitely milder than any other leading brand. That's why when you inhale you're better off smoking Philip Morris. . . . And now Lucille Ball and Desi Arnaz in *I Love Lucy.*"

The first episode was characteristic of what was to come. Ricky and his sidekick, Fred, want to go to the fights even though it is Fred and Ethel's wedding anniversary; Lucy and Ethel want to go to a nightclub. The men arrange for blind dates. Lucy and Ethel find out, dress up in outrageous costumes, and pose as the dates. The reviews were generally good, although *The New York Times* critic was dubious—he thought it was all a bit lowbrow. That alone was enough to make the head of Philip Morris nervous, and the next day he called the people at his advertising agency to get out of the sponsorship. But he was advised to give the show a little time: He did, and it was not long before it was in the Nielsen top ten.

In fact, the show had perfect pitch. Broad in its humor yet able to appeal to a wide variety of tastes, it was number one in New York within four months. Soon, as many as two out of three television sets were tuned to her. Marshall Field, the prominent Chicago department store, which had used Monday as its clearance sale night, surrendered and switched to Thursday by putting a sign in its window: "We love Lucy too so we're closing on Monday nights."

Lucy insisted the show be shot before a live audience—her experience in film and radio had taught her that she performed better when there was an audience she could see and reach out to. Opposite her, on NBC, there was a program called *Lights Out,* a mystery anthology that was a top-rated show. As Mike Dann, the NBC programmer who had so proudly made it so, remembered, "We were wiped out very quickly. We never knew what had happened, but it happened and it happened fast. And it happened without promotion—it wasn't because CBS went in and spent hundreds of thousands of dollars promoting this new show with a wacky redhead. It happened because it happened." It did not matter what show Lucy went against: She triumphed. As such, she began to redefine the nature of sitcoms. Previously, they existed as carryovers from radio, in which old-fashioned storytelling and sound effects were emphasized. The great strength of the Lucy show, a television writer named Jack Sher and his wife, Marilyn, pointed out, was the mirror it held up to every married couple in America: "Not a regular mirror that reflects the truth, nor a magic mirror that portrays fantasy. But a Coney Island kind of mirror that distorts, exaggerates and makes vastly amusing every little incident, foible, and idiosyncrasy of married life."

Lucy cut across all age groups. Children loved her, could readily understand her routines, and seemed to like the idea of an adult who seemed so childlike. In later years her shows would probably have been deemed sexist, and actually they were. In one way or another they were all a takeoff on women-driver jokes. Lucy could not really do anything right; she had a God-given instinct to get into trouble. There was Lucy trying to make wine by crushing grapes with her feet, Lucy shoving too many marshmallows in her mouth, Lucy trying on the wrong size slippers, Lucy being crunched in the face with a pie. No one was ever better at such stunts, and no one sacrificed her body and her face more readily to them. Onstage she became the dippy person she was playing, and yet it was a show starring not just one wacko but *two*.

To everybody's surprise, Desi was just as good, the straight man who was anything but straight. He knew exactly when to be appalled, and irritated or amazed, by her, by the fact *that she had done it again*. Traditionally, straight men did not get laughs, they were there to be the foil, but with Desi there was always some word or phrase he could mispronounce. That seemed also to soften the humor of the show; it was not just Lucy who was screwy, it was the two of them—and their neighbors, too. At the end, though, there was Desi embracing her, understanding her. All was forgiven, and everything came out all right.

By April 7, 1952, 10.6 million households were tuning in, the first time in history that a television show had reached so many people. By 1954, as many as 50 million people watched certain segments. The show was so popular that it lifted not just its advertisers but CBS and the entire industry; in 1953 CBS-TV showed a net profit for the first time, in no small part because of her, and a year later television became the largest advertising medium in the world.

Reality and show business continued to intersect when Lucy got pregnant in real life in the spring of 1952. The producers and writers were delighted and immediately decided to incorporate the pregnancy into the story line. But CBS, the Milton Biow advertising agency, and Philip Morris were not so sure. These were more puritanical times. Previously, pregnant women had just not been seen in films or on television. A pregnant comedienne seemed in especially bad taste. The network and Philip Morris thought it might be all right for one or two shows to be based on Lucy's pregnancy, but that was all. From then on, they would have to hide her behind tables and chairs. Nor should there be any talk of it.

But Desi went to Alfred Lyons, the head of Philip Morris, and suggested that if he and Lucy could not control the content, the show, then number-one, might slip. Lyons was so impressed he sent a note to Jim Aubrey, the president of CBS: "Dear Jim," it began. "Don't fuck around with the Cuban." But they were not to use the word *pregnancy*. CBS held the line on that. Lucy instead was an expectant mother. That was more genteel. The first show on Lucy's pregnancy aired on December 8, 1952. It was a typical episode: Lucy wanted to tell Desi in the most romantic way possible, but he did not seem to have time to listen. "I want to tell you something," she says. "Uh-oh, how much are you overdrawn?" he replies. There are endless interruptions. In the end she shows up at his club, passes him a note that a member of the audience is about to have a baby, and asks him to serenade her. As the crowded nightclub audience watches, he realizes that he is the father, and his wife the expectant mother. CBS lined up a priest, a minister, and a rabbi to review all pregnancy scripts to be sure that they were in good taste. "It looked like a revival meeting around the place," Lucy once said.

Week by week the entire nation watched with fascination as Lucy grew larger, the real-life event paralleling the television script. She was allowed to have morning sickness on the air as she had it in real life. Finally, at exactly the time that she was due to deliver, the show (entitled "Lucy Goes to the Hospital") called for her to go to the hospital. Again the show was filled with misunderstandings and slapstick. Lucy is calm as she waits for the big moment, but Desi is an emotional wreck. One scene shows them arriving at the hospital with Lucy pushing Desi in a wheelchair. Desi Arnaz, Jr., was born on January 19, 1953—right on schedule. By some estimates, 68 percent of the television sets in the country were tuned to the show, which meant that 44 million people saw it. That was twice the number who watched the inauguration of Dwight Eisenhower the next day, a President who was uneasy with television but who presided over the years in which it became an ever more dominant force in American life.

During its first years the *I Love Lucy* show, like most of the early shows, had an urban setting; but a few years down the line, as their ratings slipped a bit, Lucy and Desi were forced to follow much of their audience to the suburbs. How, otherwise, could the housewives of America sympathize with Lucy? Fred and Ethel with them, they moved to Westport, Connecticut.

Their real lives were not quite so idyllic as their television existence. It was always a difficult relationship: Desi was a drinker and a womanizer. "If I stayed mad at every woman that Desi had an affair with, I'd have been angry with half of the nicest girls in Hollywood," Lucy once said. As Desi Arnaz, Jr., the true child of television, once noted, "I learned pretty early to relate to *I Love Lucy* as a television show and to my parents as actors on it. . . . There wasn't much relationship between what I saw on TV and what was really going on at home. Those were difficult years—all those funny things happening on television each week to people who looked like my parents, then the same people agonizing through some terrible, unhappy times at home, and each of them trying to convince my sister and me separately that the other was in the wrong."

Television was a fickle instrument, as Fred Allen had found out. It could grant instant fame to a person or popularity to a fad and just as quickly withdraw that fame or popularity. This was a lesson that all kinds of comics, actors, and politicians were just beginning to learn the hard way. The great danger of this new medium, which favored the new at the expense of the old, was overexposure.

Television changed the relationship of the nation with its politicians: Where once the President had been a distant figure few Americans had ever seen and whose voice, even during the radio era, was rarely heard, television brought him into the home. At such close range there was a danger the President would lose the illusion of heroic proportions that distance created. At the same time, television brought an immediacy to events and demanded, as well, that they entertain. Slowly, as the power of television journalism grew, the national agenda would begin to respond to such changes. It was the comedians who first came to understand the darker side of television—such men as Fred Allen, Milton Berle, and, eventually, Allen's long-running radio adversary, Jack Benny. Like Berle, Benny was first a beneficiary of the new medium: His success was considerable, and he had a fifteen-year run, beginning in 1950. But as he began to be pushed aside by other shows, he wrote an astute analysis not only of his own experience but that of many other entertainers, politicians, and athletes as well: "By my second year in television I saw the camera was a man-eating monster. It gave a performer a close-up exposure that week after week threatened his existence as an interesting entertainer. I don't care who you are. Finally you'll get on people's nerves if they get too much of you. I don't care how wonderful or handsome or brilliant or charming you are—if the public gets too much of you, they'll be bored. Given that kind of magnification combined with intimacy that's characteristic of television, the essence of a comedian's art becomes inevitably stale. The audience gets to know you inside and outside. Your tone of voice, your gestures, and your little tricks, the rhythm of your delivery, your way of reacting to another performer's moves, your facial mannerisms—all of these things, so exciting to an audience when you are a novelty, soon become tedious and flat." In radio, he said, people had loved him in a different way. "I came at them gently—quietly, through their ears. I suggested subtle images to them, picture jokes. I was like a friendly uncle, a slightly eccentric, mad uncle—now I became something too much. The television camera is like a magnifying glass and you can't enjoy looking at anything blown up for too long."

SIXTEEN

After his return, General MacArthur waited for political lightning to strike. It never did. The polls reflected both his personal triumph and the wariness of the American people toward his policies: 54 percent of those polled by Gallup favored MacArthur's more aggressive tactics against China, but only 30 percent favored them if they meant escalating the war. Even as the congressional cheers for MacArthur were continuing, Senator Robert Kerr went on the floor of the Senate and suggested that the general and his Republican supporters were more than a little hypocritical. Let them, he said, be honest about it and call for a declaration of war with China and open warfare with the Chinese as well. "If they do not," he said, "their support of MacArthur is a mockery." His challenge was answered with silence. The Senate hearings that followed MacArthur's speech had been sobering, particularly when Omar Bradley, the Chairman of the Joint Chiefs, had declared that MacArthur's politics "would involve us in the wrong war at the wrong place at the wrong time with the wrong enemy." That one sentence had cut to the heart of the argument.

MacArthur's political decline was quick indeed. Part of it was due to the nation's wariness of men on horseback: It might cheer them, but it hesitated to vote for them. If it must choose a general for civilian office, then it preferred the quieter, more modest, more diplomatic Eisenhower. For a short time the crowds remained big, and MacArthur spoke all over the country. But since he did it still wearing his uniform, there was something unsettling about his attacks on the President of the United States. Gradually, his crowds grew smaller and less enthusiastic; his supporters diminished to a coterie of powerful, wealthy, conservative isolationists. His attempt at the Republican nomination was surprisingly leaden. Robert Taft was the true choice of the grass-roots conservatives. MacArthur's last great chance came when he keynoted the Republican convention in 1952; his most ardent admirers hoped that he would ignite that convention with a speech similar to the one he had given before Congress. But it was not a success. He seemed uncomfortable trying to thread his way through the minefield of a divided Republican party. His audience shared his lack of enthusiasm, and many delegates in the audience left their seats to gossip with each other. The electricity was gone. To his own surprise, he did just what he had promised—he faded away. As the excitement he'd bottled the year before died, he was left with a job as chairman of the board of Remington Rand. A cartoon in *The New Yorker* captured the banality of his fall: It pictured the general's office at Rand, and hanging on the doorknob was a sign that said: "Out to lunch. I shall return."

Truman's firing of MacArthur had a profound effect on the 1952 presidential race, wounding the President even more than it had the general. It also advanced the political chances of Dwight Eisenhower. The country was not in the mood to return to isolationism. It wanted to be reassured, not threatened. Who better to do that than a general who was a hero and an internationalist and who had successfully made the transition to being a civilian. Eisenhower was MacArthur's sworn enemy. As William Manchester wrote, MacArthur's feelings toward Ike were very much like those of Cain toward Abel. Eisenhower had made the supreme mistake of being a MacArthur aide who had gone on to surpass his boss. MacArthur still, on occasion, referred to Ike as "the best clerk I ever had." It was the final irony that Douglas MacArthur's desperate desire for the White

House eased the way there for Dwight Eisenhower, who did not seem to want it at all.

Yet by all rights the 1952 Republican nomination belonged to Robert Taft, and if Eisenhower was the only man who could stop him, no one, in late 1951, knew whether he was even a Republican, let alone a politician. Taft had waited twelve years and had been exceptionally loyal to his party. But his strengths were also his weaknesses. He appealed to a narrow slice of the electorate, and it was said that he could not win a national election. Before Taft announced, he wrote down the pros and cons. Perhaps, he noted, he was a little old and his health was not quite as good as it should be. But on the pro side, he wrote down, "Opportunity to save liberty in U.S."

The Easterners might have captured the previous three nominations in a row, but Bob Taft believed in his heart that he was closer to what the average Republican believed in than Tom Dewey—twice the candidate, twice defeated—was. But Taft was a prisoner of his own past and had little appeal to younger voters, many of them veterans of World War Two. That year, Herblock, the *Washington Post* cartoonist, caught him in an image he seemed unable to escape, despite his considerable intelligence. It was a cartoon of a dinosaur bearing Taft's face, telling Uncle Sam, "Don't be ridiculous. Nobody is a dinosaur anymore."

Taft was the last major isolationist of American politics, and his political base was rooted in an America of the past—pre-war, pre-superpower. John Franklin Carter, a friend of Dewey's, wrote of him: "I believe he would make a splendid President for a stable prosperous country in an orderly world—say, in 1925. I suspect, however, that as has happened to many other able and patriotic men, his political serviceability has been repealed by World War II and the rise of the Third International [that is, Joseph Stalin]."

Taft was highly intelligent, commanding the respect of even those who disagreed with him completely. Yet he made no effort to charm or win over his colleagues; he was a man apart, almost rude, certainly standoffish. By all rights his personal manner should have cost him dearly in the Senate, which was one of the great old-boys' clubs of all time. By its standards Taft was almost prissy. But even as partisan a figure as Harry Truman thought him "a high-class man . . . honest, intelligent and extremely capable . . ."

He was the scion of a great political family—the Tafts of Ohio—that included a solicitor general, a chief justice of the Supreme Court, and a President of the United States. Rooted as it was in the Midwest, the family valued responsibility and obligation over wealth. (Taft's uncle Alphonso had made a brief tour of New York in the previous century as a young man and had been appalled by the selfishness and greed he found there, and the fact that in New York, "money is the all and all.")

Robert had gone off to prep school—the Taft School, of course, run by Uncle Horace, his father's brother. He finished first in his class and then went to Yale, the preferred choice of both the Taft School and the Taft family—of his graduating class of twenty-five at Taft, twenty-one members went on to Yale. He was first in his class at Yale, too. His matriculation at Harvard Law caused something of a stir, because he was the son of the President. On the first day he was forced to answer reporters who showed up at his residence: "I'm here to study, I do not intend to go into athletics or to be a social lion, or to do missionary work, or to be interviewed." Even then, noted his biographer, James Patterson, tact was not his forte. A classmate noted: "Have I mentioned anything of the Taft boy? . . . He is very quiet, appears not to be even the slightest swell headed, yet seems not to care at all what people think or don't think, but does exactly as he pleases. He gives the appearance of a person with lofty ideals, and the courage of his convictions and to spare. He dresses in very plain and sober clothes, which strike me as somewhat out of date . . ."

At Harvard Law he was again first in his class, and after graduation he returned to Ohio, where he ran for the legislature and won. He married, typically, not merely within his class but within his remarkably circumscribed world: Martha Bowers—bright, engaging, highly political—was the daughter of a Yale classmate of Will Taft, who had served as the elder Taft's solicitor general.

In those early days everything he did seemed right. Because his name was so powerful in the Midwest and particularly in Ohio, he never needed to court popularity in the traditional political sense. His skill with voters, especially voters who did not already agree with him, was limited. He was stiff, shy rather than arrogant. His speeches were intelligent but dry. Small courtesies seemed beyond him. He might spend several hours with a Capitol Hill reporter one day and two weeks later run into him without giving the slightest sign that they had ever met before.

The Robert Taft who finally showed up as a senator in Washington in 1938 was quite possibly the most cerebral politician of his era. His views were not likely to be influenced by the results of polls and were, by contemporary standards, libertarian. He hated the draft, not merely because he saw it as an escalating step toward militarism but because he believed it limited a young man's freedom of choice. He opposed federal aid to education, not because he did not value education but because he thought it yet another intrusion of the federal government into the rights of the states.

As the shadows of war in Europe began to fall on American politics, his reservations grew. "Modern war," he said, opposing any escalation which would bring us into the Second World War, "has none of the glamour which we were taught to associate with war in our childhood. It is nothing but horror and mechanical destruction. It leaves the victor as exhausted as the vanquished." He even opposed Lend Lease aid to England during England's darkest hour. His lack of concern for traditional allies in Europe shocked even his family. "One of the best fellows in the world," Uncle Horace Taft said of him, "but dead wrong on our foreign policy." The pressure on him to change, to become more internationalist, was immense. One of his few friends in the press corps, Turner Catledge of *The New York Times,* saw him on a train in 1940, his glasses slipped halfway down his face, repeating to himself, "I'm just not going to do it . . ."

Of course, he had hated the idea of Luce's American Century. Luce, a leader in the internationalist wing of the Republican party, had defined the new postwar era, even while the war was being fought, with the vision of an all-powerful America spreading democracy and riches across the globe. This was contrary to the ideals of the American people, Taft said, adding with more than a touch of prophecy, "It is based on the theory that we know better what is good for the world than the world itself. It assumes that we are always right and that anyone who disagrees with us is wrong. It reminds me of the idealism of the bureaucrats in Washington who want to regulate the lives of every American along the lines that the bureaucrats think best for them. . . . Other people simply do not like to be dominated and we would be in the same position of suppressing rebellions by force in which the British found themselves during the nineteenth century."

The crisis of the postwar years was for him still the crisis of isolationism versus internationalism. Taft had no use for Soviet Communism, but his innate isolationism and fear of military involvement were so powerful that he would not join the broad bipartisan consensus of containment, which bound both parties together in the years immediately after World War Two. In 1946–47 *Fortune* magazine (a Luce publication) described his image as "one of that vast group of Americans to whom other countries seem merely odd places full of uncertain plumbing, funny-colored money, and people talking languages one can't understand."

In 1948 he was at the height of his political powers, so dominating a figure in the Senate that *The New Republic* wrote that "Congress now consists of the House, the Senate, and Bob Taft." His career was also on a collision course with political realities. Despite others' attempts to make him better at public relations, he retained a basic wariness of any attempts to shape his public image. Photo opportunities were arranged to show him with a dead turkey, which readers were apparently to believe he had shot. He posed in a business suit with the dead bird; he and the turkey seemed to have no connection to each other. On another occasion he was photographed landing a very dead sailfish from a boat still obviously tied to a wharf. Why are all these people complaining about "Bob's lack of color?" asked his uncle, Horace Taft. "They seem to think he should be standing on his head or turning somersaults."

He tried for the nomination in 1948, but Dewey crushed him at the convention. There had been a clear regional division: Taft with his true-blue conservatives from the Midwest and a good number of delegates from the South; Dewey with New England, New York, and the Middle Atlantic states. Dewey's eventual defeat did nothing to bring the party closer together; if anything it inflamed both wings. Dewey's people believed he had been sabotaged by the conservative congressional leadership, which had given Truman his issues; Taft and his people were convinced Dewey had failed to offer the voters a real choice.

It seemed Taft's best chance was in 1952. The others who had taken the nomination away before were gone. Willkie had been a comet, fueled by the approach of World War Two; Dewey had had his chance twice. On the liberal side there was no strong opposition: Stassen was already beginning to show the political promiscuity that would later make him a joke on late-night television, and Earl Warren was formidable in his own territory, California, but had no discernible base outside it.

The only cloud on the political horizon was General Dwight David Eisenhower. Who was Ike? Was he a Republican? Did he want the presidency? On these questions the general himself was coy. Right after the war, MacArthur had given a large dinner for him in Tokyo, and after the guests had all left, MacArthur predicted that one or the other of them was bound to be President. But the Pacific commander speculated it would not be himself: He had been away too long and was too out of touch with the Republican leadership.

Eisenhower was irritated by his words and by the suggestion that he had a covert political agenda. He launched into a long lecture about the separation of the military from civilian politics, as well as his own lack of desire to run for office. When he was finished, MacArthur patted him on the knee and said, "That's all right, Ike. You go on like that and you'll get it for sure."

The heads of both parties wanted Eisenhower as their candidate. In 1948, immediately following his defeat, Tom Dewey told the general's brother Milton Eisenhower that Ike's appeal was so great that he was "a public possession." In the four years that followed, Eisenhower issued no Sherman-like disclaimer. But just as he'd told MacArthur, there was no driving desire for the job. After all, he had already handled a more important one—the invasion of Europe: He had commanded the mighty force that eventually defeated Nazi Germany. As for politics, in his own mind, it turned out, he *was* a Republican, conservative at heart, more comfortable with powerful businessmen than with their liberal critics. Yet he had strong ideas about internationalism, and he was reluctant to turn the Republican party, and possibly the country, over to isolationism.

By late 1951, the Eastern wing of the party was working harder than ever to bring him home from Paris, where he served as the first commander of NATO. His supplicants explained that it was not going to be that easy, that he could win the Republican nomination, particularly if he got in early enough, but in fact the nominating process would most likely be harder than the general election—an all-out battle against passionate, well-entrenched Republican conservatives. Slowly, Eisenhower began to inch toward running. There were signs that his hesitation was not entirely uncalculated. He told his friend Bill Robinson, one of the many Eastern Republican power brokers who came to court him: "The seeker is never so popular as the sought. People want what they can't get." In addition, he was pushed by his intense dislike of two other potential Republican candidates, Douglas MacArthur ("now as always an opportunist," he told Cy Sulzberger) and Robert Taft ("a very stupid man . . . he has no intellectual ability, nor any comprehension of the issues of the world").

In May 1951, Eisenhower wrote his brother Milton a letter that reflected his continuing uncertainty: He did not want a political career, he said, and he had no intention of "voluntarily abandoning this critical duty [NATO] unless I reach a conviction that an even larger *duty* compels me to do so." As he was being pulled into the political arena by forces outside his control, his reservations remained strong: "Anybody is a damn fool if he actually seeks to be President," he told friends. "You give up four of the very best years of your life. Lord knows it's a sacrifice. Some people think there is a lot of power and glory attached to the job. On the contrary the very workings of a democratic system see to it that the job has very little power."

Nevertheless, it was gradually leaking out that he was a Republican, had voted against Franklin Roosevelt in 1932, 1936, and 1940, voting for him only in 1944 because the war was on; in addition he had voted for Dewey over Truman. A representative from *McCall's* came to see him and offered him $40,000 for a yes-or-no answer to the question Are you a Republican? As the political pressure grew, Ike became increasingly tense, and Dr. Howard Snyder, the general's personal physician and a member of his bridge-playing inner circle, started mixing stronger cocktails in order to relax him. But even as he came nearer and nearer to announcing, the question of whether he was actually a Republican was still not entirely settled. Sherman Adams, the governor of New Hampshire, needed by law to be able to show that his candidate was, in fact, a Republican in order to enter Ike's name in that first, crucial primary. Adams asked his attorney general to write to the county clerk in Abilene, Kansas—Eisenhower's hometown—to see if Ike had ever registered with either party. In return he got a memorable letter of regret from a crusty old clerk, C. F. Moore, who wrote that Eisenhower had not voted in the county since 1927, and then added: "Dwight's father was a Republican and always voted the Republican ticket up until his death, however that has nothing to do with the son as many differ from the fathers of which I am sorry to see. . . . I don't think he has any politics."

In early January, Eisenhower gave Cabot Lodge permission to enter his name in the New Hampshire primary, and on January 27, he finally announced that he was a Republican. On March 11, the night of the New Hampshire primary, he got together as usual with his pals in Paris for a game of bridge. Dr. Snyder left early so that he could go home and listen to the returns. Snyder promised to call if there was any important news. "Don't call me," Eisenhower said. "I'm not interested. Call Al [Gruenther, a man who bet on almost everything] if you want to speak to anyone. He's got some money on it." In New Hampshire, without even showing up, he beat Taft 46,661 to 35,838. The race was on, like it or not.

. . . .

The real driving force behind getting Ike to run was Dewey, whose talents, it turned out, were far better suited to being campaign manager than candidate. He spoke regularly to Ike via transatlantic phone. He knew exactly which buttons to push with Ike and finally got him into the campaign by suggesting in early April that if he did not enter, the nomination might well go to Douglas MacArthur. A week later, on April 12, 1952, Dwight Eisenhower asked to be relieved of his military command so he could come home to fight for the Republican nomination.

Ike came home to Abilene in early June, knowing that he would not get the nomination by acclamation and that he was getting a late start. The homecoming did not go well; it was virtually obliterated by a downpour. CBS covered the homecoming live and the camera caught Ike buttoned up in his slicker, with his rain hat on. Perhaps it was not only the weather but the strain of the arduous new role of politician that seemed to dim Ike's ever-present grin and immense aura of personal vitality. Instead, he looked like a tired, somewhat dispirited old man doing something he did not want to do. When he took his rain hat off, what little remained of his hair blew in the wind, making him seem even more forlorn and lost. The next day he held a live press conference, which did not go much better. Whenever he was asked questions about the chasm within the Republican party, he answered that he was not going to engage in personalities. In general he appeared just short of querulous. The aura of warmth and confidence that had always endeared him to others suddenly seemed to have deserted him. The charm, the ruddy good looks, the almost tangible inner strength disappeared on television. Instead of the heroic conqueror of Nazi Germany, he seemed a rather shaky, elderly Midwestern Republican. In fact, he resembled no one so much as Robert A. Taft.

What followed was one of the most bitterly contested struggles for a nomination in American history: Taft against Eisenhower, with Warren and Stassen hoping for a deadlocked convention. Politics seemed uglier than usual; the Korean War dragged on; McCarthy was in full bloom.

A few weeks before the convention, the Associated Press showed Taft with a lead of 458 delegates to Eisenhower's 402, with 604 needed to nominate. On the very eve of the convention, Taft had 504 votes. The problem was that after that, it got very hard. There was no capacity to grow; if you were for Taft, you were already for him. He could not make a deal with California, committed to Warren as a favorite son and where a young senator named Richard

Nixon was already challenging Warren's hold on behalf of Eisenhower. Warren had already run for Vice-President and had not much liked the experience.

In the end, the Taft people were crushed by a combination of Eisenhower's popularity and Dewey's muscle. Eisenhower's supporters were better organized and better on the floor, and their communications gear was more modern than that of their opponents. They knew how to play to the media, including television. But the mood was nasty. At one point John Wayne, who was a Taft man, jumped out of his cab to shout at an old mess sergeant running an Ike sound truck, "Why don't you get a red flag?" The issue, as the Taft forces saw it, was what did the general stand for. "I like Ike," said Eisenhower's buttons, so the Taft people countered with buttons of their own that said, "But what does Ike like?" On the floor, during a struggle over rules, Senator Everett Dirksen announced that he was addressing himself to "all our good friends from the Eastern seacoast." Then he turned bitterly on Dewey. "We followed you before," he said, looking right at the New York governor, "and you took us down the path to defeat." It was as if Dirksen had ignited all the anger in the room; suddenly people were shouting at each other and fistfights even broke out. Taft himself seemed immobilized by the events: Just before the first ballot started, he turned to an aide and suggested he talk to Senator Bill Knowland, a conservative in the California delegation. Perhaps, said Taft, he and Knowland could meet after the first ballot and strike some kind of deal. Back came the message: "Knowland says there isn't going to be any second ballot." The nomination was Ike's.

It was a bitter moment for Taft. He would never be President, and he would fall short of his father's accomplishments. Embody the Republican party's heart and soul he might, but his own colleagues believed he could not win. Yet he was gracious when Eisenhower called on him. A short time after, John Foster Dulles visited him as well and tried to lighten the mood in the room by saying, "How many of you can remember who was President when Webster, Clay, and Calhoun were functioning?" Taft was amused and replied, "Some of my friends have been trying to retire me to the vice-presidency, but, Foster, you're trying to retire me to history." In fact, he was already seriously ill with cancer and had less than a year to live.

Richard Nixon was nominated as Vice-President on Eisenhower's ticket. He reflected the duality of the Republican party. His fierce anti-Communism, as manifested in his 1946 victory over Jerry

Voorhis, his relentless pursuit of Alger Hiss, and his unusually harsh Senate victory over Helen Gahagan Douglas had made him immensely popular with the Republican right. If Nixon had a record of being highly partisan on the issue of domestic subversion, he was not an isolationist. He had grown up not in the Midwest, but in California—the new America—and had served in the Navy during World War Two. As such he reflected all the contradictions of a party that had been out of power for so long. Though he was popular with the anti-Communist right, his champion within the highest circles of the party was Tom Dewey. In early May 1952, Nixon was invited to speak at the annual Republican fund-raiser in New York, and he argued forcefully for the nomination of a Republican candidate who would appeal to Democrats and independents. It was, in effect, an audition for the Vice-President spot on Eisenhower's ticket, and Dewey was impressed. Afterward, he shook Nixon's hand and said, "That was a terrific speech. Make me a promise: Don't get fat, don't lose your zeal, and you can be President someday." Dewey invited Nixon up for a drink in his room later that night and told him that the Eisenhower people were interested in him. From then on, Nixon became Dewey's man: He was good on the anti-Communist issue, Dewey would say, and yet he was "someone who knew the world was round." Nixon had already figured out that his best chance for national office was to balance a ticket with Ike. California might be locked up for its favorite son, Earl Warren, but Nixon covertly worked hard for Eisenhower in the weeks before the convention. He was, in the words of Dewey's own people, "a fifth column" for Ike among the Warren forces. It was the first example of his talent for bridging difficult gaps, for bringing together factions that were bitterly divided.

Eisenhower himself had no clear preference of a running mate. The night he was nominated, Herbert Brownell, one of his top people, asked whom he would pick as his Vice-President. "I thought the convention had to do that," Ike answered. At the first meeting the Eisenhower staff held after the nomination they discussed the vice-presidency. "What about Nixon?" Dewey asked. He held the exact center of a bitterly divided party and was acceptable to virtually everyone, including McCarthy. Henry Cabot Lodge, Ike's official campaign manager, had to herd Nixon past reporters to avert a premature press conference, but he put his arm around Nixon and told the reporters, "He has done as much to rid this country of Communists as any man I know." So it was that Richard Nixon was introduced to the country for the first time as a national candidate.

It was not by chance that so much of the resistance to America's new internationalism came from the great center of the country. In some ways the heartland was still apart, instinctively resistant to any greater American involvement in Europe and wary of those Eastern leaders who would tie us closer to any nation in Europe, traditional ally or not. Part of the reason for the resistance was geographic, for the American Midwest remained a vast insular landmass that bordered on no ocean and still felt confident and protected by its own size. As a region it was, wrote Graham Hulton, "surrounded, shielded, [and] insulated" by the rest of the country. The Midwesterners were supremely confident that theirs was the more *American* culture, one less imitative of the English and less sullied by foreign entanglements and obligations than those in the East. To them the Midwest was "the center of the American spirit," in Colonel Robert McCormick's phrase. The people back East, they believed, were essentially parasitic—they went around making money, while the good Midwesterners, purer of spirit but dirtier of hand, went around making products for the Midwest. Those resentments were deep and bitter and they were not unlike the resentments of people in a distant colony toward the leaders back in the colonial power.

Some of it was the region's ethnicity, and a wariness of events in Europe on the part of the people who had settled the Midwest and were glad to leave Europe behind them; some of it came from Scandinavians who were essentially pacifist; some of it came from German-Americans sympathetic to Germany; some of the region's Irish were anti-British and some were Germans who did not want to fight on the side of the British, and some were Poles did not want to fight alongside Russia.

The leading voice of Midwestern isolationism was Colonel Robert McCormick, publisher of the *Chicago Tribune,* a paper that modestly referred to itself as "The World's Great Newspaper." The *Chicago Tribune* shared and orchestrated those same isolationist feelings, even as technological change ended any remaining possibility of isolation. When John Gunther, one of the great foreign correspondents of his generation, had come back to America after the war to write on changes wrought in his native land, he believed that the issue of isolation had been settled once and for all. Nobody, he had thought, "can easily be an isolationist in an era when you can cross the Atlantic between lunch and dinner and when the atomic bomb can make mincemeat of an ideology. Chicago is as near Moscow as New York. Foreign policy is, or at least should be, as much a matter or survival in the Middle West as the price of corn." Gunther was soon to learn that he was wrong, that the forces of reaction were still powerful and that there were deeper roots to the regional isolation than he had expected, in no small part because of the intransigence of its foremost propagandist and publisher, Colonel McCormick.

In the years immediately after World War One, the *Trib*'s circulation and its influence in its region were seemingly limitless. It sold over 1 million copies daily and 1.5 million on Sunday. There was no comparable voice in the region. Within the folkways of the Midwest, the *Trib* was more than a mere newspaper; it was something larger, a critical part of the culture that unerringly reflected the attitudes and preferences and prejudices of the region. It brought a daily reaffirmation of the regional commandments, reminding the faithful of what they believed, who were their friends and, most important, who were their enemies. The singular power of Colonel McCormick and his paper within the region reminded Gunther of nothing so much as Stalin's Russia. Not only was there, as in the Soviet Union, "a fixed dogma," but it was, Gunther wrote, "big, totalitarian, successful, dominated by one man as of the moment, suspicious of outsiders, cranky, and with great natural resources not fully developed . . ." As Gunther noted, McCormick's power went far beyond the sheer numbers of his paper's circulation. The paper profoundly affected many who had never read it, particularly in the smaller cities within its greater circulation area, where it functioned as something of a bible for those members of the Rotary and Kiwanis clubs whose members made up the core of the Republican party. "Even if you don't actually read it, you feel its permeating influence," Gunther wrote. "Its potency is subcutaneous."

The *Trib* filtered the news carefully, passing on those items that confirmed its prejudices and omitting many of those that might have caused doubt among the faithful. During World War One, when television did not exist and radio was just beginning to become an alternative source of information, the *Trib*'s voice was a dominating one. For a time its publisher expressed the region's prejudices and fears with singular accuracy. Later, as World War Two approached, and even more when it was over, a new dimension of internationalism began to surface among younger people in the region, particularly those who had returned from fighting in World War Two. The *Trib* still remained influential, but its influence was on the decline, and its editors were gradually losing touch with a changing region. The colonel's bitter break with Roosevelt, his hatred of the New Deal, and his unyielding postwar isolationism cost him severely with younger readers, particularly as they had radio and television to turn to. His xenophobia seemed on occasion like a caricature. He did not like Europe, which he regarded as a lesser continent, populated with people significantly greedier and more materialistic than Americans. It was a place, he noted, where everyone always seemed to want to go to war. But as much as he disliked Europe, he disliked England even more, not just merely because he thought it a snobbish and foppish place, but because he was sure that the entire American foreign service was filled with Anglophiles eager to serve England's purpose rather than that of their own citizens. The British were not only perfidious (with the Americans their favorite dupes), they worked hand in hand with the Soviets. A typical *Trib* cartoon of the postwar era showed Clement Atlee, the British prime minister, with an exhausted and somewhat witless Uncle Sam and Atlee saying, "Let's bribe Stalin with your two billion atomic bomb so Russia will let England rule Europe with the five billions you're going to lend us without interest." The colonel thought of himself as the prototype of a more patriotic America, uncontaminated by foreign influence as so many others back East were. Near the end of his life, the colonel was interviewed by a British journalist: "Isolationist? Anglophobe?" he said, "No, I'm just a patriot." His, wrote John Gunther, was "a furious Americanism and patriotism." Anglophobe he might be, but he fancied English clothes made by English tailors, English hatters, and English shoemakers; he affected a slight British accent; he drove a Rolls-Royce and lived in a British country house outside Chicago. His father had been a diplomat, serving for a time in London, and the young McCormick had not only attended British schools, but when he returned to America he had gone to the schools of the Eastern elite: Groton, which he found provincial, and Yale. At Groton, McCormick noted with disgust, with the exception of Washington and Lincoln, "all the rest of their heroes were New Englanders. Their sectional patriotism," he noted, "was also evidenced by the reading of mediocre New England poets."

He had disliked Hoover (on the occasion of Hoover's inaugural in 1929, the colonel had listened to his speech and immediately cabled his Washington bureau "THIS MAN WON'T DO"), but it was nothing like the feeling he soon came to have for Franklin Roosevelt. That feeling was hatred, pure and simple. He despised Roosevelt personally, the New Deal politically (all New Deal institutions were to be referred to as "so-called"; thus the NRA was, in the *Trib* columns, "the so-called NRA"). He had been somewhat neutral during Franklin Roosevelt's first run for the presidency; they had been, after all, at Groton at the same time, and for a time there were even Dear Frank/Dear Bertie letters. But he quickly turned on Roosevelt as the direction of the New Deal became constantly more clear. It was anathema to him. In time his hatred of Roosevelt and the New Deal became like a virus. He seemed to differentiate little between Roosevelt's administration and those of Hitler and Stalin. His vendetta was finally far more poisonous to the colonel himself, given the essential popularity of most of Roosevelt's reforms. Their feud became ever more bitter, ever more personal, and ever more obsessive on his part. (Roosevelt seemed almost amused by it, and when a *Trib* reporter would ask a question at a Roosevelt press conference, the President would tell him to tell Bertie to stop seeing things under the bed.) Late in his life, a decade after Roosevelt's death, as McCormick himself lay dying, all he could do was talk about was Roosevelt.

During the Roosevelt years, he liked to say—and he most definitely was not joking—that he had kept the Republican party alive. By the Republican party he did not mean the party of Dewey and Willkie and Cabot Lodge, he meant the old Republican party—one rooted in small Midwestern towns, one that was antilabor, conservative on all fiscal matters, wary of government intervention in any public matter, and one that did not see the world as becoming more dangerous. His opposition was expressed not only on the editorial page but in every aspect of the paper. The colonel was in his own way a rather pure man; he was simply a propagandist, not a journalist. His views were as likely to appear in the news columns as on the editorial page. He was famous for having his editors take the copy of the Associated Press (which was never supposed to be rewritten) and rewrite it to suit his prejudices, inserting whatever they wanted; thereupon, the *Trib* would print the report, still under the AP logo. For this and other sins, there were periodic attempts to have him kicked out of the AP. That meant that the backing of the *Trib,* given all its prejudices, was something of a two-edged sword. It stirred passions deeply on both sides. It was often said of the *Trib*'s political power that you could not afford to have it for you in a political campaign (because so many people hated it), but you also could not afford to have it against you.

Others who disliked the New Deal gradually became a part of a larger coalition that understood that the events in Europe now had a great impact on America and that America, like it or not, was tied to the fate of England and France. McCormick did not accept that premise, the anger burned too deeply in him. His answers about what he would do to stop the mounting German aggression were, for so dogmatic and forthright a man, curiously soft. When he had testified before a Senate committee, Claude Pepper had pushed him about what he would do, and McCormick had answered, "Those Germans are not so tough. I have been up against them and there is no use in being scared of them." He seemed more and more, with the approach of the war—and even more after it—a man out of touch with reality. "One of the finest minds of the fourteenth century," a former *Trib* foreign correspondent called Jay Cooke Allen called him. The America that had entered the war was different from the America that emerged from it. His isolationism during so critical and patriotic a time had hurt him. His ego had become more and more of a joke. Colonel McCosmic, the rival *Chicago Daily News* called him and had made fun of all of his boasts about how much he had done to modernize the American military, bringing ROTC to college campuses and making available machine guns for the Army. A *Daily News* cartoon showed him on a horse being pulled by a van and saying, "I was the first to mechanize the cavalry." Another cartoon showed him kicking Uncle Sam in the pants and saying, "A powerful man like you can be of considerable assistance to me in winning the war."

Landlocked the region might be, and conservative it might be, but there were generational changes taking place; the younger men who had fought in the war believed in their cause and did not accept McCormick's isolationism. He was, in the years after the war, a man overtaken by events. His last great political moment came when Everett Dirksen, one of his protégés, savaged Tom Dewey at the 1952 Republican convention for him. It was a last sweet moment in one more lost campaign, one more defeat within his own party. Taft's defeat by Eisenhower in 1952 was the final straw: "I can see no benefit in changing 'Me Too' Dewey for 'I, Too' Ike, who was nominated and is entirely surrounded by men who know exactly what they want—which is not the good of this country," he wrote. He called for a third party, but it was all too late.

The Democrats were nothing less than desperate. They had been in power for too long—twenty years—and while the record of the sitting President, Harry Truman, might one day provide fertile territory for revisionist historians to take a second look at a courageous man operating in an extremely difficult time, there was no escaping the fact that at the time he was an unpopular President in an unpopular party burdened by an unpopular war. That year the Democrats turned to a short, slightly overweight, rather aristocratic figure named Adlai Stevenson, just completing his first term as the reform-minded governor of Illinois.

Ironically, Stevenson had been launched by one of the toughest, most unsentimental political organizations ever put together in American politics, the Cook County machine in Chicago. The machine had been looking to upgrade its image, and Jake Arvey, its most enlightened leader, had come back from World War Two determined to bring a higher tone to Chicago politics. Stevenson himself had worked in the Roosevelt administration in the early days of the New Deal and as an aide to George Marshall during the war and had been a delegate to the conference that founded the United Nations after the war. Arvey first heard of Stevenson from James Byrnes, then secretary of state. "Why don't you grab this fellow Stevenson—he's a gold nugget," Byrnes said.

At around the same time, Stevenson was examining his life and was not satisfied. He wrote in his journal: "Am 47 today—still restless; dissatisfied with myself. What's the matter? Have everything. Wife, children, money, success—but not in the law profession. Too much ambition for public recognition; too scattered in interests; how can I reconcile life in Chicago as a lawyer with consuming interest in foreign affairs—public affairs and desire for recognition and position in that field?"

Arvey was intrigued by the idea of a high-gloss candidate, but he checked further and was appalled to hear that the candidate, in addition to being wealthy, had allegedly gone to *Oxford*. Word of these misgivings reached Stevenson, and he cabled Arvey: "Never went to Oxford, not even to Eton." It was Arvey's first taste of the candidate's wry and often self-deprecating wit. When they met, Arvey was enormously impressed and sensed not only that he would add significant prestige to the ticket but that he might be a formidable candidate as well, attracting not only the usual Democratic votes, but those of upper-class Republicans as well. Initially, Stevenson believed he was scheduled to run for the Senate, while Paul Douglas, a professor of economics at the University of Chicago, a city councilman, and a highly decorated Marine hero from World War Two, would be governor. But suddenly the roles were switched and the machine decided to put the energy behind Douglas, who was something of a maverick, for *Senate* (where he could not do anything to damage the machine) and Stevenson for the more delicate job of governor.

Stevenson worried that he had no particular qualifications to be governor of Illinois, but the machine did not clear its decisions with the candidates. When Arvey came by, Stevenson asked him, "Jack, I'm a little worried about this governor thing. What's expected of me? Everybody says you don't trust Douglas on patronage." That, of course, was true. For a time Stevenson hedged on Arvey's offer; it was Stevenson's friend Herman (Dutch) Smith, a formidable figure in Chicago business circles, who convinced him: "They need you this year. If you say no when they need you, they won't take you when they don't need you." Stevenson was from the start a stunning success. When Arvey read Stevenson's first speech—the candidate had tried to get a professional speechwriter to do it for him but had ended up doing it himself—Arvey told his colleagues, "Don't let anyone change a word of it."

He was forty-eight when he ran for his first office in 1948. He was bright, funny, and literate, and he seemed incapable of uttering a sentence that did not sound polished. He seemed immune to the clichés of professional politics; if canned, warmed-over thoughts did not offend his audience, they most certainly offended *him.* He was a snob about many things—particularly in his choice of friends and in his social attitudes (there was a touch of covert anti-Semitism to him). He was quick to give credit to others, except in the area of speechwriting; there, he became highly irate when other Democrats even so much as suggested that their words had come from Adlai Stevenson's mouth. He had a bitter break with the writer Bill Attwood, a close friend, because he believed Attwood had claimed to write one of his speeches.

Stevenson's ancestors were part of Illinois's landed gentry and no strangers to politics. His great-grandfather Jesse Fell had been Lincoln's campaign manager, and the first Adlai Stevenson had served as Vice-President of the United States. The current Adlai was the adored son of parents who were somewhat disappointed in themselves; Lewis Stevenson, his father, had never quite lived up to his own ambitions or those of his rather wealthy wife, and there was considerable tension in the marriage. During one fight Lewis had said to Helen Stevenson, "Well, you took me for better or worse," and she had answered, "Well, you are worse than I took you for!"

For all his self-effacing qualities, Adlai Stevenson had a certain sense of political entitlement, thanks to his privileged background. A typical political beginner might run for a spot on the city council or for assemblyman, yet Stevenson seemed to think it perfectly normal when the people in charge of the political process tapped him for the important job of governor. George Ball, one of the bright young men in politics of the era, thought Stevenson had an exceptional quality for self-dramatization: "The thing that fascinated me about Adlai was that he accepted so early the idea that he was a great historical figure moving back and forth on the scene," Ball said. "I think he always had Abraham Lincoln on his mind . . . ."

For much of his adult career, Stevenson practiced law in Illinois, but foreign policy was his first love, and he liked to dream of the day when he hoped to make enough money—$25,000 in those preinflation days—to hand to the head of the Democratic National Committee and say, "Here's $25,000. I want to be an ambassador." As he ran for governor, though, he had to be careful about his interest in foreign affairs and his earlier experience at the United Nations. Chicago was the base of Colonel McCormick, and the colonel was more than delighted to represent such experience as a political liability. Arvey's management of the Stevenson campaign for governor was brilliant: He and the other pros held on to the hard-core Democratic voters, who still voted their pocketbook and their ethnic alienation, while Stevenson, with his appeals for a higher civic virtue and his wariness about overemphasizing economic issues, was unusually successful in cutting into Republican and independent votes. Underdog at the start, he won by a plurality of *572,067 votes,* some 170,000 more than Douglas and over half a million more than President Truman, who carried the state by only 33,000 votes. The dimensions of the victory instantly made him a national figure and a contender for the 1952 Democratic presidential candidacy.

He became quickly sought after as a speaker for large fundraisers. He was funny, unpredictable, irreverent, and self-deprecating. Going into a Cook County fund-raiser, he once said: "Ah, the deep, rich smell of democracy in Cook County." Asked about the role of America's newspaper publishers, later, when they opposed him editorially, he answered, "Their job is to separate the wheat from the chaff and then print the chaff." When Drew Pearson wrote that Stevenson would marry Dorothy Fosdick, one of a series of prominent women to whom Stevenson was linked after his early marriage ended in divorce, Stevenson issued a statement: "The newspapers have married me to three ladies in the last three months. I guess they think the plural of spouse is spice—and now Mr. Pearson has added still another. It is all very flattering to me—if not to the ladies! I apologize to them for any embarrassment the writers may have caused them."

Slowly and relentlessly, the pressure built for him to run for President. As early as 1951 every time that Arvey talked to Truman about political matters, the President would ask, "How's your governor doing?" Essentially, Stevenson had walked into a vacuum. Truman's popularity was at a low ebb. The other candidates were marginal. Richard Russell, a Southerner, was a segregationist; Averell Harriman was a formidable figure in foreign policy but had little popular appeal; and Estes Kefauver, who was doing very well in the polls, had enraged the party machinery by dint of his crime investigations. In addition, he was a poor public speaker.

After Supreme Court justice Fred Vinson rejected the President's offer of the nomination, Truman decided to tap Stevenson. He was the most reluctant of candidates; he liked being governor of Illinois, had promised the voters he would serve a second term, and tended to agree with his Republican friends that the Democrats had been in power for too long and that a change of parties in the White House was probably a good thing. Early on, he suspected that the Republican candidate would be not Robert A. Taft but Dwight Eisenhower, whom he thought might make a good President and who was self-evidently an internationalist, and he did not think he could beat Eisenhower. He wanted to run for the presidency one day, but he wanted to wait.

When the President offered the governor the nomination, the governor told him he did not want it. At first the President tried to convince him. "Adlai," Truman said. "If a knuckle-head like me can be President and not do too badly, think what a really educated, smart guy could do in the job." But when it became clear that Stevenson truly did not want the job, Truman became enraged. Here he was, not merely the President, but a devoted man of the party, offering the highest position in the country to a mere one-term governor and he was being rebuffed. Arvey later reported: "He couldn't understand it. How a man could dillydally around with a thing like the presidential nomination." When Scotty Reston, *The New York Times'* most influential Washington reporter, talked to Stevenson right after he had met with Truman, he found the noncandidate both stunned and irritable, certain that he had botched a critical moment in his career, but believing it was not his fault. "What are you trying to tell me?" he asked Reston. "That it's my duty to save Western civilization from Ike Eisenhower?" But the pressure did not abate. If anything, his reluctance made him even more attractive. Suddenly, he was the candidate everyone wanted. Wherever he went he was asked whether he was going to run. In late March he went on one of the early *Meet the Press* shows, and Ed Lahey of the Chicago *Daily News* asked him: "Wouldn't your grandfather, Vice-President Stevenson, twirl in his grave if he saw you running away from a chance to be the Democratic nominee in 1952?" "I think we have to leave Grandfather lie," Stevenson answered.

Curiously, Stevenson was now able to have it both ways, to campaign without campaigning, to be the candidate produced by the party professionals who nonetheless excited the independents and reformers. If he ended up with the nomination, it would be not as the candidate of the Truman administration but a candidate in his own right. He was not unaware of the process he had set in motion. His strategy was simple: He would not enter the primaries, but if the party so decided, he would accept its nomination at the convention. In fact, that was pretty much how it turned out. Estes Kefauver came to the convention with the largest number of delegates, 340, but in addition he had by far the greatest number of powerful sworn enemies. Truman had switched his allegiance to Alben Barkley, but in the end, to the annoyance of the sitting President, the convention nominated Stevenson on the third ballot.

He had been spared the bruising fight in the primaries, but unfortunately, that played into his weakest side as a politician. As he was nominated as an independent, he came to believe himself one, implying that there was no need to court the various groups and blocs that made up the Democratic party. He had never had to do it in his apprenticeship within the party; indeed, he hated the part of politics that called for the candidate to court special-interest groups, and later in his career he liked to joke about the many times he had "bitterly denounced that Japanese beetle and fearlessly attacked the Mediterranean fruit fly."

One of the biggest problems, remembered Arthur Schlesinger, Jr., the Harvard historian and an early speechwriter for Stevenson, was moving him left, toward the traditional Democratic voters and away from his conservative social circles. If Stevenson attacked the Republicans, Schlesinger thought, his close friends would reproach him the next day for unseemly partisanship. As far as Schlesinger was concerned, Stevenson was the most conservative Democratic candidate since John W. Davis. The biggest job was getting him to overcome his patrician upbringing.

SEVENTEEN

The people at Batton, Barton, Durstine and Osborn (BBD&O) were appalled by Eisenhower's initial failure to come across well on television. Ben Duffy, the head of the agency and a close personal friend of the general, was particularly unhappy. BBD&O, then the third-largest advertising firm in the country, was more or less the Republican house firm. Duffy decided that they had to recast Ike. He was stiff and awkward in his formal presentations; therefore it was important to show him in commercials and in quasi-spontaneous appearances, reacting to other people, becoming more like the attractive, magnetic Ike everyone knew and loved. In addition they had to change the harsh television lighting, which was generally set up by the newsreels people, who still dominated the technical logistics. It made Ike look old and gray. The word went out that no Eisenhower television appearance was to be scheduled without BBD&O clearing it.

Since every good advertising campaign needed a theme, BBD&O decided to develop one: It wanted to maximize the idea of Ike the returning hero, welcomed home by a grateful nation, in order to minimize Ike the political candidate, who had a responsibility to speak on his own behalf. His thirty-minute television specials would not be thirty-minute speeches, as campaign specials in the radio era had been. In television, drama was as important as ideas; images were as important as substance. That was fortunate for Ike, because he could never be a better speaker than Adlai Stevenson. In fact, when the Democrats purchased television time that fall, Stevenson seemed so much a prisoner of his own speeches that he was generally in midsentence when his time ran out. By contrast, Eisenhower's appearances were scripted: Ike arrives at the hall, with flags everywhere; the crowd starts cheering; people stand on their seats in order to see him—then shots of Ike going to the rostrum, then shots of Mamie, properly proud, then cut to a brief segment of the speech, then at the end, the hero's departure amidst the adoring crowd: he had come, he had seen and been seen, and he had conquered. This signaled the emergence of television as a force in American political campaigns—much to the regret of both candidates, it turned out.

As BBD&O was developing the overall theme for Ike's campaign, Rosser Reeves, of the Ted Bates Agency, was working on Ike's television spots. If it was a campaign in which the American people carefully studied Dwight Eisenhower and Adlai Stevenson, it was also a campaign in which they did not study Rosser Reeves, who became a critical adviser to Ike that fall. Rather, he studied them, and he became, in the process, one of the two or three most influential men to emerge in politics in 1952—yet his name rarely appeared in the millions of words written about the campaign. Rosser Reeves was not a politician and he had little use for politicians in general; he was an advertising man, and in 1952 he helped change the nature of American politics by introducing the television spot. He was the head of the Ted Bates Agency and a dominating presence, perhaps the most successful advertising man of his time in terms of reaching a mass audience. He had grown up in Danville, Virginia, gone to the University of Virginia to study history, and subsequently drifted in and out of journalism and banking before ending up as an advertising man in New York in 1934. He wrote poetry, often under another name, and after his retirement he wrote a novel about a Greenwich Village eccentric who rejects a life of privilege and wanders the universe speculating about religion and philosophy—"my secret self," he later explained. But if others were making a name in advertising with the elegance and sophistication of their work in the exciting new medium of television, then Reeves was a throwback to the more primitive days of advertising, when the main idea was to hit people over the head with the product as bluntly as possible. It was not to be beautiful; it was not to be artistic. It was not to amuse viewers, who might not even buy the product. It was to sell. Rosser Reeves had decided early in his career that the most effective advertising campaigns were not the ones with the biggest budgets but the ones that held relentlessly to a single theme. Advertising, he believed, particularly in the age of television, was primal. Reeves liked to tell the story of the mule trainer, called in to deal with a recalcitrant mule, who had begun the treatment by first hitting the mule in the head with a two-by-four, explaining to the astonished owner, "Well, first I've got to get his attention." One of his campaigns for Anacin was a classic example of this. It portrayed the inside of the head of a headache sufferer. Inside were a pounding hammer, a coiled spring, and a jagged electric bolt, but they were relieved by little bubbles making their way up the body from the stomach. The Anacin ads, he later admitted, "were the most hated commercials in the history of advertising." But they increased Anacin sales from $18 million to $54 million a year in an eighteen-month period. "Not bad," Reeves once said, "for something written between cocktails at lunch."

While his brother-in-law, David Ogilvy, was doing campaigns for Schweppes tonic, Rolls-Royce, and Hathaway shirts (the last of which featured the man wearing an eyepatch), Reeves was working with mass-consumer items: soap, toothpaste, and deodorants. As far as Reeves was concerned, the difference between him and Ogilvy was the difference between doing snobbish ads for the elite that ran in *The New Yorker* and running mass campaigns for America's most important consumer merchandise. When Ogilvy once mentioned that he had learned much about advertising from Reeves but that it was a shame he had never been able to teach Reeves anything, Reeves replied, "If we ever get out of packaged goods and into luxury items, I'll be glad to go sit at David's feet and listen." When his friends complained about the crude quality of his commercials, Reeves would go into their bathrooms, open up their medicine chests, and take out several brand-name products as evidence that his campaigns worked, even with them. One of his more genteel competitors, Fairfax Cone, said that Reeves delivered advertising "without subtlety, and without concern for anyone's gentler feelings. He also proves that advertising works."

Reeves had admired Ted Bates, whose agency he eventually took over, because Bates had, in his words, "the most unconfused mind" he had ever seen. What he had learned from Bates more than anything else, he would say, was that a commercial should be cut to the essentials: Most commercials were too long and too repetitious, wasting viewer time (and goodwill) and advertiser money. Years later he looked back on the early television commercials as colossally wasteful. Sponsors would pick up an entire program, to do one long commercial at the beginning, one long one in the middle, and one at the end. Far more effective, he eventually decided, was the spot: in quick, out quick, and done. This new medium of television was so powerful that less could easily be more. He gradually evolved the principle of USP, or the unique selling proposition. Reeves had an uncanny ability to determine the essence of a product and then make it seem dramatically different from its competitors (when in fact the difference was often negligible). At the heart of USP was finding one feature about the product that was allegedly unique and pummeling the public with it. "The prince of hard sell," he was called. Advertising without illusion, his campaigns might have been called. They were simple and repetitive: If the claims were not always true, they were never exactly untrue, either.

In an age in which advertising in general prospered from the growing affluence of the society, Reeves prospered more; he took Ted Bates from $16 million in billings in 1945, and no place among the top ten firms, to number five, with $130 million in billings in 1960. Reeves often depicted products the way heroes and villains were depicted in Hollywood in B movies: His product would be, in effect, in the white hat, and the other product, lesser medicinal strength or cleaning capacity, wore the black; on occasion it would be known to the entire nation only as brand X. Reeves's commercials for over-the-counter medical items generally featured pseudomedical testimony delivered by someone wearing a white jacket, playing the role of the doctor. Some competitors, not so amused, spoke of his fondness for "the uncheckable claim."

For the 1948 campaign, Reeves had proposed a series of radio spots to Tom Dewey, who had turned them down, saying he felt they would not be dignified. His decision not to use them had left Reeves convinced that if Dewey had been a bit more modern and a bit less of a prig, he might have been elected President that year. So in 1952, when a group of Texas oilmen ("I had some oil interests at the time,"

Reeves once noted) who supported Eisenhower asked him to come up with a retaliatory slogan to the Democrats' "You Never Had It So Good," he told them that what they needed was not a slogan but a campaign of quick television spots, featuring the general speaking to the American people on a vast range of issues—in short, punchy, unanswerable takes. Some of Reeves's people got together and came up with a plan called "How to Insure an Eisenhower Victory in November." It recommended that $2 million be spent in the last three weeks on spots, "the quickest, most effective and cheapest means of getting across a message in the shortest possible time." With that, American politics and American television advertising were about to be married by a man who did not believe in overestimating the intelligence and attention span of his audience.

Reeves, who was relatively new to politics, went out and did his homework. He read a popular book by Samuel Lubell, one of the early analysts on ethnic voting in America, and came away with the belief that the Dewey people had been incalculably stupid in their campaign. A shift of very few votes in just a few critical states would have won the election for him. Reeves was so impressed by the Lubell study that he hired a brilliant young man named Michael Levin, a disciple of Lubell's and a firm believer in the value of polling. The Lubell study and Levin's research convinced Reeves even more that spots were the answer for the Republicans. The election was going to be close, so they had to concentrate their best efforts on key areas in the swing states—forty-nine counties in twelve key states, he decided. The spots had many advantages, he argued: They were a relatively low-cost way to exploit an expensive new medium; they could be fine-tuned to reach undecided voters; there was a vital element of control to them—the candidate never ended up saying things that surprised his backers or himself; and finally, they allowed the campaign manager to concentrate money and effort in critical areas. If they did them in the last few weeks of the campaign, the Democrats would be hard-pressed to answer them. The oilmen liked the idea, and shortly thereafter, the forty-two-year-old Reeves, under the aegis of Citizens for Eisenhower, took a six-week unpaid leave from Ted Bates to work for the Eisenhower campaign.

Earlier in the year Reeves had sat with some friends, including liberal columnist Drew Pearson, when Douglas MacArthur had keynoted the Republican convention. Pearson and others had thought MacArthur's speech powerful, but Reeves thought the prose too purple and that MacArthur had wandered all over the map, failing to dramatize the very issues he stood for in American life. To make his point, Reeves sent out a research team to interview 250 people about the speech. Only 2 percent of the people had any idea of what the general had said. That, as far as Reeves was concerned, proved his point. In September, as he sat in the St. Regis Hotel reading Ike's clips from newspapers across the country, he concluded Ike was as bad as MacArthur. He was doing a terrible job of packaging and selling himself. He had the advantage of a popular, recognizable name, but he was letting it all slip away, talking in all kinds of directions about too many different things. This was a disaster. "You don't do that in advertising," he said. "You lose penetration." Reeves zeroed in on three essential themes: Ike cleaning up corruption; Ike the soldier who was, in truth, a man of peace; or Ike who would clean out the Communists in government. Then he went to the *Reader's Digest,* which had what were considered the best mailing lists for middle-of-the-road, mainstream Americans. He did three mailings of ten thousand each, asking the subscribers to say which theme would be most effective. Most people responded to Ike as a man who knew war but who would now bring peace. Reeves also met with George Gallup and had him do some polling. The results were similar: The American people were worried about Korea above all. With that, Reeves thought he had his USP, so to speak: "Eisenhower, the man who will bring us peace." That slogan was brought to the general for his approval, and much to the surprise of Reeves and his group, the general demurred. He, no more than anyone else in the world, could guarantee peace. So the slogan was made even simpler and better: "Eisenhower, man of peace."

Soon Reeves had worked out an entire strategy for the spots. He wanted them to air at critical times, between two highly popular regular shows ("You get the audience built up at huge costs by other people," he wrote in a memo to the Eisenhower people). The announcer would say, "Eisenhower answers the nation!" Then an ordinary citizen would ask a question and Ike would answer it, in words crafted by Reeves from Eisenhower's speeches. The candidate approved of the idea but was not entirely comfortable with it; it was something, he made clear, that the people who knew more about this game of politics were insisting he do. Most assuredly, he did not like the fact that these same people were running around telling him that his forehead shone too much.

The subject of the relationship between his bald dome and the television camera had already considerably irritated the candidate. It had first arisen back in Paris, when David Schoenbrun, a CBS correspondent, had pointed out that he had something of a problem. Ike had told him he knew he was bald, but what could he do about it? Schoenbrun told him, "You tend to lower your head and that elongates it and makes it seem longer and balder, like an egghead. Maybe you can tilt your head the other way, back a little." So Ike had tried, but he had clearly disliked his television appearances. Once when Schoenbrun had suggested the use of makeup to take some of the shine off his head, Ike had said, "Why don't you just get an actor. That's what you really want." But gradually Reeves and his people persuaded Ike to overcome his reservations.

In order to film the spots, Ike and his closest aides decided to give Reeves only one day, in early September, which was a reflection of how seriously the candidate took it all. Reeves knew he was working with a reluctant candidate and that he would have to accept the limitations imposed on him. He had wanted to do fifty spots, each twenty seconds long; but given his limited time frame, he decided to do only twenty-two. He wrote them all himself. When Ike arrived at the studio, it was obvious he was uncomfortable in this alien place. He had brought along his trusted brother Milton to act as censor. It was Milton's job to look through proposed spots and announce which ones the candidate would and would not do. "No," Milton would say, to Reeves's annoyance, about words taken verbatim from one of Ike's speeches. "Ike will never say this." But he had already said it in a speech, Reeves would protest. "He's not going to say it again," Milton would answer with finality.

Technically, everything was quite primitive: This was before the coming of the TelePrompTer, and Reeves had wanted to shoot Ike without his glasses, but Ike could not see the prompter board. So Reeves improvised a giant handwritten board, which Eisenhower could see without glasses. Now, at least, Ike would look like he did in his photos—hale and hearty, not like some aging, tired politician or banker. If the candidate initially had some misgivings, once he started doing the spots he relaxed. Seeing that things were going better than expected, Reeves wrote an additional eighteen spots and the general did them. The general was still not pleased by all this; at one point he sat shaking his head and saying, "To think that an old soldier should come to this."

Now that he had Ike's answers in the can, Reeves needed to get the questions. He sent film crews to Radio City Music Hall to search out the most typical-looking and -sounding Americans they could find—"real people in their own clothes, with wonderful native accents." Typically, a woman would be directed to say: "You know what things cost today. High prices are driving me crazy." Then Ike answers: "Yes, my Mamie gets after me about the high cost of living. It's another reason why I say it's time for a change. Time to get back to an honest dollar and an honest dollar's work." Or a man asks: "Mr. Eisenhower, are we going to have to fight another war?" Then Ike answers: "No, not if we have a sound program for peace. And I'll add this: We won't spend hundreds of billions and still not have enough tanks and planes for Korea."

When Reeves had finished the spots, he showed them to David Ogilvy, one of the few Stevenson loyalists on Madison Avenue. He thought they represented the worst abuse imaginable of the advertising man's skills. "Rosser," Ogilvy said. "I hope for your sake it all goes well and for the country's sake it goes terribly." The spots were typical of Rosser Reeves's style—primitive and effective. They showed Ike as a good, ordinary heartland American. Stevenson (brand X in this case) was never mentioned at all.

It was pioneer work, Rosser Reeves liked to say, in the art of penetrating a specific market with a high-density campaign and yet using a minimal amount of time and money. The campaign spent $1.5 million on the spots in those states where the campaign was perceived as being close. The Democrats were furious. George Ball, then a young Stevenson speechwriter, said the Republican crisis was that they had all the money but no real candidate. "Faced with this dilemma they have invented a new kind of campaign—conceived not by men who want us to face the crucial issues of this crucial day, but by the high-power hucksters of Madison Avenue." Marya Mannes, writing in the liberal *Reporter,* had mocked this new marriage of Madison Avenue with the American political system: "Eisenhower hits the spot/One full General, that's a lot/Feeling sluggish, feeling sick?/Take a dose of Ike and Dick./Philip Morris, Lucky Strike,/ Alka Seltzer, I like Ike." By chance the executive editor of the *Reporter,* Harlan Cleveland, lived next door to Reeves. One day Reeves asked Cleveland what his magazine's objection was. "It was selling the President like toothpaste," Cleveland answered. Reeves answered that the essence of democracy was an informed public. "Is there anything wrong with a twenty-minute speech? Or a ten-minute speech? Or a five-minute speech?" "No." "Then what's wrong with a one-minute speech or a fifteen-second speech?" Reeves replied. " 'You can't say anything in a fifteen-second speech,' " Reeves quoted Cleveland as saying. Then Reeves dissented: "As a man who had been responsible for five hundred million dollars' worth of advertising I know more about this than you do." There was a pause in their conversation; Reeves was sure he had his man now. "Harlan," he asked. "Do you remember that old radio speech of Franklin Roosevelt—his first acceptance speech?" Cleveland said he remembered it. "And the phrase about the only thing we have to fear is fear itself?" Again Cleveland assented. "Harlan," Reeves said, locking the trap. "That's a fifteen-second spot." Now he pushed forward. "Do you remember the speech that Churchill gave at Westminster College in Fulton, Missouri? What did he say there?" "That an Iron Curtain had descended on Europe," Cleveland said. What else did he say? Reeves pushed. Cleveland could not remember. "That was a fifteen-second spot from Churchill," Reeves said, "just like the one during the war about 'never have so many owed so much to so few.' That was a Churchill spot, too. He was very good at spots." Reeves remembered Cleveland as being very uncomfortable. "This can lead to demagoguery," Cleveland said. "An uninformed electorate can lead to demagoguery faster," Reeves said, confident that what he was doing was helping to inform the electorate.

If Ike adapted, albeit somewhat uneasily, to the new communications technology, Stevenson did not. He hated the idea of using advertising with the political process. "This is the worst thing I've ever heard of," he told Lou Cowan (a CBS executive on loan to the campaign) when he heard of the Eisenhower spots, "selling the presidency like cereal. Merchandising the presidency. How can you talk seriously about issues with one-minute spots!" Though there were already 17 million television sets in the country, Stevenson essentially refused to recognize the medium. Ironically, he was quite good at it: The medium caught him as he was—his lack of false airs, his natural grace and, above all, his charm. Because he did not seek television exposure, and did not take it seriously, he was not stilted when he went on. In early September, John Crosby, then the premier daily critic of television, wrote, "To both Republicans and Democrats it is now fairly obvious that Gov. Adlai Stevenson is a television personality the like of which has not been seen before." Still, he did not like speaking to an invisible audience of millions. No amount of pressure and cajoling from his staff could convince him of the new medium's importance. He did not watch television himself—he bore it the snobbery of the elite class.

It was hard for the men around him to get him to change. Part of the reason was generational and part of it was snobbery. Many of the people in his circle refused to admit that they even watched television, let alone owned one. On one occasion when Stevenson was scheduled to give a major televised speech, Lou Cowan came up with an idea on how to soften the troubling issue of Stevenson's divorce. How about, he suggested, having the camera pan to his three loyal sons, onstage. Just before a speech, they would say something nice and folksy, like "Good luck, Dad." Stevenson quickly rejected the plan. "Lou old boy, we don't do things like that in our family." The network correspondents assigned to him tried to humanize him by suggesting informal shots. Perhaps he would allow their cameras into his car as he was campaigning or into his workroom as he was writing a speech. His answer always the same: "Certainly not."

Yet Stevenson's very resistance to such attempts to focus on things other than the issues and the seriousness of his speeches lent the campaign its special dignity. Years later his enthusiasts would remember his speeches as eloquent, fearless, and forceful. Curiously, when they took the time to go back and read them, they were often disappointed. The speeches were good, there was no doubt about that, but what had made them seem so exhilarating was their context. For here was a courageous man in a bad time. He was speaking at the very height of the McCarthy period and the terrible fear generated by nuclear peril and the postwar confrontation between the two great powers. Public discourse in America at that point was at its nadir. The chemical formula for victory, Karl Mundt had said, was KC_2: Korea, Communism, and corruption. Many politicians of the period gave speeches that were crude and accusatory. Others simply waffled on the issue of individual liberties, so much under assault by McCarthy. Eisenhower was, regrettably, silent. But Stevenson remained calm and unafraid; he seemed to find strength in America where others saw only decline, vulnerability, and, indeed, betrayal.

A speech he gave at the Mormon Tabernacle in Salt Lake City in mid-October was typical. He was tired after a long day of traveling and he had argued with his assistants over whether or not he had to go to the reception that preceded the speech. He preferred to sit in his room and work on his speech, shortening it so he would not once again run over the allotted time. In the end, he went to the reception and then returned to his room. He was so tired that he said he decided to have a second drink. "I won't know what I'm saying tonight," he joked.

That night, fatigue or no, he was at his best. He began: "Tonight I want to talk to the great confident majority of Americans, the generous, and the unfrightened, those who are proud of our strength, and sure of our goodness and who want to work with each other in trust." Regrettably, he said, that confident majority did not include the Republican speechmakers in the campaign. How did they see America? "They call sections of us dupes, and fellow travelers, a man without a purpose and without a mind. But at all times they picture us as unworthy, scared, stupid, heartless. They thus betray the hopeful, practical, yet deeply moral America which you and I know." He then spoke about the danger of McCarthyism. There was, in a society like ours, he said, a rightful division between what was the province of God and what was the province of Caesar. The freedom of the mind and of conscience, the freedom from attempts of the state to impose thought control, was God's province; things like minimum wage, farm prices, and military spending were under the jurisdiction of Caesar. "Those among us who would bar us from attempting our economic and social duty are quick with accusations, with defamatory hints and whispering campaigns when they see a chance to scare or silence those with whom they disagree. Rudely, carelessly, they invade the field of conscience, of thought, the field which belongs to God, and not to senators." The Founding Fathers, he claimed, thought of government as a benign force, not a force of bullies, and as such they permitted great freedoms to those who would govern us. "So if their conscience permits, they [McCarthy and men like him] can say almost anything, and if my opponent's conscience permits, he can try to help all of them get reelected." In this most conservative state, he was interrupted again and again by thunderous applause.

In no small way, there were certain new class lines forming during the campaign. Stevenson was immensely popular with the new emerging postwar intellectual elite, what writer Michael Arlen years later termed "the new G.I. Bill intellectuals." It seemed for the moment as if the country were dividing along intellectual lines. On the night of Stevenson's nomination, Eisenhower had watched his opponent's acceptance speech with his friend George Allen at a ranch in Colorado, and when it was over, Allen turned to him and said: "He's too accomplished an orator; he'll be easy to beat." The general appealed to the squarer America—the traditional wealthy Republicans and the good, solid citizens of the small towns. If Stevenson was the candidate of the readers of *The New Yorker, Harper's,* and the *Atlantic,* then, as Arlen added, Ike was the candidate of the *Saturday Evening Post* and *Reader's Digest.*

There was a belief in certain parts of the country that Stevenson was not manly enough to be President; indeed there was a good deal of carefully orchestrated background noise about his sexuality. The New York *Daily News,* staunchly conservative, referred to him as Adelaide. On the contrary, he had a number of passionate affairs, both as governor and as candidate. He seemed to be surrounded by so many adoring women that they came to be known as Adlai's harem.

The difference between the two men's appeals to the electorate was shrewdly caught that fall by CBS commentator Eric Sevareid in a letter, which clearly reflected the elitism of class and education that had surfaced during the campaigning: "In his almost painful honesty, he . . . has been analyzing, not asserting; he has been projecting not an image of the big, competent father or brother, but the moral and intellectual proctor, the gadfly called conscience. In so doing he has revealed an integrity rare in American politics, a luminosity of intelligence unmatched on the political scene today; he has caught the imagination of intellectuals, of all those who are really informed; he has excited the passions of the *mind;* he has not excited the emotions of the great bulk of half-informed voters, nor among these has he created a feeling of Trust, of Authority, of Certainty that he knows where he is going and what must be done. Eisenhower does create that feeling, or that illusion, because, God knows, he is empty of ideas or certitude himself."

The Republicans were hardly bothered by Stevenson's appeal to intellectuals and journalists. That September columnist Stewart Alsop called his younger brother John, a powerful figure in the Connecticut Republican party, to suggest that Stevenson was doing well among the people he ran into. "Sure," answered John Alsop. "All the eggheads are for Stevenson, but how many eggheads are there?" Thus Stevenson became the candidate of the eggheads.

It was nonetheless a handsome campaign in a bad time. For all of the squalid background noise of McCarthyism (the Wisconsin senator, expert in all forms of democratic behavior, said he would like to get on the Stevenson campaign trail with a club and thereby make a good and loyal American out of the governor) (and Nixon working the Republican right wing), Eisenhower was a decent man and Stevenson an elegant campaigner who elevated the political discourse. Right-wing accusations against George Marshall, Stevenson noted, reflected a "middle of the gutter approach." Among some who thought Stevenson the superior candidate there was a feeling that the country needed to elect Eisenhower in order to make the Republican party accept responsibility for McCarthy. Others feared that if the Republicans remained out of power very much longer, the two-party system would be in jeopardy. No one articulated it better than the columnist Joe Alsop in a letter to Isaiah Berlin. The campaign had convinced him that Stevenson was admirably qualified to be President and Eisenhower was not, and yet, Alsop added: "I find myself constantly blackmailed by the virtual certainty that we shall have a first-class fascist party in the United States if the Republicans don't win. The real need for a change in this country arises, not from the decay of the Democrats, but from the need to give the Republicans the sobering experience of responsibility."

If Stevenson had thought he had even the smallest chance of winning, he might have been more tempted to compromise. Right after he gained the nomination, he was told by his advisers to make some kind of accommodation with Texas conservatives on the issue of offshore oil rights; otherwise, he was warned, he would probably lose Texas and the election. "But I don't *have* to win," he answered. Instead, he went before the American Legion, a citadel of jingoism and political reaction, and told the audience that McCarthy's kind of patriotism was a disgrace. Besides his own inevitable defeat, the result was that at a moment when the Democratic party, having been in power for more than twenty years, should have been in complete disrepute, Stevenson reinvigorated it and made it seem an open and exciting place for a generation of younger Americans who might otherwise never have thought of working for a political candidate.

"When an American says he loves his country," he said in one memorable speech, "he means not only that he loves the New England hills, the prairies glistening in the sun, or the wide, rising plains, the mountains or the seas. He means that he loves an inner air, an inner light in which freedom lives and in which a man can draw the breath of self-respect." In a speech he gave to the Liberal party, he spoke of the right-wingers who hoped to ride into power with Eisenhower, "the men who hunt Communists in the Bureau of Wild Life and Fisheries while hesitating to aid the gallant men and women who are resisting the real thing in the front lines of Europe and Asia. . . . They are finally the men who seemingly believe that we can confound the Kremlin by frightening ourselves to death." Stevenson's gift to the nation was his language, elegant and well crafted, thoughtful and calming.

The campaign, as courteous as it was, did not make the candidates like each other. Stevenson was angered by Eisenhower's failure to disassociate himself from the McCarthy wing of the party and for his willingness to be packaged in television advertisements. Early in the campaign he stopped referring to Eisenhower as his distinguished opponent and started calling him the general. Eisenhower was equally disenchanted with his opponent. In the beginning he was inclined to be impressed by Stevenson—after all, they both had connections to George Marshall—but as the campaign progressed, he decided that Stevenson, for all his high-mindedness, was just another politician, not a profession greatly admired by the general.

· · ·

The most dramatic moment in the campaign came early, and it was also connected with television. In mid-September, it was discovered that a group of wealthy California businessmen had created a fund designed to alleviate the financial pressures on Richard Nixon, a politician without financial resources of his own. The idea was that the money be used for the young senator's travel, for his Christmas cards and other small expenses. "They are so poor that they haven't a maid and we must see to it that they have a maid," said Dana Smith, one of the chief organizers. The Nixon fund was not unique. Similar funds had been used by other politicians, including Adlai Stevenson, it would turn out. Many congressmen enhanced their salaries by placing their wives on the payroll in various administrative or secretarial positions, something that Nixon, to his credit, had not done. Neither Nixon nor the organizers were particularly secretive about it. In mid-September, when reporters first asked Nixon about it, he was quite open and relaxed about it and suggested that they go see Dana Smith. Smith, in turn, spoke enthusiastically about what they were doing and suggested that it might be a model for others. He also used the opportunity to go on a tirade against the New Deal, which he said was "full of Commies. . . . Our thinking," he added, "was that we had to fight selling with selling and for that job Dick Nixon seemed to be the best salesman against socialization available. That's his gift, really—salesmanship."

The fund apparently had a total of over $16,000. The contributions ranged from $100 to $500. The early stories did not seem to cause much of a stir. Most newspapers played the story inside if at all. Then on September 18, the *New York Post,* a liberal left newspaper decidedly unsympathetic to Nixon, played the story big. "SECRET NIXON FUND," screamed the banner headline. "SECRET RICH MEN'S TRUST FUND KEEPS NIXON IN STYLE FAR BEYOND HIS SALARY," said the head. Nixon responded in typical fashion. He was doing whistle-stop speeches from the back of a train in Northern California when a voice rang out, "Tell them about the $16,000!" Nixon started visibly: "Now I heard a question over there—hold the train! Hold the train!" The train came to a stop several hundred feet down the track. "The Alger Hiss crowd," Nixon said to the reporters with him in an aside as he waited for the crowd to catch up and reassemble. Then he began again: "I heard a question over there. He said, 'Tell them about the $16,000.' And now I am going to talk about that on this score. You folks know the work I did investigating the Communists in the United States. Ever since I have done that work, the Communists and the left-wingers have been fighting me with every smear they have been able to do . . ." The *Post* story could easily have been the end of it: The fund might be somewhat questionable, but there was no evidence of anyone buying a vote. In addition, the *Post* was obviously hostile. "We never comment on a *New York Post* story," Jim Hagerty, Ike's press secretary, said immediately. But with that the Eisenhower people froze. The whole campaign was premised on his cleanliness: He was the man who was going to, as the saying went, clean up the mess in Washington. A decision was taken aboard the Eisenhower train that the general must be protected and not tainted by this, even if it meant letting Nixon take the heat. The general himself soon held a press briefing, supposedly off the record, in which he asked rhetorically, "Of what avail is it for us to carry on this crusade against this business of what has been going on in Washington if we ourselves aren't clean as a hound's tooth?"

With that, the burden was on Nixon to clear himself in Ike's eyes. How he was going to do this was unclear. Nor were the candidates' logistics much given to coming up with a coherent mutual strategy. Ike was on his train, traveling in the Midwest, surrounded largely by people from the liberal, Eastern wing of the party, men who had never wanted Nixon on the ticket in the first place; Nixon was on *his* train, whistle-stopping in California, surrounded by people who were fast becoming angry at the general for his lack of political acumen. Communication between the two trains was sparse. Ike was sitting back waiting for Nixon to save himself, and in the resulting vacuum the story grew.

Each candidate was now behaving exactly in character: Ike, the commanding general, was aloof, so carefully sheltered by his own staff that he did not sense that his very inaction was giving the story momentum and validity (in fact, his people were leaking their irritation with Nixon and the fact that the general barely knew him); on the Nixon train the candidate, always given to black moods and periods of despair, fell to brooding and self-pity. His staff cursed the general, who could have put the entire thing behind them in a minute and had chosen not to do so. Nixon later said that Ike had made him feel like "the little boy caught with jam on his face."

As the story fed on itself, the newsmen covering the trains had a field day. It was the first flaw in an otherwise perfectly orchestrated campaign. Even BBD&O was not able to handle it, and the newsmen took some pleasure in showing that the leader of the greatest invasion in the history of mankind was not necessarily adept at domestic politics. More and more, Nixon's place on the ticket seemed in jeopardy. Bill Knowland, on vacation in Hawaii, was alerted to get back to the mainland and to be prepared to replace Nixon on the ticket; this news was soon leaked, spurring even more rumors about Nixon's demise. The one Easterner sympathetic to Nixon, Governor Dewey, privately reported to the vice-presidential candidate that the men around Ike were by and large a hanging jury. Gradually, the idea was born among those sympathetic to Nixon that Nixon should make a special television appearance to clear himself.

Nixon himself was angry over what he considered Eisenhower's waffling. "General," Nixon said to him at one point in desperation. "I never thought someone of my rank would be saying something like this to someone of your rank, but there comes a time when you have to shit or get off the pot." So Nixon decided to seize the initiative with a television appearance. Arthur Summerfield and Bob Humphreys were told to raise $75,000 for the television hookup—a pathwork of 64 NBC television stations and 194 CBS radio stations and, in addition, almost all of the 560 radio stations of the Mutual Broadcasting System. The decision to go ahead with the television broadcast was made on Sunday, September 21. There was some debate over time slot: The television people wanted to piggy-back after the *Lucy* show on Monday night, which would guarantee a huge audience. But Nixon did not think he could be ready in only twenty-four hours, so they decided to come in on the back of Milton Berle, on Tuesday, September 23, even though Berle did not have the audience that Lucy had.

That night Nixon seemed to bare his soul to the entire nation—at least, his financial soul. He had everything to gain and nothing to lose, with his political career hanging in the balance. He was, it appeared, to be judged by a hostile jury; he had been told by Dewey to conclude his speech by resigning from the ticket, thus leaving the decision up to the general. Ike's people wanted copies of the speech before Nixon went on, but the vice-presidential candidate was not about to give them anything. Murray Chotiner, Nixon's top political operative, finally told Sherman Adams, his counterpart on the Eisenhower train, "Sherm, if you want to know what's going to be said, you do what I'm going to do. You sit in front of the television set and listen." For Nixon, it was all rather exhilarating—it was the kind of challenge he could understand and rise to. The speech was thereafter known as the Checkers speech, after a reference to his dog, Checkers—although Nixon himself, who loved the speech and thought of it as one of the high-water marks of his career, much preferred to refer to it as the Fund speech. Still, Nixon was proud of the reference to his girls' dog because it was a version of a famous Roosevelt speech that featured Roosevelt's little dog, Fala.

He knew exactly how he wanted to portray himself: as the ordinary American, like so many other veterans back from World War Two, just starting out in life, more than a little modest about his service to his country ("Let me say that my service record was not a particularly unusual one. I went to the South Pacific. I guess I'm entitled to a couple of battle stars. I got a couple of letters of commendation, but I was just there when the bombs started falling"). He wanted his audience to know he had never been rich and that he was being smeared in the process of fighting Communists for ordinary Americans (which he would continue to do, no matter how this all came out). There was no advance copy of the speech; he spoke from notes.

Ted Rogers, who was in charge of television for Nixon, told the people at the broadcast studio to make the setting as natural as possible. Rogers wanted to make the candidates comfortable with the American people, into whose homes he was going. There were to be no flags, no gimmicks. Nixon was the one who insisted that Pat go on with him. She was his only prop, a reminder that they were a typical young American couple. Rogers was dubious about putting her on—he thought it might be in bad taste—but Nixon was firm. It was not just politics for him, Rogers realized; it was as if he were fighting some kind of war—Nixon against the world. The director kept asking Rogers how he would know when Nixon was through. Rogers could answer only, "You'll know. You'll just know." Rogers drew an arc on the floor with a piece of chalk and told Nixon to stay within it so the camera could shoot him.

Nixon spoke to the nation for thirty minutes. He outlined his family's finances in exceptional detail. Pat Nixon came to hate the speech because in her eyes it unveiled the poverty of their past. "Why do we have to tell people how little we have and how much we owe?" she had asked. The speech itself was extremely maudlin: "Pat doesn't have a mink coat. But she does have a perfectly respectable Republican cloth coat. And I always tell her that she'd look good in anything." Then there was the dog: "And you know the kids love that dog, and I just want to say this right now—that regardless of what they say about it, we're going to keep it . . ." But above all there was the respect and obedience to Eisenhower ("And remember, folks, Eisenhower is a great man, believe me. He is a great man . . ."), while telling his listeners to send telegrams to the Republican National

Committee, a conservative group hostile to Ike and sympathetic to Nixon. He cast the issue not in political terms but in personal ones. He had come to the American people and told them he was drowning and asked them to save him: Most surely they would now reach out.

He was in tears as he finished, sure that he had blown it and that he had not even gotten in the Republican National Committee's address in time. Rogers, though, was dazzled by how well it had worked, how Nixon had ended just on the right note without even knowing it, "walking off the set into the Warner Brothers sunset," as Rogers later said. The phone response showed that Rogers was right. Ike, watching in Cleveland, was not amused by the way in which Nixon had taken the play away from him. He turned to Summerfield and said, "Well, Arthur, you surely got your $75,000 worth."

If the advertising people around Ike had not known how to deal with the news of Nixon's fund, they were ready well in advance to deal with Nixon's speech. Bruce Barton, one of the more senior people at BBD&O, had cabled Ben Duffy: "Ben, tonight will make history. This will be the turning point of the campaign. The general must be expertly stage managed and when he speaks it must be with the understanding and the mercy and the faith of God. My suggestion is that . . . at the conclusion of Nixon's speech . . . the General come out with the following memo in his own handwriting: 'I have seen many brave men perform brave duties. But I do not think I have ever known a braver act than I witnessed tonight, when a young Marine private [Barton was apparently under the impression that Nixon had been an enlisted man in the Marine Corps rather than an officer in the Navy], lifted suddenly to the height of national prominence, marched up to the TV screen and bared his soul . . .' " That was in fact very close to what Ike later said: "I have seen many brave men in tough situations. I have never seen anyone come through in better fashion than Senator Nixon did tonight . . ."

Nixon had saved his spot on the ticket. There was a price, of course. Ike never entirely trusted him again, and Nixon became increasingly contemptuous of Eisenhower's political judgment. There was also the belief on the part of the nation's tastemakers that there was something more than a little unsavory about the entire episode: the self-pity, the willingness to use wife, children, and dog. "He may aspire to the grace and nobility of Quakerism but if so he has yet to comprehend the core of the faith," Richard Rovere wrote. "It would be hard to think of anything more wildly at variance with the spirit of the Society of Friends than his appeal for the pity and sympathy of his countrymen . . . on the ground that his wife did not own a mink coat." Walter Lippmann was equally bothered; it was, he wrote, "a disturbing experience . . . with all the amplification of modern electronics, simply mob law." A few days after the speech, Fred Seaton, Bernard Shanley, and a few of Eisenhower's other people were having drinks when Tom Stephens, a Dewey man working for the general, joined them. "There was just one thing he left out of the program," Stephens said. What was that? one of the men asked. "It was the portion when Checkers, the Nixon dog, crawled up on Dick's lap and licked the tears off his face."

The big winner in the whole episode was not Nixon but television. Nixon had given a powerful demonstration of what it could do. In effect, Richard Nixon had summoned his own instant convention, deputizing millions of Americans sitting in their homes as the delegates to it. With a shrewd, emotional speech, he had gone over Eisenhower's head, forced his hand, and rehabilitated himself. The old political bosses could provide an audience of several thousand; television could provide one of millions, without the risk of hostile questioning.

The person who learned this lesson best was Nixon himself. The entire tone of his campaign began to change. If his bus was ready to roll and the print reporters, to his mind his principal enemies in the fund scandal, were not ready, his attitude now was, thought Ted Rogers, "Fuck 'em; we don't need them." He had become convinced that television could carry him above any obstacles the print reporters might put in his way. He was the new electronic man in the new electronic age.

EIGHTEEN

Those years are sometimes called the Eisenhower era, and his presidency spanned much of the decade. When used by critics, the label is pejorative, implying a complacent, self-satisfied time ("looking down the long green fairways of indifference," Frank Clement, the governor of Tennessee, sneered when he keynoted the Democratic convention in 1956—a reference to the fact that the President played golf primarily, it seemed, in the company of America's wealthiest corporate figures). The truth was the country was changing at a remarkable rate, and a generation would soon come to power whose confidence and ambition had been intensified by both World War Two and the dynamism of the postwar economy. Still, it was Dwight Eisenhower and the men of his generation who were actually running the country, and the America they governed was the one they remembered from their childhoods, during the turn of the century. Thus, while the country was exploding in terms of science, technology, and business, and had assumed a new international role as the most powerful nation on earth, the minds of the governing class were rooted in a simpler day. Many of the tensions of the era stemmed from this contradiction.

Dwight Eisenhower was the last American President born in the nineteenth century. The fifties had not shaped him; rather, he was the product of small-town life in America at the turn of the century. He was the best of that generation—educated, intelligent, ambitious. He had considerable ego, but he also had exceptional control of it. That allowed him to deal successfully with such immensely egocentric generals as Patton and Montgomery without losing his temper, and also to handle with great skill such delicate tasks as overseeing the transfer of power from a declining England to an ascending America. At a moment when feelings in both countries were raw (reflected most notably in Eisenhower's constant problems with General Montgomery, who was not only unbearably egocentric but also openly insulting), Ike always managed to control his temper. After one particularly egregious offense, Ike had put his hand on Monty's knee and said, "Steady, Monty. You can't speak to me like that. I'm your boss." Eisenhower never lost sight of the fact that he had to hold the alliance together, a job that was greater than one man's ego. To ordinary British citizens he came to represent the embodiment of the new America just coming of age—fresh, strong, modern, decent, and generous.

He was ten years old when the new century began. His hometown, Abilene, Kansas, was a simple place then. In the center of town there were still hitching posts and watering troughs for the horses that drew the buggies. When his family had arrived in Abilene from Texas in 1891, the town did not yet have streetlights or paved streets. The mud made the streets virtually impassable after heavy rains. During Ike's boyhood the town began to change. First there were sidewalks, made of lumber. Hard pavement on the streets came around 1904. Other amenities soon followed, like electricity and running water and then sewers. Abilene had but one policeman, who patrolled the town not for local crime, of which there was none, but for visiting hustlers and card sharks. The proprietors of the town's handful of shops knew, Eisenhower later noted, that their customers came in to buy only what they needed and nothing more. (Later, as President of the United States, with some money in his pocket for the first time, Eisenhower became a shopper of legendary proportions.) There were no radios, and the local telegraph operator, as a favor to his neighbors, kept the wire open late during the World Series so that he could pass on the scores every half-inning to the boys at the Smoke House, the local pool hall. As a boy, Eisenhower had seen a tennis court, but he had never seen anyone play on it. He had never even heard of golf.

Taxes were almost nonexistent. People took care of their own, as the saying went. Almost everyone voted Republican. The Midwest was isolated from the rest of America, as in a subsequent age of radio, television, automobiles, and highway systems it was not. "The isolation," Milton Eisenhower once said "was political and economic as well as a prevailing state of mind. Self-sufficiency was the watchword; personal initiative and responsibility were prized; radicalism was unheard of." Abilene was a town with its own subtle class distinctions. The railroad tracks divided the town. On the north side were the leading merchants and doctors and lawyers, in their expansive Victorian houses with huge porches; on the south side of the tracks were the people who served them—the railroad workers, carpenters, and bricklayers. The Eisenhowers were respectable but not part of the gentry.

Religion, not entertainment, was the focal point of the town's life. "Everyone I knew went to church," Eisenhower wrote years later. "The only exception were people we thought of as the toughs—pool room sharks, we called them." The Eisenhowers were Mennonites from the Rhineland who had been persecuted for their faith and had come to America in the middle of the eighteenth century. They settled in a Mennonite community in Pennsylvania. In 1878 Jacob Eisenhower—the name means hewer, or artist, of steel—hearing of rich land further west, led his family and other Mennonites to Kansas. He sold his farm in Pennsylvania for eighty-five hundred dollars to pay for the trip. Tales of the fertile quality of the land in Kansas turned out to be true: Within a year his butter production was a thousand pounds, six times what it had been back in Pennsylvania. In addition, land on this new frontier was cheap. In Pennsylvania it went for $175 an acre; in Kansas, for $7.50 an acre.

Dwight's father, David Eisenhower, hated farming. Instead, he loved tinkering with machinery and wanted to be an engineer. His father insisted farming was God's work but eventually relented and allowed David to attend a nearby Mennonite college. There, David met and married Ida Stover, who came from a similar background. She was even more religious than he and had once won a prize for memorizing 1,325 biblical verses. As a wedding present Jacob gave his son a farm of 160 acres (as he had done with his other children) and two thousand dollars, but David mortgaged the land and bought a general store in Hope, Kansas, twenty-eight miles south of Abilene. Soon thereafter the region's farmers were hit by a plague of grass-hoppers, which devastated the local economy. David's partner ran off with what little money they had, and the store went bankrupt. He had been carrying all the local farmers on credit, and now, as they went broke, so did he.

It was a bitter failure, and the shadow of it hung over the Eisenhower family. David became dour, pessimistic, and wary of granting anyone his trust. At first he went to work for the railroads in Texas, at ten dollars a week, and then returned to work at a creamery run by his brother-in-law. It was not an easy life. There was never extra money. Everyone in the family had to work hard. The Eisenhowers grew most of their own food. Nothing was to be bought on credit. After his bankruptcy, David never wanted to owe anything to anybody. Once, Ike did not have enough money to buy a pair of pants from a local storekeeper and he agreed to pay the balance later. He swore the storekeeper to secrecy, but somehow a bill was sent out. David Eisenhower was furious, but to his son's surprise there was no punishment for once.

The chores were rotated by Ida Eisenhower among her six sons. Each boy had his own vegetable garden. So humiliated by his failure, David remained distant and aloof. No one ever dissented from any-thing he said. His sons took turns getting up at 5 A.M. to build a fire in the cookstove and to fix their father's breakfast. He went to work every morning at six-thirty and came home at five. Every day one of the boys would bring him a hot lunch.

It was a seriously religious family. David read from the Bible before meals, and after dinner he brought the Bible out again and read it again. There was no discussion of the meaning of these biblical stories; the word of God was sufficient unto itself, David thought. Were it not for Ida Eisenhower's ebullience and generosity of spirit, it might have been a grim boyhood. But she was both religious and gay, softening the family's harsh circumstances for her children.

Dwight Eisenhower was known as Little Ike, a mutation of his last name. His older brother was Big Ike. As a boy, he had a fero-cious temper. One Halloween night when he was ten years old, he was not allowed to go out trick-or-treating with his two brothers. Enraged, he pounded his hands against an old apple tree until they were bloody. His father was furious and used a hickory switch on him. Later that night Ida Eisenhower took him to his room and bandaged his hands while she quoted to him from the Bible: "He that conquereth his own soul is greater than he who takes a city." It was an important lesson for the man who would lead the mightiest army in the history of mankind.

Although Ike's father provided little in the way of companionship and emotional warmth, the young Eisenhower did befriend a local trapper named Bob Davis. An illiterate man, Davis shared his superb hunting and fishing skills—some of them legal, some not—with Ike and also taught him how to play poker. Ike, it turned out, had a natural talent for the latter, and he played it so ruthlessly, coldly calculating the mathematical odds, that later in his life, as a young Army officer, he had to give it up lest his phenomenal success stir up resentment among his fellow officers.

If Ike was not rich, he was popular and admired. He had an engaging grin and natural charm. The word most often used to describe him throughout his life was *winning*. He was ambitious in an old-fashioned, straightforward way, without being a toady. He did well in school when the subject matter interested him. Military history was his first love, to the horror of his pacifist mother, and he read everything he could, at first about the military battles of the Greeks and Romans and then of modern European and American warfare. For a time his mother hid his books, locking them in a closet, but he managed to find the key. This was one battle she was destined to lose.

Ike aspired to attend the University of Michigan, where his brother Edgar had gone. Then a friend told him about Annapolis. He applied there but did not get in. Eventually he was accepted at West Point. Ida Eisenhower was not pleased: The day Ike set off on the three-day train trip to New York, his mother returned home from the station and broke into tears. It was the first time, Milton Eisenhower, Ike's younger brother, noted, that he had ever heard his mother cry. She must have realized he would never come back. There was nothing for him in Abilene—at best he might end up as a clerk in a store.

At West Point Ike was surrounded by small-town boys very much like himself. Freed from the strictness of David Eisenhower's rules, he constantly perpetrated such minor infractions as smoking, and he did not apply himself to his studies with any great seriousness. The one thing he seemed to care about was football. Before he tore up his knee he seemed on the verge of becoming an All-Eastern halfback. He graduated 125th in a class of 162, entering a professional army of 120,000 men. Europe was already embroiled in what was to become the First World War. He asked for duty in the Philippines, but instead he was assigned to Fort Sam Houston in 1915. That year he met a young woman named Mamie Doud, who was spending the season with her family in San Antonio. The Douds were wealthy: John Doud was the son of a Chicago meatpacker who had made millions through shrewd investments. He had retired from his day-to-day business in his early thirties and moved his family to the frontier town of Denver. They had a chauffeur and a maid, and John charged his wife with keeping the books, it was said, down to the penny they spent.

When Ike called Mamie for a date, the maid told her, "Mister I-something called all day." Mamie had already noticed how striking he looked in his uniform. Who's that handsome young man? she asked one of her friends. The woman-hater of the post, her friend answered. She told him she was busy. He asked her out for the night after that. She had a full social life but granted him a date four weeks in the future. Eventually, he talked her into canceling some of her overloaded social schedule. He was making $141.67 a month, which he supplemented by coaching football and playing poker. They caught a jitney and had a Mexican meal in San Antonio, where two people could eat for $1.25, including tip. A few months later he proposed to her. He was still a second lieutenant, but he told John Doud that he expected a promotion soon. Doud liked Eisenhower but was worried because his daughter was accustomed to servants and a generous allowance. Mrs. Doud warned that they would have to live within Ike's income. They wed in July 1916, as the signs mounted that America would soon be drawn into the European war.

The life of a young Army wife was not easy for Mamie. She had to devote her life entirely to her husband, living on an endless series of Army bases, with little in the way of creative comforts. In the first thirty-five years of their marriage, they moved thirty-five times. Not until 1953, when he was sixty-three and President of the United States and she was fifty-six, did they own a house. In the Army, Dwight Eisenhower was immediately drawn to the new weaponry that was reshaping modern warfare. At first he had sought a position with the new Army Air Corps, but John Doud thought it far too dangerous and announced that he would oppose the marriage if Ike intended to spend his life flying airplanes. Instead Ike opted for tank warfare. As war spread throughout Europe, he was desperate to get a command, preferably of a tank battalion. On several occasions he seemed about to get one, only to be transferred to a training unit. In October 1918, at the age of twenty-eight, he was finally given orders for France. His tank unit would be part of the big spring offensive of 1919. But the Germans surrendered before Ike saw any action. "I suppose," he told one of his friends, "we'll spend the rest of our lives explaining why we didn't get into this war."

In the postwar years, the Army shrank to its prewar norms; in July 1920, Ike was made captain and three years later he became a major, a rank he held for sixteen years. Promotion in the Army between wars was excruciatingly slow. Still, he was known as a talented young comer; he became friendly with George Patton, Jr., at the Infantry Tank School at Camp Meade, and also Fox Conner, possibly the most talented and cerebral officer in the Army at the time. Both Eisenhower and Patton felt the Army was underestimating the future importance of tanks. Ike eventually served as Conner's executive officer in Panama; there, Conner taught Ike to take his career more seriously. From then on, Eisenhower was never the same officer. He entered the command and general-staff school at Fort Leavenworth, the Army's most important school for mid-level officers, and finished first in his class.

But for all of that, life in the peacetime Army was hard, particularly on Mamie. For her, Panama was a world of bugs, tropical storms, and brutal heat. She was never quite able to enforce her rule that the chicken for dinner be killed out of her earshot. Their housing was dreadful. "Roofed-over camping out," was the way she described it. There were certain hardy, adventurous women who were ideal for the role of Army wife; Mamie was not one of them. "She was," wrote Stephen Ambrose, "an authentic American and like many native Iowans she considered the world a wonderful place, especially when she was living neatly between New York and San Francisco." To make things even more painful, they lost their first son, Dwight David Junior (Icky), to scarlet fever. But Mamie endured those years. As he was frugal from the legacy of his father's failure, so she became frugal as well. She was furious when they bought furniture for their post housing at Fort Sam and did not get reimbursed.

If the younger officers, like Eisenhower and Patton, were already thinking in terms of the next war, many old-fashioned Army rituals were still emphasized. Ike disliked such ceremonies as the Sunday morning protocol visits to superiors in which he had to dress in striped pants and derby hat. The modern Army was about tanks and airplanes and he knew it. Yet he served and waited, never in a rush. Patience and hard work would be rewarded; his biographer Stephen Ambrose shrewdly noted that Ike was different in this respect from his younger brother Milton. Milton had worked in Washington for years and thought in terms of what government should do for the citizens. Dwight Eisenhower, whose life was spent mostly in the Army, was wary of politicians and believed in what the citizen should do for the country. Those years of sacrifice made him a somewhat hard and unsentimental man. At the start of World War Two, when he had finally begun to rise above men who had long been his superiors, George Marshall suggested making Troy Middleton a two-star general. Middleton was an old friend of Ike's who had left the Army just before World War Two to become comptroller of Louisiana State University. Ike said no. "He left us when the going was tough," Eisenhower said.

For McCarthy, Eisenhower's election was the beginning of the end. On election night, as the returns came in, Phil Graham, the publisher of *The Washington Post,* turned to Murrey Marder, the *Post* reporter who had distinguished himself with his intelligent and thorough coverage of the senator, and told him he was going to lose his beat. Graham was sure that Ike's presidency would eventually mean McCarthy's isolation; now that the Republicans had the White House, they would not need McCarthy any longer. But Marder knew McCarthy's recklessness and his hatred of authority. Party loyalty was not even an issue with him—it would not matter who was in the White House. No, Marder speculated, his beat was not finished; instead they would now need two people to cover the senator. They were both right.

What would take place, of course, was the denouement. McCarthy did not understand, of course, that his real value was not in uncovering spy rings (which he had most certainly not been doing) but as a partisan ploy, allowing worthier men to keep their hands clean. "Joe, you're a real SOB," Senator John Bricker of Ohio once said, "but sometimes it's useful to have SOBs around to do the dirty work." The McCarthy show had been playing for too long. By the time Eisenhower was inaugurated, three years of endless charges with little proof were wearing thin. McCarthy was losing the center, as represented by Dwight Eisenhower, who hated him. "A pimple on the path of progress," Eisenhower called him, and there were epithets far harsher as well. McCarthy's virulent attacks on George Marshall, Ike's great benefactor, had prompted Eisenhower to attempt to square the record at a campaign stop in Wisconsin. Eisenhower had already been appalled at a campaign stop in Indiana, where he had been embraced on the platform by William Jenner. It had caused Eisenhower to recoil physically and leave as quickly as possible. The attempt to defend George Marshall, whom McCarthy had accused of treason, was for Eisenhower the saddest day of his campaign. He directed his speechwriters to craft a ringing defense of General Marshall and his patriotism: "I know that charges of disloyalty have, in the past, been leveled against General George C. Marshall. I have been privileged for thirty-five years to know General Marshall personally. I know him, as a man and as a soldier, to be dedicated with singular selflessness and the profoundest patriotism to the service of America. And this episode is a sobering lesson in the way freedom must *not* defend itself." Ringing words that never rang. Ike's advisers, fearing McCarthy's retaliation against their candidate, talked him into dropping the remarks. Ike cut them out, but he was furious—at his advisers, at McCarthy, above all at himself.

More than anything, his handling of McCarthy during the campaign marked Dwight Eisenhower's loss of innocence, his decision, for reasons of political expediency, to be less of a man than he really was. Not just his Democratic opponents, but some of his oldest and closest friends, such as General Omar Bradley, were appalled by his failure to defend Marshall, whose relationship to Eisenhower was described by Ike's close aide Harry Butcher as "that of father and son." "It turned my stomach," Bradley wrote years later of Ike's failure to speak up for the man he had once revered now that he was a political candidate. "No man was more beholden to Marshall than Ike." Moreover, Bradley noted that Ike as a candidate in 1952 seemed again and again to be "hypocritically calling into question policies that he himself had helped formulate or approved or had carried out." The one person who did not seem particularly bothered by the fuss was Marshall, a stoic man with an overwhelming sense of personal duty and marginal expectations of the political process. He told his goddaughter at the time, quoting Will Rogers, that there was no more independence in politics than there was in jail.

But Eisenhower's hatred of McCarthy was virulent. At one point during the Army-McCarthy hearings, he remarked that the Kremlin ought to put McCarthy on its payroll. "He don't take shovin'!" Jerry Persons, Ike's longtime aide, once said of his boss. Eisenhower viewed McCarthy as someone who always shoved, and in private, embittered tirades he raged against him to his closest associates—how McCarthy was kept going by Texas oil money, how McCarthy wanted to be President. At one cabinet meeting in which

Arthur Larsen was describing a new kind of life insurance, a sudden-death policy you could take out on someone else, Eisenhower observed grimly, "I know one fellow I'd like to take that policy out for." But when aides suggested that he personally take on McCarthy, he would always say, "I will not get in the gutter with that guy."

McCarthy had not only alienated Eisenhower; his power was waning in the Senate as well. Taft, with little time left to live, began to distance himself. He gave the Internal Security subcommittee to William Jenner as a means of heading McCarthy off; McCarthy countered simply by using the Committee on Government Operations as his forum. Taft demanded that all investigations be cleared with him, but of course McCarthy had no intention of clearing anything with anybody. The first major break came in early March 1953, when Eisenhower nominated Chip Bohlen to be ambassador to Moscow. Though clearly the most competent man available for the job, Bohlen had been a minor official at Yalta. John Foster Dulles, the new secretary of state, was not enthusiastic about the nomination. Couldn't you tell them that you were only an interpreter at Yalta? Dulles asked the nominee. On the morning of their appearance before Congress, Dulles suggested to Bohlen that they travel in separate cars so there could not be photographs of them together.

McCarthy, of course, went after the Bohlen nomination from the day Ike announced it, which meant that in the end he was forced to go after Dulles, whose duty it was to vouch for Bohlen. McCarthy demanded that Dulles testify under oath. It was the first time McCarthy had turned on his own party. Taft was furious. "So far as I am concerned Mr. Dulles's statement not under oath is just as good as Mr. Dulles's statement under oath," he said. Afterward, reporters asked Taft if this represented a break with McCarthy. "No, no, no, no," he quickly said. But, of course, it did.

The end came sooner than anyone expected. McCarthy went after the United States Army, and the resulting confrontation was carried live on ABC television; the nation watched and when it was over, McCarthy had done himself in with his ugliness. Somehow the Army-McCarthy hearings managed to show that he was in decline. And this to no less an authority on winners and losers than the head of the FBI, J. Edgar Hoover. Hoover, an important ally in the past, always backed winners; during the hearings he unceremoniously dumped McCarthy. McCarthy overplayed his hand and became an embarrassment. He began to drink more heavily than ever. "You're killing yourself, goddamnit," his old friend Urban Van Susteren would tell him, and he would answer, "Kiss my ass, Van." In 1954 the Senate censured him. But worse for him than the censure was what the press did: it began to ignore him. He could not understand what had happened. Why, he kept asking Dion Henderson, an out-doors writer for the AP in Milwaukee and a close friend, was a statement that had been news in 1950 not news in 1955? Finally, in 1955, he decided to make an about-face and give a pro-civil-liberties speech in which he would say that his entire career as a red-baiter had been a mistake. He had been reading Thomas Jefferson, McCarthy told Henderson, and had been influenced by him; but above all, he was anxious to make headlines, especially in *The Milwaukee Journal,* his most relentless journalistic opponent. McCarthy bet Henderson that the *Journal* would not use the story. Both Henderson and Ed Bayley of the *Journal* filed it, and Henderson's story was used in a few papers, but Bayley's story died on the copy desk. It had been McCarthy's last chance to grab headlines: Joe McCarthy the born-again civil libertarian. Three years after being censured by the Senate and some seven years after his first speech, he died of cirrhosis of the liver. He was only forty-eight. If nothing else, he had illuminated the timidity of his fellow man.

NINETEEN

In the summer of 1951 Marlon Brando opened in his first big film, the cinematic version of Tennessee Williams's *A Streetcar Named Desire*. There was never any doubt he would get the part after his Broadway performance; he exuded a raw sexual power onstage that could only translate into box-office power. Brando was paid $75,000, reasonably good money at that time for a first starring role.

It would be hard to imagine an actor more wary of going from the legitimate stage to Hollywood than Brando. When he was a young, struggling actor in New York, he liked to boast that the theater was his real love and he would never sell out to become a movie star, something he viewed as a less exalted calling. After finishing *Streetcar* on Broadway, he received a letter from Stanley Kramer, who asked him to star in a movie called *The Men,* about a group of paraplegic veterans. Kramer was the rare producer whom Brando respected, and the theme intrigued him. Somewhat reluctantly, he accepted. He installed himself in a ward at a real veterans' hospital for six weeks, to get some firsthand experience of these men's lives. He was on his best behavior, and the movie was excellent, but he did manage to offend the Hollywood press, particularly the two powerful gossip columnists of that era, both of them rightwingers, Hedda Hopper and Louella Parsons. Hopper, he liked to say, was the one in the hat, and Parsons was the fat one. They reciprocated his contempt.

If he found Hollywood an alien place, he was reassured by the fact that Elia Kazan, who had directed *Streetcar* on Broadway, was going to direct the movie. Vivien Leigh would play Blanche. When Miss Leigh, then married to Lord Laurence Olivier, arrived, the local journalists kept referring to her as Lady Olivier. "Her ladyship," she noted at an early press conference, "is fucking bored with such formality and prefers to be known as Miss Vivien Leigh!" That should have augered well for her relations with Brando. But from the start he was suspicious of her, as much as anything else put off by her good manners; she *was* British and she *was* polite to everyone. That irritated him. His manners were at best flexible and at worst appalling; in the decade ahead, he would frequently exercise his inalienable right to be rude, especially to powerful people. "Why are you so fucking polite? Why do you have to say fucking good morning to everyone?" he asked Ms. Leigh early on. There were other problems on the set—the struggle between Olivier and Kazan over Ms. Leigh's reading, for instance. Kazan would prepare her one way, and she would be his Blanche, then she would go home, work with Olivier, and return as *his* Blanche. But perhaps the more serious problem was getting certain aspects of Williams's play past the Hollywood censors. On Broadway the elite audience was ever more willing to break new ground with sexual subjects in this new and more open postwar era. But Hollywood was a different story. Kazan and Williams, who wrote the screenplay, had to contend with the Breen office, the guardians of public morals, whose standards had been set in another time. Kazan had to negotiate each cut reluctantly and painfully with Joseph Breen. All references to homosexuality would have to be cut; Blanche was no longer to be interested in young boys. Then Breen demanded the rape scene be cut. On this Kazan stood his ground. He would not do the film unless the rape scene, in some form, was left in. The Breen office relented, but only if Stanley was punished by losing his wife's love at the end. It was an appalling process, repugnant to Kazan and to Williams. As for Brando, it merely confirmed his worst fears about Hollywood. What kept Kazan going was the knowledge of how much he was saving—the play was so strong, the performances so powerful, that Kazan was certain the movie was going to be an immense success. But when it was finished Kazan was stunned to find that Warner Bros., in order to win approval from the Catholic Church's Legion of Decency, had made additional, serious cuts without telling him. It was a done deal and he had not even been consulted. Kazan was enraged. He was also powerless. He told Jack Warner he would never make a picture for him again. He wrote a bitter piece for the Sunday *New York Times,* but it was over. But Kazan's instincts about making the film in the first place, and the compromises that it entailed, still proved to be true: The raw power of Williams's play and the performances were beyond the reach of the censor. The film became a classic, but one cannot help but wonder what it might have been if the censors had not had their way.

A Streetcar Named Desire was not just a play—it was an event. Its frank treatment of sophisticated sexual themes marked it as part of a powerful new current in American society and cultural life. Even the plot seemed emblematic—the brutal assault on Blanche's prim, Victorian pretensions by Stanley's primal sexuality. Every night on Broadway the audience would leave the theater visibly shaken—not only in response to Blanche's tragic breakdown, but also in some small way, perhaps, because they had gotten a glimpse of the violent changes just beginning to transform their own culture and lives.

That *Streetcar,* first on Broadway and then on film, seemed to transcend a mere theatrical triumph to become a cultural benchmark was due to three remarkable talents, all then at that zenith of their powers: Tennessee Williams, perhaps the greatest American playwright; Marlon Brando, the most original American actor of his time; and finally Elia Kazan, the great director. The cumulative force of these three men caused an explosion that shattered the pleasant conventions of American life. Different though they were in many ways, all three were outsiders, liberated by the changing times and eager to assault existing conventions.

Williams was gay, his private life an open secret. Kazan was a Greek-American, driven by the feverish energy of the outsider looking in. Brando was a self-invented outsider, a middle-class American who scorned the conventions of middle-class life. *Streetcar* derived its vitality from the talents of all three, and the person who realized that from the start was Williams. After a long, arduous apprenticeship as a playwright, he achieved a major success with *The Glass*

Menagerie. For *Streetcar* he passionately pursued Kazan, although at that point hardly the best known or preeminent director on Broadway. Still, Williams was certain he could put over the poetic vision of his play. Williams recognized his own limitations, and in a letter to Kazan he wrote: ". . . The cloudy dream type, which I admit to being, needs the complementary eye of the more objective and dynamic worker. I believe you are also a dreamer. There are dreamy touches in your direction which are vastly provocative, but you have the dynamism my works need."

With *Streetcar,* Williams made the unsayable sayable, the forbidden legitimate. The playwright seemed to have a natural instinct for violating convention: On the eve of the New Haven opening of *Streetcar* he went to the home of Thornton Wilder, then a formidable if rather conservative figure in the American theater. There, Williams remembered, Wilder explained (as if holding "a papal audience") that the play was "based on a fatally mistaken premise. No female who has ever been such a lady [he was referring to Stella] could possibly marry a vulgarian such as Stanley." Listening to this dismissal of his work, Williams thought to himself of Wilder, "This character has never had a good lay."

Tennessee Williams was born in Mississippi. His mother, Edwina Dakin, was the daughter of an Episcopalian minister. She was reared, at least in her own mind, to be a great Southern lady, without, regrettably, the financial means the role necessitated.

In the small towns where her father held the ministry, Edwina was regarded as something of a catch; even though she had no money, she had a good family, looks, and grace. She filled her diaries with innocent, vain reports of the young men who courted her, to whom she referred as gentlemen callers, a term Williams was later to appropriate for *The Glass Menagerie.* One day Cornelius Coffin Williams showed up. As people with pretensions are often fooled by their own kind, Edwina was taken immediately by his charm, probably in no small part because she sensed he was a rogue, a drinker, a gambler, and a carouser on those occasions when he was away from her. She wrote in her diary on June 1, 1907: "Many men have said I love you, but only three have said Will you marry me. I will marry one next Monday. Finis. Goodbye."

The marriage was a disaster from the start. C. C. Williams did not intend that marriage would change his life. His job as a traveling salesman gave him the freedom of the road, the freedom not to be home, and he seized on it. Inevitably, husband and wife fought, and when Edwina gave birth, she moved from their first apartment, in southern Mississippi, back to Columbus to be with her parents. Their first child, Rose, was born there. Divorce was unthinkable—so this was a solution of sorts. C. C. spent most of his time on the road, and Edwina became once again the rector's daughter. As her father moved, so did her family, which would soon include a son, Thomas Lanier Williams, born in March 1911, in the church vestry.

When C. C. made his periodic visits home, he treated his family with contempt. His son came to despise the kind of blustery macho his father exhibited: Years later, talking about the kind of men who made antigay remarks in locker rooms, Williams said, "They're all the same, shoe salesmen with bad territories and wives they can't abide. So they take it out on us."

For the first seven years of Tennessee Williams's life, his parents' marriage survived. Then C. C. was made sales manager of an International Shoe branch in St. Louis. It was a crushing moment for everyone: C. C. had lost his freedom, and Edwina had gained an unwanted husband. From then on, young Tennessee's life was a horror. The family moved constantly as Edwina sought better neighborhoods in a hopeless attempt to regain the one thing that mattered to her—social status. Her husband drank and gambled away his salary. Edwina began to drift into the fantasy world of her girlhood, twenty years earlier. She romanticized a world of privilege and genteel manners. External appearances became desperately important. She smothered her children with love, finding unsuitable almost every potential playmate for them. The other boys were too rough, the girls too common. Self-knowledge was not her strong suit. When *The Glass Menagerie* opened in Chicago, with its portrait of the mother who lived in a fantasy world of her own making, Edwina attended the opening night party. Laurette Taylor, who played the character based on Mrs. Williams, asked her, "Well, how did you like you'seff, Miz' Williams?" "Myself?" answered the shocked Edwina Williams.

Young Thomas Lanier Williams (aka Tennessee Williams) struggled terribly with the secret knowledge that he was sexually different. "Miss Nancy," C. C. sometimes called him, with cruel contempt. As a boy he could not conquer an uncontrollable blush whenever someone looked him directly in the eye. "Somewhere deep in my nerves there was imprisoned a young girl, a sort of blushing school maiden," he wrote. The Great Crash of 1929 had almost prevented him from going off to college, but with a thousand dollars borrowed from his grandparents he enrolled at the University of Missouri in Columbia, a place he quickly came to loathe. There he saw himself as a social failure: "I was not a young man who would turn many heads on the street. . . . The pupil of my left eye had turned grey with that remarkably early cataract. And I was still very shy except when drunk. Oh, I was quite the opposite when I had a couple of drinks under the belt," he later wrote. He put in three years at Missouri before his father brought him back to St. Louis and got him a job at International Shoe for sixty-five dollars a month as an accountant.

Back in St. Louis, he would have to face the terrible experience of watching his sister, Rose, mentally come apart. The problems of the family fell heaviest on her. Tennessee and his sister had always been close. Deprived of other playmates, they had taken to each other; he had loved her gentleness and the vivid quality of her imagination. She had always known that her mother's plans for her were hopeless—she would never be a popular Southern belle pursued by the handsome young men from Vanderbilt and Sewanee. As a young woman she had gone to Knoxville to stay with two of her aunts and to make her debut; it was a dismal failure. When she returned to Memphis, Tennessee asked her how it had gone. "Aunt Ella and Aunt Belle only like charming people," she had told him, "and I'm not charming."

Slowly, the seriousness of her mental illness became obvious. The more fragile and alienated she became, the more Edwina Williams pushed for her to be the belle she could never be. "If I could only get Rose into her right senses," Edwina wrote her own mother. By the mid-thirties Rose was a distant, elusive creature, moving steadily toward true madness. She decided that she would eat only Campbell's tomato soup, and saved the labels from them. She became dangerous to herself and to others. Once, her mother happened to see that she was going off to a doctor's appointment with a carving knife, quite possibly to murder him. Rose knew what was happening to her. At one point her brother made light of mental illness, and she chided him. "It's worse than death." By 1937 she had become a violent schizophrenic and a frontal lobotomy was done on her.

What saved Tennessee was his writing. When he was still a young boy, Edwina had given him a typewriter: "It immediately became my place of retreat, my cave, my refuge," he wrote. Here he could escape, create his own reality. It also gave him a hope that he might get out of that home and out of St. Louis. His family life had been rich in material for someone who managed to escape it. In his ability to look back, examine that life, and write about it, Williams showed a rare emotional strength.

Elia Kazan always believed that he and Williams both survived because of their ability to work. "He did it every morning and nothing was allowed to interfere," Kazan wrote of his friend. "He would get up, silent and remote from whoever happened to be with him, dress in a bathrobe, mix himself a double dry martini, put a cigarette in his long white holder, sit before his typewriter, grind in a blank sheet of paper, and so become Tennessee Williams. Up until then he'd been nothing but 'an aging faggot' (his phrase to me) alone in a world he had always believed and still believed hostile."

Success came slowly. During his twenties and thirties, he waited on tables and worked as an elevator operator and as an usher (he got the job because the previous usher's uniform fit him). For a time he was a chicken plucker in Los Angeles—for every one he plucked, he put a feather in a bottle, which would show at the end of the day how much he was owed. But he was always writing. Slowly, there were small signs of success. Then in March 1939 his breakthrough came. He entered a playwriting contest sponsored by the Group Theater in New York. All writers were supposed to be under twenty-five, but he altered his birthday by three years in order to enter. One of the committee members, Molly Day Thacher Kazan, wife of a young actor-director named Elia Kazan, was so impressed by Williams's work she lobbied for a special award of a hundred dollars for him. She also suggested that Audrey Wood, a young New York agent, represent him. "There's a wonderful young playwright riding around Southern California on a bicycle," Molly told her husband. Soon there was a one-thousand-dollar grant from the Rockefeller Foundation ("my friends the Rockefellers," he liked to say afterward). But even then things were hard. An early play, *Battle of Angels,* was produced in Boston, but the themes were too explicit for the time. The play provoked a negative response among critics and theatergoers, and the local censor was anxious to sanitize it. Scared of the controversy, the producers paid Williams a hundred dollars for the right to close it.

He was rootless. He lived in New Orleans, New York, Los Angeles, Provincetown, Key West—almost anywhere he could but St. Louis. Like Faulkner's, his best work is rooted in the South, and his characters often seem to represent certain Southern archetypes. But he had no desire to live again among his roots. Sometimes he rented a small place of his own, sometimes he stayed with friends. His personal habits were eccentric. Yet he never lost sight of the need to write. "He put writing before knowing where he was going to sleep or where his next meal was coming from," his friend Donald Windham noted. In the midst of the worst kind of personal chaos, he always remained wildly productive.

Audrey Wood got him a job as a screenwriter for MGM at $250. Two hundred and fifty a month? he asked, thinking it a princely sum. "Two hundred and fifty a week," she answered. That brief time in Hollywood was, he later reflected, one of the happiest in his life, even though he and the studio had nothing in common. He spent most of the time doing his own work and enjoying the West Coast and feeling wealthy. He finished the play that became *The Glass Menagerie* during that period. Laurette Taylor, a great actress who had been an alcoholic for more than a decade, was cast in it; she seemed unable to memorize her lines and unable to stop drinking. As opening night approached, disaster loomed. Then miraculously, just on opening night, it all came together and she gave an inspired performance. The audience nonetheless was uneasy, for this play was different. But two local critics relentlessly championed it, and it stayed alive and became a hit. It had even greater success when it moved to New York. Finally the door had begun to open for him.

He was lucky to find as his first producer Irene Selznick, who was at that time attempting to establish herself as a Broadway producer. The daughter of the fabled and feared Louis B. Mayer, she was in the midst of a long and arduous divorce from Hollywood producer David Selznick. In New York she courted a number of agents who represented younger writers, among them Audrey Wood. Wood said to her, "My most cherished and important client has a play I would like to put in your hands. It is his best play yet. His name is Tennessee Williams." Ms. Selznick was excited but puzzled. After all, she was a mere novice. "Why me? Why me?" she asked Ms. Wood. "Find me someone else," she answered the agent. For it had remained hard going for Williams. His work was not commercial, and his themes were difficult; he was said to be difficult to deal with personally as well. Ms. Selznick read and loved the play but was immediately concerned that she was not experienced enough to handle it. She met with Williams, and their only conversation seemed to be about the title. Did she like the original title, *Poker Night,* or the backup, *A Streetcar Named Desire*? But they did agree that she would produce it.

She was touched by him. She had a sense that his was not merely a worthy talent but a great one. In addition, as someone who had known nothing but affluence her whole life, she was touched by his poverty. At one point just as they were going into production, he told Ms. Selznick that he would waive all rights and royalties to the play if he could just be guaranteed $250 a week for the rest of his life. But she told him she was certain that greater material wealth lay ahead for him.

For Ms. Selznick the primary job, and it quite terrified her, was to raise the $100,000 required to put on the play. Then she and Williams had to agree on a director. Williams wanted Kazan—he had seen Kazan's production of Arthur Miller's *All My Sons*. Kazan was uncertain whether to accept. In desperation, Williams wrote him a letter, pleading with him to take it: "I am sure that you must have had reservations about the script. I will try to clarify my intentions in this play. I think its best quality is its authenticity or its fidelity to life. There are no 'good' or 'bad' people. Some are a little better or a little worse, but all are activated more by misunderstanding than malice. A blindness to what is going on in each other's hearts. Stanley sees Blanche not as a desperate, driven creature backed into a corner to make a last desperate stand—but as a calculating bitch with 'round heels.' . . . Nobody sees anybody truly but all through the flaws of their own egos. That is the way we all see each other in life. Vanity, fear, desire, competition—all such distortions within our own egos—condition our vision of those in relation to us. Add to those distortions in our *own* egos the corresponding distortions in the egos of *others* and you see how cloudy the glass must become through which we look at each other. That's how it is in all living relationships except when there is that rare case of two people who love intensely enough to burn through all those layers of opacity and see each other's naked hearts. Such cases seem purely theoretical to me."

That clinched it for Kazan. When he took the job, he was thirty-seven and just beginning to emerge as the most important young director in America, first in the theater and later in movies. With *Streetcar*'s success, he became a force on both Broadway and in Hollywood, the director that everyone wanted for any important production—especially one that challenged conventional morality. Tennessee Williams had been absolutely right. Kazan knew how to turn his poetic images into powerful drama. He could, his wife once said, make a hit out of the telephone book.

Like Williams, Elia Kazan was driven by his work and the need to excel, to avenge old slights. His autobiography, published in 1988, is a conquest-by-conquest record of his professional and personal success. It is an odd book, at once exceptionally honest and self-revealing and at the same time a bit like a locker-room boast in its many tales of sexual conquests. He had no use for the conventions of American life; he was the outsider, the son of Greek immigrants. Of his home and its rules, only the address was American. "I come from a family of voyagers; my uncle and my father were transients, less from disposition than from necessity," he wrote. "They were slippery, had to be. Raised in a world of memories, they grew up distrustful of fate. 'Don't worry,' my uncle used to say, 'everything will turn out bad.' . . . This instinct was in me at birth."

Kazan and Williams, as different in manner and sexuality as two men could be, shared a sense of being different, Kazan thought. They got on so well, so naturally, because they were both, in Kazan's phrase, "freaks." What, after all, could be freakier in 1950s America than being the son of George Kazan—Yiorgos Kazanjioglou—who was not merely a Greek immigrant but a Greek immigrant who had grown up in Turkey, where Greeks had learned to dissemble as a way of life. George Kazan was a man of the old world, wary of the corruptions of the new. In the old world, women were bound by prearranged marriages. Mrs. Kazan had pleased her husband on their first meeting in Turkey by not suggesting, as so many of his friends had, that he shave off his mustache. "It's fine, leave it," she had said. "That's the first thing I remember about her," he later told his son. In his world the men set the rules; they worked, came home, were served dinner, and then played cards with their friends. When one of George Kazan's American friends came to their home and made a remark about how nice Mrs. Kazan was, George answered, "She's all right, minds her business."

Yet early on, Athena Kazan entered into a conspiracy against her husband. The conspiracy was dangerous, for it involved the most sacred thing imaginable: the disposition of a male heir. Athena Kazan had made the journey to the new world, and while she might not have been able to save herself and determine her own fate, she intended to bestow upon her son some of the freedom for which the new world was famous. Her husband was preoccupied with business, so she took care of the schooling, sending her son to a Montessori school, which was not, so to speak, in the Turkish-Greek tradition. Then Mrs. Kazan joined with a high school teacher in a secret plan to send young Elia to Williams, a patrician liberal arts college, rather than a business school as her husband clearly preferred. Not a word of this was said to George Kazan, and in time Elia applied to Williams and was accepted. When Athena Kazan broke the news to George, he hit her in the mouth and knocked her to the ground. When Kazan came back from college for the first time during his freshman year, he found that his parents had begun to sleep in

separate bedrooms—a situation provoked by his father's view that
his wife had betrayed him in the matter of Elia's education. When
Elia described his courses, most of them in the humanities, George
asked, "Why you not learning something useful?" His father, Elia
knew, had probably given up on him long before. Once, working for
his father during the summer, he had tried to fold a rug instead of
rolling it. An uncle had yelled over to his father, "Hey, George, you
got a dead one here!" The two worlds had diverged. He was no
longer a Greek. The question was whether he was yet an American.

Williams College, in Williamstown, Massachusetts, was not a
particularly hospitable place for the son of immigrants in those days.
In the late twenties, it was a citadel of the American upper class. To
Kazan everyone seemed tall, blond, and socially graceful. He was
short, dark, and socially inept. Never before had he felt his foreign-
ness so intensely nor had he ever felt so vulnerable because of it. He
loved to watch the football players at games and at practice, and he
even ate at a particular local short-order restaurant where they hung
out so he could sit in the corner and admire them: "How confident
they were, how glamorous, how awesome. They looked as if their
glory would never die." (Years later he returned to Williams as the
famous movie director and found that the former football players
now sought him out. One even confided how empty his life had been,
and Kazan found that vengeance was his.)

At first he mistakenly believed he would be asked to join a
fraternity. He was soon disabused of that notion; he would enter a
fraternity the hard way, as someone who waited on tables. He found
himself virtually friendless, and it seemed to him that days would
pass without anyone talking to him. On the Williams campus, he
deliberately chose routes that would spare him from meeting people.
His only close relationship seemed to be with his mother, who dutifully shipped him his clean laundry once a week. He left Williams
feeling farther than ever from the American dream: "Every time I
saw privilege from then on I wanted to tear it down or possess it,"
he wrote.

He went from college to Yale Drama School. It was an unlikely
move; he had not been that interested in the theater previously, but
one of his few friends from Williams, a young man named Alan
Baxter, was going there. For lack of anything better to do, Kazan,
who wanted no part of the traditional American business world,
decided to try it too. It was a decision expedited by the fact that Yale
had a job for someone who could operate a dishwashing machine.
When George Kazan heard of this latest impractical decision on the

part of his hopeless son, he was appalled. "Four years over in Massachusetts there, looks like he learn nothing," he told Elia's brother.

At Yale he wanted to be an actor, but his looks were against him. But he was ambitious, and he quickly became skilled in the areas disdained by more affluent students—stagecraft and production. He could make things and fix things, do lighting, build sets. That was to be his trademark in the early days, and from it came his nickname, Gadge, is a diminutive of Gadget. His role as an outsider made him attractive in a way he did not understand; he brought a certain energy and purpose to everything he did. As a young man, noted his friend Clifford Odets, he seemed like a hungry wolf. He was never bored; he took nothing for granted. He married Molly Day Thacher, a Yale classmate, who appreciated the energy he brought to living; she thought him gifted and bedeviled. From a patrician family, she became his bridge to mainstream America. "Very high class," George Kazan said of her in a somewhat dubious voice. "Looks like society."

Not surprisingly, Kazan utterly rejected the prevailing vision of theater as a pleasant, mannerly place where handsome upper-class types acted out drawing-room plays. It bore no relevance to the world he saw around him. He signed on with the experimental Group Theater, a left-wing assemblage of talented, egocentric people in New York City who were trying at once to build a new theater and a new left-wing America at the same time. The dominant figures there were Harold Clurman, the great director-critic and Lee Strasberg, one of the foremost drama teachers of his time. When Kazan went for his audition with Clurman and Strasberg, the latter had turned to him and asked, "Tell us what you want." "What I want is your job," Kazan answered. On ego alone Kazan qualified. The Group was nothing if not a place for ideas and adventure. By instinct, the people there were rebellious; they were out to break rules.

At the height of the Depression and the height of his own personal dissidence, Kazan also joined the Communist party for a brief time. But he was much too iconoclastic and original to be a dutiful member of the Party. He saw himself as a working-class radical whereas in truth, as he later noted, no one could have been more middle-class. Work was, he later wrote, his drug. "It held me together. It kept me together. When I wasn't working I didn't know who I was or what I was supposed to do. . . . Work made it impossible for me to dwell on my personal problems. I forgot them. As soon as I stop work, my uncertainties swarm back—even now with all the flattery I've received."

"All they want is a stagehand," complained Molly Kazan of the Group leadership. "Okay, I'll be a stagehand," he answered. Eventually, he began to get small roles. Again he ran into a ceiling because of his looks. "What I could play successfully was a man-boy, angry at the world and turned to violence," he noted.

Then Robert Ardrey, a young playwright in the Group, asked him to direct his play. Kazan had already begun to develop his own vision of what theater should be. The professionals at Yale were inadequate because they came to the theater without vision and emotion; the people at the Group were inadequate because they were all emotion but no craft. "I," he wrote, "could bring these two opposite and often conflicting traditions together, as they should be brought together."

Of his talent there was no doubt from the start. He had a genius for bringing drama out on the page, for finding the emotion in words. Because he was the outsider, he saw challenge and conflict where others did not. When World War Two started, there were fewer directors around. Soon he was being asked to handle increasingly important plays. In December 1941 he was offered Thornton Wilder's new play, *The Skin of Our Teeth*.

The play featured Fredric March, Florence Eldridge March, Tallulah Bankhead, and a young actor named Montgomery Clift. Characteristically, Ms. Bankhead was a source of constant dissidence. She unrelentingly tried to provoke Kazan. Finally, he blew. "I won't take any more of your shit," he told her. Later he was sure that was the making of him as a director. The play was a great success; now even Hollywood wanted him. He had won. He had created his own version of the American dream.

When he started on *Streetcar,* he had thought of conventional casting and offered the part to John Garfield, the quintessential craggy but tough good guy. But Garfield set down terms that were impossible: He would play Kowalski for only four months, and he demanded a guarantee of the movie role. Kazan thought it was Garfield's somewhat polite Hollywood way of saying he did not want the part. That brought him to Brando. Kazan had used him for a bit part in a play called *Truckline* and had witnessed the raw sexual energy he projected onstage. He began thinking of him as Stanley. But a traditional audition was out of the question. Kazan already knew Brando well enough to know that he needed time to absorb the essence of a role. He had a bad reputation for auditions, where he mumbled and strayed emotionally. An additional problem was that Brando, at twenty-four, was significantly younger than the Stanley that Williams had envisioned. Since Brando disdained telephone ownership, Kazan had to send out word through the Village underground that he was searching for the actor. Then he passed him the script. At first Brando was uneasy with it; he hated the Kowalski character—it was just the kind of male brutality that offended him. He tried to call Kazan and tell him he didn't want the part, but he was unable to get through. But there was a power to the play that was irresistible. Finally, they got in touch. "Well, what is it, yes or no?" Kazan asked. Yes, said Brando. Kazan lent him twenty dollars and sent him to do an informal reading for Williams, then in Provincetown.

Three days later Kazan called Williams to see what he thought of the young actor he had sent up. "What actor?" Williams asked. Brando had not yet shown up. He had used the borrowed money to eat and, in the company of a girlfriend, was hitchhiking up. He finally arrived in the middle of a crisis. Williams's plumbing was clogged, the toilet was overflowing, and the electricity was out because a fuse had blown. In came Brando, wearing blue jeans and a T-shirt. Men in blue jeans and T-shirts knew how to fix toilets (or at least they did back then), and he unclogged the plumbing and put in a new fuse. "He was about the best-looking young man I had ever seen with one or two exceptions," Williams later wrote. Having performed like Stanley Kowalski in real life, Brando thereupon gave an exceptional reading as well; Williams was in awe. His friend Margo Jones, a Dallas producer, yelled, "Get Kazan on the phone right away! This is the greatest reading I've ever heard—in or outside of Texas!" A day later Williams called Kazan, so enthusiastic as to be "near hysteria." Brando was in. Back in New York City, he tried to insult Mrs. Selznick by putting down the world of Hollywood. But she remained immune to his provocation, and she signed him to the part at $550 a week.

Brando was, of course, always a great original. He was the new American rebel, rebelling not against physical hardship or harsh economic conditions but rather against conventionality and the boredom engendered by his boyhood in the Midwest and a strict father. Marlon Brando, Sr., a limestone salesman in Omaha, was a man much given to setting strict rules at home. Yet when he himself was off on sales trips in Chicago or elsewhere, he strayed from his puritan ethic to drink and chase women. Brando's mother, Dodie, was talented, charming, and almost fey—a would-be actress who was a leader in local amateur theater. Caught in this unsuccessful marriage, she found her own manner of freedom in alcohol. Later when

Dodie would visit her children in New York, they would hide her liquor. But she always foiled them by sneaking the bottles under the bath towels they had dropped on the bathroom floor. This, she said, was the perfect hiding place: "One thing I know, none of my children ever picks up the towels from the bathroom floor." The respective influence of the parents on their three children can be judged by the fact that Marlon became an actor, Jocelyn became an actress, and Frances became a painter. No one went into conventional careers in business or sales.

Brando's resentment of his father's authoritarianism would stay with him throughout his life. "I hate ultimatums," Marlon would say later. That would be obvious in his work and his career from the start. At school he appeared in a number of plays, and in 1943, at the age of nineteen, he came to New York City. He intended to be an actor. Though most young men his age were eager to have their chance to fight against Germany and Japan, Brando was definitely not: "I watched the war in the Trans-Lux at 42nd and Broadway," he told friends. To him the real war was not that taking place overseas, but the one that took place in so many homes, between generations.

If a counterculture existed anywhere in America in the forties and early fifties, it was in Greenwich Village. Here were Italian restaurants with candles stuck in old Chianti bottles, coffeehouses with poets and artists, small theaters and clubs that featured modern jazz; here were interracial couples and homosexual and lesbian couples living rather openly. The battle cry was the rejection of commercialism and materialism. In one of his first important films, *The Wild One,* Brando plays a member of a motorcycle club. "What are you rebelling against?" asks a girl in the small town. "Waddya got?" asks Brando.

He loved the Village from the start. It was everything that Omaha was not. Here he could get by in T-shirts, blue jeans, ragged sneakers and, if necessary, a leather jacket. Even for the Village he lived like a gypsy, moving around constantly, rarely having an apartment of his own. Anyone who wanted him would have to find him. There were always women, but his relationships were casual, a forerunner of the kind that would flower in the sixties. If by chance he had money, he spent it or gave it away. If he didn't have money, he borrowed it. Material possessions seemed to mean little to him. He seemed to covet something different: personal freedom. That meant, for him, a lack of personal possessions and obligations. His was not so much a political rebellion as a restlessness with the conventions of the American middle class. He was suspicious of the world around him and broke the rules at every opportunity. Years later, he liked to boast that he had been expelled from every school he ever attended. He scorned authority not so much because he wanted to replace it with something else, but because he instinctively disliked authority.

But at this point in his career there was already a sense that he was going to make it. From the very start he got work, more, it sometimes seemed, than he needed or wanted. "This puppy thing will be the best actor on the American stage," Stella Adler, the actress and teacher, said. Unlike most young actors, he quickly found a first-rate agent, Edith Van Cleve. A year after arriving, he was working in a play called *Hannele's Way to Heaven,* and shortly after that he got a good part in *I Remember Mama.*

Yet he was oddly ambivalent about his talent and the search for success. He hated auditions, for they meant pleasing a person in authority. He was at once ambitious and not ambitious. He was almost deliberately provocative at readings—it was almost as if he tried to read as poorly as he could, and sometimes he would even join his friends after a reading and boast of how badly he had done.

The ambivalence came from both fear of failure and fear of success, which might force him toward a place in a world he was already rejecting and present him with too many choices. Success led inevitably to materialism, he was sure, and that was not something he sought. Thus he was the first in a tradition of new American rebels that would include James Dean and Jack Kerouac. Essentially, the dissidence of Brando and the other rebels was social rather than political. By staying outside traditional straight society, they projected how much they were misunderstood. Implicit in this was the need for more love. "Marlon," said Truman Capote, who wrote knowingly about him, "always turns against whatever he's working on. Some element of it. Either the script or the director or somebody in the cast. Not because of something very rational—just because it seems to comfort him to be dissatisfied, let steam off about something. It's part of his pattern . . ."

Brando brought a new dimension to narcissism as well: The rules did not please him, so he reinvented a society in which he set the rules. Inevitably, it all led to becoming only more self-obsessed. In his mind he owed nothing to anyone, and accepted no larger obligations. At one point Robert Mitchum was asked on a talk show if he had ever made a movie with Brando. He answered mordantly, "Brando's never made a movie with anyone."

On some level, though, he knew it all worked for him, and his provocative behavior made his looks and sexuality seem even more remarkable and powerful. The overall effect assured that he was going to get what he wanted, if perhaps, in his own mind, for the wrong reason. As such he was disrespectful of both the very charisma that enabled him to succeed so easily and of those upon whom it worked so readily. He was like a beautiful girl who wants to be known for her intelligence but instead is known for her looks.

Yet no one doubted his talent and appeal, which was due to an almost perfect balance between toughness and angelic beauty. His powerful muscular physique belied an oddly delicate sensibility. Self-obsessed he might be, but he was aware of the foibles of others, and he was a brilliant mimic. Stella Adler once said of him, "Marlon never really had to learn to act. He knew. Right from the start he was a universal actor. Nothing human was foreign to him." Indeed, she later said of him, "I taught him nothing. I opened up possibilities of thinking, feeling, experience, and I opened these doors, he walked right through. He never needed me after that. . . . He lives the life of an actor, twenty-four hours a day. If he is talking to you he will absorb everything about you, your smile, the way your teeth grow. His style is the perfect marriage of intuition and intelligence." For the New York theater world he was a breath of fresh air, the man who broke the rules and thereby achieved a more natural kind of acting. Not everyone, of course, understood. When Stella Adler told Clifford Odets of Brando's genius, he was completely puzzled. "He looks to me like a kid who delivers groceries."

Streetcar opened in December 1947. The confluence of these three outsiders reflected a changing America and changing sensibilities. It represented a new and more tolerant social order, where words and images once banned were now permitted. Ten years earlier America might not have been ready for Williams's plays, an immigrant like Kazan might not have been able to have gone to the best colleges and then found his way to Broadway, and Brando might have been rejected by those running the theater. But now they had all arrived at the same place at the same time.

The synergy of talents was extraordinary. Each strengthened and amplified the others' talent: Williams without Kazan might have been too poetic and not sufficiently dramatic; Kazan without Williams might have been too political and raw; and both without Brando might have lacked the star who brought their work to the very center of American cultural life, first in the theater and even more remarkably in Hollywood, which reached far beyond a narrow cultural elite. Each of the three was in his own way rebelling against the puritanism of American life and the conventional quality of the American dream. Thanks to Hollywood, they could now bring it to an audience of millions.

TWENTY

Among those deeply moved by *A Streetcar Named Desire* was a college professor from Bloomington, Indiana. His name was Alfred Kinsey, and in 1950, when he first saw it on Broadway, he had already published the first of his two pioneering works, *Sexual Behavior in the Human Male,* in fact popularly known as the Kinsey Report. Kinsey knew immediately that he and Williams were, in different ways, doing something very similar—they were tearing away the facade that Americans used to hide their sexual selves. As a result of his work, Kinsey was both fascinated and troubled by the vast difference between American sexual behavior the society wanted to believe existed and American sexual practices as they actually existed; in other words it was one thing to do it, but it was quite another thing to admit doing it. For example, at least 80 percent of successful businessmen, his interviews had shown, had

had extramarital affairs. "God," he noted. "What a gap between social front and reality!"

Therefore, his response to Williams's play was not merely emotional. He proposed that he and Williams get together, and the two began a steady correspondence. "As you may know we are making an extensive study of the erotic element in the arts," he wrote Williams. "This covers painting, music, writing, the stage, etc. One of the plays we have studied in some detail has been your *Streetcar*. We have been fortunate enough to obtain histories from a high proportion of the actors and two of the companies which have put on the play and it has made it possible to correlate their acting with their sexual backgrounds. There are a great many points in the play which we should like to discuss with the author to find out his original ideas and intentions. This is one of the reasons why we should get together." Eventually, Kinsey and Williams became good friends. Though he was in many way the very embodiment of the Middle American square, Kinsey had no problem with Williams's homosexuality. He was immensely tolerant of all sexual variations, but he was prudish enough to keep the interviews that his staff did on homosexuality under a file that was known as the H-histories, and he could not bring himself to actually write the word *homosexual*.

Alfred Kinsey was no bohemian. He lived in the Midwest, had married the first woman he ever dated, and stayed married to her for his entire life. Almost surely, his close friends thought, he had had no extramarital affairs. Because he was an entomologist and loved to collect bugs, he and his bride went camping on their honeymoon. In his classes at the University of Indiana he always sported a bow tie and a crew cut. He drove the same old Buick for most of his lifetime and was immensely proud of the fact that he had more than 100,000 miles on it. On Sundays, he and his wife invited faculty and graduate-student friends to their home to listen to records of classical music. There, the Kinseys served such homey desserts as persimmon pudding. They took these evenings very seriously—Kinsey was immensely proud of his record collection. When the wife of one faculty member suggested that they play some boogie-woogie, the couple was never invited back.

His values were old-fashioned, and he did not like debt. His house was the only thing he had not paid hard cash for. He bought it with a small down payment and took on a mortgage of $3,500. He boasted at the time of the publication of his landmark book, *Sexual Behavior in the Human Male,* that he had never been paid more than $5,000 from the University of Indiana; indeed, doing his income tax at the very last minute one year, he could not remember what his salary was (this was before W-2 forms) and he had to wake the head of his department to find out. He was extremely careful about money and almost everything else. He once gave some wonderfully Victorian advice to Ralph Voris, a younger colleague who was about to get married: "Years ago my banker . . . gave me this advice about investments and savings. Diversify. Buy life insurance and annuities. Pay for your home. Have a thousand dollars in cash or instantly convertible securities on which you can draw for emergencies. After each and every one of these items has been achieved (in order), put the next few thousand in sound 3% investments (do not look for bigger returns; if buying stocks or bonds, put it all in investment trust shares which give the small investor the same diversification that the big investor enjoys). For you and Geraldine I should hesitate to advise any serious inroads on your savings until you are well along on the above program." He once told a colleague, Wardell Pomeroy, to drive back from New York at 35 MPH with some large models showing the reproductive process: "Anything faster than that is not safe for such a heavy load. You cannot stop in a hurry and you dare not bounce on roads that have been damaged by winter freezes." The mother superior, Pomeroy called him.

Kinsey did not smoke and he rarely drank. Relatively late in his career he decided to try smoking, since it might make him more like the men he was interviewing and help put them at their ease. Try as he might, he never quite got it right and his assistants finally suggested that the prop was hurting rather than helping him. When he drank it was much the same. After his death, Wardell Pomeroy wrote, "To see him bringing in a tray of sweet liqueurs before dinner was a wry and happy reminder that Alfred Charles Kinsey, the genius, the world figure, was a simple and unsophisticated man in the true sense of that word."

As a boy he was seriously religious and he walked to church with his family every Sunday, though as he grew older he distanced himself from organized religion and a belief in God. Nonetheless, his children were made to go regularly to Sunday School. Still, the scientist in him was always present. Once his son Bruce pointed to a flower and told his father that God had made it. "Now, Bruce," Kinsey said. "Where did that flower really come from?" "From a seed," Bruce Kinsey admitted. Kinsey was driven by curiosity, not prejudice. He rejected those who came to him with preconceptions. To one young man who applied for a job as a researcher, he said, "Well, you have just said that premarital intercourse might lead to

THE FIFTIES / 275

later difficulties in marriage, that extramarital relations would break up a marriage, that homosexuality is abnormal, and intercourse with animals is ludicrous. Apparently you have all the answers. Why do you want to do research?"

His greatest passion was his work. He approached it with an intensity that was rooted in the Calvinist zeal of his forefathers. As a young man he had gone on vacation with friends but complained later that the time might have been better spent working, and in fact he generally worked every day of the year except Christmas Day. He had always been, his biographer Pomeroy shrewdly noted, a *collector*. As a boy he collected stamps, but it was the only collection he ever made that was not designed to be useful. Sickly as a child from rheumatic fever, he had not been able to play among his peers; instead, he became a student of nature. He wrote his first book in his teens, a small monograph entitled, "What Do Birds Do When It Rains?" By the time he was in college at Bowdoin, he had come to love collecting plants and animals; the Bowdoin College yearbook notes that "on entering his room one never knows whether Mr. Kinsey or a large able-bodied snake is going to greet him."

As a graduate student at Harvard, he won a fellowship that allowed him to travel around the country. He later wrote a high school teacher of the pleasure of that fellowship: "In all, counting the summertime that I spent at either end of the trip, I got fifteen solid months out-of-doors! Think of that—for a life! I am more and more satisfied that no other occupation in the world could give me the pleasure that this job of bug-hunting is giving. I shall never cease to thank you for leading me into it!" From the start he had proven to be a first-rate scholar, and he never failed to see the beauty in plants and in animals. Earle March, a San Francisco gynecologist, once spoke of his rare ability to "look through the ugliness to something lovely beyond. I often," Marsh added, "thought about him as an athlete of the spirit."

He seemed by this time to be the least likely candidate to become one of the most controversial figures of his generation. During the early forties he published *Edible Wild Plants of North America,* which was voted the most important book of the year by the trustees of the Massachusetts Horticultural Society. He was a highly respected professor of zoology in a good department at Indiana University. Esteemed by his colleagues for his world-class collection of gall wasps, he was also popular with his students, a kind and humane teacher who was always generous with his time.

Then, in 1938, a group of his students came to him and asked questions about marriage. He was touched by their innocence. At first he refrained from answering, fearing he knew too little. He went out and read everything he could on the subject and was appalled by the inadequate available material—both in quantity and quality. Some of the students petitioned the university to start a course on sexuality and marriage. From the start it was Kinsey's course. He was one of eight faculty members who taught it and he gave three of the basic lectures. The course was a huge success. It soon became his obsession. Clara Kinsey was known on occasion to tell friends, "I hardly see him at night anymore since he took up sex." What was probably true, some of his colleagues thought, was that he was already a little restless with the study of insects and was looking for a larger challenge—a new area in which to start collecting.

When he began his studies of human sexuality, one of his oldest friends, Edgar Anderson, by then the director of Missouri Botanical Garden in St. Louis, wrote him: "It was heartwarming to see you settling down into what I suppose will be your real life work. One would never have believed that all sides of you could have found a project big enough to need them all. I was amused to see how the Scotch Presbyterian reformer in you had finally got together with the scientific fanatic with his zeal for masses of neat data in orderly boxes and drawers. The monographer Kinsey, the naturalist Kinsey, and the camp counsellor Kinsey all rolling into one at last and going full steam ahead. Well, I am glad to have a seat for the performance. It's great to have it done, and great to know that you are doing it."

He began by taking sexual histories of his students. He conducted the interviews in his tiny office, locked the door, and sent his assistant elsewhere. The enrollment for the class grew every year, and first juniors and then freshmen and sophomores were allowed in. Soon four hundred students were signing up for it. But more and more his heart was in the research. By 1939 he wrote to a friend that the interviews were "a scientific gold mine." Soon he was taking the sexual histories of not only his students but traveling out of town on weekends, at first to Chicago and then to other communities in the Midwest, to find additional subjects. As the project took an increasing amount of his time, there was an inevitable conservative reaction against him in Indiana. Complaints began to come in, from parents and local ministers. One of his early critics, Professor Thurman Rice of the University of Indiana Medical School, was enraged because Kinsey had not, in the course of teaching, denounced premarital sex.

In 1940 Herman Wells, the president of Indiana University, who was largely sympathetic to Kinsey and his work, called in Kinsey and, citing complaints from local ministers, told him that he would have to make a choice: He could either teach the course or take his histories, but he could not do both. Wells assumed, since he loved the course, that he would give up the case histories. Kinsey, sure that his critics feared the research more than the sex-education course, resigned from the course. Those who thought he would do otherwise, he noted, "do not know me." From then on, he devoted himself exclusively to his research.

The study of American sexual habits was a delicate business. Kinsey wanted a certain bland neutrality to his researchers. He did not want them to wear beards and mustaches, and he worried when one of them looked too young and therefore might not inspire the proper amount of confidence. Though he was a generous, abidingly tolerant man, he did not hire Jews or blacks or those with names that were not distinctly Anglo-Saxon. He was sensitive to the prejudices of the time and wanted his interviewers to cause no distractions among the subjects from whom they were eliciting such sensitive information.

During the forties, while much of the rest of the country was going off to war, Alfred Kinsey and a handful of assistants set off to interview as many men and women as they could on their sexual habits. At first they had limited resources: Kinsey used part of his own small salary to hire others. The war made things harder, and he worried whether he could get enough miles from the thinning treads of his tires ("I am well fixed for tires right now. I think I can get perhaps 30 or 40,000 out of what I have, but if retreads are not available then, my traveling after case histories will be at an end . . .").

In 1941 he got his first grant from a foundation, for $1,600; in 1943 he received his first grant from the Medical Sciences Division of the Rockefeller Foundation, a gift of $23,000; by 1947 that figure was $40,000. The foundation thereby became the principal financial backer of his studies. By 1947 he was preparing to publish the first book of his results—a simple report on the human animal studied in one of its highest-priority biologic acts. His conclusions do not seem startling today: that healthy sex led to a healthy marriage; that there was more extramarital sex on the part of both men and women than they wanted to admit; that petting and premarital sex tended to produce better marriages; that masturbation did not cause mental problems as superstition held; that there was more homosexuality than people wanted to admit.

Herman Wells, the president of Indiana University, had made a

278 / DAVID HALBERSTAM

few minor requests of him: He asked Kinsey not to publish during the sixty-one days that the Indiana legislature was in session—or for that matter immediately before it convened—and he asked him to use a medical publisher, in order to minimize sensationalism. Kinsey chose W. B. Saunders, an old-line firm in Philadelphia. The original printing was slated for 10,000, but as prepublication interest grew, Saunders increased it to 25,000. The book cost $6.50, which made it expensive for those days, had 804 pages, and weighed three pounds. Kinsey had received no advance against royalties from the publisher, and whatever money he made, he turned back to his own think tank, which by then was known as the Institute for Sex Research of Indiana University.

Though he continued to sign himself on letters "Alfred Kinsey, professor of zoology," his days as a mere professor were behind him. His name was suddenly a household word; everyone knew of him as the sex doctor. There was a famous Peter Arno cartoon in *The New Yorker* showing a woman reading the report and asking her husband with a horrified expression, "Is there a *Mrs.* Kinsey?" Within ten days of the book's release, the publisher had to order a sixth printing, making a phenomenal 185,000 copies in print. To the astonishment of everyone, particularly Kinsey, the book roared up the best-seller lists, a fact somewhat embarrassing to *The New York Times,* which at first neither accepted advertising for Kinsey's book nor reviewed it. The early critical response was good. The first reviews saw his samples adequate, his scientific judgments modest, his tone serious. Polls taken of ordinary Americans showed that not only did they agree with his evidence, but they believed such studies were helpful.

Then his critics weighed in. They furiously disagreed with almost everything: his figures on premarital sex; his figures on extramarital sex; his figures on homosexuality; above all, his failure to condemn what he had found. Not only had he angered the traditional conservative bastions of social mores—the Protestant churches on the right and the Catholic Church—but to his surprise, he had enraged the most powerful voices in the liberal Protestant clergy as well. Henry Pitney Van Dusen, the head of Union Theological Seminary, and Reinhold Niebuhr attacked. Harry Emerson Fosdick, the head of Riverside Church and the brother of the head of the Rockefeller Foundation, complained that the advertising for the book was not sufficiently sedate. Harold Dodds, the president of Princeton, said, "Perhaps the undergraduate newspaper that likened the report to the work of small boys writing dirty words on fences touched a more profound scientific truth than is revealed in the surfeit of rather trivial graphs with which the reports are loaded." By trying to study our sexual patterns, he was accused instead of trying to lower our moral standards.

Kinsey was at first stunned, then angered by the response, but he was never embittered. He was appalled by the failure of other scientists and doctors to come to his defense. He sensed in certain cases that the lack of support stemmed from professional jealousy. In time, as the attacks grew more strident, he did not hesitate, when talking with friends, to compare himself with such scientists as Galileo, who had been pilloried in the past for challenging the myths and the ignorance of their age. What surprised him most was the absence of scientific standards in most of the assaults. His critics were, he noted, merely "exposing their emotional (not their scientific) selves in their attacks."

Soon his friends began to worry about his reaction to criticism. It was as if even the mildest dissent in a review bothered him—someone either supported him completely or had become an enemy. But he held back from revealing his dismay in public. He treated most critics the way he treated one would-be heckler at a lecture at Berkeley. It was a marvelous moment: Several thousand people had turned out to hear him. As he reached the most delicate part of his lecture—that a person might need a sexual outlet as many as seven times a week—a long, low wolf-whistle came from someone in the audience. "And then there are some whose outlet is as low as that of the man who just whistled." The audience roared with laughter. It was his last interruption of the night.

The attacks wounded Kinsey, yet he refused to show it in public. Besides, there was a second book to finish. His biggest fear was that he might lose his key source of support, the Rockefeller Foundation. Unfortunately, Henry Pitney Van Dusen was not just the head of Union Theological, he was a member of the Rockefeller Foundation board. It seemed to Kinsey that a systematic attack was being aimed toward the Rockefeller people, designed to get them to cut off their support to him.

At first the Rockefeller Foundation stood firm. The criticism from Van Dusen, Fosdick, and the others had not damaged Kinsey's standing there. Alan Gregg, who was in effect Kinsey's man at the foundation, congratulated Kinsey for handling himself so well in the face of such venomous criticism. But soon Gregg's tone began to change, reflecting, Kinsey was sure, mounting pressures on the foundation. Gregg started suggesting that Kinsey show more statistical evidence in the next volume. Soon there were warnings from Gregg that it might be harder than he had expected to sustain the funding. Perhaps the royalties from the book could pay for the research, Gregg suggested. To Kinsey that was a spurious argument. If the Rockefeller people wavered in their support or cut it back, Kinsey wrote Gregg, it would be the equivalent of a vote of no confidence in him. There was only a limited amount the royalties could do in terms of support. If anything, Kinsey wanted to expand the budget—there was always so much more to do.

The trouble, Kinsey learned, was the new head of the Rockefeller Foundation, Dean Rusk. Rusk had come over after serving as assistant secretary of state for Far Eastern affairs. Cautious to a fault, wary of the power of conservatives in Congress, he was not anxious to take serious political risks on behalf of something that must have seemed as peripheral to him as Kinsey's sex research. B. Carroll Reece, a conservative Republican from Tennessee, was threatening to investigate the Rockefeller Foundation and one of the reasons was the Kinsey report. Kinsey sensed that Rusk was quietly distancing himself from the institute.

The second book, *Sexual Behavior in the Human Female,* was published in the fall of 1953. Kinsey was well aware that it was even more explosive than the first—he was, after all, discussing wives, mothers, and daughters. As a precaution, Kinsey invited journalists to come to Bloomington for several days to have the data explained and interpreted. Ed Murrow asked Kinsey to come on his television program *Person to Person.* Kinsey turned him down, noting in a letter to *Edgar* R. Murrow that it was the policy of the institute not to appear on radio, television, or in the movies.

Like the first book, it was a sensation. The first printing was 25,000 copies. Within ten days the publishers were in their sixth printing, for a total of 185,000. It would eventually sell some 250,000 copies. Again, the initial reception was essentially positive: Some of the magazine reporting was thoughtful. Then the firestorm began again: "It is impossible to estimate the damage this book will do to the already deteriorating morals of America," Billy Graham pronounced. The worst thing about the report, Van Dusen said, was not Kinsey's facts, if they were indeed trustworthy, but that they revealed "a prevailing degradation in American morality approximating the worst decadence of the Roman Empire. The most disturbing thing is the absence of a spontaneous ethical revulsion from the premises of the study and the inability on the part of the readers to put their fingers on the falsity of its premises. For the presuppositions of the Kinsey Report are strictly animalistic . . ." Again Kinsey was disheartened: "I am still uncertain what the basic reason for the bitter attack on us may be. The attack is evidently much more intense with this publication of the Female. Their arguments become absurd when they attempt to find specific flaws in the book and basically I think they are attacking on general principles."

The new book was the final straw for the Rockefeller Foundation. In November 1953, Kinsey's supporters there made passionate presentations on his behalf. His work, they argued, was among the most important the foundation was sponsoring. They put in a request for $80,000. An unsympathetic Rusk rejected it. It was a shattering moment. Kinsey wrote a note to Rusk pleading with him to come out to Bloomington and see what they were doing and telling of how well things looked for the future. Later, in another letter to Rusk, he noted, "To have fifteen years of accumulated data in this area fail to reach publication would constitute an indictment of the Institute, its sponsors, and all others who have contributed time and material resources to the work." Rusk was unmoved by his pleas. Instead, the Rockefeller Foundation made a grant of $520,000 to Union Theological Seminary. Kinsey was devastated. "Damn that Rusk!" he would say from time to time.

Kinsey merely redoubled his efforts. If he had been a workaholic before, now there was a manic quality to his work. His friends began to worry about his health. His friend Edgar Anderson warned him that the institute needed him for another decade, not just another year or two. Anderson pleaded with him to see a doctor and work out what he called "a rational way of living under the circumstances." He suffered from insomnia, began to take sleeping pills, and started showing up groggy at work in the morning. The problems with his heart grew more serious. On several occasions he was hospitalized, and by the middle of 1956 he was forced to stay home and rest. In the summer of 1956 he conducted interviews number 7,984 and 7,985. "It is a shame, " he noted, "that there comes a time that you have to work up data and publish it instead of continuing gathering. Frankly, I very much enjoy the gathering." He was ever the scientist, delighted by discovery. On August 25, 1956, he died, at the age of sixty-two.

TWENTY-ONE

The revolution in birth control had begun in 1950, when Margaret Sanger, the great warrior for that cause, renewed an old friendship with a formidable dowager named Katharine McCormick. Much of both women's lives had been about fighting to advance the cause of sex education and birth control and fighting against the Catholic Church, which sought to stop such efforts. For most of her life Sanger had been on the radical fringe, constantly living with harassment and the threat of jail. But after forty years of leading the struggle, her ideas on sexual hygiene and population control had moved so much into the mainstream of social opinion that she was even featured in *Reader's Digest,* the bible of middle-class America. At this point in her life she was anxious to launch an all-out scientific drive for her greatest dream: a birth-control pill. What she needed, first of all, was a wealthy contributor, and that was where Katherine McCormick came in.

There was nothing conventional about Sanger's life. As a mother she was, at best, erratic and distant—when her son Grant was ten he wrote from boarding school, asking what to do at Thanksgiving, since all the other boys were going home. He should, she answered, come home to Greenwich Village and Daisy, the maid, would cook him a fine dinner. She had little time for such minor intrusions as children and holiday dinners. She was an American samurai, and she had spent her life on a wartime footing. Her passion was the right of women to control their own bodies. Her principal enemies (and she had many enemies) were the Catholic Church and clergy, because in her struggle to inform women about birth control, they did much to prevent her from reaching the urban poor, who were often Catholic.

She came honestly by radicalism. She was born in Corning, New York, in 1879, one of eleven children; her mother suffered from tuberculosis and died at fifty. She believed her father's sexual appetite had expedited her mother's death. Her father was an audacious, old-fashioned Irish radical whose iconoclasm did not include women's issues; fight the establishment he might, but when it came to his family, his daughters were virtually indentured servants. At nineteen she started nurses' training in White Plains, New York. She considered marriage as equivalent to suicide, but at age twenty-two she met a charming painter and architect named Bill Sanger. He pursued her ardently, and six months after meeting him, despite her promises to herself, she found herself married and soon pregnant. Because her health, like her mother's, was frail, she spent much of her first pregnancy in a sanatorium. Two more children followed.

But Bill and Margaret Sanger soon tired of White Plains and moved to New York City. For Bill, the draw was all those other young men who hoped to be artists, but his young wife was attracted to the political ferment of Greenwich Village. Everywhere there were meetings, parties, and demonstrations. She became deeply involved with such radicals as Big Bill Haywood of the IWW and yet quickly established her own agenda; it was radical, not in the conventional political sense, but in sexual terms.

As Mabel Dodge, who ran one of the great radical salons of the period, wrote of her, "It was she who introduced us all to the idea of Birth Control and it, along with other related ideas about sex, became her passion. It was as if she had been more or less arbitrarily chosen by the powers that be to voice a new gospel of not only sex-knowledge in regard to contraception, but sex-knowledge about copulation and its intrinsic importance. She was the first person I ever knew who was openly an ardent propagandist for the joys of the flesh. This, in those days, was radical indeed . . . Margaret Sanger personally set out to rehabilitate sex."

By 1913, her marriage was beginning to break up. She wanted to put theory into practice regarding greater sexual freedom, but Bill Sanger did not. She increasingly began to regard him as a bore and even suggested that he take a mistress. He was appalled. "I am an anarchist, true, but I am also a monogamist. And if that makes me a conservative, then I am a conservative." Her zeal and sense of urgency increased as she encountered the lives of the poor urban women of New York City. They bore the full brunt of the misery of being new immigrants, and she experienced their plight by walking the tenements of the Lower East Side. The depth of the poverty and misery overwhelmed her: In one Jewish section of the Lower East Side, known as New Israel, there were 76,000 people crowded into 1,179 tenements. "Oh, Juliet, there never was such a Cause," she wrote to a friend of the urban poor a few years later. "These poor, pale-faced, wretched wives. The men beat them. They cringe before their blows, but pick up the baby, dirty and unkempt, and return to serve him." Their only method of family planning was to line up on Saturdays with five dollars and submit to hack abortionists. She was amazed to find they knew virtually nothing about contraception and basic sanitation. They were strangers to their own bodies. She started writing for a radical paper, The Call, and announced a series of articles about venereal disease, and other reproductive issues to be called "What Every Girl Should Know." She was promptly told by postal authorities that the entire issue would be suppressed for violating the Comstock laws.

These were named after Anthony Comstock, a fundamentalist who had waged an uncommonly successful campaign in the latter part of the nineteenth century to suppress all information about sex in this country. Comstock was so puritanical that, among other things, he got the courts to arrest store owners who left naked dummies in their store windows. The laws, slipped through a lame-duck Congress on the last day of its session, were designed to prohibit the use of the mail for transporting pornographic materials, in particular obscene postcards. But Comstock expanded the definition of pornography to include all information about sex, including information on birth control.

By 1914, Sanger started her own newspaper, The Woman Rebel. "No Gods, No Masters," announced the masthead. Women, she wrote in the first issue, should "look the whole world in the face with a go-to-hell look in the eyes; to have an ideal; to speak and act in defiance of convention." The paper would primarily contain articles on birth control, and Sanger spent a considerable amount of time in the library studying all the information available on the subject. From the start, Comstock himself went after her paper and demanded that the postmaster suppress it.

That was to set the tone for the next forty years. She would see her lectures closed, herself and her associates arrested, her clinics sacked. A few months after she started publishing, she was indicted for violating the Comstock laws. As her trial approached, she sent a copy of her birth-control pamphlet to the judge and then fled the country. In Europe she had a passionate affair with Havelock Ellis, one of the early sex researchers. She traveled widely, studying contraception as it was used in more tolerant countries. She returned in the fall of 1915, because Bill Sanger had stayed behind and been arrested. She did not want her husband to steal the glory. As she faced trial, she got a bit of public relations advice from John Reed, the famous radical. Because she was so lovely, he suggested she should have a prominent photographer take her portrait. Most people thought crusaders looked like Amazons, Reed told her. So she wore a plain dress with a wide Quaker collar, her hair was up, and her two young sons posed with her. The photo was extremely effective, appearing in hundreds of newspapers. With the publicity about the case going her way, the district attorney began to ask for postponements. Soon he dropped the case, perhaps to prevent her from becoming a martyr.

Her cause was gaining respectability and she began to attract new allies—society wives instead of radicals. They were, more often than not, college-educated women from old families and good homes, with a bent toward social work. She helped form the "Committee of One Hundred," and Gertrude (Mrs. Amos) Pinchot, the wife of the governor of Pennsylvania, was her chairwoman. In 1916 she embarked on a major speaking tour throughout the country. She attracted large crowds everywhere she went. In St. Louis the theater at which she was to speak was locked. In Portland, Oregon, she was arrested. In Boston, where authorities had threatened to close any meeting at which she spoke, she stood on the stage with a gag around her mouth while Arthur Schlesinger, Sr., read her speech.

In late 1916, she opened the first of her birth-control clinics, designed to provide information for all women on birth control. Flyers were passed out among the poor, in English, Yiddish, and Italian. The police moved immediately: She and her sister were arrested. But each new arrest was seen now as a victory. Slowly, steadily, she was shifting the focus from herself to those who threatened our most basic liberties.

In 1921, she sponsored a three-day conference on birth control at the Plaza Hotel and Town Hall in New York City. On the final day, Sanger and a British speaker named Harold Cox, a former member of Parliament, were to appear. They arrived to find a huge crowd gathered outside. The doors to Town Hall had been locked by New York City police, who also had formed a tight circle around the building. When the police opened the doors momentarily to let out those who were already inside, Sanger and Cox were swept inside. She tried to speak but was carried out of the hall by the police. Police reserves had to be called up to protect the station from an increasingly angry crowd. It was the turning point in her struggle: The manner in which her right to free speech had been abridged shocked the city and the nation. According to the policemen involved, New York's Roman Catholic archbishop had not even bothered to call the mayor or any other municipal figure to see what could be done. He had merely called the local precinct captain, who, on his own authority, had shut down the meeting.

The New York Times ran a story about it. Later, Mrs. Sanger said of the incident, "It was no longer my lone fight. It was now a battle of a republic against the machinations of the hierarchy of the Roman Catholic Church."

Her singularity of purpose was remarkable: "If you like my religion—birth control—we shall be friends," she once told a friend. She hated that many of her colleagues hid behind the title "Planned Parenthood." That was a euphemism. "It irks my very soul and all that is Irish in me to acquiesce to the appeasement group that is so prevalent in our beloved organization," she wrote.

Despite the opposition of the Catholic Church, the popularity of her cause continued to grow. At her sixth annual birth-control conference, in 1925, more than a thousand doctors sought admission. In 1931 she ordered a hundred Japanese diaphragms through the mail as a means of testing customs. In the court case that followed she won a significant victory. Judge Augustus Hand ruled that even though the Comstock laws were clear in intent, Congress in 1873 had not had access to modern information on the danger of pregnancy and the potential usefulness of contraception. That decision opened the mails to the sale of contraceptive devices. By 1937 the business of contraception reached sales of $250 million annually.

By the forties she was like a commander who had won but did

not know it, in part because her enemies were still on the battlefield. But even within Catholic middle-class circles, the questions of how to limit the size of a family, how to have a normal sex life, and how to remain a good Catholic were ever more troubling.

By 1950 she occupied the center of thinking on the issue and her opponents were increasingly regarded as fringe elements. A new urban young middle class was evolving, one that was independent of the ways of their parents and increasingly sympathetic to social and scientific advances. Now she regularly railed against the fact that contraception remained, in her mind, appallingly primitive and that there had not been any significant developments in a century. That was proof to her that men dominated the world of science and medicine.

It was around this time that she renewed an old friendship with Katharine Dexter McCormick, a woman who had admired her for some forty years. McCormick, Dr. John Rock once noted, was "rich as Croesus. She had a *vast* fortune. Her lawyer told me she couldn't even spend the interest on her interest." She was a member of a distinguished family and her father, who understood her intelligence, had pushed her to go to MIT, where, in 1904, she became the second woman to graduate.

Soon thereafter she married Stanley McCormick, son of Cyrus McCormick, founder of International Harvester. They must have seemed the perfect couple, combining brains, breeding, and good looks. But Stanley McCormick was stricken by acute schizophrenia, which shattered any chance for happiness. Katharine's interest in birth control may have come from her belief that schizophrenia was genetic and her fear that she might conceive children who bore the same illness as her husband. She remained married to Stanley McCormick until his death in 1954.

She started corresponding with Sanger in 1948. As soon as she gained control over her husband's estate, she started giving generously: $5,000 in 1951 and then $150,000 annually. Like Sanger, Katharine McCormick saw the issue of birth control as part of a woman's right to control her own body and life and thus escape the kind of servitude that came with poverty and unwanted children. She was not interested in birth control per se; she was interested in it only as it affected women. When in 1958 a scientist mentioned to her the possibility of creating a pill that men could swallow, she wrote Sanger, "He was rather shocked when I told him I didn't give a hoot about a male contraception, that only female research interested me."

In March 1952, Sanger brought McCormick together with Gregory Goodwin (Goody) Pincus. ("No," she had written Sanger in answer to an inquiry. "I have heard nothing of the research of Dr. Pincus . . . I am glad to see anything about this line . . .") Pincus was a brilliant pathfinder in the field of genetics, and Sanger's challenge, his colleague Oscar Hechter thought, was meant to appeal to his most basic instincts: "You have the power to change the world by doing this." Then in his late forties, Goody Pincus was never a man to turn down a challenge. He loved to compete, and he hated to lose. His gracious, charming manner concealed an almost steely hardness that guided him professionally. In fact, he wanted to succeed not just in science but in everything he did. When he played Monopoly or gin rummy with his son, the games would often end in comical arguments or good-natured mutual accusations of cheating. He learned to drive only when he was in his mid-forties (before that he had not been able to afford a car, one friend noted), but then he drove with a vengeance. He saw all other cars as potential challengers and felt compelled to pass them. When his wife would complain and tell him to slow down, he would say, "But this is just a cruising speed."

Born in 1903 in Woodbine, New Jersey, Goody Pincus was the son of Russian Jewish immigrants who lived in a Jewish farm colony founded by the Baron de Hirsch Fund, a German-Jewish philanthropy. The fund aimed to spare Russian Jewish immigrants potentially grim lives as peddlers, but the recipients of its largess were somewhat uneasy about the future their benefactors had planned for them as part of "a contented Jewish peasantry." Joseph Pincus, Goody's father, ran the local farm, lectured to Jewish farmers all over the East, and for a time was editor of the Yiddish-language newspaper *The Jewish Farmer*. Joseph's wife, Elizabeth Lipman Pincus, was the secretary to the superintendent of agronomy on the colony. As a boy, Goody was fascinated by animals and told his father he wanted to be a farmer when he grew up; his father told him there was no money in farming. The oldest of six children, Goody was always studying or reading and usually seemed pleasantly preoccupied. "What time is it, Goody?" his sister Sophie once asked him. Without looking up from his books, he answered, "What time is what?" The Pincus home was filled with intellectual energy and curiosity and Goody always seemed to be at the center of it. Evelyn Isaacson, a cousin, remembered a typical evening: John, the youngest of the children, then about six, turned to Goody, then about sixteen, and said, "Goody, I have three questions for you." "What are they, John?" asked the obliging older brother. "One, why are we here? Two, why were we born? And three, there is no God." The family believed Goody was a genius. His I.Q. was said to be 210. He remained fond of animals and eventually majored in biology at Cornell. He continued his studies at Harvard graduate school under William Castle, the leader of the first generation of American geneticists, and W. J. Crozier, a protégé of the famed biologist Jacques Loeb. Genetics seemed a perfect vocation for someone with Pincus's immense talents. The field was just beginning to explode as scientists forged breakthrough after breakthrough.

Goody Pincus's early work involved parthenogenic (that is, fatherless) rabbits. In 1934 Pincus announced that he had achieved *in vitro* (that is, inside a test tube) fertilization of rabbit eggs. Pincus took great joy in his work and was uncommonly candid about it. That candor might have served him well in other fields, but in genetics it got him into trouble. His work, as James Reed has written, "scared people, creating visions of Frankenstein-Brave New World nightmares." The *New York Times* headline ran: "RABBITS BORN IN GLASS: HALDANE-HUXLEY FANTASY MADE REAL BY HARVARD BIOLOGISTS." The *Times,* as Reed noted, "pictured Pincus as a sinister character bent on hatching humans in bottles."

But that was nothing compared to an article in *Colliers* entitled "No Father to Guide Them." The article managed, as Reed noted, to combine antifeminism, anti-Semitism, and a phobia of science. Pincus was depicted as a kind of Rasputin of the science lab, bent on evil deeds. A photo showed him, with a cigarette dangling from his lip, holding up a rabbit that was clearly soon to be sacrificed. In Pincus's world, the author, J. D. Ratcliff, wrote, "man's value would shrink. It is conceivable that the process would not even produce males. The mythical land of the Amazons would then come to life. A world where women would be self-sufficient; man's value precisely zero."

In reality, Pincus was the gentlest and most orthodox of men, a devoted husband and father, who left little poems behind on the pillow for his wife when he went to the lab in the morning. Still, the publicity did not sit well at Harvard. Pincus was already something of a controversial figure: He was Jewish in an age when American academia was still largely anti-Semitic; and his critics claimed he was too ambitious for his own good (and theirs). In 1936 Harvard, celebrating its tercentenary, cited Pincus's work as one of the university's outstanding scientific achievements in its entire history. The next year, when Pincus was thirty-two, it denied him tenure. He was devastated, even though he knew university politics were responsible. Fortunately, his old colleague Hudson Hoagland had just gone to Clark University, in Worcester, Massachusetts, as the chairman of its biology department. Clark was a small school with a long tradition of scientific excellence. Enraged by Harvard's cowardice and pettiness, Hoagland invited Pincus to come as a visiting professor.

From the start Hoagland had a vision that went far beyond the tiny three-man biology department at Clark. He began to build a research center with talented young scientists who were drawn by his and Pincus's reputations. M. C. Chang, for example, was delighted to come to Worcester. A talented young Chinese who received a Ph.D. from Cambridge in 1941, he had read Pincus's book *The Eggs of Mammals* in 1936. "A path-finding book, done when he was only thirty-three years old," Chang said years later. "*Everyone* in our field knew about him. You must remember that until then no one knew mammals had eggs." Soon Clark's research team numbered fifteen scientists, all of them considered brilliant by their peers and many of them nationally renowned. Their salaries were underwritten by dint of Hoagland's vigorous fund-raising in the Worcester community. Their lab was a converted barn. Hoagland's people did not, however, have faculty status and could not eat at the faculty dining room. Wallace Atwood, Clark's relatively conservative president, hated Hoagland's end runs, and he got back at him by denying Hoagland's staff, generally the most distinguished people on campus, such small privileges.

Atwood preferred the kind of academic atmosphere—with its committee meetings, departmental politics, and academic pettiness and jealousies—that Hoagland and Pincus wanted to leave behind. Since Clark's only contribution to their work was Hoagland's rather small salary and a limited amount of space, they became independent of the university in 1944 and founded the Worcester Foundation for Experimental Biology. As its co-directors, they estimated an annual budget of about $100,000, and declared its purpose to connect new biology to practical medicine.

The two men complemented each other. Hoagland's son noted years later that his father never seemed as happy as when he was working directly with Goody Pincus. Hoagland was immensely skillful in tapping into the Worcester establishment for money. He persuaded businessmen to contribute $25,000 for an old mansion, which became their headquarters. Much of their funding came from a patent held by a local businessman for the hard ties that held shoelaces together at the end; the running joke in Worcester was that they were operating on a shoestring. The staff was young and confident, full of the excitement that comes with having no limits.

Pincus served as father figure and mentor by dint of his remarkable scientific accomplishment and curiosity. Once, a staff member found him operating on a rabbit and asked what he was doing. "Putting cow's eggs in the rabbit," Pincus answered. "Why?" the friend asked. "I'm curious to see what will happen," answered Pincus. At first their funds were so limited that Pincus cleaned the animal labs, Mrs. Hoagland was the bookkeeper, Hoagland cut the lawn, and Chang was the night watchman. When a local Worcester businessman saw Hoagland, stripped to the waist, cutting the lawn, he added a groundskeeper's salary to the budget. In 1950, Chang won an award of a thousand dollars for a paper on fertilization of rabbit eggs from the American Sterility Society. The award allowed him to buy his first car. That same year Oscar Hechter, another research associate, won an award from the Endocrinological Society. "We don't have to worry about money and salaries anymore," an enthusiastic Pincus told Hoagland. "Our staff members can live on their awards."

They were among the early leaders in this country in steroid research. In the late forties, Hechter had won the CIBA award for a paper on producing adrenal hormones, but in the race to produce cortisone, the Worcester group was beaten by the scientists at Upjohn—at least partly because Worcester's major benefactor, the Searle Pharmaceutical Company, was not particularly supportive. When the next great challenge came—the development of a drug for contraception—the intensely competitive Pincus swore they would not be beaten again.

Pincus already had a sense that hormones could be used to control reproduction, from his work in mammalian reproduction. As a young lab assistant he had been intrigued by what happened when too many rats were placed in the same cage—they attacked each other. His own ideas about the problems of human overcrowding, friends thought, stemmed from those experiments. He asked the people at Searle to finance research in contraception, but again the answer was not encouraging. In fact Albert Raymond, Searle's director of research, came down hard on him. According to Pincus's notes of the meeting, Raymond told him: "You haven't given us a thing to justify the half-million that we have invested in you . . . yet you have the nerve to ask for more for research. You will get more only if a lucky chance gives us something originating from your group which will make us a profit. If I had unlimited funds I would undertake a large program in the steroid field, but I don't have such funds and the record to date does not justify a large program."

If the attitude at Searle reflected the wariness of a large corporation to be involved in something as sensitive as contraceptive research, still the Worcester Foundation was remarkably isolated from the prejudices of the era. Its funding sources were varied, the contributors in the local community were generally liberal, and it had no board to answer to. That did not mean that the people at the foundation were not wary. One night in the early fifties a woman knocked on the door of Pincus's house. She was desperate, almost out of control. She was pregnant, she said, and needed help. Could he help her? Pincus was very gentle with her, his son John noted, but kept his distance. It was, he was sure, a setup; he knew of other such incidents.

So when Mrs. Sanger and Mrs. McCormick came along, it was a godsend. From the start, Pincus was optimistic about what could be accomplished and how soon. He had met Mrs. Sanger, it was believed, at the home of friends and colleagues in Planned Parenthood in the winter of 1950, and Mrs. Sanger had asked him if some sort of drug was possible to stop conception. He hedged slightly and said that yes, there was. Out of that conversation came the first grant from Planned Parenthood. It was after an early meeting with Mrs. Sanger and Mrs. McCormick that Pincus first envisioned the device as a pill, and one that would probably use progesterone in some manner to block ovulation. When he arrived home, he was so excited that he told his wife he had discovered a new device for contraception. She tried to caution him: Women like Mrs. Sanger were bright and intelligent, but they were living in a fantasy world. "Lizuska," he said, using the Russian diminutive for Elizabeth. "Everything is possible in science."

Pincus became the driving figure of the team that made the assault, the leader who kept everyone aligned and whose vision guided the search from the start. His friend Chang thought that his brain had the ability to function on two tracks simultaneously. He could carry on a conversation with a colleague at the very highest level and at the same time be thinking of something else entirely, Chang was certain. A sure sign that this was happening, Chang thought, was when Pincus would begin tugging nervously at his mustache.

Personal politics did not matter to him—only science did. To that end, he could be quite cold-blooded. He was capable of secretly undermining the attempts of a valued assistant to get a better position elsewhere. He could cut loose a staffer he particularly liked and promote another he loathed if he thought it would benefit the project. Once Oscar Hechter asked him about the capacity to make such hard decisions: "Goody, how did you get to be the way you are?" "I had to learn," he answered. "I had to learn to be amoral."

He had the ability to remain focused on the central issue, no matter how complicated the problem. Some scientists have vision but lack the ability to attack the problem analytically. Pincus had vision and analytic ability. He was like a great detective who had envisioned exactly what he was looking for. He envisioned a pill that would prevent conception by mimicking the hormonal condition of pregnancy, when the body blocked ovulation of its own natural instincts. If you could suppress ovulation, he believed, you could suppress fertilization. There were significant earlier studies that suggested progesterone might be an effective inhibitor of ovulation and that it might be taken orally.

Progesterone was then available in large part because of the earlier work of an eccentric maverick scientist named Russell Marker, who in 1940 discovered a cheap and plentiful source in the root of a wild yam that grew in the Mexican desert. Previously, progesterone had been obtained only in minute amounts from animal sources and, as a result, was fabulously expensive—too expensive, in fact, to be wasted on humans; it was used exclusively to improve fertility in world-class racehorses. But with virtually no support or encouragement from others, Marker set up a primitive lab and by 1943 he was able to walk into a small wholesale pharmaceutical company in Mexico City with two pickle jars filled with powder worth about $150,000 on the open market. Did the owners want some progesterone, he asked. The first tests, on the effect of progesterone on rabbit ovulation, were started on April 25, 1951. The actual lab work was carried out by Chang. Chang was still so poorly paid he liked to joke that he lived in the laboratory, giving rise to persistent (and racist) rumors among the neighbors that a Chinaman was kept chained in the basement by the mad scientists.

Both Mrs. Sanger and Mrs. McCormick kept pushing Pincus for quick results; science, he tried to explain, does not necessarily work that way. Even so, the work went surprisingly well. Because of Mrs. McCormick, there was always enough money. Chang was a brilliant lab man, the perfect counterpart to Pincus. He had the patience to endure the seemingly endless lab work required. When Mrs. McCormick told him that she envied him for getting to stay in the lab all day long and have such fun, Chang had to grit his teeth—it was backbreaking work. One day it might lead to a great scientific breakthrough, but from his perspective at the time, it was just one endless series of experiments.

From the start Pincus was optimistic; Chang was, in his own words, equally pessimistic—he was, after all, a man who had had the good fortune to receive his Ph.D. on December 7, 1941. Even when test after test succeeded, he remained dubious. Sometimes when the work was boring, Change remembered, he would ponder the social benefits of what they were doing. In fact, everyone in the group understood the importance of the undertaking in terms of the world population explosion.

TWENTY-TWO

They were the first to protest what they considered to be the blandness, conformity, and lack of serious social and cultural purpose in middle-class life in America. If much of the rest of the nation was enthusiastically joining the great migration to the suburbs, they consciously rejected this new life of middle-class affluence and were creating a new, alternative life-style; they were the pioneers of what would eventually become the counterculture. If other young people of their generation gloried in getting married, having children, owning property and cars, and socializing with neighbors much like themselves, these young men and women saw suburbia as a prison. They wanted no future of guaranteed pensions but instead sought freedom—freedom to pick up and go across the country at a moment's notice, if they so chose. They saw themselves as poets in a land of philistines, men seeking spiritual destinies rather than material ones.

Their protest would have significant political implications, but its content was essentially social and cultural. The politics of the era had little meaning for them, and they saw little difference between the two main parties. If there was one figure who symbolized their discontent, though, it was Dwight Eisenhower. One night during the mid-fifties, the writer Jack Kerouac and a friend got drunk and drafted a message to the President: "Dear Eisenhower, We love you—You're the great white father. We'd like to fuck you."

The original group had come together at Columbia University in upper Manhattan. The most successful students at Columbia—those who fit in easily at an elite Ivy League school—regarded them as outcasts. Everything about them was wrong: their clothes, their manners, their backgrounds. In truth, they were a rather unlikely amalgam of friends. Allen Ginsberg was an awkward, shy but enthusiastic seventeen-year-old from New Jersey who couldn't quite decide whether to be impressed by Columbia or to make fun of it. In December 1943 he met Lucien Carr, who had recently transferred from the University of Chicago. Carr was playing Brahms on a player in his room, and Ginsberg, lonesome and bored, knocked on Carr's door. "I heard music," Ginsberg began. "Did you like it?" asked Carr. "I thought it might be the Brahms Clarinet Quartet," Ginsberg said. "Well, well!" Carr said. "A little oasis in this wasteland." Carr opened a bottle of wine. Ginsberg was dazzled, not least by Carr's blond good looks.

Carr, at the grand age of nineteen, must have seemed a man of the world to the innocent and impressionable Ginsberg. He came from an upper-class St. Louis family, his father had walked out on his mother when he was an infant, and he had been in and out of various secondary schools for bright but difficult students. He was smart and cynical, and already there was to him a kind of harsh self-knowledge that the young and observant Ginsberg noted in his journal: "He [Carr] said he could not write, he was a perfectionist. He compared himself not with those around him but with a high imagined self. He feared that he was not creative, that he could not achieve his imagined potential. He rationalized his failure, but adopted the postures and attitudes of the intellectual for recognition. Carr and his scarred ego. He had to be a genius or nothing and since he couldn't be creative, he turned to bohemianism, eccentricity, social versatility, conquests."

Carr held the key to the door of the bohemian world Ginsberg so desperately wanted to enter. His conversation was filled with references to Dostoyevsky, Flaubert, Baudelaire, and Rimbaud. Ginsberg wrote in his journal: "Know these words and you speak the Carr language: fruit, phallus, prurience, clitoris, cacoethes (a bad

habit or itch, as in 'itch for writing'), feces, foetus, womb, Rimbaud."
Carr seemed to know everyone worth knowing, including a strikingly handsome young man named Jack Kerouac, who had come to Columbia on a football scholarship. Kerouac had injured his knee as a freshman and quit first the football team and then Columbia. Determined to be a writer, he was seen by Carr "in very romantic terms as a seaman who was a novelist or a poet, or a writer, Jack Londonesque in style." That someone who so easily could have been a jock chose instead to belong to the world of poets and writers was thrilling to Ginsberg, who was instantly smitten. Kerouac's first impression of the young Ginsberg was of "this spindly Jewish kid with horn-rimmed glasses and tremendous ears sticking out, seventeen years old, burning black eyes . . ." Somewhat to the surprise of both, they became friends.

Carr had already done some off-campus exploring in New York City, and he invited Ginsberg to accompany him to Greenwich Village—the epicenter of bohemian life in America since the early part of the century. Ginsberg wrote his older brother: "Saturday I plan to go down to Greenwich Village with a friend of mine who claims to be an 'intellectual' (that has a musty flavor, hasn't it?) and knows queers and interesting people there. I plan to get drunk Saturday evening if I can. I'll tell you the issue."

Carr also introduced Ginsberg to William Burroughs, an eccentric friend from St. Louis then living in the Village. Burroughs came from a prominent family—his grandfather had invented the adding machine—and he had graduated from Harvard in 1936. But propelled by his own deep alienation and his homosexuality, he had resorted to a kind of subterranean life of mental hospitals, prison, and a drug habit. The others thought him rich because he received a $200-a-month allowance from his family, on the condition that he go regularly to a psychiatrist. When Ginsberg first met him in 1943, Burroughs was tending bar in the Village, one of a series of marginal jobs he held in search of what he called "experience."

Burroughs was older than the others and affected a certain snobbism. He usually wore three-piece suits, a costume not exactly *de rigueur* in this new counterculture they were creating. Brilliant and coldly logical, he was more confident than these new young friends of his. Ginsberg was so impressed by his book collection that he took a pencil and wrote down some titles so he could read them himself. Burroughs, Ginsberg and Kerouac decided, was "a big seeker of souls and searcher through cities. I think Kerouac said 'the last of the Faustian men.' "

It was no surprise that Ginsberg soon ran into problems with

the Columbia administration. In a creative writing class, he chose to
novelize an incident within their group about which Columbia was
particularly sensitive and which had become something of a cause
célèbre. It centered on Lucien Carr. When Carr had come east he had
been followed by a man fourteen years older, named Dave Kammerer. Kammerer had run a play group for young boys in St. Louis
in which Carr had been enrolled. Infatuated with Carr ever since,
Kammerer had followed him, first to Chicago, and then to New
York. One night in August 1944, Kammerer pressed his attentions
too far, and Carr stabbed him to death. Carr confessed the crime to
Kerouac, the two dropped the knife down a subway grating, went to
a movie, and then Carr turned himself in to the police. Carr eventually spent two years in the Elmira, New York, reformatory.

Ginsberg's efforts to fictionalize these sensational events greatly
offended his professor, who called his writing "smutty" and told the
assistant dean about it. The dean ordered Ginsberg not to write
about the incident and also questioned his right to hang out with
such friends as Kerouac. That was just the beginning. A few months
later, Ginsberg further aggravated the situation with a dumb prank.
Suspecting that his maid was anti-Semitic, he wrote "Fuck the Jews"
on his window and drew a skull and crossbones. The maid reported
the graffiti to the dean, who went by Ginsberg's room that night and
found not just Ginsberg, but Kerouac (no longer a student), sleeping
there as well. They were not, it should be added, sleeping together—
Ginsberg was still a virgin. Ginsberg was summoned to the dean's
office to discuss the incident. The dean looked at him and said, "Mr.
Ginsberg, I hope you realize the *enormity* of what you've done!"
Columbia charged him $2.35 for housing an overnight guest and
suspended him for a year. He could not return until he had seen a
psychiatrist. Some of his friends thought that Columbia had acted so
harshly because of rumors he was a homosexual and because of his
friendship with Kerouac, who was by this time persona non grata. It
was a reflection of the time that when Lionel Trilling, the first Jewish
member of the English department to gain tenure at Columbia, went
to the dean to protest the suspension, the dean was so embarrassed
that he could not utter the words of Ginsberg's offending graffiti but
instead chose to write them down.

These young rebels did not so much want to learn, thought Hal
Chase, a member of the group, as "they wanted to emote, to soak up
the world." They aspired to become, as Allen Ginsberg put it, "intelligent, Melvillean street wanderers of the night." Several of them
were to become writers: Ginsberg, Kerouac, Burroughs, and John

Clellon Holmes, whose first book, *Go,* is often called the first Beat novel. The initial response from straight society was to try to send them to psychiatrists: Burroughs believed that the healthier you were, the more the straight world, which he considered inherently sick, wanted to see you as sick. Therefore it was obvious that psychiatrists were part of the conspiracy. "These jerks," Burroughs once said, "feel that anyone who is with it at all belongs in a nuthouse. What they want is some beat clerk who feels with some reason that other people don't like him . . ."

There was a great intensity to their lives in those days; they talked endlessly about what life should be, of how they would escape the mundane. They were, even by the usual standard of restless young men, exceptionally self-absorbed: They recorded their thoughts, dreams, and emotions meticulously, as if they were the first who had ever had them. As such, there is a remarkable record of those days. Kerouac was among the most prolix, writing his books in manic all-night sessions on reams of paper borrowed from a wire-service teletype machine. Truman Capote later said of him that he did not so much write as *type.* Writers they might have been, but in the end their lives tended to be more important than their books. They spoke of a New Vision, an idea taken from Yeats, of a society of artist-citizens, in which they would be the leaders.

Their roots were generally middle-class. Ginsberg's father, Louis, who was a moderately successful poet, kept exhorting him to get rid of his ne'er-do-well friends and do something with his life. "Where is your former, fine zeal for a liberal, progressive, democratic society?" Louis Ginsberg wrote Allen while the latter was still in college. Ginsberg replaced Carr as the social glue of the group after Carr went to the reformatory. He was intelligent, generous, interested in everybody and everything; and he was awed, after the loneliness and self-doubt of his adolescent years, to find himself a part of such an extraordinary group of talented friends.

Yet if anyone was the center of the group, it was Kerouac. He hungered to be a writer, not so much for fame, but for people to listen to him, to take his words and his ideas seriously. He would go around the city all day long with his notebooks, writing down observations on life around him. Sketching, he called it. When the others would read what he had written, they were moved by his natural instinct for words and phrases.

He was the son of French Canadian parents in Lowell, Massachusetts. English was his second language; as a boy he had spoken joual, the dialect of the French Canadians. In his next-to-last year in high school, his football coach noted that one reason he did not use Kerouac very much as a player was that Kerouac had trouble understanding the language and therefore could not learn the plays. His was a harsh childhood, the Depression was difficult, and the Jansenist Catholicism of his home was particularly oppressive. He had experienced not merely the prejudice of a New England town but also his father's endless rage about being a second-class citizen in America. This paranoia became deeply embedded in Jack Kerouac as well, and when things went badly for him as an adult, the same fears and angers that had driven his father surfaced in him. In effect he became a divided man—on one hand, the heroic prototype of the modern hipster nonconformist who lives on the road, unburdened by family and responsibility; on the other hand, he was unable to shed the deeply rooted fears and prejudices of his parents.

In his novel *Go,* John Clellon Holmes describes his hero on an all-night outing in the Village, followed by a groggy subway ride back to his apartment in the morning. Sharing the subway car with him is a happy, bouncy troop of Girl Scouts, on their way to a picnic. The antihero looks at these upbeat, optimistic emissaries of traditional wholesome American values and wonders: "To be like them or like us, is there another position?"

The Beats, as they came to be known, revered those who were different, those who lived outside the system, and particularly those who lived outside the law. They were fascinated by the criminal life and believed that men who had been to prison had experienced the essence of freedom from the system. In *Go,* Holmes described their world as "one of dingy backstairs 'pads,' Times Square cafeterias, bebop joints, nightlong wanderings, meetings on street corners, hitchhiking, a myriad of 'hip' bars all over the city, and the streets themselves. It was inhabited by people 'hung up' with drugs and other habits, searching out a new degree of craziness; and connected by the invisible threads of need, petty crimes of long ago, or the strange recognition of affinity. They were going all the time, living by night, rushing around to 'make contact,' suddenly disappearing into jail or on the road, only to turn up again and search one another out. They had a view that life was underground, mysterious, and they seemed unaware of anything outside the realities of deals, a pad to stay in, 'digging the frantic jazz,' and keeping everything going."

They were fascinated also by urban black culture, and they appropriated phrases from it: *dig* and *cool* and *man* and *split.* They saw themselves as white bopsters. They believed that blacks were somehow freer, less burdened by the restraints of straight America, and they sought to emulate this aspect of the black condition. An interest in African-American music of the time—the new sounds of Charlie Parker, Miles Davis, and others now seen as legends among jazz musicians—was almost a passport into Beat society.

The first words that Neal Cassady, who was to become a mythic figure of the group, spoke to a young woman named Carolyn Robinson when they met in Denver were, "Bill [Tomson] tells me you have an unusually large collection of Lester Young records." Ms. Robinson understood in some instinctive way that this was a test. Unfortunately, she did not have a single Lester Young record, and worse, she had never even heard of him. She apologized, noting that she had some swing albums left over from her college days at Bennington.

Drugs were also important. They were viewed as the key to the spiritual world. The cheapest and easiest (although often trickiest) high was benzedrine, imperfect but available from the local drugstore. Marijuana, then known as tea, was preferable to a benny. In *Go,* Hart Kennedy (a figure based quite deliberately on Neal Cassady) ruminates on the difference between a benny high and a tea high: "Yes, yes, man! That's right! You got it! But *everything's* great on tea! Everything's the greatest. That's the point, you see? You're just digging everything all the time. Hell, when I was on benny, two years ago or so, I got all mean and . . . compulsive, you know? Always worried and hung up. Sure. I was a real big serious intellectual then, toting books around all the time, thinking in all those big psycho-logical terms and everything . . ."

Their name, the Beats, was borrowed from Herbert Huncke, a Times Square thief and male prostitute, who had used the word *beat* in regular conversation. As Barry Gifford and Lawrence Lee note in *Jack's Book,* an oral biography of Kerouac, the word came from the drug culture and has special meaning: "cheated, robbed or emotionally or physically exhausted." Later, the definition was reinvented by Kerouac to mean "beatific," to describe those who went against the prevailing tide of materialism and personal ambition.

Malcolm Cowley, the distinguished editor and critic, more sympathetic to them than critics at the time, wrote that they were "looking for something to believe, an essentially religious faith that would permit them to live at peace with their world." It was no small irony that the magic ingredient that allowed them to forgo regular jobs and still manage reasonably comfortable lives was the sheer affluence of the mainstream culture that they so disdained; the country was so rich that even those who chose not to play by its rules were protected. No one pointed up the contradictions in their lives more vividly than

Kerouac. Throughout his adult life he continued to live with his mother, Mémère, as she was known to his friends, who loathed her and whom by and large she loathed in return. Kerouac was extremely sensitive on this subject; in *On the Road,* a book which he wanted to be brutally honest, it is his *aunt,* not his mother, that the narrator lives with. Mémère disliked Ginsberg particularly, because he was both Jewish and homosexual. He was not really allowed in the house, and when he wrote Kerouac letters, he had to use false names and return addresses—otherwise she would read and destroy them. Kerouac himself could only write his fiction once Mémère went to sleep. Then he would smoke a marijuana cigarette with the window wide open and pour his words into the typewriter. On reason that the sentences in *On the Road* were so long, John Clellon Holmes believed, was the rush of sensation Kerouac got from the dope.

Hedonism stopped inside the doors of the house. Visiting friends were allowed to use the bed in his home for sex only if they were married. That, Gregory Corso liked to say, was Jack's puritanism, not Mémère's. Holmes noted that deep down, Kerouac was more than anything else "a very, very proper middle-class boy from a mill town in New England. He believed that life could break open somehow. He wanted it to break open, but he didn't have the guts to do it himself. He didn't have the way to do it himself." Certainly, Kerouac himself understood how little he had really experienced. In the early days, he desperately sought a real adventurer to use as a role model. He found it in Neal Cassady.

Cassady was to Kerouac what Kerouac was to others: someone who had escaped the shackles of middle-class America. Kerouac described him in *On the Road* as a "young Gene Autry—trim, thin hipped, blue-eyed with a real Oklahoma accent—a sideburned hero of the snowy West." On occasion when Kerouac and Cassady posed together, they looked like brothers. Cassady came honestly to the kind of life that Kerouac so admired and wanted. His parents' marriage had broken up when he was six, and he had stayed on with his skid-row alcoholic father: He got himself ready for school in the morning while his father slept off the whiskey from the previous night's drinking. He learned to survive by his wits at an astonishingly early age, cadging food and money, and stealing cars before he was legally old enough to drive. By the time he showed up in New York he was twenty, four years younger than Kerouac, and had already, by his own account, stolen some five hundred cars.

He made his connection to Kerouac's group through Hal Chase, a Beat from Denver. Everyone in New York had heard of

Cassady long before he arrived, of this golden young man who could throw a football seventy yards, run the 100 in under ten seconds, and have his way with any woman he wanted. To those immune to his macho charm, he was merely a small-time con artist; but to the group, he was a romantic Zen hipster of the road. The more conventional the setting, the more vulnerable Cassady felt with his sad background, so he always experienced an almost manic need to keep moving. What he exemplified, Ted Morgan wrote, was "pure, abstract, meaningless motion. Compulsive and dedicated, he was ready to sacrifice family, friends, even his very car itself to the necessity of careening from place to place. Wife and child might starve, friends existed only to be exploited for gas money, but Neal must move." He was in awe of the New York group's sophistication, for he was obviously bright and had spent long hours at the Denver public library trying to educate himself. He longed to be a writer, and he spoke of going to Columbia. Hal Chase even arranged with several professors for him to take special oral entrance exams. He never showed.

He was powerfully attractive to both sexes and he used that power indiscriminately. All sorts of men and women were in love with him. He changed wives often; by his late twenties, he had been married three times and had three children, none of whom he knew very well. He sensed that Ginsberg, with his wonderful mind and great generosity of spirit, was someone who could teach him a great deal, so he slept readily with him. Ginsberg, in turn, fell desperately in love. "When Neal came to town, that was total, man," John Clellon Holmes noted. "The wives of people and the girlfriends of people looked upon Neal as an enemy, perhaps because their men were so attracted to him. I don't mean homosexually, but attracted to the pole of this vigor and this energy and the simplicity that he seemed to offer. I mean, 'Let's roll up to Harlem and see what's going on!' Neal had a capacity to make—he didn't intend this, I don't think—some kinds of people feel inauthentic. I was always afraid I wouldn't respond in the right way . . . Neal never said, 'Oh, come on, man, you're a square.' "

Kerouac was mesmerized by him from their first meeting. Kerouac wanted to travel with him and to write someday what he called his "Neal" book. An odd relationship developed, Holmes thought. Kerouac seemed a man without a center, for whom Cassady offered, "not a center, but a trajectory." Cassady wanted to write a book, and Kerouac wanted to be Cassady and in the end did Cassady's book, which did not entirely please Cassady. In 1949 they embarked on the first of their several journeys together. In 1950 the first of Kerouac's books, *The Town and the City,* for which he received an advance of a thousand dollars, was published to modest reviews and negligible sales. It was a derivative book, strongly influenced by Thomas Wolfe, rambling and poorly focused, but not without merit. Kerouac was embittered by its failure and still wrestling with the question of how he was going to translate his experience with Cassady into a book.

In early 1951 John Clellon Holmes finished *Go,* which Scribner's planned to release in the fall of 1952. Holmes wrangled with his editors and the publishing house's lawyers over language. The editors and lawyers demanded that Holmes cut three of the six times that a character named Agatson says, "Fuck you." On this point Holmes held his ground: "What's the difference between three and six?" he asked. Although *Go* was a far more traditional novel than *The Town and the City,* it still had a tough time of it in the bookstores, with a printing of only 2,500 copies. The climate was obviously not yet right for books with eccentric language and characters challenging mainstream culture by talking about drug use and the sexual netherworld of that time.

But spurred by Holmes's work (and his own belief, frequently stated, that he was a better writer), Kerouac started what would eventually become *On the Road.* He was twenty-eight at the time, not gainfully employed, already twice married. He wrote it in a fury—it was one long paragraph, and it was fiction as nonfiction; he changed nothing, not even the names of his friends. He wrote it, his friend John Clellon Holmes said, "simply following the movie in his head." Within a week of finishing it, he had handed it to Holmes, not even having reread it himself. It was, in Holmes's words, "a roll like a big piece of salami." Kerouac's great talent was an ability to catch precisely the moods and feelings of characters far outside the reach of traditional novelists. Holmes thought the book was brilliant; he also thought it was going to be almost impossible to convince the traditional, conservative publishing world of its value.

Not everyone thought it was that good. Ginsberg, who was usually generous about his colleagues' work, wrote to Cassady that it was "a holy mess—it's great all right but he did everything he could to fuck it up with a lot of meaningless bullshit." The problem, he added, was that it had "page after page of surrealist free association that doesn't make sense except to someone that has blown Jack. I don't think it can be published in its present state . . ." That seemed almost a prophecy. Kerouac seemed unable to interest publishers, even though Malcolm Cowley, the venerable recorder of the Lost Generation, sensed that Kerouac's was a new and interesting voice. It would take some five years to publish *On the Road*.

But slowly things were beginning to open up. Gil Millstein, a talented and eccentric young editor and writer at *The New York Times Book Review*, called Holmes and asked him, "What in the hell is this whole 'Beat Generation' thing? What is this? Come in and let's talk about it." The result of their conversation was a piece on the Beat Generation in the *Times Magazine* in November 1952. Under Cowley's auspices two sections of *On the Road* were published, one in the *Paris Review* and the other by Arabelle Porter at *New World Writing*, an important forum for experimental writing in those days.

At almost the same time Ginsberg's career began to advance. He had gone to San Francisco to be near Neal Cassady. At that moment San Francisco was becoming the West Coast center of Beat culture. Its literary headquarters was the City Lights Bookstore. Named after the great Chaplin movie, it was the first bookstore in the country devoted to quality paperbacks. City Lights stayed open until midnight during the week and until 2 A.M. on weekends. Lawrence Ferlinghetti, one of the owners, was a considerable poet himself and he also wanted to tie the bookstore to a publishing venture. In August 1955, he published the first of his Pocket Poets series.

That year Ginsberg had reached a critical moment in his life. It was time, he decided, to stop being an ingenue; he was twenty-nine, and he was tired of holding on to such casual jobs as market researcher, trying to find out which was likely to be the more successful advertising campaign for a toothpaste: "Ipana makes your teeth sparkle," or "Ipana makes your teeth glamorous." He wrote Kerouac, "I am passing, like all others, out of youth, into the world . . . faced with financial problems that must be solved. How the hell are we going to get the $s to get to Europe, and when that $'s gone, what are we going to do? How can we live with no future abuilding? That's what's bothering me." That summer he started to attend graduate classes at Berkeley for a master's degree in English. He sent a copy of one of his poems to Kenneth Rexroth, a major figure in the San Francisco poetry world, who wrote him back that he had gone to Columbia too long and that his work was too formal—in effect, he was telling Ginsberg he had not yet found his voice.

Ginsberg decided that Rexroth was right; he would just let go, not think of a *poem* as such, but let his thoughts and feelings pour out. The result was poetry as if done to the rhythms and phrases of modern jazz, in his own words, "a tragic custard-pie comedy of wild phrasing, meaningless images for the beauty of abstract poetry of mind, running along, making awkward combination (of images) like Charlie Chaplin's walk, long saxophone-line chorus lines I knew Kerouac would hear *sound* of—taking off from his own inspired prose line, really a new poetry." (In hindsight, there seems more than a passing kinship to the poems of Walt Whitman.) Ferlinghetti agreed to publish it, and Ginsberg, thrilled, wrote Kerouac joyously, "City Lights Bookstore here . . . will put out 'Howl' (under that title) next year, one booklet for that poem, nothing else, it will fill a booklet."

So it was that on October 13, 1955 Allen Ginsberg gave his historic reading of "Howl" at Gallery Six, a converted auto repair shop. The first line, now one of the most famous in American poetry, was a veritable Beat anthem: "I saw the best minds of my generation/destroyed by madness/starving, mystical, naked,/who dragged themselves thru the angry streets at/dawn looking for a negro fix . . ." Ginsberg was dazzling as a performer that night. Kerouac was in the audience, with a bottle of jug wine, cheering Ginsberg on, shouting, *"Go, go,"* throughout the evening. "It had," Ted Morgan later wrote, "an absolutely compelling incantatory quality, and seemed to be a manifesto for all the misfits of the fifties, the rejected, the deviants, the criminals, and the insane, who could unite under his banner." "Ginsberg," a joyous Kerouac told him afterward. "This poem will make you famous in San Francisco." "No," Kenneth Rexroth said. "This poem will make you famous from bridge to bridge." Ferlinghetti sent Ginsberg a cable paraphrasing what Emerson had said to Whitman after reading "Leaves of Grass": "I greet you at the start of a great career."

It was not merely a triumph for Ginsberg, it was a larger victory as well for the Beats. Ginsberg, always generous, pushed Malcolm Cowley again on Kerouac, and in December 1955 Viking decided to publish *On the Road,* eventually bringing it out in 1957. *On the Road* offered a new vision of American life, from its hip opening sentence: "I first met Dean not long after my wife and I split up. I had just gotten over a serious illness that I won't bother to talk about, except that it had something to do with the miserably weary split-up and my feeling that everything was dead." It was to be a celebration of an alternative life-style. What Kerouac did, wrote Ted Morgan, "was to assert possession of a birth right—not through ownership, but through mobility. The book was a pamphlet of lyrical instructions for crisscrossing the great American landscape, geographical and spiritual."

The old order tried to strike back. In May 1957, two officers of the San Francisco police, acting on orders from Captain William Hanrahan, walked into the City Lights store and bought a copy of "Howl." They also had a warrant for the arrest of Ferlinghetti and the store's manager. But Ginsberg and Ferlinghetti could already call on powerful supporters. There had been a positive review in *The New York Times* by the influential critic Richard Eberhart, and there was an introduction to the poem by William Carlos Williams, a towering traditional poet. All sorts of well-known figures in the world of letters were ready to testify to the poem's importance, power, and legitimacy. In October 1957, Judge W. J. Clayton Horn decided that "Howl" was not obscene. Quite the contrary: "The first part of 'Howl' presents a picture of a nightmare world; the second part is an indictment of those elements of modern society destructive of the best qualities of human nature; such elements are predominantly identified as materialism, conformity, and the mechanization leading to war. . . . It ends with a plea for holy living . . ."

It was all beginning to come their way—publishing contracts, requests to write for magazines, lecture offers for the unheard-of sum of five hundred dollars a night. Kerouac ultimately found fame hard and destructive, ending his life in a cloud of alcoholic rage and bitterness, but Ginsberg, who had felt so ugly and unattractive as a boy, loved flirting with success. Their success, above all, was a sure sign that the old order was changing. The walls were tumbling down.

TWO

TWENTY-THREE

Isolationism as an end in itself was finished. The Republican party had put on its international face and had chosen the man most identified with collective security and involvement with Europe as its leader. And yet internationalism—in the true sense of involvement in the world—was less the driving force than an international policy geared up to contain Communism.

The division within the Republican party, though, did not end with Eisenhower's election. There were many in the Republican party who had gone along with the decision to nominate Eisenhower only because victory, any victory, was preferable to the sixth Republican defeat in a row. But that did not mean they *liked* Ike. They regarded him, Ike himself sometimes felt, as a figurehead, a sort of pretty girl with no mind of her own. At his first meeting with Republican professionals, in August 1952, Sherman Adams had seen a hard look cross Ike's face, and Adams knew the candidate was becoming increasingly irritated with their condescension. When the others left the room, Adams asked what was the matter. "All they talked about was how they would win with my popularity. Nobody said I had a brain in my head," Eisenhower answered. It was, in fact, Eisenhower's independence and the fact that he was new on the political scene that made him an ideal candidate: He served as healer to a badly divided and frightened nation.

Richard Nixon was assigned the job of reconciling the irreconcilable within the Republican Party. Dewey had recognized in him the ability to balance the internationalism of the Eastern wing with the anti-Communism and conservatism of the old isolationist wing. His economic policies were essentially Republican centrist leaning toward liberal. If there were occasional doubts about him in some of the old isolationist circles—a belief that he had sold out to the Eastern wing or that he was too pragmatic—then he immediately set out to silence such criticism by being a party workhorse, by going out and making endless speeches at county Republican dinners, by collecting due bills, becoming the ultimate party loyalist. In that he was successful, but the end result was that the contradictions of the Grand Old Party became his own.

If there was any politician in America who reflected the Cold War and what it did to the country, it was Richard Nixon—the man and the era were made for each other. The anger and resentment that were a critical part of his temperament were not unlike the tensions running through the nation as its new anxieties grew. He himself seized on the anti-Communist issue earlier and more tenaciously than any other centrist politician in the country. In fact that was why he had been put on the ticket in the first place. His first congressional race in 1946, against a pleasant liberal incumbent named Jerry Voorhis, was marked by red-baiting so savage that it took Voorhis completely by surprise. Upon getting elected, Nixon wasted no time in asking for membership in the House Un-American Activities Committee. He was the committee member who first spotted the contradictions in Hiss's seemingly impeccable case; in later years he was inclined to think of the case as one of his greatest victories, in which he had challenged and defeated a man who was not what he seemed, and represented the hated Eastern establishment.

His career, though, was riddled with contradictions. Like many of his conservative colleagues, he had few reservations about implying that some fellow Americans, including perhaps the highest officials in the opposition party, were loyal to a hostile foreign power and willing to betray their fellow citizens. Yet by the end of his career, he became the man who opened the door to normalized relations with China (perhaps, thought some critics, he was the only politician in America who could do that without being attacked by Richard Nixon), and he was a pal of both the Soviet and Chinese Communist leadership.

If he later surprised many long-standing critics with his trips to Moscow and Peking, he had shown his genuine diplomatic skills much earlier in the way he balanced the demands of the warring factions within his own party. He never asked to be well liked or popular; he asked only to be accepted. There were many Republicans who hated him, particularly in California. Earl Warren feuded with him for years. Even Bill Knowland, the state's senior senator and an old-fashioned reactionary, despised him. At the 1952 convention, Knowland had remained loyal to Warren despite Nixon's attempts to help Eisenhower in the California delegation. When Knowland was asked to give a nominating speech for Nixon, he was not pleased: "I have to nominate the dirty son of a bitch," he told friends.

Nixon bridged the gap because his politics were never about ideology: They were the politics of self. Never popular with either wing, he managed to negotiate a delicate position acceptable to both. He did not bring warmth or friendship to the task; when he made attempts at these, he was, more often than not, stilted and artificial. Instead, he offered a stark choice: If you don't like me, find someone who is closer to your position and who is also likely to win. If he tilted to either side, it was because that side seemed a little stronger at the moment or seemed to present a more formidable candidate with whom he had to deal. A classic example of this came early in 1960, when he told Barry Goldwater, the conservative Republican leader, that he would advocate a right-to-work plank at the convention; a few weeks later in a secret meeting with Nelson Rockefeller, the liberal Republican leader—then a more formidable national figure than Goldwater—Nixon not only reversed himself but agreed to call for its repeal under the Taft-Hartley act. "The man," Goldwater noted of Nixon in his personal journal at the time, "is a two-fisted four-square liar."

Nixon's unwavering pragmatism did not work with everyone. From the moment he arrived in Washington, he exuded such odor of personal ambition that the old order was offended. Bob Taft never forgave him for helping to tilt the nomination to Ike. But that personal grievance aside, Taft had not liked him anyway—for Nixon seemed to represent something new and raw in the Senate. To Taft, he was "a little man in a big hurry." Goldwater later wrote that he was "the most dishonest individual I ever met in my life." Even J. Edgar Hoover, who was so helpful to Nixon during the Hiss case and whom Nixon worked hard courting, decided early on that Nixon tended to take too much credit for himself. Hoover's closest aide, Clyde Tolson, wrote in a memo to the director that Nixon "plays both sides against the middle." Hoover noted on the same memo, "I agree."

If Nixon set out to be the man who redefined the Republican political center in the post–New Deal, post–Fair Deal age, he did not, nor did any other young Republican politician, dare campaign by suggesting a return to the America that had existed before the New Deal. The phrase "creeping socialism" was about as close as they got to attacking the New Deal on its domestic reforms. Rather, the catchphrases were about a need to return to Americanism. It was better to attack Communism and speak of domestic treason than it was to be specific about reversing the economic redistribution of the New Deal. In fact, Nixon's essential response to all issues was to raise the specter of Communism: "The commies," Nixon told the *Chicago Tribune*'s Seymour Korman during his harsh 1950 senatorial campaign against Helen Gahagan Douglas, "don't like it when I smash into Truman for his attempted cover-up of the Hiss case . . . but the more the commies yell, the surer I am that I'm waging an honest American campaign." He was, he liked to say, the number one target of the Communists in America. In those early campaigns, he was, it seemed, a man who needed an enemy and who seemed almost to feel that he functioned best when the world was against him. Such men, almost surely, eventually do get the enemies they so desperately want.

If the leaders of a nation as powerful as the United States needed, above all, personal confidence—Oliver Wendell Holmes once said of the young Franklin Roosevelt that he had a third-rate intellect but a first-rate temperament—Nixon was ill-prepared for his long journey in American politics. Emotional strength and self-confidence were missing from him. Everything with Nixon was personal. When others disagreed with him, it was as if they wanted to strip away his hard-won veneer of success and reduce him to the unhappy boy he had once been. In political terms that had bitter consequences: He would lash out at others in attacks that seemed to go far beyond the acceptable norms of partisanship; if others struck back at him, he saw himself as a victim. Just beneath the surface of this modern young politician was a man who, in Bob Taft's phrase, seemed "to radiate tension and conflict." He was filled with the resentments of class one would have expected in a New Deal Democrat.

He was a very private man, a true loner, who lacked the instinctive affability and gregariousness of most successful politicians. One thought of him more easily as a strategist than a candidate. He hated meeting ordinary people, shaking their hands, and making small talk with them. He was always awkward at the clubby male bonding of Congress. When he succeeded it was because he worked harder and thought something out more shrewdly than an opponent and, above all, because he was someone who always wanted it more. Nixon had to win. To lose a race meant losing everything—so much was at stake, and it was all so personal. Taft, if not exactly jolly and extroverted, won the admiration of his peers because he was intellectually sterling. Ike inspired other men because of his looks, his athletic ability, his natural charm. Nixon was always the outsider; his television adviser in his successful 1968 presidential campaign, Roger Ailes, once said of him that he had the least control of atmosphere of any politician that Ailes had ever met. By that Ailes meant charisma, the capacity to walk into a room and hold the attention of those assembled there. Even success did not really bring him confidence. There is a 1952 photo that is a testimonial to Nixon's terrible awkwardness: Nixon, recently nominated for the vice-presidency, had visited Eisenhower at a fishing camp in Colorado. There was Ike in his fishing gear, glowing and looking very much at home; and there was Nixon, who had shown up without any informal clothes, looking absurdly stiff in jacket, suit, and tie. The curriculum vitae for success had never included a list of items to wear for fishing photo opportunities. Years later when he was President, there was a comparable photo of him self-consciously walking on the beach at San Clemente, much as Kennedy had done at Hyannisport—Kennedy had walked barefoot, Nixon was still in streetclothes and shoes.

His childhood was sad. As Stephen Ambrose, one of Nixon's biographers, pointed out, though the family lived on a farm, the Nixon boys never had a dog or cat or any other kind of pet. Whittier, his hometown, was a small town, founded by Quakers, outside Los Angeles; it was isolated quite deliberately by its religious and civic leaders and was extremely conservative: Typically, when a teacher was hired by the local public school, she had to promise that she did not smoke, and there was a major struggle in town when the first cocktail lounge opened at the Hoover Hotel. Because the town's population came mostly from one ethnic group, it was an extremely hierarchical society, with explicit standards of success and failure.

Nixon's mother, Hannah, was a Milhous, and the Milhouses were a large, affluent, and somewhat snobbish clan, one of the leading families of Whittier. As Nixon's cousin Jessamyn West, the writer, once noted, the Milhouses thought it rather a pity that for biological reasons there had to be the admission of non-Milhous blood into their family line. Hannah Milhous married Frank Nixon against her family's wishes. He was not a Quaker, and although he converted, he was still regarded by most of her family as an outsider, louder and more argumentative than a Quaker should be. To make matters worse, Frank, despite a handsome bequest from his wealthy father-in-law, did not make a success at first. He invested in ten acres of a lemon grove. The land was poor: "The hardest piece of soil in Yorba Linda," said Paul Ryan, a neighbor. "Red clay. You irrigate it but it doesn't help." It took a long time for lemon trees to turn a profit; most of the successful citrus farmers in the area had more money, better land, and already established groves, so they could wait for their new trees to grow. Frank had to take a variety of odd jobs to make extra money, and Hannah cooked for boarders. After a decade of backbreaking labor, Frank went bust and sold the land at a loss. "He never made a penny," said another contemporary, Ralph Shook. "He was a jack-of-all-trades." He bought a small gas station on the Whittier highway, gradually turned it into a market as well, and finally enjoyed considerable success, albeit success that required the participation of every member of the family. Young Richard had to get up at 4 A.M. to drive to Los Angeles to buy the fruit and vegetables; Hannah baked ten pies a day. All members of the family had to work in the store. Richard did not mind the early-morning runs to Los Angeles and he liked to do the store's books, but he was extremely sensitive to social slights. He hated working in the store and waiting on customers—years later, when he was running for President, he would mention those days and how every time he passed a vegetable stand, he felt sympathy for the person who had to pick out the rotten produce.

Even though the gas station and market became increasingly successful, the Nixons had slipped socially by Milhous standards. Frank Nixon began to avoid Milhous family gatherings, and Richard Nixon was acutely aware of how his father had fallen in the eyes of in-laws and the local community in this closed and rigid little universe. Frank Nixon, under the best of conditions a difficult man with a volatile temper, became angrier than ever. Aware of how his father reacted to slights from his in-laws, Richard learned to recognize when a particularly dark spell was coming on, and he would warn his brothers to avoid any confrontations with him. Frank Nixon remained combative and suspicious throughout his life. (At his son's inauguration as Vice-President of the United States, he complained that he would not wear the requisite white tails: "I am not going to wear these blasted things.") When the oil boom struck the region, neighboring farmers sold their land and oil was found there. Frank refused handsome offers for his land, hoping that oil would be found—but in his case, of course, it was not. Hannah, a gentle but strong-willed Quaker woman, accepted the hard times without a word of complaint. She was, as Nixon would refer to her later, "a saint," but a controlling saint at that. She never raised her voice, but it was she who set the norms and the goals for the children. Two of her children died from tuberculosis, which created an aura of even greater sadness in the house. Richard Nixon, the eldest of the three surviving children and self-evidently the most intelligent and talented, felt a great burden to succeed and validate the family's sacrifices. After Harold, his older brother, died, Hannah Nixon noted, "From that time on it seemed that Richard was trying to be *three* sons in one, striving even harder than before to make up to his father and me for our loss. . . . Unconsciously, too, I think that Richard may have felt a kind of guilt that Harold and Arthur were dead and that he was alive." As a child, Richard was usually remembered as either working or studying, trying to achieve, trying to live up to his mother's expectations of him. "He always carried such a weight," his mother once said of him. There were, she thought, too many burdens; there was too much hardship for someone so young. She wished that he and his brothers had been able to have more fun.

Old friends who knew the family, including Paul Smith, Nixon's professor at Whittier College, were fascinated by the vastly disparate characters of the two parents: Frank, with his anger and rage, Hannah, with her beatific gentleness and quiet, unbending sense of purpose. To her, a Milhous was still special and her son was a Milhous, destined to be extremely successful and yet highly moral. The effect of that on Nixon, Smith thought, was powerful: He was a young man caught between his father's rage and sense of injustice and his mother's high moral purpose, ambition, and concern for correct behavior. In Smith's view, this was the key to his character—his inability to reconcile the two sides. Certainly, it was Hannah who sent him off to school in starched shirts every day when none of the other children wore them, Hannah who insisted from the beginning that the teachers and other children call him *Richard,* not Dick, and Hannah who during the Checkers episode, when Ike had not yet made up his mind, sent the general a telegram saying that Richard was honest and clean, signing it, "one who has known Richard longer than anyone. his mother Hannah Nixon."

In high school, he had none of the qualities that make boys popular—charm, looks, athletic prowess—so he worked harder, earning if not the liking of his peers, at least their respect. In elections for class offices, he almost always won, because he seemed to have given so much of himself. That was to set a pattern: In both college and law school, he was largely regarded as a lonely, immensely competent striver; yet at both Whittier, the local college, and Duke Law School, he was nonetheless elected student-body president.

At Duke, to which he won a scholarship for that university's first law-school class, he finished third in his class, working once again tirelessly, making few friends, above all *achieving.* After graduation he ventured to New York to try the great law firms, but despite his flawless academic record, he could not get across the moat. Typically, when he had applied at Sullivan and Cromwell, New York's mightiest corporate firm, David Hawkins, the partner in charge of interviewing young men, made note of his "shifty-eyed" manner. (Years later, during Watergate, someone at Sullivan found the notes and, to everyone's amusement, read them aloud during a partners' dinner.) Others in his class received offers; Nixon did not. He tried for a job with the FBI but was turned down there as well; he was not considered aggressive enough. If Duke Law School had promised to be an escape from the airless small-town life in Whittier, his postgraduate experiences dashed any such hopes. That was in no small part what drove him so relentlessly in later life: There were men of power in the world who seemed to have gathered in the elite New York law firms, and they would not give someone like him a break. He had wanted to escape Whittier and had failed.

Failing to get a job in New York or Washington, he returned to Whittier, where Hannah had already visited Tom Bewley, the town's leading lawyer, and called in a chit or two. Richard was less than eager to work for Bewley; nor for that matter was Bewley at all sure he wanted to hire Nixon—he asked Paul Smith, the president of Whittier College, whether it was worthwhile to hire this young man. Richard stayed in Whittier for four years, becoming a partner in Bewley's firm in two. It was during this period that he met and wed Pat Ryan, an extremely attractive young teacher whose ambitions matched his own; she was trying to escape a childhood of grinding poverty, infinitely harsher than his own. She taught commercial subjects in the Whittier school system and earned around two thousand dollars a year, which seemed to her a magnificent sum at that time.

They met in February 1938, at a try-out for the Whittier Community Players. (The play called for someone to play the district attorney, and a friend suggested to Nixon that if he played an attorney convincingly onstage, it might help bring in some business.) He was immediately smitten; she was not. When the play opened, he invited his parents to come and take a look at the young woman he hoped to marry. When her son asked what she thought of her, Hannah, a formidable mother who knew a rival when she saw one, could comment only that "she did her part nicely."

The first two times he asked Pat out, she turned him down, even though she liked his ambition and drive. She tried to fix him up with her roommate, but he spent the entire evening with the roommate talking of nothing but Pat. When she tried to shake him off by pleading she had work, he volunteered to help grade papers with her. When she pretended not to be home, he saw the door bolted and knew she was there. He was nothing if not persistent. At one point he wrote her a letter full of schoolboy gush, which ended, "Yes—I know I'm crazy and that this is old stuff and that I don't take hints, but you see, Miss Pat, I like you!"

Persistence won out. She had always vowed that she would live a better life than that of her parents. Though she was so attractive that a few years earlier, when she was working in a Los Angeles department store, there had been several offers for her to take screen tests, she was not the kind of young woman to go into the movies. Richard Nixon's relentless ambition finally overcame her doubts, and whatever else, he had no intention of spending the rest of his life in Whittier—and neither did she. His letter to her at the time of their engagement was filled with their mutual plans: "It is our job to go forth together and accomplish great ends and we shall do it too." Just before they were married, they decided to buy a car; Nixon found that the least expensive way was for him to take a bus to Detroit, buy the car there, and drive it back. He did, buying the car with money from *her* savings (because she was making four times as much money as he was then). Their wedding ring cost $324.75, which was most of the rest of their combined savings. Their honeymoon was in Mexico, and they carried a suitcase full of canned food to eat for breakfast and lunch, to save money. But while they were dressing to go on their honeymoon, friends opened the luggage and took all the labels off the cans—so when they opened them, they never knew quite what they were going to eat.

The next year, when he received a letter from a friend in Washington offering him an early job with the Office of Price Administration, it was Pat Nixon who concinced him to take it. They could reinvent themselves in Washington and leave their small-town pasts behind. They had no money or family connections; their only fuel was their own ambition, their willingness to work hard and sacrifice for their future. He went into the Navy during World War Two, and as it was winding down, he wrote her from overseas making it clear that they would not settle down in Whittier: "Too many restrictions etc. A little freedom is far more important than security, don't you agree?" They would be glad to leave behind familiar landmarks, old friends, even their families. What was familiar was also limiting. They sought the new, modern life-style of the middle class, freed from constraints of geography and background. They were always a little stilted with each other. As he prepared to return from the Navy, he wrote her: "Whether it's the lobby of the Grand Central or the St. Francis bar—I'm going to walk right up to you and kiss you—but good. Will you mind such a public demonstration?"

They were like millions of other couples, trying new jobs in new cities and finding out that they were as able as the people who had always been in charge of things in the past. They were filled with optimism for the future. But even before they could decide what he would do next, Nixon was being asked to audition for the Republican congressional nomination to run against Jerry Voorhis in his old home district; there was an advertisement in local papers asking for bright young candidates to apply, and in addition, Nixon got a letter from Herman Perry, a local banker, leader of the Whittier establishment and father of one of Nixon's friends. The letter seemed to offer the inside track to a local boy: "I am writing you this short note to ask if you would like to be a candidate on the Republican ticket in 1946. Jerry Voorhis expects to run—registration is about fifty-fifty. The Republicans are gaining. Please air mail your reply if you are interested." He was a Republican, he decided, for he had voted for Dewey in 1944 while in the South Pacific. Yes, he was very interested.

At first, Pat was ambivalent about politics; it was a public profession and she was, after a terrible childhood, a very private person. This implied a different kind of career than she had in mind, almost a joint career, and she was uneasy with the demands it might place upon her. They flew out to meet the conservative Republican group that was going to choose the candidate. Dick met with the men while Pat lunched with their wives, affluent ladies of the upper middle class. She did not make a good impression; to their eyes she was poorly dressed and did not, one of the women complained, even know what color nail polish to use. But wearing his naval uniform, he made a good impression. From his years living in Whittier he knew exactly who these men were, what their fears and prejudices were, and what they wanted to hear. They were small-town businessmen, they hated the New Deal (as he did not; he might have thought it was going too far, but it was hardly an emotional thing with him), so he talked about free enterprise and how much the returning veterans wanted it. He was their choice.

Once he started in politics, he could never stop: There would always be one more office to run for. Nothing could be allowed to stand in his way. He was a man consumed. He wanted, needed, success because it meant vindication—perhaps even revenge. Defeat meant only one more mark on the slate to wipe out. Her ambitions were very different; she sought merely respectability, a gentler environment for her children than the one she had known.

Thus he gravitated toward his first political race. So instead of all of their savings going for a house, as they had planned, half of it went for his campaign and half went for a house. Pat became, almost without realizing it, the prototype of the new political wife, always campaigning and sharing the spotlight with him. She asked only one thing—for the right not to have to make any speeches. She would work for him, but she was too shy to speak. So they campaigned together, although she was already pregnant. In February 1946, Tricia, their first child, was born; within a few weeks the baby was in the care of Hannah Nixon and Pat was out again with her husband, handing out Nixon thimbles to women, shaking hands, attending coffee hours, and running his campaign office. She also sold her share of her family's Artesia property for three thousand dollars, which she immediately put into the campaign. Her participation helped greatly. She was young and pretty, as if cast by Hollywood for the part of the young politician's wife. If at first it was instinctive, then as his career proceeded, their public partnership became more deliberate, particularly in 1950, when he ran for the Senate against Helen Gahagan Douglas, a former actress who was married to an actor perceived as left-wing; the Nixons, because of the simplicity of their backgrounds, seemed more the American norm: "NIXON LIFE STORY LIKE FILM SCENARIO," ran a headline that fall in the *Los Angeles Examiner*. The candidate was "so average an American," wrote Carl

Greenberg in the paper, "that unless you found out for yourself, it would smack of a campaign manager's imagination."

The new American candidate, it appeared, was more and more part of a team. Thanks to television, the entire family was on display. The Nixons, as much as any couple, helped pioneer this. People often liked him because they felt at home with her; if the older wives of the ruling elite in Whittier had looked down on her a bit in 1946, then she was very much someone that the wives of the young couples moving to California right after the war could identify with. They were, in those early years, showcased politically as an all-American couple doing all-American things. In particular, they shared the same financial hardships as other young couples just returning to civilian life. She learned her role as well or better than he did his. She became an expert at rolling her hair in a car while traveling from one campaign stop to another. She learned to keep a notebook to record which clothes she wore to which function in case she ever went back. In those days, she later reflected, she bought all her clothes not so much according to her own taste, but with her political appearances in mind. "I think: Will it pack? Is it conservative enough? Can I wear it for a long time? Can I doll it up with accessories?" She also mastered the art of sitting next to him on the podium and hearing him give for the umpteenth time, the same speech, while still managing to look adoring, as if she had never heard any of it before. She adored him equally in print. "I Say He's a Wonderful Guy," was the title of her 1952 article in the *Reader's Digest*. They became so much the ideal young American couple that in the late fifties, Mort Sahl, the nightclub comic, joked about them sitting home at night, Pat knitting the American flag and Dick carefully reading the Constitution, "looking," Sahl said after pausing for a moment, "for loopholes."

In the early years she was by far the stronger of the two: She would sleep with the baby in a separate room so that he would not be disturbed if Tricia woke up. In those days she accepted, and on occasion even enjoyed, the political life. When he sank into one of his dark moods she, better than anyone else, could bring him out. When he got angry at her in front of others, she could turn away from it, even though such incidents embarrassed his associates. Gradually, she became poised and professional at the business of politics.

Her father's emotional outbursts had terrified her, and she kept her own emotions to herself. Later, when she was First Lady, Jessamyn West interviewed her on a day when Pat Nixon had been to so many functions that she had barely eaten. Ms. West apologized for taking her time and said that she must be very tired. "I'm never tired," Pat Nixon answered. That, reflected Ms. West, must have come out of that hard childhood—running a family, earning a salary, and going to school—as if she had told herself: "You cannot be tired, you dare not be tired. Everything depends on you. You are *not* tired."

She was one of the most photographed and written about women of the decade and at the same time one of the least known. She sat by his side and smiled. She could not have been at once more public and yet more private. She told an endless number of inquiring reporters that she believed in what he believed in and supported him, that they were together in all this. It was a performance so relentless that it was numbing: Her smile seemed glued on, her expression immune to all the usual signs of pain and stress. A reporter for the *London Spectator* wrote in 1958, after one of her appearances in London: "She chatters, answers questions, smiles and smiles all with a doll's terrifying pose. There is too little comprehension. Like a doll she would still be smiling when the world broke. Only her eyes, dark, darting, and strained, signal that inside the black suit and pearls there is a human being, content not to get out." It seemed to the *Spectator* writer an almost inhuman human performance: "One grey hair, one hint of fear, one gold teacup overturned on the Persian carpet and one would have loved her . . ." She later told her own children, "I detest temper, I detest scenes. I just can't be that way. I saw it with my father. And so to avoid scenes of unhappiness I suppose I accommodated to others."

One of the few times her public facade slipped was when her husband was running for President in 1968. On board her plane was a young journalist named Gloria Steinem, one of the leaders in the women's movement and obviously a supporter of her husband's opponent. Though Ms. Steinem, a strikingly attractive young woman, had suffered through considerable adversity herself as a child, she must have seemed at that moment for Pat Nixon to epitomize the new liberated American woman, someone who enjoyed all the pleasures of success on her own terms, not derivatively through her husband's accomplishments. Ms. Steinem led a highly visible life as a celebrity, and the list of her boyfriends was dazzling. Between her and Pat Nixon was not just the usual generation gap of twenty years—it was a chasm.

It was a memorable moment. Perhaps it was Ms. Steinem's composure at 7 A.M., so early in the day; perhaps her cool and elegant manner struck Mrs. Nixon as condescension; perhaps it was the certainty that she was there to do nothing so much as damage her husband, but when Ms. Steinem asked Mrs. Nixon about her own youth, her role models and life-style, Pat Nixon, always so cool, blew: "I never had time to think about things like that, who I wanted to be, or who I admired, or to have ideas. I never had time to dream about being anyone else. I had to work. I haven't just sat back and thought of myself or my ideas or what I wanted to do . . . I've kept working. I don't have time to worry about who I admire or who I identify with. I never had it easy. I'm not at all like you . . . all those people who had it easy."

It would be difficult, in that rather comfortable period in America in the fifties and sixties, to imagine a harder childhood than Pat Nixon's. She was born on March 16, 1912, in a miner's shack in Ely, Nevada. (The nickname Pat, which eventually became her legal name, came from the proximity of her birthday to St. Patrick's Day.) Her father was a prospector, Will Ryan, born in 1866 in Connecticut. His fortune always seemed just one step ahead of him. He had worked on a whaling ship, been a surveyor, and spent much of his life prospecting for gold. At the time of Pat's birth he was a timekeeper in a silver mine. Her mother, Kate Halberstadt Bender, had been born in Germany and had lost her first husband in a mining accident. When Kate met Will Ryan, she was a widow with two very young children. She knew a good deal about hard times herself; she had had to give up a child from her first marriage to her own parents to raise. She and Ryan eventually had three children of their own, including Pat, the youngest.

Kate Ryan, exhausted by the harshness of mining life in Nevada, pushed constantly for Will to take the family to California and farm, which he finally did. Settling in Artesia, eighteen miles southeast of Los Angeles, he spoke of himself as a rancher. In reality he was a small-time truck farmer. The house was without electricity or running water. The family lived on the very margin of poverty. He grew peppers, beets, cauliflowers, cabbage, corn, and tomatoes. His cabbages were so big he was known as the "cabbage king." Sometimes when her father went into town to sell them, Pat went with him. There he would joke with his friends, pretending that he was going to sell her to the highest bidder. To a small child already in a vulnerable situation, this was truly frightening. She was absolutely terrified that he would actually sell her. If he made a little extra money, he would buy her an ice-cream cone at the local drugstore. For her, that was an exhilarating moment, for hers was a childhood largely without indulgences.

Will was a man who wore his disappointments openly. When

things went badly, he drank. His wife feared the days when he came back too soon, which meant that he had done poorly and had gone to have a few drinks. On days like that he would turn on her and their children. Her mother, Kate, the one kind soul in her young daughter's life, died of liver cancer when Pat was barely in her teens. Pat had to take over, do the cooking and cleaning and take care of the house. When her mother died she realized that she had barely known her, that they had never had the time to talk. With the death of her mother, her hard life became even harder. In the mornings she did the farm chores and cooked breakfast for herself and her brothers. Only then did she head off to school. When she came home in the afternoon she cleaned the house, did the wash, and prepared dinner. With all that, she still managed to do well in school.

Soon after Kate's death, Will Ryan was diagnosed with tuberculosis; in truth it was black lung, the miners' disease. As he became weaker and weaker, Pat took care of him while attending nearby Fullerton Junior College and working as a janitor at the local bank in the afternoon for thirty dollars a month. She and her two brothers made a pact to work together so the local authorities wouldn't place them in the hands of a guardian. All three graduated from high school and won scholarships, but there was enough money for only one to go to college. They decided they would take turns and support each other. Tom Ryan had a football scholarship, so he would go first. Pat took a job at the bank to pay for the hospitalization of their father. In May 1930, Will Ryan died. Pat was still only eighteen.

In the fall of 1934, she entered USC. Living with her brothers in a tiny apartment in Los Angeles near the USC campus, she was determined, strong, unusually attractive, and very quiet. At USC she held several jobs, among them working at Bullock's, a Los Angeles department store, doing some modeling. She wrote, "The manager of our department is always telling or describing how I drape the lovely velvet robes, etc., around me, grin at the fat, rich customers, and pff! they buy. But this is true—and I sell more than any of the other girls. Saturday I sold over $200. . . . Really, business is good—it makes one feel good to see people really *buying* instead of looking as in the past few years." When she graduated from college and landed a job as a schoolteacher in Whittier, being able to put her childhood behind her was an immense relief.

Richard Nixon's rise in politics was in a way meteoric, but it was not without a terrible price. There was in the Voorhis and Douglas races a savagery, a willingness to blur the truth in charges against opponents. In the process, Nixon made real and lasting enemies: Sam Rayburn, the longtime Democratic House Speaker, who was angered by Nixon's insinuations that the Democratic party was one of treason, liked to say that Nixon had the most hateful face of the five thousand people he had served with in the House. Why he pushed such charges so far is a fascinating question: It was as if he believed that all rich and powerful men had adjusted the rules to succeed and he was going to do the same. During the 1950 campaign Ted Rogers, who handled television appearances for him, was struck by Nixon's almost obsessive fear of the television technicians and his belief that because they were union members, they were going to pull a plug or kill a mike on him. Rogers would point out that they were professionals, but Nixon would have none of it. It was, Rogers later decided, a fascinating insight—that Nixon thought *others* would behave as if there were no rules, because, on occasion, he behaved as if there were none.

Helen Douglas said years later that it had been foolish of him to run so dirty a race. He was going to win anyway. Everything was against her. Because of the Tidelands issue, the oil money was pouring into the state against her; all those new young voters saw her as an older, too liberal figure, and the outbreak of the Korean War sealed her fate, she was sure. What drove him to such excess, she suspected, was not politics but his own anger—that everyone else got away with something, so finally he should too. He was most comfortable, she thought, when he was on the attack, even when he did not need to be.

The vice-presidential nomination in 1952 was something he had courted, even though Pat had at first strongly opposed it. Eventually, she came around. "I guess I can make it through another campaign," she said. What had ended the pleasure for her once and for all was the Checkers speech, though. Pat had told him to press forward, and on the eve of the speech she had allayed his doubts. "I don't think I can go through with this," he had said. "Of course you can," she had answered. But she hated it. She felt her privacy had been completely violated. He had gone on national television and opened their bank account; he had shown the entire nation the haunting poverty from which she had barely escaped and which was still so painful to her. She remained the good soldier or, more accurately, the good trooper, but their professional associates could feel a chill in the marriage. Such old-time colleagues as Jim Bassett, a *Los Angeles Times* reporter who served as a Nixon press secretary, was appalled by the way he began to treat her. He was cold, almost rude to her, lashing out on occasion, yet he was quick in all public appearances to refer to her glowingly as his wonderful wife. Thus developed an odd pattern that was to mark their campaign appearances for the next twenty years: In public he would always praise her lavishly, but once the public appearance was over and they were back in the airplane, he would go about his business as if she did not exist. When he left the White House in disgrace in 1974, he gave an impromptu speech in which he paid homage to his parents, yet he failed to mention Pat: Given how much pain she had been through and how little pleasure she had taken from the latter part of his political career, it was an omission that offended many of those who knew him best.

Her face, under the pressure of his career, gradually turned from a movie star's to American Gothic. It was as if she had gone full circle. Whatever success she had once enjoyed in her husband's career had been stolen from her bit by bit. In the end their heartbreak was caught, live and in color, for the entire world to see on television: the disgraced President leaving the White House in order to escape impeachment. A family photo was taken on their last night in the White House, and Pat particularly hated the photo: It was the final indignity of politics intruding into her personal life. "Our hearts," she told her daughter of the photo, "were breaking and there we are smiling."

Once in office as Vice-President, he became a prisoner of his own past—handling the Republican right, keeping McCarthy on a short leash, and playing the partisan role for a President who had little taste for partisan politics. All in all, Ike got the high ground, Nixon the low. The President grandly disdained the uglier side of politics, yet he accepted the fact that it had to be done although he did not particularly like the man who did it for him. In fact, the more Nixon did for Ike, the more he became, in the President's eyes, a politician, a breed not to be greatly respected. The White House staff, led by Sherman Adams, exacerbated his usual resentments; as far as Nixon was concerned, the staff wanted to keep him as far from policy as possible and to summon him only when it had some odious task to be attended to. In the early years that meant trying to baby-sit McCarthy, and then eventually filling the vacuum created as McCarthy self-destructed.

In December 1953, he and Bill Rogers, on orders from the White House, tried to get McCarthy to let up on the Communist issue (which was placing McCarthy on a collision course with his own party in the White House). In March 1954, after Adlai Stevenson went on national television and accused the Republican party of being "half Eisenhower, half McCarthy," it was Nixon who was chosen to answer Stevenson, for he was, Ike thought, perfectly situated as the victor in the Hiss case. Nixon hated the idea of giving the response; that was a part of his past that he was quite willing to let go of. At first he flatly refused, but then Ike called him to the White House and ordered him to do it. Jim Bassett, who worked with Nixon on the speech, had rarely seen him so angry. He was already aware that he was being perceived as the administration hatchet man, Bassett thought, that it was becoming harder to escape the stigma of that role, and that there would almost surely be a price to pay later. In a phrase that had not yet entered the language, he was caught in Catch-22. The more loyal he was, the less respect he got from the man he served. His political advice, which was often shrewder than that of Eisenhower's inner political circle, was rarely sought.

In 1956 Eisenhower wanted to squeeze Nixon off the ticket; he asked Len Hall, then the head of the Republican party, to break the bad news to Nixon. When Nixon heard, he was shattered. His face, Hall remembered, turned very dark. "He's never liked me," Nixon had told Hall. "He's always been against me." Hall had decided that the decision to drop Nixon from the ticket would be a disaster, it might split an already divided party. He set out to save Nixon's job by commissioning a series of polls that showed Nixon running ahead of anyone else as Vice-President. With that, the threat to get Nixon off the ticket was turned back.

But the damage was done, and it added to Nixon's feeling that he was a second-class citizen in this White House. In truth he was. The social distinctions in the Eisenhower years were not inconsiderable, and the Nixons were treated somehow more as servants than as peers. He felt that he and his wife were outcasts. On occasion Nixon complained bitterly that even though he was Vice-President, he had never been invited into the social quarters of the White House. The Eisenhowers *did* look down on the Nixons. When, in 1958, the Nixons were about to go on a multination tour of Latin America, Pat Nixon called Mollie Parnis, a prominent dress designer who catered to the wives of many of Washington and New York's most powerful men, including Mamie Eisenhower, about doing some clothes for her. Ms. Parnis mentioned this to Mamie Eisenhower, who immediately vetoed the idea. "No, no, dear, don't do that. Let the poor thing go to Garfinckel's and buy something off the rack."

Eisenhower never could really understand Nixon. He couldn't fathom how a grown man could have so few friends. In that way, as in so many others, the two men could not have been more different. Friendship came easily to Ike; by contrast, Nixon was wary and distrustful of most of his peers. He sought alliances, most of them temporary, rather than friendships. Once Eisenhower visited Nixon in the hospital, and when he returned to the White House, he remarked how lonely his Vice-President had seemed. How could that be so, he wondered aloud to his secretary, Ann Whitman, with a man at the top of his profession?

TWENTY-FOUR

J. Robert Oppenheimer's security file had always been something of a nightmare. Whereas he was the ultimate sophisticate as far as science went, in political matters he was totally naive. He had been the prototypical fellow traveler of the thirties, belonging, he once joked, to every Communist front organization on the West Coast. But the McCarthy era had so changed the political climate that there was little sympathy or understanding for youthful and careless Depression-era politics. He had tried to justify the past and protect old friends with small lies. That had been tolerated during the war because of his immense contribution to the important work at Los Alamos. Still, some of the security men there had believed him to be a security risk; they kept him under constant surveillance, bugged meetings he attended, and tapped his phone. Indeed, Oppenheimer later joked that the government had spent more money watching him for security violations than it had paid him in salary—and he was almost surely right.

The move to strip Oppenheimer of his security clearance took place in the spring of 1954, at the same time as the Army-McCarthy hearings. With McCarthy's censure looming, it seemed that McCarthyism was over; and yet, ironically, the key players who moved against Oppenheimer (including, eventually, Eisenhower himself) prided themselves on being opposed to McCarthy and were moving to head him off. Obviously, they were still making significant accommodations to the norms he had established; a certain ugliness had entered America's bloodstream.

By 1954, Robert Oppenheimer had become a target of various conservative groups, not merely because of his security lapses in the thirties and forties, but because of his virtually unchallenged position in the political scientific world and because he was emerging as a powerful opponent to administration policy on the hydrogen bomb. He was not, in the vernacular of the time, on the team. He offended not just the political conservatives but also, increasingly, the Air Force, which saw itself as the nuclear delivery arm of the military.

Oppenheimer's own politics had come a long way since his days as a vaguely radical student and young academic. He had come to recognize the cruelty and brutality of Stalin, and he had little confidence left in Russian intentions. If anything, in the years after the war, he had become something of an establishment figure. He had even apologized lightly for his left-wing days in a 1948 *Time* magazine cover piece celebrating him as America's scientist laureate: "Most of what I believed then now seems complete nonsense, but it was an essential part of becoming a whole man. If it hadn't been for this late but indispensable education I couldn't have done the job at Los Alamos." His opposition to the H bomb was a curious blend of moral and pragmatic concerns. On the moral side, he was exhausted and spiritually depleted by the making of the atomic bomb; on the pragmatic side, he, like Conant and Kennan, wondered if the Super might divert energy from more usable weaponry and whether we were devoting too much of our resources to a weapon that might, in the end, turn out to be unusable. It was easier for opponents to challenge his past than his logic.

Some of his old colleagues felt that Oppenheimer had become, by this time, a prisoner of his own myth. Even at Los Alamos, Victor Weisskopf thought, he had believed that the other scientists should not debate or even think about the political consequences of the bomb. They should leave this to Oppie, who was their ambassador to the world of politics and who knew how to deal with politicians. After the war, old friends complained that Oppenheimer had changed, that he had become self-important, constantly dropping the names of the high officials with whom he had just visited. He turned out to be a surprisingly hierarchical man, Weisskopf thought, and he seemed to be unduly impressed by the wisdom of the politicians with whom he dealt. "He was," Weisskopf said dryly, "impressed by their need to come to him."

"Oppie, in terms of politics, always wanted to do the impossible," I. I. Rabi, his friend and colleague, once said. "The difference with me is that I have always managed to stay within the possible." His old-time friend Philip Morrison thought Oppie began to play God in the years after the war. Even some of those who supported him had doubts about the course he had charted and his reasons for it. Ulam thought Oppenheimer had, in his own mind at least, exaggerated his role in the making of the atomic bomb and, correspondingly, exaggerated his guilt, seeing himself as, in the *Bhagavad-Gita,* Death the destroyer of worlds. Von Neumann agreed. "Some people profess guilt to claim credit for the sin," von Neumann liked to tell Ulam.

For all of that, no one thought that this distinguished man, who had given such invaluable service to his country, would soon be defending his patriotism before the nation's security apparatus— even though there had been earlier encounters with the security forces. In June 1949, Oppenheimer had gone before the House Un-American Activities Committee, and afterward the candor of his testimony had been praised by the committee's most enterprising young member, Richard Nixon. But by the early fifties, one man who held a very important job at the epicenter of atomic politics was beginning to believe that J. Robert Oppenheimer was not merely a political problem but also a security problem.

That man was William Borden, who was chief staff aide to Brien McMahon on the Joint Committee on Atomic Energy. Borden, a graduate of Yale and Yale Law School, had been a bomber pilot during World War Two when he had glimpsed his first V-2 rocket in the air. "Our plane seemed to stand still," he later said. It made a profound impression on Borden, who saw the coming of modern rocketry as an end to the security America had previously enjoyed. The oceans no longer offered protection, as they had in the past. A Soviet bomber would require two and a half hours to hit targets in Europe; a rocket might cover the same distance in five or six minutes. He wrote a book on the subject, *There Will Be No Time: The Revolu-*

tion in Strategy, and believed as a matter of faith that we should move ahead as quickly as possible on the hydrogen bomb.

Borden's interest turned into an obsession, and he became more and more suspicious of Oppenheimer. Obsessed himself, he could not comprehend how a man of Oppenheimer's intelligence could come to different conclusions. He soon concluded it was not simply a simple disagreement between two men of goodwill. Instead, he decided that there was something sinister to Oppenheimer's behavior and his opposition to the Super. In 1950 Borden began to study Oppenheimer's security file. At that point, his attitude hardened from suspicion to conviction. Borden had always believed that there was someone in a high place in the American nuclear program who had allowed Fuchs to operate. For Borden, Oppenheimer now became that man.

In July 1953, Lewis Strauss became the chairman of the AEC. He arrived with an agenda of his own, not the least of which, some thought, was to separate the AEC from the influence of Robert Oppenheimer. At the time Herbert Marks, a former AEC attorney and a close friend of Oppenheimer's, received a call from an old friend on the AEC staff: "You'd better tell your friend Oppie to batten down the hatches and prepare for some stormy weather," he said.

In the summer and fall of 1953, Harold Green was a young lawyer doing security checks at the AEC. He was thirty-one years old and had been at the AEC for some three years. He loved his job and he was at ease with the way cases were handled. The commission, unlike some other agencies in the government, used what he called "the whole-man concept." It meant an official had the right to answer derogatory charges; in addition, no one episode was isolated from the totality of a man's life. Critical to this view was a belief that everyone, at some point in his or her life, made a mistake—got drunk publicly, bounced a check, had a friend who was not worthy of him.

Green saw his role as helping to preserve a free and decent society, in which the essential rights of the individual were balanced against the interests of the state. At one point he was summoned to argue before the Supreme Court in the Rosenberg case, and he had no doubts, having studied the private files and secret reports from the cryptographers, of their guilt. Later he came to believe that he had played a significant role in sending the Rosenbergs to their death; it was a role for which he felt little remorse.

But Green found attitudes toward security in the AEC changing after Strauss arrived. "The caesar's wife rules," Green called the new method, which he thought reflected a more anxious society—in the new era security "was a privilege and not a right." If there was significant derogatory information, clearance would not be granted. Nor was an individual always given a chance to answer his or her accusers. Since the FBI files were filled with hearsay, this posed a terrible problem. Early in the Strauss years, there was a case in which the local people recommended clearance, and Green passed their recommendation on without comment. His superior, Harry Trainer, who, Green thought, cared considerably less about individual liberties than his predecessor, was enraged. He charged into Green's office, shouting: "How can you clear him? Look who his lawyer is—he's got a Communist lawyer." The lawyer was from the American Civil Liberties Union. "Harry," Green said. "The American Civil Liberties Union is anti-Communist."

From the first, Strauss showed he was going to be a far more powerful, indeed dominating, chairman. Security was made the first order of business. Now Harold Green often started his day with an early-morning call from Ken Nichols, the AEC general manager, who would ask Green to come to his office to get a security file. "See what you can do about this," Nichols would say, and it was clear that Green was to draw up a list of charges.

Suddenly, the security staff of the commission was spending long hours going through the files of men who had been previously cleared. Strauss brooked no dissent on this: "If you disagree with Lewis about anything, he assumes you're just a fool at first," one of his fellow commissioners told the Alsop brothers, "but if you go on disagreeing with him, he concludes you must be a traitor."

It became clear soon after Strauss's takeover at the AEC that he wanted to get rid of as many of the holdovers as he could, on the assumption that they were all too liberal. Suddenly, the AEC added considerable investigative muscle to its staff. Almost overnight, there was a new connection between the AEC and the FBI. Charley Bates, the FBI's man at the AEC, became a virtual extension of the AEC staff, and it was hard at times to know whether he worked for Hoover or Strauss. He was a classic FBI man, unusually privileged because he had a direct line to Speaker Sam Rayburn's office—his aunt was the Speaker's secretary. Unlike most FBI agents at his level, he did not have to leave Washington and serve in the Bureau's field offices periodically. Bates made constant references to Hoover—"the director wants," or "the boss wants"—that seemed to underline the immediacy of the Hoover/Strauss connection. Harold Green decided that while Lewis Strauss was so security-minded he probably moved to tighten security procedures on his own, he was also doing this to please Hoover. Indeed, thought Green, who was in an unusually good position to monitor such things, it was almost eerie. What the FBI knew, Strauss knew almost immediately thereafter, and vice versa. There was such an assumption of collegiality that to his astonishment, Green found himself looking at FBI transcripts of illegal wiretaps of Oppenheimer. Normally, Hoover took great care that no one outside his inner circle ever saw such illegal evidence, which was far more damning to the FBI than the subjects.

Strauss was a tough bureaucratic infighter. Whenever possible, he preferred to wield the ax in a genteel fashion; his favorite ploy was to get powerful friends in the business world to offer irresistible jobs in the private sector to the men he wanted to get rid of. No one in that era of government greased as many palms (or as many skids) as Lewis Strauss; he was wealthy in a town where few had money, and he knew how to silence potential enemies. Was there a former AEC lawyer who had left the commission feeling less than warmly about Lewis Strauss? Strauss, knowing that he was just starting out in legal practice, sent him a lot of business. Was there someone who might surface as a knowing and hostile critic to Strauss's autobiography? Strauss made sure that the potential critic was paid well, ostensibly to correct mistakes (which were not corrected, of course) in the manuscript. Yet what was taking place at the AEC was nothing less than a purge, Green noted, done "with consummate artistry."

The notable exception, Green noted, came to be Robert Oppenheimer. Oppenheimer had shown himself as one not lightly bought off. But J. Edgar Hoover wanted him out. The FBI director liked to judge people by what he defined as their Americanism—i.e. the more conventional they were, the more they thought like him and shared his prejudices, the better Americans they were. It would have been hard to find anyone less like Hoover than Robert Oppenheimer. Oppenheimer offended Hoover professionally and personally; everything about him jarred Hoover's nerves: his fellow traveling, his intellectual and moral arrogance, his left-wing Jewish background, the elegant schools he had attended, the pretentiousness of his life as Hoover saw it, the fact that he was willing to lie to protect old, left-wing friends. In recent years, Oppenheimer's defenders were ever less powerful and J. Edgar Hoover saw his chance.

Green became convinced that some kind of promise had been made by Strauss to Hoover to clean out the AEC, specifically, by getting rid of Oppenheimer. Hoover, in a different time, under a different administration, had acquiesced to Oppenheimer's security clearance, but he had become increasingly bitter about the AEC since the Klaus Fuchs case. Oppenheimer in the words of the AEC security people, was "like a bone in Hoover's throat."

Some thirty-five years after these events, it was hard to believe that at one time Hoover had been one of the two or three most powerful men in the country. His name alone struck fear in the hearts of the most powerful politicians in America, for he was the most successful of entrenched bureaucrats at a time of mounting fear, and he used that fear with great skill to expand his power. He had longevity, and he had secrets. Every year his files grew, and he added more secrets, and thus his power grew. The secrets were nothing so mundane as information about the criminal world or organized crime or even genuine cases of Communist subversion. There was some of that, to be sure, but the important information, the material that made his files so potent a weapon, concerned the moral failings of his fellow Americans, particularly those in power.

Because he was the keeper of the files, he was a man not to be crossed. He dealt in fear. In the inner circle of Washington, the very powerful (almost all of whom had in some way or another transgressed—sexually or financially) feared what his files contained on them; ordinary Americans were made to fear some great and threatening enemy by him. If the nation was afraid, be it of John Dillinger and other punk bank robbers or of the German American Bund or Communist espionage agents *next door,* it strengthened his hand, and his appropriations went through the Congress ever more readily.

He was a man who lived by ritual. Every morning at the same hour, a chauffeur-driven car picked him up. The car was bulletproof, so heavily laden with plating that it was powered by a truck engine. The chauffeur was James Crawford, a black man who had driven John Edgar Hoover for some twenty years, seven days a week, fifteen hours a day if the job so required. He could also, on the occasions that civil rights groups protested the lily-white nature of the FBI, be dressed up in a suit, posted at a desk outside Hoover's office, and described to innocent visitors as one of the Bureau's premier black agents. Already in the car by the time it reached Hoover's house was Clyde Tolson, Hoover's number-two man, as well as his closest friend.

It was Tolson's job to flatter the director of the Federal Bureau of Investigation and to make sure that others flattered him as well; he did this without subtlety, for the job did not require any. Tolson also spent much of his time telling others, when Hoover was out of hearing distance, what a great man the director was. These statements of loyalty, miraculously, almost always got back to Hoover. If the weather was pleasant, the chauffeur would let them off a short distance from the FBI office and they would walk the last few blocks at a brisk pace.

The two men lunched together every day at the same restaurant—Harvey's. No one else was asked to join them. (Once, a man named Lee Boardman was moved into the number-three slot at the Bureau, and he had the effrontery to suggest that he join them at Harvey's. His job was soon dissolved.) Hoover and Tolson sat at the same table, surrounded by empty tables to fend off well-wishers and gawkers, and for additional protection, the owner strategically placed a large serving cart to block access. His lunch rarely varied: grapefruit, cottage cheese, and black coffee; at dinner he and Tolson usually ate again at Harvey's: prime ribs and whiskey from miniature bottles that could be hidden from view by large napkins. Hoover was comped every day by the owner, a considerable favor, which he did not refuse. He did, however, faithfully leave a tip each day of 10 percent of the tab. The director did not like to be seen drinking or gambling in public. When he went to the racetrack (his passion), he boasted that he placed only two-dollar bets. In truth, he often bet a hundred dollars or more, but those larger bets were placed discreetly by FBI agents.

He also liked to boast that he never took a vacation. In fact, his vacations, with Tolson in tow, were as ritualized as his lunches and cost him about the same. They were pegged to the racing seasons. Famous for his frugality (repair work on his house was done by FBI agents; his income tax was done by yet another agent), he and Tolson traveled by train at government expense. The cover story was that they were inspecting FBI field offices. They would stay at hotels belonging to friends who comped them—in San Diego they stayed at the Hotel Del Charro, owned by right-wing oil millionaire Clint Murchison. Hoover would stay in the same bungalow every year, one built especially for him and Tolson by an admiring Murchison. Every afternoon he went to the Del Mar track.

The political and social prejudices of the era were his by instinct, and he waged a relentless struggle against those who might challenge them or, more important, might challenge him. He enshrined the American family and gave frequent speeches extolling its virtues (indeed, in his book *Masters of Deceit,* which tells of the evils of Communism, he quoted information excoriating Karl Marx for running a dirty household: "In the entire apartment there is not a single piece of clean and good furniture. Everything is broken, tattered and ragged; everything is covered with a finger-thick dust, everywhere there is the greatest disorder . . ."). In reality he knew remarkably little about the American family. He never married and had virtually no contact with his nieces and nephews. The families he knew were those idealized in Hollywood movies. No women entered his life if he could help it. The things he did, only men did; the places he went, only men went to. He was the lonely puritan, a morally fierce man, on red alert, fulminating to protect something he knew nothing of. He was also phobic, so frightened of infection that he kept an ultraviolet light in his bathroom to battle the armies of subversive germs.

He lived his entire life in Washington, D.C. His mother was strong and domineering; his father, fragile and weak, lapsed into depression and died of "melancholia" while Hoover was still young. In no small part because of his mother's will and ambition, he was always eager and hardworking; as a boy he delivered groceries and earned the nickname Speed for his quickness and efficiency. He worked all day to put himself through law school at night. Starting his career with nothing save his ambition and nimbleness—no family money, no fancy college degree—he joined the Justice Department as a clerk in 1917 without illusion and prospered because of that.

He lived with his mother until he was forty-three, when she died. During World War One he worked as part of the War Emergency Division's alien-enemy bureau. His efficiency and ability to master the bureaucracy were noticed by his superiors, and after the war he was appointed head of the FBI's Radical division. Working with Attorney General Mitchell Palmer, he led the assault upon the radicals of the twenties. He became assistant director of the Bureau in 1921, when he was only twenty-six.

In the late forties and fifties, there would be considerable political benefit in going after the radical left, but when Hoover began in the twenties, he was led by pure instinct, for he did not like people who were different, people who opposed the values in which he believed, people whose names were different. Intellectually, it was as if he was a survivior of a simpler America that existed mostly in myth; Richard Gid Powers has described Hoover's ethos as "a turn-of-the-century vision of America as a small community of like-minded neighbors proud of their achievements, resentful of criticism, fiercely opposed to change. As twentieth-century standards of the mass society swept over traditional America, subverting old values, disrupting old customs and dislodging old leaders, Americans who were frightened by the loss of their community saw in Hoover a man who understood their concerns and shared their anger, a powerful defender who would guard their America of memory against a world of alien forces, strange people and dangerous ideas."

It was John Dillinger who made Hoover famous. The FBI gunned down the celebrated bank robber in 1934 in a sensational publicity coup. Thereafter, the anteroom to Hoover's office was a kind of Dillinger museum. Powerful men waiting to see the director would have ample time to spend among the relics of Hoover's finest hour: a plaster facsimile of Dillinger's death mask; the straw hat he was wearing at the time of his death; a partially crumpled photo of a girl that Dillinger had been carrying; the glasses he had been wearing as a disguise; the cigar he had been carrying in his shirt pocket and which he never got to smoke, still wrapped in its cellophane. Thirty years later, talking with strangers in his office, Hoover would always manage somehow to bring the subject around to Dillinger.

The Dillinger case was the crucial link between the public imagination and Hoover and his Bureau. Publicity, Hoover learned, was power. In reality, a talented agent named Melvin Purvis was the key figure in taking Dillinger. Later, he killed Pretty Boy Floyd. But Hoover fought off any attempts by the press to lionize Purvis; his success in wresting the glory himself, noted Powers, "may well have been J. Edgar Hoover's greatest public relations triumph."

The lesson from this and similar incidents was not lost on others in the Bureau. The Bureau was to be a gray place, with a vast, dedicated *anonymous* team; only one person at the Bureau had a name. So great was Hoover's thirst for publicity that by 1940 Senator George Norris called him "the greatest publicity hound on the American continent." "No organization that I know of meets in Washington," Norris said, "without having some person appear before it to tell what a great organization the FBI is. The greatest man of all, who stands at the head of it, never made a mistake, never made a blunder. In his hands lie the future and the perpetuity of our institutions and our Government."

All announcements came from him. All publicity releases from the Bureau began by using his name—and had to mention his name at least twice more. When William Sullivan joined the Bureau as a young man, he was paired with a veteran agent named Charlie Winstead, who advised him: "Never initiate a meeting with Hoover for any reason [because if the director was less than impressed for any reason], your career would end on that very day. If Hoover ever calls you in, dress like a dandy, carry a notebook, and write in it furiously whenever Hoover opens his mouth. You can throw the notes away afterwards if you like. And flatter him, everyone at headquarters knows Hoover's an egomaniac, and they all flatter him constantly. If you don't, you'll be noticed."

Those reporters who played ball with him, who took their information dutifully and put the appropriate spin on it, were rewarded with more inside information. The FBI files on criminal cases could, on occasion, give a friendly reporter a beat, and Bureau cooperation could sometimes help with the sale of a movie or a book. In that way, Hoover gradually built up a coterie of favored reporters. They traveled with him and had complete access to Bureau files and personnel. Their work always met with his approval; they knew by instinct how to practice self-censorship.

Hoover worked easily with Franklin Roosevelt, who allowed him to expand his capacity to do illegal surveillance (albeit primarily against pro-German groups). Still, he never entirely trusted Roosevelt, whom he regarded as too liberal and manipulative, and he hated Eleanor Roosevelt and her associations with black people and other left-wingers. When Hoover was asked in later years why he never married, he would answer, "Because God had made a woman like Eleanor Roosevelt."

When Roosevelt died, Hoover, for once, was caught unprepared, for he had no link to the Vice-President. He searched his staff until he found a man named Morris Chiles III, the son of an old friend of Truman's. Hoover dispatched him to see the new President. Truman greeted Chiles by asking why he was there. To offer Hoover's and the Bureau's cooperation, Chiles answered. "Anytime I need the services of the FBI," said Truman, "I will ask for it through my attorney general." From that moment on, wrote William C. Sullivan, who eventually rose to be the number-three man under Hoover, the director's hatred of Truman knew no bounds. He became the one President Hoover did not have a special line to, and Truman's personal life was spotless.

In the late forties, Hoover challenged Truman on the issue of domestic security and won. Hit by a combination of scandals and a growing anti-Communist mood in the country, the President was under siege on the issue. Believing that the President was not sufficiently vigilant on the issue and sensing that the tide was going the other way, Hoover abandoned his usual nonpartisan stance and joined up with the Republican right. As early as 1947 he went before the House Un-American Activities Committee and gave testimony so hostile to Truman that it was nothing less than a declaration of war. The Bureau's files were made available to the new investigators—and, more often than not, were a source of McCarthy's charges. "We gave McCarthy everything we had," Sullivan said later, "but all we had were fragments, nothing that could prove his accusations."

Aiding McCarthy was a natural step: He had always been the defender of the existing order against alien threats. When a reporter from the *San Diego Evening Tribune* asked Hoover what he thought of McCarthy, Hoover was almost paternalistic: "McCarthy is a former Marine. He was an amateur boxer. He's Irish. Combine those and you're going to have a vigorous individual who is not going to be pushed around. . . . The investigating committees do a valuable job. They have subpoena rights without which some vital investigations could not be accomplished. . . . I view him as a friend and believe he so views me. Certainly he is a controversial man. He is earnest and he is honest. He has enemies. Whenever you attack subversives of any kind, Communists, Fascists, even the Ku Klux Klan, you are going to be the victim of the most extremely vicious criticism that can be made."

By the time Eisenhower was elected, Hoover was untouchable, based on his length of office, the lack of constitutional limits on his authority, and the fear of the average congressman of what was in his files. Since the fear of his files was such that he rarely, if ever, had to use them, there was an ongoing debate in Washington over whether they were as extensive as some people thought. The House Subcommittee on the Judiciary reported in February 1972 that the bureau held *883* files on senators and *722* on congressmen, this despite Hoover's official denials that he kept such files.

Washington was a city, after all, where it was true that the more powerful the man, the greater his sense of entitlement. In a city of powerful men whose lives were filled with more than the normal indiscretions of the human species—sexual, alcoholic, and financial—the mere threat of the existence of files was enough. There was, Hoover believed, a certain amount of scandal to almost everyone. He might have fancied himself the guardian of the greatness, strength, and *moral decency* of the American system, but his true power came from the very human deviations from morality on the part of the men who governed the country.

There was a certain symbolic value to Hoover driving through the streets of a democratic society in his armored car, which, because of its immense weight, far too heavy for the poor engine, frequently broke down. His visitors were carefully screened, and to the degree that his aides could control it, he saw only people who already agreed with him and came to pay homage to him. When he read his mail, it was deliberately arranged so that the letters he saw would be those that most fulsomely praised his activities. He was, in fact, surprisingly like the chief of a totalitarian state. He fit perfectly, Victor Navasky once noted, the authoritarian personality as defined by Fred Greenstein. He was obsequious to superiors, absolutely domineering to subordinates. He was director for life.

In the case of Oppenheimer, Hoover was, as ever, the cautious bureaucrat. He did not like to lose a case, and he was always sensitive to anything that might bring the Bureau criticism. He did not want anyone to know the extent of the FBI's illegal wiretaps, and he did not want the FBI blamed if this case somehow backfired and drove talented scientists from defense work. However, Strauss was out in front; Hoover was merely supplying the support troops—the files and the taps. Nor were they alone. By 1953 a number of Oppenheimer's enemies had begun to join forces. Powerful figures on the Hill and in journalism were beginning to single him out as the enemy.

In the summer of 1952 there was a *Wall Street Journal* story about the H bomb that seemed to be sourced by high Air Force officials. It divided the *good* scientists, those who wanted to move ahead quickly with nuclear weaponry (Ernest Lawrence and Harold Urey, for instance) from *bad* scientists like Oppenheimer, Conant, and Lee DuBridge. In the fall of 1952, Robert Lovett, the secretary of defense, turned to a colleague and said: "Have you read Oppenheimer's security file? I've just been through it and it's a nightmare." Then he added: "The quicker we get Oppenheimer out of the country, the better off we'll be." By 1953, McCarthy, McCarran, and Jenner were said to be tracking him. The White House began to fear McCarthy would launch an investigation of the atomic-bomb program. Some of Oppenheimer's friends were certain the senator was being fed material by Hoover.

In May 1953, *Fortune* magazine published a piece, written by Charles J. V. Murphy, an Air Force reservist: "The Hidden Struggle for the H-Bomb: The Story of Dr. Oppenheimer's Persistent Campaign to Reverse U.S. Military Strategy." Reading it, David Lillienthal was sure that it signaled an all-out campaign against Oppenheimer. The drumbeat was getting louder and louder. In August 1953, Strauss met with William Borden to express his doubts about Oppenheimer. Borden assured Strauss that he was not alone.

Oppenheimer, he decided, was clearly the enemy, and something would have to be done about him. Shortly thereafter, Borden hired an old law-school classmate, John Wheeler, whose assignment was to study Oppenheimer's security file. Wheeler soon decided Oppenheimer was responsible for the lack of enthusiasm among the scientists working on the Super.

The truth was Oppenheimer had become too dovish for the policies of his country, or at least certain institutions within that country. What made Oppenheimer so formidable a figure was not merely his immense intellect but his ability to articulate his knowledge in terms lay people could understand and his standing among his fellow scientists. To his opponents, and to the enthusiasts of the H bomb, he was someone who had to be brought down a few notches. It was not enough to remove him from the government, which had already decided to go after the Super. It was important to discredit him as a voice on public policy. If anything, there was now a race for the honor of taking him on. Some Republican senators, like Karl Mundt, discussed whether or not McCarthy should take a shot at Oppenheimer. McCarthy apparently was interested, but held off after being told by the White House that the matter would be looked into. The middleman between Eisenhower and the Republican right was apparently Richard Nixon.

Soon Strauss and the AEC announced that at the chairman's request, all classified material would be removed from Oppenheimer's files. Strauss said it was only a technical matter, but there was an ominous ring to it. In the fall of 1953, William Borden, who was planning to leave the Joint Committee Staff soon, had decided that J. Robert Oppenheimer represented his one unfinished piece of business. He spent long nights in 1953 going over everything he had on Oppenheimer. By the time he finished, he'd compiled over four hundred suspicious questions.

More the trigger man than a central player in the drama, Borden put his material into a letter and on November 7, 1953, he mailed a copy to J. Edgar Hoover and one to the Joint Committee on Atomic Energy. In the copy to Hoover, he wrote "more probably than not, J. Robert Oppenheimer is an agent of the Soviet Union." Hoover forwarded his copy to the White House. Eisenhower's position was fairly simple and essentially defensive: He wanted to separate himself from Oppenheimer as quickly as possible. He did not want a major investigation led by someone like McCarthy, and he did not want a scandal that might tear apart the nation's nuclear-weapon apparatus. Eisenhower ordered that "a 'blank wall' should be placed between Oppenheimer and information of a sensitive or classified nature." The matter could have ended there. Oppenheimer was no longer a member of the GAC but merely a consultant to the AEC, a consultant with whom the AEC might choose not to consult. But Strauss wanted blood. Jack Lansdale, who had been one of the top security people at Los Alamos and knew Oppie was no security risk, heard that Oppenheimer's clearance was to be revoked and asked his old colleague Ken Nichols to intervene. "There must be some way to stop this, Ken," he said. "Oppie's contract with the commission only has a short time to run, so why not just let it lapse and then not renew it." "Jack, I'm sorry," Nichols answered. "There is nothing I can do."

As the AEC began to move on Oppenheimer, it was difficult to tell where the commission let off and the FBI began. In the past when the FBI had done a security dossier on a person, it sent in the file and that was the end of it. Not in the Oppenheimer case. FBI surveillance of the scientist was constant. So close was the cooperation between the FBI and Strauss that by the time Oppenheimer was first presented with the charges against him, the FBI had already managed to bug two places he was almost sure to go to next: the law offices of both Joe Volpe and Herbert Marks, the former AEC general counsels.

For Harold Green, the Oppenheimer case was the one episode in his government career that he came not merely to regret but to hate. He sensed he was preparing charges for a hanging jury and a kangaroo court. Still, Green was surprised by Oppie's prolonged history of fellow traveling during the late thirties and the disingenuous answers Oppenheimer had given to questions from security officers during the Los Alamos years. Above all, Green was fascinated by the charges that Oppenheimer had deliberately slowed down the attempt to produce a hydrogen bomb. One document seemed to jump out at him—an FBI interview with Edward Teller some eighteen months earlier. In this secret conversation, Teller portrayed Oppenheimer as a once great scientist who was able, by using deft psychological tricks and considerable powers of persuasion, to persuade other, more patriotic physicists not to work on the Super. Teller believed that Oppenheimer was motivated not by subversive attitudes but by jealousy and his fear that Teller was about to build an even bigger bomb and thus achieve even greater scientific success.

On December 21, 1953, Lewis Strauss summoned J. Robert Oppenheimer to tell him that the AEC believed he was a security risk. Strauss gave him twenty-four hours either to challenge the AEC charge or to concur in his own repudiation. Oppenheimer, for all his awareness of the growing resentment of him in high places, was stunned. He sat that first day with his two lawyers (with the FBI listening in on electronic bugs), shaking his head and saying, "I can't believe what is happening to me!"

The lines were drawn. "Don't fight it, you can't win," his old friend Victor Weisskopf told Oppenheimer. "What you should say, if they take away your clearance, is that it's their loss." But Oppenheimer felt cornered. The charges cut to the core of his integrity as a scientist. He had had some sense of how painful the hearings would be. He did not, he wrote Lewis Strauss, accept the idea that he was unworthy to serve his government: "If I were this unworthy I could hardly have served our country as I have tried, or been the Director of our Institute in Princeton, or have spoken, as on more than one occasion I have found myself speaking, in the name of science and our country." Of course, he would fight the charges.

There was a curious duality to events now. As America was moving ahead to test the Super, lawyers hired by the Atomic Energy Commission were preparing to put J. Robert Oppenheimer on trial as a security risk.

The case against J. Robert Oppenheimer seemed likely to begin in April 1954; the test of the Super took place on March 1, 1954, at Bikini, in the Marshall Islands. It was the first hydrogen bomb to be exploded, and it was dropped not from a plane but from a 150-foot tower so that scientists could calibrate the damage with precision. The men controlling the explosion believed that it would detonate 7 megatons of explosion. Instead, it was twice as powerful, with a yield of 15 megatons. That made it a thousand times more powerful than the bomb dropped on Hiroshima.

The government's best meteorologists had studied the prevailing winds in the area in order to predict what the radioactive fallout would do after the explosion. But instead of blowing to the northeast as expected, the winds shifted to an area south of the projected course. Fallout blew across an American destroyer, whose seamen had been well schooled in what precautions to take: They buttoned up their clothes and quickly went belowdecks; later, they hosed down the ship for hours to wash away any of the ash from the fallout. No one on the ship was seriously ill.

Not everyone was so lucky. Three tiny islands some hundred miles to the east of Bikini were hit hard. On the island of Rongerik, twenty-six American sailors stationed to make weather observations knew enough to wash immediately, put on extra clothes, and stay inside their tents. But no one had bothered to tell the Marshall Islanders about their vulnerability to the most terrible of modern weapons. American medical teams were rushed to all three islands. Luckily on Rongerik, the worst radiation occurred in unpopulated areas.

The most unfortunate victims turned out to be a group of fishermen aboard a small Japanese fishing trawler called the *Fukuryu Maru* or *The Lucky Dragon*. The *Dragon* on this trip was anything but lucky. From the start of its cruise, five weeks earlier, almost everything had gone wrong. The regular captain was ill, there was constant engine trouble, the catch was marginal, and the fishermen lost half their lines to coral. Trying desperately to salvage their disastrous trip, they decided to try the waters east of the Marshalls. Forty tons of tuna was considered a good catch. So far they had taken only nine. On March 1, they decided to cast their nets for the last time on this trip. The men in charge of *The Lucky Dragon* were wary of the area around the Marshalls, where in the past the Americans had conducted atomic tests. They did not so much fear for their health as worry about offending the authorities of a great foreign power. A notice had been issued by the Japanese Maritime Safety Board warning of the possibility of a test around March 1, but this news, while it reached some Japanese boats in the major ports, did not reach *The Lucky Dragon,* which was out of the minor port of Yaizu.

Just before dawn on March 1, the *Dragon* was about a hundred miles east of Bikini. Unable to sleep, a young seaman named Shinzo Suyuki was walking on the deck and chanced to look toward the west. There he saw a giant whitish-yellow glow that turned orange. He raced belowdecks to tell his shipmates. "The sun's rising in the west!" he yelled. They woke to see the flaming orange light. "It a *pika-don*!" one of the seamen said, using the new Japanese phrase for an atomic bomb: Born on the morning of Hiroshima, it meant "thunder and flash." A few minutes later there was a great seismic shock in the ocean, followed by two enormous concussionlike explosions. Soon the crew could see a giant cloud reaching far into the stratosphere. Some of the fishermen wanted to get out of the area immediately, but others felt that their catch was so small that they needed to spend one more day fishing. So they unfurled their net. Aikichi Kuboyama, the radioman and the most educated man of the crew, wondered what had happened and pulled from among the books in his cabin one that gave the speed of sound. He estimated that some seven minutes had elapsed between the sight of the explosion and the sound from it. Calibrating as best he could, Kuboyama figured that seven minutes equaled roughly eighty-seven miles. He looked on the map and placed the boat exactly eighty-seven miles from the island of Bikini. The fishermen were nervous now, and they quickly pulled their nets in. Their luck had not changed. They caught only nine fish that day.

Two hours later the sky changed. Suddenly a giant fog appeared and a light drizzle began. But this was no ordinary rain, for it contained tiny bits of ash. "Some kind of white sand is falling from the heavens," said Takashi Suzuki, one of the seamen. The ash got in their hair and in their eyes, and the men tentatively tasted it. Some said it tasted like salt, others, like sand. The crew found, to their surprise, that they had little appetite that afternoon. Some experienced severe nausea. Others found that their eyes ached and the next morning they could barely open them. Their hands began to hurt where they had handled the ropes. By the third day some felt feverish. Their skin began to turn darker and they began to get sores on their fingers and necks, which had been exposed to the rain of ash. Still, they were mostly relieved to have gotten out of the Bikini area without being caught by the Americans.

On March 13, the AEC issued a quiet announcement of the test, not notable for its candor ("during the course of a routine atomic test in the Marshall Islands") and mentioning briefly that twenty-eight Americans and 236 Marshall Island residents had been treated for radiation ("The individuals were unexpectedly exposed to some radiation. There were no burns. All are reported well . . ."). The story made page-one news in Japan, though it was of no help to the *Dragon*'s crew who pulled into port the next day. Though many of the men aboard were very sick, it had not radioed for help on its return trip to Japan, for its men still feared notifying the Americans authorities. Kuboyama, the man who had the best sense of what had happened, went to see a friend named Ootsuka: "Ootsuka-san, look at me, I am done for." His friend took one look at his dark skin. "You look like a Negro," he said.

The crew was taken to a hospital, many of them seriously ill by this time. When he found out about his radiation sickness, Kuboyama wrote in his journal: "From this day on, unhappiness in our family began." At first the seamen were outcasts: No barber in Yaizu would cut their hair; young women, interviewed on television news shows, said they would never marry them. One of the seamen told a German journalist, "Our fate menaces mankind. God grant that it may listen."

Kuboyama became the central figure as the drama continued to unfold. He was the most articulate of the men, and, as it turned out, the sickest as well. Perhaps, Japanese newspapers pointed out at this time, his illness was a cautionary tale for millions. He was sure the Americans were being disingenious; for those who had been killed or had become sick at Hiroshima had been relatively near the epicenter, whereas his boat had been nearly ninety miles from where the explosion had taken place.

Japanese authorities found the American officials less than forthcoming about the nature of the explosion, and the Japanese doctors regarded the preliminary visits of American doctors warily; the Americans, they thought, seemed prone to arrive, make pronouncements, immediately dismiss the seriousness of the illness, and then go on to other matters. When the fishermen were eventually asked if they wanted to be examined by a team of American medical experts, they, led by Kuboyama, rejected the offer, because they felt the Americans were far more interested in studying them like guinea pigs than in helping them.

That summer Aikichi Kuboyama's health continued to decline. He was terribly weak. His white-blood-cell count was low, and he suffered from hepatitis. By September the entire nation took up a vigil as he hovered near death. At one point he cried out that the pain was unusually severe: "My body feels like it is being burned with electricity. Under my body there must be a high-tension wire." On September 23 he died. American authorities, speaking without attribution, told journalists that Kuboyama had died of hepatitis. More and more often, it seemed, the cover-up was a critical part of American policy.

As additional reports emanated from Japan on the terrible hardships endured by the crewmen of *The Lucky Dragon,* Lewis Strauss became so angry that he started to believe—it was a reflection of the paranoia of the age—that he, rather than the fishermen, was the victim. Those Japanese fishermen, he told Eisenhower, were part of a Communist plot to spy on and to embarrass the U.S. "If I were the Reds," he told Eisenhower's press secretary Jim Hagerty, "I would fill the oceans all over the world with radioactive fish. It would be so easy to do!"

On April 2, 1954, James Hagerty made a note in his diary that presented a remarkable insight into the increasing isolation from reality that was coming with the Cold War: "Here is good place to put down story on Japanese fishing boat who claims fishermen were 'burned' by fallout of March 1 H-bomb explosion. Lewis Strauss and others suspect this boat was a Red spy outfit. Here are the reasons (1) The fish, supposedly radioactivized, were in refrigerators when the fallout occurred. (2) The Japanese government has refused to let our people examine the fishermen. (3) Their reported blood count same as those of our own weather station personnel who were also caught in fallout, and who were not burned. (4) The 'captain' is twenty-two years old, with no known background of seamanship. Suspect this part of Russian espionage system, but we don't want to say so publicly. Would tip our hand on other stuff we also know about. Interesting story and hope it will come out some day."

At the same time a three-man board was being selected to hear the evidence against Oppenheimer, not on the basis of its experience in security cases but rather for political tilt. Those suspected of having any sympathy for Oppenheimer were vetoed. Strauss busied himself rounding up the anti-Oppenheimer forces. He reminded Teller how he had helped get him the lab and backed him when his was a lonely voice of opposition. Also, some thought Teller was personally indebted because Strauss had tried to help shepherd Teller's aged parents out of Communist Hungary in a clandestine operation after World War Two. Luis Alvarez, another Oppenheimer opponent, did not want to testify, but as Alvarez later wrote, "I had a duty to serve my country, Lewis countered. I said I had served my country during the war. Lewis' emotional intensity increased as he ran out of arguments. As a parting shot he prophesied that if I didn't come to Washington the next day I wouldn't be able to look myself in the mirror for the rest of my life."

There was, Oppenheimer's friends Lilienthal and Weisskopf thought, an insanity to the proceedings. "Somehow," Weisskopf wrote Oppenheimer, "Fate has chosen you as the one who has to bear the heaviest load in this struggle. . . . If I had to choose whom to select for the man who has to take this on I could not but choose you. Who else in this country could represent better than you the spirit and the philosophy of all that for which we are living. Please think of us when you are feeling low. Think of all your friends who are going to remain your friends and who rely upon you . . . ."

That turned out not to be true. The hearing—a trial, really, with a prosecution and a defense—was one of the lowest moments in American politics. The rules of evidence greatly favored the prosecution. Strauss did not use a lawyer from inside the AEC to conduct the hearing, as normal procedure might have mandated. Instead, he got a fierce trial lawyer named Roger Robb, prominent in conservative causes and a close friend of the right-wing commentator Fulton Lewis, Jr. Robb behaved as a savage prosecutor, but Oppenheimer was not particularly well represented; his lawyer was far too genteel. The elite of the scientific and political community testified to Oppenheimer's loyalty and dedication—Fermi, Rabi, von Neumann, McCloy, Kennan, Conant. But it was to no avail. Quite possibly no American public figure had been bugged and shadowed by the FBI more relentlessly than Robert Oppenheimer. There were wiretaps of Oppenheimer going back some fourteen years. Gone was the context in which things were said. Gone, as well, was any sense of his years at Los Alamos, during which he had sacrificed so much for his country. It was as if he was caught in a maze from which he could not escape. Asked why he had told a minor lie to a security officer a decade earlier, he answered, "Because I was an idiot."

On certain questions Oppenheimer's lawyers were forced to leave the room because they did not have sufficiently high security clearances. "There hadn't been a proceeding like this since the Spanish Inquisition," Lilienthal noted. Oppenheimer stood on the witness stand for some twenty exhausting hours, including three brutal days of cross-examination. In the end, to the surprise of his friends, he was not the powerful witness for freedom of scientific opinion that they had expected but a man diminished by tiny misdeeds from the past.

In the end it was probably Edward Teller's testimony that brought Oppenheimer down. Right after the accusations against Oppenheimer had surfaced, the two had met at a scientific conference in Rochester, New York. He was sorry to hear about his trouble, Teller told Oppenheimer. Oppenheimer asked Teller if he thought there was anything sinister in what he had done in those years. Teller answered no. Oppenheimer thereupon suggested that Teller talk to Lloyd Garrison, his lawyer. Perhaps Teller might be a witness for him. The meeting between Garrison and Teller did not go well. Garrison came away with the belief that Teller viewed Oppenheimer not only as dangerously wrong, but with virulent dislike. Teller told Garrison he did not, however, have any doubts about Oppenheimer's patriotism.

After being recruited by Strauss, Teller was confused and ambivalent about his role, it was later clear from FBI documents—not so much about testifying against Oppenheimer, but because he feared that in so doing he would become a pariah among American scientists.

Teller later claimed that he arrived in Washington unsure of whether or not he would testify, and it was only when Robb showed him Oppenheimer's security files that he decided to go ahead. The record is different: It shows that almost certainly a deal was worked out among Strauss and Robb and Teller and that much effort had gone into figuring out how Teller could best damage Oppenheimer while not rupturing his relationship with other scientists. A very delicate line had to be walked. When Robb asked Teller whether he wanted to suggest that Oppenheimer was disloyal to the United States, Teller answered quickly, "I do not want to suggest anything of the kind. I know Oppenheimer as an intellectually most alert and a very complicated person, and I think it would be presumptuous and wrong on my part if I would try in any way to analyze his motives. But I have always assumed, and I now assume that he is loyal to the United States. I believe this and I shall continue to believe it until I see very conclusive proof to the opposite."

Robb knew exactly what he was doing and moved to maximize the effect of Teller's testimony. "Now, a question which is the corollary of that," he began. "Do you or do you not believe that Dr. Oppenheimer is a security risk?" This was the critical moment, and Robb knew from the previous night's talk what he was going to hear: "In a great number of instances I have seen Dr. Oppenheimer act—I understood that Dr. Oppenheimer acted—in a way which for me was exceedingly hard to understand. I thoroughly disagreed with him in numerous issues and his actions frankly appeared to me confused and complicated. To this intent I feel that I would like to see the vital interests of this country in hands which I understand better, and therefore trust more. In this very limited sense I would like to express a feeling that I would feel personally more secure if public matters would rest in other hands." It was deftly done—Teller had punished Oppenheimer severely while seeming not to call him a security risk.

Finally came the denouement: Teller said that while Oppenheimer would never deliberately intend to do anything against the safety of the country, "if it is a question of wisdom and judgment as demonstrated by actions since 1945, then I would say one would be wiser not to grant clearance."

He finished his testimony, walked over to the couch where Oppenheimer sat, and shook his hand. "I'm sorry," Teller said. Oppenheimer, in a polite voice that nonetheless expressed his disbelief, looked at Teller and said: "After what you've just said, I don't know what you mean."

The testimony was devastating to both men. The board ruled

two to one against Oppenheimer. Northwestern University scientist Ward Evans was the dissenter. Considered a solid anti-Oppenheimer vote at the hearing's beginning, he became a defender after sampling opinion in the academic world. When Oppenheimer had been asked to run the Manhattan Project, Evans said, "They cleared him. They took a chance on him because of his special talents and he continued to do a good job. Now when the job is done, we are asked to investigate him for practically the same derogatory information." Many in the scientific world were stunned by the decision, among them a talented scientist of German origin then working in the American space program. His name was Wernher von Braun, and at the time of Oppenheimer's supposed security lapses, he had been working for Nazi Germany. What a strange country America was, he thought; in England, Oppenheimer surely would have been knighted for his scientific achievements.

Harold Green, the young AEC security lawyer who had drawn up the security charges, was enraged by Teller's testimony. You double-dealing, lying son of a bitch, he thought to himself. You don't have the guts to say for the record what you said to the FBI, the words I helped base this procedure on. The word Green finally used to describe the hearing was a *lynching*. The hearings were supposed to be a secret, but Strauss ordered the publication of the transcript. He did it, Green noted, as a means not merely of damaging Oppenheimer personally but of bringing additional pressure on the three Truman leftovers on the AEC to uphold the two-to-one Gray board ruling.

Green resigned in August 1954. When Lewis Strauss asked him why, Green was circumspect at first. Finally, Strauss asked if his departure had anything to do with the Oppenheimer case. Yes, said Green, though that was only partly the reason—it had merely reflected the entire change in the nature of the commission.

The administration was pleased by the outcome. It wanted to remove Oppenheimer from government and yet keep the case away from McCarthy. But as the case began to appear in the newspapers and Oppenheimer counterattacked in public, Eisenhower became nervous: "We've got to handle this so that all our scientists are not made out to be Reds. That goddamn McCarthy is just likely to try such a thing . . ." Later, after the review board ruled against Oppenheimer and the scientist decided to make the panel decision public, Eisenhower was furious: "This fellow Oppenheimer is sure acting like a Communist. He is using all the rules that they use to get public sentiment in their corner on some case where they want to make an individual a martyr."

Oppenheimer was devastated. He said he would not resign from the Institute for Advanced Study in Princeton. Strauss, who was on the Institute's board, said that he had not been moved by personal animus. To show his good faith, he told reporters, he had just secured a 25 percent raise for Oppenheimer at the Institute. But essentially, having his clearance revoked severed Oppenheimer from the cutting edge of work in his field. Now he could no longer even get together with his colleagues and talk informally about their work. Inevitably, he pulled back from his old professional friendships and became something of a loner, more remote than ever, more than a little sad. He chain-smoked constantly now. The FBI watched him constantly. Once a friend ran into him at Idlewild Airport and Oppenheimer motioned to three men off to the side, noting that they, or men like them, followed him at all times. The writer John Mason Brown once suggested to Oppie that he had been subjected to a "dry crucifixion." Oppenheimer smiled and answered, "You know, it wasn't so very dry. I can still feel the warm blood on my hands."

Later that year Enrico Fermi, who had ties to all camps, lay dying of cancer. Deeply depressed by the coming of the H bomb and the political squabbles it had occasioned, Fermi gave a statement from his hospital bed. "The Los Alamos laboratory," he said, "has deserved the gratitude of this nation for its development of both A and H weapons." It was, thought Emilio Segre, a close friend of Fermi's, his way of trying to restore some sense of justice after Oppenheimer's ordeal.

Edward Teller became a pariah within the larger scientific community. The jury of his peers, those who knew best what had happened, were the angriest at him. What made things even worse, many of them believed, was the fact that if there had been any delay in the creation of the Super, it had been caused not by Oppenheimer's coolness to the project but by Teller's faulty calculations. The summer after the Oppenheimer verdict, Teller attended a conference of nuclear scientists at Los Alamos. On the first day he went to the dining room for lunch. Across the crowded room he spied Robert Christy and I. I. Rabi. He eagerly went over to join their table, hoping to join in the easy camaraderie of old colleagues reunited after a time apart. While a room full of prominent scientists looked on, both Christy and Rabi refused Teller's extended hand and Rabi congratulated him on what he termed the extremely clever way in which Teller had phrased his testimony.

As if slapped in the face, Teller retreated and went immediately to his room. There he sat for the rest of the day and wept. He did not return to Los Alamos for nine years. Once notoriously gregarious, he now seemed quieter, more removed. His distrust of the world around him grew. Before he would talk with a news reporter, he demanded to know the reporter's position on the hydrogen bomb. He developed colitis. His wife, Mici, had to warn their children to stay away when their father was in one of his dark moods. Friends heard their young daughter say on one occasion, "Don't bother Daddy, he has black bugs in his head." Some eight years later, Princeton historian Eric Goldman interviewed Teller for a television program. At one point Goldman asked Teller if he favored reinstating Oppenheimer's security clearance. Teller was dumbfounded by the question. While the film rolled he remained still, unable to utter a word. The camera seemed to emphasize the devastating silence. Later, Teller pleaded to have the question cut from the tape and Goldman obliged, but word of what had happened got out and made the nation's newspapers.

The political shift taking place in Washington, with such men as Teller and Strauss on the ascent, was also marked by the growing importance of the Strategic Air Command (SAC). In an age just before the intercontinental ballistic missile, when the Soviets still had a vast land army in Europe, the SAC was seen as the key to America's ability to retaliate against any major provocation in the world. It was commanded by Curtis Le May, a legend in military circles—a sort of airborne George Patton. He was singleminded, demanding, fearless, and original, and he oversaw SAC's great expansion, coming as it did between Joe One and *Sputnik*. For a period after the war, aeronautical technology fell short of SAC's mission, but in the fall of 1951, the first B-47 bombers started to arrive. This signaled the marriage of the jet age and the long-range bomber. It replaced the old B-36, a much heavier prop plane with six engines, which had a huge range—up to 7,500 miles—but a limited top speed of 430 miles per hour. The B-47, by contrast, was all skin and power. It could fly at speeds of up to 600 MPH, far faster than any Soviet bomber, and it could reach altitudes of up to 45,000 feet. It could only go about 3,000 miles without refueling, but it could be refueled in the air by the KC-97 tanker, which had arrived in the summer of 1951. Thus its real range was more like 6,000 miles.

From 1949 to 1955, LeMay more than quadrupled the size of SAC, increasing not only the quantity of planes and equipment but also the quality of the pilots and crews. LeMay had been appalled by the conditions he found when he took it over in late 1948. The planes were in poor shape; the pilots, he felt, had gotten fat and lazy in peacetime. They weren't, he noted, "worth a goddamn." Almost as soon as he took over in October 1948, LeMay had ordered a simulated attack on Dayton, Ohio. It became a legendary event within the small world of SAC, a disaster of epic proportions. The planes were to fly at night and select targets by use of radar. The crews were unaccustomed to flying at combat altitude, the planes were not ready, and the pressurization did not work on many of them. Not a single one of the 150 crews involved flew the mission as prescribed. The level of bombing error defied the imagination. LeMay, privately pleased that the Dayton mission had shown to the pilots that they were in every bit as bad shape as he thought, called it the darkest night in the history of American aviation.

He wanted from the start to make SAC the best unit in the American military. He busted commanders who did not perform and rewarded those who did. Because he thought that his officers were spending too much time at the officers' clubs drinking, his men were not merely lectured about the standards now going to be set at SAC, but their wives were now summoned to meetings as well, and told that promotions would henceforth be given not on the basis of seniority but on the basis of performance. An entire crew would be promoted together, and it was the job of the wives to produce each morning a husband who was not hung over but ready to provide his country a full day's work.

During those years he changed the very prototype of the modern airman. The pilots of World War Two had been glory boys of a kind, dashing and heroic, eager to fight, drink, and love, quick to break regulations, often on the verge of a court-martial, it seemed, until at the last minute they gained reprieves by shooting down more Japanese fighters or taking on more dangerous bombing runs over Germany. The old-timers regarded LeMay's new breed with disdain—as straight-arrows who went to bed early every night, who worked with slide rules and briefcases, and whose ability to do math was better than their talent for picking up an enemy fighter coming out of the sun. There was an element of truth in this, for the new planes were increasingly complicated pieces of machinery, demanding ever more sophisticated mathematical skills. The new pilots were flying ever higher, and their relationship to their targets was increasingly computerized. In addition to bombing runs, they went on humdrum practice missions that included fourteen or fifteen hours of flying; these were exhausting and they assumed a pilot who had slept well the night before and who was in prime physical condition.

But if there were criticisms of LeMay and his new breed, they were never spoken to his face. He was too formidable a figure for that. In World War Two, he had sharply improved the accuracy of bombing raids on Germany by having his men spend more time studying photographic re-creations of the cities before their missions. He became famous for his low-altitude nighttime incendiary raids on Tokyo and other Japanese cities, using stripped-down planes without guns or gunners. The low-altitude bombing, he was sure, would increase accuracy, increase the range of the lighter planes, and reduce stress on the engines. Warned by aides that he would lose 70 percent of his planes at so low a level, LeMay nevertheless went ahead; he suspected that the rate of loss would be no higher than 5 percent.

The first mission was staggeringly successful. If it was not a date of which many Americans made note, then in Japan it was a night that a generation remembered. It was as if a great hand had torched an entire city. Tokyo, constructed as it was of thousands of little wooden shacks, had burst into flame. Fires jumped the narrow streets and grew larger and larger. Some 83,000 people died and another 40,000 were injured. Later it was reported that half the casualties were from suffocation as the terrible fire sucked the oxygen out of the air. The flak greeting LeMay's planes had been light, fighter resistance negligible, and some seventeen square miles of Tokyo had been destroyed. It was one of the most complete acts of devastation ever visited upon a city; as LeMay's biographer Thomas Coffey wrote, "at the cost of only 14 B-29s, LeMay had found out how to destroy Japan's capacity to make war." Other equally devastating raids on other Japanese industrial centers followed.

No one did what he did better, and no one was more quickly out of place in situations demanding complex political analysis. Not everyone in the Air Force liked him; to many of his fellow officers he was a crude man with no social graces, incapable of conversation, a man who insisted on smoking cigars right through a meal. He saw the world in the most simplistic terms imaginable. There were two sides in a struggle and the people on his side tried to kill the people on the other side. He made most politicians extremely nervous. His ironic nickname, which even his fellow Air Force officers used, was The Diplomat. On his first trip to Omaha to look at the prospective headquarters for his command, a local reporter, thinking of what this might mean for Omaha's economy, asked him, "General, don't you think this will be a great thing for Omaha?" LeMay answered, "It doesn't mean a damned thing for Omaha and it doesn't mean a damned thing to me."

He was not a man for an age of complicated, sometimes delicate, relations between the government and the military. In 1952 he
voted for the first time, choosing Dwight Eisenhower over Adlai
Stevenson, but Ike quickly disappointed him. He was not nearly as
conservative as LeMay had hoped, not nearly as worried about the
red menace.

As he succeeded in making American air superiority so complete, LeMay seemed to long for the chance to use it, to take out the
Soviet military machinery with one terrible strike. He believed, right
up until the mid-fifties, that SAC "could have destroyed all of Russia
(I mean by that Russia's capability to wage war) without losing a
man to their defenses." He did not advocate this policy to his superiors, but he still regretted their inability to formulate it for themselves.
"Some of us," he would add, "thought it might be better to do so
then than to wait until later."

He feared a first strike by the Russians, more than anything else.
It was his ultimate nightmare. He worked to make sure that all SAC
plans called for an adequate number of bombers to be in the air if
there was a strike, so that there would be immediate retaliation. To
him the Third World War was not an unthinkable idea; SAC was on
perpetual red alert, but even if he had not commanded SAC, Curtis
LeMay would have been on guard against potential enemies, and
particularly Communist ones. If Joseph McCarthy ever had a fellow
traveler in the American armed services, it was Curtis LeMay. No
one serving at so high a level in the U.S. government or military in
those days was probably more virulently anti-Communist. He did
not, he liked to say, worry about the threat from Russia itself. That
could be leveled with one strike. What worried him was the threat of
domestic subversion, and he was convinced that if the secret Communist cells ever made a move against any American institution, it
would be SAC. He thought the base security protecting his planes
was virtually worthless. "The stupidest people we had in the Air
Force were put in the Military Police," he said. So he upgraded his
Air Police. They would wear berets, white belts, and revolvers. That
was good for morale, he believed. Soon all SAC men and officers, at
the very least, wore their side arms at all times. The Air Police always
carried loaded carbines. When ground crews worked on planes, they
carried their handguns with them. Once, LeMay toured a SAC base
and found a maintenance man who had taken a lunch break and put
aside his weapon while he ate. LeMay immediately summoned all the
ground crews on the base. "This afternoon," he told them, "I found
a man guarding a hangar with a ham sandwich. There will be no

358 / DAVID HALBERSTAM

more of that." He decided his people should have antisabotage training. This soon featured security games—attempts by trained Air Force people to test security. Carefully disguised teams would arrive at a SAC base and try to slip in and kidnap high officers, or at the very least to plant fake bombs. One team—whose passes were issued in the names, among others, of Mickey Mouse and Joseph Stalin—penetrated base security rather easily and handed an officer a coffee container that turned out to be a simulated bomb; at the same time, other members of the team were stringing rolls of toilet paper from SAC bombers, each one bearing the message that it was a bomb and would go off in fifteen minutes. LeMay was furious. The wing commander was fired, and the entire unit was ordered to take special security training for five days, starting at 5 A.M.

There were even simulated attempts to "capture" LeMay himself, one that he foiled after noticing that a telephone repairman was wearing fatigue pants. LeMay quickly pulled a revolver on him. On another occasion Mrs. LeMay was working in her backyard when the enlisted man assigned to guard the house demanded to see her identification. She said that she did not carry it every time she went out the back door. In that case, said the guard, clearly a good deal more afraid of her husband than of her, he would have to take her to the guardhouse. A very heated exchange took place, at which point Helen LeMay finally went into the house and got her identification.

TWENTY-FIVE

The underdeveloped world was turning out to be a more difficult and complicated place than Eisenhower's policymakers had ever imagined. In the 1952 campaign, the Republicans had criticized the Democrats for losing so much of the world to the Communists. But now that the Republicans were in office, they found they had inherited a world filled with trouble spots that might easily go Communist on their watch. In Indochina, the French were fighting a colonial war against an indigenous Communist-nationalist force, and despite optimism from French military headquarters, the war was obviously not going well. The French public was tiring of it, and French politicians were beginning to ask America for increasing amounts of aid. As the colonial order collapsed in other parts of the world, a process much accelerated by World War Two, which had significantly weakened the traditional colonial powers, Marxism found fertile new ground. The Republicans found themselves facing a real dilemma; they did not want to "lose" any countries to Communism, but there were obvious limits to American military and political power abroad. In addition, as the Korean War proved, there were certain domestic restraints on American military involvement in the third world. The Eisenhower administration quickly found a solution in the Central Intelligence Agency, which had developed a covert-operations capability in addition to its mandated role of gathering intelligence. This willingness to use the CIA for paramilitary and other clandestine operations was a marked contrast from the policies of the Truman years, and the first break came in June 1953, just five months after Eisenhower took office.

The final meeting on whether to topple Mohammed Mossadegh, the legally constituted but left-leaning prime minister of Iran, was held in the office of the secretary of state on June 22, 1953. Everyone there knew it was a done deal: The men in charge had already decided to go ahead, and the meeting was really a last-minute review. But Secretary of State Foster Dulles signaled his importance by remaining busily engaged on the phone while the group arrived in his office. In fact, he remained busily engaged on *two* phones. That showed clearly he was the most important person in the room.

Even as he hung up one phone, he switched to the other, while the other senior officials bided their time. They included Foster's brother, Allen, the director of the Central Intelligence Agency; the undersecretary of state; and the secretary of defense. Kermit Roosevelt, the young CIA operative who was explaining the plans for the coup and who would be in charge of it in Teheran, may have been, like almost everyone else in Washington in those days, unimpressed with Foster Dulles's manners, but at the same time he was secretly pleased that Foster was the dominating figure on this particular team. For Foster Dulles was not only a hard-liner in public, he was an enthusiastic supporter on this touchy issue—the overthrow of a seemingly legitimate government. So was his brother Allen, Roosevelt's boss. That meant that no State Department underling was likely to oppose Roosevelt that day or point out that the United States was moving into new and uncharted territory to fight international Communism—for the Dulles brothers were an imposing team, able to bypass on an issue like this the slow and tedious processes of government. "A word from one [brother] to the other substituted for weeks of inter- and intra-agency debate," Howard Hunt, the former CIA man later caught in the Watergate case, once said.

A third strong supporter of the coup was Walter Bedell (Beetle) Smith, far less well known to the general public than the Dulles brothers. His influence was belied by his title: undersecretary of state. He had served Dwight Eisenhower as chief of staff during World War Two, and in the view of many of their contemporaries, it was Beetle Smith's unbending, steely nature that had enabled Ike to withstand the constant pressures on him from all sides. "The general manager of the war," Ike had called him. When, at one point, Field Marshall Sir Alan Brooke, chief of the British General Staff, had tried to have Ike removed, it was Beetle Smith who had taken on Brooke, telling him, "Goddamnit, let's have it out here and now." Perhaps only Al Gruenther, another of Ike's wartime associates, was closer to the President. No man admired Ike more than Beetle Smith: "I love that man . . . the sun rises and sets on him for me," he once said. It was Smith's job to be Ike's son of a bitch, to represent his rough and meaner side. Kim Philby, the British double agent, described Smith as a man with a "cold fishy eye and a precision tool brain." Smith alone among Ike's top aides had not been to West Point, but instead had come from the Indiana National Guard. He took over the CIA at Truman's request in 1950, understanding instinctively the high expectations for the fledgling intelligence organization. "America's people expect you to be on a communing level with God and Joe Stalin," he told his staff at an early meeting. "They expect you to say that a war will start next Tuesday at 5:32 P.M." Always irascible, he became downright belligerent in the years after World War Two, when he developed terrible ulcers. An operation was performed to remove half of his stomach, but the pain never went away. In no small part because he served as ambassador to Moscow from 1947 to 1950, the worst period of the Cold War, he became a true hard-liner. It was said that he considered Nelson Rockefeller something of a radical leftist, because Rockefeller had once said something in favor of labor unions.

Kermit Roosevelt, the young CIA operative in charge of the coup in Iran, did not personally like Beetle Smith; as far as he was concerned, he was a small man with a sour face and a personality to match. They were neighbors, and a year earlier Roosevelt's beagles had dug up Smith's lawn. Smith, then Roosevelt's boss at the CIA, had fixed his subordinate with a hard look and said, "Roosevelt, if you can't keep your goddamn dogs out of my garden, I'll shoot them." Roosevelt thought that Smith might as well have added he would shoot Roosevelt as well.

At a meeting such as this, Smith was Eisenhower's proxy. Foster Dulles, both of his phone calls finally completed, held up the report

Kermit Roosevelt had prepared and signaled the meeting had begun by saying, "So this is how we get rid of that madman Mossadegh!" The plan was based on a simple premise: If the Iranian people had to choose between the Shah and Mossadegh, they would prefer their historical leader over a mere politician. Therefore, the plan called for the Shah to fire Mossadegh and replace him with a man acceptable to the West. At a critical moment, the CIA intended to fill the streets with a pro-Shah mob in order to block any retaliatory demonstrations by Mossadegh and his allies in the Tudeh, or Communist party. Roosevelt had outlined the increasing Soviet influence in the area and the growing potential for a Soviet coup, like the one that had taken place in Czechoslovakia in 1948, within the country. The stakes were high: the immense reserves of Iranian oil and the critical strategic location of the country. Roosevelt thought the risk of failure negligible. He doubted the depth and strength of Mossadegh's power or that of the Tudeh. In addition, the coup would cost relatively little—perhaps $200,000—most of it for renting the mob. As the Dulles brothers had intended, there was virtually no dissent. Loy Henderson, the American ambassador to Iran ("one of a small band of distinguished foreign service officers of that era who understood the realities of the world we live in," in Roosevelt's phrase), did not particularly like operations of this kind but said that we had no choice. Henderson had decided Mossadegh was unbalanced and perhaps a maniac. "As I listened to him," Henderson wrote, "I could not but be discouraged that a person so lacking in stability and clearly dominated by emotions and prejudices should represent the only bulwark between Iran and Communism." The key representative from the Defense Department, Charlie Wilson ("inarticulate as usual but enthusiastic," in Roosevelt's disdainful words), was on board. Beetle Smith was downright eager: "We should proceed. Of course!" he said. Allen Dulles was almost paternalistic about the performance of his young agent, and Foster was particularly pleased by the tone of the meeting. "That's that then; let's get going!" he had said.

Kermit Roosevelt, known as Kim to almost everyone, was the grandson of Teddy Roosevelt and was thus extremely well connected in Washington (Franklin Roosevelt had been "cousin Franklin"; Joe Alsop was also a cousin). He had graduated from Harvard and taught history at Cal Tech just before World War Two. Like many of his contemporaries, he believed that America had to lead the Western democracies in stabilizing the world against Soviet expansionism in the postwar era. In the days just before the war he wrote an article describing the kind of clandestine propaganda organization the United States would need if it entered World War Two. Kim Roosevelt showed his article to Joseph Alsop, and Alsop implored him *not* to publish it but instead to show it to Bill Donovan, who was then organizing the OSS. Donovan, in turn, invited Roosevelt to come to work for him. In the postwar years, the Middle East became Roosevelt's venue. He visited there often, ostensibly to work on a book called *Arabs, Oil, and History*. To Kim Philby, who was the son of a famed Arabist, Roosevelt was rather unassuming. "The last person," Philby once noted, "you would expect to be up to the neck in dirty tricks." Philby even had a nickname for him, "the quiet American," which Graham Greene would later use as the title of a novel about an innocent but dangerous young CIA man in Vietnam.

Allied policy had kept Iran and its oil fields out of German hands during World War Two, but in the years after, it seemed a particularly vulnerable nation, its people poor, its modern social institutions weak. As Franklin Roosevelt once noted, "One percent of the population ruled—and they were all grafters—while the other ninety-nine percent live under the worst kind of feudalism."

By mutual agreement with the Americans, the British had remained the primary Western presence in Iran after World War Two. The British embassy in Teheran was a magnificent structure, whose compound took up sixteen city blocks; by contrast, the American embassy looked like a Midwestern secondary school, in the words of writer Barry Rubin, and in fact it was known as Henderson High, after the ambassador, Loy Henderson.

Since making the first successful oil strike in Iran in 1909, the British had taken Iranian oil as if it were theirs. In the years after World War Two, they had treated with great contempt the repeated pleas and protests from Iranian officials to make the relationship more equitable; inevitably they became the unwitting architects of a rising Iranian nationalism, which began to surface in the late forties and early fifties.

In 1950 the British made some 50 million pounds, in taxes alone, on the oil, while the Iranian government managed to take only a third of that in profits. The Iranians were not even allowed to look at the books kept by the British, nor were they allowed to use such company facilities as restaurants, hospitals, and swimming pools. Clearly, the times were changing, though, and in February 1951, the American oil companies worked out a new relationship with the Saudis which gave the Saudis 50 percent of the profits from their own oil fields. When the British finally accepted the idea that the old system of economic domination would no longer work and offered the Iranians a fifty-fifty split, it was too late. The negotiations between the British and the Iranians grew increasingly acrimonious, and in May 1951 the Iranians, thoroughly disgusted with the British, nationalized the oil company.

The politician who arose to lead Iranian nationalism was the volatile Mohammed Mossadegh, who became prime minister, and who was far more adept than the young Shah (the West's leaders in those days privately thought of the Shah as weak; the CIA's code name for him was Boy Scout). In October 1951, Mossadegh ordered all British oil employees home while Iranian troops occupied the huge refinery at Abadan. The Americans, fearing the Soviets would sense an opportunity, urged the British and Iranians to work out a settlement.

As tensions mounted, Averell Harriman led an American team to meet with Mossadegh and the Shah. The contrast between the lushness of the Shah's palace, the vodka and the caviar so readily available there, and the simplicity of Mossadegh's life-style struck the American team. Mossadegh was so frail that he was confined to his bed, and Vernon Walters, Harriman's aide and translator, had to sit as near Mossadegh as possible in order to hear him. "You do not know how crafty they [the British] are. You do not know how evil they are. You do not know how they sully everything they touch," Mossadegh said. The American team did not leave optimistic about the future.

Soon after, Mossadegh visited the United States, where hopes still existed that some kind of settlement could be achieved. But on his last evening in Washington, Mossadegh was visited in his hotel room by Vernon Walters, who reiterated the need for an accord. "Don't you realize," the prime minister answered, "that returning to Iran empty-handed, I return in a much stronger position than if I returned with an agreement which I would have to sell to my fanatics?"

A Western boycott of Iranian oil followed. Mossadegh broke diplomatic relationships with the British. Americans feared he was moving ever leftward. Mossadegh was a highly dramatic political figure. Many in the West mocked him because of the provocative nature of his speeches and also because he often went around in his pajamas. But even that was calculated. He used his histrionics, as Barry Rubin wrote, "to embody Iran personally, its problems and its requirements. The highly emotional component in his nationalist cause took hold among urban Iranians especially; his charisma could never be matched by the shy, stilted Shah." He was easy to underestimate. "Old Mossy," Anthony Eden called him.

Dean Acheson liked to describe a wonderful scene when Mossadegh first arrived in Washington: He was "small and frail, with not a shred of hair on his billiard-ball head; a thin face protruded into a long beak of a nose flanked by two bright shoe-button eyes. His whole manner and appearance was birdlike, marked by quick and nervous movements as he seemed to jump about on a perch." As he got off the train, he supported himself with a stick and on the arm of his son, but when he spotted Acheson, he threw down the stick and skipped over to greet him. Later, Mossadegh spoke in piteous tones: "I am speaking for a very poor country—a country all desert—just sand, a few camels, a few sheep." Acheson interrupted him to note that his country had, just like Texas, sand *and* oil. But being called on so obvious a ploy had seemed only to delight Mossadegh. Truman and Acheson had been somewhat charmed by his performance. Later, they felt they had underestimated his darker side; he was, in Acheson's words, "essentially a rich reactionary, a feudal-minded Persian inspired by a fanatical hatred of the British and a desire to expel them and all their works from the country regardless of cost." In fact, his family was immensely wealthy, among the largest landowners in Iran.

In November 1952, British intelligence sought out Kim Roosevelt, who, unlike them, still had access to Iran, and presented him with surprisingly detailed plans for a coup against Mossadegh. For a time Roosevelt held them off because he felt that the Truman administration was not sufficiently concerned about the threat in the area. But, he told them, it was likely that the Republicans would soon gain the White House, and he suspected American policy on covert operations was likely to change dramatically.

Roosevelt was right: Even as the Eisenhower administration was preparing to take office, Beetle Smith began pushing him to put together a covert operation against Mossadegh. Smith was extremely aggressive about it, Roosevelt thought. "When are those blanking British coming to talk to us? And when is our goddam operation going to get under way?" he asked. "As soon after Inauguration Day as you and JFD [Foster Dulles] can see them," Roosevelt answered. "They're every bit as eager to get going as you are. But we still have considerable studying to do before we'll be sure, reasonably sure, that we can pull it off." Beetle Smith was not a man greatly burdened by self-doubts. "Of course we can," he told Roosevelt irritably. "Pull up your socks and get going, young man," he answered. The key to success, Roosevelt thought, was the loyalty of the army. The Shah was young and immature, but he was connected to the nation's past. Mossadegh's popularity was thin—the mullahs were wary of him, the Tudeh was merely using him, the students were volatile, and only a few top military men supported him.

By this time, all sides were becoming edgy. In Iran, Mossadegh's popularity was slipping during the hard months of the economic boycott, and he was becoming increasingly dependent on the support of the Tudeh. The British were impatient and anxious to topple him. It was obvious from the start, Roosevelt thought, that the two Western allies had very different interests in the region: The British were driven by their desire to get back on line with Iranian oil, but the Americans, with their own large domestic oil deposits and their tight connections to the Saudis, were primarily interested in keeping the country out of the Soviet orbit. Starting in early February 1953, meetings between intelligence agents from Britain and America began taking place regularly on the subject.

Ajax was the name of the operation, and it took ever clearer shape, with Roosevelt and British intelligence in constant contact. On a regular visit to Teheran, Roosevelt noted that the gap between the Shah and Mossadegh seemed to be widening. A new Soviet ambassador had arrived, the same man who had been in charge of the Soviet embassy in Prague when the Czech coup had taken place in 1948. As the summer began, it seemed more and more a matter of who would strike first—the West and the Shah against Mossadegh, or perhaps Mossadegh and the Soviets against the Shah, or perhaps another party backed by the Soviets would act.

On July 19, 1953, Kermit Roosevelt drove from Beirut to Baghdad to lead the covert operation. He went under the name of James Lochridge, one of several aliases he used. He felt excited and ready to embark on the great adventure he had long been looking forward to. He recalled something that his father had written when he had arrived in East Africa in 1909 with *his* father, Teddy Roosevelt: " 'It was a great adventure and all the world was young!' I felt as he must have then. My nerves tingled, my spirits soared as we moved up the mountain road to Damascus." The guard at the Iranian border post at Khanequin seemed, Roosevelt thought, unusually listless. He was barely literate and mistook the description on the immigration sheet as Roosevelt's name: "Mr. Scar on Right Forehead," he wrote down.

From then on, it was a matter of moving quietly around Teheran and readying his Iranian agents to create the requisite pro-

Shah mob. It was also necessary for Roosevelt to meet with the Shah, who could not easily move around the city, particularly to a CIA safe house. Roosevelt had himself smuggled into the palace. An ordinary black car showed up at his agency house. Roosevelt got in the back and sat on the floor. A blanket was spread over him. The car drove off to the palace grounds and pulled inside the gate, but Roosevelt never got out. Instead, the Shah came out of the palace and slipped into the car. Roosevelt explained that he was the personal representative of Dwight Eisenhower and Winston Churchill. As proof of the Anglo-American commitment, he said, there would be certain signals given over the radio for which the Shah was to listen. The next night on the BBC overseas broadcast, for example, instead of saying, "It is now midnight," the announcer would say, "It is now . . ." then pause for a moment, and conclude, *"exactly* midnight." There would be a similar secret message contained in a speech Eisenhower was about to give in San Francisco.

This was the kind of intrigue that Allen Dulles and Roosevelt loved: It brought back memories of OSS during World War Two. Roosevelt's cryptonym was RNMAKER, for Rainmaker. The Shah's cryptonym was KGSAVOY; his nickname ("I hope it won't offend you," Roosevelt had told him) was Boy Scout. Mossadegh's nickname was The Old Bugger. Roosevelt also brought with him $1 million, in Iranian currency, of which about $100,000 was subsequently used to rent a mob and pay off key people.

It was important for the Shah to be out of the country when the coup was taking place, both to reduce his responsibility for events and also to get him out of harm's way in case things went wrong. Everything was set. The Shah was ready and eager. At his final clandestine meeting with the emperor at the palace, Roosevelt told the Shah of a cable from Ike (an imaginary cable, actually, as Roosevelt noted in his book: the occasion had called for a presidential blessing from Washington, but since Ike had neglected to mark the moment with his own words, Roosevelt made up what Ike would have said): "I wish your Imperial Majesty goodspeed. If the Pahlavis and the Roosevelts working together cannot solve this little problem, then there is no hope anywhere. I have complete faith that you will get this done!"

The coup itself began inauspiciously. Messages were not delivered on time, and on August 16, the Teheran radio did not, as the CIA had hoped, announce the Shah's firing of Mossadegh; rather, Mossadegh appeared to get in the first strike, announcing that the Shah, "encouraged by foreign elements," had tried to oust him as prime minister. Therefore, he announced, he was seizing all power to himself. The Tudeh rallied to him, and for a day the Mossadegh-Tudeh forces seemed to control the streets. The fate of the coup hung in the balance. Then on August 19, the pro-Shah mob, recruited by Roosevelt's man out of gyms and wrestling clubs, began to gather and shout slogans. The tide quickly turned. Roosevelt later took great pleasure in publishing a cable to him from Beetle Smith, written at the moment that the coup seemed to have stalled. "Give up and get out." By the time the cable arrived, though, the coup was a success. "Yours of August 18 received," Roosevelt cabled back to Washington. "Happy to report . . . KGSAVOY will be returning to Teheran in triumph shortly. Love and kisses from all on the team." When the pro-Shah forces made their move, the army remained loyal to the Shah and Mossadegh fled. It had all seemed so easy: Roosevelt, who was hardly an area expert and did not speak Farsi, had had only five American agents and a handful of Iranian organizers working for him.

It was a triumphant moment for Roosevelt. On August 23, the Shah received him. "I owe my throne to God, my people, my army—and to you!" By that, Roosevelt thought, he did not mean Roosevelt personally but the intervention of both America and the British. With that the Shah gave him a golden cigarette case, "as a souvenir of our recent adventure." A cable, apparently from Roosevelt, was sent back to Beetle Smith and passed on to Eisenhower. It was, given the intervention by Western powers, not without its irony: "The Shah is a new man. For the first time he believes in himself because he feels that he is King by his people's choice and not by arbitrary decision of a foreign power." Everyone connected with the operation was delighted: It had been done quickly, cleanly, and on the cheap. (Nine years later, Allen Dulles made a rare appearance on a CBS television show and was asked about the Iranian coup and whether it was true that we had spent millions of dollars toppling Mossadegh. "Well," he answered, "I can say that the statement that we spent many dollars doing that is utterly false.")

Kim Roosevelt flew to London, where he met Churchill. "Young man, if I had been but a few years younger, I would have loved nothing better than to have served under your command in this great venture!" the aging prime minister told him. On September 23, 1953, Dwight Eisenhower, in a private ceremony, pinned the National Security Medal on Roosevelt. Two weeks later Ike noted in his diary: "Our agent there, a member of the C.I.A., worked intelligently, courageously, and tirelessly! I listened to his detailed report and it seemed more like a dime novel than an historical fact."

In the meantime the British were back in business: Under the new charter the Anglo-Iranian (later known as British Petroleum) retained 40 percent of the Iranian oil and an American syndicate composed of Jersey Standard, Mobil, Texaco, Gulf, and Standard of California got the rights to 40 percent. Mohammed Mossadegh was tried by a military court on a series of charges: that he had not been loyal to the Shah, that he had tolerated the rise of the Tudeh, and that he had weakened the Shah's relationship with the military. He was sentenced to three years in prison, and served two and a half of them.

In the years that followed, the Shah became increasingly grandiose in his view of Iran's geopolitical importance and its military might; in that he was encouraged by Washington, which generally offered him the latest in American military hardware. But he was perceived by many in his own country as a mere pawn of the West, and his government finally collapsed in 1979. Though he had spent billions to create an army and air force loyal to himself, barely a shot would be fired in his defense.

The easy success of the coup in Iran was a powerful inducement to the Eisenhower administration to run more covert operations. If the Cold War was at a stalemate in Europe, then third world countries, with their vulnerable political institutions and comparatively strong military organizations, became irresistible targets for American policymakers, thereby offering an expanded role for the CIA.

TWENTY-SIX

Kim Roosevelt sensed the problem created by his success the moment he returned home in triumph. He was asked to brief the original group, plus Eisenhower (who had been shielded from the planning meetings, so if the coup was botched he could deny his involvement in the whole thing). Roosevelt's report was well received by everyone in the room; in fact if anything, he thought it was *too* well received. Foster Dulles was leaning back in his chair, "his eyes . . . gleaming; . . . he was not only enjoying what he was hearing, but my instincts told me that he was planning ahead as well. What was in his mind I could not guess. Would it be a future employment of the same counterrevolutionary—or revolutionary—approach?"

In fact, Foster Dulles's enthusiasm made Roosevelt so uneasy that he ended the briefing on a cautionary note: The endeavor had gone so smoothly, he pointed out, because local conditions were favorable—the Shah's historical legitimacy had proved far more compelling than Mossadegh's popularity, which was shaky at best. But Roosevelt sensed that Dulles was not terribly interested in *that* part of his report.

In fact, even as Roosevelt was briefing the top national security people about Iran, planning was going ahead on the next coup—one that they hoped would topple the leftist government of Jacobo Arbenz in Guatemala. In fact, soon after Roosevelt's return, he was offered the job of running the new covert operation, which confirmed his earlier suspicions about Foster Dulles's eagerness to proceed in this sphere. The success of the coup in Iran, Roosevelt sensed, had provided an irresistible inducement for the Eisenhower administration: It had been quick, painless, and inexpensive. A potential adversary had been taken out with almost ridiculous ease. American newspapers had all carried the cover story, although the press elsewhere and the Iranian people talked openly about the CIA role.

Administration officials had few moral qualms either about their role or about deceiving the American press and people. They saw themselves in an apocalyptic struggle with Communism in which normal rules of fair play did not apply. The Soviet Union was run by a dictator, and its newspapers were controlled by the government; there was no free speech or public debate as it existed in the West. To allow such democratic scrutiny of clandestine operations in America could put the country at a considerable disadvantage. The national security complex became, in the Eisenhower years, a fast-growing apparatus to allow us to do in secret what we could not do in the open. This was not just an isolated phenomenon but part of something larger going on in Washington—the transition from an isolationist America to America the international superpower; from Jeffersonian democracy to imperial colossus. A true democracy had no need for a vast, secret security apparatus, but an imperial country did. As America's international reach and sense of obligation increased, so decreased the instinct to adhere to traditional democratic procedures among the inner circle of Washington policymakers. Our new role in the world had put us in conflict not only with the Communists but with our own traditions. What was evolving was a closed state within an open state.

The Guatemala plan, Roosevelt found, was already well advanced. He checked around a bit on his own and decided that the conditions for success in Guatemala were not so favorable as in Iran. He turned down the offer and eventually resigned from the CIA—

just before the Bay of Pigs disaster, which, he liked to say, was compelling proof that his earlier warnings had been justified.

What was happening at this moment, as the coup against Arbenz gradually took shape, was that American foreign policy was changing. It was doing so very quietly, with very little debate taking place—in fact almost no public debate, for that was seen as something that aided the enemy. The President himself, and many of the men around him, like those who had served Truman earlier, believed they were operating in a period that was, in any true sense, a continuation of the wartime period, when America had struggled against totalitarian governments in both Germany and Japan; now, they believed, the same struggle continued against Soviet expansionism. Because the enemy was cruel and totalitarian, we were justified in responding in kind. Our survival demanded it. There were no restraints on the other side; therefore there should be no restraints on us.

The men who were the driving forces of this new philosophy, the Dulles brothers, Beetle Smith, and their various deputies, as well as the President himself, were from a generation profoundly affected by the vulnerability of an isolationist America to attack by foreign powers—as Pearl Harbor had proved. They worried endlessly that the very nature of a democracy, the need for the consent of the governed, made this nation vulnerable to a totalitarian adversary. Therefore, in order to combat the enemy, the leaders of the democracies would have to sacrifice some of their nation's freedoms and emulate their adversary. The national security apparatus in Washington was, in effect, created so America could compete with the Communist world and do so without the unwanted clumsy scrutiny of the Congress and the press.

Given the nature of the Cold War and domestic political anxieties, the national security apparatus gradually grew richer and more powerful, operating under a separate set of laws (on occasion, it would become clear, under no laws at all). In any crisis, if there was an element of doubt about legality, it was best to press ahead because that was what the other side would do. The laws for the secret regime were being set by our sworn adversaries, who, we were sure, followed no laws at all.

The key men of this world, the real insiders from the CIA and the other semicovert parts of the government, soon developed their own culture and customs: They might be more or less invisible in terms of the ongoing public debate about foreign policy, but that simply made them all the more powerful. They were the real players in a real world as opposed to the world that newspapers wrote about and Congress debated. They might be pleasant and affable and did not lightly boast of their power, but it was always there—to make or break kings and prime ministers and strongman generals if need be. At one State Department meeting on Nasser of Egypt, Allen Dulles reportedly told a colleague, "If that colonel of yours pushes us too far, we'll break him in half." A man who could talk like that had real power. When, during the planning for the Guatemalan coup, one State Department official questioned the wisdom of a CIA-sponsored coup to Beetle Smith, the latter brought him up quickly. "You don't know what you're talking about," he said. "Forget those stupid ideas and let's get on with our work."

Nor, in those earlier years, did the Congress or the press push the secret government very hard to know what was going on; they accepted the governing rationale that there were things one should know and things best kept secret. "I'll tell the truth to Dick [Russell]. I always do," Dulles once said before an appearance before Russell's Senate Armed Services Committee. "That is, if Dick wants to know!" So the temptation to do things covertly grew; it was easier, less messy. In this netherworld of power and secrecy it was particularly comforting to the more established figures of Washington to have a man like Allen Dulles as head of the CIA. His job so readily lent itself to the abuse of power, but he was a comforting figure in the Washington of the fifties, a kind of shadow secretary of state, he once joked, "for unfriendly countries." He was as affable as his brother, Foster, was not. Even more importantly, he lacked Foster's dogmatism and righteousness and rigid certitudes. If anything, he seemed more a figure from academe than one from the world of espionage. He was tall, attractive, craggy. He smoked a pipe, wore tweeds, and played tennis, the game of choice in Washington's clubby circles. No one in Washington was better connected socially. A friend once said to him, "Allen, can't I ever mention a name that you haven't played tennis with?" His book on his experiences in the CIA was typically titled *The* Craft *of Intelligence* (written in collaboration with E. Howard Hunt, a key operator in the Arbenz coup; later, a key organizer in the clandestine Bay of Pigs assault; and ending up as one of the key operatives in the clandestine Watergate burglary). Dulles was gregarious and he loved good food, good wine, and attractive women. He was a regular on the A-list Georgetown dinner circuit, a Washington hostess's delight. Indeed he was a bit of a flirt. (Someone once asked Rebecca West, the writer, if she had been Allen Dulles's mistress, and she had answered, "Alas no, but I wish I had been.") "He refueled himself on parties after an exhausting day at the office," one CIA aide said of him. That very visibility helped his image and seemed to diminish the idea that he could be a sinister figure from the clandestine world; a man that accessible, that open and gregarious, could hardly be a part of a world of invisible men with false identities who worked in the darkness. Rather, he seemed a thoughtful, fairminded, humane public servant, who seemed to offer reassurance that whatever things his men were doing, they were the kind of things that everyone at the party would approve of. He was not only the head of the closed society, he was its ambassador to the open one.

The two brothers were different emotionally, their sister, Eleanor, thought: Foster, righteous and unbending, as if always on a mission for God; Allen, a charmer of men and women alike. (His affairs were so notorious that whenever he had one, his wife, Clover, simply went to Cartier's and bought herself an expensive gift. It was her compensation, she liked to say.) Sometimes Eleanor Dulles felt that Allen remained religious only for the "delicious sense of sin" when he broke a Commandment or two. Allen was more shrewd, some believed, than intelligent. By contrast with Beetle Smith, Kim Philby thought, there was a certain sluggishness to Dulles, when he had to discuss broader intellectual subjects—except, of course, when he was talking about covert operations, a subject which excited him, so that he might talk long into the night about it. Allen Dulles, Philby thought, was guilty of intellectual carelessness. He tended to answer certain questions by saying, " 'I can make an educated guess,' which Philby thought, usually meant, 'I don't know but. . .' "

His happiest years had been those during World War Two, when he was posted with the OSS in Geneva, a city filled with intrigue—of Americans and Germans watching each other, of Germans watching Germans. After the war he had gone back into private legal practice but was brought back to the Agency by Beetle Smith. Smith promised Dulles that he would succeed him at the Agency, but in 1953, when Smith, somewhat bored, was about to switch and go over to State as number two to Foster Dulles, he apparently had doubts as to whether Allen Dulles should succeed him. Smith apparently thought Dulles too caught up in the love of covert operations for the job—the real substance of which was long hours spent working on research and analysis.

By the early fifties, Allen Dulles was so popular and respected that there was a broad general perception in Washington that the CIA was something of a liberal institution. That view existed, in part, because there were a significant number of bright people working there who had been to elite colleges and had liberal friends, and because Allen Dulles, unlike Foster, had protected his people from Joe McCarthy. But how deep that liberalism really went is another question.

Guatemala, the next CIA target, was a small, very poor Central American country that the administration's top officials, including the President himself, had already decided had gone Communist. Tensions between the United States and Guatemala had been on the rise since the late forties, when a harsh and brutal dictatorship under Jorge Ubico Castaneda had been overthrown and the Guatemalan government had begun to experiment with democracy. An inevitable byproduct of the Guatemalan social revolution was a new sense of nationalism, whose economic component was aimed at the United Fruit Company. Some called United Fruit *La Frutera,* others called it *el pulpo*—the octopus. In a country that was poor and weak, United Fruit was rich and strong—the largest employer in the entire country.

Allen Dulles was enthusiastic from the start about a coup against the troublesome Arbenz. Both Dulles brothers, and Beetle Smith as well, had close ties to United Fruit, and the top United Fruit lobbyist, Tommy ("Tommy the Cork") Corcoran, was a prominent New Dealer and Washington insider. Smith himself, on occasion, suggested that when he finished his government service he might make an excellent president of the fruit company, a suggestion Corcoran passed on enthusiastically to his clients. "He's had a great background with his CIA associations," Corcoran said, thinking that the people at United Fruit would understand immediately the value of having so important a connection. But United Fruit wondered if Smith knew enough about bananas. "For Chrissakes, your problem is not bananas," Corcoran told the Fruit people. "But you've got to handle your political problem." Though the United Fruit people did not give Smith the presidency of their company, they did clear a place for him on the board when he left the State Department in 1955. "The last thing I did for the Fruit Company," Corcoran later said, "was to get Beetle to go on the board."

From the start, Eisenhower was on board for a CIA-sponsored coup in Guatemala. More and more he saw Communism as a monolithic force that had to be combatted with extralegal means. This hard-line side of Ike was rarely revealed to the public. Genial, fair-minded, even-tempered, he never seemed a Cold War enthusiast or a jingoist; rather, he was the man who went before the world and called for an "Open Skies" approach to end the arms race. He was not unaware that poverty and nationalism were powerful forces in the third world, and he understood, especially in the later part of his administration, that the arms race was not only dangerous but that it needlessly used up billions of dollars that might better be spent among the world's poorer nations. Yet privately and in small groups, he seemed to subscribe to the prevailing simplistic view of the world as either part of the Communist or part of the free world.

But in this case Eisenhower was convinced that Guatemala had moved too far left and represented a potential bridgehead for Communism in the continent. He sent his brother Milton, more liberal than he, to the region and Milton seemed to concur. What Ike heard from both Dulles brothers and Beetle Smith was that Guatemala had irredeemably broken with the policy of the United States. The proof of it, clearly, was in Arbenz's land reform decree that allowed for expropriation of United Fruit property. The Washington government consistently hardened its line and came to the conclusion that Arbenz was beyond saving and had to go, that his government was in the hands of Communists.

In one of the early planning sessions, Eisenhower asked Allen Dulles what the chances of success in Guatemala were. Better than 40 percent, Dulles answered, but less than even. That was good enough as far as Eisenhower was concerned, and he told Dulles to go forward. As in the past, he reserved the right to cancel the operation if at the last minute it did not feel right to him.

In August 1953 the CIA went ahead with training several hundred Guatemalan exiles and mercenaries at a camp in Opa-Locka, Florida, and in Honduras, while putting together a small air force for this "national liberation force." By mid-June 1954, all the pieces of the coup were in place: the airplanes readied, a radio station set to broadcast on behalf of the rebels, and the liberator of Guatemala chosen—a military man named Carlos Enrique Castillo Armas, who had "that good Indian look about him . . . which was great for the people," Howard Hunt noted. All that was needed was Eisenhower's final approval, which he gave at a meeting on June 16. Foster Dulles, Allen Dulles, Charlie Wilson, and other top officials were at the meeting. Allen Dulles went over the plan; Eisenhower listened carefully and finally asked, "Are you sure this is going to succeed?" All of his advisers seemed confident. "I want you all to be damn good and sure you succeed," he continued. "I'm prepared to take any steps that are necessary to see that it succeeds. When you commit the flag, you commit to win." Two days later Operation Success began.

. . .

Guatemala was one of the poorest places in the Western Hemisphere. No wonder American policymakers feared that it was a fertile place for Communism to take hold. A small oligarchy owned most of the land, wages were desperately low (in recent months there had been strikes by workers on United Fruit's banana plantations seeking wages of $1.50 a day), and United Fruit, with the help of bribes and payoffs, controlled the political process of the country. It also controlled, either directly or indirectly, as Stephen Schlesinger and Stephen Kinzer note in their book *Bitter Fruit,* some 40,000 jobs in Guatemala, and its investment there was valued at $60 million. Almost all of Guatemala's railroad tracks belonged to a subsidiary of United Fruit; and in addition, United Fruit owned the telephone and telegraph facilities and ran the most important Atlantic port. Virtually anything that was modern belonged to La Frutera; what was old and broken-down belonged to the nation.

Of La Frutera's vast acreage of land, a relatively small percentage was kept under cultivation, in order not to flood the market with bananas and bring the price down. By 1950 the company reported an annual profit of $65 million, a figure that represented twice the total revenue of the Guatemalan government. No one important in the Guatemalan government existed without the approval of United Fruit. As such the country was traditionally run by anti-Communist dictators, plucked out of the military, who liked to use their police powers to suppress any domestic social unrest. It was not by chance that the names of Central American and Caribbean dictators came to read like a rogue's list of the region's most despised despots: Somoza, Trujillo, Batista, Ubico of Guatemala, and Galvez of Honduras. All of them were backed by the American government and its partner in the area, United Fruit.

The Ubico regime had come to power in Guatemala in 1930. It was a cruel, almost sadistic government, particularly brutal in the way it treated the Indian peasantry. Paranoid and ignorant, Ubico seemed to glory in the fear his name inspired and delighted in the popular image of himself as a "wild and dangerous beast." Once when a minor official named Miguel Ydigoras Fuentes, a rather conservative man, suggested that Guatemala's truck drivers, who were often on the road for three days at a time, receive some traveling expenses, Ubico screamed at him, "So! You too are a Communist!" On another occasion he accused Ydigoras of reading Communist literature: When the latter protested that he had been reading a papal encyclical and showed it to Ubico, Ubico skimmed it and said, "Then it's true! There *was* a Communist Pope!"

When conservative American political advisers suggested to Sam Zemurray, United Fruit's head (Sam the Banana Man was the nickname he had gotten as a poor boy working the New Orleans port when he had managed to corner the banana market), that the company's repressive policies put it on some sort of political collision course with its poorest workers, he waved them aside. Political revolution was no problem, he liked to say; the peasants were too ignorant.

In 1944 the country's fledgling middle class had revolted and brought back from exile the popular Juan Jose Arevalo Bermejo, a schoolteacher and writer who had been living in self-imposed exile for almost a decade because of his open opposition to Ubico. He was a true democrat, with a passionate belief that economic progress came through the political participation of ordinary people; his heroes were Bolivar, Lincoln, and Franklin Roosevelt.

Arevalo was, as Richard Immerman, the historian, noted, almost too idealistic, a kind of latter-day Don Quixote, yet "his idealism coincided with the revolutionary fervor so prevalent in his country." If his orientation was essentially liberal, the results of his administration were somewhat mixed. There was so far to go: 70 percent of the country (and 90 percent of the Indians) was illiterate when he took office. Yet every move he had made on behalf of ending ignorance and injustice was viewed with growing uneasiness by powerful interests by United Fruit. Particularly suspect were the labor laws borrowed from the New Deal, which sought to improve working conditions and provide some kind of compensation for work-related injuries. Even worse, the new laws gave workers the right to form unions and, if necessary, to strike. To the top executives of United Fruit, accustomed to having their every whim turned into law in Guatemala (and unhappy with Roosevelt's domestic reforms anyway), the idea of sharing economic power in Central America was unthinkable. Their resistance to reforms, and their belief that the people of Guatemala were not entitled to the same freedoms as the citizens of the United States, eventually embittered Arevalo. In his valedictory speech in March 1951, he had noted with no small amount of scorn the irony of this opposition from "the banana magnates, co-nationals of Roosevelt, [who] rebelled against the audacity of a Central American president who gave to his fellow citizens a legal equality with the honorable families of the exporters . . ."

The tensions of the Arevalo years came quickly to a head during the administration of his successor, Jacobo Arbenz. If Arevalo had focused on improving educational opportunities, Arbenz wanted land reform. Even before he took over, he announced that United Fruit would have to respect the Guatemalan government as the arbiter in any disputes between labor and management. That was a truly revolutionary concept, for it took the right to regulate economic disputes from the company and awarded it to the country. Arbenz put forth a number of other demands, that made clear he was a new and obstinate foe. There was a strike between workers and the company, which the company was unwilling to settle. The Guatemalan courts ruled in favor of the workers, but anxious to show that it was bound by no jurisdiction save its own, United Fruit laid off the four thousand workers. The Guatemalan court responded by suggesting that a 26,000-acre farm belonging to United Fruit be confiscated as a guarantee for the workers' back wages. This marked an escalation of grievance on both sides. In March 1952 the company agreed to pay $650,000 to the workers.

There was almost a coup attempt in 1952. It was called Operation Fortune, and it was originally promoted by Nicaragua's Somoza, who was extremely unhappy with the new direction taken by the Guatemalan government, which he saw as threatening his own autocratic rule. He told the Americans, "Just give me the arms and I'll clean up Guatemala for you in no time." Beetle Smith, at the CIA, and Truman apparently approved the idea. The plan called for arms to be shipped from the United States to Nicaragua by United Fruit company ships in boxes labeled AGRICULTURAL MACHINERY. But shortly after the ship left for Nicaragua, a CIA operative approached Edward Miller, the assistant secretary of state for inter-American affairs, and asked him to sign a receipt for the arms, on behalf of State's munitions department. Miller immediately got in touch with David Bruce, the undersecretary of state, who brought it to Acheson, who in turn went to Truman and stopped the operation.

Arbenz's critical land reform, known as Decree 900, was passed by the Guatemalan national assembly in June 1952. To his supporters it was the key to the future. Fertile cultivated land was to be given in packets from 8.5 to 17 acres for a peasant family, and in lots from 26 to 33 acres if it had lain fallow. In the succeeding eighteen months, despite the opposition of large landholders, some 100,000 Guatemalan families (almost all of them Indian) received 1.5 million acres of land, for which the government paid $8.3 million in long-term bonds. Arbenz himself gave up 1,700 acres.

Arbenz refused to heed the warnings of various American officials that the land expropriation would be viewed in the north almost as declaration of war. By February 1953, some 234,000 acres on the Pacific coast had been expropriated from United Fruit. That was enough for Washington. From then on, the coup plotting went into high gear. In February 1954 the government expropriated an additional 173,000 acres from the Caribbean coast. Worse, the government decided to pay only $1.185 million in compensation—the exact figure at which the company, in its own devious way, had chosen to value the same land for tax purposes. United Fruit was furious, and in April 1954 the U.S. State Department, acting on its behalf, presented Arbenz with a bill of $15.8 million for the land.

In all of this there was precious little evidence that the Arbenz government was dominated by Communists. But Washington began to gradually tighten the screws on Arbenz. It moved to isolate him by refusing to sell him any arms. In October 1953 Jack Peurifoy was sent down as ambassador. It was an important signal a coup might be in the works, for not only had Peurifoy played an important role in crushing the Communists in Greece, he had helped hammer different, fractious right-wing groups in that country into an anti-Communist coalition. In addition, he was a Democrat, in case the operation failed. If anyone had to take the fall, let it be someone with close connections to Acheson. Peurifoy was conservative, a hard-line anti-Communist, in his own words, "a Star-Spangled Banner guy."

He was not a man much given to the subtleties of policy, and his marching orders, as far as he was concerned, were to get rid of Arbenz. Almost the first question he asked Marian Lopez-Herrarte, a wealthy Guatemalan landowner with ties to the CIA, was what it would take to topple Arbenz. Would an American boycott of Guatemalan coffee do it? No, said Lopez-Herrarte, the government would still manage to smuggle out enough through El Salvador. But if the Americans cut off all Guatemala's oil, "the government will fall in a week." Peurifoy, Lopez-Herrarte thought admiringly, "seemed much more C.I.A. than State Department to me."

Peurifoy took his time in meeting with Arbenz, as he cabled back to Washington, because, "I had the psychological advantage of being new and government feels I have come to Guatemala to use the big stick. We have been letting them stew . . ." What Washington felt about the Arbenz government's land reform was made clear from Peurifoy's first warning to foreign minister Toriello: "Agrarian reform had been instituted in China and that today China was a Communist country." Essentially, the Guatemalan government had no room to maneuver other than to end its social revolution. The

United States had handed an unspeakably poor country a tough ultimatum.

Actually, the United States did not think Arbenz would change, and it was not unhappy with the idea of using Guatemala to show other Latin-American countries the limits of their freedom. A few months after Peurifoy arrived, someone asked him about Arbenz's future, and the ambassador answered, "We are making out our Fourth of July reception invitations, and we are not including any of the present administration." From then on, he openly encouraged dissident military leaders to rise up against Arbenz. In December he sent a long cable to Eisenhower, which removed any of the President's remaining doubts. "If Arbenz is not a Communist," he cabled, "he will certainly do until one comes along." Nothing could be done to change the Arbenz policies, he reported. "The candle is burning slowly and surely, and it is only a matter of time before the large American interests will be forced out completely."

All that was left was for the administration to find a rationale that would justify American action. It came in mid-April 1954, when a CIA agent in Poland noted the suspicious manner in which a Swedish ship named the *Alfhem* was loaded in the Polish port of Szczecin. The agent thought its cargo was Czech arms. Allen Dulles had another agent check the ship as it passed through the Kiel Canal, and the Agency became convinced that it was carrying arms. On May 17, the *Alfhem* reached Puerto Barrios, Guatemala's main port on the eastern coast. There Peurifoy and his staff were at the dock waiting for it. Unable to buy arms from the West, despite a series of desperate pleas to Washington, and fearing the mounting pressure from hostile surrounding dictatorships, the Arbenz government had secretly moved to buy arms from the East bloc. It was a critical mistake: That, if anything, was the smoking gun Washington wanted, proof that Arbenz was playing with Communists. The Congress was enraged.

That a coup was coming was by now an open secret in Guatemala. Mercenaries at the two CIA training camps were so well paid—about three hundred dollars a month, or ten times the going wage for United Fruit workers—that they had boasted rather openly and told of their plan to invade the capital. The day before the coup occurred, Peurifoy greeted his staff in the morning by saying, "Well, boys, tomorrow at this time we'll have ourselves a party." In fact, the news was so public that Peurifoy's son came home early from school, announcing that there would be no school in the afternoon because there was going to be a revolution at 5:00 P.M.

There was one crucial ingredient left for the success of the coup and that was the cooperation, voluntary and involuntary, of the American press. This meant it was necessary for the press corps to tell the public that the coup was the work of an indigenous Guatemalan force. In general, given the tensions of the Cold War, the obvious sins of Eastern European Communism, and the fear of being accused of being soft on Communism, most editors and reporters tended to accept Washington's side in any dispute involving Communism. In effect, the men controlling an operation like this wanted the same trust that had existed between journalists and public officials during World War Two. United Fruit had already achieved considerable success in putting out its side of events, thanks principally to the skills of Edward Bernays, a pioneer in public relations who was well connected in the world of print media. He convinced United Fruit to sponsor a series of press junkets for selected reporters to Guatemala: These emphasized the benign aspect of the fruit company and the sinister purpose of the Arbenz government.

But in 1954, however, the administration hit a snag with the press when it barred a talented *New York Times* reporter from the venue. Sydney Gruson was then thirty-eight years old and he was based in Mexico City, which meant that his beat included Guatemala. Gruson had no particular ideological bent: He had previously reported from Eastern Europe, and watching the harsh ways of the Communists as they solidified their power there had made him something of a hard-liner. Both Irish and Jewish, born in Dublin, Gruson was a man of unusual personal charm, with a joie de vivre rarely seen in *Times* correspondents. In fact, if in the past he had ever gotten in trouble with his bosses, it was not because there was a radical bent to his reporting but rather because his employers felt he was having altogether too much of a good time. When Gruson had first arrived in Mexico City, the *Times* was not particularly interested in Central America, so he could cover it, he assumed, without great exertion. Mexico City was not, he once noted, "an onerous assignment." He began to live the high life, rubbing shoulders with a number of the city's wealthiest citizens, including a member of the Du Pont family who owned a string of horses and who had decided to buy the local racetrack. Since that meant she could not own her horses anymore, she gave one, Candice Ann, to Gruson as a gift: "You're crazy," Gruson's wife, the journalist Flora Lewis, told him. "You know you won't be satisfied owning just one." She was absolutely right— Gruson quickly went out and bought four more. Shortly after that, Turner Catledge, the *Times* managing editor, showed up for an inspection tour of his man in the field. Gruson greeted Catledge at the airport, drove him to the palatial residence where he lived, and then said, "Turner, we can do this one of two ways. We can go to the office every day and I can make a lot of phone calls to Mexican bureaucrats whom I would not be interviewing if you were not here, for stories I would not be filing if you were not here, or you can do what I do, which is go to the racetrack every day because I own five racehorses, play golf four days a week, and go to the bullfights once a week." Catledge chose authentic Mexican life as Gruson lived it; he had a thoroughly good time, and upon his departure, he warmly praised Gruson for showing him such a good time. But soon Gruson was recalled to New York.

During his sojourn in Mexico City, Gruson had written several stories about the Arbenz government that had pleased the embassy and irritated the government, and he had been expelled from Guatemala by Arbenz in November 1953. Peurifoy himself had argued for Gruson's readmission, and in time, he was readmitted to the country. This time, however, his stories angered Peurifoy, particularly those implying that Latin American nations were rallying to Arbenz's side after the *Alfhem* incident. That directly contradicted the embassy line. American attacks on Arbenz, Gruson reported, did not necessarily hurt the Guatemalan leader in Latin America, and "the reaction [to them] has served to remind observers that the dominant feeling among articulate Guatemalans is not pro- or anti-Communism, or pro- or anti-Yankeeism, but fervent nationalism." In the eyes of the embassy people, that made Gruson a radical.

After filing the stories, Gruson eventually returned to Mexico, but as the date for the coup neared, he asked permission to return to Guatemala. He found, much to his surprise, that his foreign editor, Emmanuel Freedman, ordered him to stay in Mexico to cover the Mexican angle on the story. Gruson knew there was no Mexican angle to the story. His phone conversations with Freedman over the subject became heated: "Sydney," Freedman said. "We want you to stay in Mexico to cover the spillover there." "Manny," he answered. "I know Mexico and I know Guatemala, and there isn't going to be any spillover in Mexico." "But the *publisher* wants you to cover the spillover," Freedman said. Suddenly, Gruson became aware that he was being iced on a very big story—a story that quite properly was his. "Goddamnit, Manny, I know more than the publisher about both Guatemala and Mexico, and I want to go back to Guatemala," Gruson said. "Sydney," Freedman had said, closing the case. "There is nothing I can do. This is beyond my control. I cannot let you go back."

There was a reason why Manny Freedman's decision was set in stone. Unknown to Gruson, Allen Dulles of the CIA was wary of his reporting and a series of cables from Peurifoy had made him even warier. Dulles had gone to his main contact at the *Times,* his Princeton classmate General Julius Ochs Adler, the nephew of the founder and the cousin of the then publisher, Arthur Hays Sulzberger. Adler worked on the business side of the *Times* and was rarely involved in news decisions. A company commander during World War One, he had served with Douglas MacArthur during World War Two and had ended the war with the rank of major general, a title he still liked. In his postwar incarnation, he was, Harrison Salisbury once noted, "a major general, a no-nonsense patriot, an ardent anti-Communist, sometimes coming on like an American Colonel Blimp, but with an inner warmth which made him dear to his children despite the fact that, as a close friend once said, 'he treated his family as he would his regiment in battle.' " Julie Adler was less than impressed with many of the *Times* foreign correspondents, and he sometimes let the publisher know he thought they might as well have been in collusion with the enemy.

Dulles invited Adler to meet with him in Washington in early June, some two weeks before the coup was supposed to start. At dinner, Dulles had explained that some very delicate events were coming up in Guatemala and that he and his brother, Foster, would feel a good deal more comfortable if Sydney Gruson did not cover the story. Dulles added that the CIA had certain information about Gruson that had caused its top people to question Gruson's political reliability. Nothing that Dulles said greatly surprised Adler: He himself had already decided that Gruson was a dangerous radical. Adler passed on his information to Sulzberger, who was very upset by the charges, and in a rare act of interference with the news division, he ordered Manny Freedman to keep Gruson out of Guatemala.

Gruson was furious about being kicked out of Guatemala and missing the story, and when the coup took place a few days later he was sure that Peurifoy had been behind the *Times*'s strange behavior. Sulzberger, having accepted Dulles's very serious charges at face value, began to feel uneasy with them. He began to press the head of the CIA for more information, as Harrison Salisbury later noted, politely and sympathetically. He did this even before the coup took place, and he made it clear that the matter was not going to rest until he got more information. If Gruson was really a subversive, Sulzberger did not want him on the paper, and if he was not a subversive, then there was no reason he should be barred from Guatemala or any other country.

. . .

The CIA coup began on June 18 and was acted out by a ragtag army that seemed ill prepared to conquer. In fact, the liberator, Castillo Armas, moved a few miles across the border from Honduras and then did not budge. One of the CIA's main responsibilities was to keep American journalists out of the area lest they find out how pathetic Castillo Armas's army really was. Two of the three airplanes from the liberation air force were soon out of action, one of them downed after its American pilot failed to pay attention to his gas gauge and had to crash-land. The CIA air force was puny and extremely primitive; in once case a CIA pilot leaned out of the cabin of his aged plane to lob hand grenades on military installations below. Against the forces of any developed country, the invading forces would have quickly collapsed. But Guatemala's institutions were so weak that Arbenz was largely paralyzed and could not even get his (equally puny) air force into the air. Nevertheless, three days into the coup it appeared likely to collapse. The CIA people on location had to demand more planes—without which they would surely fall.

A meeting was called in the White House to deal with the request. Henry Holland, a State Department official who opposed the coup, showed up lugging three tomes on international law. But in the end, Ike decided to go with Allen Dulles's request for the additional fighter bombers. "Mr. President," Dulles said with a grin on the way out. "When I saw Henry walk into your office with those three big law books under his arm, I knew he'd lost his case already."

Two new airplanes were assigned on June 23, and that reinforcement, marginal though it was, helped turn the tide. Day after day, as the old-fashioned planes made their runs over Guatemala City, the powerless residents watched in fear. Arbenz's army neither joined the rebels nor fought them, and almost no one was killed. Later, Ike asked the CIA operatives how many men they had lost. One, an agent answered, a courier who had infiltrated Guatemala before the invasion and had tried to join a partisan group. Thinking of the terrible losses in war as he knew it, Eisenhower paused a moment and said, "Incredible."

The key to the victory was the CIA's radio station, based outside the country. The Agency had jammed the government station and deftly created a fictional war over the airwaves, one in which the government troops faltered and refused to fight and in which the liberation troops were relentlessly moving toward Guatemala City. If anyone was a hero of the coup, it was David Atlee Phillips, a former actor, recruited by the Agency for his good looks and his ability to speak Spanish. The broadcast war became all the more important because the real war barely took place. By the night of June 27, the radio claimed that two huge columns of Castillo Armas's soldiers were almost on top of Guatemala City and that the final battle was about to take place. Arbenz promptly resigned.

Peurifoy loved it all. He spent the coup running around Guatemala City, brandishing his pistol and demonstrating his courage and fearlessness to the handful of foreign journalists in the city. (Peurifoy had little reason to be afraid, since he knew what was happening at all times and where the bombings would take place.) "People are complaining that I was 45 minutes off schedule," he boasted after it was all over. He played his official role to the hilt, though. When Toriello came to negotiate surrender terms and accused Peurifoy and the United States of complicity in the coup—after all, the weapons used by the rebels were American-made—Peurifoy was properly indignant, he later boasted to Washington. He pointed out angrily that these weapons could be purchased anywhere in the world, and "that if he had brought me to his house to make accusations against my government, I would leave immediately."

For a brief time it appeared that Colonel Carlos Enrique Diaz, the army chief of staff and transition leader, might succeed Arbenz. He promised Peurifoy that he would outlaw the Communist party and exile all its leaders, but after Diaz gave his first speech, the Americans decided that he was insufficiently anti-Communist and anti-Arbenz. John Doherty, one of the CIA men, was deputized to tell Diaz he was stepping down. Doherty lectured Diaz on the evils of Arbenz's rule. Diaz began to argue back, but it had been a long day already and the other Agency man, Enno Hobbing, was tired and in no mood to prolong the discussion: "Colonel," he told Diaz. "You're just not convenient for the requirements of American foreign policy." When Diaz protested to Peurifoy, Peurifoy handed him a list of Communists he wanted shot in the next twenty-four hours. "It would be better in that case that you actually sit on the presidential chair and that the Stars and Stripes fly over the Palace," Diaz later claimed he had told Peurifoy.

In the United States there was little sense of outrage over the coup. Few Americans, after all, knew what really had happened. The CIA laundered the operation, in the early days at least, with considerable success. The coup was widely seen as the work of pro-Western anti-Communists against agents of the Kremlin, witting or unwitting. Dwight Eisenhower liked to refer to the Guatemalan coup as the model of its kind. Foster Dulles was so pleased that he ordered Carl McCardle, his press officer, to line up all the networks and radio stations so he could broadcast to the entire nation. He told McCardle it was "the chance to talk about the biggest success in the last five years against Communism." He told the people of the United States that the coup represented "a new and glorious chapter for all the people of the Americas." He expressed his gratitude to all "the loyal citizens of Guatemala who, in the face of terrorism and violence and against what seemed insuperable odds, had the courage and the will to eliminate the traitorous tools of foreign despots." Dulles later asked C. D. Jackson, the administration's psychological warfare expert, to arrange for some writer to do a major historical novel based on events in Guatemala, along the lines "of Uncle Tom's Cabin or Ida Tarbell." He would, he said, make everything available to such a writer, except, of course, the CIA's role in the affair.

A year after the coup, Foster Dulles asked Park Armstrong, the assistant secretary of state, whether his shop had ever found anything connecting Arbenz with Moscow. There was nothing conclusive, Armstrong had answered.

In New York, Arthur Hays Sulzberger was not happy about the way his paper had been used and the fact that he had kept one of his best people away from a legitimate story. He wrote Allen Dulles that he had kept Gruson out of Guatemala, "because of my respect for your judgment and Foster's." But he was not going to let the issue stop there. He wanted more information. There had been, he pointed out, two incidents in the past when members of the *Times* staff had been accused of disloyalty, and in one case the charge had not been true and in the other it had concerned a much earlier and long severed association. Therefore, he felt it was very important to settle the issues of Sydney Gruson's loyalty and his reputation.

Dulles weaseled. He did not like the idea, he wrote Sulzberger, that "a man having his (Gruson's) particular nationality, background, and connections should be representing you at a particular place and a particular juncture." Beyond that, he had nothing more to offer. As Sulzberger realized he had been used, Harrison Salisbury noted, his correspondence with the head of the CIA grew chillier. His last note to Dulles on the subject said: "My judgment, formed on the basis of our experience with the man and on Cy's report [the report of his nephew, Cyrus Sulzberger, who believed Gruson the ablest foreign correspondent on the staff] to me of what he learned, is that he is a good newspaperman who happened upon some stories which the people reporting to you did not like because they did not want them published." It was an important moment, a warning to the paper's top executives about the potential difference between the agenda of the secret government and that of serious journalists.

TWENTY-SEVEN

In years to come, students of American foreign policy would have considerable difficulty deciding which secretary of state had been more militantly anti-Communist—Dean Acheson or John Foster Dulles. But in the era of Dulles's reign at the State Department, anyone could have told who was more self-righteous and who more prone to bombastic rhetoric about the justness of the American cause. As Reinhold Niebuhr said of him, "Mr. Dulles's moral universe makes everything quite clear, too clear. . . . Self-righteousness is the inevitable fruit of simple moral judgments."

It was the unfortunate responsibility of John Foster Dulles to bridge the gap between the excesses of the recent Republican campaign speeches, particularly those that catered to the sensibilities of the Republican right, and the limits of American power abroad. In addition, he had to soothe the ruffled feathers of those traditional

Republican conservatives, the bedrock loyalists who had supported Taft and who still felt guilty about rejecting their own for an outsider who seemed dangerously internationalist, perhaps even liberal. A lesser man might have shied away from so daunting a task, but not Foster Dulles.

Dulles had emerged by the end of the war as the principal foreign policy spokesman for the Republican party, the shadow secretary of state. He had been close to Tom Dewey in 1948, and Dewey's defeat that year had come as a considerable shock to him. Dulles had, after all, spent the entire preceding year being described by all as the next secretary of state. Dulles happened to be in Paris on Election Day in 1948, and he had promised to do an interview with David Schoenbrun of CBS on the day after the election. It was projected as an interview with the new secretary of state-designate. When Dewey lost, Schoenbrun asked if Dulles would still appear on the show. Yes, said Dulles—and he added in a rare burst of humor— if Schoenbrun would introduce him as "a former future secretary of state."

His roots in the party went deep. He had skillfully managed to steer a middle course in the bitter feud between Dewey and Taft, no small achievement in itself, and he had close relationships with many of the Midwestern conservatives. After that, if a Republican was ever elected President, Dulles seemed to come with the territory as secretary of state; in fact, he had been apprenticing for some thirty years. He might be the prototype of a powerful Eastern establishment lawyer, but he had always been able to convince the conservatives of his own intense partisanship. After Eisenhower's election there were reports that at the last minute, Eisenhower had considered John J. McCloy, an Eastern establishment insider, for the job, but he decided against it, fearing the reaction of the Taft wing, which still needed to be appeased.

The contrast between Dulles's and Eisenhower's style could not have been greater: Eisenhower was cautious, pragmatic, modest, and given to understatement; Dulles, bombastic, arrogant, and self-important. He tended to underestimate even the intelligence of the President he served, and there was no doubt among his aides that on occasion he believed his principal job was to save the President from his more trusting self, that is, the side that might be exploited by the Soviets, on occasion. He complained to close aides of Ike's lack of a sense of crisis. Still, he honored Eisenhower for the wise choice of himself: "With my understanding of the intricate relationships between the peoples of the world and your sensitiveness to the political considerations involved, we will make the most successful team in history," he told Eisenhower early on.

In public at least, Dulles did not seem a man much given to nuance. Instead, he thundered out his own certitudes, oblivious to others, in a voice that seemed to threaten anyone who did not accept his idea that American goodness included the use of nuclear weapons. As Townsend Hoopes, Dulles's critical biographer, noted, "There are times when style makes all the difference. Stentorian warnings appeared to be a compulsive element of the Dulles theory of deterrence. Eisenhower, on the other hand, tended to view the nuclear force as a quietly unassailable backdrop, whose relation to policy should be more subtly communicated." Dulles's version of American foreign policy was an ongoing sermon, which exhausted friend and foe alike. "Mr. Dulles makes a speech every day, holds a press conference every other day and preaches on Sunday," Winston Churchill once noted. "All of this tends to rob his utterances of real significance." Even in a town known for its stuffiness, sanctimony, deviousness, and partisanship, Foster Dulles stood out.

The strength of the relationship between the President and Dulles surprised people who knew how different the two men were. Emmet John Hughes, a senior *Life* writer who worked closely with both, observed Ike's face as Dulles droned on and on at one of their early meetings and thought that Eisenhower could barely conceal his boredom. That, Hughes thought with glee, is a relationship that won't last long. But much to Hughes' surprise, the partnership worked quite well and the two became close professionally, if not personally. Perhaps Eisenhower regarded Dulles as a buffer between him and the Republican right; perhaps he valued Dulles for taking the heat off of him, thereby creating the illusion of the good Ike and the bad Foster for the media and the Democrats. After all, there was an inherent political contradiction at work, for underneath all the rhetoric Ike was, in essence, merely continuing the same Democratic policies of containment that the Republicans had been so bitterly attacking.

Dulles in particular specialized in assailing the weakness of containment under Truman and Acheson. Such talk was all very well, and certainly almost everyone wanted a world without Communists. But the Red Army in Eastern Europe *did* look formidable, and using American forces in Asia might get us into a quagmire. In early 1952, Emmet Hughes was assigned to do an article with Dulles that would outline the dramatic differences between the aggressive new foreign policy of the Republicans as opposed to the quite soft defensive policies of the Democrats. There was, Hughes noted, much talk about liberation of Europe, all of it curiously vague. "What are you proposing that we *do*?" Hughes kept asking Dulles. Hughes noted drily in his memoir that it was "extraordinarily difficult to persuade him to give clarity and substance to his critiques of 'containment' or to his exhortations on 'liberation.' " The writer came away, as many had before him, with the belief that Dulles was both the most righteous and the most relentlessly devious man he had ever met in his life.

That very vagueness about liberation got Dulles into trouble even during the 1952 campaign, when he debated Averell Harriman on a television program hosted by the young Walter Cronkite. Dulles began by talking about switching American foreign policy under Ike "from a purely defensive policy to a psychological offensive, a liberation policy which will try and give hope and a resistance mood within the Soviet empire . . ." "Those are very fine words," Harriman answered, "but I don't understand the meaning of them." At that point Dulles mentioned that he had written "quite a little piece" on the subject for *Life* (the very piece Emmet Hughes had worked on). "I read it twice," Harriman said, "but I couldn't understand what you meant." "You should have read it a third time," Dulles said. "I did," Harriman said. "I still didn't understand it." At that point Cronkite noted, "Mr. Harriman, being impartial, we don't know whether Mr. Dulles can't write or you can't read."

The British had disliked him from his first minor missions to England during World War Two. In July 1942, he went to lunch with Anthony Eden. Alexander Cadogan, an assistant to Eden, noted later that Dulles was "the wooliest type of pontificating American . . . Heaven help us!" Hearing that Eisenhower was thinking of choosing him as secretary of state, the British passed a number of private messages to the President-elect, asking him not to. Ike later said he answered those notes by saying, "No, look, I know something about this man and he's a little abrupt and some people think he's intellectually arrogant and that sort of thing. It's not true. He's a very modest man and very reasonable and he wants to use logic and reason and good sense and not force . . ." The British remained unconvinced; with their own power shrinking, Dulles seemed to them the worst possible manifestation of the new American hegemony. He tended to divide the world along relatively predictable but rather rigid criteria: the free world was, of course, better than the Communist; the white world was more reliable and valuable than the nonwhite; the Christian better than the heathen.

Even Europe was not without its flaws for Dulles. He tended to admire the Germans as solid, hardworking, religious, and good anti-Communists. "Those people have cut the throat of the world twice in a generation," he told a House committee, "but they're a vital piece of real estate." Of the French he was wary: "France was the one place where they have all those mistresses and sell dirty postcards, but it's a damned important piece of real estate because it's got all those canals and highways leading to Germany." The Italians, of course, were even worse than the French, "an asset to their enemies in every war." He was the purest of chauvinists.

He grew up in spare surroundings. The son of a clergyman, he bathed in cold water for much of his boyhood. His father, the Rev. Allen Macy Dulles, was a Presbyterian minister, first in Watertown, New York, and then in Auburn, New York. The Rev. Dulles was surprisingly liberal for his time, taking the side of the modernists in the then-burning question of whether to accommodate the manifestations of modern science as they encroached on the literal teachings of the Bible. On two occasions he was almost expelled from the ministry, first for questioning the virgin birth and later for permitting a divorced woman to marry in his church.

The Rev. Dulles was a gentle, contemplative man. The drive and ambition came from his wife, Edith Foster Dulles, whose father, John Watson Foster, was secretary of state under Benjamin Harrison. In her mind, even though her husband made only $3,500 a year as a small-town minister, they were still *people,* and she was confident that her own children would bear out their distinguished lineage. When Edith was pregnant with Foster, her first son, she moved temporarily from their modest home in New York State to her father's far grander home in Washington. Her father, upon leaving State, had joined the boards of several powerful corporations and built himself a summer lodge on Lake Ontario, to which he often invited such close friends and associates as Andrew Carnegie, William Howard Taft, John W. Davis, and Bernard Baruch. Edith Dulles made sure that young Foster was there to help out and go along on the fishing trips.

When Foster was five, his mother wrote, "Mentally he is remarkable for his age. His logical acumen betokens a career as a thinker . . . he reasons with a clearness far beyond his age." As a boy Foster was precocious, unsentimental, and priggish. Seeing his younger sister, Eleanor, crying because she couldn't buy a hatband she wanted, he told her, "You are not crying because you're sad, you're sad because you're crying." Years later, as a father, he hated it when his own children cried. To cry was to be emotional; to be emotional was to be weak; to be weak was to be unworthy. That stoicism ran through the family, which did not tolerate weakness or imperfection. Allen Dulles, Foster's brother, was born with a club foot. In the beginning it was a family secret. He was quietly taken to a doctor in Syracuse, where he was operated on.

Awkward and arrogant with his peers, Foster spent much of his childhood among the adults. A prodigious reader, he graduated from high school at fifteen and went to Princeton at sixteen. There he disdained popularity, refusing to join an eating club, the symbol of social success at Princeton. He could have been popular at Princeton, he liked to say, but it would have taken up too much of his time. He graduated Phi Beta Kappa and second in the class of 1908. For a time he pondered what his future should be—the ministry or law and politics. It was as if he were caught between the world of his mother and that of his father. In the end, he decided to combine the two: he would be not merely a lawyer but "a Christian lawyer."

At George Washington Law School (which he finished in two years rather than the usual three), he met and decided to marry Janet Avery, a young woman from Auburn, New York, near Syracuse. At first, her parents were less than thrilled with the match. The Dulleses were poor by their standards. But Miss Avery was completely in love with Foster; her assessment of his exceptional abilities equaled his own. Years later, when she was asked to describe him, warts and all, she answered, "What warts? Foster was perfect." Her life was completely about serving him so, naturally, he adored her. When his sister, Eleanor, an intellectually gifted and ambitious young woman, told him that she wanted to go to college, he was appalled. He did not think women should go to college. "It made them bossy, gad-about, assertive," he later told others, "like Eleanor."

George Washington Law School was not prestigious enough, so after graduation his grandfather had to pull a few strings to get him a job at Sullivan and Cromwell, the great establishment law firm of its era; its primary function was to remove all possible legal barriers for the nation's most powerful corporate titans so they could operate with as few restrictions as possible. Its lawyers were eventually handsomely rewarded, but not at the beginning of their careers. Foster Dulles started at fifty dollars a month. He was successful from the start: Endlessly hardworking and tightly focused, he did not bring to his work any moral ambivalence. "He knew," his sister later wrote of him, "that if he wasn't right in his opinion on life, he was as right as most people he knew. He had few doubts. He was sure of himself in everything he did."

The connections were always there. At the end of World War One, Bernard Baruch took his old friend John Foster's grandson along with him to Europe as an aide. It was Foster Dulles's introduction to international politics. He did well, making his reputation as a rising young internationalist, and making connections to Jean Monnet and John Maynard Keynes. Back in New York, he rose quickly at Sullivan and Cromwell. He mastered early a trick of the successful lawyer: to speak last, after others were tired, and to sum up their arguments while tilting the presentation in his own direction. In 1925–26, Sullivan's two top people at Sullivan died suddenly and the firm turned to Foster Dulles, then only thirty-eight, to head it. Soon he was a formidable figure in New York's cultural life, even though he was never fully comfortable with the city's elite. He remained "a man of Watertown rather than of New York," his sister thought.

For a man who burned by then to be a major foreign policy figure, he was curiously insensitive to the rise of Hitler, perhaps because Sullivan and Cromwell had many close ties with the leaders of German industry. Others warned him that the times were changing, that something terrible was happening in Germany, and that Sullivan and Cromwell's connections there were giving it a reputation for anti-Semitism. He thought that preposterous. "How could anyone think that we're anti-Jewish? Do you realize that Sullivan and Cromwell is the first big law firm to have a Jewish partner?" he asked friends.

His brother, Allen, posted in Europe between the wars, was appalled by his older brother's indifference to the deteriorating international situation. Foster Dulles even wrote a small book that seemed to Allen to rationalize the rise of Hitler. At home Foster worked covertly to ensure a free flow of nickel to Germany, a critical ingredient in its re-armament. But gradually, as war came, he moved to the center and served Roosevelt ("the architect of victory," Dulles later called the President sarcastically) during the war on several missions.

He was phenomenally successful as a corporate lawyer even during the worst of the Depression. In the mid-thirties his annual salary was $377,000. As the war wound down, he was already looking forward to a government post. His worldview was steadily emerging, and it was similar to that of the other great Calvinist of the era, Henry Luce—it was the voice of Christian capitalism, American internationalism, and fierce anti-Communism. He thought Republicans more trustworthy than Democrats—they, after all, made more money and therefore were more successful in the real world; the Democrats had to be watched closely for they tended, for reasons of demographics, to pander to lesser groups. In addition, they had been in power too long and had been insufficiently aggressive in combating Soviet adventurism.

By the fall of 1953, the Eisenhower administration was formulating what it would later call "the New Look," a reformulation of American foreign policy and military posture. It reflected the President's belief that the true strength of America came from a healthy economy and that a heavy defense budget would diminish that strength. Cutting defense spending inevitably meant a greater dependence on atomic weapons. Ike had arrived in office with the Korean War inflating the military budget to $42 billion. As they stepped down, Acheson, Lovett, and Harriman had recommended an additional $7 to $9 billion for air defense against the Soviets. One of the first things George Humphrey, the secretary of the treasury, did—with the help of Taft—was to help pare the defense budget down to $34.5 billion.

Humphrey, with Ike's backing, wanted to give the country a tax break in February 1955, by cutting an additional $4.5 billion from defense and more from other departments. Instead, in October 1953, Charlie Wilson, the secretary of defense, and Admiral Arthur Radford, the new head of the Joint Chiefs, produced a Pentagon budget of $35 billion, a small increase, to be sure. Both Eisenhower and Humphrey, who had hoped for a defense budget of $30 billion, were disappointed. Radford shrewdly suggested that the desired cuts might be possible if the JCS could narrow its options, plan for fewer contingencies, and assume that in almost any conflict nuclear weapons would quickly be used. A few weeks later Eisenhower approved a new National Security Council (NSC) paper that, in effect, assumed nuclear weapons would be used in limited-war situations—as they had not been used in Korea. Humphrey seemed to speak for Eisenhower's fiscal conservatism at an October 30, 1953, NSC meeting: "There would be no defense," he said, but only "disaster in a military program that scorned the resources and the problems of our economy—erecting majestic defenses and battlements for the protection of a country that was bankrupt."

The adjunct to the New Look, first identified by Dulles in January 1954, was the doctrine of "massive retaliation." (What Dulles actually said was that local defense measures would now be replaced throughout the world "by the further deterrence of massive retaliatory power.") That meant we would react instantaneously, to even the smallest provocation, with nuclear weapons; therefore, an enemy would most assuredly not dare provoke us. The policy seemed to guarantee that all future wars would be short and inexpensive. But such military critics as Matt Ridgway were hardly impressed. He saw the world as far more disorderly, with all kinds of threats and enemies, requiring flexibility in the ways we might respond. Nor did he see nuclear weapons as a practical option in the many messy situations that were already developing around the world.

The great powers were already locked in what was a de facto atomic stalemate, Ridgway and others argued. But what about insurgencies and brushfire wars that did not necessarily fit into the superpower nuclear equation? Was the New Look a viable strategy there, or was it primarily a bluff? Dulles's speech about massive retaliation was not a great success abroad. Our allies were terrified by it. We seemed to them to threaten turning small wars into much larger ones. Soon there were a variety of attempts by the administration to explain Dulles's speech, so many in fact that Walter Lippmann wrote, "Official explanations of the new look have become so voluminous that it is almost a career in itself to keep up with them."

There was one additional critical change in the American military establishment that had occurred the previous summer, and it reflected no small accommodation to the Republican right: Admiral Arthur Radford had replaced Omar Bradley as Chairman of the Joint Chiefs. Bradley was, ostensibly, a mild-mannered man who seemed more a schoolteacher than a warrior (but who sacked more battalion commanders than any general in modern American history). One of the great generals of World War Two, he was closely associated in the public mind with Eisenhower, but he was also, as far as the Republican right was concerned, a man of Europe and containment. Worse for them, he had dissented from MacArthur more than anyone else. The final straw, though, turned out to be his refusal to support Eisenhower as he cut back traditional military forces and bet everything on a nuclear response.

In early May 1953, Ike appointed new Chiefs and he had worked them out in conjunction with Taft, who had approved them all; Arthur Radford, the embodiment of what the Republican right wanted, became Chairman of the Joint Chiefs. There was, it would turn out, a world of difference between the old-fashioned Bradley and the modern, eager young Arthur Radford.

Radford was a product of the modern Navy, a man of both Annapolis and of aircraft carriers, whose career had raced ahead, propelled by the force of modern technology. He had been very successful as the head of air operations for Task Force 58 in the naval action in the Marshall and Gilbert islands. That success in using naval air power against Japan had given him a limitless vision of what that strategy could do, particularly if nuclear weapons were harnessed to it. He was unusually interested in Southeast Asia and had decided it was the coming battleground between the West and Communism; he considered himself something of an expert on the region.

If the critics of the Truman-Acheson years had seemed to envision a simpler world, in which nothing limited American power and the atomic weapon offered an easy answer to every military dilemma, they now had, in Admiral Radford, a Chairman of the JCS who shared their views. Both assumed that the Communist world was a monolith, and easily bluffed by nuclear threats. The problem with military policies that are built to domestic specifications and do not take into account the complexity of the real world is that eventually the real world intrudes. So it happened to Eisenhower, Dulles, and Admiral Radford in the spring of 1954, in the most unlikely of places: Indochina, where the French were still fighting an exhausting colonial war. In the spring of 1954, it seemed they were about to suffer a decisive defeat at Dien Bien Phu, a cluster of small Montagnard villages in the Thai mountains along the Laotian border.

The French Expeditionary force of some 500,000 men—some French, some Vietnamese, some North Africans, and some Europeans in the French Foreign Legion—was being swallowed up in the rice paddies and jungles. Their opponents, the Vietminh—the Communist-nationalist insurgents—were gaining confidence and fighting with greater audacity. That inevitably posed something of a problem for the new Republican administration. French Indochina—later to be known as Vietnam—was not yet an American war, but it was in many ways increasingly an American-sponsored war; even before the outbreak of hostilities in Korea, Truman, anxious to take a stronger stand against Asian Communism, had started helping finance the French war. By the end of 1953 we had spent over $1 billion in aid and escalated our rhetoric to classify the struggle between the Vietminh and the French not as a colonial war, but as part of the larger struggle of the Western democracies against Communism; by 1953 we had more interest in continuing the Indochina war than the French did.

More, in the view of American policymakers, the source of all evil was not even the Vietminh but an aggressive, militaristic, imperialist, Communist China. By 1954 it was increasingly obvious that French and American interests in Indochina, which had been seemingly compatible for the preceding four years, were now about to diverge; the Americans now had more interest in continuing the Indochina war than did the French, who increasingly wanted out. In late May 1953, the French had sent General Henri Navarre, one of their top staff officers, to take command there. Navarre's orders were to bring home some kind of settlement. But Navarre was by no means ready to admit defeat. Using the kind of words that would come back to haunt Americans in Vietnam, *Time* magazine quoted an aide to Navarre as saying, "A year ago none of us could see victory. There wasn't a prayer. Now we can see it clearly—like light at the end of a tunnel."

The reality was that the French had systematically underestimated the capacity of the Vietminh to wage a guerrilla war. In fact, the Vietminh had never set out to defeat the French in any given battle, or on a rigid timetable; instead, they decided to exhaust them and force them to win pyrrhic victories. Time was on their side, they believed, and they were succeeding handsomely. Lacking the airplanes, tanks, and artillery of the French, the Vietminh had learned to conserve their forces, to strike only when they had numerical superiority, and when the French were vulnerable, preferably in well-prepared ambushes and at night. In these strategies they had followed the joint dictates of Ho Chi Minh and his immensely skilled military commander, Vo Nguyen Giap.

"La guerre sale," it was called by this time back in France, "the dirty war." The longer it went on, the less popular it became. As early as 1950 the French parliament voted to stop sending draftees to Indochina; instead, it was to be a war fought by European professional soldiers and poor Asian enlistees. A professional's war it was: Every year in Vietnam, France lost a third of the graduating class from St. Cyr, its military college. There had always been a wariness on the part of some French officers that Indochina would prove to be nothing more than a quagmire at a time when the colonial impulse was clearly exhausted in France. In 1946 General Jacques Philippe Leclerc had been sent to Indochina by de Gaulle; he surveyed the country and then told Paul Mus, his political adviser, "It would take 500,000 men to do it and even then it couldn't be done." By mid-1953 it was clear to most military observers that the French were on the defensive, as the hemorrhaging of French forces continued, and as domestic support for the war continued to shrink.

Some informed estimates placed Vietminh total forces at seven full divisions, in the unlikely event that they chose to mass them. Even worse, there were signs that with the Korean War over, the Chinese Communists (despite historic tension between them and the

Vietnamese nationalists) were supplying heavy weaponry. Navarre
was not enthusiastic about his assignment, the less so when his old
St. Cyr classmate Gonzales de Linares greeted him by saying, "Henri
old boy, what have you come to this shithole for? I'm clearing out."
Even more ominous was a warning from the general Navarre was
replacing, Raoul Salan: "General, you must take care, for the Vietminh is organizing its big units and giving them a European character." "In that case they are done for," Navarre immediately
answered with the arrogance that marked French officers who were
new in the country. The warning from Salan did not seem to bother
Navarre, and later he spoke to his staff about the future with a
certain Gallic swagger: "Victory is a woman who gives herself only
to those who know how to take her."

Navarre wasted no time in developing a plan that minimized
contact with the Vietminh for more than a year while he rebuilt his
forces, with significant reinforcements from France. Starting in the
fall of 1954, he intended to strike against the Vietminh with these
beefed-up units. Significantly, he did not aim for victory; rather, he
hoped to demonstrate a French presence so strong that the Vietminh
would finally come to the negotiating table. The Navarre plan immediately ran into trouble as the French cabinet balked at sending
additional troops and spending any more money for Indochina.
What Navarre wanted would cost an extra $300 million. "Not one
sou for the Navarre plan," Finance Minister Faure told his fellow
ministers.

The Americans were becoming extremely nervous that the
French would pull out of Indochina. The National Security Council
met on September 9, 1953, to deal with the Joint Chiefs' recommendation to help fund the Navarre plan. Dulles began by giving a fairly
pessimistic appraisal: All in all, he thought French chances were
poor. But we might as well pay the money, he argued, because the
Laniel government was as good as we were likely to get. George
Humphrey, the secretary of the treasury, spoke like a small businessman: "Well look, we've got a proposition here in which we've put an
awful lot of money in the past. Mr. Dulles says this is the last hope
of salvaging the investment. Therefore I think we should go ahead
and make the further funds available." With that the Americans
decided to pay for much of the Navarre plan.

By all rights the Navarre plan should have excluded a battle for
a small and not particularly valuable outpost along the Laotian
border. Yet a plan for Dien Bien Phu had existed for some time
before Navarre arrived. Slowly, almost inevitably, Navarre and his

command incorporated it into his larger plan, deciding to send several French battalions into Dien Bien Phu and hoping that the Viets would attack them there. It would be the set-piece battle the French had wanted for some time; instead of fighting an army of ghosts who disappeared into the night time and again, the Vietminh would be tricked into standing and fighting, and the French would finally be able to use their superior weaponry. The French believed they were setting the trap; the Vietminh would rise to the bait, would attack the well-fortified French position, and in time would be worn down by the superior fire from the well-entrenched French positions. It would be, the French thought, men against boys, professionals against amateurs.

In a way the very concept was a study in Western arrogance, for the war had already been going on for seven years, and even casual study of the other side should have given the French commander a healthy respect for the Vietminh's bravery, combat skills, and, above all, their ability to conserve resources. Navarre believed that General Giap, the Vietminh commander, could bring at most a reinforced division to bear upon this distant position. It proved to be a terrible miscalculation, one of the worst of many such in this war, for Giap eventually moved three divisions into play. It would be a trap all right, but for which side was the question.

Had the French command been less prejudiced, it would have understood, as others who studied the war did, that the Vietminh boasted a world-class infantry force, extremely well led and accustomed to the difficult natural terrain. The Vietminh soldiers were physically tough, able to travel as much as twenty miles a day. They had the most primitive footwear, often only rubber sandals cut from tires, but "our feet are made of iron," the soldiers used to say. Like the Chinese who had fought the Americans in Korea, they traveled lightly, carrying only their weapons, some water, and some salt.

Giap would eventually be viewed as one of the two or three greatest military strategists of the twentieth century, but General Salan regarded him, in effect, as a noncommissioned officer who had not even been to a military staff college. When Giap's name was mentioned in French dispatches, the title "General" was put in quotation marks, as if to mock him. Speaking of the French arrogance, Jules Roy, an officer in and a historian of the war, later wrote, "Navarre should have kept a photograph of Giap before him at all times as Montgomery kept a photo of Rommel before him during the Egyptian campaign . . ."

The name Dien Bien Phu means "large administrative center on the frontier," and this cluster of villages stretched some eight miles along a north-south axis and about five miles from east to west. It was isolated in the midst of rough mountainous terrain, and thus was hard to resupply and exceptionally vulnerable to attack. Worst of all, it was in a valley, so the French forces there were essentially immobilized. Its original importance to the French had been as an air base used to resupply other points in the area, but as the French need to conserve forces grew, its strategic value had diminished. In fact, at this point it had no strategic value whatsoever.

By no means was the French high command unanimously enthusiastic about engaging the enemy there. General René Cogny, the French commander for the northern part of the country, was well acquainted with the terrain and was absolutely appalled by the idea. In November 1953, responding to warnings from his staff, Cogny sent Navarre a memo suggesting that it was a dubious venture in all ways: "In that kind of country," he wrote, "you can't interdict a road. This is a European type notion without any value here. The Viets can get through anywhere. . . . I am persuaded that Dien Bien Phu shall become, whether we like it or not, a battalion meat grinder, with no possibility of large-scale [French operations] radiating out from it as soon as it is blocked by a single Vietminh regiment." As Bernard Fall, the historian, pointed out, Cogny felt that the use of his best troops as bait was not merely a military mistake but also a personal betrayal of them. But even if he expressed doubts to his superiors, he never told them an outright no, that he would not do it.

On November 20, 1953, two battalions of French forces parachuted into Dien Bien Phu. The post was notorious for its bad weather, and given a bad forecast, the jump and the entire operation would have been canceled. Years later, Major Marcel Bigeard, a famed French paratroop commander captain who jumped into the post, cursed the good weather: "Oh, why did it not rain that day!" The jump took place as planned. A terrible tragedy was beginning to be unveiled. For weeks before the battle, various visitors to the post noted that the French unit seemed to be encircled and that the surrounding high ground belonged to the Vietminh. When they pointed this out to the garrison's artillery commander, Colonel Charles Piroth, he treated the idea with ridicule. He claimed the Vietminh could never get their artillery through to this distant outpost, and even if they did somehow manage, they would never be able to supply them with enough ammunition. The French would smash them, he added. Asked a few weeks before the battle began whether he wanted additional artillery pieces, Piroth scorned the idea; he had all the weapons he needed, he answered. When Navarre himself visited the camp and raised the same question, Piroth reassured him: "*Mon général,* no Vietminh cannon will be able to fire three rounds before being destroyed by my artillery."

Among other things, the French believed that the Vietminh had almost no capacity to resupply their troops. Once again they had made a fatal mistake, even though the French calibrated their capacity to resupply in thousands of tons by airplane while Giap figured "in pounds carried by a single man." But Giap's ability was far greater than the French realized, though, thanks to a secret new, if rather primitive, weapon: the bicycle. The Viets had reinforced two thousand of them with extra supports so that peasants could load and push them through the primitive trails to Dien Bien Phu. They could carry up to five hundred pounds, more than five times the weight of most of the peasants themselves and more than twice what an elephant could carry. Resupply was less of a problem for them than the French imagined. Slowly, steadily, usually by moving at night, some 50,000 Vietminh soldiers gathered on the high ground around the French post—four times as many men as the French had assembled and four times as many as Navarre thought they were capable of gathering. An additional 100,000 peasants were there to help supply the combat soldiers. In addition, they had four times the number of heavy weapons, including 105 20 mm howitzers. Pierre de Chevigne, a high official in the French ministry of war, landed at Dien Bien Phu on February 7, 1954, some five weeks before the siege, and he was appalled by the French stronghold. It was nothing of the sort, he decided; rather, it was more like a chamberpot, with the French garrison at the bottom and the Vietminh force poised on the rim above. To Robert Guillain, a *Le Monde* correspondent, it resembled a football stadium in which the French were on the bottom and the Vietminh in the top rows. So eerie was the feeling of the French position that René Pleven, the French defense minister, begged General Pierre Fay, the French air force chief of staff, to evacuate the post.

On March 13 the siege of Dien Bien Phu began. "Hell in a very small place," Bernard Fall called it. Within two days, Colonel Piroth was desperate; he could not believe that he was so badly outgunned. When one of his superiors asked him where the Vietminh guns were, he pointed to a spot on the headquarters map and said, "They may be there." Then he quickly pointed to another spot. "Or there . . ." Can you silence them? he was asked. He shrugged his shoulders and refused to eat. "I am completely dishonored," he told one friend. "I have guaranteed deCastries [the camp commander] that the enemy artillery couldn't touch us, but now we are going to lose the battle. I'm leaving." Soon thereafter, Piroth pulled a pin on a grenade and committed suicide.

On the first night a major stronghold on the northeast sector, Beatrice, fell, and on the second night, so did another, Gabrielle. That gave the Vietminh two of three key points on the northern rim of the valley; on the third night they gained the third when the Thai tribesmen deserted at Anne Marie. "Let's have no illusions," Navarre told his staff officers the second night. "I hope the Viets aren't going to start again tonight. We shall have to find some other solution."

It was to prove a nightmare; there was little in the way of food, water, or medical support, and little cover. The Viets did, contrary to Colonel Piroth's opinion, know how to use their artillery pieces, and in fact they had positioned them brilliantly. They did not put them on the reverse side of the hills as some of the French officers had expected; instead, by using immensely skillful excavation and camouflage, they placed them under the very noses of the French, facing the garrison. Their gunnery crews had a perfect view of the French, below in the bowl, while they themselves were invulnerable to the French artillery below and to the French bombers trying to protect the garrison. The Vietminh had wrought something of a peasant engineering miracle. As such the battle was over almost before it started.

Suddenly, this war with its thousand little skirmishes was focused on one dramatic and poignant battle. Dien Bien Phu became a household word, and the question of whether the embattled French garrison would survive was taken up as an international issue. The French lacked the resources to rescue the surrounded troops. The only hope was some form of American intervention, but even conservative congressional leaders were wary of getting involved. John Stennis, of Mississippi, a Democrat and a member of the Senate Armed Services Committee, had been very unhappy when we began to send a few ground crew to service American aircraft being used by the French in February 1954. "First we send them planes," he warned, "then we send them men."

Here then was the first test of the New Look and of the new Eisenhower-Dulles doctrine, the keystone of which was that no additional Asian country should fall to the Communists. For the next two months John Foster Dulles was a man constantly in motion, cajoling, pushing, and stroking allies, telling them half truths about each other, almost like a socially ambitious dinner party hostess who tells one prized would-be guest that another (who has not yet accepted) is coming in order to get the first guest to come. Ostensibly, he wanted some kind of joint Allied intervention in Indochina to rescue the French garrison, most likely by pounding the general area with the American Air Force, perhaps even using, if need be, atomic weapons. (At one meeting Air Force chief of staff Gen. Nathan Twining apparently thought that just one atomic bomb might do the job: "You could take all day to drop a bomb, make sure you put it in the right place . . . and clean those Commies out of there and the band would play the 'Marseillaise' and the French could come marching out . . . in great shape," he later said of the Dien Bien Phu dilemma.)

But the problems of putting together some sort of joint action were immense. The French, stunned by the tragedy facing them at Dien Bien Phu, seemed to have lost all taste for battle. The British were just finishing up their own hard war in Malaya, and having given up India without firing a shot, they had little interest in shedding British blood for what was to them very clearly a colonial war for a French cause. Under no condition did they intend to come in. Nor was Eisenhower eager for another Asian war. He had just finished in Korea, for which there had been little public support from the start. Indochina promised, if anything, to be even worse. The Democrats in Congress, seeing the approach of a Republican dilemma and just having been attacked for being soft on Communism, sat back and watched with no small amount of glee as the administration juggled this. "The damn Republicans blamed us for losing China and now we can blame them for losing Southeast Asia," Franklin Roosevelt, Jr., then a congressman, was heard to say after one congressional briefing.

At a meeting between the administration leaders and congressional leaders in early April, Senate minority leader Lyndon Johnson pointed out that the United States had carried some 90 percent of the burden in Korea in terms of both men and finances. How many other allies had Dulles consulted with, he asked, other than the French? There was a pause and Dulles admitted that he had consulted with none.

Dulles was now in the process of performing a very difficult and delicate balancing act. What he himself actually wanted to happen has always intrigued historians of the period. Certainly, those who opposed intervention—General Matt Ridgway, for instance—

thought he did want to intervene. What was clear is that he did not want the administration to be blamed for being soft on Communism or for losing Indochina. Therefore, the most important thing was to make sure that if the worst happened, the blame was assigned elsewhere, either to the Allies or to Congress.

Thus began an elaborate shadow dance: Perhaps we would go in, perhaps we would not. Perhaps we wanted to help the French, perhaps we did not. Perhaps we made them an offer of unconditional military aid, particularly of American aircraft, then again perhaps we did not. Perhaps we had offered the French atomic weapons, perhaps we had not. In all of this John Foster Dulles was the featured performer. Ostensibly, he seemed to favor intervention, and he spoke passionately at the meetings convened on the subject; evidently, he even asked the French foreign minister if they wanted atomic weapons. But the French demurred, pointing out that atomic weapons would not be helpful, since they would destroy the French garrison as well as the Vietminh.

The idea of intervention did not die lightly. Radford, more than anyone else, seemed to be pushing for it. At a meeting with congressional leaders from both parties, Radford pushed for a massive American air commitment in Indochina. Senator Earle Clements asked if the other Chiefs agreed with him, and Radford somewhat reluctantly admitted that no, they did not. How many agreed? Clements pursued. None, Radford admitted. Why was that? Clements asked. "I have spent more time in the Far East than any of them and I understand this situation better," he had answered.

Radford seemed on more than one occasion to make commitments to the French that he was not authorized to. Eisenhower, in all this, remained ambivalent. At one point in early April, he wrote Churchill a surprisingly passionate letter asking him to join in united action: "If I may refer again to history; we failed to halt Hirohito, Mussolini and Hitler by not acting in unity and in time. That marked the beginning of many years of stark tragedy and desperate peril. May it not be that our nations have learned something from that lesson?" A few days later, at a press conference, he outlined for the first time what became known as the domino theory. In response to a question about Indochina he answered: "You have a row of dominoes set up, you knock over the first one, and what will happen to the last one is the certainty that it will go over very quickly. So you could have the beginning of a disintegration that would have the most profound consequences." The loss of Dien Bien Phu, he said, would have dire consequences for Australia, New Zealand, and even Japan.

Gradually, Dulles was forcing others to make the case against intervention and thereby take the blame. For if Eisenhower had really wanted to go into Indochina, he could easily have gotten congressional support, and Dulles and others may have asked for such support, but they never *pushed* for it. The real question, then, was not about using American ground troops; it was about using American air power.

General Matt Ridgway was unyielding in his opposition to the idea of intervention. He was also unalterably opposed to the New Look and the implication that wars could be fought quickly, easily, and antiseptically. He had witnessed the worst fighting in both World War Two and Korea, and in Korea, particularly, he had seen what the Air Force had promised to do with strategic bombing and how limited, in fact, strategic bombing was as an instrument of policy. If we bombed, he argued, we would end up inevitably using ground troops. Ridgway saw air power as a sort of high-tech aspirin; it gave some immediate relief, but it did not cure the underlying problem.

Ridgway thought the war in Indochina was a complete political and military mess. He did not merely dissent on such general terms, though. Since his President was a soldier, he made the case against intervention in terms that a soldier would understand: He sent a team of planners to Vietnam to find out what victory would take in terms of manpower. The answer was devastating: minimally, five divisions and quite possibly ten (there had been six divisions in Korea), plus fifty-five engineering battalions. Altogether, that meant between 500,000 and 1 million men. Draft calls would be far greater than those for Korea. The existing infrastructure was horrendous, and the construction costs would be immense. Worse, political conditions on the ground would be much worse than in Korea. There the indigenous population had generally supported American intervention. That would not be true in Indochina.

No one ordered the Ridgway report; he did it on his own because of a profound conviction that if you were going to send young men into battle, you had better know exactly what you were getting into. When he briefed Eisenhower on what the cost would be, a groan seemed to come from the President. Ike was, Ridgway noted laconically years later, a much better listener than Lyndon Johnson.

The other restraining influence was the British resistance to the idea. No matter how much Dulles pushed, neither Churchill nor Anthony Eden, the foreign secretary, would bend. The pressure, much of it from Radford, continued all through the month of April; since Radford seemed to imply to the French that the Americans were hell-bent to make a major commitment if only the British would come in, the French also applied significant pressure on the British. On April 26, Radford dined with Churchill. If Radford did not get exactly what he wanted—a British commitment to send troops—he got something more important: a wise lecture on the limits of power from one of the great men of the era who was watching his own nation's power contract in the twilight of his career.

Churchill had begun by talking about the British decision to give up India in 1947. He had been in opposition then, he said, and he had hated the idea of giving up so important a country, one Britain had ruled for 250 years. He had regarded this as one of the most painful decisions of a long career, but he had come to accept it. Radford had to understand this when he viewed the British decision on Indochina. He was asking a nation that had given up the most valuable part of its own empire without firing a shot to fight to preserve French colonialism. That could not be done. The British people, he said, would not accept the idea of investing any of their limited resources in Indochina. When Radford tried to make the case about the danger to the entire area, Churchill accepted that there might be serious regional consequences, but he warned Radford, prophetically, that the most important thing was to defuse the tensions with the Soviets and not "to squander our limited resources around the fringes."

As the idea of intervention began to die, Dulles continued to speak publicly of the importance of the garrison, but in a private cable to Eisenhower from Paris on April 23, he noted that the situation there was hopeless but that there was "no military or logical reason why loss of Dien Bien Phu should lead to collapse of the French . . ." Then Dulles finally went on national television and blamed the British; we would have gone in, he seemed to be saying, but for the Allies. That took care of the domestic politics. We had not lost the war, our allies had. The post fell on May 7. The news reached Paris in the late morning of that day, and the prime minister, Joseph Laniel, dressed entirely in black, barely able to control his voice, broke the news to the national assembly. It was a terrible moment, filled with the deep, bitter shame of a nation betraying fighting men halfway around the world. That night all French television and radio networks canceled their regularly scheduled programs and instead played the Berlioz "Requiem."

It was over. There was great bitterness among America's most important allies, most particularly the French, whose garrison had been forced to surrender. The British felt the Americans had not merely tried to initiate a policy beyond their reach but behaved arrogantly. In April that year The Times of London had shrewdly written of one of Dulles's speeches that seemed to call for American intervention at Dien Bien Phu: "It has not always been easy to let Mr. Dulles' speeches speak for themselves because, since he became Secretary of State, he has often seemed to be reversing the normal tactics for a Foreign Minister, and, instead of using his public statement to hint at policies, has made them stronger than the policies themselves."

At a conference in Geneva, Vietnam was divided up, with the North becoming a Communist state under Ho Chi Minh and the South an anti-Communist society under Ngo Dinh Diem, a Catholic mandarin who had sat out the war in America and was now being installed by the Americans. Both sides, ironically, resented the Geneva settlement; the North, with good reason, felt it had been on the verge of a total victory but had been pressured by the Soviets to settle for half the pie. By contrast, in America there was a feeling that somehow the French had sold out and given the Communists a victory at the conference table. Dulles had dodged a bullet and came to believe that Dien Bien Phu was a boon to us. "We have a clean base there now without the taint of colonialism," he told Emmet Hughes with stunning innocence during the 1956 campaigns. "Dien Bien Phu was a blessing in disguise." Some blessing, some disguise.

Not all the Republicans were appeased by Dulles's speeches. There were rumblings on the right that the new administration had not strengthened America's position in the world. Thus in late 1955 it was decided that a major defense of administration policies should be made and that Dulles should do it in the friendly forum of *Life* magazine, in an article by a particularly friendly writer, James Shepley. Published in January 1956, it was called: "How Dulles Averted War." The theme of the article was that foreign policy under Eisenhower and Dulles had not been merely a bland continuation of past (cowardly) policies, as some critics had charged, but that Dulles, backed by the atomic weapon, had walked to the very brink of war, had stared down the country's enemies, and thereby brought back an otherwise unattainable peace.

In Indochina (one of the three places where Dulles had apparently rescued the peace—the other two were in Korea and the island of Quemoy), he had succeeded by sending two aircraft carriers steaming into the South China Sea. It was, he noted, "a modern version of the classical show of force designed to deter any Red Chinese attack against Indochina, and to provide weapons for instant retaliation . . ." In fact, the aircraft carriers had been a bluff that did not work and had absolutely no effect on the Vietminh. "You have to take chances for peace," Dulles told Shepley, "just as you must take chances in war. Some say we were brought to the verge of war. Of course, we were brought to the verge of war. The ability to get to the verge without getting into war is the necessary art. If you cannot master it, you inevitably get into war. If you try and run away from it, if you are scared to go to the brink, you are lost. . . . We walked to the brink and we looked it in the face. We took strong action." From the article came the famous term for Dulles's foreign policy, *brinkmanship*. Hearing later of Dulles's boasts about his trips to the brink and the calculated risk involved, Georges Bidault, the former French foreign minister, noted with no small degree of bitterness that "It involved a great deal of calculation but no risks."

How wrong Dulles was to claim that we had escaped the taint of colonialism, the next generation of American policymakers would find out. For in the minds of Ho and General Giap, only half the battle had been won. Of what eight years of revolutionary war had done to Vietnam, of the fateful future political alignments it had produced, Americans had no comprehension. We had given nearly $3 billion in aid to the French, yet it might as well have gone into a black hole. The Vietminh had emerged with a modern, confident army, in which young men had risen through the ranks, despite peasant origins, by ability alone; the army in the South, soon to be created by the Americans, was an extension of the colonial age, reflecting class and privilege. It was virtually impossible for a peasant to rise to any kind of command in it. Our side reflected the old feudal order; their side released the nationalism so powerful in an anticolonial war. Our side was nationalist because the Americans *said* that Diem was a nationalist; we even hired public relations experts to sell the American public on the idea. The other side did not have to announce its nationalism; it had earned the title by dint of hard and long fighting.

We could not see the affairs of Vietnam as they really were, mired as we were in prejudices generated by our own domestic politics. Rhetoric, repeated by Foster Dulles, emphasized that Vietnam was part of the larger struggle with *China*. We did not pause to understand why a peasant army had defeated a powerful Western army. Anyone who tried to talk about why the other side had won was vulnerable to charges of being soft on Communism. We had to see the struggle in Vietnam through the prism of the Cold War and had, in effect, already begun the process of making a commitment to a small, artificial country where the other side held complete title to nationalism. We thought the war in Indochina was over; the other side knew it had just begun.

TWENTY-EIGHT

By the early 1950s the Supreme Court was in chaos, racked, ironically, by long-simmering divisions among the four judges appointed by Roosevelt; if nothing else, the conflict reflected something of the political contradictions and deviousness of the man who had appointed them. The personal squabbles among the four intellectually towering figures—Felix Frankfurter, Robert Jackson, Hugo Black, and William O. Douglas—sometimes seemed more serious than the political ones. When Harlan Fiske Stone, the Chief Justice, died in 1946, Jackson was so bitter about being passed over as his successor that he went public with the accusation that Black was the mastermind of a plot to deny him the high office he so desperately wanted. For his part, Black believed that Jackson and Frankfurter (a relentless networker and political schemer) had worked behind the scenes to block his chances for the same position. Since the Court was the one institution in government that was supposed to embody civility and courtesy, the rancor among these men was particularly unattractive.

There were two clear political factions on the Court, the more liberal Black/Douglas wing and the conservative Jackson/Frankfurter one—Frankfurter, a great liberal as a young man, believed that the Court was a conservative institution and seemed to want to reaffirm precedent as if his vote belonged more to the Court's past than to his own instincts. Frankfurter referred to Black and Douglas sarcastically in his letters as the "great libertarians," and his close friend Judge Learned Hand (who longed to be on the Court himself) referred to them in letters to Frankfurter as "the Jesus Choir," and "the Holy Ones." Jackson was hardly less virulent: He said of Black that "I simply give up trying to understand our colleague and begin to think he is a case for a psychiatrist." Of a Black opinion, Frankfurter once noted, "It makes me puke." Black, who was aware of the degree he irritated Frankfurter, once noted, "I thought Felix was going to hit me today, he got so mad, but he'll get over it." Nor was it only Black that Frankfurter (and Jackson) hated. In a letter to Hand in 1954, Frankfurter called Douglas "the most cynical, shamelessly immoral character I've ever known." Douglas returned the sentiments and called Frankfurter "a prevaricator"; once after hearing an unusually long Frankfurter lecture, Douglas walked into the conference room and announced that he had been prepared to vote for the conclusion Frankfurter supported, "but he's just talked me out of it." The general atmosphere was poisonous. The Truman appointees, Harold Burton, Sherman Minton, and Tom Clark, more modest in talent, but more generous by nature, looked on aghast as these battles took place.

Truman, trying to make the Court more collegial, chose his old friend Fred Vinson to replace Stone in 1946 as Chief Justice, because he believed Vinson to be gregarious, likable, and extremely skilled as a conciliator. Like the President, Vinson was a small-town boy from the mid-South (Kentucky), where he had practiced law; like Truman, he had come to Washington as a New Dealer to serve in the Congress. Welcome in the back rooms of Capitol Hill, where the real decisions were made, he drafted some important early New Deal legislation and during the war he had served as a kind of domestic economic czar.

But Vinson's skill of bringing people together, which had served him so well in the Congress, deserted him on the Court, where he faced questions too complicated and subtle for the old-fashioned compromise solutions he was accustomed to in the Congress. Moreover, the men he was now dealing with did not have to run for reelection, and they were different by temperament than the kind of men Vinson had dealt with in the past. Frankfurter, Black, Jackson, and Douglas were men of formidable talent and intellect, matched only by their overwhelming egos. They did not welcome Vinson as a kindred spirit; instead, they looked down on him as second-rate; his former political strengths became liabilities. "This man," Philip Elman, an influential Frankfurter clerk, wrote his boss, "is a pygmy, morally and mentally. And so uncouth." Not that Frankfurter, a great intellectual snob, needed a great deal of convincing. If anything, the Court under Vinson fragmented even further, and in the early McCarthy years, as the issues of civil liberties came before the Court, Vinson took a simplistic (some might say craven) view toward protecting them. He believed that, with an enemy as terrible as the Communists, the President and the Congress knew best and that it was the job of the Court to defer to them. Hugo Black, one of the great free-speech advocates of his era, regarded Vinson's views on this subject with great disdain. They were, he thought, laced with superstition and ignorance—we had to sacrifice our liberties in the struggle with Communism or, "the goblins'll get you."

The most unfortunate aspect in all this was that a number of transcending questions were wending their way toward the Court docket. The most important of these dealt with the question of separate-but-equal school facilities in the South. Indeed, Frankfurter tried to slow down the segregation cases, not only because he felt that Vinson was unsympathetic but worse, he lacked the capacity to lead the Court in dealing with the most emotional and broad-ranging cluster of cases it had faced in this century. By this time a number of cases challenging the right of states to segregate their schools, including one filed in (of all unlikely but highly segregated places) Topeka, Kansas, had worked their way through the judicial process and had reached the Supreme Court. The Kansas case had been filed in 1951 by a black welder named Oliver Brown, who objected to the fact that his eight-year-old daughter, Linda, had to go twenty-one blocks by bus to a black school when there was a white school only seven blocks from her house. Brown, a mild, religious man, was hardly a local radical: He had tried hard to register his daughter at the all-white Sumner School but finally decided to sue the local school board. The case was filed under the title *Brown* v. *Board of Education* of Topeka.

In the South, the concept of separate but equal had always been a sham: It might have been separate, but it never was equal. Before

World War Two, black groups pressing their case were weak, under-manned, and underfinanced. Nonetheless, the process of chipping away at segregation had begun in the thirties and forties. Gunnar Myrdal's *An American Dilemma*, a devastating indictment of segregation, was published in 1944. Myrdal revealed the terrible fiction of separate-but-equal facilities: The Southern states were spending twice as much to educate white children as they were black children and four times as much for school facilities; white teacher salaries were 30 percent higher; and there was virtually no transportation for black children to and from school. The disparity was even greater at the college level, where the Southern states spent $86 million on white colleges and $5 million on black colleges. A study by Ralph Bunche showed that the poll tax was highly effective in keeping blacks out of the political process; only 2.5 percent of the black population voted in the presidential election of 1940 in the deep South.

If the pace with which the challenge to segregation moved through the courts was, in the words of Richard Kluger, "a glacially slow process," then there was finally a sense of steady progress in the postwar years. Thurgood Marshall, the shrewd, folksy black lawyer, had started working for the NAACP in 1936 for the grand sum of $2,400 a year, plus expenses, and he carried the burden of much of the litigation. Marshall argued most of the early civil rights cases in small Southern courtrooms and suffered the worst indignities of segregation himself, not to mention the threat of physical danger. No town in which he argued seemed to be large enough to have a hotel or restaurant for black people. Most often he stayed in the homes of local blacks. In court he was rarely referred to as Mr. Marshall; instead, according to the custom of the South, he was addressed by his first name, as if he were still a boy. On occasion, he liked to reminisce about the small town in Mississippi where a local resident had told him, "Nigguh, I thought you oughta know the sun ain't nevah set on a live nigguh in this town." So, he noted, he had "wrapped my constitutional rights in cellophane, tucked 'em in my hip pocket," and caught the next train out of there. Marshall and a handful of colleagues attacked the segregationists where they were most vulnerable—in the border and Southwestern states, where racism was less virulent. Always waiting in the background was the larger question: Even if a state provided truly equal facilities, was it not still discriminatory, nonetheless, to shunt one segment of the population off to separate schools?

By 1950, the Supreme Court began to tilt away from segregation and had outlawed it in graduate schools. Marshall and his handful of colleagues had carefully and indeed cautiously escalated what had begun as piecemeal raids on the periphery of segregation into a full-scale assault upon its very core. That meant taking on the critical precedent of *Plessy* v. *Ferguson,* the critical decision made some sixty years earlier. In the aftermath of the Civil War there had been considerable impetus to give blacks full citizenship. The Thirteenth Amendment had outlawed slavery, and the Fourteenth Amendment ruled that state governments could not deny black citizens due process or equal protection. "The Fourteenth Amendment," Thurgood Marshall liked to say, "was no more or less than a codification of the Judeo-Christian ethic." But slowly and steadily after that, the pendulum had swung back to reflect the prejudices of the white power establishment. By the latter part of the nineteenth century, a series of separate-but-equal laws authorized segregation throughout the South: Most of these seemed in direct conflict, legally and spiritually, with the Fourteenth Amendment. Among these was a Louisiana law that said all railroad trains should have separate-but-equal accommodations. In June 1892 a light-skinned black man named Homer Adolph Plessy deliberately tested the law on a trip from New Orleans to Covington, Louisiana. He was asked to leave by the conductor, then arrested and tried before Judge John Ferguson in New Orleans. Plessy argued that the arrest had violated his rights under the Fourteenth Amendment, but Judge Ferguson ruled against him. The case eventually found its way to the Supreme Court, where Justice Henry Billings Brown (a rather bland Massachusetts judge who had paid someone to take his place in the Union Army) handed down the decision against Plessy. Brown argued that it was not clear which rights were actually covered by the Fourteenth Amendment, and he noted that the government could not force citizens to commingle. Somewhat disingenuously, Brown argued that segregation laws did not necessarily imply the inferiority of either race. It was a remarkably insensitive decision, reversing the tide of legal equality begun after the Civil War. "Justice Brown, in short would make no provision for the fact or purpose or result of the Civil War," wrote Richard Kluger, a historian of the segregation decisions. "He [Justice Brown] wrote as if the South had won." The vote against Plessy was seven to one, the one dissenting cast by John Marshall Harlan, the leading intellect of the Court and himself a very conservative man. In a passionate dissent, he noted that if the state could do this to blacks on railroad cars, could it not do it elsewhere to other groups, "of native and naturalized citizens of the United States, or of Protestants and Roman Catholics?" He added: "The white race deems itself to be the dominant race in this country. And so it is, in prestige, in achievements, in education, in wealth and in power. . . . But in view of the Constitution, in the eye of the law, there is in this country no superior, dominant, ruling class of citizens. In respect of civil rights, all citizens are equal before the law. The humblest is the peer of the most powerful."

For the next fifty years a legal, political, and social crisis built. In the vacuum of presidential and congressional inaction on the subject—the Democratic party, after all, was paralyzed by the power of its Southern wing in the Congress—the issue was finally passed on to the Supreme Court. Whether Chief Justice Vinson himself would be willing to help reverse the *Plessy* decision was a serious question among those who knew him well. When the Court met in conference in December 1952, he observed, "However we construe it, Congress did not pass a statute deterring or ordering no segregation." He was clearly very nervous about the course ahead: "We can't close our eyes to the seriousness of the problem. We face the complete abolition of the public school system." Since Clark tended to vote with Vinson on such issues, Frankfurter, a conservative who nevertheless was convinced that segregation had to end, foresaw a decision that would end segregation, but only by a five-to-four vote. Such a narrow margin would make implementation difficult, if not impossible. As a delaying tactic, Frankfurter suggested rehearing the arguments. The new hearings were scheduled for December 1953, but in September Vinson suddenly died of a heart attack. "This is the first indication I have ever had that there is a God," said Frankfurter.

The question now was who Dwight Eisenhower would pick as the new Chief Justice. The President announced that his choice would be a political moderate like himself. He offered the job to Foster Dulles, knowing almost surely that Dulles would turn it down—taking on international Communism was a big enough job for him. Speculation began to center on Earl Warren, the liberal governor of California, who was coming to the end of his third term. ("He's a Democrat and doesn't know it," Harry Truman once said of him.) In the 1952 Republican convention, Warren had thrown his support to Eisenhower in the early procedural confrontations, thereby stopping Taft. Whether Ike owed Warren after that is debatable, but for a while there had been talk of a place for Warren in the Eisenhower cabinet.

He was born in California in 1891. The name was originally Varran and was Americanized to Warren; his father had emigrated from Norway as an infant. Like many Scandinavians, his family headed for the Midwest. The poverty of his father's life was crushing; years later Earl Warren said that when he read Dickens's *Oliver Twist,* the first thing he thought of was his father's life. Matt Warren became a railroad car repairman. In an age of bitter labor divisions, he had taken part in union activities, for which he had been duly punished. Matt Warren taught his children to be careful and thrifty: "Earl, saving is a habit, like drinking, smoking, or spending. Always save part of what you earn." As a boy Earl held a series of demanding jobs—delivering ice and groceries among them—and he managed to save eight hundred dollars, enough money to go to Berkeley. He loved Berkeley, where if he was not a brilliant student, he was an enthusiastic one.

He went to law school and entered the army during World War One, but saw no service. When he returned he began a career in government, first as an assistant to a legislator. Eventually, he became attorney general of the state, during which time he won a reputation for being clean and incorruptible. He was part of the Republican Progressive movement, which was about to blend with the embryonic forces of the New Deal. Subsequently, as governor, he came to be viewed as a model for the best in government in America—intelligent, decent, and fair. His political successor in almost every job, Pat Brown, thought that being governor greatly expanded Warren's vision, that he had been a good prosecutor and state attorney, but somewhat narrow, with little sense of the complexities of people's lives: As governor, he grew with the demands of the job. The one blot on his record was his leading role in interning Japanese-Americans in detention camps during World War Two. He was playing to the growing fear of sabotage and the country's anger against the Japanese, particularly in California. The Japanese-Americans, he said, had not assimilated or embraced American values and traditions. That they had not yet risen up to perform acts of sabotage, he said shortly after Pearl Harbor, was merely proof that they were awaiting some kind of "zero hour" to act. Warren signed the order to evict 110,000 Japanese-Americans from their homes, which others took over at bargain-basement prices. In June 1943, Warren, in his first year as governor of California, told the other American governors, "If the Japs are released, no one will be able to tell a saboteur from any other Jap. We are now producing approximately half of the ships and airplanes on the West Coast. To cripple these industries or the facilities that serve them would be a body blow to the war effort. We don't want to have a second Pearl Harbor in

California. We don't propose to have the Japs back in California during this war if there is any lawful means of preventing it." Later he expressed considerable regret for his actions, although he was somewhat defensive in his memoirs: In 1972, when he was interviewed on the subject, he broke down in tears as he spoke of little children being taken from their homes and schools, and the interview had to be stopped while he recovered his composure. That a record otherwise so admirable had a blot so serious was a reminder, the California writer and professor A. J. Langguth once said, that even in the very best politicians there is always some fatal imperfection.

It was easy to underestimate Warren. He was not particularly articulate, and he prided himself on being homespun. His critics thought him a very ordinary man, just "that big dumb Swede," in the words of Judge Learned Hand. He may have been born in California, but he looked like his Scandinavian ancestors. When he ran his first statewide race, he mentioned in a speech that he had been born in California. There was no reaction from the crowd. Then he said his father, like so many of them, had come from Iowa. There was, in his words, tumultuous applause. From then on, he included the remark in all his campaign speeches, and he was often regarded as Earl Warren of Iowa.

He was quite comfortable with his own squareness. He hated the pornography cases he had to review, and after reading some of the books and magazines involved, he often needed to get out and take some fresh air. When his law clerks twitted him about this, he would respond, "You boys don't have any daughters yet." He was a member of both the Moose and Masons. "Warren's great strength," said Justice Potter Stewart years later, "was his simple belief in the things we now laugh at—motherhood, marriage, family and the flag."

He was above all an excellent listener, and his years as a prosecutor had served him well. He liked to get different people to tell him everything in order to expand his horizons. Edgar Patterson, his driver when he was governor of California, was convinced that *Brown* v. *Board of Education* was the result of Patterson's own conversations with the governor about what it had been like to grow up black in segregated Louisiana. Warren did not need to dominate in meetings, and he was as comfortable listening to others as he was hearing his own voice. He seemed so relaxed and agreeable that it was easy for new acquaintances to underestimate his ferocious sense of purpose.

John Gunther, one of the very best reporters America ever produced, wrote of him in 1947: "Earl Warren is honest, likeable and clean; he will never set the world on fire or even make it smoke; he has the limitations of all Americans of his type with little intellectual background, little genuine depth, or coherent political philosophy; a man who has probably never bothered with abstract thought twice in his life; a kindly man with the best of social instincts, stable, and well balanced . . ." He was not a man who worried if other people thought they were smarter than he was.

He was also a more astute politician than even his admirers realized. During his rise to power, he constructed his own base as an independent candidate not beholden to the oil interests in Southern California. For party loyalty, he substituted personal connections to the state's two most important (and quite conservative) publishers— Joe Knowland in Oakland, and Harry Chandler in Los Angeles. At the very least, these friendships helped neutralize papers that might otherwise have rejected his increasingly liberal agenda.

He was a distinguished governor of California. The state was growing by as many as ten thousand new residents a week, and the pressures on the state's schools, roads, and its water resources were enormous. Facing that challenge had made him tough-minded and pragmatic about government, its limits, and how best it could benefit ordinary people. He was both an optimist and an activist: If he did not exactly bring an ideology to the Court, then he brought the faith of someone who had seen personally what government could and should do to ameliorate the lives of ordinary people.

That the great figures on the bench had so much more judicial experience—Black with sixteen years of service on the Court, Frankfurter and Douglas with fourteen each, and Jackson with twelve— did not daunt him. As he saw it, they knew more about the law, but he knew more about the consequences of the law and its effect on ordinary citizens. His law clerk, Earl Pollock, said years later that there were three things that mattered to Earl Warren: The first was the concept of equality; the second was education; and the third was the right of young people to a decent life. He had spent a lifetime refining his view of the role of government, and he came to the Court ready to implement it.

He made an excellent first impression on his colleagues, who were not by any means easy to impress. Warren, Hugo Black wrote soon after the governor's arrival, "is a very attractive, fine man. Just a short acquaintance with him explains why it was possible for him to get votes in both parties in California. He is a novice here, of course, but a man with his intelligence should be able to give good service. I am by no means sure that an intelligent man with practiced hard common sense and integrity like he has is not as good a type to select as could be found in the country."

At first, because of his small-town manner, most people did not comprehend his intense sense of purpose. "Earl Warren," Anthony Lewis wrote years later, "was the closest thing the United States has had to a Platonic Guardian, dispensing law from a throne without any sensed limits of power except what was seen as the good of the society. Fortunately, he was a decent, humane, honorable, democratic Guardian." If Dwight Eisenhower had decided from Earl Warren's record that the two of them shared similar attitudes and values, then he was wrong. They could not have been more different. They might have come from similar backgrounds, but Eisenhower had long ago removed himself from the complexities of contemporary American life by going off to the military; there he was largely isolated from the changes in the society.

Warren's greatest skill, perhaps, was his ability to cut to the core of an issue. He immediately came to the conclusion that the Court had to confront *Plessy* directly. Previous cases, he later told the writer Richard Kluger, had all but stripped *Plessy* down and the concept of separate but equal had, in his words, "been so eroded that only the *fact* of segregation itself remained unconsidered. On the merits, the natural, the logical, and practically the only way the case could be decided was clear. The question was how the decision was to be reached." *Plessy,* he believed, could only exist based on the idea of Negro inferiority. He was not eager to overturn so important a law from the past, but he did not want to continue punishing black children by sending them to inferior schools. That had to end. The law, he said in one meeting and in words noted by Frankfurter, "cannot in 'this day and age' set them apart."

At this point it was all a matter of tactics and strategy. Warren wanted "a minimum of emotion and strife." He did not want to inflame the South or to divide the country unnecessarily. Justice Tom Clark had pointed out the vulnerability of the Court as an instrument of social policy: "We don't have money at the Court for an army and we can't take ads in the newspapers, and we don't want to go out on a picket line in our robes. We have to convince the nation by force of our opinions." Warren wanted, if at all possible, to make this a unanimous decision. He wanted the Court to speak with one voice, and he saw it as his job to bring the Court together to balance liberals and conservatives on this issue, to convince those who might otherwise have doubts about whether the Court was exceeding its limits. He shrewdly framed the Court's internal dialogue so that

It was one of Harry Truman's memorable moments—holding up the front page of his archenemy, *The Chicago Tribune,* which claimed that Dewey had won. Truman's victory embittered many in the Republican party and made the decision of many Republican politicians to use the issue of domestic subversion against the Democrats almost inevitable. BLACK STAR

He was the poet as scientist: Robert Oppenheimer's face always seemed to reflect some kind of inner anguish, but when he took his doubts about the hydrogen bomb public, he became a target of a vast array of conservative forces and was judged a security risk.
ALFRED EISENSTAEDT/*LIFE*/TIME WARNER, INC.

Dr. Edward Teller, the father of the H-bomb, testifying before the Senate Disarmament Subcommittee in 1958 against what he thought were overly cautious controls on weapons testing. UPI/BETTMANN

A group of ordinary citizens gathers on a Las Vegas Street in 1952 to watch an immense mushroom cloud from a particularly powerful nuclear explosion. UPI/BETTMANN

Corporal Lake Hodge carries a home-made regimental sign to the top of Heartbreak Ridge. The hill was the scene of fierce fighting between U.N. forces and North Koreans, who lost an estimated four divisions in the twenty-nine days of battle. CULVER PICTURES

Soldiers of the 11th Airborne Division watching an atomic explosion at the Atomic Energy Commission's testing grounds near Las Vegas in 1951 during the first-ever deployment of troops on maneuvers involving a nuclear weapon. UPI/BETTMANN

General Douglas MacArthur barks out his orders during the Inchon landing. It was his last great victory, an operation carried out against the advice of most pundits. American forces came to be haunted by Inchon, for it convinced MacArthur that he was beyond civilian control and made almost inevitable his subsequent terrible defeat near the Yalu in late November 1950. CARL MYDANS/*LIFE*/TIME WARNER, INC.

Matt Ridgway (left) was one of the true heroes of the Korean War. After the American forces' reversal of fortune at the Yalu, Ridgway took over, steadied the line, made his soldiers get out of their vehicles, and gave them back their pride. He is seen here with Vice Admiral C. Turner Joy.
BLACK STAR

Douglas MacArthur's return to America after Harry Truman had fired him was one of the most dramatic moments of the decade. Rarely had the nation been so divided in opinion along ethnic and class lines, but his support soon slipped away— no one wanted a larger war.
WAYNE MILLER, MAGNUM PHOTOS, INC.

Joseph McCarthy on the attack. He was the most prominent demagogue of the Cold War period, and his name was used to describe a larger phenomenon, McCarthyism, in which politicians attacked not the wisdom of policies they disliked, but the loyalty of the architects of those policies.
HANK WALKER/*LIFE*/TIME WARNER, INC.

McCarthy made a fatal mistake when he failed to realize that his usefulness to the Republican party had come to an end with Dwight Eisenhower's election, when the Republicans reclaimed the White House. He is seen with his nemesis Joseph Welch during the climax of the Army-McCarthy hearings. ROBERT PHILLIPS, BLACK STAR

Levittown was one of the great success stories of the postwar years; ultimately, 17,000 homes were built, and although critics bemoaned the homogenization of taste, the young buyers were delighted with their purchases. BURT GLINN, MAGNUM PHOTOS, INC.

Alger Hiss was the epitome of Establishment sophistication: He had attended the best schools and had been a Frankfurter law clerk. Whittaker Chambers named him as a former Communist conspirator. Tried twice on charges of perjury, Hiss was convicted the second time. ELLIOT ERWITT, MAGNUM PHOTOS, INC.

Charlie Wilson, shown with models of some of the Pentagon's best toys, went from being head of General Motors to a job that seemed much the same—head of the defense department. At his confirmation hearings, he was thought to have said that what was good for General Motors was good for the country. He didn't actually say it, but surely he believed it. HANK WALKER/*LIFE*/TIME WARNER, INC.

When it was time for Frank Costello, allegedly the head of organized crime in the United States, to testify, his lawyers asked that the camera not show his face. An enterprising cameraman showed Costello's hands instead, producing dramatic footage as they writhed, sweated, tore up pieces of paper, and shook. ALFRED EISENSTAEDT/*LIFE*/TIME WARNER, INC.

Mickey Spillane was a self-taught writer whose tough-guy detective stories, featuring a character named Mike Hammer, became the bestselling paperbacks of the era. Hammer was a two-fisted street guy on the lookout for crooked pols; at the height of the Cold War, he turned his attention away from taking down the usual rats to cleanse the country of commies. PETER STACKPOLE/*LIFE*/TIME WARNER, INC.

The early computers were big, clunky, and slow. However, their invention and increasingly frequent use was not only of exceptional value to the defense department and some large corporations, but promised an eventual technological revolution for smaller companies and ordinary people. CULVER PICTURES.

The Motorama shows were the brainchild of General Motors' domineering chief designer, Harley Earl, and were a great success. Buyers not only could get a look at the company's latest models, but could enjoy the modernist look of cars of the future. DENNIS STOCK, MAGNUM PHOTOS, INC.

The McDonald brothers, Dick and Mac, had not been very successful in their business ventures until they opened this small fast-food restaurant in San Bernadino, California. Almost overnight, they became the country's reigning geniuses on the mass production of the American hamburger. *TIME*

Kemmons Wilson, founder of Holiday Inn, at Holiday City, the Holiday Inns of America Headquarters in Memphis, Tennessee, circa 1958. COURTESY OF KEMMONS WILSON, INC.

C. Wright Mills in his study in 1950. COURTESY OF COLUMBIA UNIVERSITY, COLUMBIANA COLLECTION

Allen Ginsberg and Gregory Corso were among the first Beat poets, and Barney Rosset, right, of Grove Press, was one of the first publishers who encouraged them. Founding fathers of a counterculture, the Beats deliberately rejected any possibility of success in traditional society. BURT GLINN, MAGNUM PHOTOS, INC.

Writer William S. Burroughs with his assistant, Alene Lee, in 1953 on top of Allen Ginsberg's roof. ALLEN GINSBERG/ALLEN GINSBERG ARCHIVES

Tennessee Williams attending the 1956
world premiere of *Baby Doll.* The film,
which was made from his screenplay, was
attacked by Francis Cardinal Spellman
and the Legion of Decency. UPI/BETTMANN

Neal Cassady, the inspiration for *On the
Road,* and author Jack Kerouac in San
Jose, California, during their 1949 trip
together. CAROLINE CASSADY/ALLEN
GINSBERG ARCHIVES

Marlon Brando and Vivien Leigh in a scene from the movie *A Streetcar Named Desire*. Much to Kazan's anger, the movie was heavily censored, but Brando's sensuality still came through. THE BETTMANN ARCHIVE

Elia Kazan and Marlon Brando, here filming *On the Waterfront,* were among the key artistic figures of the era. Kazan's direction in both theater and film brought a new dimension of realism to both, while Brando's tangible power and obvious sexuality stood in marked contrast to the more conservative attitudes of the era. CULVER PICTURES

James Dean was Marlon Brando's heir-apparent. Dean's great skill was his ability to project a sense of being wounded by life and, despite his short career, he became a lasting American folk hero to the young. DENNIS STOCK, MAGNUM PHOTOS, INC.

Milton Berle, the early superstar of television, in full regalia performing on an early Texaco Show program. It was Berle's background in vaudeville that allowed him to make such an easy entry into television. UPI/BETTMANN

Lucille Ball, here with Desi Arnaz, had to work hard to convince CBS executives that a sitcom in which her real-life husband co-starred would be a success. UPI/BETTMANN

The Nelsons seemed to embody every virtue of the all-American family, but Ozzie's dictatorial rules increasingly left Ricky alienated. KEN GALENTE, THE SILVER SCREEN

The Kefauver hearings gave the nation its first experience with the political power of television. Until he began his investigation into organized crime, Kefauver was a little-known senator from Tennessee. However, his hearings proved hypnotic viewing and much of the nation was transfixed. Here a movie theater advertises them on its marquee. MICHAEL ROUGIER/*LIFE*/TIME WARNER, INC.

Kefauver himself (second from right), became a national celebrity overnight. Although he denied at first that he had any larger ambitions, Kefauver made a strong run for the Democratic nomination in 1952, and again in 1956 when he received the Vice-Presidential nomination. ALFRED EISENSTAEDT/*LIFE*/TIME WARNER, INC.

Rosser Reeves was one of the early successes in television advertising, a man who believed that the more primitive the message, the more successful it was likely to be.

Thanks to the power of television, Betty Furness, the Lady from Westinghouse, became as well known a national figure as many of the country's top politicians during the 1952 and 1956 conventions.

Harry Truman and Adlai Stevenson at the 1952 Democratic Convention. Truman had personally offered Stevenson the nomination, but Stevenson, who had no desire to run against Eisenhower, had demurred, angering Truman. Stevenson later gained the nomination on his own. GEORGE SKADDING/*LIFE*/TIME WARNER, INC.

Dwight Eisenhower's popularity was immediate and visceral, here at a 1952 appearance in Manhasset, Long Island. UPI/BETTMANN

The 1952 Republican Convention was a bitter one, as the conservative old guard favoring Bob Taft lost once again. Here the victors celebrate on the podium: Ike and Mamie, and Ike's choice for Vice-President, Richard Nixon, with his wife, Pat. GEORGE SKADDING/*LIFE*/TIME WARNER, INC.

Network television was still something relatively new in 1952 but the political process had made the television set a mandatory household item. Here a large crowd gathers outside a New York store to watch the election results in November 1952. EVE ARNOLD, MAGNUM PHOTOS, INC.

Pat Nixon, never comfortable or happy with her public role, smiles determinedly at a 1956 meeting of Republican women. She dutifully went through the motions of being a public person, but in truth she longed for a simpler life with greater privacy. CORNELL CAPA, MAGNUM PHOTOS, INC.

John Foster Dulles, U.S. secretary of state, at a news conference in 1956 rejecting suggestions by Russia and India that the United States suspend further H-bomb tests. UPI/BETTMANN

Allen W. Dulles, director of the Central Intelligence Agency, after appearing at an executive session of the Joint Congressional Atomic Energy Committee in 1958. UPI/BETTMANN

J. Edgar Hoover (right) and his friend Clyde Tolson cheering on the FBI baseball team during a 1955 game. The closeness of their friendship and their constant companionship amused observers aware of Hoover's intense homophobia.
UPI/BETTMANN

Dwight D. Eisenhower in the official photograph for his presidency. UPI/BETTMANN

Alfred Kinsey, shown here in 1953, was pilloried by many for trying to bring scientific standards to the study of America's sexual habits. UPI/BETTMANN

Gregory Pincus, the driving scientific force behind the invention of the birth-control pill, was wary of attempts to entrap him by those seeking advice on abortions. UPI/BETTMANN

Margaret Sanger was one of the great crusaders of the era for greater sexual freedom for women. THE BETTMANN ARCHIVE

Katharine Dexter McCormick
supplied the badly needed
money for the revolution in
contraceptives.
THE MIT MUSEUM

Joe DiMaggio and Marilyn
Monroe: It was the tabloids'
dream wedding—the nation's
greatest baseball player
marrying its sexiest actress.
UPI/BETTMANN

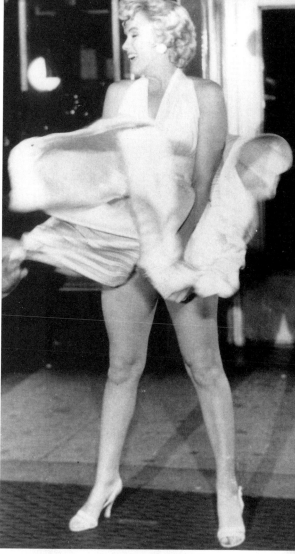

Marilyn Monroe in a scene from *The Seven Year Itch;* DiMaggio was enraged, and a bitter domestic fight followed.
UPI/BETTMANN

Hugh Hefner, sensing that his own sexual obsessions were similar to those of other males of his generation, founded a magazine empire in the fifties.
THE BETTMANN ARCHIVE

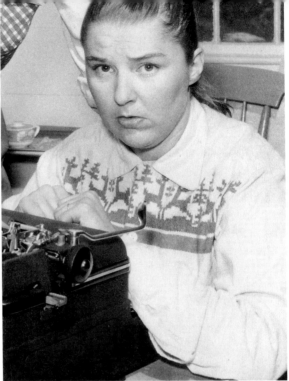

Grace Metalious's accurate portrait of small-town New England life made her a bestselling author, but she had problems dealing with her new-found success. UPI/BETTMANN

Betty Friedan, assigned to do a magazine article on her fifteenth college reunion, found that she was hardly alone in her career disappointments. She is pictured here with her daughter Emily. THE SCHLESINGER LIBRARY, RADCLIFFE COLLEGE

American-backed supporters of the shah of Iran ride through Teheran aboard a tank, holding up a portrait of their leader. A 1953 CIA coup toppled the government of Prime Minister Mohammed Mossadegh and installed the shah as Iran's sole ruler. UPI/BETTMANN

Mohammed Mossadegh being led into Iranian court in 1953 for a session of his trial for treason.
UPI/BETTMANN

A soldier stands guard while supporters of Colonel Carlos Castillo Armas make broadcasts outside of his headquarters in Chiquimulilla, Guatemala. Armas was installed by a CIA coup after American authorities decided the government of Jacobo Arbenz was too left-wing. UPI/BETTMANN

Earl Warren posing for the first time in his black silk judicial robe after being sworn in as the fourteenth chief justice of the United States in 1953. He immediately set out to make the Supreme Court's decision on the landmark Brown case a unanimous one. UPI/BETTMANN

Emmett Till was fourteen years old when he allegedly whistled at a white woman in Money, Mississippi. He was beaten and then killed, his body thrown into the Tallahatchie River weighted down by a heavy cotton-gin fan. UPI/BETTMANN

His was a powerful voice in a powerful cause: Martin Luther King, Jr., scion of one of Atlanta's most prominent black families, became the symbol for a generation. DON UHRBROCK/ *LIFE*/TIME WARNER, INC.

Mrs. Rosa Parks sits in the front seat of a Montgomery, Alabama, bus, more than a year after she was arrested for violating the city's segregation laws. In December 1956, the Supreme Court ruled the laws unconstitutional. UPI/BETTMANN

Little Rock became the first great battleground of the civil rights struggle when Arkansas governor Orval Faubus defied a court order to integrate Little Rock Central High (some of whose students are shown here). Riots provoked by Faubus and his allies followed, and President Eisenhower reluctantly sent in elite airborne troops and federalized the Arkansas National Guard. BURT GLINN, MAGNUM PHOTOS, INC.

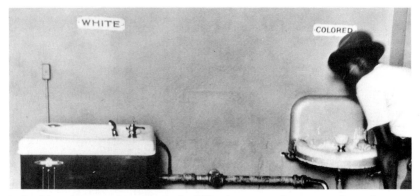

In the rising affluence of America in the fifties, it was sometimes easy to forget that the society's blessings did not extend to everyone. The South was still segregated by law and custom (as shown here at drinking fountains in North Carolina in 1950), though a series of Supreme Court rulings undermined the idea of separate but equal facilities. ELLIOTT ERWITT, MAGNUM PHOTOS, INC.

Supporters of Faubus rallied behind their man in 1958 and the lines were drawn at Little Rock. Federal officials had to push integration almost at gunpoint, helping the governor politically. Faubus, whose chances of reelection had once seemed slim, now presented himself to white voters as a victim of integrationists and was reelected several times. COSTA MANOS, MAGNUM PHOTOS, INC.

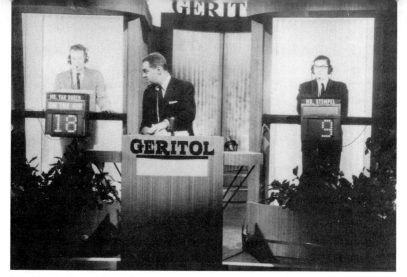

Nothing captivated the nation like the quiz shows of the late fifties, and no one was a bigger hero than Charles Van Doren, a graceful, charming young Columbia English instructor from a famed literary family. Here he beats Herb Stempel, right, in *Twenty-One*. Millions of Americans were later shocked to find that Van Doren had been given the answers. TIME

Van Doren and *Twenty-One* M.C. Jack Barry show their pleasure as Barry adds up Van Doren's record-breaking winnings. THE BETTMANN ARCHIVE

Though the striking success of Elvis Presley produced many imitators, there was nothing artificial about Presley. His success was immediate and powerful. The night that a Memphis radio station played his songs for the first time, its switchboard lit up; the deejay sent for Presley and interviewed him that night; he also made sure that the singer gave the name of his high school so listeners would know he was white.
FRED WARD, BLACK STAR

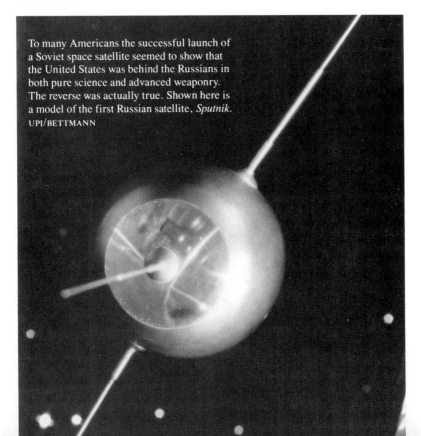

To many Americans the successful launch of a Soviet space satellite seemed to show that the United States was behind the Russians in both pure science and advanced weaponry. The reverse was actually true. Shown here is a model of the first Russian satellite, *Sputnik*.
UPI/BETTMANN

Powers, released after serving time in a Russian prison, holds up a model of the U-2 as he testifies before the Senate Armed Services Committee. UPI/BETTMANN

Russian peasants survey the wreckage of Francis Gary Powers' U-2 spy plane. More than the plane was shot down, for the U-2 incident damaged any hopes for a greater American-Soviet détente, and undermined Nikita Khrushchev's ability to hold power. UPI/BETTMANN

In 1959, Nikita Khrushchev barnstormed Hollywood during the first visit of a Soviet
premier to the United States. Khrushchev's prudish side showed when he met a
number of Hollywood actresses—here Shirley MacLaine—in skimpy outfits.
BOB HENRIQUES, MAGNUM PHOTOS, INC.

During his 1959 march on Havana, Fidel Castro became leader of all forces
opposed to the hated Batista regime and his movement's strength greatly increased.
UPI/BETTMANN

anyone who did not go along with him seemed a racist. The job with Frankfurter was to keep him from writing a long concurring opinion that would weaken the force of a single, powerful decision. Jackson, in any case, was likely to write his own opinion. Tom Clark, with roots in Texas and Mississippi, was perceived as a segregationist, but he would, he signaled the new Chief, be willing to end segregation as long as the decision reflected the complexity of the problem ahead, region by region, and was not punitive to the South. Stanley Reed appeared to be the only true segregationist on the Court.

The one jarring moment for Warren came shortly after his arrival in Washington, when he was invited to the White House for a dinner. The President sat the new Chief Justice next to John W. Davis, then acting as chief counsel for the defendants in the segregation cases. This seating arrangement did not exactly thrill Warren. Davis, the President told Warren, "is a great man." Later after the dinner was over, Ike took Warren by the arm and walked with him to the sitting room. "These are not bad people," he said of the Southerners who were defending themselves in the segregation cases. "All they are concerned about is to see that their sweet little girls are not required to sit in schools alongside some big black bucks." It was the first sign that the President and the Chief Justice were going to part ways on the most important case before the Supreme Court.

The process of bringing this particular court together for a unanimous decision was not an easy one. After the first conference of the judges, on December 13, 1953, Warren moved with great political skill. The stakes were so great that the justices were unusually secretive, in many cases holding back information even from their clerks, lest word leak out of the divisions that existed within. When Frankfurter circulated a memo on the case, he wrote on it, "I need hardly add that the typewriting was done under the condition of strictest security."

Jackson still needed some convincing. He was scornful of the briefs by the NAACP—they were sociology, not law, he thought. But gradually he was won over in conferences. He accepted the political purpose of a decision; the dilemma, he suggested, was how to "make a judicial decision out of a political conclusion." But he would go along with the right kind of decision, to make it 8–1. Still, he wanted to write his own concurring opinion. He even prepared a draft, which was one of the more illuminating documents of the time. The time was ripe for an assault on legal segregation, he wrote. The racism of the Nazis had caused a broad and powerful sense of revulsion among the American people, which extended even to our own treatment of the Japanese-Americans. It was foolish to say that blacks were not ready for greater political freedom, and it was a mistake to cite the Constitution of the United States as the reason to deny those freedoms. It was not the Constitution that had changed in the past sixty years but the blacks themselves; according to Jackson, they had shown a far greater capacity for assimilation than had been thought possible in the days of Plessy. Then—in words that would have greatly offended the South—he touched on the most emotional issue of all: blood, or miscegenation, as it came to be called. The mixing of the races, Jackson said, had already far outstripped the speed of the courts, and "an increasing part of what is called colored population has as much claim to white as to colored blood."

The possibility that Jackson would offer this separate concurring opinion ended on March 30, when he suffered a major heart attack. Warren now went after Stanley Reed for a unanimous decision. By early December Reed was aware of his increasing isolation, and he started his clerks working on a dissent. He told one of them, John Fassett, that it was likely that he would end up alone. Fassett, who was also from the South, wondered aloud to his boss if a dissent on this issue had any real purpose and whether it might damage the Court as an institution. He also spoke deftly to his superior about the importance of this case to America's role in a divided world, with the Communists on one side and with much of the world's population being nonwhite. There was no doubt in Fassett's mind that Reed took him seriously. By late February, the Court met again in conference and the vote was still eight to one, with Reed in dissent.

Reed was Southern gentry from a border state—Kentucky. He had gone to Yale as an undergraduate and to the University of Virginia and Columbia for his law degree. He was a moderately liberal legislator who helped introduce laws on workmen's compensation and child labor in the Kentucky legislature; in Washington during the Hoover years, he was a government lawyer at the Federal Farm Board. He also served as counsel to the Reconstruction Finance Corporation, an institution charged with trying to keep banks and businesses afloat during the worst of the Depression. His work so impressed Roosevelt that he was asked to serve as solicitor general. For arguing the early New Deal cases before a hostile Supreme Court, he received Roosevelt's second Court appointment, and other than Jimmy Byrnes, he was widely regarded as Roosevelt's most conservative Court appointment. In 1947, the law clerks at the Supreme Court decided to have an office Christmas party—a first—and they invited everybody connected with the Court, including the janitorial staff, which was mostly black. That being the case, Reed decided he would prefer not to attend, and so the party was shelved.

As late as April, Reed was still holding out, but Warren was lunching regularly with him, and often including Burton and Minton, Truman appointees who were closer to Reed than the others. Finally, the Chief Justice made his move: "Stan, you're all by yourself in this now," he said. "You've got to decide whether it's really the best thing for the country." In the end he caved in; all he asked was for a decision that made the dismantling gradual, rather than violent and quick. "There were many considerations that pointed to a dissent. They did not add up to a balance against the Court's opinion. The factors looking toward a fair treatment for Negroes are more important than the weight of history," Reed wrote Frankfurter a few days after the *Brown* decision.

Warren's decision reflected the nature of compromise. It sacrificed brilliance for simplicity and deliberately sought not to offend. Jackson's clerk, Barrett Prettyman, thought it the work of a skilled politician who knew exactly how far he could push people before their backs were up. The 9–0 decision was a great personal triumph. Frankfurter, not often given to praise, wrote: "Dear Chief: This is a day that will live in glory. It's also a great day in the history of the court, and not the least for the course of deliberation which brought about the result. I congratulate you." (Frankfurter's benign view of Warren did not last long; soon he decided that Warren was going too far in the cause of civil liberties.) So it was that on May 17, 1954, Earl Warren read the unanimous opinion of the Supreme Court on an issue that had haunted America for almost a century: "We conclude that in the field of public opinion the doctrine of 'separate but equal' has no place. Separate educational facilities are inherently unequal." Not all black leaders were satisfied, although almost everyone was stunned that it was a unanimous decision. The question of compliance still existed, and a year later in a second case, largely known as *Brown II,* the Court outlined what it expected.

The *Brown* v. *Board of Education* decision not only legally ended segregation, it deprived segregationist practices of their moral legitimacy as well. It was therefore perhaps the single most important moment in the decade, the moment that separated the old order from the new and helped create the tumultuous era just arriving. It instantaneously broadened the concept of freedom, and by and large it placed the Court on a path that tilted it to establish rights to outsiders; it granted them not only greater rights and freedoms but moral legitimacy, which they had previously lacked. This had a profound effect on the growing and increasingly powerful communications industry in the United States. Because of *Brown,* reporters for the national press, print and now television, felt emboldened to cover stories of racial prejudice. Those blacks who went into the streets in search of greater freedom found that in this new era, they were not only covered but treated with respect and courtesy by journalists. *Brown* v. *Board of Education* was just the beginning of a startling new period of change, not just in the area of civil rights, but in all aspects of social behavior. One era was ending and another beginning.

That Earl Warren found the President less than enthusiastic about the cause of civil rights in the South would have come as no surprise to Frederic Morrow, the first black special assistant ever to work in the White House. Morrow had worked for the NAACP as a field secretary and then for CBS in the public affairs department. After twenty years of the liberal policies of Roosevelt and Truman, he was the rarest of things—a black Republican.

In 1952 he had been asked to be the liaison between the black community and the campaign of Dwight Eisenhower. Morrow had some doubts about the job, but had accepted it, only to endure a series of endless humiliations, some large and some small, during the campaign. In Los Angeles, the rest of the campaign party was placed in the Ambassador Hotel's best rooms, but he was given a virtual closet, obviously reserved for chauffeurs and servants of guests; in San Francisco, hotel security men, watching him leave for dinner with a group of Republican co-workers, decided that Morrow had snuck a white woman into his room, and literally smashed open his door at 3 A.M. to uncover the evidence—only to find him sleeping alone. In Salt Lake City, a young white woman running the elevator again and again refused to let him on. He was, he later reflected, angry; but given the attitude of the people he worked for, he felt it important not to embarrass a man who might be President of the United States.

He stayed with the campaign because he believed in the historic process itself. He was the grandson of people who had fled slavery and someone had to carry this special burden, someone had to be first. For some reason, he decided, he was chosen. In addition, he liked the candidate himself. That was not to say that he had a lot of contact with Eisenhower. His role was not so much to offer advice—

for this was a campaign largely run by men who did not want advice from a black man on behalf of other blacks—but rather it was to be visible at certain times and invisible at others. Yet Morrow was determined at some point to take up with the candidate his testimony, just before the invasion of Japan began, that the Army fought better as a segregated entity and that it was the wrong time to integrate the Army. He finally had a chance to talk with Ike about it one day in October 1952 on a train ride back from an appearance at West Point. Morrow told Eisenhower of his own bitterness at having had to serve in segregated units and how much other blacks resented the way in which they had been treated in what was ostensibly a war fought on behalf of democratic ideals. Ike answered that his field commanders had convinced him that the battle of Japan was about to take place and that it was not a time for social experiments. They were, of course, Eisenhower seemed to note with regret, almost all Southerners. Then he looked at Morrow and asked if it was true that his father was a minister. Yes, said Morrow. His father as well as his grandfather. "Does he ever talk to you about forgiveness?" Ike asked. Yes, Morrow answered. Often. "Well, that's what I'm doing now," Dwight Eisenhower said. Then the candidate talked about his own prejudice toward black soldiers early in his career. It was rooted in an assignment right after his graduation from West Point, when he had been in charge of a black Illinois National Guard unit. Poorly trained, poorly educated, often led by second-rate white officers, they had performed poorly for him. Dwight Eisenhower said that he was working to overcome his own prejudices, and Morrow finally decided he was a good man, a prisoner of his own isolation and the beliefs of his generation, but decent nonetheless.

After Ike was elected, Morrow believed he had been promised a job in the White House. He duly resigned from CBS, was given a warm farewell party, and moved to Washington. He was stunned by what he found in Washington. New York City in early 1953 might not have been, in racial terms, the most enlightened city in the world, but it was nonetheless relatively open and legally integrated. There was a general belief that life for black people was getting better there. Washington, by contrast, was a Southern city, segregated not just by tradition and culture but by law. White cab drivers would not pick up a black man: When Morrow went to Washington from New York, he had to have a friend meet him with a car at Union Station. Blacks could not eat in white restaurants or stay at white hotels. There was virtually no integrated housing, as he soon discovered from a prolonged search for a decent apartment. Even when the resources of the White House were summoned on his behalf, little turned up. Finally it was decided to pressure the owner of a big residential hotel, who was said to be a major contributor to the Eisenhower campaign. The owner said that yes, he would offer Morrow an apartment but Morrow would have to use the freight elevator to get to his room and he could not use the main lobby, nor could he eat in the building's restaurant. I am supposed to work in the White House, for the President of the United States, and I can barely find a place to live and eat, Morrow thought. In the end, with a great deal of effort, he found a small room in a rare integrated building on Rhode Island and Thirteenth.

Another thing he found, to his shock, was that the promised job with the Eisenhower administration did not exist. There were powerful men in the new administration who were sharply opposed to the idea of a black presidential assistant. At first there was some haggling over money, and then even when that had been ironed out, the job offer was not forthcoming. Eventually, a call came to Morrow from the White House: Nothing was available. Some of the opposition to him, he thought, was generational—men of a certain age did not want a black peer; some was political, for Ike had done surprisingly well in breaking into the Democratic South, virtually doubling the number of votes the GOP had received during the Democratic thirties and forties.

It was, Morrow later said, one of the most humiliating moments in his life. He had announced to all his friends that he was going to be in the White House and now found himself outside it. Eventually, he took a minor position as an adviser in the Commerce Department; he was told there was still a possibility that something might open up in the White House. It did—two years later. In the summer of 1955 he was given a job in the Executive Office Building. Almost from the first, he found himself walking on eggshells. He was isolated and given little encouragement from the administration. None of the young women in the office stenographic pool wanted to serve as his secretary, and when one young woman volunteered, in Morrow's phrase, "impelled by a sense of Christian duty," she arrived in his office and burst into tears. That was not an auspicious beginning. When staff members from the White House came by to see him at his apartment, he asked them to come in pairs so there would be as little gossip as possible and so it would not seem that white women were visiting him.

He quickly found that there were certain rules for survival in his new, precarious position. It was important *not* to presume anything:

That is, if he was invited to be with a certain White House official or group one day, he was not to presume that he would be invited the next day. It also meant that if he was invited to ride in a certain car, he should not presume that the other passengers all wanted him to be in the car nor did they agree that the White House should have a black aide.

He always had to be prepared to be insulted. When Morrow represented the President at a Lincoln Day ceremony in Topeka, Kansas, a woman came over near the end of the reception and told him, "Boy, I am ready to go now; go outside and get me a taxi." When he went to a social gathering at Vice-President Nixon's, another woman, slightly under the influence of liquor, in Morrow's view, asked him to get her coat and complained sharply when he seemed slow about it. When in 1958 he asked to go over and hear the final arguments being held before the Supreme Court on the Little Rock school integration case, at first he could not get in. He was told to see J. Lee Rankin, the solicitor general, who would get him in. Morrow did as requested, and Rankin immediately handed him his briefcase and said, "You are now my messenger." Even his colleagues in the White House, he noticed, tended to ignore him when their wives were present.

Morrow was willing to accept the personal indignities, for he believed he was opening one more door. He was all too aware of the administration's lack of true interest in the advancement of black people. What was most difficult for him was his lack of access to the President, as an ever widening gulf separated the President from the dramatic changes taking place in civil rights. Ike's growing isolation, his unwillingness to meet with moderate, legitimate black leaders, only made Morrow's job more difficult. Morrow found himself constantly having to defend administration actions he did not necessarily agree with in order to keep what little legitimacy he had in the White House. More and more, the national black leadership was writing off Eisenhower. At times Morrow felt he was being used by the White House as a kind of pacifier for black people.

His closest friend in the White House was Max Rabb, the White House man on minorities, yet even Rabb could be hard on him. "Max," Morrow wrote in early 1956, "gave me a tongue-lashing on the Negro's attitude on securing his civil rights. He felt that despite what the administration has done in this area, Negroes had not demonstrated any kind of gratitude and that most of the responsible officials in the White House had become completely disgusted with the whole matter. He said that there was a feeling that Negroes were being too aggressive in their demands; that an ugliness and surliness of manner was beginning to show through. He felt the leaders' demands were intemperate ones and had driven most of the liberals to cover. He said Negroes had made no effort to carry along with them the white friends they had gained and that what they were insisting on at the present time so far exceeded what reasonable white people would grant that he was afraid their white friends were becoming few and far between . . ." That from the administration man most sensitive to minority issues.

When it came time to leave the White House, Morrow did not, as most White House assistants do, have an easy time finding a job. No jobs seemed to be available for a man with his experience. He was sent by a colleague to see a Washington lawyer who was a prominent power broker of the time and who was a close friend of the President. The lawyer wanted to know how much Morrow made. At that time his salary was around ten thousand dollars a year. The idea, Morrow later reflected, that a black could make more than fifty dollars a week seemed to surprise and offend the lawyer. It was clearly one more sign to him that the racial thing was getting out of control, and the lawyer took time out to lecture Morrow on the evils of the *Brown* decision and the fact that white people like himself, normally inclined to think kindly of black progress, were now turning away from integration. Nor was there a lot of help in finding a job for someone the power broker called a "nice colored boy." Perhaps selling used cars? Perhaps working for Coke in public relations? He knew of three Negro boys who had jobs like this, although their combined salaries did not equal, as he quickly pointed out, Morrow's White House pay. Morrow left the man's office badly shaken. It was, he thought, as if the Civil War had never taken place. Some three years later he found a job in the private sector with Bank of America. Some thirty years later, by then in his eighties, Frederic Morrow, living in retirement in New York City, could not control the anger he felt over the hard times of prolonged unemployment in the early 1960s. He often could not sleep as he pondered how those years had burned up a large part of his limited savings.

TWENTY-NINE

Brown v. *Board of Education* had been the first great step in giving equality to blacks, but nonetheless only one of the three branches of government had acted. And yet the law, it soon became clear, was not merely an abstract concept—it possessed a moral and social weight of its own. So it was that the country, without even knowing it, had passed on to the next phase of the civil-rights struggle: education. The educational process began as a journalistic one. It took place first in the nation's newspapers and then, even more dramatically, on the nation's television screens. Those two forces—a powerful surge among American blacks toward greater freedom, mostly inspired by the *Brown* decision, and a quantum leap in the power of the media—fed each other; each made the other more vital, and the combination created what became known as the Movement. Together, the Movement and the media educated America about civil rights.

In Mississippi, the most reactionary of the Southern states, the resistance to integration was immediate and overwhelming on the part of whites. The moment the Supreme Court ruled in *Brown,* the existing white power structure moved to defy the law. White Citizens' Councils, often made up of the most respectable people in town, were formed to stop any attempts to integrate the schools. When blacks filed petitions in several Delta towns asking the local school boards to implement the law of the land, the citizens' councils struck back harshly. Their main weapon was economic power. For example, a local weekly, the *Yazoo City Herald,* printed the names, addresses, and phone numbers of blacks who signed such a petition, in an advertisement taken out by the local citizens' council. The result was the complete crushing of even this most tentative gesture. The blacks who had held jobs lost them. Their credit was cut off. One grocer who had a little money in the local bank was told to take it elsewhere. Of the fifty-three people who put their names on the list, fifty-one took their names off. Even then many of them did not get their jobs back. They had strayed. There was no forgiveness. It was the same in other Delta towns.

Elsewhere, the white response was open violence. Belzoni was known in the parlance of the day as "a real son of a bitch town." White people in other Delta towns marveled that in Belzoni "the local peckerwoods would shoot down every nigger in town before they let one, mind you just one, enter a damn white school." The Rev. George Lee and Gus Courts, officials of the NAACP, had gotten themselves on the local voter registration list, no small achievement in itself. But when they had tried to vote in 1955, they were turned away by Ike Shelton, the sheriff, who refused to accept their poll-tax payments. Lee was a minister, and both he and Courts owned grocery stores. Lee was a man of particular courage. He seemed immune to the threats of the racists, though by local custom, people openly boasted what they would do to him if he continued his uppity ways. In Belzoni, as in many other Mississippi towns, the most violent racists frequently led dual lives: They were men who broke the law even though they were often officers of the law. No one knew this better than Lee. Nonetheless, he proceeded to threaten suit against Shelton unless the sheriff accepted his poll-tax payments in the future. With that he had crossed a critical line. There was a good deal of talk around town that something had to be done to stop him. Late on the night of May 7, 1955, Lee was driving alone in his car when he was killed. There was no autopsy. At first Sheriff Shelton said that Lee had died because he lost control of the car. The fact that there were powder burns on Lee's face and shotgun pellets in his car disproved that. Later, other people pieced together what had happened: Lee had been followed by another car, one of whose passengers shot out his right rear tire. As he slowed down, a second car pulled alongside and someone fired twice with a shotgun at point-blank range, blowing half his face away.

With the accident theory disproved, Sheriff Shelton told reporters that it was surely a sexual thing, that he had heard that the Rev. Lee was playing around. The murderer, he said, was surely "some jealous nigger." No one was arrested. Though the murder seemed directly linked to the civil rights movement, the nation's press paid no attention. A few weeks later in Brookhaven, a black man named Lamar Smith was shot down in cold blood in the middle of the day in front of the county courthouse. Smith was a registered voter who had just voted in the state's primary election, and he had encouraged others to vote as well. A white farmer was arrested but not indicted. Again the national press did not cover the story. The traditional covenants of Mississippi seemed more powerful than the new law of the land. This was what Mississippi white men had always done, and therefore it was not news. Blacks in Mississippi seemed not only outside the legal protection of the police, but also outside the moral protection of the press.

Then just a few weeks after Lamar Smith was murdered, Emmett Till was killed in Tallahatchie County. It was this event that at last galvanized the national press corps, and eventually the nation. Emmett Till was a fourteen-year-old black boy from Chicago who had gone south for the summer; it was his second trip back to his family's home. His mother, Mamie Bradley, worked for the Air Force as a civilian procurement officer for $3,900 a year and had already been divorced from his father when he had died during World War Two. His father, it would turn out later, much to the embarrassment of some liberal journals who had proclaimed him a war hero, had actually been hanged by his superiors for raping two Italian women and killing a third. Mamie Bradley was a native Mississippian who joined the black migration from the Deep South to the great cities of the North. As Till and his cousin Curtis Jones had prepared to return to the Delta for a visit, she warned her son that the customs were very different in rural Mississippi than in urban Chicago, where Till had grown up. He had better behave himself at all times, she warned, even if he did not feel like it. Till and Jones were staying with Curtis's great-uncle, an aged sharecropper named Moses Wright, near Money, a hamlet on the edge of the Delta in Tallahatchie County.

Mississippi was a poor state, perennially either forty-seventh or forty-eighth in the union in education and per capita income ("Thank God for Mississippi," officials in Alabama and Arkansas allegedly claimed after the results of every census were published), and Tallahatchie, a county that was half Delta and half hill country, was one of the poorest areas in the state. Four fifths of its inhabitants earned under two thousand dollars a year. The educational levels were the third worst in the state. The average white adult had completed only 5.7 years of school, and the average black only 3.9. The largest town was Charleston, one of its two capitals, which had 2,629 people.

Emmett Till was rather short but already possessed the body of a man and weighed 160 pounds. It was said by some who knew him that he was a sharp dresser and perhaps a little cocky. Neither of these qualities seemed criminal back in Chicago, but in Money, Mississippi, they were the kind of things that could easily get a young black in trouble. On Wednesday evening, August 24, 1955, Till and Jones drove in Moses Wright's 1946 Ford to a little grocery store called Bryant's Grocery and Meat Market. Indistinguishable from a thousand other tiny stores in the Delta whose customers were almost exclusively poor blacks, it sold fatback, snuff, and canned goods. Most of the sales were on credit. Business picked up on Saturday, when the blacks left the plantations and came in to do their meager shopping. The store, which had recently come on hard times because of increased federal food aid to blacks, was run by Roy and Carolyn Bryant, white people so poor that they did not even have their own car.

Even by Mississippi standards, the Bryants' life was hard. Roy Bryant worked as a trucker with his half brother, J. W. Milam, carting shrimp from the Gulf Coast to Texas, while Carolyn ran the store. The feelings about blacks and white women being what they were, there was a strict rule that Carolyn Bryant was not to be in the store alone at night by herself. Moreover, when her husband was away, she and her children were to stay with in-laws. She was twenty-one years old that summer, a pretty high-school dropout from nearby Indianola. "A crossroads Marilyn Monroe," the French newspaper *Aurore* called her.

The initial incident is still the subject of some debate. Apparently, on Thursday Till and his cousin were playing with some boys outside the store. According to Jones, at one point Till pulled a photo of a young white girl from his wallet and boasted that she was his girlfriend. It was regarded by the others merely as the boast of a city slicker to his country cousins. At that point one of the other youths said that there was a white woman inside the store—if Till was so good with white women, why didn't he go in and talk to her? Emmett Till did. According to some accounts, he whistled at Carolyn Bryant; according to others, he bought two cents' worth of bubble gum and as he left, he grabbed her, suggesting that they get together and that he had had white women back up north. According to the testimony of Mrs. Bryant herself during the trial (heard with the jury out of the room because it was so inflammatory in nature, it was disallowed by the judge), he grabbed her wrist and then made a lewd suggestion. "Don't be afraid of me, baby. I been with white girls before," she quoted him as saying. Then he left. An older black man who was playing checkers outside knew at once that something was desperately wrong, and he told Jones and Till that the woman would come out after them with a pistol and blow Emmett's brains out. The two quickly jumped in the car and drove away. As they did, Carolyn Bryant came out of the store looking for Emmett Till.

Mrs. Bryant told her sister-in-law, Juanita Milam, J. W.'s wife, what had happened. The women, fearing the consequences might turn violent, at first decided not to tell their husbands. Roy Bryant did not get home from his shrimp run until about 5 A.M. Friday. By then it was clear within the small universe of rural Tallahatchie that this was a major incident. The blacks were talking about it among themselves. Some relatives were already telling Till to get out of town as quickly as he could, that he was not safe. When Roy Bryant got to the store on Friday afternoon, a black outlined what had happened. In almost any other region of the country the incident would have passed quickly; but in the deep South a deadly serious code had been violated. Bryant would have been regarded as a lesser man had he not stood up for his woman and his own kind; the shame would be his.

Bryant and Milam were not men to cross anyway. Milam, who was six feet two inches and weighed 235 pounds, was nicknamed Big. A highly decorated veteran of World War Two, he was considered even meaner and more dangerous than Bryant. Everyone locally tried hard not to cross the two. Because he had no car, Roy Bryant told Milam that he would need his help. Could Milam come by with the pickup truck later? At first Milam balked. Saturday, he said, was the only day he could sleep late. Then Bryant told him what had happened. Milam was enraged. He said he would be by early on Sunday morning. He drove home, pondered what had happened, and decided not to go to bed. He packed his .45 Colt automatic pistol, drove by Bryant's house, and woke him. Bryant got his pistol, and off they went to Preacher Wright's house. There they demanded that Wright give up "the boy from Chicago." One of the two men, Wright later testified, asked him how old he was. Wright said he was sixty-four. "If you cause any trouble," the white man responded, "you'll never live to be sixty-five."

There is a relatively clear picture of what happened next, thanks not only to several black witnesses who, despite the threats against them, came forward to testify, but also because remarkably enough, Bryant and Milam later sold their version of the story to a somewhat roguish journalist named William Bradford Huie. Huie, who was considered more talented than respectable by many of his peers (whom he regularly scooped), represented *Look* magazine. And for the sum of about four thousand dollars, the two men, who had never taken the stand at their own trial, told the inside story of what had happened that fateful night.

Huie, who specialized in such eccentric journalism, was from Alabama. Shrewd, iconoclastic, he was proud of the fact that he was not, as he liked to point out, a liberal. He was looking for a story, not a cause. He had gone to Sumner after the trial, hoping to speak to a few of the defense attorneys and thereby piece together what had actually happened. He and the white Mississippi defense team had played cat and mouse for a while and shared more than a few drinks. One of the defense attorneys, John Whitten, said that he didn't know if the two men committed the crime. His partner, J. J. Breland, was more outspoken. Both men, he told Huie, were nothing but rednecks and peckerwoods. Bryant, he said, was a "scrappin' pine-knot with nuthin'." As for Milam, Breland said, "We've sued Milam a couple of times for debt. He's bootlegged all his life. He comes from a big, mean, overbearing family. Got a chip on his shoulder. That's how he got that battlefield promotion in Europe; he likes to kill folks. [But] hell, we've got to have our Milams to fight our wars and keep the niggahs in line." The lawyers had cooperated, Breland told Huie, because they wanted the rest of the country to know that integration was not going to work: "The whites own all the property in Tallahatchie County. We don't need the niggers no more. And there ain't gonna be no integration. There ain't gonna be no nigger votin'. *And the sooner everybody in this country realizes it, the better.*"

With that, the lawyers gave Huie access to the two men and told Milam and Bryant to tell Huie what had happened. Huie explained to them that because they had been acquitted, they could never be tried again. They were free men and his project would in no way change that. Then he suggested that he write an article based on their version of the events. Because the article would surely libel them—it would portray them as murderers—Huie said he would agree to make them a libel settlement in advance of four thousand dollars. This was not a payoff for their story, he emphasized. But just in case a film was made and the film libeled them as well, he made sure that they signed away the rights for would-be film libel, too. This was one of the most intriguing examples of checkbook journalism on record, and many people were appalled. "Others," Huie noted, "find this sort of thing distasteful and I have not found it particularly pleasing." Nevertheless, Huie hung around and talked with the two men over four nights, boasting to his editors, "I am capable of drinking out of the same jug with Milam and letting him drink first." Almost a decade later he would use the same method to get the cooperation of the two men who killed three young civil rights workers in Philadelphia, Mississippi.

There were no surprises in the story they told Huie: Moses Wright had produced Till. Milam had shined his flashlight in Till's eyes. "You the nigger who did the talking?" he asked. "Yeah," Till answered. "Don't say 'Yeah' to me: I'll blow your head off. Get your clothes on," Milam had said. Then they drove away with Till. They told Huie they did not intend to kill Till, they wanted merely to scare him and teach him a lesson. But when he proved to be unrepentant, only then, much to their sorrow, did they realize that they had to kill him. "What else could we do?" Milam explained to Huie. "He was hopeless. I'm no bully; I never hurt a nigger in my life. I like niggers in their place. I know how to work 'em. But I just decided it was time to put a few people on notice. As long as I live and can do anything about it, niggers are going to stay in their place. Niggers ain't gonna vote where I live. If they did, they'd control the government. They ain't gonna go to school with my kids. And when a nigger even gets close to mention sex with a white woman, he's tired of livin'. Me and my folks fought for this country and we've got some rights. I stood there in that shed and listened to that nigger throw that poison at me and I just made up my mind. 'Chicago boy,' I said. 'I'm tired of 'em sending your kind down here to stir up trouble. Goddamn you, I'm going to make an example of you—just so everybody can know how me and my folks stand.' "

They decided to kill the boy and throw the body in the Tallahatchie River. What Milam needed most was a weight. There was a cotton gin nearby where they had just brought in some new equipment, and he remembered some workers carrying out the old gin fan, about three feet long: the perfect anchor. They drove over to the cotton gin and found the fan. By then it was daylight and Milam boasted to Huie, for the first time, that he was a little nervous. "Somebody might see us and accuse us of stealing the fan," he said. Then he and Bryant took Till to a deserted bank of the Tallahatchie. Milam made the boy strip naked. "You still as good as I am?" "Yeah," Till answered. At that point, Milam shot him in the head with the .45. Then they wired him to the gin fan, which weighed seventy-four pounds, and they tossed the body in the Tallahatchie River.

Moses Wright did not call the police, as ordered by the two white men, but Curtis Jones did. The next day Jones went to the home of the plantation owner and called the sheriff to say that Emmett Till was missing. He also called Till's mother in Chicago. The local authorities began to dredge the river. It took them three days to find the body, heavily weighted as it was and snarled in tree roots. It was the body of a boy who had been badly abused: There was a bullet hole in his head, which had been bashed in. The body was so badly mangled that Moses Wright identified it primarily from Emmett's ring. The body was shipped north to Chicago, where Mamie Bradley opened the coffin and decided to hold an open-casket funeral. "Have you ever sent a loved son on vacation and had him returned to you in a pine box so horribly battered and waterlogged that this sickening sight is your son—lynched?" she told reporters. She delayed the burial for four days, so that the world could see "what they did to my boy." Thousands lined the black funeral home to see the body.

The murder electrified the large black communities in the nation's Northern industrial cities. White newspapers, aware of this new constituency and of the magnitude of the black emotional response, began to pay attention. White readers, as well, were stunned by the sheer brutality of the act and the idea of vigilante justice at work. In Mississippi, Milam and Bryant were arrested and charged with the murder of Emmett Till. For whatever reason—the brutality of the murder of a child, the public funeral in Chicago, or the vague sense among many in the North that something like this was bound to happen—the case became a cause célèbre. Here was what the Northern press had been waiting for: a rare glimpse beneath the deep South's genteel surface, at how the white power structure kept the blacks in line—using the rawest violence, if necessary.

The Till case marked a critical junction for the national media. Obviously, the Supreme Court decision had made a critical difference morally and socially; for the first time there was a national agenda on civil rights. The national media was going to cover not just the killers but the entire South. The editors of the nation's most important newspapers were men in their fifties, who by and large held traditional views of race but who, because of the *Brown* decision, were going to pay more attention to the race issue. Their reporters were different. They were younger men in their thirties, often Southern by birth, more often than not men who had fought in World War Two and who thought segregation odious. Moreover, they thought World War Two was, among other things, about changing America and the South, where things like this could happen. They had long been ready to cover the South. Now they had their chance. The educational process had begun: The murder of Emmett Till and the trial of the two men accused of murdering him became the first great media event of the civil rights movement. The nation was ready; indeed, it wanted to read what had happened.

Into the tiny Tallahatchie County seat of Sumner poured the elite of the Northern press, more than a little nervous to be in such alien and hostile territory. The reporters were easily recognized. They wore the journalists' uniform of the day: lightweight seersucker suits, button-down shirts, and striped ties, which advertised their former attendance at the nation's better schools. As the day wore on, the jackets might be shed and the ties loosened, but in the beginning those young men seemed to take their signals from one slim, graceful man.

Until then John Popham, of *The New York Times,* was the only full-time national newspaper correspondent working the South. Popham, then forty-five, had been covering the beat for eight years, at the request of the *Times'* managing editor, Turner Catledge, who was from Mississippi and who knew that profound changes were about to take place. Popham was a true American original: a Virginia aristocrat with a secret radical heart. Educated by the Jesuits, he was the son of a professional Marine officer and had served as an officer in the Marines himself. He was an utterly beguiling man, which was fortunate because his was clearly the most delicate of missions. He was endowed with such natural dignity that he seemed to bestow it on others. It was said that in the courtrooms of the South, all of them without air-conditioning in those days, the judge would give permission to the lawyers and members of the jury to take their jackets off. The judge would even take his jacket off. The only person left in the courtroom still wearing a jacket would be Mr. Popham, obvious to all as the gentleman from *The New York Times.* He had become, however involuntarily, the pioneer covering the region. When other reporters came down at the last minute, their contact, inevitably, was John Popham. Popham, by contrast, was connected throughout the region, and when a major event was breaking, he would arrive a week in advance to visit with local officials he knew, men from his vast network of connections; everyone in the South knew someone or had been to law school with someone who knew Popham. As such he was never a stranger. So a week before the Till trial began, he called a prominent businessman in Oxford, Mississippi, who had been a fraternity brother of the Till trial judge, Curtis Swango. Popham had visited Oxford, had dined with the businessman, and ended up, of course, staying the night. So when he set off to Sumner, he was already well connected. On his first day, he went to lunch with Judge Swango.

Actually, Swango was almost desperate to see him. "I've got all these reporters coming in—seems like there must be one hundred of them," the judge complained, "and I've never dealt with anything like this before. I can pledge to you that as far as I can, I'll run a fair and honest trial, but I'd like your help in dealing with the press." So Popham agreed to be the liaison to the press, with the judge setting the ground rules. In accordance with the segregation of the times, he created one press area for whites and one for blacks, finding nonetheless that he was in constant conflict with H. C. Strider, the local sheriff. He also became the unofficial head of security for all reporters. Sumner was not merely a community without motels, it was, after sundown, an extremely dangerous venue for journalists. Filled as it was with smoldering resentments toward all these outsiders, it could explode at any time and a reporter might easily disappear, not to be seen again. Rule number one was: No reporter was to hang around the town at night. Instead, Popham decided, the white reporters should all stay in Clarksdale, some fifty miles away. He also instructed his colleagues on dress codes (once, Murray Kempton, of the *New York Post,* possibly the most talented man covering the trial, came down to dinner in British walking shorts. Popham went over and gently suggested that this was not the time or the place for shorts). He also made sure that the black reporters had a place to stay in Mound Bayou, an all-black community. When one of the blacks was arrested and put in jail for a minor parking violation by Sheriff Strider, it was Popham who got the judge to let him out.

The man who invariably embodied white political power in such small Southern towns was the county sheriff. His job was to protect the economic order for the ruling class and to maintain the racial and political balance, such as it was (but not to come down so hard on black field hands that they might miss a day of work). That was true all over Mississippi, but it was particularly true in the Delta. Sheriffs were rewarded for their stewardship: It was one of the highest paid jobs in the state, the salary coming from a percentage of the ad valorem tax and, also, payoffs from bootleggers (Mississippi was ostensibly a dry state). A Delta sheriff could officially make as much as forty to fifty thousand dollars in those days, and he could make almost as much again by permitting a certain amount of bootlegging and gambling. In a state where five thousand dollars a year was considered a good salary, that was an unusually handsome income.

Sheriff Clarence Strider seemed perfectly cast for the role of this showpiece trial. Even more than Milam and Bryant, he reflected the white-power establishment in the deep South. He tried, despite the decision of Judge Swango, to keep the black reporters from covering the trial and wanted to put the white press as far back in the court-room as possible. Almost every other word out of Strider's mouth, in conversation with reporters and others, seemed to be *nigger*. "There ain't going to be any nigger reporters in my courtroom," he told Popham in their first struggle over media privileges. "Talk to Judge Swango," Popham answered. Strider did and only reluctantly allowed the blacks to be seated.

Strider was a giant man, weighing at least 270 pounds. He was not pleased when Judge Swango ruled against him on the black reporters, and he was not pleased when others in the local white establishment told him his behavior was not helping the county's reputation and he should be more polite, especially to the black reporters. After being told this several times, he finally walked over to the black press table one day. "Morning' niggers," he said. In fact, Strider was regarded as something of an embarrassment among the local planters; he had managed to accumulate land, money, and power, but he was crude; and he did not know how to behave in someone's home or, even more important, how to accomplish the unpleasant parts of his job with a little finesse. Clarence, as former governor Bill Winter said years later, was the kind of man who felt threatened by the idea of a black man in a shirt and tie. Other sections of the country, after all, had their rednecks, but here was one who was the chief law enforcement officer. He listed himself in the yellow pages under the letter *P,* for plantation, and he housed his own sharecroppers in a series of shacks, painting S-T-R-I-D-E-R on their roofs. He had 1,500 acres of cotton, and thirty-five black fami-lies lived on his land. His sharecroppers bought their necessities from his own company store. He had three planes for crop dusting. As far as he was concerned, Strider told reporters, the entire case was rigged. Probably, it was all set up by the NAACP. Emmett Till was not dead, he said; rather, he had been whisked out of the county by the NAACP. Not only was he sheriff, he was a key witness for the defense. On the stand he testified that he could not identify the body because it had deteriorated so badly. Of course, he had done none of the elementary police work that would confirm whether or not it was Till's body.

When Charles Diggs, a black congressman from Detroit, showed up to witness the trial, Strider was furious. His deputies refused to believe that Diggs was actually a congressman. Jim Hicks, a black reporter, took Diggs's congressional ID card to show one of his deputies in order to get Diggs a seat. "This nigger said there's a nigger outside who says he's a congressman," one deputy said to another. "A nigger congressman?" the other deputy asked. "That's what this nigger said," the first deputy added.

In the face of such behavior, the national press corps was prepared to judge Mississippi by the actions of Milam, Bryant, and Strider. That quickly caused a backlash. Soon there were bumper stickers that said: "Mississippi: The Most Lied About State in the Union." A defense fund easily raised money for the defendants. Racist jokes circulated: Wasn't it just like that little nigger to try and steal a gin fan when it was more than he could carry. Everyone knew the two men would go free. That was a given. As the trial wore on, the defendants and their families sometimes sat on the courthouse steps eating ice cream and playing with their kids, as if this were all a picnic. Portents of violence seemed to hang in the air. The real drama of the trial never involved acquittal or conviction but whether Moses Wright would have the courage to name in court, at the possible risk of his own life, the two white men who had come and taken his nephew from his shack. He was scared, and there was a good deal of talk early in the case that he might skip town. Only considerable effort on the part of Medgar Evers, the local NAACP agent (who would himself be murdered a few years later), kept him from fleeing. Wright received a number of threats saying that he would be killed if he took the witness stand. But without his testimony there was no prosecution case. Showing exceptional courage, he took the stand and named both Milam and Bryant. The trial lasted five days. Mamie Bradley took the stand and identified the body as that of her son. At one point she took off her glasses and dabbed at her eyes with a handkerchief. The all-white, all-male jury (nine farmers, two carpenters, and one insurance salesman) was not moved. "If she tried a little harder she might have gotten out a tear," the foreman, J. A. Shaw, said later. When a Clarksdale radio station referred to her as Mrs. Bradley (in the local lingo for blacks she should have been called "the Bradley woman"), people called for the rest of the day to complain.

The prosecutor, Gerald Chatham, told the court in summation there had been no need to kill Till. "The most he needed was a whipping if he had done anything wrong." In his summation John Whitten, one of the defense lawyers, told the jury: "Your ancestors will turn over in their graves [if Milam and Bryant] are found guilty and I'm sure every last Anglo-Saxon one of you has the courage to free these men in the face of that [outside] pressure." The jury deliberated sixty-seven minutes and then set them free. "Well," said Clarence Strider to reporters. "I hope the Chicago niggers and the NAACP are happy." It would have been a quicker decision, said the foreman, if we hadn't stopped to drink a bottle of pop. Later it was said that the jury deliberately prolonged its decision at the request of sheriff-elect Harry Dogan, in order to make it look better to outsiders.

The trial was over. Milam and Bryant stood acquitted in Mississippi and convicted by most of the nation. Their white neighbors, who had stood by them during the trial, now turned on them almost immediately afterward, when the two men took money from Huie and bought themselves new cars. They were told in effect to get out of town. Milam was refused a loan by the Bank of Tallahatchie the next year, which limited his ability to rent land. The Money store was one of three owned by the Milam-Bryant family, and soon after the trial it was boycotted by blacks in the area. Within fifteen months all three stores were closed.

If Milam's and Bryant's trial was over, a different and larger trial had just begun. John Popham left Sumner as stunned as the local residents at the size and power of the national press there. Other events in the past had drawn a large press corps, but this was something different, Popham thought, in the talent and professionalism of the journalists. With as many racial incidents taking place throughout the South as there were, and with more surely about to happen as blacks pressed for greater freedom and whites resisted, Popham had a sense that the pace of life and the pace of change in the region was beginning to accelerate. In much of the past eight years he had worked alone, but he thought that would now be the case less and less. Something new was being created, the civil rights beat it was called, for this new and aggressive young press corps.

THIRTY

Moses Wright had not slept at home since the kidnapping of Emmett Till. In fact, he never even went back to his sharecropper's shack in Money. Right after the trial, he gave away his dog, drove his car to the train station, left it there, and boarded a train to Chicago. He no longer wanted to be a terrified, celebrity witness; instead, he became one more anonymous figure among millions of other blacks who were part of one of the greatest but least reported migrations in American history. If the dramatic and historic process of ending legal segregation was by journalistic definitions a major story, the migration of poor rural blacks from the rural South to the urban North, which was taking place at the same time, was not. Journalists, as the noted *New York Times* columnist James Reston once noted, do a better job covering revolution than they do evolution. Most of the reporters from the

North who came south to cover this story arrived by airplane in whatever Southern city was momentarily under siege, rented a car, and sped off to the center of conflict. They did not, by and large, travel by bus or train; but if they had, they might have noticed another story: At the Memphis bus and train stations every day, large families of poor blacks clustered, often two or three generations huddling together. They were dressed in their best, but their poverty was plainly visible. They carried everything they owned, lugging their belongings in cardboard suitcases or wrapped in bundles of old newspapers and tied together by string; they carried food in shoe boxes. They behaved tentatively, as if they did not belong and were vulnerable to whatever authority was in charge. They went north largely without possessions and yet they left behind almost nothing.

This mass journey, which had begun at the time of World War One, marked the beginning of the end of a kind of domestic American colonialism. The other great industrial powers, like Britain and France and Holland, had established their exploitive economic system in distance places inhabited by people of color. America prided itself that it was not a colonial power, but, if fact, our colonialism was unofficial, practiced upon powerless black people who lived within our borders. When Britain and France ended their colonial rules in the middle of this century, they merely cut all ties to the regions they had exploited. In America, the exploited were American citizens living on American soil, mostly in the South. Thus a great migration began from the rural South—the colonial region—to the great metropolitan centers of the North, which they saw as a new homeland. But they came north with terrible disadvantages; most particularly, they had been denied the education that would allow them to make an easy transition to a more prosperous life.

They were going to Chicago, Detroit, Toledo, and Cleveland, where the work force had previously always been made up of immigrants—Slavs and Germans and Italians. In the late nineteenth and early twentieth centuries, European immigrants had poured into America at an annual rate greater than the entire black population of the North. But when the supply of Europeans finally dried up, America's great employers turned quickly to the blacks in the South. The migration had been going on for some four decades, accelerating greatly during World War One, when the war virtually stopped immigration. World War Two saw the next big surge as white workers left in the hundreds of thousands to fight overseas. During the thirties and forties, the political and economic establishment of the South fought back desperately to hold on to its cheap black labor and there was an all-out effort to stop the flow North, which meant arresting, if need be, those representatives of the Northern factories who were there trying to enlist workers.

For much of the century the *Chicago Defender* was their voice. A black weekly, founded by Robert S. Abbott in 1905, it had been the driving force behind the early part of the black migration. Until then Southern blacks had had no form of public communication save word of mouth, but the *Defender* changed that. Below the Mason-Dixon line it had been regarded by whites as a subversive publication, for it printed the news, banned from Southern papers, about lynchings and murders, and it also printed help-wanted ads. If blacks joined the migration and came north, pledged Abbott, "they could get the wrinkle out of their bellies and live like men."

Abbott and others like him believed that in the South a black man was not treated as a human but as a mere economic possession. In Chicago during World War One, he liked to report, black men just off the train went to employment shops, where the jobs paid $2 and $2.50 a day. Why, the minimum wage in the packing houses in 1918 was 27 cents an hour, soon to go to 40 cents. That was a high wage for men who were accustomed to long hours of back-breaking work for subsistence wages. A black man working on a cotton plantation might make that in a month, and even then there was a chance that his boss would somehow manage *not* to pay him and to show, through the magic of white Southern bookkeeping, that the black employee in fact owed the boss money.

Abbott caught the feeling of rage that many blacks felt about their lives, and the stories he printed, from a large number of correspondents throughout the South, told of the almost daily violent racial incidents. The word *Negro* was not used in the paper, because it was too close to the pejorative *nigger;* instead, in his pages a black man was a *race man.* Critical to his success was his skill in distributing the paper through a vast network of black Pullman car porters. There were periodic attempts on the part of local Southern officials to suppress it, and much of its circulation in rural areas was accomplished clandestinely. When Abbott visited his home in Georgia, he always went in disguise, lest he be arrested. In many parts of the South it was dangerous even to be found with a copy of the paper in one's possession: "A colored man caught with a copy in his possession," wrote Carl Sandburg in the *Chicago Daily News,* "was suspected of having 'Northern fever' and other so-called disloyalties." Its circulation grew parallel to the migration: in early 1916, the circulation was 33,000; by 1919, it was 130,000. Abbott's biographer

Roi Ottley thought the numbers were even higher, that by 1919 it was 230,000. It was estimated that two thirds of the readers lived outside Chicago, most of them in the rural South.

The more that white Southerners tried to suppress the *Defender*, the greater its legitimacy grew with blacks: They reasoned, and not wrongly, that what the white man feared so much and wanted to stop must contain the truth. The most important thing that Abbott did was to articulate the case for the migration from the South to the North. To Abbott, it was like the great biblical flight out of Egypt, and Ottley called it nothing less than "a religious pilgrimage." The Great Northern Drive, Abbott called it. "Come North where there is more humanity, some justice, and fairness," he wrote. The voyage was terrifying. Southern blacks were hardly prepared for the urban condition. They left the South, the *Defender* wrote in 1918, "with trembling and fear. They were going—they didn't know where—among strange people, with strange customs. The people [the white Southerners] who claimed to know best how to treat them painted frightful pictures of what would befall the migrators if they left the land of cotton and sugar cane."

As the migration gathered force, local Southern towns tried to stop it by arresting work-force recruiters. But the migration was too powerful a force for local police to stop: a work-force agent need only walk down the street of a small Southern town, never turn his head, and yet say in a low tone, "Anybody who wants to go to Chicago, see me." That was it. They had lived close to the land, but Southern blacks were hardly rooted in any material sense; they had no homes and possessions to sell, few cars to get rid of in those days. All they had to do was pack a few belongings, some clothes, a photograph or two, and slip onto a late-night Illinois Central train to Chicago when no one was looking. So they went: first a few adventurous individuals, then whole families, church groups, sometimes it seemed, whole towns. Thanks to Abbott's negotiations with the railroads, there were better rates on the trains for large groups. One member of a family usually had gone ahead, and when others arrived later, they at least had a room waiting. The pioneer member of each family usually knew of work.

Chicago the great railhead, became, more than any other city in the country, the beacon for black Americans during the first half of the century: It had not only steel mills and other heavy metal shops, but it had the great meat-packing houses. Often there were grisly work conditions; factories were poorly lit, too cold in the winter and too hot in the summer. During World War Two, there had been a desperate need for labor and labor agents continued to scour the South, handing out free railroad and bus tickets to prospective black employees. But it was after World War Two that the migration began to accelerate even faster. There were a number of forces contributing to the change. Some of it was the reluctance of black workers to go back to a colonial agrarian economy after serving in the Army, or perhaps black people sensed that the repeated election of Franklin Roosevelt meant they had a right to greater freedoms. But the greatest impetus was a technological innovation that ended Southern resistance overnight. In fact, the very Southerners who had fought the migration hardest suddenly wanted only to speed it up. The reason was the invention of the mechanical cotton picker.

The list of technological and scientific changes that transformed America in those years is an extraordinary one—the coming of network television to almost every single home in the country changed America's politics, its leisure habits, and its racial attitudes; the arrival of air-conditioning opened up Southern and Southwestern regions; the early computers were transforming business and the military; the coming of jet planes revolutionized transportation. But perhaps no invention had so profound an effect on the future of American life and was written about so little as the mechanical cotton picker.

As with many inventions, many people worked on it over a long period of time and there was no single inventor. But the inventor of record is John Daniel Rust. As *Fortune* magazine noted, if Rust was not the first man to invent a cotton picker, his early prototypes were so much better than anything that had gone before that "he was the first one to show the world that the idea would work." For more than a century, a machine to separate cotton from the boll without destroying the cotton had eluded inventors. In the end, that breakthrough was Rust's. He was a wonderfully eccentric genius, with more than a touch of the older Henry Ford to him; he was one of those uniquely American dreamers, and for much of his career he seemed more a dreamer than an inventor.

John Rust was born in Texas in 1892, the son of a poor farmer who had fought in the Civil War. One of his jobs as a boy was to help pick the cotton on his farm; it was, he confided to his brother, Mack, the worst job in the world. He was always a tinkerer, though almost never a successful one. As *Fortune* magazine once noted of him, "at an early age he built an unworkable steam engine, later an unworkable airplane with a clockwork motor, patiently went on to invent a cotton chopper (to thin out cotton plants) and a suction device that would not only catch boll weevils but harvest cotton bolls. None of these things quite worked out either." But none of his early failures stopped him.

Rust spent his youth drifting: He worked as a migrant hand, and he took classes from correspondence schools on mechanical drawing and engineering. Gradually, the engine-driven cotton picker became his obsession; he knew from his own experience that there was a desperate need for one. He knew some eight hundred patents had been taken out on cotton pickers since the Civil War, none of them successful. If anything, that simply made his pursuit even more dogged. Like others, he conceived of a long spindle with teeth that would, while spinning, hit the boll and tear the cotton out. The problem was how to get the cotton off the spindle. It got caught in the machine's teeth and remained stuck there.

His own early designs featured a serrated or barbed spindle that would pull the cotton off. That, he finally decided after a long series of failures, was not the way to go. For the cotton seemed to obey its own laws and not the laws of man-made machines. It was not so much a machine that picked cotton as a machine that made a mess of cotton. Then one night in 1927, Rust lay in bed pondering his dilemma. There had to be, he was sure, some simple answer. Then he remembered his own experiences back in Texas picking cotton. In the morning when he had picked the bolls, his hands were still wet from the dew and the cotton had tended *to stick to his fingers.* He got out of bed, went downstairs, found a nail, wet it, and stuck it into a clump of cotton. The cotton stuck to the nail. He was stunned that it was all so simple. "I knew I had hold of something good," he said years later. "I was so sure of it, I thought I'd be able to build a salable machine inside of five years." Not everyone else was so confident. One hardware-store clerk who sold him parts asked him what he needed them for. When he explained, the clerk answered, "Good heavens, Rust. You can't do that! Some of the biggest companies in the world have been working on that for years and they haven't got anywhere yet. If they can't build a cotton picker, what makes you think you can?" The big companies, Rust answered, were all going in the wrong direction. With that the clerk sold him the material. "But I still think you're wasting your time," he noted.

Rust had budgeted five years for the task, but it turned out to take much longer than that. As he worked on the machine, he survived on the kindness of friends and relatives (but always kept a careful record of his debts). By the time his machine came to market, he had spent perhaps $200,000—but the mighty Harvester Co., his chief rival, had spent an estimated $5 million. He was always underfinanced; he was essentially a tinkerer, working out of his own garage. His one partner during this long, difficult search was his brother, Mack. Like many inventors, he was fiercely independent and wary of big corporations, which he was sure were corrupt. Though he could easily have sold his idea to a large company and seen his machine go to market more readily, he would not even consider the idea. A group of local businessmen once offered him $50,000 for a half interest in his invention, but he preferred to go it alone with his brother.

It was a long, hard journey from drawing board to production. The picker was, in fact, an engineer's nightmare: a complicated and delicate machine that had to work on rugged terrain. The possibilities of things going wrong were endless. When the Rust machine first went to market in 1927, it contained some 25,000 parts—3,000 in the spindles alone. It worked well in theory, but it was not dependable in the field. Small parts constantly broke down, and if there had been too much rain, the early machines were so incredibly heavy that they sank in the mud. The sixth Rust prototype, completed in 1933, was the first significant success; it was shown at an agricultural station in Stoneville, Mississippi, and it picked more cotton in one hour than an ordinary worker could pick in a week. W. E. Ayres, the director of the station, called it "the missing link in the mechanical production of cotton." With that the future was assured for someone to mass-produce a mechanical picker; by 1936 he had completed the prototype, and it was now just a matter of time. Ayres later told Rust, "I sincerely hope that you can market your machine shortly. Lincoln emancipated the Southern Negro. It remains for the cotton harvesting machine to emancipate the Southern cotton (tenant) farmer."

Rust had finally succeeded—at the height of the Depression. Already, millions of men and women were out of work. Did anyone want a machine that would quite possibly create even more unemployment? E. H. Crump, the political boss of Memphis, talked of passing a law to make it illegal to produce the machine. The *Memphis Commercial-Appeal* ran a cartoon of a black field hand with an empty sack saying, "If it does my work—whose work am I going to do?" The *Jackson (Mississippi Daily) News* suggested that the machine be thrown in the Mississippi River.

By 1940, John Rust was desperate. He had the basics of a good machine, but he still had bugs to work out. He was also broke: His home was mortgaged and he had been forced to sell his shop equipment to pay his debts. He, his wife, his brother, Mack, and his wife had all taken jobs to help pay for their very survival. "There was a long time there," said G. E. Powell, who worked with Rust, "when he and his wife and his brother and his wife lived in this tiny apartment together, and they essentially lived on starvation wages." Worst of all, it was rumored that Harvester had its machine down pat and was ready to go into production the minute the war was over. His brother, Mack, finally took off to customize cotton pickers in the Southwest, but at his wife's urging, John Rust decided to give his machine one more shot: He sat down and for three months all he did was redraw the machine. He cashed his war bonds, went to Washington, and filed his new patents. At the same time Allis-Chalmers, a large company, decided that Rust's old patents were feasible and was trying to contact him.

He sold Allis-Chalmers permission to use his patents, and the company in turn put him on contract as a consultant; during the war it built six machines for experimental use in the Delta. With the war over, Harvester was ready to go into production and by 1948 it was building a plant to manufacture the picker in Memphis, capital of the cotton belt. But Allis-Chalmers faced strikes and shortages of material after the war and was slower to go into production. When, in 1949, it finally did get going, it manufactured so few machines that it lost exclusive rights to Rust's designs.

The cotton planters were ready for the arrival of the mechanical picker—rumors of which had been floating around for some twenty years. They saw it as the answer to their growing labor shortage. During the war, many crops had not been fully picked because there were not enough hands. Now the war was over, and to the growers' shock, the manpower shortage still existed. In addition, the planters realized that they could no longer set the price of labor themselves, because of the growing number of job opportunities for blacks in the North. The cost of labor had tripled in just one decade: In 1940 the price for picking a hundred pounds of seed cotton was 62 cents; by 1945, it was $1.93, and what was worse, after the war it did not go down, as some planters had assumed it would. It kept going up, reaching $2.90 by 1948. At the same time they were suddenly competing with such synthetic fabrics as rayon, for the manufacturing of synthetics had been expedited by the wartime shortages. "COTTON

PICKERS, WHERE ARE YOU?" read a headline in the *Memphis Press Scimitar* a year after the end of the war. The local director of the federal employment service was appalled because farmers were begging for pickers, even at $2.10 for a hundred pounds of cotton. "A good picker can average 300 or 400 pounds a day," said Mrs. Clara Kitts. "A whole family can bring home lots of money. The weather has been warm and beautiful. There are lots of people idle. But still nobody comes out to pick. I don't understand why." In the days before the war, she added, her office sent out some 16,000 short-term pickers every day. Now that number was down to 3,000.

Worse, and this was something the planters spoke about privately, there were now attitude problems. The war, it was said locally, had ruined many of the black people, particularly the young men. They had become uppity. There were stories about black people sassing their white bosses, or just walking off their jobs one day and never showing up again. The future lay, everyone seemed to agree, with the new machines. Some planters had actually seen demonstrations. In addition, everyone knew Harvester had built a factory in Memphis after the war—a sure sign of confidence. That showed that the company was making a commitment. By 1948 Harvester was in production, turning out 1,000 machines annually, priced at $7,600 (mounted on a tractor)—but it was tax deductible. It was the 1948 crop, more than anything, that convinced the farmers to go mechanical. That had been a particularly good crop, but almost everyone was having trouble getting it picked. By the end of the year some farmers on the Arkansas side of the Mississippi suggested that the Ben Pearson company, which made archery equipment in Pine Bluff, go into the manufacture of cotton pickers. They arranged for Carl Hahn, the head of Pearson, to attend a meeting of planters in January 1949. One of them had seen a demonstration of one of Rust's machines, and the machine was just waiting for Hahn to take a look. Would Pearson build it, they asked? Hahn thought it a good risk and promised to take it on, if the farmers could guarantee him fifty orders, noncancellable, with $1,000 of the full $3,750 price down. Everyone was enthusiastic, and he quickly raised the necessary money from the men present. By July 1949, they had their first machines out.

It was not exactly a perfect machine, and in that first year, it proved to be better picking cotton in the Southwest and California, because the cotton fields there were irrigated; that meant an easier place to work than the rich, often muddy Delta land. The stress on the machine in the Delta was far greater; in some cases the Pearson company ended up giving the $1,000 down payment back to the Arkansas farmers and selling the machine out West. Still, of the one hundred machines the Pearson company made that year, ninety-nine were sold. Within eighteen months the Pearson people, working with Rust, improved the spindle on the Rust machine so that it could work the rougher Delta farms.

Billy Pearson grew up in Tallahatchie County and went off to the University of North Carolina, thinking perhaps he would be a lawyer. But his uncle died in 1945 when he was twenty-three, and he came back to take over the family place: 1,500 acres of fertile alluvial soil. The Rainbow Plantation, it was called, because it was shaped like a rainbow. Pearson had never really intended to be a cotton planter, but in later years, he decided that everyone in life has some form of predestination that dictates how his or her life will be spent, and he had been chosen to be a cotton farmer. His mother's family, the Simpsons, had been in the Delta since the latter part of the nineteenth century: His maternal grandfather, William Marion Simpson, had arrived without money or land but was a shrewd businessman. Some twenty-five years after he arrived in the Delta, he found a partner and bought the Rainbow Plantation, then a handsome spread of 2,300 acres. Those were boom years for agriculture in the Delta; the total price even then was $300,000 with a down payment of $75,000. Within five years, as the price of cotton remained stable, Simpson and his partner had wiped out their indebtedness, at which point they split the land evenly and formed separate plantations. By the mid-twenties, times had become very hard. The price of cotton began an uninterrupted decline, and each spring William Simpson would announce, "Well, the only thing I can do this year is lose some more money." For almost a decade the Simpsons lived well but accumulated heavy debts, and William Simpson's considerable shrewdness was required to keep his spread going— essentially, he traded parcels of land against its own indebtedness. By the time cotton farming began to be viable again, at the beginning of World War Two, the plantation had shrunk considerably, from 3,500 acres down to 1,800.

As soon as Pearson returned from the war, he heard about the imminent arrival of the mechanical pickers. In fact, when he took over the family place, he believed machines were the future, and most of the other men his age felt the same way. It was only the older men who looked at the price of the machines—about eight thousand dollars in all, with the tractor—and thought they themselves were so old and had been around so long that there was no point in changing at this late date. Instead, they would do as they had always done. But the younger men thought of the future, and the future was clearly in the machines. The labor shortages were so acute there had even been some stealing of hands among planters desperate to get their cotton in—a practice so frowned on by most Delta planters that it would have been unthinkable in the past. Pearson bought his first machine, a Harvester, in 1948. He decided on a one-row machine because the spindle seemed stronger, and there was already a good deal of talk about spindle problems with the Rust machines. The problem with the Harvester was that it picked dirty cotton—that is, it pulled in more trash than either the Rust machine or hand labor did: Because the cotton gins were not yet sophisticated enough to separate the trash, Pearson and others like him had to sell their cotton at a discount price, roughly one third off.

Delta planters knew they had only a brief window of time in which to pick their cotton, from the instant it was mature, in late September, to around October 20th, when the rains always came— about four weeks. Pearson's one-row picker could pick somewhere between 150 and 175 acres in the time allotted, so eventually he went to two-row machines, which could do about 350 acres. A decade later, he had as many as three or four machines on the place. Pearson had only the vaguest sense of the great black migration that was taking place: He was so preoccupied with his cotton that he had not stopped to think about the larger social implications.

From the time that he had come back from the war, he had employed more people than he had needed, and he had watched the migration taking place as people no longer able to make an acceptable living opted to go north, often in the middle of the night without even a farewell. It was a terrible time for these men and their families, he realized; they existed on the edge of solvency and when they got behind and borrowed, as they regularly did, they could rarely climb out of debt. He thought often about one family whose journey had reflected the general hardship of black field hands caught by a dying agricultural way of life. The husband had silently gone off to Detroit one night, leaving behind a wife and seven children. A few months later the rest of the family departed. What shocked Pearson was the manner of their departure: One winter night a pickup truck had shown up and the entire family got in the open back and drove to Detroit in the cold. It was, Pearson thought later, not unlike Eliza going across the ice.

In 1991 he would read a book by a young writer named Nicholas Lemann about the great migration, and although he disagreed with some of Lemann's conclusions, he was impressed by the authority and sensitivity of the book. Billy Pearson was intrigued that he, a man who cared so much about the past and about history, and who took such pleasure reading about it, had been part of so profound a social movement and had never even been aware of it. But he had realized at the time the vulnerability of the black people, of how little they got from so much hard work, and he had been disturbed by the rising anger he had felt among the white people in the years after the *Brown* decision.

During the Till trial in 1955, his wife, Betty, and her friend Florence Mars had gone into Sumner every day to watch the trial, and they had been stunned by what they saw; Clarence Strider had not wanted them to attend, but sheriff-elect Harry Dogan had given them both press passes for the local paper, the *Summer Sentinel*. They were shocked by what had taken place. It was like watching a community you thought you knew reveal itself as something else entirely.

Much later in his life, Billy Pearson's thoughts often went back to a day during the Emmett Till trial when he had gone into town to take a look around. He had been appalled by the tension he had found in a small town he thought he knew well. Clarence Strider had hired a number of extra deputies, and they seemed to be bully-boys, young men with long sideburns and pistols who delighted in pushing people around, particularly the blacks. Pearson had gone there with Nathan Kern, who was a black employee Pearson admired greatly, and Kern had clearly been upset by what he saw: He said it was something new, this cruelty and violence toward black people. "Mr. Pearson," Kern had said. "Those of us that are still here, we're here because we chose to be here. We don't have to stay. We've all got cousins and kin up north and all we have to do is send a postcard saying save me a room, and we're gone. We stayed here because this was our home and now we wonder if it's our home anymore."

Gradually, over the years the number of black people on the Rainbow Plantation dwindled until Pearson was left with only eight full-time employees. It was, he thought, a world without easy answers—the forces of change had proved more powerful than any of them, white or black. Though his land was rich—as rich as any land in America, with the possible exception of the San Joacquin Valley, he thought—he was not a wealthy man except in the value of his land. The only way to survive was through mechanization, which of course required fewer field workers. But he had sensed the workers were probably going to leave the land anyway—the machine merely accelerated the process. The one money crop for a long time was cotton, which was a wonderful crop but heartbreaking in some ways—for there was so much that could go wrong. Yet there was a special pleasure in doing it right, in fighting and coming up with a successful crop. Cotton farming was, he liked to muse when he reached the age of seventy, a bad business but a good life. The government now set strict limits on cotton acreage. There had been talk of soybeans, but for a long time it was not a valuable crop. Then in the mid-fifties, a new variety of soybean that did not shatter was developed. Some men he knew eventually went to rice as well and some finally turned to catfish, but he remained with cotton and soybeans.

During the fifties the race for dominance among the great farm-implement companies was on: There was the Rust machine, there was Harvester, and the John Deere people were said to be working on a machine that eventually many would consider the best of the three. By 1952 there were some ten thousand machines in use, and by 1955 there would be almost twice that number. Some estimated that by 1955, 25 percent of the cotton crop was harvested by machine, by 1960, 55 percent. In addition, it was believed that where it had taken 130 hours to pick a bale of cotton before the mechanization, it now took only 45 hours with it. In 1952 the National Cotton Council estimated that the entire operation of producing cotton, from sowing to harvesting, could be done with 15 man-hours of work per acre using machines, compared with 155 hours using hand labor and a mule.

The Pearson Company paid Rust $100,000 on the sale of the first one hundred machines, which allowed Rust to pay back his creditors at a rate of two dollars for every dollar borrowed. He died in 1954. John Rust, who had invented the cotton picker to help small farmers, did live to see the machine of his dreams roll off several assembly lines, and he did escape the grinding poverty that had dogged him for so long. His picker did not, though, become an instrument that helped small farmers; indeed, it predictably played a role in the trend that saw plantations grow ever larger as small farms fell by the wayside. His widow, Thelma, who did not share her husband's utopian dreams, managed to divert the royalties from a foundation he had established to her private estate and to buy a motel in Pine Bluff. In all, the Pearson Company paid some $3.7 million to the Rusts in royalties.

Before he died, Sheriff Clarence Strider did not come around on the issue of integration, and he left a piece of his own plantation to be used for an all-white academy, which was named after him, the Strider School. His nephew Jesse was also a big man—about six feet four inches and 250 pounds—and was known, deservedly enough, as Big Daddy Strider. Elected sheriff of nearby Grenada County, Jesse Strider changed with the laws of the land. He helped rescue his county from the Klan, and he hired black deputies. When a young black man named Mike Espy was running for Congress in that part of Mississippi, Chuck Robb came down from Virginia to speak at an Espy rally in Vicksburg. Robb suggested to Espy that he could help defuse the race question by getting a big old redneck sheriff to come out for him. Espy said, he knew just the man. So Espy's television people shot a commercial of Big Daddy Strider leaning against a tree saying that he was for Mike Espy, and it turned the election around and helped send Espy to the House.

THIRTY-ONE

T he Supreme Court ruling on *Brown* v. *Board of Education,* which occurred in the middle of the decade, was the first important break between the older, more staid America that existed at the start of the era and the new, fast-paced, tumultuous America that saw the decade's end. The second was Elvis Presley. In cultural terms, his coming was nothing less than the start of a revolution. Once, in the late sixties, Leonard Bernstein, the distinguished American composer and conductor, turned to a friend of his named Dick Clurman, an editor at *Time* magazine. They were by chance discussing political and social trends. "Elvis Presley," said Bernstein, "is the greatest cultural force in the twentieth century." Clurman thought of the sultry-faced young man from the South in tight clothes and an excessive haircut who wiggled his body while he sang about hound dogs. Bernstein's statement seemed a bit much.

"What about Picasso?" he began, trying at the same time to think of other major cultural forces of the century. "No," Bernstein insisted, and Clurman could tell that he was deadly serious, "it's Elvis. He introduced the beat to everything and he changed everything— music, language, clothes, it's a whole new social revolution—the Sixties comes from it. Because of him a man like me barely knows his musical grammar anymore." Or, as John Lennon, one of Elvis's admirers, once said, "Before Elvis there was nothing."

If he was a revolutionary, then he was an accidental one, an innately talented young man who arrived at the right place at the right time. He had no political interests at all, and though his music symbolized the coming together of black and white cultures into the mainstream in a way that had never happened before, that seemed to hold little interest for him. Though much of his music had its roots among blacks, he, unlike many young white musicians, seemed to have little interest in the black world and the dramatic changes then taking place there. Indeed, he often seemed to have little interest in music at all. What he really wanted from the start was to go to Hollywood and be a movie star like James Dean or Marlon Brando, a rebel up on the screen. It was almost as if the music that shook the world was incidental. Brando and Dean were his role models, and when he finally got to Hollywood and met Nicholas Ray, who had directed Dean in *Rebel Without a Cause,* he got down on his knees and started reciting whole pages from the script. He had, Ray realized, seen *Rebel* at least a dozen times and memorized every line that Dean spoke. If he would never rival Brando and Dean as a movie actor, he learned from them one critical lesson: never to smile. That was the key to their success, he was sure. He was sure he could manage the same kind of sultry good looks they had. As a teenager he spent hours in front of a mirror working on that look, and he used it to maximum effect, later, in his own appearances.

Sam Phillips, Memphis recording man, enthusiast of black music, had been looking for years for someone like Elvis—a white boy who could sing like a black boy and catch the beat of black music. Elvis, Phillips later said, "knew I was there a long time before he finally walked into my studio. I saw that Crown Electric Company truck that he was driving pull up a number of times outside the studio. He would sit in it and try to get his courage up. I saw him waiting there long before he got the nerve to come in." Elvis Presley walked into that studio in the summer of 1953. He had been sent there by another talent scout, who had not wanted anything to do with him—and those awful pegged pants, the pink and black clothes.

He was an odd mixture of a hood—the haircut, the clothes, the sullen, alienated look; and a sweet little boy—curiously gentle and respectful, indeed willing and anxious to try whatever anyone wanted. Everyone was sir or ma'am. Few young Americans, before or after, have looked so rebellious and been so polite.

Sam Phillips immediately liked Presley's early greaser style. The clothes came from Lansky's, a store more likely to be visited by flashy black men about town then by young white males. "And the sideburns, I liked that too. Everyone in town thought *I* was weird, and here was this kid and he was as weird as I was," Phillips recalled. There is some dispute as to whether Sam Phillips was in the studio the day that Elvis first walked in. Marion Kreisker, Phillips's secretary, believes he was not, and in her account she takes credit for his first recording. Phillips insisted that he *was* there, and that while Ms. Kreisker may have spoken to him first, he actually cut Presley's first disc. "It's a very expensive piece of equipment and I wasn't about to let a secretary use it," he noted. "What do you sing?" Marion Kreisker asked. "I sing all kinds," she remembered him answering. "Well, who do you sound like?" she prodded. "I don't sound like nobody," he replied. He told her he wanted to cut a record for his mother's birthday, which was still several months away.

So he sang into Sam Phillips's little record machine, getting his three dollars' worth. He sang two Ink Spots songs, "My Happiness" and "That's When Your Heartaches Begin." Presley himself was disappointed with the results. "Sounded like someone beating on a bucket lid," he said years later. Sam Phillips later said that he heard Elvis sing and thought to himself, *Oh man, that is distinctive. There is something there, something original and different.*

Sam Phillips listened to Presley a few times and was sure that Elvis had some kind of special talent, but he just wasn't sure what it was. He was not a particularly good guitar picker, but there was a sound almost buried in there that was distinctive. Part of it was Elvis's musical promiscuity: He did not really know who he was. After one frustrating session, Phillips asked him what he could do. "I can do anything," he said. He sang everything: white, black, gospel, country, crooners. If anything, thought Phillips, he seemed to see himself as a country Dean Martin. "Do you have any friends you woodshed with?" Phillips asked him. Woodshedding was a term to mean musicians going off and working together. Elvis replied, no. Phillips said he had two friends, and he called Scotty Moore at his brother's dry-cleaning shop. Moore was an electric-guitar player and Phillips suggested he and Bill Black, a bassist, work out with Elvis.

They were to try to bring forth whatever it was that was there. Elvis, Moore thought—that's a science fiction name. After a few weeks of working together, the three of them went to Phillips's studio to record. Phillips by chance entered the date in his log: July 5, 1954. For a time the session did not go particularly well. Elvis's voice was good, but it was too sweet, thought Phillips. Then Elvis started picking on a piece, by a famed black bluesman named Arthur Crudup, called "I'm All Right, Mama." Crudup was a Mississippi blues singer who had made his way to Chicago with an electric guitar. He was well known within the narrow audience for black blues. He had recorded this particular song seven years earlier, and nothing had happened with it. Suddenly, Elvis Presley let go: He was playing and jumping around in the studio like all the gospel singers, black and white, he had watched onstage. Soon his two sidemen joined him. "What the hell are you doing?" Phillips asked. Scotty Moore said he didn't know. "Well, find out real quick and don't lose it. Run through it again and let's put it on tape," Phillips said. They turned it into a record. Having covered a black blues singer for one side, it seemed only fitting to use Presley's version of bluegrass singer Bill Monroe's "Blue Moon of Kentucky" on the other.

Country blended with black blues was a strain that some would come to call rock-a-billy, something so powerful that it would go right to the center of American popular culture. Crudup, one of the legendary pure black blues singers of his time, was not thrilled by the number of white singers who seemed to make so much money off work he had pioneered. "I was makin' everybody rich and I was poor," he once said. "I was born poor, I live poor, and I'm going to die poor." Bo Diddley, the great black rocker, was more philosophical. Someone later asked Diddley if he thought Presley had copied his style. "If he copied me, I don't care—more power to him," Diddley said. "I'm not starving."

Phillips was sure the record was a winner and he sent it to a local disc jockey named Dewey Phillips (no relation), who had a show called *Red, Hot and Blue,* on WHBQ. He was very big with the young white kids—Elvis himself had listened faithfully to him almost every night since he was fourteen years old. Dewey Phillips played traditional white artists all the time, but just as regularly, he played the great black singers, blues and gospel. "Dewey was not white," the black blues singer Rufus Thomas once said in the ultimate accolade. "Dewey *had* no color." Dewey and Sam, spiritually at least, were kin. If Sam was a man who subscribed to very few local conventions, then Dewey openly liked to flaunt them. He had ended up at WHBQ, as much as anything else, by being very unsuccessful at anything else he tried. He came from Adamsville, in west Tennessee. As a boy he had loved listening to black music, although he had been assured by his elders that it was the work of the devil. He had visited Memphis as a boy once when he was ten to sing in a Baptist church choir. The lady in charge had taken them to their hotel, the Gayoso, and explained to them that there were two rules: first, they were not to order from room service, since they would eat at churches; second, they were not to wander over to Beale Street. Dewey immediately took a younger boy and went to Beale Street. It had not disappointed him, with its rich black life and music. Eventually, after serving in the army, he came back home and migrated to Memphis. There he had started out working in a bakery. He was fired when he convinced the other bakers that instead of making the regular bread, they should all make loaves shaped like little gingerbread men. Baking, obviously, was not his calling. He next went to work as a stockboy for the W.T. Grant store downtown. There he managed to get himself in the store's music department and soon was beaming his department's records over loudspeakers into the street at top volume. That, of course, stopped downtown traffic. He also accompanied them with his own patter by plugging a microphone into the store's record player. He had invented himself as a disc jockey. All he needed was a radio station.

At the time Memphis had a radio show called *Red, Hot and Blue,* which consisted of fifteen minutes of popular music on WHBQ. Dewey Phillips often told friends that he would do the show for nothing if they would let him try. He went down to WHBQ, asked for a job, and miraculously got it. He was so different, so original, that the management did not know at first whether to fire him or expand the show; within a year he had three hours to himself. He was, in the words of his friend Stanley Booth, both brilliant and terrible as a disc jockey. He could not read a line of copy, and he could not put a record on without scratching it. But he had perfect taste in the music that young people wanted to hear. Soon he was the conduit that hip young white Memphis kids used to hear black music with its powerful beat. Political boss Ed Crump might keep the streets and schools and public buildings segregated, but at night Dewey Phillips integrated the airwaves. Daddy-O-Dewey, he was soon called. Phrases he tossed away casually at night on his show became part of the teenage slang of Memphis the next day. Stumble he might while doing the commercials (and he might even do commercials for people who had not bothered to buy time—he was always suggesting that his listeners go out and buy a fur-lined Lincoln, even if Lincoln was not an advertiser), but he was wildly inventive.

There were always surprises on his show. He loved having contests as well, and all three of his sons were named during radio contests. He was a man driven by a kind of wonderful madness and an almost sweet desire to provoke the existing establishment, and to turn the world gently upside down. Memphis in those days still had a powerful movie censor, Lloyd Binford, and when Binford had banned an early teen movie, Phillips had played its theme song, Bill Haley's "Rock Around the Clock," and dedicated it to Binford: "And this goes out to Lloyd Binford. . . . How you *doin'*, Lloyd? . . . Anyway . . ." There he was in clean, well-ordered Memphis, tapping beneath the polite, white surface into the wildness of the city.

On one occasion he decided he wanted to find out how large his listenership was. Nothing as clumsy as demographic polls for Dewey Phillips, particularly since Memphis had just won an award for being the nation's quietest city—instead, he just told everyone listening to him to blow their horns at 9 P.M. If they were in their cars they could blow their horns, and if they were in their homes they should go out to their cars and blow the horns. At 9:05 the police chief called the station and told him, "Dewey, you just can't do this to us—the whole city's gone crazy, everybody out there is blowing horns." So Dewey Phillips went back on the air and told his listeners what the chief had just told him. "So I can't tell you to blow your horns at 11:30." The faithful went back out and blew their horns at 11:30.

Dewey Phillips had, in his friend Sam Phillips's words, "a platinum ear" and was connected to young listeners like no other adult. Therefore, he was the first person Sam Phillips thought of when he had Elvis's first disc. Dewey agreed to play it. The night he did, Elvis was so nervous that he went to a movie by himself. The two songs were such a success that all Dewey Phillips did that night was flip the record back and forth. The switchboard started lighting up immediately. Finally the disc jockey decided he wanted to interview Elvis on the air, and he called Sam Phillips and told him to bring the boy in. The Presleys did not have a phone, but Sam called over to their neighbors and they got Elvis's mother. Gladys and Vernon Presley had to go looking for their elusive son in the movie theater. "Mama, what's happening?" he asked. "Plenty, son," she answered, "but it's all good." Off they went to the station. There he was introduced to Dewey Phillips, who was going to interview him. "Mr. Phillips," he said. "I don't know nothin' about being interviewed." "Just don't say nothing' dirty," Phillips said. So they talked. Among other things, Phillips deftly asked Elvis where he had gone to high school, and Elvis answered Humes, which proved to the entire audience that yes, he was white. At the end Phillips thanked him. "Aren't you going to interview me?" Presley asked. "I already have," Phillips said.

Elvis Aron Presley was born in the hill country of northeast Mississippi in January 1935. It was a particularly poor part of a poor region in a nation still suffering through the Depression; in contrast to other parts of Mississippi, it was poor cotton land, far from the lush Delta 150 miles further west. Yet the local farmers still resolutely tried to bring cotton from it (only when, some thirty years later, they started planting soybeans did the land become valuable), and it was largely outside the reach of the industrial revolution. Presley's parents were typical country people fighting a daily struggle for survival. Gladys Smith until her marriage and her pregnancy operated a sewing machine and did piecework for a garment company, a rare factory job in the area. Vernon Presley—a man so poorly educated that he often misspelled his own name, signing it Virnon—was the child of a family of drifters and was employed irregularly, taking whatever work he was offered: perhaps a little farming, perhaps a little truck driving. He lived on the very fringes of the American economy; he was the kind of American who in the thirties did not show up on government employment statistics. At the time of their marriage Gladys was twenty-one, four years older than Vernon. Because they were slightly embarrassed by the fact that she was older, they switched ages on their marriage certificate. Elvis was one of twins, but his brother, Jessie Garon Presley, was stillborn, a death that weighed heavily on both mother and son.

When Gladys became pregnant, Vernon Presley borrowed $180 from Orville Bean, a dairy farmer he worked for, and bought the lumber to build his family a two-room cabin. The cabin was known as a shotgun shack—because a man could stand at the front door and fire a shotgun and the pellets would go straight out the back door. When Elvis was two years old, Vernon Presley was picked up for doctoring a check from Bean. It had been an ill-conceived, pathetic attempt to get a few more dollars, at most. Friends of Vernon's pleaded with Bean not to press charges. They would make up the difference. But Bean was nothing if not rigid, and he held firm against their pleas. Vernon Presley could not make bail, and he waited seven months in the local jail before the trial even took place.

He was convicted and sent to Parchman prison in the middle of the Depression for two and a half years. It was a considerable sentence for a small crime, but those were hard times. When he came out times were still hard; he worked in a lumberyard and then for one of the New Deal aid programs for the unemployed, the WPA.

During World War Two he got a job doing defense work in Memphis, eighty miles away. That at least was steady work, even if he was away from home much of the time. After the war, returning veterans had priority for any jobs. Vernon had no skills and was soon out of work again. In the late forties the new affluence rolling quickly across much of the country barely touched people like Vernon and Gladys Presley. They were poor whites. Their possibilities had always been limited. They were people who lived on the margin. Religion was important to them, and when Elvis was nine he was baptized in the Pentecostal church. As a symbol of Christian charity, he was supposed to give away some of his prized possessions, so he gave his comic books to other children.

Because a city like Memphis held out more hope of employment, Vernon Presley moved his family to Memphis in the late forties. There he took a job in a paint factory for $38.50 a week. They had made the move, Elvis said later, because "we were broke, man, broke." The family was still so poor that it had to live in federal housing—the projects, as they were known. The Presleys paid thirty-five dollars a month for rent, the equivalent of a week's salary. To some whites, living in the projects was an unspeakable idea, for it was housing that placed them at the same level as blacks; for the Presleys, the projects were the best housing they had ever had.

Even in a high school of his peers, Elvis Presley was something of a misfit. He went to Humes, an all-white high school where he majored in shop. There was no thought of college for him. Not surprisingly, he was shy and unsure of himself. He was bothered by the way his teeth looked. He worried that he was too short. As an adult he always wore lifts in his shoes. He did, however, have a sense that his hair worked for him. Soon he started using pomade; his style, black clothes, shirt collar up in back, hair pomaded into a major wave, was an early form of American punk. His heroes—Brando and Dean—were narcissistic, so too by nature was he. His social life was so limited that he did not know how to slow-dance with a girl; rather, in the new more modern style, he knew how to dance only by himself. His peers deemed him effeminate and different. Everyone, it seemed, wanted a shot at him, particularly the football players. Years later he would tell a Las Vegas audience, "They would see me coming down the street and they'd say, 'Hot dog! Let's get him! He's a squirrel! He just come down outta the trees!' " His one friend was Red West, a more popular Humes student and a football player. West stopped about five other boys from cutting off Elvis's hair in the boys' room one day. "He looked like a frightened little animal," West said.

The one thing he had was his music. He could play a guitar and play it well. He could not read a note of music, but he had an ear that, in the words of Chet Atkins, the guitarist who supervised many of his early RCA recordings, was not only pure but had almost perfect pitch. He could imitate any other voice he chose. That was his great gift. Some of the other kids suggested he play his guitar at a school picnic, and he did, with surprising success. His homeroom teacher asked him to play it at the school variety show. He did, playing the Red Foley country favorite "Old Shep," about a boy and his dog. When the dog dies and goes to heaven, the boy does not feel too badly, for "old Shep has a wonderful friend." For the first time he gained some popularity.

On the surface, the Mississippi he grew up in was a completely segregated world. That was seemingly true even in music. Among the many musical subcultures that flowed across the Mississippi Delta were black rhythm and blues music (called race music in the trade), black gospel, white gospel, which in no small part was imitative of black gospel, and country, or hillbilly, music. Because whites were more influential and affluent than blacks, the last was the dominant strain in the region.

For Elvis Presley, living in a completely segregated world, the one thing that was not segregated was the radio dial. There was WDIA ("the Mother Station of the Negroes," run, of course, by white executives), which was the black station, on which a young white boy could listen to, among other people, the Rev. Herbert Brewster, a powerful figure in the world of Memphis black churches. A songwriter of note, he composed "Move On Up a Little Higher," the first black gospel song to sell over a million copies. What was clear about the black gospel music was that it had a power of its own, missing from the tamer white church music, and that power seemed to come as much as anything else from the beat. In addition there was the immensely popular Dewey Phillips. When Elvis listened to the black radio station at home, his family was not pleased. "Sinful music," it was called, he once noted. But even as Elvis Presley was coming on the scene, the musical world was changing. Certainly, whites had traditionally exploited the work of black musicians, taking their music, softening and sweetening it and making it theirs. The trade phrase for that was "covering" a black record. It was thievery in broad daylight, but black musicians had no power to protect themselves or their music.

As the decade began, there were signs that young white kids were buying black rhythm and blues records; this was happening in pockets throughout the country, but no one sensed it as a trend until early 1951. In that year a man named Lee Mintz who owned a record store in Cleveland told a local disc jockey named Alan Freed about this dramatic new trend. Young white kids with more money than one might expect were coming into his store and buying what had been considered exclusively Negro music just a year or two before. Freed, something of a disc jockey and vagabond, had a late-night classical music show, and Mintz was pushing him to switch over to a new show catering exclusively to these wayward kids. Mintz told Freed he knew the reason why the taste was changing: It was all about the beat. The beat was so strong in black music, he said, that anyone could dance to it without a lesson. Mintz promised he would advertise himself on Freed's new program and that he would help find other advertisers if Freed would switch.

Alan Freed was hardly locked into classical music. He was a smart, free-spirited man, who like many of the nation's best disc jockeys, seemed to be two people: one a rather insecure, ordinary person who went angrily through everyday life and the other, a man in front of an open mike who exploded into a secret confident and audacious self before listeners he could not see. His career, at that moment, had not been exactly brilliant. Even within a profession given over to a significant excess of ego, Freed was considered difficult and abrasive by various employers. At one point he had worked for a station in Akron, had asked for a raise, and had been turned down, so he went to a competing station and offered his services. Unfortunately, his contract with the first station had not yet expired; the first station took him to court and a judge ordered him not to broadcast within seventy-five miles of Akron for a year. Such was the life of a disc jockey who has not yet found his special niche. When his period of disbarment expired he eventually showed up in Cleveland. So when Mintz suggested the new show, he was amenable.

In the summer of 1951, Freed inaugurated the *The Moondog Show* on a 50,000-watt clear channel station in Cleveland, a station so powerful it reached a vast area of the Midwest. His success was immediate. It was as if an entire generation of young white kids in

that area had been waiting for someone to catch up with them. For
Freed it was what he had been waiting for; he seemed to come alive
as a new hip personality. He was the Moondog. He kept the beat
himself in his live chamber, adding to it by hitting on a Cleveland
phone book. He became one of them, the kids, on their side as
opposed to that of their parents, the first grown-up who understood
them and what they wanted. By his choice of music alone, the Moondog had instantly earned their trust. Soon he was doing live rock
shows. The response was remarkable. No one in the local music
business had ever seen anything like it before: Two or three thousand
kids would buy tickets, and sometimes, depending on the level of
talent, thousands of others would be turned away—all for performers that adults had never even heard of.

At virtually the same time, Elvis Presley began to hang out at
all-night white gospel shows. White gospel singing reflected the region's schizophrenia: It allowed white fundamentalist groups, whose
members were often hard-core segregationists and who wanted nothing to do with black culture—to co-opt the black beat into their
white music. Presley gradually got to know some of the gospel singers, and by the time he graduated from high school in 1953, he had
decided to become one himself. He was eighteen, with extremely
limited options. For a country boy with his background, the possibilities were few: He could drive a truck or hope for a job in a nearby
plant—and he could dream of being a singer. Soon he was singing
with a local group from his church called the Songfellows. But a few
random singing dates were hardly a career, so he was also working
at a small plant in Memphis where artillery shell casings were made.
By the standards of the time and the region, the pay was not bad—
$1.65 an hour—and he made about sixty dollars a week with over-
time. Soon he left that job for another that excited him
more—driving a truck for Crown Electric. Driving a truck seemed
infinitely freer than working in a defense factory. It seemed at that
moment he would be driving a truck for the rest of his life. In
September 1956, a year after he had exploded into the consciousness
of his fellow Americans, he tried to explain the secret of his success
to a writer for the *Saturday Evening Post*. "I don't know what it is
. . . I just fell into it, really. My daddy and I were laughing about it
the other day. He looked at me and said, 'What happened, E? The
last thing I can remember is I was working in a can factory and you
were drivin' a truck.' . . . It just caught us up."

. . .

The Memphis of 1954 was a strictly segregated city. Its officials were white and its juries were white, and as late as 1947 there had been no black police in the city (when the first few were finally hired in 1948, they could not arrest white people). In 1947 *Annie Get Your Gun* was banned from Memphis because it included a black railroad conductor, and as the local censor Lloyd Binford said, "We don't have any Negro conductors in the South." That same year the American Heritage Foundation, which sponsored the Freedom Train, a traveling exhibition filled with historic documents about American history, took Memphis off its itinerary because local officials there insisted that the train be segregated.

Sam Phillips thought the city's segregation was absurd. He was not a liberal in the traditional sense and he was not interested in social issues, as many of the activists of the period were. He was a raw, rough man, with an eleventh-grade education, pure redneck in all outward manifestations, such as his love of used Cadillacs. A good country boy, Sam saw Cadillacs as the surest sign of status and comfort, and he would buy a used one and get a good deal and drive it for a few years and then turn it over and get a used but newer one and drive that for a few years. But he was different in one sense: his love of the blues. He had been drawn to Memphis in the first place because he *knew* it was a great center for black music, and he intended to capture some of it on record. Sam Phillips hated the hypocrisy of a city that denied the richness of its own heritage. Sam Phillips, thought his friend Stanley Booth, a talented music writer, was drawn to what he was doing not because he was a liberal and felt that the social order ought to be changed: "It wasn't a humanitarian gesture, and people like Sam weren't social activists," Booth said. "You did it because of the power of the music—you were drawn to the music. It made you hip and a little different, and in addition, in a life which was often very hard, it was the one thing which gave you a little grace." What others thought about his passion mattered little to him. He held a job as an engineer at the Peabody Hotel, working on a radio show broadcast from there; at the same time he began to record some of the region's black singers in a small studio he had created. He generally did this on the weekends, and it was great sport among his colleagues at the Peabody to tease him on Monday mornings, "Well, Sam, I guess you didn't spend the weekend recording all those niggers of yours like you usually do because you don't smell so bad today."

He never for a second doubted his own ear. Nor, for that matter, did he doubt his purpose. He wanted to be a pioneer and an explorer. "I have my faults in the world, a lot of faults, I guess," he once said, "but I have one real gift and that gift is to look another person in the eye and be able to tell if he has anything to contribute, and if he does, I have the additional gift to free him from whatever is restraining him." It was a description, his friends thought, that was remarkably accurate.

He had grown up poor in northern Alabama, aware of the tensions between blacks and whites. The whites had their music, country music, and in those years, when poor whites did not yet have radios, they would gather at someone's home on a Saturday night, put the furniture aside, and have square dances. But their music had none of the power of black music. Every Sunday Sam Phillips went to a white Baptist church in town. About a block and a half away was a black Methodist church. In those days before air-conditioning, the windows of both churches were open during the summer, and the power of the music in the black church was transcendent. "There was something there I had never heard before or since," he said years later. "Those men and women singing the *Amen*. Not the choir singing it. I mean the congregation. It was a heaven on earth to hear it. A jubilation. The Amen and the rhythm. They never missed a downbeat." There was, he thought, so much more power in their music than his own, so much more feeling and so much more love. He felt pulled toward it, and he would leave his own church and linger outside the black church to listen.

As he came to adulthood, he began to follow the music, to ever bigger cities, working as a disc jockey. He finally made it to a big, powerful station in Nashville, but he was still restless. Nashville was the capital of white country music, but that music cast no spell on him. He knew he had to go to Memphis. It seemed to be his destiny. Phillips knew that the best and richest soil was in the bend of the Tennessee River near where he grew up and that where there was rich soil, the people were also rich—in sorrow and joy and, above all, in music. Fertile land somehow produced fertile people as well, he believed. "There was going to be no stopping something as big as Memphis and the Mississippi River. I always knew that, *knew that*. I'd driven to Memphis, and the closer I'd gotten to the Mississippi, I knew that there was something rich ahead, this totally untamed place, all those people who had these hard hard lives, and the only way they could express themselves was through their music. You had to be a dunce not to know that."

He reached Memphis in 1945, and he was not disappointed. "I'd never seen such a gulf between two words. One side white, the other side black. One world all white, the other world, a few blocks away, all black. There was no street like Beale Street, no street I'd ever seen. It had a flavor all its own, entirely black. Lined with clubs and dives and pawnshops. Lord there were pawnshops! All these black people, some of them rich and some of them poor, they'd come from Mississippi and Arkansas and Tennessee, saved up all their money, determined to spend every bit of it there. No one tried to save money when they came to Beale Street. It was wonderful, all that energy, all those men and women dressed in their best, the country people from those hamlets, black hicks a lot of them trying to pretend that they're not hicks, that they're men of the street. It was amazing, there were these people who were rich, and who had saved all their money and were celebrating, and the people who had nothing, who were down and out, they were celebrating, too, and the one thing that was different from white folks was that it was impossible to tell who was rich and who was poor on Beale Street."

He built his own studio, a small storefront out at 706 Union Street. He laid the tile on the floor and on the walls himself, to maximize the acoustics, and created a raised control room so he could see the musicians who were recording, and finally installed an air conditioner, which always dripped. It cost about $1,000 to fix the place up, and he was paying about $75 a month rent.

In January 1950 he quit his job at the Peabody to record full-time himself. Almost all his white friends thought he was crazy, giving up a good solid job at the grandest hotel in the entire region to go off and record black music. "Hell, Sam," one friend told him. "You're not only recording them, you're going to shake hands with them too." As a white man recording black singers he offended local mores. Phillips himself, however, was absolutely sure of his mission. In Memphis there was all kinds of talent around: B.B. King, Phineas Newborn, Howling Wolf. B.B. King was typical of the music and the region: His real name was Riley B. King, and he came from Indianola, in the Delta. He had grown up picking cotton (he once noted that he could pick four hundred pounds a day and make as much as 35 cents a hundred pounds—no one, he thought, could pick more cotton than he could). He had driven tractors, sung spirituals, and had finally ended up in Memphis in 1947, where he had worked his way up and down Beale Street playing in different clubs. He was good, authentic; everyone knew it—no one had to be told. It was even in his nickname—Beale Street Blues Boy, which eventually was shortened to B.B. There was nothing smooth about his sound: It was raw and harsh—almost angry. Eventually, he got a job on

WDIA. It was not an auspicious beginning. He started by singing commercials for Peptikon, a patent medicine guaranteed to cure all the things that ailed you and a few things that did not. Soon he got his own half-hour in the midafternoon, the "Sepia Swing Club," and his popularity began to grow. In those days B.B. King was young and shy, particularly around white people. The first time he recorded for Sam Phillips, he revealed that he could not play the guitar and sing at the same time, which made him different from most singers. "Can't you sing and play at the same time?" Phillips asked him. "Mr. Phillips, that's the only way I ever played," he answered. "Whatever you do," Phillips told him, "don't change it. Just keep it natural."

The last thing Phillips wanted was sweeteners: "I didn't build that studio to record a big band. The big bands didn't need me. I wanted to record the local talent. I knew the talent was there. I didn't have to look it up to know B.B. King was talented. And I knew what I wanted. I wanted something *ugly*. Ugly and honest. I knew that these people were disenfranchised. They were politically disenfranchised and economically disenfranchised, and to tell the truth they were musically disenfranchised. . . . The big trouble in those days, if you were recording black musicians, was that they would start changing what they were doing for you because you were white. They did it unconsciously. They were adapting to you and to the people they thought were going to be their audience. They'd look up in the recording booth and see a white man and they'd start trying to be like Billy Eckstine and Nat King Cole. I didn't want that. The things that RCA and Capitol winced at, I loved. I didn't want anyone who had ever recorded before, and I didn't want to do what other recording studios did."

So word got out that there was this slightly crazy man who had set up his own studio and was taping black people. B.B. King told Ike Turner, who was from Clarksdale, Mississippi. Phillips recorded Turner and his band, and soon Turner became a kind of one-man talent scout for Phillips, finding people throughout the region. One memorable receipt in Sam Phillips's office for the early fifties was for one hundred dollars paid out to a small town in Mississippi for bailing Ike Turner and his band out of jail for driving an overloaded auto—Ike had strapped his bass on top of the car, and that had been enough to enrage the local authorities.

It was a simple operation. He called it the Memphis Record Service. The studio was so small that Phillips did not even have a real office. His office, his friends like to point out, was the simple café next door, Miss Taylor's, third table back. That's where he'd meet someone who wanted to do a business deal. When he recorded black musicians he could not take them to Miss Taylor's, so he would take the food out himself and bring it back for them. To make enough money to survive, he also advertised that he recorded weddings, banquets, bar mitzvahs. "We Record Anything-Anytime-Any-where," was his motto. His gear was portable, and he hustled around Memphis in those days, recording happy occasions for posterity and grieving with loved ones. He even did funerals, which cost about eighteen dollars—that is to wire it, tape it, and then transfer the tape to a disc. A wedding cost a little less.

He also hired out his studio to any person who wanted to record. It was a good way of hearing new talent and making a little money on the side. The price was three dollars a shot. He sensed, long before the major record companies located far away in New York did, that the traditional musical barriers that had always sepa-rated the musician constituencies no longer held. He often told his assistant, Marion Kreisker, "If I could find a white man with a Negro sound I could make a billion dollars." In addition, he said, "I knew that for black music to come to its rightful place in this country we had to have some white singers come over and do black music—not copy it, not change, not sweeten it. Just *do* it."

It would turn out that he would engineer an entire musical migration of whites into black music. In addition to Elvis, he discov-ered Johnny Cash, Carl Perkins, Roy Orbison, and Jerry Lee Lewis, all major talents and all, in different ways, American originals.

Even as Sam Phillips was inventing himseif as a producer, the musical world was changing dramatically. The old order was frag-menting. The traditional giants, RCA, Columbia, and Decca, had dominated in the past. They had the big names, the crooners. But they were hardly entrepreneurial; the bigger they were, the more conservative they inevitably were as well. They watched the world of country-and-western and rhythm-and-blues with disdain, bordering on disapproval. It was music that came from the wrong side of the tracks. Some companies in fact even referred to black music as the "sepia market." It was not an important slice of the market, obvi-ously, because sepia people did not have very much money. Re-corded music, in fact, until the fifties bore the label of class. People from the upper middle class and upper class had the money for phonographs with which they listened to classical and high pop, the crooners and the big bands. The people who liked country and black listened to the radio. But the forces of change were far more powerful than anyone at the big companies realized. Technology was democratizing the business of music—phonographs and records alike were becoming much cheaper. It was only a matter of time before the artists began to cross over on the traditionally racially segregated charts. In 1954 a white musician named Bill Haley did a version of "Shake Rattle and Roll." By February 1955 it sold 1 million copies; by the summer of 1955 it was number one on the white chart and number four on the rhythm and blues (or black) chart. In that same year Chuck Berry brought out "Maybellene," which was the first successful assault on the main chart by a black musician; "Maybellene" went to the top of the rhythm and blues chart and went to number five on the white chart. Soon there was "Tutti Frutti," by Little Richard.

After Elvis Presley's sensational debut on Dewey Phillips's show, his career skyrocketed. He was what first the region and then the nation wanted: a white boy to explode into the beat, to capture it for the whites. The success spread steadily: Deejays in Texas soon picked up on it, and soon after that Elvis was making regular appearances on the Louisiana Hayride, which was second only to the Grand Ole Opry as a showcase of country white talent. He began traveling the South with a company of country musicians, headlined by Hank Snow. But almost overnight he became the star of the touring group, something that did not escape the attention of Snow's manager, Colonel Tom Parker. Parker, it appeared, though he did not own Presley's contract, was encouraging the large companies to move in and buy it from Sam Phillips. In the beginning Phillips probably would have sold it for $5,000 or $10,000, for he lacked the resources to promote and sustain a major success. But interest constantly escalated. Mitch Miller at Columbia called. Phillips asked $20,000. Miller replied, "Forget it. No artist is worth that kind of money." Ahmet Ertegun, the head of Atlantic, a label that was coming on quickly because of its owners' exceptional early awareness of rock and roll, was probably the one record executive who personally knew how valuable Presley was. He made an offer of $25,000, which, as Ertegun told Phillips, was everything Atlantic had, including the desk he was using. It was too low, said Phillips. By then Colonel Parker was in on the game, and the Colonel had friends at RCA, the traditional recording powerhouse. Phillips was fairly sure he ought to sell Elvis's contract, but just to be sure he was doing the right thing he had called his friend Kemmons Wilson, the local contractor who was just beginning to enjoy success in his own amazing career as the builder of America's first great motel chain, Holiday Inns. Sam Phillips had been smart enough to be an early investor, and he would eventually become a millionaire from his investments with Wilson. Phillips asked whether he should sell Elvis's contract. "I wouldn't hesitate," Wilson said. "That boy isn't even a professional." So Phillips went ahead. When the negotiations were over, Sam Phillips had $35,000 and Elvis was the property of RCA.

Presley's timing was nearly perfect. The crossover, led by Bill Haley, Chuck Berry, and Little Richard, was in full force. Parents might disapprove of the beat and of their children listening to what they *knew* was black music. But their disapproval only added to Presley's popularity and made him more of a hero among the young. Local ministers might get up in their churches (almost always well covered by local newspapers) and attack demon rock as jungle music and threaten to lead a crusade to have this Presley boy arrested if he dared set foot in their community (generally, there was no problem, their towns were too small for him to play). It did not matter: Elvis Presley and rock music were *happening*.

A new young generation of Americans was breaking away from the habits of its parents and defining itself by its music. There was nothing the parents could do: This new generation was armed with both money and the new inexpensive appliances with which to listen to it. This was the new, wealthier America. Elvis Presley began to make it in 1955, after ten years of rare broad-based middle-class prosperity. Among the principal beneficiaries of that prosperity were the teenagers. They had almost no memory of a Depression and the great war that followed it. There was no instinct on their part to save money. In the past when American teenagers had made money, their earnings, more often than not, had gone to help support their parents or had been saved for one treasured and long-desired purchase, like a baseball glove or a bike, or it had been set aside for college.

But now, as the new middle class emerged in the country, it was creating as a byproduct a brand-new consuming class: the young. *Scholastic* magazine's Institute of Student Opinion showed that by early 1956 there were 13 million teenagers in the country, with a total income of $7 billion a year, which was 26 percent more than only three years earlier. The average teenager, the magazine said, had an income of $10.55 a week. That figure seemed remarkable at the time; it was close to what the average American family had had in disposable income, after all essential bills were paid, fifteen years earlier.

In addition, technology favored the young. The only possible family control was over a home's one radio or record player. There, parental rule and edicts could still be exercised. But the young no longer needed to depend on the family's appliances. In the early

fifties a series of technological breakthroughs brought small transis-
torized radios that sold for $25 to $50. Soon an Elvis Presley model
record player was selling for $47.95. Teenagers were asked to put $1
down and pay only $1 a week. Credit buying had reached the young.
By the late fifties, American companies sold 10 million portable
record players a year.

In this new subculture of rock and roll the important figures of
authority were no longer mayors and selectmen or parents; they were
disc jockeys, who reaffirmed the right to youthful independence and
guided teenagers to their new rock heroes. The young formed their
own community. For the first time in American life they were becoming a separate, defined part of the culture: As they had money, they
were a market, and as they were a market they were listened to and
catered to. Elvis was the first beneficiary. In effect, he was entering
millions of American homes on the sly; if the parents had had their
way, he would most assuredly have been barred.

Certainly, Ed Sullivan would have liked to have kept him out.
Ed Sullivan, in 1955 and 1956, hosted the most successful variety
show in America on this strange new piece of turf called network
television. The official title of his show was *The Toast of the Town.*
Sullivan made his way to television from the world of print, where
he'd worked as a Broadway gossip columnist, first on the old *New
York Graphic* and eventually making his way to the *New York Daily
News.* His column, in the city's largest paper, was one of considerable influence. In 1947 he had served as master of ceremonies for an
annual amateur dance contest sponsored by the *News* called the
"Harvest Moon Ball." Unbeknownst to Sullivan, CBS was televising
the show. A CBS executive was impressed at how graciously Sullivan
treated everyone he dealt with that evening and how natural his skills
as an emcee were. He seemed completely comfortable with himself
despite the fact that the show was being televised; the reason he was
so comfortable was that he didn't realize it was going on television:
He thought all those cameras around the hall were simply movie
cameras. CBS was in the process of putting together a Sunday-night
variety program, and Sullivan was offered the show. The show
opened a year later, and much to everyone's surprise, it was a stunning success. Certainly, part of the reason was the leverage of Sullivan's column. Those who went on his show were likely to get plugs
in the column, and it was for that reason that on his opening broadcast, Dean Martin and Jerry Lewis clowned, Eugene List played the
piano, and Rodgers and Hammerstein happened to drop in just to
say hello.

Eight years later, Ed Sullivan was the unofficial Minister of Culture in America. His was the great national variety theater where one could find the famous. Broadcast at 8 P.M. on Sundays—an hour when families were likely to have gathered together—Sullivan's show provided a pleasant, safe blend of acts, including some performers of exceptional talent. In addition there seemed to be a guarantee that nothing would happen that was at all threatening. Sullivan was, after all, involved in the most delicate business imaginable: selecting acts to perform live in millions of American living rooms, a place where no one had ever performed before. There was something there for everyone, and Sullivan made sure that there was always one act for the children. He stressed the importance of variety, and few acts got more than a couple of minutes. Mark Leddy, who did the booking for the show, once told Jim Bishop, the writer, "You want to know the day Christ died. It was on the Ed Sullivan Show and Ed gave him three minutes." Sullivan himself was shrewd enough to minimize his own appearances, since his style was widely perceived as being exceptionally wooden. He would introduce a number, get off the stage, and reappear in time to lead the applause. "Let's hear it for . . ." he would say, and then give the name of the act. Once, after Sergio Franchi had sung the Lord's Prayer, Sullivan turned to his audience and said, "Let's hear it for the Lord's Prayer." A mimic named Will Jordan once went on and did an imitation of Sullivan, the idea for which, Jordan said, came from watching mechanical ducks in a shooting gallery. Jordan walked on and said: "Tonight on our really big show we have 702 Polish dentists who will be here in a few moments doing their marvelous extractions . . ."

The popularity of Sullivan's show was remarkable because the master of ceremonies was, on the screen and in real life, a stiff—a staid, humorless, rather puritanical man. As a print journalist he once attacked Marlene Dietrich because she had appeared in a Broadway show wearing slacks. His charm was at best marginal. His body language was that of someone frozen and not yet thawed out. He was almost completely expressionless. His voice was sharp and high-pitched, with what the rest of the country judged to be a New York accent. John Crosby, the best television critic in the country, wrote as early as December 1948, "One of the small but vexing questions confronting anyone in this area with a television set is: 'Why is Ed Sullivan on it every Sunday night?' " The question, Crosby went on, "seems to baffle Mr. Sullivan as much as anyone else." Later, Jack Paar said of him, "Who can bring to a simple English sentence suspense and mystery and drama? Who but Ed Sullivan can introduce a basketball player with the reverence once reserved for Dr. (Albert) Schweitzer?" Slightly offended by all the criticism of her husband, Sylvia Sullivan once sought to write a piece answering all the criticism of his wooden manner. Unfortunately, the article was titled "I'm Married to the Great Stone Face." In it she proceeded to deny rumors that he seemed so stiff because he had a serious war wound or that he had been hit on the head by a golf club. "They're not true," she wrote in *Collier's*. "Nevertheless once in a while some kindly stranger will congratulate him on his courage in working despite his deformity!"

CBS, on whose network the show was carried and for whom he made a great deal of money, was never entirely happy with him. Yet miraculously, despite what the critics said, the show worked. Why, no one really knew. Perhaps it was the perfect hour for a variety show, 8 P.M. on Sunday. Perhaps it was the sheer quality of the entertainers, since almost every entertainer in the world was desperate to be showcased on so prominent a platform. Perhaps it was the fact that television was still new and there was something comforting for ordinary Americans, tuning in their first television sets, to take this adventure with so stolid and careful a man. For his taste was conservative, cautious, and traditional. When some of the blacklisting groups criticized some of the performers he put on in the late forties, Sullivan backed down immediately and gave the blacklisters a veto power over any acts or performers who might have political liabilities.

In 1956, he was at the height of his power. He was making about $200,000 a year from CBS and another $50,000 from the *News*. He was most assuredly not a man to cross. His show was at the exact center of American mass culture. And he wanted no part of Elvis Presley, who was now in the process of enraging endless ministers and parent groups by dint of his onstage gyrations and the overt sexuality of his music. Nor did Sullivan like rockers in general. There had been a somewhat unpleasant incident earlier with the great black rocker Bo Diddley. Sullivan's people had heard that Diddley was hot, that his records were rising on the charts, and they booked him without knowing very much about his music or the strength of his personality. Diddley was raw and original, and there was a lot of movement in his act. When Sullivan saw it, he was not pleased. According to his biographer, Jerry Bowles, Sullivan wandered over to the orchestra area, thumbed through some sheet music, picked out "Some Enchanted Evening," and handed it to Diddley. "Sing this," he said. That night Diddley started by singing "Some Enchanted Evening," but the audience began to giggle. Suddenly, Bo Diddley switched over to his song about the heroic Bo Diddley, and he went straight to the beat. The orchestra stayed with Rodgers and Hammerstein. Sullivan was furious. Rockers, he decided, were different from other people and did not keep their word. He wanted nothing to do with them.

Earlier, as Elvis conquered the South with regional appearances, he had begun to perfect his act. Some of it was natural instinct—he had to carry a beat, and it was hard to carry a beat while standing still. So he began to gyrate as he had seen endless gospel singers gyrate. The first time he had done it, he had been driven by pure instinct and the crowd began to shout. Later he asked a friend what had happened. The friend explained that Elvis had started jumping around on the stage and using his body and the crowd had loved it. From then it became part of his act; if you were going to do a live show, he explained, you had to have an act. That's what people came to see. Otherwise, they could just as well stay at home and play records. A country singer named Bob Luman once said of an early Elvis concert: "This cat came out in a coat and a pink shirt and socks and he had this sneer on his face and he stood behind the mike for five minutes, I'll bet, before he made a move. Then he hit his guitar a lick and he broke two strings. I'd been playing for ten years and I hadn't broken a total of two strings. So there he was, these two strings dangling, and he hadn't done anything yet, and these high school girls were screaming and fainting and running up to the stage and then he started to move his hips real slow like he had a thing for his guitar . . ."

The teeny-boppers started to maul him. They did not mean him any harm, he explained. What they wanted "was pieces of you for souvenirs." By the end of 1955 RCA was ready to push his records nationally, and he had signed to do four Saturday-night shows on a show produced by Jackie Gleason called *Stage Show.* He got $1,250 a show for the Gleason appearances plus, of course, national exposure. Gleason knew exactly what was happening. "He's a guitar-playing Marlon Brando," he said. Only part of what worked for Elvis was the music, Gleason knew. Certainly, that was important, but it was more than just the music. It was also the movement and the style. And a great deal of it was the look: sultry, alienated, a little misunderstood, the rebel who wanted to rebel without ever leaving home. He was perfect because he was the safe rebel. He never intended to cause trouble: He was a classic mama's boy, and Gladys Presley had barely let him out of her sight until he was in high school; now finally on the threshold of great success, he used his royalties in that first year to buy three new homes, each larger than the last, for his parents. He also gave each of his parents a new Cadillac, though the one he gave his mother never got license plates, since she did not drive.

By 1956 he had become both a national celebrity and a national issue. His success, amplified as it was by the newfound wealth of the nation and the new technology of radio, record players and, finally, television, defied the imagination. He quickly made a three-picture deal with Hal Wallis for $450,000. "Hound Dog" sold 2 million copies and "Don't Be Cruel," sold 3 million. His singles were not merely taking off, they were defying traditional musical categories: "Heartbreak Hotel" was number one on the white chart, number one on the country chart, and number five on the rhythm-and-blues chart; "Don't Be Cruel" and "Hound Dog" became number one on all three charts. In April 1956 he already had six of RCA's all-time top twenty-five records and was selling $75,000 worth of records a day.

That month he made a rather sedate appearance on the Milton Berle Show and in June Berle had him back. This time he cut loose, causing an immense number of protests about the vulgarity of his act. Now Elvis Presley was working the American home, and suddenly the American home was a house divided. At this point Ed Sullivan lashed out against Presley. He announced that Presley's act was so suggestive that it would never go on his show. This was Sullivan as a guardian of public morals, a man born in 1902, fifty-four years old that summer. Within three weeks Sullivan had to change his mind. His competition, the Steve Allen show, immediately called Colonel Parker and booked Presley for July 1. The problem for Allen, of course, was that, like everyone else, he wanted it both ways. He wanted Elvis on board, but he did not want a big protest on the part of the traditional segment of his audience. So he and his staff compromised: They would go high Elvis rather than low Elvis. They dressed Elvis in a tux, and they got him to limit his body movement. He did a dim-witted sketch with Allen, Imogene Coca, and Andy Griffith, in which he played a cowboy named Tumbleweed, and he sang "Hound Dog" to a live basset hound. The Presley fans hated it. After the show, Dewey Phillips called Elvis long-distance in New York: "You better call home and get straight, boy. What you doing in that monkey suit? Where's your guitar?" When Elvis returned to Memphis for a concert in Phillips's honor, he cut loose with a pure rock-a-billy performance. It was Presley at his best, and when he finished, he told the audience, "I just want to tell y'all not to worry—them people in New York and Hollywood are not going to change me none."

But the Steven Allen show had worked in one sense; it was the first time Steve Allen had beaten Ed Sullivan in the ratings. Sullivan surrendered almost immediately. His people called Colonel Parker and signed Elvis for $50,000 to do three shows. It was a figure then unheard of. It was one thing to guard public morals for the good of the nation and the good of your career; it was another thing to guard public morals at the cost of your career.

The battle was over: Ed Sullivan had conceded and the new music had entered the mainstream of American culture. Sullivan was not there for the first show; he was recuperating from an auto accident, and Charles Laughton was the host. The producers deliberately shot Elvis from the waist up. But soon he would be singing and dancing in full sweep. Sullivan was pleased; his ratings were extraordinary. He also wanted to make clear that he had not lowered America's morals. "I want to say to Elvis Presley and the country that this is a real decent, fine boy," Sullivan told his audience after the third show. "We've never had a pleasanter experience on our show with a big name than we've had with you. You're thoroughly all right." It was the deftest of surrenders; it appeared to be the generous speech of a man receiving a surrender while in fact it was the speech of a man who had just surrendered himself. Market economics had won. It augured a profound change in American taste: In the past, whites had picked up on black jazz, but that had largely been done by the elite. This was different; this was a visceral, democratic response by the masses. It was also a critical moment for the whole society: The old order had been challenged and had not held. New forces were at work, driven by technology. The young did not have to listen to their parents anymore.

Marlon Brando and Elvis Presley were only the first of the new rebels from the world of entertainment and art. Soon to come were many others. If there was a common thread, it was that they all projected the image of being misunderstood, more often than not by their parents' generation, if not their own parents themselves. There was little overt political content in their rebellion; their public personae and the characters they played were not fighting against the sinister injustices of the McCarthy era or racial injustice. Only Brando came close to politics when he confronted the mob in *On the Waterfront.*

Above all, they were young men with obvious emotional tensions—onstage, on screen, and in real life. After Brando finished in the Broadway production of *Streetcar,* he vowed that he hated Hollywood and would be back on the legitimate stage soon. In point of fact, he never returned. After a short run of remarkable films that included *Streetcar* and *On the Waterfront,* he seemed to become increasingly careless in his selection of roles and cynical about his art. If Brando was rebelling against anything, it seemed to be against the idea of his profession, of having to pursue the career, the achievements, and the honors that everyone expected of him.

Just as Brando went from doing his best work to giving surprisingly ordinary performances in surprisingly ordinary movies, a new rebel star was ascending in Hollywood: James Dean. Brando was Dean's personal hero, and like Brando, Dean was plucked from the edges of the New York theater crowd by the perceptive and vigilant Elia Kazan. Even more than Brando, Dean was a cult figure. Brando might have had a bigger career and done more distinguished work, but Dean's legend was greater, because his life was so short. He was always remembered as young, always to be mourned—the ultimate, eternal rebel, whose promise had never been fulfilled. To serious fans of the era's theater and movies, Dean's legend would eventually surpass Brando's, and that was almost heretical, because Brando was the original and Dean the imitation. In a book that was in no small part an open letter to Brando, the critic Richard Schickel wrote: "To tell you what may be a more awful truth, later generations are more interested in James Dean. Can you imagine? The kid who copied you! Who used to annoy you by calling up and trying to make friends!" For Dean had a puppy-dog infatuation with the older Brando. Kazan knew it, so one day he invited Brando on the set. Dean "was so adoring that he seemed shrunken and twisted in misery," Kazan later wrote. On occasion Dean signed his name to letters in a way that showed he was conscious of the different influences on him: "Jimmy (Brando Clift) Dean."

Dean was typecast as the rebel, and like Brando, in real life he was rebelling against an unhappy childhood and a father he had grown to hate. Even more than Brando, he came to symbolize the belief of the youth of that era that because they were young, they were misunderstood. He was good-looking, almost delicate, with a sulky, androgynous appearance that made him seem vulnerable. He was driven by his own pain and anguish. Dean was, wrote Steven Vineberg, "the most inward of actors: His performances were always about the beautiful chaos in his own soul."

Dean's life and his art were inseparable. Unlike Brando, who had considerable professional training and considerable range, Dean basically played himself—but brilliantly. Sullen and sulky, he was still worthy of redemption if only the properly tender girlfriend could be found to mother him. Either he got a part right instinctively, Kazan believed, or he didn't get it at all. At a certain point the only way to get him to improve his performance was to get him liquored up.

His career was short. There were only three films before he met his death in a car accident. The end came at the height of his fame and in the very same year of his stunning debut in *East of Eden*. That early death ensured him a place in the pantheon of artists who lived fast and died young. His poster would grace the bedroom walls of future generations of young would-be rebels. Dick Schickel noted the advantages of dying young (Dean) and the disadvantages of not (Brando): "There is much to be said for dying young in circumstances melodramatically appropriate to your public image. There is very little to be said for living long and burying that image in silence, suet and apparent cynicism."

Dean was born in small-town Indiana. His mother died of breast cancer when he was a young boy, and his father, weighted by debt, had been forced to sell the family car to pay for her final operation. The burden of rearing a family alone was too much for Winton Dean, and James was sent to live with an aunt and uncle. Both of his parents had let him down, he would sometimes say, his mother by dying so young, his father by being cold and distant. Once, when they were both young actors, Dennis Hopper asked Dean where his magic came from. Dean answered that it came from his anger: "Because I hate my mother and father. I wanted to get up onstage . . . and I wanted to *show* them. I'll tell you what made me want to become an actor, what gave me the drive to want to be the best. My mother died when I was almost nine. I used to sneak out of my uncle's house and go to her grave, and I used to cry and cry on her grave—Mother, why did you leave me? I need you . . . I want you."

In 1949 he finished high school and headed for Hollywood, hoping to become an actor. His initial success was marginal, but gradually he learned to use his charm and looks to get ahead. In effect, he became a sexual hustler on both sides of the lines; he was, at once, both innocent and predatory. He was always ambitious, although his ambitions were a bit ill defined. When he was twenty he went east to study at the Actors Studio. He also tried his hand at

television. His talent, especially his ability to show profound vulnerability, was obvious from the start, but unlike Brando, who was a
major force at the Studio, Dean never really committed himself to
the workshops and was wary of having his work critiqued by his
peers: "If I let them dissect me like a rabbit in a clinical research
laboratory or something, I might not be able to produce again. For
chrissake, they might sterilize me!" he told a friend at the time. Still,
Rod Serling, one of the foremost of the new television playwrights,
thought Dean's move to New York was a critical break for so
unusual a talent. Serling's *A Long Time Till Dawn* was Dean's first
starring vehicle. In 1953 television's theatrical productions were still
experimental. There was no powerful network bureaucracy yet to tell
directors and writers what they could not write. It was a rare time,
when unexpected talent flourished and was discovered on television—particularly young talent.

In those days, Serling thought television was well ahead of
Hollywood in social and cultural adventerousness. Movies, he believed, were lodged in another time, in an outdated reality; and when,
for example, they dealt with the young, with few exceptions they still
showed teenage girls as cheerleaders and bobby-soxers, and teenage
boys as high school athletic heroes in letter sweaters. Serling was
convinced the young had begun to change, were significantly more
alienated from the values of their parents. In *A Long Time Till Dawn*,
the hero or antihero was, in the author's words, "a terribly upset,
psyched-out kid, a precursor to the hooked generation of the sixties,
the type that became part of the drug/rock culture . . ." Serling
understood immediately that Dean was perfect for the role, and
indeed he went on to play it brilliantly. To Serling, Dean was one of
the first manifestations of a youth culture just surfacing and which
Hollywood did not yet understand. "There was a postwar mystifica-
tion of the young, a gradual erosion of confidence in their elders, in
the so-called truths, in the whole litany of moral codes," Serling said.
"They just didn't believe in them anymore. In television we were
more aware of this and more in touch with what was happening. We
could portray it immediately too—write a script one week and have
it on the air the next."

For Dean, playing a rebel was effortless; being conventional was
much harder. He seemed to have figured out during this period that
his future lay in being the outsider. David Dalton points out a
portfolio of photos taken of him in New York that reveal a young
man in metamorphosis. In the early photos he appears to be eager to
please, someone who might still be able to play an all-American boy;

in the later photos, his face and his eyes have darkened and he is clearly a rebel.

During that period Kazan, then at the height of his fame, was in the process of turning John Steinbeck's novel *East of Eden* into a film. The script was a contemporary retelling of the Cain/Abel story from the Bible. The older actors were already lined up, Raymond Massey and Jo Van Fleet as the father and mother. But casting the two boys was critical. At first Kazan had wanted Brando and Montgomery Clift as the twins, one good, the other bad. But they could not decide on who would play the bad brother. Besides, both Brando and Clift were getting a little long in the tooth for these roles. Kazan started searching for even younger talent—something he liked to do anyway, because to his mind, young actors were hungrier and had more of an edge, something they lost with success. "They're like fighters on their way up. It's a life or death struggle for them and they give their utmost to the role. This quality disappears later," he once said. "They become civilized and normal."

A friend told Kazan about Dean, whom he remembered from the Actors Studio as sullen and not very productive. At their first meeting Kazan, wanting to provoke Dean, deliberately kept him waiting; when he finally arrived, Kazan found Dean slouched down in his seat—rude, disrespectful, and shabbily dressed. The two of them were engaging in a certain kind of theatrical gamesmanship, Kazan decided. They did not talk much—conversation was not James Dean's strong suit, particularly with someone so powerful in the theater and whose good opinion he so desperately wanted. Dean offered Kazan a ride on his motorbike, and off they went. "He was showing off," Kazan later wrote, "a country boy not impressed with big city traffic."

Fortunately for Dean, his act worked. To Kazan, who bore his own resentments against *his* father, Dean *was* Cal Trask. "There was no point in trying to cast it better or nicer. Jimmy was it. He had a grudge against all fathers. He was vengeful; he had a sense of aloneness and of being persecuted. And he was uncommonly suspicious." Before heading west, Dean did one screen test with the young Paul Newman. Kazan asked Newman: "Paul, do you think Jimmy will appeal to the bobby-soxers?" Newman answered, "I don't know. Is he going to be a sex symbol?" Then, playing along with the director's question, Newman gave Dean a long flirtatious look: "I don't usually go out with boys. But with his looks, sure, sure, I think they'll flip over him." The technicians working on the set, though, were so

484 / DAVID HALBERSTAM

unimpressed by him that they thought Dean was the stand-in for the real star.

Kazan scooped Dean up and flew him out to California for shooting. Dean had never been in a plane before. He carried his clothes in two packages wrapped in paper and tied together by string. When they got to Los Angeles, Dean asked if they could stop in at the suburban Los Angeles lab where his father worked. That delighted Kazan, who was always in search of life as art; Kazan remembered Dean's father as a "man [who] had no definition and made no impression except that he had no definition. Obviously there was a strong tension between the two, and it was not friendly. I sensed the father disliked his son." Soon Dean and Kazan drove on.

Dean was his own worst enemy, often alienating those around him. "Must I always be miserable? I try so hard to make people reject me. Why? I don't want to write this letter. It would be better to remain silent. Wow! Am I fucked up," he wrote a girlfriend when he had reached California to shoot *Eden*. He resented the older actors on the set. Raymond Massey, the veteran actor who played the father, could not stand Dean's sullen manner and his tendency to improvise with the script. Rather than try to heal the breach, Kazan aggravated the tension in order to show it on screen. Kazan kept Dean moody and resentful. There was a brief affair with Pier Angeli, the young actress, but it ended soon. That pleased Kazan: "Now I had Jimmy as I wanted him, alone and miserable."

With Ms. Angeli gone on to a romance with Vic Damone, in Kazan's words, "Narcissism took over." Dean had a camera and took endless pictures of himself standing in front of a mirror, changing his expression only slightly. "He'd show me the goddamn contact sheets and ask which one I liked best," Kazan wrote. "I thought they were all the same picture, but I said nothing." Kazan used that suffocating self-absorption to good effect in Dean's performance.

The success of *Eden* was stunning. It might have been perhaps Kazan's best film. Dean's performance was a sensation. "There is a new image in American films," wrote Pauline Kael, "the young boy as beautiful, disturbed animal, so full of love he's defenseless. Maybe the father doesn't love him, but the camera does and we're supposed to; we're thrust into upsetting angles, caught in infatuated close-ups, and prodded, 'Look at all that beautiful desperation.'" After a screening of *Eden*, Dean was interviewed by Howard Thompson of *The New York Times*. It was his first interview.

Even Kazan was surprised by Dean's impact, which surpassed that of the young Brando. Dean himself was acutely aware of the niche he occupied and of why his persona worked. On the set of *Giant* he told Dennis Hopper, who had become his friend: "Y'know, I think I've got a chance to really make it because in this hand I'm holding Marlon Brando, saying, 'Fuck you!' and in the other hand, saying, 'Please forgive me,' is Montgomery Clift. 'Please forgive me.' 'Fuck you!' 'Please forgive me.' 'Fuck you!' And somewhere in between is James Dean."

He went on quickly to do *Rebel Without a Cause.* When it had first been purchased by Warner in 1946, it was thought of as a vehicle for Brando, but Brando had not been interested, so the script was put aside. Then Nicholas Ray, the director, picked up on *Rebel* because juvenile delinquency was becoming such a hot issue. The script was written and rewritten by a seemingly endless stream of writers, but in the end it was a vehicle for Dean, who was to play the son of a weak father and a nagging, complaining mother. According to the notes in the screenplay for his part, Dean was to be "the angry victim" of insensitive, careless parents: "At seventeen he is filled with confusion about his role in life. Because of his 'nowhere' father, he does not know how to be a man. Because of his wounding mother, he anticipates destruction in all women. And yet he wants to find a girl who will be willing to receive his tenderness." Dean is, once again, the tender but misunderstood young man, not getting a fair chance, and his character muses: "If I could have just one day when I wasn't all confused . . . I wasn't ashamed of everything. If I felt I belonged some place." The screenplay is weak; what power the movie has is in the performance. If Dean's acting reputation rests on *East of Eden,* his myth is largely entwined with his role in *Rebel.* The role is the prototype for the alienated youth blaming all injustice on parents and their generation.

Years later Kazan had some doubts about the image of youthful alienation that he and Ray had fostered; Dean had cast a spell over the youth of America, he said. It was not something he approved of, though he accepted his share of the responsibility: "Its essence was that all parents were insensitive idiots, who didn't understand or appreciate their kids and weren't able to help them. Parents were the enemy. . . . In contrast to these parent figures, all youngsters were supposed to be sensitive and full of 'soul.'" The more Kazan thought about it, the less he liked the character of the self-pitying, self-dramatizing youth. Nor was he happy when an endless number of Dean fans wrote him letters thanking him for what he had done for Jimmy. In truth, he was not fond of Dean and did not think him a major talent; as far as Kazan was concerned, Dean had gotten through the movie largely because of the kindness and professionalism of Julie Harris. Kazan was convinced he had gotten Dean's best work out of him.

If Dean had learned from Brando, now others would copy Dean. Elvis Presley, for one, wanted to be known as the James Dean of rock and roll. A line was beginning to run through the generations. Suddenly, *alienation* was a word that was falling lightly from his own lips and those of his friends, noted the writer Richard Schickel in an essay on the importance of Marlon Brando as a cultural figure: "*The Lonely Crowd* was anatomized in 1950, and the fear of drifting into its clutches was lively in us. *White Collar* was on our brick and board bookshelves, and we saw how the eponymous object seemed to be choking the life out of earlier generations. *The Man in the Gray Flannel Suit* stalked our nightmares and soon enough *The Organization Man* would join him there, though of course, even as we read about these cautionary figures, many of us were talking to corporate recruiters about entry-level emulation of them."

THIRTY-TWO

No one at GM could ever have dared forecast so much prosperity over such a long period of time. It was a brilliant moment, unparalleled in American corporate history. Success begat success; each year the profit expectations went higher and higher. The postwar economic boom may have benefited many Americans, but no one benefited more than General Motors. By rough estimates, 49.3 million motor vehicles were registered when the decade began, 73.8 when it ended; by some estimates, an average of 4.5 million cars, many of them that might have stayed on the road in a less prosperous economy, were scrapped annually. That means as many as 68 to 70 million cars, ever larger, ever heavier, ever more expensive, were sold, and General Motors sold virtually half of them. The average car, which had cost $1,270 at the beginning of the decade, had risen to $1,822 by the end of it; that rate, Edward Cray noted in his book *Chrome Colossus,* was twice as fast as the rest of the wholesale cost index.

There was in all of this success for General Motors a certain arrogance of power. This was not only an institution apart; it was so big, so rich, and so powerful that it was regarded in the collective psyche of the nation as something more than a mere corporation: It was like a nation unto itself, a separate entity, with laws and a culture all its own: Loyalty among employees was more important than individual brilliance. Team players were valued more highly than mavericks. It was the duty of the rare exceptional GM employee to accept the limits on his individual fame; he would be known within the company and perhaps within the larger automotive industry as a man of talent, but the rest of the country would not know his name; the corporation came first and the corporation bestowed wealth but anonymity on its most valued employees. The individual was always subordinated to the greater good of the company.

The men who ran the corporation, almost without exception, came from small towns in America and were by and large middle class, white, and Protestant or, occasionally, Catholic. If they had gone to four-year colleges they were usually land-grant colleges. They were square and proud of it, instinctively suspicious of all that was different and foreign. They were American, and above all else Americans knew cars. Everything about them reflected their confidence that they had achieved virtually all there was to achieve in life. Never knowing anyone very different from themselves when they had grown up (or certainly anyone very different from themselves worth emulating), they believed they represented what everyone else aspired to. They were sure of their accomplishments and of their taste. Others, critics, outside Detroit, might believe that these men were not such giants and might believe that they did not so much create that vast postwar economic wave as they had the good fortune to ride it; be that as it may, no one contradicted the men of GM to their faces. As for the intellectuals, if they wanted to drive small foreign cars, live in small houses, and make small salaries, why even bother to argue with them?

General Motors was Republican, not Eastern sophisticated Republican but heartland conservative Republican—insular, suspicious of anything different. Zora Arkus-Duntov, a top GM designer and an émigré, once complained to a friend of the insularity of the culture and noted that the problem in the company was that it was run in every department by men "who believe that the world is bordered on the East by Lake Huron, and on the West by Lake

Michigan." (In those days, when the nation's anti-Communism was at its height, Arkus-Duntov, the son of a White Russian engineer who had lived briefly in Belgium before coming to the United States, was described in GM promotional material as being of Belgian extraction.) Arthur Summerfield, one of the largest Chevy dealers in the country, had always seen the company, the country, and the Republican party as one and the same thing. A leading figure in the Michigan Republican party, Summerfield in the late forties devised a plan by which all Michigan GM dealers paid one dollar to the Republican party for each car they sold, upon fear of not receiving their regular shipment of cars from the company if they held back. For such loyalty Summerfield was eventually rewarded with the job of postmaster general in Eisenhower's cabinet.

As the success of the company grew, its informal rules gradually became codified. The culture was first and foremost hierarchical: An enterprising young executive tended to take all signals, share all attitudes and prejudices of the men above him, as his wife tended to play the sports and card games favored by the boss's wife, to emulate how she dressed and even to serve the same foods for dinner. The job of a junior executive was to know at all times what the senior executive desired at any given moment, what kind of snack or alcohol he wanted in his hotel room on the road, what his favorite meal at a favorite restaurant was in a given city (and to have an underling there several hours early, standing guard to make sure that nothing went wrong—that the right table was available, that the restaurant did not run out of the favorite food or wine). It was the underling's job not only to make sure that Harlow Curtice's favored hors d'oeuvre, smoked oysters, was at cocktail parties, but the underling was to stand as near as possible to Curtice, holding a tray of oysters for him as he moved through a crowd. Thus, at one of GM's famed Motorama shows in New York, a reporter named Don Silber, from the *Cleveland Press,* once asked Paul Garrett, a high-ranking GM public relations official, what time it was. Garrett did not deign to look at his watch. Instead, he turned to his aide, a man named Ken Yewl, and said, "Ken, tell him what time it is."

The essential goodness of the corporation was never questioned. It was regarded as, of all the many places to work, the best, because it was the biggest, the most respected, made the most money and, very quietly, through bonuses and stock, rewarded its top people the most handsomely. Early in his career Harlow Curtice, while still the controller at AC Champion Spark Plugs, had ventured to New York with Albert Champion, the head of AC, to meet the top GM people, including Alfred Sloan. There Curtice had undergone something of an initiation rite as the home office checked out the new boys from the Midwest. Apparently, both men met GM's standards, for at the end Mr. Sloan offered both Champion and Curtice a chance to invest in GM's prime management investment program for up-and-coming executives. They could invest about $25,000 and would in a few years' time, as Mr. Sloan promised, each get back around $1.5 million. It was, in an age of rising income taxes, the company's pioneering method of trying to protect and reward its top executives. Suddenly, Curtice realized that in addition to being successful, he might also become truly rich. As they were heading back to Flint, Curtice turned to Champion and said, "That sounds like a pretty good deal, doesn't it—as close to a sure thing as you can get." "We're not going to do that, Red," Champion answered. "I don't believe in letting New York tell us how to run our business."

Even within the closed world of General Motors, there was a feeling that Chevrolet was a world apart, perhaps a little too smug. After all, the corporation was mighty, but at Chevrolet they felt the other divisions were just window dressing, that the heart and soul of General Motors was Chevy. It was responsible for nearly 70 to 75 percent of GM's profits in most years. Chevrolets were what healthy, stable young Americans drove. Chevy belonged on the short list of certifiably *American* things, which could not be duplicated anywhere else in the world: homemade apple pie, Coke, a World Series baseball game, a Norman Rockwell cover on the *Saturday Evening Post,* a grilled hamburger in the backyard. In those years it did a brilliant job of connecting its advertising to those other American artifacts. Chevy was not just the great American car, it was something uniquely American. If there was any fear in those years, it was that the government might break General Motors up into its component parts. If there was nervousness in the rest of GM over the implications of the splitting up of Sloan's masterpiece, there was a good deal less nervousness at Chevy; indeed they were almost cocky about it, for if the feds acted, and Chevy was broken off, it would still be the largest company in the United States.

In the early fifties, no one from the corporation had any power over Chevy; in fact, in those earlier days the corporation was comparatively weak, with a small, somewhat understaffed headquarters. Chevy was a mighty industrial masterpiece that had been together by the founding giants of the corporation, such men as Sloan and his great enabler, Big Bill Knudsen. (In the late fifties and early sixties, the corporation shrewdly sought to limit Chevy's autonomy.

Knowing that the Chevy people were resistant to any change mandated from the outside, the corporation promoted former top executives of Chevy who, knowing the vulnerabilities of the division they had once served, knew exactly how to subdue and undermine this once proud and once independent kingdom. Heading the corporation after heading Chevy was not, in the eyes of some, that much of a promotion: "When you left Chevy and took over the corporation," Tom Adams, a Detroit advertising man who worked closely with GM, once noted, "it was almost like retiring.")

Yet for all of Chevrolet's great wealth and power, if there was a potential weakness in General Motors as Curtice took over (replacing Wilson who had joined Eisenhower's cabinet), it was the car itself. The basic Chevy was becoming quite stodgy. It was GM's low-end model, and the inevitable result of the company's relentless thrust to make its models bigger and heavier and to make more profit per car had gradually undermined the traditional Chevy. General Motors' great surge to increase automotive power had begun when Bill Knudsen had upgraded Chevy to take the entry-level niche away from Ford. Now it appeared that Chevy was slipping, that its cars had become dowdy, and that entry-level leadership was swinging back to Ford. Ford had introduced an eight-cylinder engine, and not only was that helping Ford at the low end, it was lending a certain ominous success to the whole line-up. Ford's cars were now regarded as hotter and sexier, and Chevy, with only six cylinders, was now trying to play catch-up. Clearly, the company had stayed too long with the old six-cylinder engine—what was called the "blue flame six." In addition, the styling of the car was boring, and one auto writer said that it looked like it had been designed "by Herbert Hoover's haberdasher." So in late 1951 Wilson, in one of his last major decisions, told his then-assistant Curtice that he had to juice Chevy up.

Curtice envisioned a racier, sportier new Chevy; he wanted an eight-cylinder engine, and he wanted it immediately. Immediately, in this instance, meant two years: Normally, a project like this—the complete redesign of engine, transmission, and body—took at least three and sometimes up to four or five years. But Curtice knew exactly what he had to do: He decided to take the best engineer the company had, Ed Cole, and put him in charge of the new Chevy.

Ed Cole was a troubleshooter and maverick extraordinaire within the organization; he was by normal standards far too idiosyncratic and outspoken for the corporation, probably the last true maverick of his generation at GM. He had always fought the bureaucracy as it got more powerful. He was disliked and distrusted by the financial people because he loved to spend the company's money, but he was tolerated by other executives because he was so driven and talented. Cole was the rare man in so large an institution who not only seemed able to deliver what the company demanded but to deliver it under exceptional pressure and crushing deadlines. He had been something of a star at the company during World War Two, working on GM's tanks, and had gone from there to be a key figure at Cadillac, where he had become chief engineer at the youthful age of thirty-six. Then, during the Korean war, he had taken over an old deserted plant in Cleveland, which was literally filled with stored-up sacks of beans, and created tanks for the Korean War. Cole, unlike many in the company, had liked the intense pressures of wartime, the sense of immediacy, and of course the leverage it gave him to do things his way and ignore those above him who told him that what he intended to do could not be done.

Ed Cole was a farm boy from Marne, Michigan, who had hated the boredom of the farm and had always vowed he would get out as quickly as he could. He had intended to be a lawyer and was on his way to a legal career, except that his great natural ability as a tinkerer convinced him that he probably ought to be an engineer. He had gone to the General Motors Institute in Flint and had done so well that he never actually graduated—instead, he was recruited by Cadillac early and went directly to work in its engineering department. From the start he was different, a man apart, driven, relentless, challenging everything around him. He made the company a great deal of money and, in the words of his friend Tom Adams, cost the company a great deal as well, because he *had to try everything*. He had 150 ideas a week and he had to make sure each actually succeeded or failed. He might well, Adams thought, have been the most driven man he had ever met—in both work and at play. If you hunted with him, he pushed himself and others so ferociously that he was out in front of the dogs. "Ed," Tom Adams used to tell him. "We don't really need the dogs when you hunt." If he fished, he fished longer and harder and had to catch not only the biggest fish but the most fish. If he was down in the Florida Keys and he hooked a mammoth tarpon on light tackle, he would fight the fish for what seemed like the entire afternoon—no matter how brutal the sun on himself, his wife, and his friends, no matter that the tarpon was sure to be released back into the water. If he took his young son, David, fishing up in northern Michigan, where there were a vast number of lakes, he did not fish only one lake every day for five or six days, getting to know it and its secrets; rather, he arranged to have a boat at a different lake every day.

Any mechanical object that was broken was a challenge to him. The idea of throwing out a broken piece of home equipment was a personal insult. If there was a coffee maker at home that did not work, Ed Cole had to fix it. If he and his pals were on a fishing trip in Canada and the motor on their generator conked out, Ed Cole stayed up all night to fix it—not because he needed to, not because they needed the generator in the morning, but because he was proving to the world that he could fix it, by working all night with a French Canadian guide holding a flashlight. If he was hunting in some farmer's field and there was a broken reaper, he had to stop and fix it. Once, when the heater in his home swimming pool went out, he did not, as others might do, call a specialty repairman. There was no need for the Yellow Pages with Ed Cole. Instead, he swam to the heater and started repairing it, until there was a small explosion and his eyebrows were singed.

He was a man utterly without sophistication. He was as good an engineer as there was, but outside of that, he had little interest or curiosity. He was not a particularly good businessman and was vulnerable to schemes—he bought, among other things, a fair number of leases from a man who claimed he was going to find vast oil fields in southern Michigan. Bud Goodman, a senior GM executive, liked to joke that he was still teaching Cole how to use a telephone.

He was not genteel or careful as most of the other men rising to power at GM were; they were a reflection of the cautiousness that comes when institutional values become enshrined by generation after generation and when cautiousness is rewarded. Cole argued too often and too loudly for doing whatever it took to build a good car, and by the mid-fifties, he was doing it in a corporation where many of the men around him were less committed to cars and to engineering every year. But they were a poor match for Ed Cole, who seemed to bring a kind of primal force to each encounter.

He was not smooth. He did un-GM things. He got divorced, which violated the then code of the company. He went out for a time with Mamie Van Doren, the flashy movie actress (if he was going to go out with an actress, as someone noted, why couldn't it be someone like Lee Remick?). He even gave her a Corvette painted a color that matched her lipstick. When he married for the second time, it was to a much younger, striking blonde, and her name was *Dolly;* Dolly Cole, most assuredly, was not a GM type of wife, content to wait her turn in the pecking order at the Bloomfield Hills Country Club.

From the moment she arrived, there was a sense on the part of the other wives that she represented not just a challenge to the culture of the company but a threat to every marriage within it.

Cole's motto, a friend noted, was the very un-GM-like "Kick the hell out of the status quo." He had played a critical part in designing the V-8 engine that had reshaped the '49 Cadillac, but this new challenge at Chevy was even greater, for it required a powerful but lighter engine, which would not load the car down. Ed Cole went on a wartime footing. He scoured the company for its best engineers, offering them the challenge of working on something entirely new. He started in May 1952 and overnight the engineer pool at Chevy grew from some 850 engineers to 3,000. Ed Cole did a brilliant job on the new V-8. It was a marvelous engine, the best, his competitors thought, that the industry had ever produced at that time. His V-8 was inherently balanced—that is, unlike the four-cylinder engine and the six cylinder-engine, the two sets of four cylinders in the V-8 balanced each other and fired at the same time and made the engine smoother and the car less shaky. The power was there, and the new technology had allowed the engine to be considerably lighter than V-8s in the past. Almost everything about the 1955 Chevy was new, in a way that Detroit cars were rarely new: of 4,500 component parts used in it, all but 675 were brand-new. It was, noted Clare MacKichan, one of its designers, designed to exemplify "youth, speed and lightness." Normally, it was Harley Earl who liked his cars low and powerful, but this time it was Ed Cole who pushed for it. Earl was excited when he got the height down to sixty-one inches. But even then Cole wasn't satisfied. "Hell, I wouldn't want to make it over sixty inches," he said. The two years creating the '55 Chevy were probably his happiest time in the company—he was dealing with something entirely new, and though he was constantly fighting the financial people, he was doing it with the top brass on his side. As such, he lived with his car; it became a part of the house, and there were meetings all the time, even on weekends. There was a prototype of it in the garage and, wrestling with a new idea, he would get up in the middle of the night, and tinker with the car. When the prototype V-8 engine was completed, he put one under the hood of a '53 Chevy and blasted off. He and his son David took it on a trip to northern Michigan. A state policeman in a Ford seemed to be tailing him, so Ed Cole simply floored the accelerator and roared away. Later, he stopped for a sandwich at a small café in Baldwin and the trooper came in. He was not angry; he was just curious. "What in God's name do you have in that Chevy?" he asked. Cole was delighted; soon almost everyone in the café had gathered around him as he opened up the hood. From then on it became a special pleasure of his—pulling into a gas station, telling the attendant to fill the car up and check on the oil and gas, and hearing the kid, who was almost always a car nut, exclaim, "That's no Chevy." "It sure as hell is," he would always answer.

By October 1954, the '55 Chevy was finished and in the showrooms and it was a tour de force. With its lightweight 4.3-liter, 265-cubic-inch V-8 it supplied 160 horsepower. It was a car buff's delight. In the first year, the company sold 1.83 million cars, plus 393,000 trucks with the V-8.

Armed now with his powerful, completely new car, Cole set out to go after not just Ford but, semicovertly, GM's own Cadillac as well. For what Ed Cole had really intended from the time he took on the car was to create a Chevrolet that competed with Cadillac, a car almost as big as a Caddy and with just as much power. A poor man's Caddy, he liked to call it. "He wanted the average guy to feel he was driving a baby Cadillac," said Bob Cadaret, a designer. Or as Harley Earl said to Harlow Curtice in the design shop one day, "Now, *there* . . . there's a car that if it had a Cadillac emblem [on it] I could sell as a Cadillac." Was there higher praise? The Chevy under Cole kept growing bigger and more powerful: The horsepower, which had once been around 90 to 100, now suddenly took off in quantum leaps: from 160 to 250 and, finally, to 325 and 410. Inside were such options as power steering, power brakes, and air-conditioning. In the end he had done what he set out to do—produced a Chevy that was the virtual automotive equivalent of a Cadillac. That was what the public wanted, he liked to say, "austere mink."

Ed Cole had stunned the corporation by putting the car together in such a short time, and not only had he successfully challenged an ever more confident Ford Company (and in the process been part of a year in which some $65 billion was spent on motor vehicles—one fifth of the national GNP), but it had set the stage for the next decade, for ever bigger more powerful cars. The next year the advertising slogan was: "The hot one's even hotter."

THIRTY-THREE

In the home it was to be a new, even easier age, the good life without sweat. "Never before so much for so few," wrote *Life* in 1954. Poppy Cannon, a food writer of that period, agreed: "Never before has so much been available to so many of us as now," she wrote in 1953, singling out as the key to the new American dream, the can opener—in her words, "that *open sesame* to wealth and freedom . . . freedom from tedium, space, work and your own inexperience." "Never has a whole people spent so much money on so many expensive things in such an easy way as Americans are doing today," reported *Fortune* in October 1956 in a glowing account of the consumer-driven economy entitled "What A Country!" It was, in fact, an astonishing age of abundance, an age of wondrous kitchen and household aids, ever bigger, but not ever more expensive as in the auto industry—the very success of the item meant that the price kept coming down: consumers were buying more for less).

Life in America, it appeared, was in all ways going to get better: A new car could replace an old one, and a larger, more modern refrigerator would take the place of one bought three years earlier, just as a new car had replaced an old one. Thus, the great fear of manufacturers, as they watched their markets reach saturation points, was that their sales would decline; this proved to be false. So did another of the retailers' fears—that people might save too much. Of the many things to be concerned about in postwar America, the idea of Americans saving too much was not one of them. The market was saturated, but people kept on buying—newer, improved products that were easier to handle, that produced cleaner laundry, washed more dishes and glasses, and housed more frozen steaks. What the leaders of the auto industry had done in autos with the annual model change, now, on a somewhat different scale, the manufacturers of home appliances and furniture were doing in their businesses. No wonder people bought more appliances. Suddenly, the old ones seemed inconvenient and outdated. That was, as much as anything else, a reflection of the new fantasy kitchen, as portrayed in endless women's magazines. Virtually every house had a refrigerator. Yet in 1955 alone, for example, *Fortune* reported, consumers had spent $1.3 billion buying 4 million new units, a significant increase over the previous year. The explanation was simple: frozen food. The old refrigerators had tiny freezers—enough space only to freeze a few trays of ice. The new refrigerators were designed for a wondrous, new world of frozen foods and TV dinners.

If there was one figure who came to symbolize the dazzling new American kitchen and all its astonishing appliances, as well as the revolution in selling and advertising that was taking place, it was Betty Furness—the Lady from Westinghouse. In 1949 Betty Furness was thirty-three, an ingenue whose career was winding down after thirty-six films in five years (most of them B films). In those days, the people who did television commercials usually had come from radio, which meant they were good at reading lines but not at memorizing them, and they had no earthly idea of how to look at the camera. One poor woman who was directed to stand at a Westinghouse stove and heat some chocolate had been so terrified by the idea of talking and demonstrating at the same time that she had spilled melted chocolate all over the stove.

Furness had been doing some live television acting on *Studio One* at the time, and she had been appalled by these performers' lack of professionalism, and she spoke out indignantly on the set about incompetent radio amateurs intruding in a visual medium. The next thing she knew, someone from the ad agency asked her to try a commercial. She gamely gave it a try, found that she was good at it, and got the job, which paid $150 a week—good money in 1949. It was, she soon discovered, hard work. On each episode of *Studio One,* where Westinghouse was the sole sponsor, she had to deliver one three-minute commercial and two one-and-a-half-minute commercials. They were live, and different each week, so the lines had to be memorized.

She soon discovered her chief asset was that she was attractive, but not in a way that made women jealous. Men liked her looks, but even more important, women, the prime targets of these commercials, liked her too. She came across, in fact, very much like the women portrayed in photos and ads in women's magazines—bright, upbeat, and confident, and modern without looking too glamorous. She was the all-American wife in the all-American kitchen. She exuded confidence that she could handle anything in this sparkling new workplace that promised to make household chores, if not downright obsolete, at least easy and glamorous. The advertising people wanted her to appear even more housewifely, and they pressured her to put on a wedding ring: There was even serious talk of having her take an assumed name under which she would in effect become the living Westinghouse logo. "We want you to be like Betty Crocker," someone from the ad agency told her. "But I'm not, I'm Betty Furness," she answered. "Well," he said. "What about wearing an apron when you do these commercials? That seems more kitcheny." "I don't want to wear an apron, and I don't want to seem more a part of the kitchen," she said. She had a strong sense of her own identity, and they were smart enough to let her alone after that.

She became a celebrity of significant proportions for the first time during the 1952 political conventions. Westinghouse had bought an immense amount of time, and she was on air constantly, almost as much as Walter Cronkite, it seemed, who also made his reputation during that campaign. There was an agreement not to put her on more than three times an hour, but she noted later, since the networks were on all day, she made as many as twenty to twenty-five appearances every day for a week. Add on an additional week for the other convention, and that was a lot more time on the air than any American politician was getting. Mercifully, the TelePrompTer had arrived by then and she did not have to spend all her spare time learning her lines.

Her clothes became something of an issue. She had to change minimally three times a day in order to stay fresh for herself and her viewers. She had an intuitive sense about her role, which was to keep as many people as possible from going to the bathroom during the commercial break. Therefore, she had to be interesting and unpredictable. If she changed her clothes constantly, housewives would be curious about what she was going to wear next. At the 1956 conventions she showed up with twenty-eight different outfits, so many that *Life* magazine later did a panel of photos showing her in each outfit. She bought all her clothes herself. There was a reason for this. If she let Westinghouse pay for the clothes, then the company would decide what she should wear and she was sure that she would have to look more like the wives of Westinghouse executives. But she knew exactly the look she wanted: modern, neat, no frills, sophisticated but modest.

Suddenly, she not only was famous, but all sorts of people she did not know seemed to think of her as a friend. Whenever she went out people recognized her and wanted to talk to her. To her surprise, she was Betty to them; they did not feel the need to use her last name, since she had been in their homes and, indeed, had helped them out in their kitchens. The sale of Westinghouse appliances boomed, and there was no doubt that there was a connection to this pleasant, attractive woman's appearances as the Westinghouse hostess. "You can be sure if it's Westinghouse," she said at the end of each commercial, and it became her trademark. One small incident alone demonstrated her power. In June 1952 she presented the American people with the Mobilair fan. In retrospect, she thought, it was a clunky machine, larger than most fans and mounted on wheels so it could be wheeled from room to room. It cost $89. It could blow air into a room or suck it out. Why anyone would have wanted one was beyond her. But the day after she went on television with one, the Mobilairs sold out in a number of major cities.

The Westinghouse people realized they had a star on their hands, and they asked her to sign a three-year, noncancellable contract to represent Westinghouse exclusively, for $100,000 a year. With that she became the queen of American appliances, standing between a great faceless industrial company and American housewives. She knew little about the machines themselves except that they seemed well made and that the people who made them seemed like solid Americans from Ohio.

The one thing she did notice about the appliances, as she continued to promote them, was her sense that she was beginning to shrink—because the machines were getting bigger. When she started in 1950, the first refrigerators came up to her shoulders, which made them about fifty-eight inches high, on average. Gradually, they began to gain on her and became ever fancier, with enormous "frost-free" freezers. In this new wonder age, she mused at the time, people were being swallowed up by their kitchen appliances.

The only appliance she represented for Westinghouse that did not sell well was the dishwasher. For a long time the people at Westinghouse, as well as at other companies, were both surprised and disappointed by that appliance's poor showing. Persistent research with consumers finally showed that women were wary of buying dishwashers because the modern kitchen had become so automated that they feared if they stopped doing the dishes by hand, they would lose their last toehold in the kitchen and husbands would start wondering why they needed wives at all.

Furness did not take her new fame too seriously. Once, Westinghouse decided that she should do an institutional advertisement explaining how jet engines worked. She was appalled by the idea. They're going to laugh at me, she told her colleagues, but they insisted she do it. So the ad was written, and she stood there with what to her nonetheless seemed like a complicated explanation. "The way these engines work," she began and then quickly inserted her own words, "they tell me . . ."

Near the end of her eleven-year stint, there was a new president of Westinghouse who was clearly unhappy with her work—in part, she suspected, because he had not invented her. Immediately, he began casting doubts on her—and suggesting that perhaps Westinghouse needed a new and younger woman for its image. Gil Baird, the Westinghouse executive in charge of dealing with her, was told he should get a new person for the ads. Baird said he did not think it a particularly good idea. Why not? the new president asked. "Because," said Baird, "when you walk down the street no one knows who you are, but when Betty Furness walks down the street, everyone thinks Westinghouse."

The power that Betty Furness had as a commercial symbol for Westinghouse was a reflection of the growing power of television as a vehicle for advertising and also of the growing power of advertising in American life. For the fifties was a decade that revolutionized Madison Avenue. At the turn of the century, the home had been a reasonably safe haven from the purveyors of goods (among other

THE FIFTIES / 501

reasons, because there was so little disposable income) other than the occasional traveling salesman. Radio advertising had been clever and deft and had greatly expanded the possibilities for reaching the consumer; but television opened up the field even more dramatically and offered a vast array of new techniques, from the subtle and sophisticated to hammering away with a brief, repetitive message. At first the television departments of the major agencies were small, understaffed, and lost money. That changed quickly enough. "We discovered," said Rosser Reeves, one of the prime architects and beneficiaries of television advertising, "that this was no tame kitten; we had a ferocious man-eating tiger. We could take the same advertising campaign from print or radio and put it on TV, and even when there were very few sets, sales would go through the roof." The speed with which television's power ascended awed even those who prophesied it: In 1949, Madison Avenue's total television billings were $12.3 million; the next year, it jumped to $40.8 million; and the year after that, it jumped to $128 million. Television, of course, could do what radio never could, for it was visual. "Show the product," said Ben Duffy, one of the men who was writing the rules even as he learned them, "and show it in use." Many advertisers did that and more: A Remington razor shaved the fuzz off a peach, as Stephen Fox noted in *The Mirror Makers,* and a Band-Aid was used to show it was strong enough to lift an egg.

It was a salesman's dream: The nation had not only been wired to sell, but it was wired to sell through pictures, going right into the home. It was, Rosser Reeves said, like "shooting fish in a barrel." The advertising firms that adapted most readily to television tripled and quadrupled their annual billings; BBD&O, where Ben Duffy was an early booster of television, shifted 80 percent of its media buys to television, and by 1950 the television department had grown from twelve people to 150; Duffy was well ahead of the curve, and he was rewarded for his foresight: The firm went from billings of $40 million to $235 million in the fifteen-year period from 1945 to 1960.

Advertising men became the new heroes, or antiheroes, of American life. Novels and movies appeared about them. They were said to dress more stylishly than the mere businessmen they served: They lived somewhat unconventional, even racy lives and were supposedly torn between guarding the public good and using their great gifts to manipulate people for profit. In effect, it was seen to be a profession where talented young men traded their ideals for an even higher life-style, with luxurious suburban homes in Greenwich and Darien. In the film version of the Frederic Wakeman novel *The*

Hucksters, one of the early novels that helped give Madison Avenue its dubious reputation, Deborah Kerr tells Clark Gable that he does not have to sell out, that he can be an honorable man in advertising. "Why don't you be one of those who sells only what he believes in? Sell good things, things that people should have, and sell them with dignity—and taste. That's a career for any man, a career to be proud of."

If ad men were not more esteemed in this new era, no one doubted that they were more influential. The Yale historian David Potter noted in his book *People of Plenty* that in a culture of so many choices, as America was in the fifties, it was inevitable that advertising would come to play an increasingly important role. "Advertising," he wrote, "now compares with such long-standing institutions as the school and the church in the magnitude of its social influence. It dominates the media, it has vast power in the shaping of popular standards and it is really one of the very limited groups of institutions which exercise social control."

Rather than glamorous, it was in fact a job of long hours and high turnover that bred ulcers and heart attacks and children who barely knew their fathers. Studies comparing the health of men in advertising with that of executives in other professions showed them to be consistently in poorer health than their peers. It was an enormously stressful calling; if the rewards were great, so were the pitfalls. Advertising executives were at the beck and call of large, powerful companies whose chief executives rarely understood the market. The big companies could switch firms in a minute, and even within the advertising agencies themselves competition was extreme. "I sold my interest in Benton and Bowles when I was thirty-five," said Bill Benton, "and I'd been taking $300,000 to $400,000 a year out of it. Any business where a kid can make that kind of money is no business for old men."

As for television, it was all on-the-job training and, at first, almost everyone was getting it wrong. A handful of firms—like Ted Bates, and Young and Rubicam, Ogilvy and Mather, and Doyle Dane—were somewhat more nimble than the others in making the transition from radio to television and came to understand the obvious early on: The new medium was visual. But even at Young and Rubicam, the first instinct was to transfer people who had done radio to the television department, whereas what was needed was a miniature movie production team.

Previously advertising, like many professions, had depended on a sort of Ivy League old-boy network, in which heads of companies could be counted on to patronize their school chums. The largest and perhaps most famous agency, J. Walter Thompson, reached its zenith in the thirties and forties, largely because its account executives did most of their business at the Harvard and Yale clubs. But in the new age of television advertising, talent was everything, and by the fifties J. Walter Thompson was regarded as so stodgy by the bright young men on Madison Avenue that it was called J. Walter Tombstone.

It was a heady time. Everything was a risk. It was quite possible to do a campaign that succeeded brilliantly by mistake: It was equally possible to do a brilliant campaign and have it turn out to be a disaster. A young ad man just starting out at Young and Rubicam named David McCall was assigned in the early fifties to do a campaign for Rinso soap, a Lever Brothers product. Rinso had been one of the great brand names in the old radio days, but it had come on hard times, for two reasons: Its producers had not mastered the art of television advertising, and it was being challenged by the new more powerful detergents. In retrospect, probably nothing could have saved Rinso, McCall decided, but if it was possible for a campaign to hasten the demise of an ailing product, his campaign had done it: fifty-two weeks of full-page ads in *Life* magazine, beautifully illustrated by the top photographers in the country, including Richard Avedon. One ad alone showed sixteen different kinds of stains in full color. Everything was executed perfectly, and not even a ripple in sales resulted to show that someone out there had paid attention.

Thanks to the power of television, selling and marketing became ever more important within companies—the sizzle was becoming as important as the steak. Some auto executives later decided that television advertising tilted the balance within their companies, making marketing and sales gradually more important than engineering and manufacturing. A kind of misguided ethic began to take root, one of great and dangerous hubris—that it did not really matter how well made the cars were; if the styling was halfway decent and the ad campaign was good enough, the marketing department could sell them.

In the case of cigarettes, Madison Avenue faced a particularly stiff challenge, though. The tobacco industry was in crisis by this time. There was growing evidence that smoking was in fact injurious to one's health. (Rosser Reeves tried to calm doubts with a particularly ingenious slogan for Tarryton: "All the tars and nicotine trapped in the filter are guaranteed not to reach your throat.") The beginnings of consumer resistance were already apparent; even though Philip Morris sponsored *I Love Lucy,* it received less of a boost in sales than the company hoped. Indeed, along Madison Avenue the general belief was that a cigarette company was the wrong sponsor for the show, that it was ill-positioned to extract maximum benefit from Lucy's success. At the height of Lucy's success, in 1952, Philip Morris's sales slipped slightly, in fact.

The dilemma grew worse in the mid-fifties as the government began to close in on the tobacco companies. The Federal Trade Commission ordered Philip Morris to stop using the claim that its cigarettes were "recognized as being less irritating to the nose and throat by eminent nose and throat doctors." Soon after, in July 1954, the *Reader's Digest,* one of the great barometers of life in the American heartland (and, because of its lack of advertising, a magazine immune to commercial pressures), published an article on the possible connection between smoking and cancer. The industry, feeling cornered, was beginning to introduce filter-tip cigarettes. Philip Morris made its commitment with a brand called Marlboro. It was developed initially as a cigarette for women, but in the mid-fifties, the company decided to push Marlboro for men as well. The problem was that filter cigarettes were regarded at the time as effeminate. Real men didn't smoke filter cigarettes and didn't worry about lung cancer. The Philip Morris people took their problem to the Leo Burnett agency in Chicago. Burnett was a crusty old advertising hand who prided himself on keeping his agency in Chicago and away from New York. New York was too smooth and its people tended to be too highbrow. He wanted none of that. He wanted his copy simple, almost corny. In fact he kept a file in his desk, called "Corny Language," into which he placed simply folksy Americanisms. "Our sod-busting delivery, our loose-limbed stand, and our wide-eyed perspective make it easier for us to create ads that talk turkey to the majority of Americans. I like to think that we Chicago ad-makers are all working stiffs. I like to imagine that Chicago copywriters spit on their hands before picking up the big black pencils," he once said. Certainly, Burnett himself was a working stiff. He worked seven days a week and kept two full-time secretaries busy. He took only Christmas Day off. He often arrived home after his family had gone to bed. His children barely saw him: "It must be disconcerting for three highly intelligent children to see their father only if they happen to get up for a glass of water during the night," one colleague, William Tyler, said of him.

Burnett trusted his instincts and was wary of the new research departments just then springing up at various ad agencies. These featured polling, in an attempt to understand why people wanted certain goods. He was scornful of what he regarded as the pseudo-scientific approach to selling. Advertising was not a science, he thought. It was a skill that took talent and experience. He was particularly accomplished at creating folklorish figures for his campaigns—the Jolly Green Giant and the Pillsbury Doughboy, for example.

Now when Philip Morris asked for a campaign to make Marlboro more masculine, he pondered the problem with his top people. They asked themselves which was the most masculine symbol in American life. The answer was the tattoo. A series of ads was drawn up with rugged men, from different walks of life, sporting prominent tattoos on their hands, readily visible when they lit up. Of the original ads, the one with the cowboy was by far the most effective, and gradually the theme became the cowboy instead of the tattoo. At a time when many Americans feared losing their individualism to the norms of suburbia, the myth of the cowboy, celebrated by Hollywood in a thousand films, was powerful stuff.

The first ad ran in January 1955. The Burnett people also suggested changing the packaging to a stronger red color. But the key to the campaign became the craggy-faced cowboy. It was an immense success, and it changed the market for filter cigarettes. The ads began to talk about "man-sized flavor," and suggested that Marlboro was, "[a] man's cigarette that women like too." Pierre Martineau, one of the pioneer market-research people and pop psychologists in advertising, praised the Marlboro ads and the macho quality of the campaign, which placed the cigarette "right in the heart of core meanings of smoking: masculinity, adulthood, vigor, and potency. Quite obviously these meanings cannot be expressed openly. The consumer would reject them quite violently. The difference between a topflight creative man and the hack is this ability to express powerful meanings indirectly . . ."

The cowboy was so successful for Marlboro that it was not long before other cigarettes tried to get in on the act. Soon there was a Chesterfield commercial that showed cowboys on a roundup smoking Chesterfields. There was a new Western song to go with it: "Chessss——ter——fiieeelddd," it began: "Drivin' cattle/ desert sun a-blaze/ Poundin' leather/ roundin' up the strays/ Herdin' steers/ Across the range/ You'll find a man/ Who stops and takes big pleasure/ When and where he can." It was a nice try and the cowboys all looked like they ought to be riding with Gary Cooper, but it was in vain: Cowboys and the West belonged to Marlboro.

There was in all this new and seemingly instant affluence the making of a crisis of the American spirit. For this was not simple old prewar capitalism, this was something new—capitalism that was driven by a ferocious consumerism, where the impulse was not so much about what people *needed* in their lives but what they needed to consume in order to keep up with their neighbors and, of course, to drive the GNP endlessly upward. "Capitalism is dead—consumerism is king," said the president of the National Sales Executives, defining the difference between prewar America and the new America orchestrated by Madison Avenue. The people surging into the middle class were the target market, and they were supposed to buy any way they could—if necessary, indeed preferably, on credit. This was an important new development, for the country was prosperous, but it was not *that* prosperous; the new consumerism depended not merely on mercantile seduction but on credit as well, and ordinary buyers were extended levels of credit never enjoyed by such people before. The auto companies lengthened the credit period on buying new cars from twenty-four to thirty-six months. As that happened, the old puritanism was dramatically weakened: Expectations and attitudes were being rapidly changed. (Not everyone was so enthusiastic about easier access to credit; Winthrop Aldrich, then the head of the Chase bank, expressed his doubts at one meeting with younger employees who wanted to ease requirements: "I'm just not sure that we should offer the ability to borrow and to have easy credit to the kind of people who are clearly going to have serious problems paying us back," he said.)

Few others shared his wariness. For most Americans, the idea of buying luxury items was a relatively new concept, as was the idea of buying on time. Their parents and their grandparents had lived in a world in which they bought only what was essential, because they could afford little more. They did not like to buy on time, because they tended to be pessimistic rather than optimistic about economic trends, and they knew too many stories of banks foreclosing on houses and stores repossessing items that were only half paid for. It was not so much that they did not like being in debt; they *feared* being in debt. But in the new, affluent America even blue-collar jobs brought middle-class salaries. Young Americans, though, if they had one foot in the future and responded eagerly to the cornucopia of goods around them, still knew of a Calvinist past. The dilemma for them, and thus for Madison Avenue, was the question of how to balance the cautiousness of the past with the comparative opulence of the present.

Ernest Dichter, one of the first and most influential of the motivational research experts, was a pioneer in trying to explain to companies the complicated subterranean psychological reasons on which people based their choices. He picked up on this theme very quickly, deciding that one of the main tasks advertisers had to deal with in the mid-fifties was resolving what he called "the conflict between pleasure and guilt," among those now more affluent than their parents. The job for the advertiser, he said, was therefore not so much to just sell the product "as to give moral permission to have fun without guilt." This was, he believed, a major psychological crisis in American life: the conflict between American puritanism and appetites whetted by the new consumerism. Every time a company sold some item that offered a new level of gratification, he argued, it had to assuage the buyer's guilt and, in his words, "offer absolution."

No one understood that better than the people at Cadillac, and they hadn't needed motivational-research people to figure it out for them. For years in their advertising they had pushed Cadillacs not just as the top-of-the-line car, the best that money could buy but, equally important, as a reward for a life of hard work: "Here is the man who has earned the right to sit at this wheel," the ads said. Classically, the Cadillac ad pitched the Horatio Alger part of the American dream: "Let's say it was thirty-one years ago on a beautiful morning in June. A boy stood by a rack of papers on a busy street and heard the friendly horn of a Cadillac. 'Keep the change.' The driver smiled as he took his paper and rolled out into the traffic. 'There,' thought the boy as he clutched the coin, 'is the car for me!' And since this is America, where dreams make sense in the heart of a boy, he is now an industrialist. He has fought—without interruption—for the place in the world he wants his family to occupy. Few would deny him some taste of the fruits of his labor. No compromise this time!"

That ad set the tone for much of the advertising that was to follow. The head of the family had worked hard and *selflessly,* and he had earned the right to bestow these hard-earned fruits upon his loyal family. It worked for grand and expensive products like the Cadillac, and also for small and inexpensive ones like the McDonald's ten-cent hamburger. McDonald's slogans began as "Give Mom a Break" and ended with the classic "You Deserve a Break Today." America, it appeared, was slowly but surely learning to live with affluence, convincing itself that it had earned the right to its new appliances and cars. Each year seemed to take the country further from its old puritan restraints; each year, it was a little easier to sell than in the past.

THIRTY-FOUR

By the mid-fifties television portrayed a wonderfully anti-septic world of idealized homes in an idealized, unflawed America. There were no economic crises, no class divisions or resentments, no ethnic tensions, few if any hyphenated Americans, few if any minority characters. Indeed there were no intrusions from other cultures. Nik Venet, a young record producer who grew up in a Greek-American immigrant family, remembered going to the real-life home of Ozzie and Harriet Nelson (which was strikingly like their television home) and being struck by the absence of odors. His had been a home where garlic and other powerful aromas from cooking wafted through the entire apartment; by contrast, the Nelsons' home seemed to reflect a different, cleaner culture. Invented by writers, producers, and directors, that America was the province of the television family sitcom of the mid- and late fifties.

There were no Greeks, no Italians, or no Jews in this world, only Americans, with names that were obviously Anglo-Saxon and Protestant; it was a world of Andersons and Nelsons and Cleavers.

Since there were no members of ethnic groups, with the unlikely and eccentric exception of Desi Arnaz/Ricky Ricardo, whom Lucille Ball had virtually blackmailed CBS into accepting and who existed as a kind of running gag, there was no discrimination. Everyone belonged to the political and economic center, and no one doubted that American values worked and that anyone with even an iota of common sense would want to admire them. In that sense the family sitcoms reflected—and reinforced—much of the social conformity of the period. There was no divorce. There was no serious sickness, particularly mental illness. Families *liked* each other, and they tolerated each other's idiosyncracies. Dads were good dads whose worst sin was that they did not know their way around the house and could not find common household objects or that they were prone to give lectures about how much tougher things had been when they were boys. The dads were, above all else, steady and steadfast. They symbolized a secure world. Moms in the sitcoms were, if anything, more interesting; they were at once more comforting and the perfect mistresses of their household premises, although the farther they ventured from their houses the less competent they seemed. Running a house perfectly was one thing; driving a car one block from home on an errand was another. Then things went wrong, although never in a serious way. Above all else, the moms loved the dads, and vice versa, and they never questioned whether they had made the right choice. Ward Cleaver once asked June, "What type of girl would you have Wally [their older son] marry?" "Oh," answered June. "Some very sensible girl from a nice family . . . one with both feet on the ground, who's a good cook, and can keep a nice house, and see that he's happy." "Dear," answers Ward. "I got the last one of those." Parents were never unjust or unwise in the way they treated their children.

Moms and dads never raised their voices at each other in anger. Perhaps the dads thought the moms were not good drivers, and the moms thought the dads were absentminded when it came to following instructions in the kitchen, but this was a peaceable kingdom. There were no drugs. Keeping a family car out too late at night seemed to be the height of insubordination. No family difference was so irreconcilable that it could not be cleared up and straightened out within the allotted twenty-two minutes. Moms and dads never stopped loving each other. Sibling love was always greater than sibling rivalry. No child was favored, no one was stunted. None of the dads hated what they did, though it was often unclear what they actually did. Whatever it was, it was respectable and valuable; it was white-collar and it allowed them to live in the suburbs (the networks were well aware of modern demographics) and not to worry very much about money. Money was never discussed, and the dark shadow of poverty never fell over their homes, but no one made too much or they might lose their connection with the pleasantly comfortable middle-class families who watched the show and who were considered the best consumers in the country. These television families were to be not merely a reflection of their viewers but role models for them as well.

They were to be as much like their fellow citizens as possible and certainly not better than them. There was no need for even the slightest extra dimension of ambition which might put them ahead of the curve. Being ordinary was being better. Ozzie Nelson of *Ozzie and Harriet,* who had been, in an earlier incarnation, a successful radio bandleader, changed professions when he took his family to television in order to create the model all-American family. But a bandleader was a show-business person and show-business people were different: They were Hollywood, they made money and hung out with a fast crowd. Therefore, when Ozzie and Harriet, his wife and the band's singer, left radio to go on television, the band was gone. Instead, he took some kind of middle-class job.

He was pleasant and loving and also something of a bumbler, on occasion stumbling over things, often getting his children's simplest intentions wrong, when for example he decided that David, his older son, was going to elope with his girlfriend, Ozzie raced to the justice of the peace's office only to learn that David was there to pay a speeding ticket. Ozzie was clearly no genius; but then it was not his job to be smarter than the people watching him, it was his job to be just a little less smart than the average dad. He worked at a pleasant, unspecified white-collar job. In a way, Ozzie and other sitcom dads seemed to have it both ways compared to the new breed of real-life suburban dads, who had to go off every day very early to commute to work and often returned late at night, when the children were ready for bed. By contrast, Ozzie seemed to work such flexible hours that he was home all the time. He never seemed to be at work, and yet he was successful.

If sitcom parents were just like the same upbeat, optimistic people whose faces now peopled the advertisements of magazines, then it was the duty of sitcom kids to be happy and healthy, too.

They were permitted to be feisty—which was better than being a goody-two-shoes—for the latter were not only distinctly unlikable to millions of young people across the nation, but they offered far too little chance for a scriptwriter to get them into the kind of minor trouble that could be solved in the last few minutes. After all, things could go wrong in a small way, but never in a way that threatened the families watching at home or cut too close to the nerve in dealing with the real issues of real American homes, where all kinds of problems lay just beneath the surface. Things in sitcoms never took a turn for the worse, into the dangerous realm of social pathology. Things went wrong because a package was delivered to the wrong house, because a child tried to help a parent but did so ineptly, because a dad ventured into a mom's terrain, or because a mom, out of the goodness of her heart, ventured into a dad's terrain. When people did things badly, they almost always did them badly with good intentions.

In this world the moms never worked. These were most decidedly one-income homes. The idea of a strike at a factory was completely alien. Equally alien was the idea that the greater world of politics might intrude. These families were living the new social contract as created by Bill Levitt and other suburban developers like him and were surrounded by new neighbors who were just like *them*. The American dream was now located in the suburbs, and for millions of Americans, still living in urban apartments, where families were crunched up against each other and where, more often than not, two or more siblings shared the same bedroom, these shows often seemed to be beamed from a foreign country, but one that the viewers longed to be part of. One young urban viewer, hearing that Beaver Cleaver was being threatened yet again with the punishment of being sent upstairs to his room, could only think to wish for a home of his own with an upstairs room to go to. But neither he nor anyone he knew had a home with an upstairs, let alone a room of his own.

These families were optimistic. There was a conviction, unstated but always there, that life was good and was going to get better. Family members might argue, but they never fought; even when they argued, voices were never raised. In the Cleaver family of *Leave It To Beaver,* the family always seemed to eat together and the pies were homemade. June Cleaver, it was noted, prepared two hot meals a day. The Cleavers were not that different from the Nelsons, who had preceded them into television suburbia: No one knew in which state or suburb they lived, and no one knew what Ward Cleaver, like Ozzie

Nelson, did for a living, except that it was respectable and that it demanded a shirt, tie, and suit.

To millions of other Americans, coming from flawed homes, it often seemed hopelessly unfair to look in on families like this. Millions of kids growing up in homes filled with anger and tension often felt the failure was theirs. It was their fault that their homes were messier, their parents less human (in fact they were, of course, more human) and less understanding than the television parents in whose homes they so often longed to live. As Beaver Cleaver (a rascal, with a predilection for trouble, but harmless and engaging trouble) once told June Cleaver (who was almost always well turned out in sweater and skirts), "You know, Mom, when we're in a mess, you kind of make things seem not so messy." "Well," answered June, "isn't that sort of what mothers are for?"

The Adventures of Ozzie and Harriet was hardly the most brilliant show, hardly the best written (looking back on some of the scripts, which were always written by Ozzie Nelson, it seems amazing that the show succeeded), but it lasted the longest—fourteen years. *Leave It To Beaver,* arguably a more interesting, better written show, lasted only six years, and *Father Knows Best* lasted nine. But *Ozzie and Harriet* had the added fascination of using the Nelson family members playing themselves; therefore, ordinary viewers had the benefit of watching the Nelson boys grow up in real life in their own living rooms. Harriet was a television mom right up there with June Cleaver, a wonderful all-purpose homemaker. In truth, because she had grown up as the child of show-business parents and she herself had been an entertainer at an early age, most chores in her home had always been done by servants. If she had not always been the person portrayed on television, she gradually became that person in real life. She was genuinely nice in real life. Her family came first, and she became, particularly as her younger son reached a difficult adolescence, the stabilizing influence. If, in a prefeminist era, she had doubts about who she was and how she was presented to her fellow Americans, she never showed them or talked about them. Both on television and in real life, she accepted her life, for it was a good one, far better than what anyone who had grown up in the Depression had any right to expect. Ozzie Nelson's decision to use the family as a performing troupe did not bother her much; for this was a show-business family that, unlike the one of her childhood, never had to go on the road. As a girl she had traveled all over the country with her show-business parents, who had not made a particularly good living and who had eventually divorced; now, without traveling, without leaving their home—all they had to do was drive a few minutes to a studio and inhabit a set that was a virtual replica of their real home—she and her husband and her children were being well paid and for a long time they seemed a family very much like the one they portrayed.

She did not seem, even in her home, as strong a personality as June Cleaver. She cooked and she cleaned. She seemed to approve of what the others did, and she might say near the end of a show that whatever had been proposed was a good idea as far as she was concerned. She was certainly a good sport, but why shouldn't she be, with a family as easy as this to deal with? Her own personality was never that clearly defined; her role was to make life better for her husband and children. When she was on the phone (her phone calls, by Ozzie's orders, were limited to thirty seconds, though of course, Ozzie always interrupted her), her calls, as Diana Meehan pointed out, were never revealing of her own personality but were always updates on what Ozzie and the boys were doing. She knew her role and accepted it gladly and without complaint. She did not challenge the accepted sexism of the time, most specifically her husband's vision of what a woman could do. At one point on a show she suggested that if she could join the local volunteer fire department, to which Ozzie already belonged, she would see a good deal more of him. "Are you kidding?" Ozzie answered. "You gals take too long to dress." "Oh, I don't know," she said. "We can be pretty quick." But Ozzie would have none of it: "By the time you got your makeup on, the fire would be out." The only housewife who fought back— but by doing so only served to prove that men were right and that women had no place in the serious world of business and commerce—was Lucy. Indeed, it was the very manic, incompetent quality of her rebellion that showed she should be at home burning the dinner and that women were somehow different than men, less steady, and less capable.

Of the Nelson sons, David was the good, steady, reliable older son, and Ricky was the younger son, more likely to get into trouble and to challenge, albeit lightly, the authority of the house. The Nelsons, were, of course, wonderfully attractive; the parents were handsome without being too sexy. Ozzie, after all, had been a star quarterback at Rutgers and later he and Harriet had been performers—theirs was an entertainment marriage. The boys seemed to embody pleasant American good looks. They looked as if they had been bred to be on a show about a typical American family: They were handsome, likable, seemingly virtuous and normal. They were the kids that ordinary American kids wanted to emulate. Popularity seemed to come easily to them, just as popularity came easily to their parents. Ricky was, if anything, better-looking and more natural than his older brother on air; it was toward his talents that the show was soon to be directed.

One reason that Americans as a people became nostalgic about the fifties more than twenty-five years later was not so much that life was better in the fifties (though in some ways it was), but because at the time it had been portrayed so idyllically on television. It was the television images of the era that remained so remarkably sharp in people's memories, often fresher than memories of real life. Television reflected a world of warm-hearted, sensitive, tolerant Americans, a world devoid of anger and meanness of spirit and, of course, failure. If Ozzie spawned imitators with the success of his rather bland family, then eventually the different families all seemed interchangeable, as if one could pluck a dad or a mom or even a child from one show and transplant him or her to another.

In February 1979 *Saturday Night Live,* reflecting the more cynical edge of a new era, did exactly that on the occasion of an appearance by Ricky Nelson. The skit turned the suburban world into a Twilight Zone, with Dan Aykroyd playing Rod Serling. Serling/Ackroyd began as the narrator: "Meet Ricky Nelson, age sixteen. A typical American kid, in a typical American kitchen in a typical American black-and-white-TV family home. But what's about to happen to Ricky is far from typical unless you happen to live in the Twilight Zone." At which point Ricky, on his way home from school, wanders into the home of the *Cleavers.* But he is treated warmly there. June offers him a brownie but warns him against spoiling his appetite. Ricky tells June his name. "Nelson," she says. "What a lovely name." But surrounded by all this warmth, he remains lost and cannot find his home. Again we hear Serling/Aykroyd: "Submitted for your approval. A sixteen-year-old teenager walking through Anytown, USA, past endless Elm Streets, Oak Streets, and Maple Streets, unable to distinguish one house from the other . . ." The next house he enters is that of the Andersons, of *Father Knows Best.* The Andersons immediately decide he is Betty's blind date. He tells them his name. Bill Anderson, the resident dad, says, "Nelson? What a nice name. Presbyterian?" Ricky answers: "My father is, sir. My mother is Episcopal." Bill says: "Well, I certainly hope you'll stay for dinner." And Jane chimes in, "You'll want to wash up and have a brownie first." On he continues through the family of *Make Room For Daddy,* and then on to the Ricardos', where he arrives just in time to see Lucy burn the turkey in the oven.

The world of the Nelsons was not, in reality, art imitating life. The low-key Ozzie Nelson of the sitcoms had little in common with the real-life Ozzie, who was a workaholic. He wrote, produced, and directed the shows and was an authoritarian, almost dictatorial presence on the set who monitored every aspect of his children's lives. He placed both of them in the television series when they were quite young, and constantly reminded them of their obligation to the family and to all the people who worked on the show. The incomes of all these people, he kept pointing out, depended on the success of the show, and he demanded that both boys not only perform well but that they live up to their squeaky-clean images off camera. If they got in trouble, he reminded them, they might not only damage their own personal reputations but undermine the show as well. That was no small burden to place on teenagers growing up in the late fifties. Ricky, said his friend Jimmie Haskell, "had been raised to know that there were certain rules that applied to his family. They were on television. They represented the wonderful, sweet, kind, good family that lived next door, and that Ricky could not do anything that would upset that image. He knew those were the rules."

Ozzie Nelson was not merely a man who put great pressure on his children, but in contrast to the readily available Ozzie of the show, who always seemed to be around, he was gone much of the time—albeit at home, but gone. He would retire after dinner to his office and work all night writing the scripts and the directorial notes for the coming episode, sleeping late and coming downstairs around noon. The Nelsons were, therefore, for all their professional success, very different from the family depicted on the show, they lived with an immense amount of pressure and unreconciled issues. Chief among those issues was the fact that Ozzie Nelson had in effect stolen the childhood of both of his sons and used it for commercial purposes; he had taken what was most private and made it terribly public. After all, the children cast in the other family sitcoms of the era, despite the pressure of being teenage stars and celebrities, at least had a chance to get back to their own normal lives under their own different names; but in the case of the Nelsons, the show merged the identities of the children in real life with those portrayed on television.

If Ozzie Nelson was by no means a talented writer, he was nonetheless shrewd and intuitive, with a fine instinct for how the rest of the country wanted to see itself in terms of a middle-class family portrait; if he did not like and did not understand the increasingly sharp divisions beginning to separate the young from their parents in America, then he understood how to offer a comforting alternative to it. American families, he understood, did not want at that moment a weekly program to reflect (and, worse, encourage) teenage rebellion. There was too much of that already. Americans did not want to come home and watch a warring family. People were just beginning to worry about juvenile delinquency in inner cities, and the disturbing phenomenon of rock musicians like Elvis Presley was growing ever larger.

On the show, David was good and obedient, the classic first-born, and Ricky, if written as the more contentious younger brother, was not defiant, or openly rebellious. This was a home where there was still plenty of respect for parents and Dad and Mom knew best. "Ozzie," wrote Joel Selvin in his biography of Ricky, "knew he had a gold mine in his cottage industry, fashioning a mythic American family out of a real one. If the two young boys ever felt the pressure of living up to roles created for them by an omniscient father, there was no escape. Anything the boys did could wind up on the show."

Ricky Nelson, whose identity was being shaped by scripts written by his father, found the search for his identity far more difficult than an ordinary child would. What part of him was real? What part of him was the person in the script? Did he dare be the person he thought he was, or did that go too far outside the parameters of Ozzie's scripts? The Nelsons were no more an all-American family than any other family; the generational tensions that ran through so many others ran through theirs as well, albeit they remained largely unrecognized. Moreover, the kind of mistakes that were normal, indeed mandatory, for most boys stumbling through adolescence were unacceptable in this tightly run family. The boys were always to be well groomed, they were always to be polite; they were to make no mistakes. A mishap that was minor for another child might land on the front pages of newspapers if it happened to a Nelson.

Ricky started on the television show when he was twelve, and by thirteen he was giving interviews to the *Los Angeles Times* on the role of the child actor ("I think the first requirement for a young actor, or any actor for that matter, is to lose his self-consciousness and be himself. People who are ill at ease and self-conscious are people who are thinking too much of themselves and worrying about the impression they are making on others. The best actors lose themselves in their parts and read their dialogue as naturally as possibly . . ."). What any adolescent needs is the chance to be himself, to have a childhood and stumble into adolescence; what Ricky and David had were scripts portraying them and their lives as they were supposed to be.

Ozzie Nelson had always ruled the real home with an unbending authority, one that was not to be questioned. When one of his sons displeased him, he did not exactly raise his voice, but his tone changed. Ricky might be in the room with some of his friends only to hear Ozzie's voice of displeasure: "... Rick ... *son!* ... could you come in here for a minute." Although there was no anger yet showing in his voice, there was no mistaking the measured tone, that it was a command and that something had gone wrong. Ricky seemed to change almost instantly when Ozzie's voice showed irritation, his friends thought. As Ricky moved into his middle teens, the contradictions in his life were becoming greater and greater. He was supposed to be a normal teenager, a fantasy model for millions of other teenagers, but even his mistakes had to be invented by his father and written into the script. He was making as much as $150,000 a year, but he was existing on a $5-a-week allowance. And when he took a girlfriend to a drive-in movie, he sometimes had to back in, to save the cost of the ticket. It was, thought one friend, as if Ricky longed to be his own person with his own life but Ozzie would not let him. In effect, because Ricky could not make his mistakes when he was young, he had to make them when he was an adult.

Gradually, the tensions between Ricky and Ozzie began to grow. Ricky was a naturally gifted tennis player, and Ozzie wanted him to play tennis; his way of rebelling was to give up tennis. He cruised the neighborhood in his car, a mandatory rite of California adolescence, but his parents were uneasy with it. ("I was," he later noted, "a nice greaser.") There were as he hit his mid-teens, as the first signs of the coming of a new youth culture were surfacing, frequent arguments between father and son about hair length and about smoking. "Goddamnit," Ozzie would say, "I told you to cut your hair," and Ricky would answer that he had cut it. It was a struggle for identity, and in the beginning Ozzie Nelson always won, for the obligations to the family and to the show always came first. But Ozzie and Harriet were uneasy—such tensions had never been experienced with David.

Friends who were believed to be a bad influence on him were banished. It was never done overtly—no one was ever ordered out of the house—but if Ozzie did not like someone, if he thought a friend was a bad influence, that his hair was a little long, he deftly put obstacles in the way of the friendship. As such, noted one friend, Ozzie was extremely skillful at whittling down Ricky's list of friends.

Eventually, Ozzie made what may have been his critical mistake. He decided to seize on Ricky's genuine love of rock music and annex it for the show. In a way it was a success, and one could not at the time argue with the choice, for overnight he turned a young man who longed to be like Elvis Presley into a sanitized middle-class version of him. Ricky Nelson as a rock star—combining so naturally the two most powerful forces affecting the young in those days, television and rock—was an instant entertainment success.

At age sixteen, Ricky loved rock and wanted to cut a record for his girlfriend. Ozzie, understanding the commercial possibilities—after all, Ricky was good-looking, the right age, and was clean and therefore acceptable in millions of homes where parents loathed the idea of the more sinister Elvis—shrewdly arranged for him to do a song on the show. Ricky was reluctant. He did not think he was ready yet—and musically, he was right. His singing and guitar-playing abilities were limited. Ozzie disagreed and simply went ahead and did it. The show was about the family going by ship on a vacation to Europe; near the end of it, Ozzie says to the bandleader, quite casually, "How about Ricky singing a rhythm and blues tune and the rest of us will give him a little moral support?" Ricky thereupon picked up an old Fats Domino song, "I'm Walkin'." The show aired on April 10, 1957.

The results were phenomenal. He was an instant sensation. He was a rock star before he was any good. Elvis Presley's success had been genuine: The young had understood that he was theirs, and television had been forced in the person of Ed Sullivan to capitulate, however reluctantly, and to accept him. In effect, the establishment had fought the coming of Elvis and fought his success; in the case of Ricky, it was the reverse. He was the artificial invention of conventional middle-class taste makers in a show that conventional Americans loved; his success therefore threatened no one. If anything, it seemed to sanitize rock. Yet music was important to Ricky in a way that his television career was not. The television show represented duty and obligation, something he did for his family because he had to and about which he had no choice. The show belonged to Ozzie, not to him; the person on the show, he felt, was not him, and he longed to escape from the shadow of cute little Ricky. But in the line dividing the generations in America, rock was the critical issue with which the young could define themselves and show that they were different from their parents. Now here was his father taking what was truly his and incorporating it into the show, giving it, in effect, an *Ozzie and Harriet* parental seal of approval. Ricky wanted to be

Carl Perkins, noted Selvin, his biographer, but because his father had pushed him so quickly and made him play on the show before he was ready, he was a joke to real musicians—whose approval he desperately sought. A few years later Elvis Presley, having been away from live performances for a while, was planning his return to the stage but was worried about how he would look and how he should handle his hair. At that point, Priscilla, his wife, mentioned a billboard featuring Ricky Nelson, who looked particularly attractive. Perhaps, she suggested, Elvis could take a look at it. "Are you goddamn crazy," he told her. "After all these years Ricky Nelson and Fabian and that whole group have more or less followed in my footsteps and now I'm supposed to copy them. You gotta be out of your mind, woman."

Later in his life, as his early fame as a singer and television star began to fade and, ironically, as his music became far more interesting, Ricky Nelson never received proper credit for it. Indeed, even those who showed up at his later concerts at the Palomino, in which he was playing an interesting and original version of California white rock-a-billy, seemed to want him to be Ricky from the television show. When he would play his latest songs, the audience would yell out for their favorites from his early days, such as "Poor Little Fool." When they did, said his friend Sharon Sheeley, he would wince. It was as if the public would not let him grow up and wanted him forever to be as he was cast as a boy.

He had gone, he once noted, from singing in the bathroom to the recording studio, with nothing in between. All the ingredients to make a star were there: He already had a huge ready-made constituency because of the television show; he was uncommonly attractive; he had a nice, if untrained voice. His first record sold 60,000 copies in three weeks, shot up the charts, and stayed there for five months. Eventually, it sold 700,000 copies. It was to be the start of a remarkable but unhappy career, in which his success outstripped his talent and his place in the pecking order of rock cast a shadow that always hung over him professionally. In 1958 he was the top-selling rock-and-roll artist in the country. He went on tours that summer, and the crowds were enormous. In those early years of rock, only Elvis Presley was selling more records and had more consistent hits. Yet his father was still masterminding the entire operation, serving as his manager, arranging better record contracts for him, bringing in Barney Kessel, the famed jazz guitarist, to help him with his sound, making sure his backup group was worthy of him and thereby using the Jordanaires, Elvis's backup, with him. Rock, his friends thought, was his one source of freedom, his way of escaping the public image forced on him by the television show. Ironically, his success as a teen musical idol lent additional vitality to the show; it should have been slowing down by the late fifties, but because of his new success as a rocker, the show was renewed in 1959 for five more years. He, who had wanted to escape it, had carried it forward with his means of escape.

He became rich (he made a lot of money from the television show, and now he was making much more from records and appearances—all of which was put aside for him), successful, attractive, and incomplete. As such he grew up in a kind of covert rebellion; he and Ozzie worked out an unacknowledged quid pro quo, Ozzie indulged him, offered him extra privileges, and limited Ricky's rebellion; Ricky in turn stayed on the show and remained dependent on Ozzie. He had grown up as a teen idol, but he had not had a real boyhood and now he was passing through adolescence still unsure of himself, his professional career with almost all of his major decisions still dominated by his father.

His adult life was, not surprisingly, unhappy—a marriage that seemed perfect on paper soon went sour; excessive drug use followed. Finally, the harshest truth could not be suppressed: Ricky Nelson, the charming, handsome all-American boy was, to all intents and purposes, the unhappy product of a dysfunctional family.

THIRTY-FIVE

Among those who were extremely ambivalent about their pursuit of the American dream were Tom and Betsy Rath. In 1955, when they first appeared on the scene, they should have been, by all rights, the quintessential upwardly mobile modern American family. But in this society of consumption, they were always in debt—not heavily, but consistently so; every month there was a stack of unpaid bills, which Betsy had to juggle skillfully in order not to have their credit cut off. Worse still, the house in which they had lived for seven years was too small and seemed to be disintegrating beneath them. The front door had been badly scratched by a dog; the hot-water faucet in the bathroom dripped. One of their three children had gotten ink all over a wall. Almost all of the furniture needed to be refinished, reupholstered, or cleaned. The neighbors who monitored such things whispered about the poorly kept yard and that the Raths could not afford a gardener.

For the Raths the house had come to symbolize all their frustrations and tensions. In the living room, a dent on a wall marked a bitter argument that had occurred when Betsy spent $40 on a cut-glass vase on the same day that, by chance, Tom spent $70 on a new suit he badly needed for business. Tom had dented the wall by throwing the vase against it. Even their 1939 Ford, a car they had driven for too long, marked them, if not exactly as failures, then as people who were not keeping up with the neighbors.

Tom and Betsy Rath were not real people, although there were plenty of young men and women who could readily identify with them. They were fictional characters, the heroes, or antiheroes, of Sloan Wilson's novel *The Man in the Gray Flannel Suit,* one of the most influential American novels of the fifties. Its theme was the struggle of young Americans against the pressures of conformity and imprisonment in suburban life. "Without talking about it much they both began to think of the house as a trap, and they no more enjoyed refurbishing it than a prisoner would delight in shining up the bars of his cell," Wilson wrote. For the Raths were victims of this modern malaise: What should have made them happy did not. "I don't know what's the matter with us," Betsy Rath said to Tom one night. "Your job is plenty good enough. We've got three nice kids and lots of people would be glad to have a house like this. We shouldn't be so *discontented* all the time."

They lived in a community of people very much like themselves; their neighbors, though pleasant and friendly, were, truth to tell, strangers, bonded by status and ambition rather than true friendship. "Few people considered Greentree Avenue a permanent stop—the place was just a crossroads where families waited until they could afford to move on to something better. The finances of almost every household were an open book. Budgets were frankly discussed, and the public celebration of increases in salary was common. The biggest parties of all were moving out parties, given by those who finally were able to buy a bigger house. . . . On Greentree Avenue contentment was an object of contempt," Wilson wrote.

It was not a bad world, Betsy Rath thought when she pondered their situation—the people around them were good and decent but they were dreamers and most of their dreams seemed to be about material progress. Sometimes she thought their lives were too dull and then she would ponder their condition a bit more and decide that it was not so much a dull world as a frantic one. But there was, she knew, a narrowness to it. Nor were they the only ones restless with their lives. When the neighbors gathered for one of their instant parties, late in the night, the dreams for the future were revealed: "usually the men and the women just sat talking about the modern houses they would like to build, or the old barns they would like to convert into dwellings. The price the small houses on Greentree Avenue were currently bringing and the question of how big a mortgage the local banks were offering on larger places were constantly discussed. As the evening wore on, the men generally fell to divulging dreams of escaping to an entirely different sort of life—to a dairy farm in Vermont, or to the management of a motel in Florida."

Tom Rath, whose biography was strikingly similar to that of Sloan Wilson, was thirty-three years old and made $7,000 a year, a seemingly substantial salary for a young man in those days, one that placed him squarely in the new middle class. He worked in Manhattan for a foundation that had been established by a millionaire for scientific research. He seemed neither satisfied nor dissatisfied with his job; to the degree that he was discontented, it was with his salary, not with what he did. His restlessness was revealed one day at lunch with some of his friends when he heard of an opening in public relations at the United Broadcasting Corporation. It paid between $8,000 and $12,000. Try for $15,000, one of his friends who worked there said: "I'd like to see somebody stick the bastards good." Ten thousand, he thought, might get them a new house. It was not a job he particularly wanted, nor was it a company he admired. When he mentioned to Betsy the possibilities of a life in public relations, she told him that she had never thought of him as a public relations man. "Would you like it?" she asked. "I'd like the money," he answered. Then she sighed. "It would be wonderful to get out of this house."

"When you come right down to it a man with three children has no damn right to say that money doesn't matter," Tom thought to himself. Naturally, he applied for the job. The last question on the application was intriguing: "The most significant thing about me is . . ." For a moment he thought of writing about his wartime stint as a paratrooper, during which time he killed seventeen men. "For four and a half years my profession was jumping out of airplanes with a gun, and now I want to go into public relations," he wanted to write. He pondered it, though. He could also have written: "The most significant fact about me is that I detest the United Broadcasting Corporation, with all its soap operas, commercials and yammering studio audiences, and the only reason I'm willing to spend my life in such a ridiculous enterprise is that I want to buy a more expensive house and a better brand of gin."

Whatever frustrations he felt with his current life were minor compared with those harbored by Betsy. She wanted a more civilized life, one where they would eat a real breakfast in the morning and talk to each other like real people, and eat, instead of hot dogs and hamburgers for dinner, something more substantial, a roast or a casserole. And above all there would be no more television. Instead, the family would read more, and perhaps they would read aloud to each other.

Eventually, in Wilson's novel, all the Raths' problems were resolved. Tom took the new job, and despite the treacherous politics of the organization, he discovered that his boss (a character based on Roy Larsen, one of the founders of Time-Life) was a superior man seriously pledged to a better world. In time Tom Rath confronted his demons (including fathering a child during World War Two with an Italian mother), simplified his life, and found that despite his earlier cynicism he could achieve both honor and a better salary in his new job (in addition, his grandmother left him a large tract of extremely valuable land, which could be developed). He and Betsy were able to hold on to their beliefs and their marriage while becoming part of the best of the new suburban world.

The novel was almost completely autobiographical. The book reflected, Sloan Wilson later said, his own frustrations with civilian life after serving as a young officer with the Coast Guard in World War Two. His wartime job had been rich, full of challenge and responsibility. He had commanded his own ship at twenty-three and dealt daily with the great danger involved in running high-octane fuel into combat areas. Every day in that exciting time of his life he had a feeling that what he did mattered. Civilian life, to his surprise, was infinitely more difficult. He had always wanted to be a reporter, and he had worked for a time on the *Providence Journal* at a job he loved. But with a wife and two children, the fifty-dollar-a-week salary was woefully inadequate.

"What we all talked about in those days was selling out," he said years later. "Selling out was doing something you did not want to do for a good deal more money than you got for doing what you loved to do." Though he wanted to write fiction, he took a job at Time-Life. Even as he joined the Luce publications, Wilson was appalled by his own decision because he hated everything Time-Life stood for—he viewed it as an institution that offered talented, liberal young men handsome salaries to dress up its own conservative politics. At first he had worked for *FYI,* the Time house organ, but that seemed beneath his dignity and he decided to quit. Somehow, his personnel file was sent to Roy Larsen, one of the company's founders and the top person on the business side. Larsen was about to head a major campaign on behalf of the nation's public schools and decided to hire Wilson as a special assistant to do publicity. The pay was good, and he would soon make $10,000 a year.

If Wilson did not like the political slant of Time-Life, he liked the internal politics among the managerial ranks even less. Another bright young man, who was his immediate superior, threw his first article on the floor with contempt. Later, the young man confessed that he always operated this way, believing that new employees did not work well unless they were frightened. But to Wilson's surprise, he had immediately liked Roy Larsen, a graceful, kind, and intelligent man, albeit a world-class workaholic. Best of all, he found that he could write short stories for *The New Yorker* on the side. But if there were advantages to the job, they still paled when compared with his exhilarating experiences during the war. He was somehow, for all of Roy Larsen's personal kindness and the handsome paycheck, something of a glorified flunky. He decided to quit the day that he accompanied Larsen to have his photo taken along with the head of the outdoor advertising council. Their photo was to be part of the announcement at the beginning of a billboard campaign to promote the nation's public schools.

It was a rainy day, and both executives arrived wearing handsome overcoats and bowler hats. Each was respectfully accompanied by his bright, up-and-coming young assistant. No executive was worth his salt unless he had his own up-and-coming young man, Wilson thought. Wilson looked at his opposite number from the outdoor advertising council and saw how eager and sycophantish he was—and wondered if he looked that way to other people. Because of the rain, both men had kept their bowler hats on, but since the photographer could not see their faces, he asked that the hats come off. Unlike Wilson, the other bright young man seemed to have anticipated the photographer's request, and in a second he not only had his own boss's hat but Roy Larsen's as well. Sloan Wilson realized he had been outhustled, in a competition he wanted no part of in the first place.

With that, he decided to write full-time. Eventually, he returned to New Canaan, Connecticut, and took a long, hard look at it. It was, he thought, a world he had come to hate. In fact, all the other men in publishing and advertising he knew who lived there hated it, too: three hours a day on the commuter trains; working in corporations where the internal politics seemed endless and where everyone was obsessed with playing up to his immediate superior. Talent, all too often, was pressed into service for pure commercial gain without regard to the larger consequences. Almost everyone he knew in New Canaan was trying to get out; it was a rat race, and all the participants dreamed of hitting the jackpot by writing the great American novel and selling the rights to Hollywood. If they did that, they would never have to get on a commuter train again. One friend came to symbolize this entire world to Wilson: He had only recently flown forty combat missions, and his uniform had been bedecked with World War Two medals. Now he worked for an advertising firm. One of his accounts was a cereal company and the question he was working on was whether the people who bought the cereal would prefer to find a tin frog or a rubber spider inside the box as the surprise.

Ironically, the greater one's success in this world, the harder it was to escape. Salaries would go up, and newly minted executives would merely find themselves paying more taxes, burdened by a more expensive life-style, and inhabiting ever larger houses. "For a time," he remembered years later, "I was insatiable myself—I wanted ever bigger houses and more cars." In New Canaan, Wilson thought people changed houses the way other Americans changed cars. The worst thing was that these fancy jobs were supposed to offer some sort of security, but in fact they did not. The more successful you were, the deeper you were in debt and the more exposed and more perilous your position often became at work. The process was the reverse of what it was supposed to be: Ostensibly, a young man would work hard to gain some measure of success; the better he did, the more secure he and his family should have been. Instead, the higher you went, the more people there were who were after your job—so work became more stressful.

When *The Man in the Gray Flannel Suit* appeared in 1955, it hit a vital nerve. "I wasn't thinking about what was happening to the country when I wrote it. The only thing I was thinking about was what was happening to me," Wilson said thirty years later. It was a major best-seller and soon became a movie starring Gregory Peck— an ideal choice, with just the right amount of decency and moral ambivalence. Even the title, *The Man in the Gray Flannel Suit,* suggested someone who was sacrificing his individuality to become a part of the new more faceless middle class. As it turned out, the book was published just as a major intellectual debate was forming on the issue of conformity in American life, particularly as the modern corporation became ever bigger and became an increasingly important force in American life. The debate seemed to focus on the question of whether, despite the significant and dramatic increase in the standard of living for many Americans, the new white-collar life was turning into something of a trap and whether the greater material benefits it promised and delivered were being exchanged for freedom and individuality. Was this what the new definition of success meant? More of everything except individuality? Were we as a nation already well on our way to becoming faceless drones, performing bland tasks that demanded no real skill save managerial obedience? Was America losing its entrepreneurial class to cautious, gray managers, men afraid to make mistakes and take chances? At the center of the debate were the writings of one of the most important intellectual figures of the period: C. Wright Mills. Though he was on the faculty of Columbia University and nominally a sociologist, he cut across many disciplines—philosophy, history, economics, journalism.

A man of fierce physical and intellectual presence, Mills was remembered by his friends (who more often than not ended up as his adversaries) first and foremost for his energy and combativeness. Academics were expected to be genteel and solicitous of their colleagues; most professors at Columbia wore the academic uniform of tweed jacket, flannel slacks, and bow ties. But Mills seemed determined to provoke and antagonize his colleagues. He dressed as a lumberjack—in khaki pants, flannel shirts, and combat boots—and would arrive for class from his house in the country (which he had built himself) astride his BMW motorcycle. His style, body language, and pronouncements seemed calculated to rebuke the more polished world around him; he was from the real world, his manner seemed to say, as the others in academe were not. Brilliant and egocentric, Mills was the classic loner. He had few close friends. "I have never known," he once wrote, "what others call 'fraternity' with any group . . . neither academic nor political. With a few individuals, yes, but with groups, however small, no." His writing was as incisive a post-Marxist critique of America's new managerial capitalism as existed in the country at the time, even if on occasion he painted with too broad a brush and was prone to exaggerate. Mills's work was important, the historian Stanley Katz later noted, because it told important truths about America's new class strata and about the development of capitalism after the war and yet could not be attacked for being Marxist.

Mills eventually became the critical link between the old left, Communist and Socialist, which had flourished during the Depression, and the New Left, which sprang up in the sixties to protest the blandness of American life. He found hope not in the grim rigidity and authoritarianism of the Soviet Union and its satellite nations in Eastern Europe, but in the underdeveloped world, which had been victimized by European colonialism and American imperialism. Cuba, as Castro came to power, fascinated him as Poland and Czechoslovakia did not. The old left had been born of the injustices of capitalism during the Great Depression and thrived because the Communists' voice in Europe, and the United States had been the first to warn of the rise of Nazism. But the movement had been badly undermined by a number of things: the Ribbentrop-Molotov pact; the domestic crimes of Joseph Stalin and his concentration camps, which only the most slavish Marxist could ignore; the imperialism of the Soviet Union as it brutally crushed its satellite states and left those countries with repressive, totalitarian regimes; and of course, the stunning success of postwar capitalism in the United States. Mills's books were hailed in the Communist world as brilliant critiques of American society, but he was hardly enthusiastic about this often unwanted praise. At one point late in his career he visited the Soviet Union and was toasted at a dinner as the foremost critic of contemporary American life. When it was his turn to respond to the toast, he rose and said, "To the day when the complete works of Leon Trotsky are published in the Soviet Union!"

The combination of the grimness of Communism as it now existed in Europe and the success of American capitalism had essentially devastated the traditional left. By the mid-1950s, only J. Edgar Hoover seemed to think Marxism was a powerful force in postwar America. With the triumph of capitalism and the threat of the Cold War, traditional American politics had, if anything, narrowed; the differences between the Republican party and the Democratic party were seen as marginal by many serious social critics of the time. Yet the success of capitalism did not mean the end of alienation; it simply meant a different kind of alienation. Alienation, Mills and others were suggesting, could be just as powerful in a comfortable white-collar existence as it was in a harsh working-class one. The battlefield was shifting: Instead of criticizing capitalism for its failures, a new kind of left, far more idiosyncratic and less predictable, was essentially criticizing America for its successes, or at least for the downside of its successes.

This new threat to the human spirit came not from poverty but from affluence, bigness, and corporate indifference from bland jobs through which the corporation subtly and often unconsciously subdued and corrupted the human spirit. As they moved into white-collar jobs, more and more people felt as Sloan Wilson had when he portrayed Tom Rath—that they had less control over their lives. Here was a world where individuality seemed to be threatened and the price of success might well be ever greater conformity.

Much of the old left's agenda had been imported from Europe and had been shaped by historical and social circumstances, which did not necessarily fit the postwar American condition, where workers had become consumers and beneficiaries of the economic system and thought of themselves as capitalists. As that happened, not only did more working people enter the middle class, but there was a vast new reevaluation of what being on the left meant. By the mid-fifties one of the great new growth industries in Wall Street was investing the pension funds of labor unions. Those who had been a critical part of the left in the past were now being incorporated into the system, not merely politically but economically; as that happened, a new left was beginning to form around very different issues. Mills was the perfect radical iconoclast to examine the new American condition. He was unmistakably American, a rough, untamed son of the Southwest, where the clash of economic forces was still raw. Alienation came naturally to him: He was raised as a Catholic in a small town in Texas, whose culture was, he liked to say, "one man, one rifle." His parents forced him to sing in a Catholic choir in Waco and that had produced, as Irving Horowitz noted, "a lifelong resentment of Christianity." It also helped guarantee, given the prejudices of the region against Catholics, that he felt a "painful sense of isolation from his peers." Certainly, he had always felt like an outsider. There was no taint of Marxism to his work. He once wrote the sociologist Kurt Wolff that people always had come to him and told him that he wrote "as if I were a European about this country. . . . I am an outlander, not only regionally but down bone deep and for good. In Orwell's phrase: I am just outside the whale and always have been. I did not really earn it; I just was it without intending to be and without doing anything about it except what I had to do from day to day."

Eventually, the family moved from West Texas to Dallas, where Mills graduated from Dallas Technical High in 1934. After an unhappy start at Texas A & M (years later he told his friend Harvey Swados, the writer, that the hazing he had received as an Aggie had turned him into a rebel), he transferred to the University of Texas at Austin. The university and the city had been an oasis of intellectual and political ferment in Texas, and that was true more than ever during the Depression. Among his professors and fellow students there was a sense from the start that Mills was different from the start, a young man whose physical and intellectual force and passion were remarkable. His energy was always ferocious: Every topic, as far as he was concerned, was to be argued, and every argument was to be won. Clarence Ayres, a professor at the University of Texas, wrote of him at the time: "He isn't a pale, precocious bookworm. He is a big strapping fellow with an athlete's energy. He looks much older than he is. For several years he has been reading everything within his reach, and he really is prodigiously learned for his years and situation. He also has acumen and the result of this combination of qualities has not been altogether to his advantage." In this letter written about Mills when he was twenty-three, Ayres continued prophetically: "The prevailing legend about him is to the effect that he takes people up and pursues them furiously until they get so tired of it they rebuff him (or until he has milked them dry and drops them). There is something in it both ways. Mills is tremendously eager and incredibly energetic. If he gets the idea that somebody has something, he goes after it like the three furies. I think he may have worn his welcome to shreds in some quarters. . . . The picture which emerges . . . is of an unusually strong student who may become a headliner. I think any department would be lucky to have him among its advanced students."

Mills acknowledged his own rough edges. Indeed, he felt as if they gave him a psychological advantage. He was often tactless in dealing with colleagues and surprised when his words wounded them; he was also thin-skinned, and when others ventured even mild criticism of his work, a new feud was often born. He did graduate work at Texas in sociology but no Ph.D. program was offered there, so in the fall of 1939 he entered the graduate program in sociology at the University of Wisconsin. There he made important intellectual connections and broadened his studies. In Madison, he seemed to make much the same impression he had in Austin: Hans Gerth, an immigrant intellectual, remembered him "with Thorstein Veblen in one hand and John Dewey in the other. He was a tall burly young man of Herculean build. He was no man with a pale cast of the intellect given to self mortification . . ." (Later when they had a squabble over whether Mills had taken too much credit for some of Gerth's work, Gerth was not so enthusiastic. Mills, he said, was "an excellent operator, whippersnapper, promising young man on the make, and Texas cowboy à la ride and shoot.")

While he was at Madison, Mills failed his Army physical because of hypertension (he suffered from chronic heart and circulatory problems). If anything, this heightened his alienation from the American political mainstream, for it put him on the sidelines at what was the defining moment for most members of his generation. He was big, powerful, and robust, yet he could not join what most of his contemporaries judged to be the nation's finest hour. Inevitably, as he had not participated in that great democratic cause, he rebelled and did not accept the propaganda and rationales that were used to justify it. He saw parallels, observed by few other contemporary intellectuals, between the corporate capitalism of Germany, which had allowed Nazism to rise, and the corporate capitalism of America. In Madison he married his first wife, Freya (the first of three, each of whom had one child with him). It was becoming clear that the pull of contemporary events was at least as powerful on him as that of academia, and some of his friends worried that he would become a pamphleteer rather than a scholar. "Hold your chin up, young man," wrote one of his few friends, Eliseo Vivas, a philosopher at Wisconsin who worried over the pull of journalism on Mills. He told Mills to "stick to the major guns with the 'long range' and don't allow your ambition to do something right now with you in the field of the freelancer and journalist. Write for decades, not for the week. Concentrate on the thesis and don't look right or left until it is done."

After Madison, he moved to the University of Maryland, which brought him nearer the nation's capital. He was taking politics more seriously now, and he wrote to his mother: "You ought to see me clipping *The New York Times* now." At a time when, because of World War Two, most young men were asking fewer political questions, he was on a very different path. His attitude, as Irving Horowitz pointed out, was something like a plague on both your houses.

He seemed to be saying that the horror of modern Nazism could not be blamed merely on an odd combination of circumstances: frenzied nationalism, the post–World War One depression, and the complete collapse of existing values and German currency and the social anarchy that followed. By his lights, the excesses of Germany were the excesses of capitalism. He saw Germany as the prototype for the modern corporate garrison state. The only thing that might stop it, he wrote, was the powerful force of organized labor. Not everyone agreed: Some thought that labor was just as readily seduced by exaggerated nationalism as any other class. (Some fifteen years later, one of his political descendants in the New Left, Abbie

Hoffman, was told to work on organizing blue-collar workers. "Organize the workers?" he exclaimed. "The workers want to beat the shit out of me!")

If nothing else, Mills helped reinvigorate the left, which was in decline after the war. Victory in World War Two, the growing awareness of Stalin's crimes, and the success of postwar capitalism had brought much of the intelligentsia back to the liberal center because fascist Germany and the Communist Soviet Union were so much worse than the United States. Other intellectuals found that America, in comparison with the rest of the world, now seemed less flawed; but Mills was not interested in a comparison with the rest of the world. He was a home-grown radical, bristling with his own native passions and his own very rugged, very American sense of independence.

The enemy, for him and many young leftists who came after him, was the liberalism of the era, so bland and corrupting, so comfortable, that it was essentially endorsed by both major political parties. People did not have to make difficult moral choices anymore. The liberalism of the society of abundance was "without coherent content; that in the process of its banalization, its goals have been so formalized as to provide no clear moral optic. The crisis of liberalism (and of American political reflection) is due to liberalism's success in becoming the official language for all public statement."

Maryland was not a particularly congenial place for him. He admired the exceptional group of young historians there—Frank Friedel, Kenneth Stampp, and Richard Hofstader—but he was hungry as ever for greater intellectual growth (on his terms), so he moved now into history, while writing more and more for national magazines, such as the *New Republic*. All of this helped enhance his reputation. Years later he told Dan Wakefield, a student of his at Columbia, that he had used his journalistic skills to escape the University of Maryland, which he found rather stultifying. "I wrote my way out of there!" he said. In 1944 he arrived at Columbia, where he had probably always wanted to be in the first place—a great Ivy League university in a great city, with access to a large and influential audience. "Mills," wrote Horowitz, "was caught in a cul-de-sac: antiprofessional in public utterances, quite professional in private desire. He coveted the status and glory of elite institutions while despising their snobbery and style." Mills would later say of *White Collar*, the first of his defining books, that it was "the story of a Texas boy who came to New York." At Columbia he managed to remain an outsider, with a series of tenuous friendships and shifting allegiances. Dwight MacDonald, the writer, became his first great friend—they were both, MacDonald pointed out, radicals at a time when it was not fashionable to be so. "We were both congenital rebels, passionately contemptuous of every received idea and established institution . . ." Mills, noted MacDonald, could argue with just about anyone on almost anything—and he could do it longer and louder than anyone else. They both had, he noted, a "mixture of innocence, and cynicism, optimism and skepticism. We were ever hopeful, ever disillusioned."

On campus, he was a memorable figure. In his office was a hot plate to warm soup and an electric espresso machine. He was, thought Wakefield, who eventually became a prominent journalist, "an exhilarating teacher. He stalked the room or pounded his fist on the table to emphasize a point, surprising us with ideas that seem utopian, except that he was so convinced of their practicality you couldn't dismiss them as mere theory." In the Columbia catalog he was listed as a sociologist, but he preferred to think of himself as a journalist—by which he meant someone like James Agee. That was real journalism—graceful and highly intellectual reportage.

He published *White Collar* in 1951 and *The Power Elite* in 1956. In these books he saw the new middle class as affluent but without purpose and cut off from its Calvinist past, from taking pride in craftsmanship. In *White Collar,* he seemed to bemoan the decline of the rugged American individualist and the growing frustration of the new America. He viewed history as a constant collision between competing forces that vied for power.

As an analyst of the stratification within the democratic society, Mills was without peer. Certainly, there were others writing about some of the same changes taking place in American society. David Riesman and Nathan Glazer published their important book *The Lonely Crowd,* about the inner-directed and the outer-directed new Americans, who increasingly seemed to take their signals, their values, and even their ambitions not from their own desires and beliefs but from a received value system around them. These people wanted to be a part of the larger community so much they would adjust their morality and ethics to those of the community almost unconsciously; in the end, they seemed to take on the coloration of their institutions and neighborhoods with frightening ease. Was it possible, Riesman and Glazer wondered, that America was producing a class whose sudden economic advancement, coming as it did within a generation, had outstripped the social and psychological preparations that might normally precede it? Had the very speed overwhelmed the capacity to enjoy and fully understand such affluence? Riesman himself clearly thought that Mills had touched on something important, but he was also dubious that the new white-collar class was as alienated as Mills suggested.

White Collar was, in general, favorably reviewed. As Horowitz noted, it hit on a powerful new theme that seemed to beguile American society: the growth of ever greater American power externally, alongside a feeling of a decrease in personal power among its citizens. Certainly, the new white-collar men in Mills's book seemed to be carried along by forces outside their control. They were voraciously ambitious without entirely knowing why. They never carefully considered their goals but simply plunged ahead to the next benchmark.

Yet Riesman felt Mills had a tendency to generalize and create pat, if convincing, stereotypes. From the outside, white-collar workers might indeed appear largely banal, frustrated with their lives as Mills might have been frustrated had he been forced to live similarly. Riesman thought there was a danger for someone like Mills in transferring his own need for intellectual stimulation into the minds and aspirations of people whose needs might be considerably different. Riesman pointed out that one should not underestimate, for example, the satisfaction generated by the pride of people who always had been blue-collar workers but who had finally moved up into the white-collar managerial world. Similar reservations were voiced in a letter that Richard Hofstader wrote to Mills about *White Collar*. There was, he said, a lot of human ugliness in the book, which he said was caught up in the jacket description of the book as a "merciless portrayal" of a whole class. There might be, Hofstader said, some people and perhaps even some classes "that may call for merciless treatment, but why be so merciless with all these little people? . . . Why no pity, no warmth? Why condemn—to paraphrase Burke—a whole class?"

In *The Power Elite* Mills went further, spotting early some of the forces that were coming together to create America the superpower. He pointed out the growing connection between the military and the industrial sectors—the military-industrial state that Eisenhower himself would warn of a few short years later. In addition, Mills had a strong intuitive sense of the dangers that might come, politically and socially, from a nation suddenly wielding so much power and affluence. But even here some critics thought he undermined his own work by being too simplistic. Yes, there were groups wielding considerable power in America, but American politics was so pluralistic that even as one group became too powerful, others came together to limit that power. Indeed some groups, supposedly with common interests, might in fact be bitterly opposed to each other; others that were supposed to be adversarial might get on well. For example, corporations and labor unions, traditional antagonists, might well want the same thing in the new power structure, and indeed labor unions, which Mills had once seen as the savior from domination of American life by the corporations, might in fact be a willing partner in the growth of too large a defense economy. But as Daniel Bell pointed out, there was not a clear community of interests in the power elite, as Mills would seem to have it. Often there were surprising conflicts. In Korea, Bell pointed out, the military, Wall Street, and the federal government were often at cross-purposes. The sands of American power shifted constantly: As soon as any one group began to overreach its place, it automatically came into conflict with some other group. Bell's criticism stung the sensitive Mills, who at one point wrote a friend, "Dan Bell is here now with *Fortune.* I've seen him only once or twice and don't look forward to meeting him again. He's full of gossip about how he met Luce for lunch and what Luce said. [Bell is a] little corkscrew drawn by power magnets; really pretty vulgar stuff."

One of the ironies of postwar American capitalism was that most owners of companies were making more money than ever before, expanding their size constantly, but that even as their wealth and their seeming influence increased, the leaders felt themselves less powerful in terms of their control of their own factory floor. As such they became ever more resentful of the society around them. They found a largely unsympathetic view of themselves in the mainstream media, which was, of course, owned by large corporations. What made America's power structure so interesting in the years after World War Two were its contradictions, most of which defied the traditional dogma of either the left or the right. Where Mills was most effective was in his journalism; where he was least effective was in his judgments and his occasionally simplistic projections of how different groups would in fact behave.

By the end of the decade, the gap had widened between him and most of the traditional academic community. He was appalled by the way altogether too many intellectuals, including many liberals, had enlisted in the Cold War and failed to criticize their own country for its excesses. The rise of Fidel Castro and the Eisenhower administration's hostile and clumsy attempts to deal with him only convinced Mills of the rightness of his vision. If its behavior toward Cuba turned out to be an appalling stereotype of the worst of American foreign policy, it was a perfect fit for Mills's view. America, he thought, was on its way to becoming something of a garrison state with the concurrence of what he called, with great contempt, "the NATO intellectuals." More and more, as the decade ended, he was drawn to the issue of Cuba and his radicalism deepened.

Late in the decade, Mills's health began to fail him. In 1958 he suffered the first of at least three heart attacks. He continued to smoke and drink heavily; he liked to boast that he had more women in one month than Don Juan had had in a lifetime.

His work had always been passionate, but now it was downright evangelical. *Listen Yankee!* was the title of his last book—on Cuba. He wrote his parents in 1961, after one heart attack, "Lying here all these weeks and having damn near died, because this thing was pretty damned close, well it's made me much stronger, and made me think about myself which I'd not had the chance to do before. I know that I have not the slightest fear of death. I know also that I have a big responsibility to thousands of people all over the world to tell the truth as I see it and tell it exactly and with drama and quit this horsing around with sociological bullshit."

In March 1962 he died, at the age of forty-five, of a heart attack. He was at the height of his powers, his audiences steadily expanding. "Mills," as Irving Horowitz wrote of him, "began to think of himself as the social bearer of mass beliefs; he became a movement unto himself. Armed with an Enlightenment faith that truth will out, he also became convinced that he was the bearer of the truth." When he died, he had already become something of a mythic figure to a new generation of young American radicals and it would turn out that his posthumous influence was to be even greater.

THREE

THIRTY-SIX

On the evening of December 1, 1955, Mrs. Rosa Parks's entire body ached—her feet, neck, and shoulders were especially sore. Parks was a tailor's assistant in a Montgomery, Alabama, department store. Hers was an exhausting job that paid a minimal salary; she made alterations and had to handle a large commercial steam press as well. On this particular day, she finished work and walked a few blocks as usual to the bus stop. The first bus on her route was so crowded she realized that there would be no place left to sit, and she desperately needed to get off her feet. She decided to wait for a less crowded bus. That gave her a little time to waste, so Parks walked over to a nearby drugstore to look for a heating pad, which might help ease the pain in her sore muscles. Not finding anything to her liking, she returned to the bus stop. Eventually, a bus arrived that had a fair number of seats available. She paid her ten cents, boarded the bus, and took a seat in the rear, or black, section of the bus, near the dividing line between the white and black sections. On Montgomery's public buses, the first ten rows were for white people, the last twenty-six for blacks. In many cities in the South, the line dividing sections on buses was fixed. This was not true in Montgomery; by custom, the driver had the power, if need be, to expand the white section and shrink the black section by ordering blacks to give up their seats to whites. First come, first served might have been the rule of public transportation in most of America, but it was not true in Montgomery, Alabama, in 1955. To the blacks, it was just one additional humiliation to be suffered—because the system did not even guarantee the minimal courtesies and rights of traditional segregation.

Three other blacks boarded the bus and sat next to Mrs. Parks in the same row. Parks had already recognized the driver as one of the meaner-spirited white men who worked for the bus line. He had once evicted her from his bus because she had refused, on paying her fare, to leave the bus and reenter the black section from the rear door—another quaint custom inflicted on black Montgomery bus riders. Gradually, as the bus continued on its rounds more whites got on. Finally, with the white section filled, a white man boarded. The driver, J. F. Blake, turned to look behind him at the first row of blacks and said, "You let him have those front seats." That was not a suggestion, it was an order. It meant that not only did one seat have to be freed, but the other three blacks would have to move as well, lest the white man have to sit next to a black. All four blacks knew what Blake meant, but no one moved. Blake looked behind him again and added, "You all better make it light on yourselves and let me have those seats." The three other blacks reluctantly got up and moved toward the back. Rosa Parks did not. She was frightened, but she was tired. She did not want to give up her seat, and she most certainly did not want to stand up the rest of the way. She had just spent her entire day working in a department store tailoring and pressing clothes for white people and now she was being told that she had no rights.

"Look, woman, I told you I wanted the seat. Are you going to stand up?" Blake said. Finally, Rosa Parks spoke. "No," she said. "If you don't stand up, I'm going to have you arrested," Blake warned her. She told him to go right ahead, but she was not going to move.

Blake got off the bus and went to phone the police, thereby involuntarily entering the nation's history books; his was the most ordinary example of a Southern white man fending off any threat to the system of segregation. If it had not been Blake, it would have been someone else. Some of the black riders, sensing trouble, or possibly irritated by the delay, started getting off the bus.

Parks continued to sit. In so doing she became the first prominent figure of what became the Movement. Perhaps the most interesting thing about her was how ordinary she was, at least on the surface, almost the prototype of the black women who toiled so hard and had so little to show for it. She had not, she later explained, thought about getting arrested that day. Later, the stunned white leaders of Montgomery repeatedly charged that Parks's refusal was part of a carefully orchestrated plan on the part of the local NAACP, of which she was an officer. But that was not true; what she did represented one person's exhaustion with a system that dehumanized all black people. Something inside her finally snapped. But if she had not planned to resist on that particular day, then it was also true that Rosa Parks had decided some time earlier that if she was ever asked to give up her seat for a white person, she would refuse to do so.

Rosa Parks was often described in newspaper reports as merely a seamstress, but she was more than that; she was a person of unusual dignity and uncommon strength of character. She was born in rural Alabama in 1913 (she was forty-two at the time of her famed ride). Her father was a carpenter, and her mother taught school for a time. The family moved to Montgomery county when she was a girl, and while educational opportunities for young black girls in those years in Alabama were virtually nonexistent, she had the good luck to go to a special school for black girls, called the Montgomery Industrial School for Girls (also known as Miss White's). There, New England schoolmarms, not unlike missionaries to foreign countries, taught young black girls who were barely literate the fundamentals of a primary education, as well as how to cook, sew, and run a home. Rosa was a serious reader, a quiet, strong woman much admired in the local community. She was an early member of the local chapter of the NAACP, eventually becoming secretary. She went to work for Clifford and Virginia Durr, a liberal couple in Montgomery (he was a former FCC commissioner in the Truman administration who left because he disagreed with its security process; Mrs. Durr was a formidable activist who frequently defied local racial mores).

Rosa Parks's relationship with the Durrs showed the complexity of human relationships in the South, for she was both employee and friend. The Durrs were friends of Ed Nixon, one of the most militant blacks of his generation, and Virginia Durr once asked Nixon, the head of the local NAACP, if he knew of anyone who "did good sewing." (She had three daughters, so a good deal of raising and lowering of hems went on in her home.) Yes, he said, and mentioned his fellow officer in the NAACP chapter. Soon Rosa Parks started to sew for the Durrs. The two women became good friends, and their friendship defied Southern custom. There was a certain formality to the way they addressed each other; they could not, after all, be Virginia and Rosa—since Rosa Parks was not allowed to call Mrs. Durr Virginia, then Virginia Durr could not in turn call her Rosa. That meant the seamstress was always Mrs. Parks and the employer was always Mrs. Durr. (Once, Virginia Durr turned to her friend Ed Nixon and casually called him Ed, but he cautioned her: Since he could not yet call her Virginia, she would have to call him Mr. Nixon.) But Virginia Durr helped Parks attend the integrated Highlander Folk School, in Monteagle, Tennessee, a school loathed by segregationists because it held workshops on how to promote integration. At Highlander she not only studied the techniques of passive resistance employed by Gandhi against the British, she also met whites who treated her with respect. The experience reinforced her sense of self-esteem, and set the stage for the bus confrontation.

As the bus driver continued to shout at her, Parks thought to herself, how odd it was that you go through life making things comfortable for white people yet they don't even treat you like a human being. There was something inevitable about this confrontation—a collision of rising black expectations with growing white resistance. At that moment in Montgomery, as in most deep South cities, school integration was still an abstract concept, something that had not yet happened and was not near happening. By contrast, riding a bus was the flashpoint, the center of daily, bitterly resented abuse.

Soon two Montgomery policemen arrived. Was it true that the driver had asked her to get up? they asked. Yes, she said. Why hadn't she obeyed? She felt she shouldn't have to. "Why do you push us around?" she asked. "I don't know, but the law is the law, and you're under arrest," one of the policemen said. Only then did she get up. The police escorted her to the patrol car. The police went back to talk to Blake. Did he want to press charges? Yes, he answered. The police took Parks to jail, where she was fingerprinted and charged with violating the city's segregation laws. She was allowed one phone call, and she called her home. Her mother answered and asked instinctively, "Did they beat you?" No, she said, she was physically all right. She was the first person ever so charged—the first of many tactical mistakes on the part of city officials, for it gave the local black community what it had been seeking: the case on which to hang a lawsuit.

After her phone call home, the news of her arrest spread quickly through the black community. E. D. Nixon, Parks's friend, called the police station to find out what had happened. Nixon was a Pullman car porter, a union man, and a powerful presence in the black community. For some twenty years he had been a black leader and activist in a town that despised the idea of racial change, and he became, in the process, absolutely fearless. There might be some blacks who did not like him, but everyone respected him, including some of the white leadership. For more than a decade, he had engaged in one of the most dangerous tasks of all—trying to register blacks to vote. On occasion, he did it carrying a shotgun under his coat. When Nixon called the police station to inquire about Rosa Parks, he was told it was none of his business. So he telephoned Clifford Durr, who said he would post bond. Nixon was not displeased by what had happened: This was the case he had been looking for. Mrs. Parks was the perfect defendant: She had worked with him in the NAACP for twelve years, and he knew she was a strong, confident person. If she said she was going to do something, she did it, and no amount of pressure from the white community would deter her. Her example would most likely give strength to others nervous about challenging the white establishment.

That night Parks, her family, the Durrs, and Ed Nixon sat around to discuss the details of her case. Nixon badly wanted to use it to test the constitutionality of the bus law. Would she agree, he asked, to be a test case? The idea frightened Raymond Parks, her husband, a local barber who knew the violence that traditionally awaited those blacks foolhardy enough to challenge the system. He warned her, "Oh, the white folks will kill you, Rosa. Don't do anything to make trouble, Rosa. Don't bring a suit. The whites will kill you." She was torn. She did not want to put her family at risk, but neither did she want herself or the younger black people who came after her to face such indignities. Nor did she want to face them anymore herself. "If you think we can get anywhere with it, I'll go along with it," she told Nixon.

Nixon went home and sketched a map of Montgomery—where blacks lived and where they worked. The distances were not, he decided, insurmountable. "You know what?" he told his wife.

"What?" she asked.

"We're going to boycott the buses," he said.

"Cold as it is?" she answered skeptically.

"Yes," he said.

"I doubt it," she said.

"Well, I'll tell you one thing: If you keep 'em off when it's cold, you won't have no trouble keeping 'em off when it gets hot," he said.

In Montgomery the majority of bus riders were black, particularly black women who went across town, from a world of black poverty to white affluence, to work as domestics. Nevertheless, a black challenge to the bus company was a formidable undertaking. Despite the earlier ruling of the Supreme Court, the deep South remained totally segregated. Whites held complete political, judicial, and psychological power. In a city like Montgomery it was as if the Court had not ruled on Brown.

Before the whites would take the blacks seriously, the blacks had to take themselves seriously—that was the task facing the black leadership of Montgomery in December 1955. The previous minister at the Dexter Avenue Baptist Church (a church that would be made famous by its young minister, Martin Luther King, Jr.) had been a forceful, articulate man named Vernon Johns. Some five years earlier, the Rev. Johns had endured a similar incident on a bus: He had misplaced his dime while trying to put it in the fare box, and the coin had dropped to the floor. Though it was an easy matter for the driver to retrieve it himself, he had ordered Johns to pick it up, in language that smacked of the plantation: "Uncle, get down and pick up that dime and put it in the box." Johns refused and asked the driver to do it. The driver again ordered him to pick it up, or he would be put off the bus. Johns turned to the other passengers, all of whom were black, and said he was leaving and asked them all to join him. No one moved. A week later he saw one of his parishioners, who had witnessed the incident and done nothing. Before he could reproach her, she told him, "You ought to knowed better." When he told the story to his close friend and fellow minister, the Rev. Ralph Abernathy, Johns had shaken his head, more, Abernathy thought, in sorrow than anger. "Even God can't free people who behave like that," the Rev. Johns had said. With that the Rev. Johns vowed never to ride the bus again and he bought a car.

For many blacks, the bus line symbolized their powerlessness: Men were powerless to protect their wives and mothers from its indignities; women were powerless to protect their children. The Montgomery bus system, with its flexible segregation line, vested all authority in the bus driver himself, which, depending on his personality and mood, allowed humiliation to be heaped upon humiliation. There were, for instance, bus drivers who took a black customer's money and then, while the customer was walking around to enter through the back door, would roar off.

The white officials of Montgomery had decided not only to resist integration in the years after the war but not even to listen to legitimate grievances from the black community. With every challenge to white authority, the city officials simply hunkered down and blamed outside agitators. Attempts on the part of black leaders to register more voters had failed, and there were estimates by the Justice Department after an investigation of Montgomery county's voting procedures that as many as ten thousand blacks had been denied their political rights over a period of years. In the summer of 1954, a few months after the *Brown* decision, an older activist black minister named Solomon Seay took a group of black children to Lee High School to register them in the all-white school and was turned away. He subsequently went before the all-white Alabama board of education and, in words that had a biblical ring to them, protested that changes were surely coming. "There is going to be a second day of judgment," the Rev. Seay warned, "and a worst day of judgment, if we don't all do what we can peacefully. . . . There are ways in which integration can be worked out in a peaceful process, and if we don't find these ways, then we will be punished. Let me emphasize I am not threatening you, just prophesizing."

Yet the most visceral anger of Montgomery blacks was reserved for the bus system. Four days after the Supreme Court had ruled on *Brown,* a black leader named Jo Ann Robinson wrote a letter to Montgomery's mayor telling him of the growing resentment blacks felt about their treatment on the buses, reminding him that more than three quarters of the system's riders were blacks and mentioning the possibility of a boycott. For Mrs. Robinson, a professor at Alabama State, a black college in Montgomery, the issue was particularly emotional. In 1949 she had boarded a bus to take her to the airport. It was near Christmas, and her arms were filled with the packages from holiday shopping. She was on her way home to Cleveland. She had gotten on the nearly empty bus, and, without thinking, sat down in the white section. Suddenly, the white bus driver appeared, his arm drawn back as if to hit her, and shouted, "Get up from there! Get up from there!" "I felt," she later said, "like a dog." She stumbled off the bus, and, in her own words, completed the trip to Cleveland largely in tears. But later, as she replayed the events in her mind, she became angrier and angrier; she was a human being too and, if anything, a better educated one than the driver. What right did any human have to treat another this way? When she returned to Montgomery after her vacation, she mentioned the incident to some of her friends, hoping to start some kind of protest. She was surprised by their lack of response: They assured her that this was life in Montgomery, Alabama. Not forever, she thought. Six years later, at the time of Rosa Parks's protest, Mrs. Robinson had become president of the Women's Political Council, an organization of black professional women. Her group had only recently won a major victory, entitling black customers to have the titles Mr., Mrs., or Miss used with their names when they received their bills from downtown white merchants.

The bus issue became the most pressing one for Mrs. Robinson's group. A few months before Rosa Parks made her stand, a fifteen-year-old black girl had refused to give up her seat to a white and had been dragged from the bus ("She insisted she was colored and just as good as white," T. J. Ward, the arresting policeman, had noted with some surprise during the local court proceedings on her arrest). She had been charged with assault and battery for resisting arrest. For a time the black leadership thought of making hers the constitutional test case it sought, but backed off when someone learned that she was pregnant. So when Rosa Parks was arrested, the obvious response was a boycott. This was the blacks' strongest lever: They were the biggest group of riders, and without them it was not going to be a very profitable bus service.

One of their great problems was the terrible divisions within the black leadership itself—by religion, by generation, by age, by class. There was no doubt that Ed Nixon was a forceful figure, willing on many occasions to take risks that few others would; but some felt that he was too abrasive, too eager for glory, and not sensitive enough to others. At the first organizational meeting, held the day after Parks was arrested, there was quick agreement on the need for a one-day boycott, starting on Monday morning. There was also a decision to hold a meeting of the black leadership, which included many ministers, on Monday afternoon, and a large public protest meeting was set for Monday night. At the Monday afternoon meeting, one of the ministers suggested that future meetings be secret, closed to the press, so that the whites would know as little as possible about what they were doing and who their leaders were. Meetings closed to the press! Ed Nixon got up and began to taunt them. "How in hell are you going to have protest meetings without letting the white folks know?" he began. Then he reminded them that those being hurt were the black women of the city, the most powerless of the powerless, the domestics who went off every day to work for whites. These were the people who suffered the greatest pain from segregation and made up the core of every black church in town. "Let me tell you gentlemen one thing. You ministers have lived off the sweat of these washwomen all these years and you have never done anything for them," he said. His contempt seemed to fill the church. "I am just ashamed of you. You said that God has called you to lead the people and now you are just afraid and gone to pieces because the man tells you that the newspapers will be here and your picture might come out in the newspaper. Somebody has got to get hurt in this thing and if you the preachers are not the leaders then we will have to pray that God will send us more leaders." That stunning assault contained all too much truth. It was a young minister named Martin Luther King, Jr., who answered Nixon and said that he was not a coward, that they should act in the open, use their own names, and not hide behind anyone else. With that, the Rev. King had at once taken a strong position for the boycott, but he had also shown he was not completely Nixon's man. Before the meeting was over, Martin Luther King, Jr., was named president of the new group, to be called the Montgomery Improvement Association (MIA). It was not a role he sought, but he was the obvious choice—in no small part because he was relatively new on the scene and belonged to no faction of the city's black leadership. There were other reasons as well: His congregation was unusually affluent and therefore less vulnerable to white reprisals. Finally, a number of people did not want Nixon to be the leader, yet King got on relatively well with Nixon, who had heard King speak earlier that year at an NAACP meeting and had been impressed. "I don't know how I'm going to do it," Nixon told a friend of his who taught at Alabama State, "but someday I'm going' to hitch him to the stars." King himself did not necessarily want to be hitched to the stars; he was wary of taking on too much responsibility and had only recently turned down an offer to head the local NAACP. After all, he was new in town, had a young family, and wanted first and foremost to do a good job at his first church.

But with a certain inevitability the movement sought him. He was a brilliant speaker. He had the ability to make complex ideas simple: By repeating phrases, he could expand an idea, blending the rational with the emotional. That gave him the great ability to move others, blacks at first and soon, remarkably enough, whites as well. He could reach people of all classes and backgrounds; he could inspire men and women with nothing but his words. On that first day, the Holt Street Baptist Church was filled by late afternoon, and a crowd estimated at between six and ten thousand gathered in the street to hear the meeting broadcast over loudspeakers. The white police watched the crowd gather with increasing nervousness, and the officer in charge finally ordered the organizers to turn off the public address system, hoping thereby to disperse the crowd. One of the black organizers answered that if the police wanted the PA system off, they could do it themselves. The cops, looking at the size of the crowd, decided to let them have their PA broadcast after all.

That night, most of the black people of Montgomery got their first taste of Martin King's oratory. He started out by making one point clear: Their boycott was different from those of the White Citizens' Councils, which were using the threat of violence to stop black political and legal progress in the deep South. "Now, let us say that we are not here advocating violence. We have overcome that. I want it to be known throughout Montgomery and throughout the nation that we are a Christian people. The only weapon that we have in our hands this evening is the weapon of protest." They were nothing less than ordinary Americans, he was saying, seeking the most ordinary of American rights in a democracy they loved as much as white people loved it. They were, in effect, setting out to make America whole. "If we are wrong, the Constitution of the United States is wrong. If we are wrong, God Almighty is wrong. If we are wrong, Jesus of Nazareth was merely a utopian dreamer and never came down to earth! If we are wrong, justice is a lie." By then the crowd was with him, cheering each incantation. "And we are determined here in Montgomery to work and fight until justice runs down like water and righteousness like a mighty stream." When it was over, it was clear that the right man had arrived in the right city at the right time; this would be no one-day boycott but one that would continue until the white community addressed black grievances.

That the black ministry at this moment was to produce an exceptional generation of leaders—of whom King was merely the most visible—was not surprising. It was the obvious repository for black talent at that moment. In the past, black leadership had tended to be fragmented and poorly educated. (Five years before the bus boycott, at the time of the 1950 census, the city of Montgomery had had some 40,000 black citizens, including three doctors, one dentist, two lawyers, one pharmacist, and 92 preachers.) There were not a lot of black lawyers around in those days, and the usual political avenues were blocked in the Deep South. Therefore, the new black ministry was where talented young black men went to learn how to lead their people: It was outside the reach of the white community, a rare place where a young, well-educated black man could rise by merit alone.

When the bus boycott began, Martin Luther King, Jr., was twenty-six years old; he had been in Montgomery only fifteen months. He was a black Baptist Brahmin, a symbol of the new, more confident, better educated black leaders now just beginning to appear in the postwar South. His maternal grandfather, A. D. Williams, had formally founded the Ebenezer Baptist Church in 1894, its eighth year of existence, and made it one of the most important black churches in Atlanta. The Rev. Williams had been a charter member of the local NAACP. When a local white newspaper criticized Atlanta's blacks as being "dirty and ignorant," he led the boycott that helped close the newspaper down. When an important school-bond issue failed to include any money for the city's first black high school, he started rallies, which resulted in the building of Booker T. Washington High. His son-in-law, Martin Luther King, Sr. (known as "Daddy" King), had led a voter-registration drive as a young minister in Atlanta and pushed the other black ministers to make their churches centers for voter-registration drives in the thirties, a move opposed by many on his board. But one thousand blacks had showed up at Ebenezer and marched to the city hall. Such activism made Atlanta, by the fifties, one of the great centers of black middle-class life, a place where black economic power had made black political power possible.

Daddy King was one of nine children of sharecroppers. As a boy he watched the vicious cycle of poverty and powerlessness destroy his father, who turned to alcohol and wife beating. Delia King farmed alongside her husband and worked in the home of the white owners. When Daddy King (whose real name was Michael and who changed his name to Martin as a man) was twelve, he accompanied his father to town when the annual accounts were being settled up. The little boy, a good student and better at numbers than his father, was aware that his father was being swindled. "Ask him about the cotton seed money, Daddy," he said, for that was an important part of the equation, and the tenant farmer got the money. The landowner was furious, but in the end he paid; but he did not forget the incident or forgive the little boy. The next day he had arrived to tell the elder King that he had to leave his land altogether. With that James King started coming apart. Beaten down by the harshness and cruelty of the system, he took his anger out on his family, particularly his wife and this son whose moment of truth had caused him even greater humiliation and revealed his true powerlessness.

Watching the disintegration of his family, Mike King could not wait to leave. He and his father had a violent fight once after his father had beaten his mother. The youth, already powerfully built, won the fight, but he heard his father shout, "I'll kill you, kill you, I'll do it, damn you . . ." Terrified, his mother told her son to hide out for a time. "A man's anger gets the best of him," Daddy King wrote, describing the scene some seven decades later. "Violence is the only thing he's got to calm him down some, or get him killed, one day."

The only place young Mike King decided he could find any kind of peace was in the church. He would feel, he wrote later, bitterness and anger descend upon him at other times of the day, but not when he was in church. He became a licensed minister at fifteen, traveling and preaching in small rural churches. At eighteen he went to Atlanta. There, he was regarded as a hick, bright but unlettered. He wanted badly to be somebody, yet he felt the awful shame of his rural ignorance, his rustic language.

He was nothing if not ambitious, though. Encouraged by an older sister, he went back to school at the age of twenty-one. He was assigned to the fifth grade, which completely shattered his confidence; never had he felt so ignorant before. But he persevered: He spent five years at the school, always working full-time as a driver for a man who sold and repaired barber-shop chairs, and taking his books with him wherever he went and, of course, preaching on weekends. Finally, he received his high school degree. During this time he saw Alberta Williams, the daughter of one of Atlanta's foremost ministers. She was, he thought, everything he was not: sophisticated, educated, genteel. He immediately fell in love with her. When he told this to some friends who were also country boys, they teased him unmercifully. "Now, King," one of them said. "You know God doesn't love ugly and that's about the worst-looking story I've heard all year—you marrying Alberta Williams. Get on away from here!" But King pursued her relentlessly. For his first date he took his best pair of pants, put them between two boards, and then put the boards under his mattress for a few days in order to ensure a crease. He asked the lady who ran the boardinghouse to iron his best shirt. "Why, Reverend King, you must be fixin' to court some nice young lady," she had said. "No, ma'am," he answered. "I'm fixin' to get married."

Their courtship lasted six years. Driven by the need to be worthy of Alberta, he had decided to enter Morehouse and get a college degree. He was twenty-seven, and the officials at Morehouse were not enthusiastic. He took their tests. "You're just not college material," the registrar told him. He told them he didn't care how poorly he tested—he *knew* he could succeed, if it was a matter of hard work. Nonetheless, they rejected him. Pushed by Alberta, he tried again and was rejected again. Finally, he begged for a trial period as a student and was rejected again. In a rage, he charged into the office of the president of the college and told his story. Then he stomped out. But because of his assertiveness, he was at last given a chance. "Apparently," said the unsympathetic registrar, "you can begin classes at Morehouse. Don't ask me why, but you can . . ." By going to summer school, he managed to get his degree in four years. A year later, his father-in-law died of a heart attack and Mike King took over the Ebenezer Baptist Church.

Martin Luther King, Jr., the second of three children, grew up in an environment far gentler than the one his father had known. He was a member of the black elite of Atlanta, perhaps not as wealthy as some, but even that in time might change, for Daddy King planned to have Martin marry a daughter of one of Atlanta's truly wealthy Atlanta families and come back home to Ebenezer and work with him. Then the Kings would presumably become *the* leading black family of Atlanta, the heiress's money attached now to the powerful social-political position that Daddy King had created at Ebenezer. Young Martin lived the odd duality of a black prince: He at once was exceptionally privileged within the black world yet virtually everything outside it was denied him. There were, for all the attempts to protect him, humiliations that occurred as he crossed over to the alien environment of white Atlanta, where he, like all other blacks, lost all status.

Though his birth had coincided with the coming of the Depression, which hit black Southerners hardest, the King family knew little deprivation. A black church as prosperous as Ebenezer was immune to the vagaries of national economics. Martin King remembered driving through Atlanta and seeing the long lines of black people waiting to buy bread as his parents tried to explain the harsh reality of the Depression to him. Martin King, Jr., grew up loved and secure; years later James Baldwin wrote that King lacked the self-doubts that burdened most blacks of their generation. "Martin," Baldwin wrote, "never went around fighting himself the way the rest of us did." He grew up with segregation, yet he saw his father's strength in the face of prejudice: Once when he was driving with his father, an Atlanta policeman stopped the car. "All right, boy," he had said. "Pull over and let me see your license." "I'm no boy," Daddy King said. He pointed at his son. "This is a boy. I'm a man and until you call me one I will not listen to you."

As a father Martin King, Sr., was unsparing. He beat his children for relatively minor infractions. (The father was surprised by the stoic quality of young Martin: "He was the most peculiar child whenever you whipped him. He'd stand there and the tears would run down and he'd never cry out.") He was a powerful preacher of the old school, all hellfire and brimstone. The Bible for him was a book of literal truths and stories that were not to be challenged, or to be interpreted to fit modern circumstances. He was uneasy when his son drank and danced as a young seminarian and ventured increasingly into the world of social gospel, which Daddy King thought at heart a world of leftists, which, if it threatened the white order, might threaten as well the existing black hierarchy in which he had so handsomely succeeded.

Martin Luther King, Jr.'s, earliest rebellion was not against his father's house rules but against his fundamentalist teachings. As a boy he shocked his Sunday School teacher by questioning the bodily resurrection of Christ; he was clearly embarrassed by the raw emotion of his father's preaching—the shouting, stomping, and wailing. It was only at Morehouse that more sophisticated men showed him the ministry could be socially valuable, intellectually respectable. At Morehouse, he would later note, "the shackles of fundamentalism were removed from my body."

Unlike his father, young Martin had been raised with choices in life—which schools he could go to and which profession he might choose. His was a world with far greater possibilities than the world of his father: Upon graduation from Morehouse in 1948 he had pondered a career at divinity school or a career at law school and finally chose the former, going to Crozer Seminary, in Chester, Pennsylvania. He was the first member of his family to be educated outside the South. Martin King did well at Crozer, extending himself intellectually for the first time, so much so that several members of the faculty encouraged him to go on with his studies. But Daddy King felt that seven years of higher education was enough. It was time to come back and help out at Ebenezer. Martin never said no to his father, but he accepted a fellowship at Boston University to get his Ph.D.

In Boston, as at Crozer, King was determined to undo the white stereotypes of blacks. Were blacks supposed to be careless about time? Martin King was the most punctual young man on campus, never late to class. Were blacks supposed to be noisy and loud? King was always sedate and respectful. Were they supposed to be a little flashy about clothes? King dressed as seriously and carefully as anyone on campus—always in a suit—and his clothes were *always* pressed, his shoes shined.

Boston, a great college town, was a delight for him socially; he was a leader among the young upper-class blacks in Boston in the early fifties, with his handsome wardrobe and his new Chevy, a gift from his father. He was, for all his theological studies, something of a young man about town, a great dancer, and very much on the lookout for the best-looking women. He was soon known in the small world of Boston black academia, Coretta Scott King later noted, as "the most eligible young black man in the Boston area at that time." The first time he called Coretta Scott, at a friend's suggestion, he talked a smooth line: "Every Napoleon has his Waterloo. I'm like Napoleon. I'm at my Waterloo and I'm on my knees." Jive, she thought, but different than most jive, because it was "intellectual jive." Meeting him on a blind date, she thought him too short. It was only as he began to talk that she got interested. After their first date, he took her home and virtually proposed to her. He demanded, he told her, four qualifications in the woman he was going to marry: character, intelligence, personality, and beauty. She had all four. Could he see her again? he asked. She would, though with some reluctance, for she had her own career as a singer and she was not thrilled by the idea of being the wife of a young minister. But gradually they became more serious, despite her doubts and despite Daddy King's attempts to get her out of the picture in favor of a wealthy young black Atlanta heiress from, he said, "a fine family . . . very talented . . . wonderful personality. We love that girl."

Intellectually, it was an exciting time for him; he was seeking a gospel that would fit the needs of a modern black minister working in the American South. He wanted to escape the raw fundamentalism he knew was so much a part of the existing black church. Instead, King sought a Christianity that allowed him to love his fellow man and yet to protest the abundant inhumanities and injustices being inflicted on blacks. He studied Marxism diligently and found it formidable as a critique of capitalism but empty as theology—shamelessly materialistic in its antimaterialism, unloving and, finally, totalitarian. But he was impressed by the writings of Walter Rauschenbusch, a turn-of-the-century social critic who had blamed society's ills on the raw, unchecked capitalism of his time. He was also im-

pressed by Reinhold Niebuhr and, more and more, by the teachings
of Gandhi. Gandhi had had not merely the ability to lead but also
to love, and to conquer inner darkness and rage. He felt that Niebuhr
had misunderstood Gandhi's notion of passive resistance. It was not,
King wrote, nonresistance to evil but rather nonviolent resistance to
evil. He was slowly finding a vision to fit the needs of his people and
with which he was comfortable enough to devote his professional
career. The faculty was impressed by him and encouraged him to
become an academic. For a time he considered that: The life was
pleasant and sheltered, and a young man could escape the ugly
segregation of the South. But his obligations were real and immediate. The closer he came to finishing, the clearer his path became: He
wanted a large Baptist church in the South. "That's where I'm
needed," he told Coretta. They were married in 1953. Daddy King
backed down from his opposition and advised Coretta of her good
fortune. "You will not be marrying any ordinary young minister," he
told her.

Martin King, Jr., began looking over several churches. One in
Chattanooga was interested in him, as was the Dexter Avenue Baptist Church in Montgomery. The Dexter Avenue offer intrigued him.
It was a famous church, built in the days of Reconstruction, in the
center of town, right across from the Alabama Supreme Court and
diagonally across from the state capitol. Many of its parishioners
were college-educated; they were the black Baptist elite of the city.
His father warned him about them: The Dexter congregation was
highly political, snobbish, and they had a reputation for devouring
their pastors. They did not like a lot of whooping and hollering in
their sermons. "At First Baptist," Vernon Johns acidly told the Rev.
Ralph Abernathy, "they don't mind the preacher talking about
Jesus, though they would never stoop so low as to talk about Him
themselves. At Dexter Avenue they would prefer that you not mention his name." King went to Montgomery and gave a guest sermon.
Slightly nervous, he reminded himself, "Keep Martin Luther King in
the background and God in the foreground and everything will be all
right. Remember you're a channel of the gospel, not a source." The
Montgomery people were so impressed they offered him their pulpit
at $4,200 a year, which would make him the best-paid black minister
in town. Coretta King had no great desire to return to Montgomery,
which was only eighty miles from Moraine, Alabama, where she had
grown up. She had seen the North and the South and her preference
was for the North. But Martin believed that the South was where his
future should be, so to Montgomery they went.

To the white leadership in Montgomery, Martin King was just another faceless preacher, surely ignorant. The popular caricature of a black minister was of a whooper and hollerer. Indeed, the whites kept calling him Preacher King at the beginning of the boycott, as if by denying him his proper title they could diminish him. He fought against such stereotyping with careful formality. One of the first local reporters to meet him, Tom Johnson of the *Montgomery Advertiser*, found him self-conscious, almost to the point of pomposity. He answered questions with references to Nietzsche and Kant. Johnson was amused when, in the middle of their long interview, an old friend of King's from Atlanta arrived and King broke effortlessly into what Johnson considered a kind of jive talk; then he switched back to his formal lecture again without breaking stride.

As in his university days, he was always well dressed, in a dark suit, a white shirt, and a conservative tie. "I don't want to look like an undertaker," he once said, describing his undertakerlike wardrobe, "but I do believe in conservative dress." As the bus boycott began, he would get up at 5:30 A.M. to work for three hours on his doctoral thesis and then join Coretta for breakfast before going off to his pastoral duties. (Critical parts of his thesis, it would turn out, were plagiarized, a reminder, like his womanizing, of the flaws in even the most exceptional of men.) From the start he became extremely close to the Rev. Ralph Abernathy, a far earthier figure. Like King, Abernathy was anxious to break with the narrowness of the preachers of the past. "They preached the gospel of 'otherworldliness,' of a better time in the sweet by and by," Abernathy later wrote. "Their ultimate solution to Jim Crow was death—when you died you were equal in the eyes of God. For such people the idea of desegregation was either frivolous or else threatening." Abernathy helped him overcome a tendency toward snobbishness. King was better educated and able to articulate a broad social vision; Abernathy was comfortable with a wide range of people.

The white community had no idea how to deal with the boycott. The city leadership thought it was dealing with the black leadership from the past—poorly educated, readily divided, lacking endurance, and without access to national publicity outlets. When the boycott proved to be remarkably successful on the first day, the mayor of Montgomery, W. A. Gayle, did not sense that something historic was taking place, nor did he move to accommodate the blacks, who were in fact not asking for integrated buses but merely a minimal level of courtesy and a fixed line between the sections. Gayle turned to a friend and said, "Comes the first rainy day and the Negroes will be back on the buses." Soon it did rain, but the boycott continued. As the movement grew stronger, the principal response of Gayle and his two commissioners was to join the White Citizens' Council. A month after the boycott began, it proved so successful that the bus-line operators were asking for permission to double the price from ten to twenty cents a ride. They were granted a five-cent raise. In late January, frustrated by the solidarity of the blacks, the white leadership went to three relatively obscure black ministers and tricked them into saying, or at least seeming to say, that they accepted the city's terms and would show up at a meeting at city hall. Then the *Montgomery Advertiser* was brought in—a disgraceful moment for a newspaper—to report on the alleged agreement and make it seem, without using the names of the three ministers, that the real black leadership had conceded. By chance the real black leadership found out, and the ploy was not successful. But it was a sign of how terrified and out of touch the white leadership was—as if it could, by means of disinformation, halt a movement as powerful as this. When the hoax was discovered, the mayor was petulant. No more Mr. Nice Guy, he threatened. "No other city in the South of our size has treated the Negroes more fairly," he said. Now he wanted his fellow whites to be made of sterner stuff and to stop helping their maids and workers to get to work by giving them transportation money and, worse, giving them rides. "The Negroes," he said, "are laughing at white people behind their backs. They think it is funny and amusing that whites who are opposed to the Negro boycott will act as chauffeurs to Negroes who are boycotting the buses."

The Montgomery authorities stopped the local black cabdrivers from ferrying people to and from work in groups of five and six for ten cents a ride (there was an old city ordinance that said the minimum fare for a ride had to be 45 cents), but money poured in from the outside to buy some fifteen new station wagons. Eventually, the MIA had some thirty cars of its own. Richard Harris, a local black pharmacist who was a crucial dispatcher in the downtown area, feared that his phone was tapped, so he spoke in comic black dialect to confuse the white authorities, and he used a code with other dispatchers—"shootin' marbles," for example, told how many people needed to be picked up.

Inevitably, the city leaders resorted to what had always worked in the past: the use of police power. The city fathers decided that it had to break the back of the carpool, and soon the police started arresting carpool drivers. On January 26, 1956, some eight weeks into the boycott, Martin Luther King, Jr., was arrested for driving 30 miles an hour in a 25-mile-an-hour zone. He was taken to the police station and fingerprinted; at first it appeared that he would be kept overnight, but because the crowd of blacks outside the station kept growing larger and noisier, the police let King go on his own recognizance. Two days later, King's house was bombed by a white extremist, the first in a series of such incidents at the homes of black leaders and at black churches.

In unity and nonviolence the blacks found new strength, particularly as the nation began to take notice. Things that had for so long terrified them—the idea of being arrested and spending the night in prison, for example—became a badge of honor. Their purpose now was greater than their terror. More, because the nation was watching, the jails were becoming safer. King was, in effect, taking a crash course in the uses of modern media and proving a fast learner. Montgomery was becoming a big story, and the longer it went on, the bigger it became. In the past it had been within the power of such papers as the *Advertiser* and its afternoon twin, the far more racist *Alabama Journal,* either to grant or not grant coverage to black protests and to slant the coverage in terms most satisfying to the whites. The power to deny coverage was a particularly important aspect of white authority, for if coverage was denied, the blacks would feel isolated and gradually lose heart (for taking such risks without anyone knowing or caring); in addition, the whites would be able to crush any protest with far fewer witnesses and far less scrutiny. But that power deserted the local newspapers now, in no small part because the Montgomery story was too important for even the most virulently segregationist newspaper to ignore completely, affecting as it did virtually every home in the city; second, because even when the local newspapers tried to control the coverage, and at the very least minimize it, the arrival of television meant that the newspapers were no longer the only potential journalistic witnesses.

The editor of the *Advertiser* was Grover Cleveland Hall, Jr., a seeming moderate, then in his mid-thirties. He was on the board of directors of the American Civil Liberties Union, a position which, with the pressure of events, he was soon to resign. Hall bore a famous name in Southern journalism: In the twenties, his father had won a Pulitzer Prize for covering the Ku Klux Klan. Grover Hall was a charming, witty man, much given to white suits, straw hats, and suspenders. He often wore a flower in his lapel, if at all possible a rose from his own prized collection. His foppish dress, arch manner, and flowery mode of speech and writing seemed calculated to recall another, more genteel, era. Visiting reporters were often much taken with him—"an almost perfect cross between Mark Twain and H. L. Mencken," said Karl Fleming, who covered the region for *Newsweek* and who took considerable pleasure in Hall's company.

He wrote archly, with a wicked bite, and little tolerance for fools. He seemed well suited for this particular city as he might so readily have been out of place in the harder, edgier Birmingham. Though on occasion he liked to mock many of his contemporaries in the local establishment, finding that they were not quite worthy of the standards he set, he was very much a member of the country-club set himself. If anything, he seemed to see himself as the voice of a city, which he believed enlightened and gracious; he regarded himself as the journalistic embodiment not only of the city, but of a region and of an age, and he once wrote of Montgomery, "We love our city here in the bend of a yellow river. We venerate its famous past. We cherish the style and the individuality of the present. And we trust not vaingloriously, the city's sunburst future we take for granted, even though it may mean a bit of factory soot on the magnolia blossoms."

Prior to the bus boycott, Hall had been able to straddle the contradictions between the pre-industrial South he loved and the new South that was beginning to take shape. The kindest thing that could be said for the *Advertiser*'s coverage of the Movement was that it was erratic and ambivalent. Hall apparently met Martin King just once, largely by accident, when Hall had escorted Peter Kihss, of *The New York Times,* to King's church. The rise of King baffled him.

The last plantation intellectual, Fleming called Hall. The way he was reared, and the way he saw himself and his region, thought one associate, did not include a place for such proud, increasingly militant black leaders as the Rev. King. Grover Hall could understand what King was doing and, having met him, could appreciate his intelligence; but nonetheless the agenda King represented remained alien to him, and he could never bring himself to like Martin King. He spoke more and more scathingly of him in private. King was, in sum, a threat to everything Hall knew and believed in.

Even though initially Hall urged an acceptance of the first-come, first-served segregated seating arrangement that the black leadership sought, he was soon to find himself allied with people he had once scorned as the implications of what was happening in Montgomery grew and as the black protest became a *movement.* For the situation did not allow a man who would be a great Southern editor to sit on the sidelines: It demanded a certain moral reckoning, as the Rev. Seay had so recently prophesized.

From the start, the *Advertiser* had been weak on the crisis. The first story, by the city editor, Joe Azbell, was written as if merely to let the white community know what the blacks were up to. He had been tipped off by E. D. Nixon. The story ran on page one by mistake. The publisher, Richard Hudson, had called in to order the story be placed inside, but it was too late. That gaffe greatly helped the black leadership publicize the boycott at first. Hudson was furious, and for a brief time Azbell's job seemed to be on the line. Azbell later said that he caught more heat for that than anything else he had ever done, including putting the death of Hank Williams, the great country singer and songwriter, on the front page (death of so exceptional a man being considered less than page-one news by Hudson). Hall had not fired Azbell, but he made it clear that from then on, there was to be a great deal of caution in how the *Advertiser* reported the boycott. Caught at once between its responsibilities to inform and its fear that honest coverage might embolden an increasingly audacious black leadership, the paper tried to ignore the story as much as possible. Its first in-depth piece on the leaders of the boycott ran some six weeks into the crisis. Its lowest moment was the attempt to trick the black public. (Some seven years later, at the height of the civil rights movement, the *Advertiser* did not even have a reporter cover the great Selma-Montgomery march in which some 25,000 people marched toward the state capitol along with representatives from almost every major journalistic institution in the country. The *Advertiser* used an AP dispatch.)

But even though the two Montgomery papers were owned by the same company, they no longer had a monopoly on news. Just a year earlier, on Christmas Day 1954, WSFA-TV had gone on the air. There had been one other local channel, but it did no local programming. From the start, it was announced, there would be active local news and weather coverage—fifteen minutes of news, and fifteen minutes of weather each evening, something almost unheard of locally in those days. Indeed, there was said to be a hot new news director arriving from Oklahoma City. The news director (and star reporter as well, of course) was a young man named Frank McGee, then in his early thirties. He was, in fact, a very good reporter, and he immediately decided that the bus boycott was a very big story. Unlike his local print counterparts, he did not take the protest as a social affront. Rather, he realized it was the kind of high drama that lent itself exceptionally well to television. Nor was McGee, like his counterparts at the two Montgomery papers, part of the town's white power establishment. He had grown up very poor in northern Louisiana and then in Oklahoma, and he sympathized with all poor

people, white and black. He liked to joke that his father, who worked
the oil rigs, might have risen up out of some back country swamp,
"and you never know what color there might be in our family if you
went back far enough." In an age when most of the nation's top
journalists seemed to be the product of the nation's elite schools,
Frank McGee had never gone to college and had a high school
degree only because he finished a high-school equivalency course
while in the service. He was not a particularly ideological man, but
like most reporters of that era, he sympathized instinctively with the
blacks, whose demands were so rudimentary. He was well aware of
the dangers of covering the story, that the television journalists were
vulnerable to attack. But although there were constant threats, both
in the streets and over the phone, no one ever assaulted him. What
surprised him most, he later would say, was that the local station
managers never cramped his style, never told him what he could and
could not put on the air. Part of the reason, he suspected, was that
his bosses thought they needed all the excitement they could get in
those early days in order to compete with the local newspapers.
Besides, his bosses were too new to be part of the establishment.

Like many of his generation, he was aware that he was riding a
very good story. That was particularly true as the whites blindly
continued to resist and the story continued to escalate. The NBC
network news show, also still in its infancy, started to use McGee
with increasing regularity on the network, with a direct feed from
Montgomery. It was not only a good story, in which ordinary Americans were asserting their demands for the most basic rights, but it
was also helping McGee's career, which for a young, tough-minded,
ambitious reporter was almost an unbeatable combination. (Within
a year of the bus settlement, Frank McGee became one of NBC's
first national network correspondents.) Events were soon beyond the
ability of the *Advertiser* to control coverage. Montgomery was soon
flooded with members of the national press, causing Grover Hall to
comment that he was "duenna and Indian guide to more than a
hundred reporters of the international press." The more coverage
there was, the more witnesses there were and the harder it was for the
white leadership to inflict physical violence upon the blacks. In addition, the more coverage there was, the more it gave courage to the
leadership and its followers. The sacrifices and the risks were worth
it, everyone sensed, because the country and the world were now
taking notice. What was at stake in the *Advertiser*'s coverage of
Martin King and the Montgomery bus boycott was, the editors of
that paper soon learned to their surprise, not King's reputation but
the *Advertiser*'s reputation.

The national press corps that had coalesced for the first time at the Emmett Till trial only a few months earlier returned in full strength, and its sympathies were not with Mayor Gayle, who appointed a committee to meet with the black ministers and added a White Citizens' Council member to it, or with police commissioner Clyde Sellers, who publicly joined the Citizens' Council in the middle of the struggle, saying, "I wouldn't trade my Southern birthright for 100 Negro votes." Rather, the national reporters were impressed with the dignity of Rosa Parks, the seriousness of the young Martin King, and the shrewd charm of Ralph Abernathy.

Ironically, it was the white leaders of Montgomery who first helped to create the singular importance of Martin King. Convinced that ordinary black people were being tricked and manipulated, they needed a villain. If they could weaken, discredit, or scare him, then their problems would be solved, they thought. Gradually, he became the focal point of the boycott. "I have the feeling," Bayard Rustin, the nation's most experienced civil rights organizer, told him at the time, "that the Lord has laid his hands on you, and that is a dangerous, dangerous thing." Still, King had no illusions about his role: "If Martin Luther King had never been born this movement would have taken place," he said early on. "I just happened to be there. You know there comes a time when time itself is ready for a change. That time has come in Montgomery and I have nothing to do with it."

For a time the role was almost too much for him. The amount of hate mail was staggering, and it was filled with threats that he had to take seriously. His father pleaded with him to leave Montgomery and return to Atlanta. "It's better to be a live dog than a dead lion," Daddy King said. The pressure on King was such that he was getting little sleep, and he was truly afraid. He realized for the first time how sheltered his existence had been, how ill prepared he was to deal with the racial violence that was waiting just beneath the surface in the South. One night, unsure of whether to continue, he thought of all his religious training and he heard the voice of Christ: "Martin Luther, stand up for righteousness. Stand up for justice. Stand up for truth' . . . the fatigue had turned into hope." (That was, Grover Hall noted acidly, Martin King's "vision in the kitchen speech.")

The boycott continued. The white leadership was paralyzed; in late February, it cited an obscure state law prohibiting boycotts and indicted eighty-nine leaders, including twenty-four ministers and all the drivers of the carpools. The real target, however, was King. He happened to be in Nashville lecturing when the indictments were announced. Back in Montgomery, many of the other leaders were giving themselves up in groups to show their defiance. King flew back to Montgomery by way of Atlanta. In Atlanta, his father pleaded with him not to go back. "They gon' to kill my boy," he told the Atlanta police chief. He brought over some of Martin's oldest friends, including Benjamin Mays, the president of Morehouse, to help talk him out of returning. But Martin Luther King, Jr., was firm now. Not to return, to desert his friends at this point, would be the height of cowardice, he told them. "I have begun the struggle," he said, "and I can't turn back. I have reached the point of no return." At that point his father broke down and began to sob. Benjamin Mays told him he was doing the right thing, and he returned to Montgomery.

On November 13, 1956, almost a year after the boycott had begun, King went to court to defend himself and the carpools against the local authorities who had declared it "a public nuisance." King was hardly optimistic about the outcome in a Montgomery court, but suddenly, during a recess, an AP reporter handed him a note that included an AP bulletin reporting that the Supreme Court had judged the Montgomery bus-segregation law to be unconstitutional. The blacks had won. King, always aware of the need to include rather than exclude people and the need to be magnanimous in victory, spoke at a mass rally to point out this should not be viewed as victory of blacks over whites but as a victory for American justice and democracy. On December 21, the city prepared to desegregate its buses. An empty bus pulled up to a corner near Dr. King's home. Martin Luther King, Jr., boarded it. The white driver smiled at him and said, "I believe you are Reverend King." "Yes, I am," Martin Luther King, Jr., said. "We are glad to have you with us this morning," the driver said.

So the battle was won. But the war was hardly over. It was a beginning rather than an end; the boycott became the Movement, with a capital *M*. The blacks might have alienated the local white leadership, but they had gained the sympathy of the white majority outside the South. In the past the whites in Montgomery had been both judge and jury: Now, as the nation responded to the events there, they became the judged.

Grover Hall, a man of considerable abilities, became with the passage of time an ever sadder figure. He turned on the Movement and become more conservative. His humor became bitter, his manner a caricature of what it had once been. The peer esteem he valued so greatly inevitably dwindled as the nation's consciousness on race changed. He was replaced in 1963 as editor of the *Advertiser* when the paper changed hands. He went for a time to Virginia, where he replaced James Jackson Kilpatrick as chief editorial writer on the *Richmond News-Leader*. That job did not last long; he did not blend in as well in Richmond as he had at home, and his health was failing. He returned to Montgomery, where he became ever more conservative, becoming extremely close to George Wallace, virtually becoming Wallace's resident intellectual during Wallace's national campaigns.

After his return to Montgomery, two old and rather more liberal colleagues, Ray Jenkins and Wayne Greenhaw, would go by to visit him occasionally. Hall, now in a wheelchair, would cry out to his black physical therapist as they approached, "Get me my chicken gun—I'm going to kill these Communists. . . . Why, hell, I thought you'd come up here with at least a regiment of niggers to capture this place."

THIRTY-SEVEN

She was so alive she seemed to jump off the screen to create a personal relationship with her growing audience. "The golden girl who was like champagne on the screen," one of her husbands, Arthur Miller, wrote of her. Even when she was a struggling starlet, photographers understood instantly that she was special and inevitably asked her to pose. She was, photographer Richard Avedon once said, more comfortable in front of the camera than away from it. The famed French photographer Henri Cartier Bresson described something vivid, fragile, and evanescent about her, something "that disappears quickly [and] that reappears again." "The first day a photographer took a picture of her, she was a genius," said the director Billy Wilder, who understood and exploited her talent better than any other director. To the studio heads she was, at first, just another dumb blonde, part of the endless stream of young women who had been voted the best-looking girls in their high school classes and who thereupon went to Hollywood and queued up at Schwab's Drug Store hoping to be discovered. Early on, she was perceived as being at once too desirable, too available, and too vulnerable. Watching the reaction of studio wives to her at an early Hollywood party, Evelyn Keyes, the actress, turned to Arthur Miller, who had only just met Miss Monroe, and said, "They'll eat her alive."

Her power to project such a luminescent personality surprised the veteran actors and actresses with whom she worked. "I thought surely she won't come over, she's so small-scale," said the great British actress Dame Sybil Thorndyke, who worked with her on *The Prince and the Showgirl,* "but when I saw her on the screen, my goodness, how it came over. She was a revelation. We theatre people tend to be so outgoing. She was the reverse. The perfect film actress, I thought. I have seen a lot of her films since then and it's always there—that perfect quality." She was a sex goddess but also so desperately needy and childlike that she aroused a powerful instinct on the part of audiences to protect her. "When you look at Marilyn on the screen, you don't want anything to happen to her. You really care that she should be all right," said Natalie Wood. She had, said Laurence Olivier, who directed her near the end of her career, a rare ability "to suggest one moment that she is the naughtiest little thing, and the next that she's perfectly innocent."

She had a keen sense of her own abilities and of men's response to them. Cast inevitably by others as the dumb blonde, she was shrewder and smarter than most directors suspected, and she often managed to deliver considerably more in a part than they had reckoned for. But only when she worked with a director as smart as Billy Wilder would she do her best work. He saw her as an uncommonly talented comedienne who mocked the sex-goddess mystique.

She was a genuine original. Her success, which looked so easy from a distance, was virtually impossible to repeat, try though Hollywood might with such pretenders as Jayne Mansfield and Mamie Van Doren. Those physically similar starlets never seemed to possess the intelligence that she had, or the vulnerability. Whereas she played the naif who somehow knew the score down deep, her imitators often tended to be hard and brittle. When she died, Wilder said later, a whole genre of comedy died with her. "People fool themselves," he said, by trying to come up with imitations and Monroe lookalikes. "They said, 'I have just bought myself a car, and it looks like a Cadillac,' but it turns out they've just bought a Pontiac."

The vulnerability she projected came from a nightmarish childhood; the naïveté, such as it was, came from shrewdly perceiving, however involuntarily, what men were like and what they really wanted from women. She operated on the edge: There was a very thin line between who she was in real life and the poignant, sexual figure she played on the screen. She took her strength as an actress from her real-life experiences; but as she became more and more successful, she always retained the fear of being abandoned, of being unloved. She was needy on the screen because she was needy in real life.

There was a strain of emotional instability that had run through her family for several generations. Her mother, Gladys Mortensen, had brought Marilyn, whose real name was Norma Jeane, into the world in 1926 in Los Angeles as an illegitimate child. Her husband seemed to have disappeared and was clearly not the father of the child. The man Marilyn believed to be her father, a co-worker of her mother's named C. Stanley Gifford, never accepted responsibility for her. That weighed heavily on her, and as an adult she put no little effort into trying to fight that rejection by pursuing Gifford and trying to make contact with him. But even as the most successful actress in the world, she found that her phone calls to him were still not accepted.

Her mother, always mentally unstable, was institutionalized when she was not yet eight. Norma Jeane was passed around to different families and moved in and out of orphanages. All of this was traumatic for a child. She knew she had a mother and somewhere out there was a father, so why was she being handed over to strangers? She pleaded, "But I'm not an orphan! I'm not an orphan!" Of the families paid by the state to take her in, she was abused by the head of at least one. Another was a harsh fundamentalist: "Jesus is supposed to be so forgiving, but they never mentioned that," she said later. "He was basically out to smack you in the head if you did something wrong." She was precocious physically, and given the rejections and insecurities of her childhood, it was hardly surprising that she soon decided that the world was not interested in her goodness or intelligence. That was particularly true in Hollywood, she decided: "In Hollywood a girl's virtue is much less important than her hair-do. You're judged on how you look, not by what you are."

As such she was always wary, for there were dangers everywhere, people who you thought you could count on who would let you down. "You'd catch glimpses," noted her first husband, James Dougherty, an airplane-factory worker she married at age sixteen as much to escape her life as anything else, "of someone who had been unloved for too long and unwanted for too many years."

Her dream had always been to become a movie star. Her mother had fantasized about Clark Gable and kept a photo of him by her bedside; Norma Jeane/Marilyn had even fantasized that Gable was her father. She wended her way inevitably toward the studios and was noticed by a variety of people on the fringes of Hollywood. She made friends with a number of photographers who worked for the seedy, sex-oriented magazines of the time. She was well aware that the men who said they would help her might or might not: There was no doubt in her mind, she later told writer Jaik Rosenstein, that trading off physical favors was part of her early career requirements. "When I started modelling, it was like part of the job. . . . They weren't shooting all those sexy pictures just to sell peanut butter in an ad or get a layout in some picture magazine. They wanted to sample the merchandise, and if you didn't go along, there were 25 girls who would. It wasn't any big dramatic tragedy."

In 1949 she agreed to do a nude shoot for a photographer friend named Tom Kelley. He paid only fifty dollars, but she was living hand to mouth and she owed him a favor—he had lent her five dollars on an earlier occasion for cab fare. Besides, fifty dollars was precisely the amount of money she needed for the monthly payment on her secondhand car. She was not nervous about the nudity, only its potential effect on her career, and she signed the model release with the name Mona Monroe. In fact, Kelley noted that once she took her clothes off, she seemed more comfortable than before—in his words, "graceful as an otter, turning sinuously with utter natural-ness. All her constraints vanished as soon as her clothes were off." Not long after, she was finally given a screen test and it was consid-ered a stunning success by those who looked at the results. But she was also stereotyped: starlet; dumb-blonde category; keep her speak-ing lines to a minimum.

Later there were those who believed that the studio had in-vented her. Certainly, with studio help, her hair became blonder, and plastic surgery was used to make her more photogenic. Her teeth were straightened, some work was done on her nose to slim it down, and additional work was done to refinish the contours of her chin. But the studios did that with hundreds of other young women and lightning did not strike them. Her success was completely hers.

By the late forties, she began to appear in the background in a number of films. Her first lines were spoken in a film with Groucho Marx called *Love Happy*, released in April 1950. Groucho played a private eye and Miss Monroe was cast as a dumb blonde who sashayed into his office (a move that later became something of a trademark): "Some men are following me," she said. Groucho did a full eye roll. "I can't imagine why," he answered. ("You have," he told her off camera, "the prettiest ass in the business.")

When she got a part in an old-fashioned crime film called *The Asphalt Jungle,* she was initially not even listed in the credits. But the early screening audiences responded so enthusiastically to her on the comment cards that the studio executives took notice and somewhat reluctantly included her name. She was the girlfriend of a corrupt lawyer, played by Louis Calhern. Her presence was electric. There she was, sexual, defenseless, with her potent body and her little-girl voice. "Some sweet kid," Calhern says about her early in the film, telling her to go to bed. "Some sweet kid."

With *The Asphalt Jungle* her career exploded. She made thirteen films in the next two years, few of them memorable. The studios seemed to have no real idea who she was, only that somehow there was something that worked. She was becoming, almost without anyone knowing exactly how, the first female superstar of the postwar years. It was Billy Wilder who once said of her, "She never flattens out on the screen. . . . She never gets lost up there. . . . You can't watch any other performer when she's playing a scene with somebody else." Her image was perfect for Hollywood, fighting new competition from television, which now offered free home entertainment. Hollywood was responding to the challenge by gradually allowing greater latitude in showing sexual matters on the screen. Her sexuality, so overt it might previously have been doomed by the censors (in such scenes as the famous blowing up of her skirt in *The Seven-Year Itch,* for example) was now not only permissible, it was desirable.

"The truth," she once said, "is that I've never fooled anyone. I've let men fool themselves. Men sometimes didn't bother to find out who I was, and what I was. Instead they would invent a character for me. I wouldn't argue with them. They were obviously loving someone I wasn't. When they found this out they would blame me for disillusioning them and fooling them."

Even as professional success came, her personal life remained in turmoil. Relationships began well but ended badly. In 1952 she was introduced by a friend to Joe DiMaggio, the greatest baseball player of his era, who had just retired. They went out intermittently, starting in March 1952, and in January 1954 they were finally married in the San Francisco city hall. The relationship thrilled the tabloid soul of America: the greatest athlete-hero of the nation going out with the greatest sex symbol. They were both shy; both had risen by dint of talent to social spheres in which they were often uncomfortable. DiMaggio was attractive but not particularly verbal. Friends noted their powerful mutual attraction but also his inability to talk to her. Her career was just taking off; his career (but not his fame) was to all intents and purposes finished. He saw her as a good and sweet girl and hated the idea that Hollywood perpetually cast her (to his mind) as a slut.

It was to be an uneasy marriage. For their honeymoon they went to Japan, where DiMaggio was doing a celebrity tour. Her passport read Norma Jean DiMaggio. On the way, though, she was asked by American military officers to entertain the troops still serving in Korea, a year after the war had finally ended. She did, though DiMaggio declined to accompany her. There were some 100,000 soldiers gathered enthusiastically in an outdoor instant amphitheater to hear her perform. Later, as Gay Talese wrote in a brilliant piece in *Esquire,* when she rejoined DiMaggio, she reported to him breathlessly, "Joe, you've never heard such cheering." "Yes I have," he answered.

Within months it was clear that the marriage was in trouble. She went to New York to film *The Seven Year Itch.* DiMaggio decided reluctantly to go with her. They shot scene of the air blowing her skirt up at 2 A.M. to avoid a crowd, but the word got out and several thousand people showed up. She stood over the subway grating, the wind blowing her skirt above her panties, the crowd cheering, applauding and shouting, *"Higher, higher."* DiMaggio, the child of Italian immigrants, a man who perhaps more than any athlete of his generation valued his *dignity,* watched from the corner, stone-faced and silent. That the movie was a marvelous celebration of her innocence did not matter; instead he saw it as exposing of her in *public* for financial exploitation. They had a bitter fight that night. The next day he flew back to California alone. The marriage was effectively over. In late 1954 they were divorced; the marriage had lasted a scant year. As DiMaggio packed his things and moved out of the house, a crowd of newspapermen gathered. Someone asked him where he was going. "Back to San Francisco. That's my home."

But they remained close friends; there was no doubt of his devotion. Years later as her third marriage, to playwright Arthur Miller, began to disintegrate, she talked wistfully to her maid about DiMaggio as the great love of her life, and she kept a large poster of him in her bedroom closet.

Her life eventually became so troubled that it began to have a serious impact on her career. Unsure of her abilities, needing reassurance, she moved to New York to be near Arthur Miller, with whom she had begun a burgeoning romance, and to be a part of the Actors Studio. She longed to be respected as a serious actress, but her work habits were becoming shakier and shakier. Miller was both father figure and intellectual legitimizer. But it wasn't long before he found that he too was failing her. In July 1956, she married Miller, but there was no peace or respite. "Nobody cares," she told her maid as her marriage to Miller was coming apart. "Nobody even knows me anymore. What good is it being Marilyn Monroe? Why can't I just be an ordinary woman. . . . Oh why do things have to work out so rotten?" By 1957, her mental health was deteriorating ever more quickly: She was using even more sleeping pills and starting the day with a Bloody Mary.

More than most actors and actresses, she was exploited by the studios and was significantly underpaid at the height of her career. The studio heads always seemed to resent her success and continued to see her as essentially the dumb blonde. When she shot *Gentlemen Prefer Blondes,* the studio executives thought she was being too demanding and one of them angrily told her, "You're not a star." "Well, gentlemen," she answered. "Whatever I am, the name of the picture is *Gentlemen Prefer Blondes* and whatever I am, I *am* the blonde."

In February 1952, just as her career was taking off, there was an anonymous phone call to Twentieth Century-Fox. The naked girl in a nude calendar, said the male caller, was its newest star, Marilyn Monroe. The caller demanded ten thousand dollars. Otherwise, he said, he would take his proof to the newspapers. The studio people were terrified by the call but decided not to pay, which, they decided, would only lead to more blackmail. But they did pressure her to deny that she was the girl. It was a terrible moment for her: She was sure that her career was over. But she also decided to tell the truth and to take the initiative by leaking the story herself to a friendly writer. It *was* her on the calendar, she said, and there was no sense lying about it. "Sure, I posed," she said. "I was hungry." The public rallied to support her.

The photo Tom Kelley had shot was soon hanging on the walls of thousands of barbershops, bars, and gas stations. It also helped launch a sexual empire. For in the fall of 1953 a young man named Hugh Hefner, anxious to start his own magazine, read in an advertising trade magazine that a local Midwestern company had the rights to the photo. Hefner drove out to suburban Chicago and bought the rights for five hundred dollars (along with a number of photos of other nudes). It was a brilliant purchase for a magazine just being born—America's newest star caught lushly in the nude, posing coyly on a red velvet drape. Her body was angled to hide her pubic area; her breasts were fully exposed.

Fittingly, given the relationships between men and women in those days, Miss Monroe got nothing additional for the use of the photograph. There was no small irony here—that Hefner's multimillion-dollar kingdom was launched by this photo. In time, Hefner the grandson of Midwestern puritans would become a committed convert to more open sexuality, and a crusader for greater sexual freedom and honesty. He took up this cause humorlessly, with the passion of the old-time religious zealot. There was, thought some of those who knew him well, a certain grimness to his pursuit of both truth and pleasure. By contrast, Miss Monroe, the object of so much unwanted admiration, treated all the fuss with a pleasant self-deprecating humor. She seemed to be puzzled that men made such a big deal out of her body and was therefore willing to go along, more to keep them from being cranky than anything else. Asked whether she had anything on during the Tom Kelley shoot, she answered yes, the radio.

Hefner was only twenty-seven when he started his magazine on a shoestring in the fall of 1953. He had been so uncertain of his chances of success that he did not even bother to put his name on the masthead; nor for that matter did he bother to put a date on the first issue—he hoped that if the initial sale was not high enough, he might be able to keep it on the newsstand for another month. All of his limited savings were tied up in the magazine, and he was extremely nervous about the possibility of failure and bankruptcy. If the magazine failed, he would owe several thousand dollars to close friends and his family. The new magazine was to be called *Playboy,* which was not Hefner's original choice; he had wanted to give it the much cruder title of *Stag Party.* Others had tried to dissuade him, with little success, but what *had* finally changed his mind was a letter from the lawyers of a hunting magazine in New York called *Stag,* suggesting that he look elsewhere and threatening legal action if he did not.

Hefner printed 70,000 copies of the first issue, hoping it would sell at least 30,000 copies, at 50 cents an issue. Instead, bolstered in no small part by the word of mouth on the Monroe photos, it sold 53,000, a huge success. Still, in the early weeks of its appearance Hefner was like a nervous parent, casing newsstands and checking sales, making sure that his magazine got proper display, covertly rearranging it in front of the other magazines. He did, it should be noted, know something about the magazine business as he put out his first issue. For the last few years he had worked on the promotional side of magazines, and he knew a good deal about magazine distribution. He had become expert in the kind of hearty exaggerated promotional letters that magazines then favored.

With the success of the first issue he was in business. Confident as he prepared his second issue, he went out and bought himself a new Studebaker, and he also put his name on the masthead as editor and publisher. Within a year, by December 1954, *Playboy*'s circulation had reached 100,000. By early 1955, less than a year and a half after the first issue was so timidly cast forth, *Playboy* had $250,000 in the bank and Hefner turned down an offer of $1 million from a group in Chicago for the magazine. Some of its stunning initial success was in part due to Hefner's native shrewdness, his perfect pitch for what his readers—often sexually insecure young men—wanted. His instinct to package ever more glossy photos and use what he considered upscale writing would make the magazine ever more legitimate.

Hefner had come from a financially comfortable, if emotionally arid, family. His home was largely devoid of warmth and openness, and it was against that Calvinist ethic that he would fight in the pages of *Playboy*. Their Christianity seemed to him a cold, emotionally sterile one, separated from all pleasures of life. His grandparents were pious Nebraska farmers, and theirs remained a God-fearing home: There was no drinking, no swearing, no smoking. Sunday was for church. Hefner's first wife, Millie, later noted that she never saw any sign of affection or anger displayed by either of his parents.

Hefner was a bright, somewhat dreamy child: In terms of social skills and popularity he was always on the outside looking in. He graduated from high school in 1944, went into the army and caught the last months of the war, although he saw no combat. When he came home he drifted for a time, unsure of his future, drawing 52–20 from the government—twenty dollars a week for fifty-two weeks. He entered the University of Illinois to be with his high school girlfriend, Millie Williams. He had been dating Millie for several years, but they still had not consummated their relationship. After they were married in 1949, Hefner continued to drift, supported by Millie, who was teaching school.

The one thing he loved was cartooning, at which he was, unfortunately, not particularly gifted; for the next two or three years he went back and forth between jobs, usually in the promotion department of different magazines. For much of the time, he and Millie lived with his parents in order to save money. At one point in his drive to become a cartoonist, he quit work and stayed at home to draw. The results tended to be pornographic reworkings of then-popular comic strips. Millie Hefner was convinced that his erotic sketching was a rebellion of sorts against his family's Calvinist roots and the emotional and sexual coldness of that household.

As a convert to the cause of more open sexuality, he crusaded for it with the passion his puritanical grandparents had espoused in their religion; it was as if one crusade had simply replaced another. The Calvinists, Hefner believed, thought sex was dark and furtive, and the other girlie magazines of the period were so cheap and crude they seemed to confirm that judgment. It was Hefner's particular genius to know that it was now, in this new era, going to be permissible to have an upscale, slick magazine of male sexual fantasies that customers might not be embarrassed to be seen buying—or even to leave out on their coffee tables.

As far as Hefner was concerned, he was a direct lineal descendant of Alfred Kinsey, whom he regarded as a hero, the man who had more than anyone else pointed out the hypocrisy in daily American life, the differences between what Americans said about sex and what they actually did. As a student he had quite favorably reviewed the Kinsey study for the University of Illinois humor magazine, and in truth the Kinsey studies were critically important for him. Before they appeared, he had felt himself essentially alone in his belief that sex was important and that society was duplicitous and punitive in its attitude toward sex. Kinsey had showed him that he was not alone, that there were millions of others who felt much the same way he did. Kinsey, as far as he was concerned, had opened the debate on sexual attitudes. Soon, in his own mind, at least, he was the person who took up Kinsey's banner. He also believed that he could become a role model for young men of his generation, not just in his sexual practices but for his life-style, as well.

In his first issue, Hefner wrote, "We like our apartment. We enjoy mixing up cocktails and an hors d'oeuvre or two, putting a little mood music on the phonograph, and inviting in a female for a quiet discussion on Picasso, Nietzsche, jazz, sex." There it was, the *Playboy* ethic: sex as not only legitimate but as a sophisticated life-style. By the end of 1956, still operating with a skeleton staff, *Playboy* was a phenomenon. Circulation was 600,000. "A lot of it," said Ray Russell, a writer and editor who was one of Hefner's first hires, "was good luck, random choice, being carried on the tides of the times rather than the leader of the times. It was a matter of being the right magazine able to take advantage of a rising economy, more than any degree of conscious planning."

Perhaps Hefner's great strength was his lack of sophistication. If he was square, he still longed to share the better world, which was now increasingly available around him; in that he mirrored the longings of millions of other young men of similar background, more affluent than their parents, wanting a better and freer life. His connection to his readers was immediate. It was not by chance that *Playboy* was born in the Midwest, not New York, like most magazines. Its most successful editors were sons of the Midwest, not Easterners and not graduates of Ivy League schools. Hefner understood his readers' lives; his squareness was their squareness; his magazine answered the right questions because they were his questions. "That magazine," said Jack Kessie, an early editor, "was written and edited for Hugh M. Hefner."

As the magazine became enormously successful, he was to all intents and purposes living in his offices. He became increasingly distant and remote, a kind of latter-day Gatsby, who opened his increasingly plush residences to an endless stream of people whom he did not know (and who did not know him). In some ways he was still an outsider looking in, partaking of the new sybaritic life-style but detached from it. "Hefner," said Don Gold, an editor at *Playboy* in the early days, "is not a very complicated man. He thinks Poe is the best writer in the world. When he buys a pipe, he buys two dozen of the same pipe. He likes his mashed potatoes to have a dimple of gravy on them. He is mid-America personified. The Marquis de Sade would have told him to wait in a corner, though he is, in a healthy way, by sex possessed." Some saw Hefner not so much liberator as exploiter of American puritanism. Frank Gibney, a former *Time* magazine writer and editor who worked briefly and unhappily for him, once compared him to the Methodist missionaries who traded firewater to the Indians. To Gibney, the more he tried to be hip, the more he failed.

In June 1957, Hefner wrote of himself for that month's issue: "His dress is conservative and casual. He always wears loafers. . . . There is an electronic entertainment wall in his office, very much like the one featured in *Playboy*'s Penthouse apartment, that includes hi-fi, AM-FM radio, tape, and television, and will store up to 2000 LPs. Brubeck, Kenton or Sinatra is usually on the turntable when Hefner is working. He is essentially an indoors man, though he discovered the pleasures of the ski slope last winter. He likes jazz, foreign films, Ivy League clothes, gin and tonic and pretty girls—the same sort of things that *Playboy* readers like—and his approach to life is as fresh, sophisticated, and yet admittedly sentimental as is the magazine."

Not everyone who knew Hugh Hefner in those days, would have accepted his own self-portrait. He was, they might agree, smart, albeit more shrewd than cerebral, an easy man for his more sophisticated Eastern colleagues to underestimate, but he was not exactly hip or cool, no matter how hard he worked at it. It didn't matter. For *Playboy* would play a critical role in the coming sexual revolution; it helped, among other things, to sell the idea that sex was pleasure, to be enjoyed, not something dark to be sought illicitly and clandestinely.

The women his magazine came to feature, seminude (and then, with the more relaxed censorship laws, completely nude) were young, preferably innocent-looking girls, more fresh-faced and bubbly than erotic or sophisticated. They seemed to have stopped off to do a *Playboy* shoot on their way to cheerleading practice or to the sorority house. That was deliberate policy, for over the years Hefner often seemed uninterested in much of the magazine's verbiage, but he monitored carefully the choices of the Playmates who would grace the magazine's centerfold; he was confident that what stirred his fantasies would stir the fantasies of his readers. This, thought those who knew him well, was when he was most alive and most engaged—when he sat in his bedroom, armed with the photographer's loops with which he could magnify thousands of contact sheets of film of beautiful, nude women, as the ultimate arbiter of American sexual fantasy. Nor did his interest in these young women extend merely to displaying explicit photos of them to millions of the opposite sex. Rather, they were the kind of women whom he sought for companionship. In the late sixties, Hefner, by then in his forties, met a young woman named Barbie Benton, who was to be one of his longest-running girlfriends. Ms. Benton, then only eighteen, was pleased but a little uneasy with the attention of this older man. "You're a nice person, but I've never dated anyone over twenty-four." "That's okay," he answered. "Neither have I."

The success of his magazines and his personal success reflected a powerful new chord in postwar American life: the changing attitudes about sex and a steadily more candid view of sexuality. Hefner was fighting that part of the Puritan ethic that condemned pleasure. He thought hard work and sexual freedom were not incompatible in this ever richer society. In the broader sense as well, *Playboy* shepherded a generation of young men to the good life. It helped explain how to buy a sportscar, what kind of hi-fi set to buy, how to order in a restaurant, what kind of wine to drink with what kind of meal. For men whose parents had not gone to college, *Playboy* served a valuable function: It provided an early and elementary tutorial on the new American life-style. For those fearful of headwaiters in fancy restaurants, wary of slick salesmen in stores and of foreign-car dealers who seemed to speak a language never heard in Detroit, *Playboy* provided a valuable consumer service: It midwifed the reader into a world of increasing plenty. "Hefner," said Arthur Kretchmer, his longtime executive editor, "helped the world to discover toys. He said 'Play, it's okay to play.'" Americans, particularly younger Americans, lived in a world of more and more toys; that was the good life, and it was fun. "We are," Kretchmer added, "more about indulgence and the celebration of frivolity than we are about envy and greed." Hefner's central message, Kretchmer said, was "Celebrate your life. Free it up. Your sexuality can be as good as anybody else's if you take the inhibitions out, if you don't destroy yourself internally."

The spectacular rise of *Playboy* reflected the postwar decline of Calvinism and puritanism in America, due as much as anything else to the very affluence of the society. Ordinary Americans could afford to live better than they ever had before, and they now wanted the things that had previously been the possessions of only the very wealthy; and they wanted the personal freedoms the rich had traditionally enjoyed too. In the onslaught, old restraints were loosened. If religion existed only as a negative force, Hefner was saying, if it spoke only of the denial of pleasure and made people feel furtive about what was natural, then it was in trouble. He preached pleasure. He touched the right chord at precisely the right moment.

THIRTY-EIGHT

Indian summer is like a woman. Ripe, hotly passionate but fickle, she comes and goes as she pleases so one is never sure whether she will come at all, nor how long she will stay."

It began in prose that threatened neither John Cheever nor John O'Hara as the most famous chroniclers of American social mores. "In Northern New England, Indian summer puts up a scarlet-tipped hand to hold winter back for a little while. She brings with her the time of the last warm spell, an unchanged season which lives until winter moves in with its backbone of ice and accoutrements of leafless trees and hard frozen ground. Those grown old, who have had the youth bled from them by the jagged edged winds of winter, know sorrowfully, that Indian summer is a sham to be met with hard-eyed cynicism . . ."

In 1956, the most surprising book on the best-seller list was

Peyton Place, by Grace Metalious, a young woman who had never published a word before. It was brought out in hardcover by Julian Messner, a small publisher, and went on to become the third best-selling hardcover novel of the year. Allan Barnard, an editor at the paperback house Dell, read the manuscript just before it was published and told his boss, Frank Taylor: "I have something I want to buy [to reprint as a mass softcover edition], but I don't want you to read it." Taylor gave Barnard permission to go ahead and he bought the softcover rights for $11,000 in an auction with other publishing houses. It turned out to be one of the great bargains of all time. A few years later, Taylor asked Barnard why he had asked him not to read it. "Because you wouldn't have let me buy it," Barnard answered, referring to the ambivalence many paperback editors felt about the commercial quality of the books they published.

Peyton Place was considered a hot book in the vernacular of the time, although Metalious was far less explicit than other, more serious writers who were then struggling with the oppressive censorship laws of the era. But *Peyton Place* was such a phenomenon that the title entered the language as a generic term for all the small towns that appeared placid on the surface but underneath were filled with dark secrets, most of them sexual. In her book, Metalious tore away the staid facade of Peyton Place/Gilmanton, New Hampshire, to reveal a hotbed of lust and sexual intrigue. "To a tourist these towns look as peaceful as a postcard," Ms. Metalious told Hal Boyle of the Associated Press in an early interview. "But if you go beneath that picture, it's like turning over a rock with your foot—all kinds of strange things crawl out. Everybody who lives in town knows what's going on—there are no secrets—but they don't want outsiders to know."

Indeed, the principal occupation of *Peyton Place* seemed not so much farming or the town's textile factory but gossip; people there not only led secret lives, they devoted most of their waking hours to sitting around and talking about them—at least about everyone else's. To wit: of Kenny Stearns, a local handyman with a green thumb whose wife runs around on him, the locals say, "Too bad Kenny don't have the same good luck with his wife as he has with his plants. Mebbe Kenny'd be better off with a green pecker."

It was a small town of some 3,700 people, still largely cut off from the rest of the society. A certain sense of loneliness pervaded it. A teacher lamented the waste of time teaching the children of this sad little town: "What sense was there in memorizing the date of the rise and fall of the Roman Empire, when the boy, grown, would milk cows for a living as had his father and grandfather before him? What logic was there in pounding decimal fractions into the head of a girl who would eventually need only to count the numbers of months of each pregnancy?" Class lines ran through the middle of Peyton Place; a handful of powerful men—the town's factory owner, the lawyer, the editor of the newspaper, and the doctor—played poker once a week and decided what was going to happen in the town. When Betty Anderson, a local girl from the wrong side of the tracks whose father worked for Leslie Harrington (the mill owner), became pregnant after a fling with Harrington's son, the senior Harrington handed his employee a check for $500. A furious Betty charged in to see Harrington in his office and announced that she planned to marry the son. But Harrington told her that it would require only six men to say that they also had had relations with her to make her legally a prostitute. He then tore up the check for $500 and gave her one for $250, promising that it would be $125 if she came by him again.

Mostly, the town's secrets stayed secret with much less fuss. Constance MacKenzie, the prim, attractive young widow who ran the town's dress shop, dreaded the idea that people might learn that in her brief time in New York she had an affair with a married man, who was the father of her daughter; another local girl was sexually assaulted and impregnated by her sinister stepfather, and the kindly local doctor decided to save the young girl's reputation by disguising an abortion as an emergency appendectomy.

If there ever was a book that reflected the changing nature of American book business as it changed to the new high-powered world of paperbacks from the more genteel old-fashioned world of hardcover publishing, it was *Peyton Place.* It was not so much a book as an event, with a force all its own. Published as a paperback in the fall of 1957, it quickly sold 3 million copies and it kept right on selling. By the middle of 1958 its sales were over 6 million. By 1966 there were some 10 million copies in print. In years to come, as the paperback industry grew and as the capacity to promote books became an ever more sophisticated industry, there were best-sellers whose path up the best-seller list was achieved with several hundred thousand dollars in promotion costs. *Peyton Place,* by contrast, was a true popular success.

At the time of publication Ms. Metalious's novel was perceived as being successful for the most basic of reasons: It told the blunt truth about the sexuality of a small town at a time when that was still sensational. Gradually, however, as the society evolved into the sixties and seventies, there was a revisionist view of that success, a sense that at least some of it had been due to Ms. Metalious's powerful and visceral comprehension of the problems faced by women in the modern world. Metalious did not exactly become a heroine or a role model to the generation of young women who emerged in the seventies determined to lead lives more independent than those of their mothers. Nonetheless, cultural detectives tracking the evolution of the feminist movement could find in her pages the emergence of independent women who dissented from the proscribed lives and limited opportunities reserved for women. Metalious, they suspected—for there was little evidence of this in the initial reviews of the book—had touched a nerve without anyone realizing it. Kenneth Davis noted in his book on the paperback revolution, *Two-Bit Culture,* that the women in *Peyton Place* "were on the cutting edge of a movement that had not yet arrived and still had no voice. They wanted more than to simply find the right man, settle down and begin breeding and keeping house."

Rather, Davis pointed out, Metalious's characters might have come right out of the Kinsey Report on women. They had sexual feelings and appetites that contrasted starkly with the attitudes women were then supposed to have, as set down in endless books written by men. Nor were Metalious's women nearly as admiring of men as they were supposed to be. In fact, they often considered men unreliable and childish. They did not want to be controlled by men; they wanted to be independent and to have careers in places like New York or, even if they remained in towns like Peyton Place, to have some control over their lives and their bodies. "For perhaps the first time in popular fiction a writer was saying that women wanted sex and enjoyed it but they wanted it on their terms," wrote Davis. "They were not passive receptacles for dominant men. To a generation fed on Mickey Spillane, for whom women counted as little more than animals, or Erskine Caldwell, whose Southern women were for the most part sluttish trash, the women of Peyton Place presented a new image. Independent, self-fulfilling, strong yet capable of love and desire, they were far from the perfect exemplars of the shining new woman that eventually followed with the onset of the feminist movement, but they were a breakthrough, a first faint glimmering that women were preparing to break out of the mold carefully prepared for them by centuries of male domination."

As Emily Toth pointed out in her book *Inside Peyton Place,* a serious feminist reappraisal of Metalious and her work, *Peyton Place* brought very different attitudes to sexual politics than the seemingly similar books that preceded it. It described rape not as an act of sexual pleasure but as violence; the doctor who performs an abortion is described as saving a life. In *Peyton Place,* Toth pointed out, the women who depend too greatly on men lose out, while the women who are independent are winners. Therefore, she noted, *Peyton Place* was a book before its time.

Metalious was, at first glance, an unlikely feminist hero. She never fully articulated her own vision and probably would have been surprised to find some thirty years later women at colleges reading her book not so much as literature but as part of the change in the politics of gender. With a few rare exceptions, she was not close to other women, and as her literary career progressed and her own life began to unravel, she wrote of the frustrations of women with less skill and perception than she had in her first book.

Metalious had written as she did—roughly, simply, but powerfully—because it could have been her own story. She was, by instinct, angrier and more rebellious than she herself realized, although she had always shown contempt for conventional female roles. Women were expected to be good housekeepers; Grace Metalious's home was littered with garbage, dirty dishes, and beer cans. Women were supposed to be good mothers, putting their children above their own ambitions; Grace Metalious loved her three children in her own erratic way, but she let them do pretty much as they wished; any real supervision tended to come from neighbors. Women were supposed to be dutiful handmaidens to their husbands' careers; Metalious made little effort in that direction. She dressed in a way that jarred small-town sensibilities—in blue jeans, checked shirts, and sneakers. She stayed home and wrote a book instead of attending polite dinner parties. She never fully articulated her own feminist vision and probably would have been surprised had someone told her that one day she would be a heroine of the women's movement. But she was not slick and she did not know how to romanticize her own story.

She was a lower-middle-class French Canadian girl who grew up in small towns in New Hampshire, living always involuntarily in a matriarchy. The men in her family were bit players; her own father deserted the family when she was young, and she was raised by her grandmother. Her mother fantasized a better life but slipped into alcoholism at a relatively early age. Grace loved to read and fancied that she would be a writer one day; at age thirteen she had already begun a historical novel.

In high school Grace was bright and different, and teachers noticed her. Nonetheless, a literary future seemed out of reach. It seemed dimmer still when in February 1943, at the age of eighteen, she married George Metalious, a high school friend, because she was pregnant. When George Metalious enlisted and went off to war, Grace was stunned by his decision—she was not caught up in the patriotic cause, and remembering her father, she saw her husband's desire to serve as an escape from family responsibility. She worked at different jobs and raised her daughter Marsha. When George Metalious came back from the war, sure that his army salary had been salted away for the down payment on a dream house, he was stunned to find that she had saved none of it. Rather, she had been supporting her extended family with his allotment checks. "How could you be so stupid!" he shouted at her.

They were not unlike many couples trying to make their way after the war. George had come back to a child and a wife he barely knew. They struggled for a time, had a second child, both of them held jobs, and yet they could save very little. Finally, it was decided that the only way to succeed was for George to go to the University of New Hampshire on the GI bill. His family would follow and his wife would take a job to support him—so common an arrangement in those days that there was even a phrase for it: PHTS, Putting Hubbies Through School. But Metalious was different; for above all she wanted to write; it was the one way she could escape the dreary world that seemed to be closing in around her.

If other young couples were caught up in the excitement of those years, living in cramped housing with young children, eating cheap meals thrown together from cans, always sure that their current sacrifice would be rewarded eventually, when the husband got his degree, Grace Metalious was having none of it. She hated being a poor student's wife. "I am trapped, I screamed silently," she later said of those years. "I am trapped in a cage of poverty and mediocrity, and if I don't get out, I'll die."

She was already writing, absolutely sure that she was going to be a novelist. Her work habits were excellent. She wrote every day. The odds against her must have seemed hopeless. She had no college education. She knew no one in the literary world. She was utterly without literary connections. She had no immediate literary role models. Her chances of success seemed ever slimmer, particularly after 1950 when their third child arrived, when by all rights she should have stopped writing and been crushed by the terrible odds against her. Yet she kept writing, feeling the loneliness of someone virtually without friends and without a support system. But she had several qualities that kept her going—a fierce drive, a belief that in writing and publishing there was liberation, an innate talent and shrewdness that were not to be underestimated, and finally a love of books.

In 1950 their third child had arrived. When George graduated, they were so poor that they had to borrow $300 to pay his debts so the university would release his degree. His first job, as a teacher at a tiny school in Belmont, paid $2,500, with an additional $1,100 thrown in for coaching the baseball team.

By 1953, she began to send manuscripts to publishers and began the search for a literary agent. She surveyed various writers' magazines and finally came up with a name, Jacques Chambrun, an agent with a good deal of charm and a most unfortunate reputation for siphoning off the earnings of his writers. By early 1955 she had sent him her first novel, a rather routine semiautobiographical story about a young couple struggling through GI-bill life at a New England college.

Entitled *The Quiet Place,* it was rejected everywhere it was sent. Around the same time, she sent off her second novel, entitled *The Tree and the Blossom.* She had read *King's Row,* an extremely popular novel of the forties that dealt with the incestuous relationship of an adolescent girl and her father. By chance a similar incident had occurred in the small town where Metalious lived: A young girl had shot her father to protect herself and the rest of her family. In that, Metalious seized on a sensational incident that would give her novel a special darkness. The novel, which was renamed *Peyton Place,* was mailed to publishers in May 1955.

It was turned down at several houses, but a young woman named Leona Nevler, who had a good eye, read it while she was working as a free-lance manuscript reader at Lippincott. It was impressive, Ms. Nevler thought: There was something poignant, vital, and authentic about the book. But it was not right for Lippincott, an unusually staid house. A few days later, Ms. Nevler was interviewed for a full-time job by Kitty Messner, the head of Julian Messner. She had founded the small publishing house with her husband, Julian Messner, and had divorced him, but she had continued to work with him. When he died she took over the company; so when Ms. Nevler mentioned the book, Kitty Messner, one of the first women to head a publishing company, was unusually receptive to the theme, which dealt with a young woman's desire for a better life. Ms. Messner, a formidable woman of very considerable independence, made a note of it, called Chambrun, got a copy, and stayed up all night reading it. She understood immediately the force of the book and made Chambrun an offer. "I know this is a big book," she told him. "I have to have it." Chambrun cabled Metalious, who was so excited that she forgot to ask how much her advance was—the answer was $1,500. He told her to come to New York as soon as she could to sign the contracts, which she did. She was awed by the fashionably elegant Kitty Messner, who wore jackets and pants— not, as one friend noted, off the rack, but beautifully tailored by a man's tailor for her. She seemed, particularly to this vulnerable young woman from a small New England town, to be the epitome of a New York career woman. It was mid-August and Metalious felt wilted by New York's steamy heat; by contrast, Messner "looked as if she had never had a hot uncomfortable moment in her life. As for me, my armpits itched, I stuck to my chair, and my hair had gone all limp."

The early editing did not go well. Nevler had made a number of notes on how she thought it could be improved and tightened, but the relationship did not work out well. Metalious took the editing as a sign that Nevler had really never liked the book. Nevler had a series of lunches and dinners where they tried to work together but where Ms. Metalious ended up drinking and not eating. Later she decided that what she had encountered was the first sign of an increasingly serious problem with alcohol. Soon Ms. Messner took over the book herself.

Messner thought the book might sell 3,000 copies—standard for a first novel—but editor Howard Goodkind, who handled the publicity, thought it could be promoted into a best-seller; he suggested spending an additional $5,000 to get a publicist to create a special promotion campaign for the book. That sum was a considerable risk in those days, but Messner agreed. A man named Bud Brandt was hired and he in turn got the AP's veteran reporter Hal Boyle to go up to Gilmanton to do a prepublication story on the author.

In the course of his visit, Metalious casually predicted to Boyle that her husband would be let go as the local school principal (as he soon was) and perhaps the reason was that a number of powerful people in town disapproved of her—she behaved differently, she dressed differently, and she was said to be writing a book. In Boyle's subsequent article, the story had been mutated sufficiently to eliminate any doubt: George Metalious had been fired from his job as a principal because of his wife's book, which tore the veneer off the respectability of this small town. The publicity machine was ready to roll. The ads for the book employed a series of headlines reflecting the controversial nature of the book. By the time it was published in late September, it shot up some best-seller lists and a number of studios were bidding for the film rights. It sold 60,000 copies in the first ten days. The reviews were generally respectful. Carlos Baker, the distinguished Hemingway scholar, placed Metalious in the tradition of American writers who had helped expose the underside of small-town American life. Interestingly enough, a critic named Sterling North, writing in the *New York World Telegram*, who had earlier praised blunt language when used by male writers, was appalled by Metalious's use of the same words: "Never before in my memory has a young mother published a book in language approximately that of a longshoreman on a bellicose binge."

Fame and success were sweet at first. The people in New York were touched by the contrast between her sweetness, and indeed vulnerability, and the harsh quality of her life as depicted in the book. All her dreams seemed to be coming true. She sold the book to the movies for $250,000, and the first check was for $75,000. She seemed to take particular pleasure in taking it to various stores in Gilmanton asking the owners to cash it for her. But if she had been well prepared to overcome the adversities of her life, she proved significantly less able to deal with the pressures of success. "This book business," she wrote friends in November 1956, "is some evil form of insanity." Everyone suddenly seemed to want something from her and wanted her to play the role of a sexy writer.

The writer of *Peyton Place* was supposed to be both sexy and glamorous, after all, and Grace Metalious was a rather plain young woman. (She would tell the makeup men and women in television studios to make her look beautiful.) She was uneasy about the press and television appearances that were a part of the book's promotion and she particularly disliked it when someone asked whether or not the book was autobiographical. She made an appearance on an early television talk show called *Night Beat,* hosted by a young man named Mike Wallace, then gaining a reputation for himself as a tough interviewer. She thought she had been assured he would not ask the autobiography question. Almost as soon as the interview began, Wallace asked her, "Grace, tell me, is *Peyton Place* your autobiography?" She struck back by calling him Myron, his real name, which she had been told beforehand he did not like to be called, and by asking him how many times he had been married, another sensitive point.

Even before the book's publication, her marriage had started falling apart. There had been an affair with a local farmer. Liberated by her success and her changed financial position, she ended her marriage, took up with a disc jockey, and married him. She began to spend money freely; at the same time she stopped writing. Years later George Metalious referred to that period in her life as "the tinsel years." Driven mostly by Hollywood producer Jerry Wald, she eventually wrote a listless sequel she was not proud of, called *Return to Peyton Place*. At the last minute a writer named Warren Miller was brought in to doctor it into a readable book. Nonetheless *Return* also sold well, though not as well as its predecessor.

For all of her fame and the attention, Metalious's emotional needs did not abate. "Our mother had to be told with the consistency of a flowing brook that echoes, 'I love you, I love you, I love you,' " her daughter Marsha remembered. "We did love her strongly, but after a while 'I love you' became a ludicrous expression—worn to its nap like a rug traveled on day after day, night after night."

Her work habits continued to deteriorate. When T. J. Martin, the disc jockey whom she had married, tried to get her to work, she would yell at him, "Who the hell are you? Who appointed you my guiding light?" Soon she was always seen with a glass in her hand, usually with Canadian Club and Seven-Up in it.

By 1960, George Metalious had come back into her life, and she published *The Tight White Collar,* which became her favorite book. It sold well, but not nearly as well as *Peyton Place.* To shrewd editors, it was obvious that her audience was beginning to slip away. Soon she had serious financial problems. When *Peyton Place* had been a success, she had worked out an agreement with her lawyer to place her and her family on a budget of $18,000 a year, a good deal of money then. But she never lived by the agreement and had paid almost nothing in taxes; she was said to owe the government $163,-400, plus 6 percent interest. Now, ever more fearful of the government, she tried to return to writing. She finished *No Adam in Eden,* a book about her French Canadian family, which was published in September 1963. Messner passed on it, albeit selling the rights to Pocket Books for $50,000, and the movie rights went for $150,000. Her unhappiness, indeed her increasing lack of self-esteem, one shrewd critic noted, now showed in her work. "It would seem that the writer hates women, individually and en masse. If she had anything kind or understanding to say about them, I confess to having forgotten what it was, so weighed down are all the female characters under a load of sin, lechery, selfishness and cruelty." The remaining year of her life was sad. Metalious left her again in the fall of 1963, and a few months later, in February 1964, she died of chronic liver disease.

THIRTY-NINE

I t was all part of a vast national phenomenon. The number of families moving into the middle class—that is, families with more than five thousand dollars in annual earnings after taxes—was increasing at the rate of 1.1 million a year, *Fortune* noted. By the end of 1956 there were 16.6 million such families in the country, and by 1959, in the rather cautious projections of *Fortune*'s editors, there would be 20 million such families—virtually half the families in America. *Fortune* hailed "an economy of abundance" never seen before in any country in the world. It reflected a world of "optimistic philoprogenitive [the word means that Americans were having a lot of children] high spending, debt-happy, bargain-conscious, upgrading, American consumers."

In all of this no one was paying very close attention to what the new home-oriented, seemingly drudgery-free life was doing to the psyche and outlook of American women. The pictures of them in magazines showed them as relentlessly happy, liberated from endless household tasks by wondrous new machines they had just bought. Since the photos showed them happy, and since there was no doubt that there were more and better household appliances every year, it was presumed that they were in fact happy. That was one of the more interesting questions of the era, for the great migration to the suburbs reflected a number of profound trends taking place in the society, not the least important of which was the changing role of women, particularly middle-class women. Up until then during this century women had made fairly constant progress in the spheres of politics, education, and employment opportunities. Much of their early struggle focused on the right of married women to work (and therefore to take jobs away from men who might be the heads of families). In the thirties a majority of states, twenty-six of forty-eight, still had laws prohibiting the employment of married women. In addition, a majority of the nation's public schools, 43 percent of its public utilities, and 13 percent of its department stores enforced rules on not hiring of wives. A poll of both men and women in the thirties that asked "Do you approve of a married woman earning money in business or industry if she has a husband capable of supporting her?" showed that 82 percent of the men and women polled disapproved.

During the Depression, large numbers of women went to work because their homes needed every bit of cash they could bring home. In addition women were always welcome in those parts of industry that offered poorer-paying jobs. At the beginning of the New Deal in the garment district of New York, where traditionally workers were the wives of immigrants, women worked forty-eight hours a week for 15 cents an hour, which meant that after a long, exhausting work week they brought home $7.20.

But in general there was an assumption that as society began to change and more and more women were better educated, there would be more women working in the professions for better wages. World War Two dramatically (if only temporarily) changed how the nation regarded the employment of women. Overnight, that which had been perceived as distinctly unfeminine—holding heavy-duty industrial jobs—became a patriotic necessity. Four million additional workers were needed in industry and in the armed forces and a great many of them had to be women. The *Ladies' Home Journal* even put a woman combat pilot on its cover. Suddenly, where women had not gone before they were very welcome indeed; some 8 million women entered the work force during the war.

That trend came to a stunning halt in the years after the war. Part of it was the traditional tilt of the society toward men—if there were good, well-paying jobs, then the jobs obviously belonged to men as they came home from the war to head families. Within two months after the end of the war, some 800,000 women had been fired from jobs in the aircraft industry; the same thing was happening in the auto industry and elsewhere. In the two years after the war, some 2 million women had lost their jobs.

In the postwar years the sheer affluence of the country meant that many families could now live a middle-class existence on only one income. In addition, the migration to the suburbs physically separated women from the workplace. The new culture of consumerism told women they should be homemakers and saw them merely as potential buyers for all the new washers and dryers, freezers, floor waxers, pressure cookers, and blenders.

There was in all this a retreat from the earlier part of the century. Now, there was little encouragement for women seeking professional careers, and in fact there was a good deal of quite deliberate discouraging of it. Not only were women now reared in homes where their mothers had no careers, but male siblings were from the start put on a very different track: The boys in the family were to learn the skills critical to supporting a family, while daughters were to be educated to get married. If they went to college at all they might spend a junior year abroad studying art or literature. Upon graduation, if they still had ideas of a professional career, the real world did not give them much to be optimistic about.

The laws about married women working might have changed, but the cultural attitudes had not. The range of what women were allowed to do professionally in those days was limited, and even in those professions where they were welcome, they were put on a lower, slower track. Gender, not talent, was the most important qualification. Men and women who graduated at the same time from the same colleges and who had received the same grades (in many cases the women received better grades), then arrived at the same publishing or journalistic companies only to be treated very differently.

Men were taken seriously. Women, by contrast, were doomed to serve as support troops. Often they worked harder and longer for less pay with lesser titles, usually with the unspoken assumption that if they were at all attractive, they would soon get married, become pregnant, and leave the company. Only someone a bit off-center emotionally would stay the course. It was a vicious circle: Because young women were well aware of this situation, there was little incentive to commit an entire life to fighting it and becoming what was then perceived of as a hard and brittle career woman. ("Nearly Half the Women in Who's Who Are Single," went one magazine title in that period trying to warn young women of the pitfalls of careerism.) If there were short stories in womens' magazines about career women, then it turned out they, by and large, portrayed women who were unhappy and felt themselves emotionally empty. Instead, the magazines and the new television sitcoms glorified dutiful mothers and wives.

Even allegedly serious books of the era (for instance, an influential book of pop sociology by a man named Ferdinand Lundberg and his psychoanalyst collaborator Marynia Farnham, entitled *Modern Woman: The Lost Sex*) attacked the idea of women with careers. "The independent woman is a contradiction in terms," Lundberg and Farnham had written. Feminism itself, in their words, "was a deep illness." "The psychosocial rule that takes form, then, is this: the more educated a woman is, the greater chance there is of sexual disorder, more or less severe. The greater the disordered sexuality in a given group of women, the fewer children they have," they wrote. They also suggested that the federal government give rewards to women for each child they bore after the first.

A postwar definition of femininity evolved. To be feminine, the American woman first and foremost did not work. If she did, that made her competitive with men, which made her hard and aggressive and almost surely doomed to loneliness. Instead, she devotedly raised her family, supported her husband, kept her house spotless and efficient, got dinner ready on time, and remained attractive and optimistic; each hair was in place. According to studies, she was prettier than her mother, she was slimmer, and she even smelled better than her mother.

At this particular moment, it was impossible to underestimate the importance and influence of the women's magazines—the *Ladies' Home Journal, Redbook, McCall's,* and *Mademoiselle*—on middle-class young woman. Isolated in the suburbs they felt uneasy and lonely and largely without guidance. More often than not, they were newly separated from their original families and the people they had grown up with. They were living new lives, different from those of their parents, with new and quite different expectations on the part of their husbands. Everything had to be learned.

In an age before the coming of midday television talk shows largely designed for housewives, womens' magazines comprised the core reading material for the new young suburban wives. If the magazines' staffs at the lower rungs were comprised mostly of women, the magazines were almost always edited by men; in addition, editorial content much more than in most general-circulation magazines, echoed the thrust of the advertising. Research showed, or seemed to show, that husbands made the critical decisions in terms of which political candidate a family might support, but the wives made the decisions on which refrigerator and which clothes washer to buy. If the advertising was designed to let women know what the newest appliances were and how to use them, then the accompanying articles were designed to show they could not live up to their destinies without them.

This was not done deliberately. There were no editorial meetings where male editors sat around and killed ideas that showed the brave new suburban world as populated with a significant percentage of tense, anxious female college graduates who wondered if they were squandering the best years of their lives. But there was an instinctive bias about what women needed to hear and that it should all be upbeat, and that any larger doubts were unworthy.

The magazines explained their new lives to them: how to live, how to dress, what to eat, why they should feel good about themselves and their husbands and their children. Their sacrifices, the women's magazines emphasized, were not really sacrifices, they were about fulfillment. All doubts were to be conquered.

The ideal fifties women were to strive for was articulated by *McCall's* in 1954: togetherness. A family was as one, its ambitions were twined. The husband was designated leader and hero, out there every day braving the treacherous corporate world to win a better life for his family; the wife was his mainstay on the domestic side, duly appreciative of the immense sacrifices being made for her and her children. There was no divergence within. A family was a single perfect universe—instead of a complicated, fragile mechanism of conflicting political and emotional pulls. Families portrayed in women's magazines exhibited no conflicts or contradictions or unfulfilled ambitions. Thanks, probably, to the drive for togetherness, the new homes all seemed to have what was called a family room. Here the family came together, ate, watched television, and possibly even talked. "When Jim comes home," said a wife in a 1954 advertisement for prefabricated homes, "our family room seems to draw us closer together." And who was responsible ultimately for togetherness if not the wife?

"The two big steps that women must take are to help their husbands decide where they are going and use their pretty heads to help them get there," wrote Mrs. Dale Carnegie, wife of one of the nation's leading experts on how to be likable, in the April 1955 *Better Homes and Gardens.* "Let's face it, girls. That wonderful guy in your house—and in mine—is building your house, your happiness and the opportunities that will come to your children." Split-level houses, Mrs. Carnegie added, were fine for the family, "but there is simply no room for split-level thinking—or doing—when Mr. and Mrs. set their sights on a happy home, a host of friends and a bright future through success in HIS job."

Those women who were not happy and did not feel fulfilled were encouraged to think that the fault was theirs and that they were the exception to blissful normality. That being the case, women of the period rarely shared their doubts, even with each other. If anything, they tended to feel guilty about any qualms they had: Here they were living better than ever—their husbands were making more money than ever, and there were ever bigger, more beautiful cars in the garage and appliances in the kitchen. Who were they to be unhappy?

One of the first women to challenge the fallacy of universal contentment among young suburban wives was a young woman from the heartland of the country. Born and reared in Peoria, Illinois, she did well enough in school to be admitted to an elite Eastern women's college, one of the Seven Sister schools. She entered Smith College in 1939, finding everything that she had longed for as a small-town girl in Peoria: a world where women were rewarded for being smart and different instead of being punished for it. She graduated in 1942, summa cum laude, full of optimism about the future even though the war was still going on. Several scholarships were offered her. Ambitious, admired by her classmates, Betty Goldstein was certain that she would lead a life dramatically different from her mother's. Miriam Goldstein had been a society-page writer for the Peoria, Illinois, paper, before marrying a local storeowner and becoming a housewife. In her daughter's eyes, she took out her own frustrated ambitions by pushing her children to achieve. But at graduation time, Betty Goldstein turned down the fellowships because she was interested in a young man; since he had not been offered a comparable scholarship, she was afraid it would tear their relationship apart if she accepted hers. That decision, she later wrote, turned her instantly into a cliché. Looking back on her life, Betty Goldstein Friedan, one of the first voices of the feminist movement, noted the young man's face was more quickly forgotten than the terms of the scholarship itself.

Instead of getting married, she moved to the exciting intellectual world of Greenwich Village and became part of a group of liberal young people involved in labor issues and civil rights before it was fashionable. The women all seemed to be graduates of Smith, Vassar, and Radcliffe; they were bright and optimistic, eager to take on a static society. Betty Goldstein worked as a reporter for a left-wing labor paper. As a journalist, she had got a reputation of knowing her way around and having lots of contacts. She became the person designated to arrange illegal abortions for involuntarily pregnant friends. This, she found, she was able to do with a few discreet phone calls. The going price was a thousand dollars. Once it was also her job to find a minister for two Protestant friends who wanted to marry. Because the groom was a divorced man, she noted with some irony, it was harder to find a willing minister than an abortionist.

When the war was over, the men returned from Europe and the South Pacific, and the women were gradually squeezed out of their jobs. Betty Goldstein, unsure of her role and her future, not liking the idea of a life alone (she had, she noted, "a pathological fear of being alone"), met a young veteran named Carl Friedan, who seemed funny and charming, and in 1947, two years after the war had ended, they were married. In 1949 they had their first child. When she was pregnant with her second child she was fired from the labor paper, whose radicalism, it appeared, did not yet extend to women's rights. When she took her grievance to the newspaper guild, she was told that the second pregnancy, which had cost her job, was her fault. There was, she later realized, no union term for sex discrimination.

Ms. Friedan soon found herself part of the great suburban migration as she moved further and further away from the Village, which had been the center of her professional and intellectual world. There, ideas had always seemed important. As she and her husband moved to larger and larger living quarters, first to Queens, where the Friedans lived in a pleasant apartment, and then to houses in the suburbs, her time was gradually more and more taken by children and family. As that happened, she was cut off, first physically, from what she had been, and then increasingly intellectually and socially as well. Betty Friedan now poured her energy into being a housewife and mother, into furnishing the apartment and houses and shopping, cooking, and cleaning for her family.

The Friedan family, she later realized, had been almost unconsciously caught up in the postwar migration to the suburbs. It was an ascent to an ever better style of living; but she also began to see it as a retreat as well from her earlier ambitions and standards. She liked doing the domestic things that Americans now did in their new, ever more informal social lives—grilling hamburgers on the outdoor barbecue, attending spur-of-the-moment cocktail parties, sharing summer rentals on Fire Island with friends. Finally, the Friedans bought an old house, worthy of Charles Addams, in Rockland County for $25,000 (with $2,500 down), where Betty Friedan, Smith summa cum laude and future feminist leader, spent her time, scraping eight layers of paint off a fireplace ("I quite liked it"), chauffeuring children to and from school, helping to run the PTA, and coming as close as someone as fiercely independent as she was could to being a good housewife, as portrayed in the women's magazines of that day. In some ways her life was full, she would later decide, and in some ways it was quite empty. She liked being a mother, and she liked her friends, but she missed the world of social and political involvement back in New York. She also worried that she had not lived up to her potential. By the time they were living in Rockland County, she had begun to write free-lance for various women's magazines. It was a clear sign, she realized later, that while the domestic side of her life was rich, it was not rich enough.

The deal she made with herself then was a revealing one. It was her job as a writer to make more money than she and Carl spent on a maid—otherwise her writing would be considered counterproductive and would be viewed as subtracting from rather than adding to the greater good of the family. Her early articles, "Millionaire's Wife" (*Cosmopolitan,* September 1956); "Now They're Proud of Peoria" (*Reader's Digest,* August 1955); "Two Are an Island" *Mademoiselle*) July 1955; and "Day Camp in the Driveways" (*Parents'* Magazine, May 1957) were not exactly the achievements she had had in mind when she left Smith.

She was also very quickly finding out the limits of what could be done in writing for women's magazines at that time. In 1956, when she was pregnant with her third child, she read in a newspaper about Julie Harris, the actress, then starring in a play called *The Lark.* Ms. Harris had had natural childbirth, something that Betty Friedan, who had undergone two cesareans, admired and even envied. She decided, with the ready agreement of the magazines, to do a piece on Ms. Harris and her childbirth. She had a glorious time interviewing the actress and was completely captivated by her. She wrote what she thought was one of her best articles on the joys of natural childbirth. To her surprise, the article was turned down at first because it was too graphic.

That was hardly her only defeat with the magazines. When she suggested an article about Beverly Pepper, just beginning to experience considerable success as a painter and sculptor, and who was also raising a family, the editors of one magazine were scornful. American women, they told her, were not interested in someone like this and would not identify with her. Their market research, of which they were extremely confident, showed that women would only read articles that explained their own roles as wives and mothers. Not many American women out there had families and were successful as artists—therefore it would have no appeal. Perhaps, one editor said, they might do the article with a photograph of Mrs. Pepper painting the family crib.

At the time one of her children was in a play group with the child of a neighboring woman scientist. Ms. Friedan and the woman talked on occasion and her friend said she believed that a new ice age was approaching. The subject had interested Friedan, not normally a science writer, and she had suggested an article for *Harper's*. The resulting article, "The Coming Ice Age" was a considerable success and won a number of prizes. In New York George Brockway, a book editor at Norton, saw the piece and liked it. He called to ask if she was interested in writing a book. She was excited by his interest but had no desire to expand the piece into a book; the scientific work was not really hers, in the sense that it did not reflect her true interests and feelings. It was, she later said, as if she had served as a ghost-writer for another person on it.

Then something happened that changed her life. She and two friends were asked to do a report on what had happened to the members of the Smith class of '42 as they returned for their fifteenth reunion in 1957. She made up a questionnaire and got an assignment from *McCall's* to pay for her time. The piece was supposed to be called "The Togetherness Woman." The questions were: "What difficulties have you found in working out your role as a woman?" "What are the chief satisfactions and frustrations of your life today?" "How do you feel about getting older?" "How have you changed inside?" "What do you wish you had done differently?" The answers stunned her: She had tapped into a great reservoir of doubt, frustration, anxiety, and resentment. The women felt unfulfilled and isolated with their children; they often viewed their husbands as visitors from a far more exciting world.

The project also emphasized Friedan's own frustrations. All those years trying to be a good wife and mother suddenly seemed wasted; it had been wrong to suppress her feelings rather than to deal with them. The surprise was that there were thousands of women like her out there. As she wrote later in *The Feminine Mystique:* "It was

596 / DAVID HALBERSTAM

a strange stirring, a sense of dissatisfaction, a yearning that women suffered in the middle of the twentieth century in the United States. Each suburban wife struggled with it alone. As she made the beds, shopped for groceries, matched slip cover materials, ate peanut butter sandwiches with her children, chauffeured Cub Scouts and Brownies, lay beside her husband at night, she was afraid to ask of herself the silent question—'Is this all?' "

As she had walked around the Smith campus during her reunion, she was struck by the passivity of the young women of the class of 1957. Upon graduation, her generation had been filled with excitement about the issues of the day: When Ms. Friedan asked these young women about their futures, they regarded her with blank looks. They were going to get engaged and married and have children, of course. She thought: This is happening at Smith, a place where I found nothing but intellectual excitement when I was their age. Something had gotten deep into the bloodstream of this generation, she decided.

She left and started to write the piece for *McCall's,* but it turned out very different from the one that she had intended to write. It reflected the despair and depression she had found among her contemporaries, and it was critical of women who lived through their husbands and children. *McCall's,* the inventor of "togetherness"— not surprisingly—turned it down. She heard that all the women editors there wanted to run it but that they had been overruled by their male superiors. That did not entirely surprise her, but she was sure someone else would want it. So she sent it to the *Ladies' Home Journal,* where it was accepted. There, to her amazement, it was rewritten so completely that it seemed to make the opposite points, so she pulled it. That left *Redbook,* where Bob Stein, an old friend, worked. He suggested that she do more interviews, particularly with younger women. She did, and sent the piece back to him. He was stunned by it. How could Betty Friedan write a piece so out of sync with what his magazine wanted? Why was she so angry? What in God's name had come over her? he wondered. He turned it down and called her agent. "Look," he said over the phone. "Only the most neurotic housewife would identify with this."

She was, she realized later, challenging the magazines themselves. She was saying that it was wrong to mislead women to think they should feel one way when in fact they often felt quite differently. She had discovered a crisis of considerable proportions, and these magazines would only deny it.

She was angry. It was censorship, she believed. Women's magazines had a single purpose, she decided—to sell a vast array of new products to American housewives—and anything that worked against that, that cast doubt about the happiness of the housewives using such products, was not going to be printed. No one from the advertising department sat in on editorial meetings saying which articles could run and which could not, she knew, but the very purpose of the magazine was to see women first and foremost as consumers, not as people.

At about that time she went to New York to attend a speech by Vance Packard, the writer. He had just finished his book *The Hidden Persuaders,* about subliminal tactics in advertising. His efforts to write about this phenomenon in magazines had been completely unsuccessful, he said, so he turned it into a book, which had become a major best-seller. The parallels between his problems and hers were obvious. Suddenly, she envisioned "The Togetherness Woman" as a book. She called George Brockway at Norton, and he seemed delighted with the idea.

The economics of publishing were significantly different from those of magazines. Books were not dependent upon ads, they were dependent upon ideas, and the more provocative the idea, the more attention and, often, the better the sales. Brockway knew there had already been a number of attacks on conformity in American society, particularly as it affected men. Here was an attack that would talk about its effect on women, who were, of course, the principal buyers of books. He was impressed by Ms. Friedan. She was focused and, to his mind, wildly ambitious.

She told Brockway she would finish it in a year; instead, it took five years. Later she wrote that no one, not her husband, her editor, or anyone who knew her, thought she would ever finish it. She did so while taking care of three children. She later described herself as being like all the other mothers in suburbia, where she "hid, like secret drinking in the morning, the book I was writing when my suburban neighbors came for coffee . . ."

Her research was prodigious. Three days a week she went to the New York City Public Library for research. The chief villains, she decided, were the women's magazines. What stunned her was the fact that this had not always been true. In the same magazines in the late thirties and forties, there had been a sense of women moving steadily into the male professional world; then women's magazines had created a very different kind of role model, of a career woman who knew how to take care of herself and who could make it on her own. But starting around 1949, these magazines changed dramatically. It was as if someone had thrown a giant switch. The new woman did not exist on her own. She was seen only in the light of supporting her husband and his career and taking care of the children.

The more Ms. Friedan investigated, the more she found that the world created in the magazines and the television sitcoms was, for many women at least, a fantasy world. Despite all the confidence and happiness among women portrayed in the magazines, there was underneath it all a crisis in the suburbs. It was the crisis of a generation of women who had left college with high idealism and who had come to feel increasingly frustrated and who had less and less a sense of self-esteem.

Nor, she found, did all the marvelous new appliances truly lighten the load of the housewife. If anything they seemed to extend it—there was some kind of Gresham's law at work here: The more time-saving machines there were, the more things there were to do with them. She had stumbled across something that a number of others, primarily psychiatrists, had noticed: a certain emotional malaise, bordering on depression, among many women of the era. One psychiatrist called it "the housewife's syndrome," another referred to it as "the housewife's blight." No one wrote about it in popular magazines, certainly not in the monthly women's magazines.

So, gathering material over several years, she began to write a book that would come out in 1963, not as *The Togetherness Woman,* but as *The Feminine Mystique.* She was approaching forty as she began, but she was regenerated by the importance of the project; it seemed to give her her own life back. The result was a seminal book on what had happened to women in America. It started selling slowly but word of it grew and grew, and eventually, with 3 million copies in print, it became a handbook for the new feminist movement that was gradually beginning to come together.

FORTY

At the Worcester Foundation, the search for an oral contraceptive pill was beginning to go surprisingly well. The breakthrough of synthetic progesterone had given them all an immense lift. Word of how well they were doing spread throughout the scientific community and eventually reached the general public; an article had even appeared in *Look* predicting that Pincus would soon succeed in his quest.

The next stage was reached when Searle passed on to Worcester a progesterone steroid called norethynodrel, which, Chang reported back to Pincus, was more powerful than natural progesterone by a factor of at least ten to one. Goody Pincus knew at that point that it was time to bring on board a distinguished medical doctor as a collaborator—for soon the Pill would have to be tried on human subjects. At first he considered Alan Guttmacher and Abraham

Stone, both doctors and leaders in the birth-control movement. But Pincus worried that their affiliation might diminish their legitimacy for the project, and in addition, both were Jewish. This might prove to be a liability, for opposition to birth control came primarily from Catholics and fundamentalist Christians. (For all its freedom from administrative control and political pressure, the Worcester people maintained cautious in publicly discussing what they were doing. The 1955 annual report was more than a little disingenuous; it spoke of work with animals to control ovulation; the 1956 report detailed the use of steroids to help control painful menstruation.)

Finally, Pincus turned to an old colleague and friend, Dr. John Rock. Rock was a distinguished doctor, chief of gynecology and obstetrics at Harvard Medical School. He was also a devout Catholic, father of five children, and grandfather of fourteen. Rock and Pincus had known each other since the thirties by dint of their common interest in hormones. Rock, however, was trying to use them to cure infertility in women. He believed progesterone and estrogen might stimulate the womb, and he sent one of his assistants to work with Pincus to learn from his experience in retrieving mammalian eggs. Gradually, their work brought Rock and Pincus closer together.

In 1953 Pincus suggested to Sanger that Planned Parenthood get Rock to do a study on the use of progesterone as a contraceptive device. Rock, whose attitudes toward contraception had been slowly changing, was finally ready to participate. Margaret Sanger was wary of Rock at first because he was a Catholic ("He would not," she said, "dare advance the cause of contraceptive research and remain a Catholic"). But Pincus convinced her that Rock's attitudes were flexible, and that he was increasingly sympathetic to the idea of birth control. Besides, he was an imposing figure—strikingly handsome, charming, and graceful—and he was also a representative of one of America's great universities. Kate McCormick agreed with Pincus; Rock, she explained to Sanger, was a "reformed Catholic." His position, she told her friend, "is that religion has nothing to do with medicine or the practice of it, and that if the Church does not interfere with him, he will not interfere with it—whatever that may mean." Eventually, Margaret Sanger finally came around on Rock because it seemed he would be able to win support from those who had rejected Sanger and her causes in the past. "Being a good R.C. and as handsome as a god, he can get away with anything," she noted. In 1954 he began experiments using the new synthetic hormone from Searle on three women.

Later, some critics claimed that Rock was no more than a front man. In fact he was a good deal more than that. He was the perfect choice, as a doctor, to take the experiment from the lab and move it into the real world of people. His was a powerful presence, a doctor of great distinction and originality whose own work and social ideas were taking him ever closer to the work of Pincus and his team. "If you went to doctors in New England in those days," said Oscar Hechter, "and asked who was the best obstetrician in the region, you would almost surely be told that it was John Rock—he was a formidable figure." He was also a man of singular independence. Rock's courage was admired by both Hoagland and Pincus, but they knew he was a brilliant clinician as well, not merely a theorist as they were. When they had created the Worcester Foundation, they had wanted more than anything else to make it a *relevant* institution (after all, they spent much of the war studying the biological aspects of fighter-pilot fatigue, and they had also done advanced work on the biochemistry of schizophrenia), so Rock was a man whom they would have invented had he not lived, a bridge from their world of the abstract to a world of real people with real medical problems.

Rock was the son of a small-town businessman in Marlborough, Massachusetts: His ancestors were Irish Catholics. He finished Harvard College in three years, went on to Harvard Medical School, and soon became a prominent professor of gynecology. When he married Anne Thorndike in 1925, the cardinal of Boston himself performed the ceremony, something he had done only once before, for Joe and Rose Kennedy. But the Catholic Church almost stopped the ceremony. The day before his wedding, Rock performed a cesarean section, an operation then forbidden by the Catholic Church. At confession, a local priest refused to absolve him and thus it was impossible for him to receive the sacrament of marriage. But William Cardinal O'Connell overruled the priest.

Rock was in many ways a very conservative man. He argued against the admission of women to Harvard Medical School and often told his own daughters that he did not think women were capable of being doctors. But his views on birth control evolved steadily. In 1943, when he was fifty-three years old, he had come out for the repeal of legal restrictions on physicians to give advice on medical birth control. But he added at the time: "I hold no brief for those young or even older husbands and wives who for no good reason refuse to bear as many children as they can properly rear and as society can properly engross." In the mid-forties, although scrupulous about not offering contraceptives to his own patients, he began to teach his young students at Harvard Medical School how to prescribe them. Years later he would pinpoint the late forties as the time when he became aware of what he called "the alarming danger of the population explosion." He began to fit some of his patients with diaphragms, which so enraged some of his Catholic colleagues that they tried to have him excommunicated. In 1949 he wrote a book with David Loth called *Voluntary Parenthood,* which was a comprehensive survey of birth-control methods available for the general public. His colleagues admired him because he so seriously wrestled with questions of morality. In many ways the transformation of his own values reflected those taking place among many in the middle class. Although he remained a serious Catholic who regularly attended mass, he became even blunter about his changing views on population control. Indeed, after the introduction of the Pill, he said, "I think it's shocking to see the big family glorified." When the Pill first came out, he received an angry letter from a Catholic woman who excoriated him for his role in its development. She told him, "You should be afraid to meet your maker." "Dear Madam," he wrote back. "In my faith we are taught that the Lord is with us always. When my time comes, there will be no need for introductions." Still, Rock's primary motivation in joining with Pincus was for the opposite problem that Pincus and his team were working to solve. He wanted to help couples who, despite all physiological evidence to the contrary, were unable to have children. In the past he had had some success injecting the women with natural progesterone.

He gave the progestin steroids to a group of fifty childless women at his clinic, starting in December 1954. The dosage was 10–40 milligrams for twenty successive days for each menstrual cycle. When the women came off the progestin, seven of the fifty, or 14 percent, were able to get pregnant. That was wonderful news for Rock. In addition, there was among the fifty a virtual 100 percent postponement of ovulation. That was wonderful news for Pincus and Chang. Pincus became so confident that he had begun to refer to "the Pill."

So these three very different men began to work together. Each of the three had his own private doubts. Rock, the good Catholic, still worried about the morality of what he was doing; Chang was wary of capitalist exploitation, uneasy about placing his scientific skills in the service of drug companies (Pincus had to reassure him constantly that what he was doing was for the good of the society and that the drug companies did not matter); and Pincus himself, constantly racing against the clock, wondered if what they were doing was safe. But even as they were making rapid progress, Kate McCormick remained impatient. On one occasion, after John Rock returned from a brief vacation, she wrote Margaret Sanger, "I was able to get hold of Dr. Rock today. . . . I did not want to leave him for fear that he would escape!" What seemed to them a speedy process was terribly slow to McCormick.

By the fall of 1955 Pincus was so optimistic that he decided to go and talk publicly about his research at the International Planned Parenthood meeting in Tokyo. He asked Rock to join him, but Rock was uneasy about it; he felt that the results while so far very positive, were not yet adequately conclusive and that Pincus was on shakier ground than he realized. He was also sensitive about making the announcement at what he considered a politicized event—a meeting of birth-control advocates. It was the closest the two men came to a break. Pincus and Chang desperately wanted Rock to add his name and considerable prestige to the announcements they intended to make in Tokyo. At the time, a disappointed Pincus felt that Rock was being too timid. Rock, by contrast, felt his colleagues were going too fast for the evidence. "He [Pincus] was a little scary," Rock told Paul Vaughan years later. "He was not a physician and he knew very little about the endometrium, though he knew a good deal about ovulation." If anything, noted Mahlon Hoagland, the son of the director, who himself later became the Worcester Foundation's director, Rock was right, and Pincus and Chang probably did exceed their evidence, by talking not just about what they had accomplished with animals, but dwelling on the implications for humans. "They did it," the young Hoagland noted, "because they were restless, talented mavericks, cocky and arrogant, very good and aware of being very good—it was what made Worcester such a wonderful place to work." Rock did not go, and in fact urged Pincus not to go.

What they all needed now were more patients and a broader selection of them: It was one thing to succeed with middle-class, college-educated women, who would be disciplined about taking the Pill, but what about poorer, less well educated women? Would they be as careful? Puerto Rico and Haiti were chosen as locales for mass testing. These places were perfect for their needs—poor and over-crowded. Public officials were more than ready for a serious study of birth control. (There was no small irony in the choice of Puerto Rico. At that time the primary birth control was for a woman to go to the hospital and demand the *operación,* which was a sterilization proce-dure. As Puerto Ricans migrated to New York, they went to New

York's hospitals with the same request, but under New York law, not every woman who wanted to be sterilized had that right. Under pressure from this growing new Hispanic population, the law was changed.)

In April 1956, the tests began on one hundred women in a poor suburb of San Juan. It had been exceptionally easy to get volunteers; the problem was keeping other women out. The pill used was Enovid, made by Searle, whose officials were nervous about being associated with Pincus in the program and whose top public relations officials warned that this activity might destroy their good name. (A few years later, as they were preparing to market Enovid publicly in America and their research showed overwhelming public acceptance, they swung around 180 degrees and considered calling it The Pill. "After all, if you could patent the word Coke for Coca-Cola why not 'The Pill' for the oral contraceptive? So we kicked the idea around. But we never took any action," said James Irwin, a Searle public relations executive.) The early returns from Puerto Rico were very good: In the first eight months, 221 patients took the Pill without a single pregnancy. There were some side effects, primarily nausea, but Pincus was able to reduce them, by adding an anti-acid. Soon the tests were being expanded to other areas in Puerto Rico, and to Haiti as well.

Pincus's daughter, Laura, took some time off from her studies at Radcliffe to help with the tests in Puerto Rico. Upon her return to Boston she was sent to brief Kate McCormick, who lived in a grand mansion in Back Bay, a foreboding house that seemed to have neither lights nor life to it. Laura Pincus was, in her own words, rather naive about sex and she got a little flustered talking to this old woman about the experiments then taking place. But Kate McCormick did not become unsettled: She talked openly and frankly. The sex drive in humans was so strong, she kept insisting, that it was critical that it be separated from reproductive functions. She followed that with a brief discussion of the pleasures of sex and then added rather casually that sex between women might be more meaningful. This was spoken dispassionately, not suggestively. Nonetheless, young Ms. Pincus was stunned. Here she was in this nineteenth-century setting hearing words that seemed to come from the twenty-first century. Then, knowing that her visitor had to take the subway back to college, Mrs. McCormick summoned her butler, who brought her a silver tray with coins. She reached down and picked out two dimes and handed them to her visitor. Later, after she left, Laura Pincus looked down at the coins and noticed they were minted in 1929.

But if the breakthrough was near, Margaret Sanger remained on a wartime footing. In 1957 she made her first television appearance, on the Mike Wallace show, and the reaction stunned even Sanger. There was so much hostile mail that for the first time in her life, she was wary of reading it. "The R.C. Church," she wrote in her diary at the time, "is getting more defiant and arrogant. I'm disgusted and worried. No one who was a worker in defense of our Protestant rights has got to accept the Black Hand from Catholic influence. Young Kennedy from Boston is on the Stage for President in 1960. God help America if his father's millions can push him into the White House."

It was an extraordinary triumph for Pincus. Pincus, claimed Oscar Hechter, was the prototype of a new kind of biologist, the engineer of "a conscious use of science to effect social change in the interests of man and civilization." By so doing he was able to "liberate humanity from an immediate social threat and to remove restraints from the full development of uniqueness of men and women alike." Pincus began to travel around the world, talking with great enthusiasm of the coming breakthrough in contraception. He would tell his audiences "how a few precious facts obscurely come to in the laboratory may resonate into the lives of men everywhere, bring order to disorder, hope to the hopeless, life to the dying. That this is the magic and mystery of our time is sometimes grasped and often missed, but to expound it is inevitable." It was, his friends thought, the great validating moment of his professional life.

Some people in Planned Parenthood still thought Pincus was too optimistic and precipitous, but his optimism was now shared by Rock. They were both now pushing for acceptances of the Pill, and they were getting results: In 1957, the U.S. Food and Drug Administration authorized the marketing of the Pill for treatment of miscarriages and some menstrual disorders. By 1959 both Pincus and Rock were convinced that Enovid was safe for long-term use by women. In 1959 Pincus completed a paper on the uses of Enovid for oral contraception and sent it to Margaret Sanger. "To Margaret Sanger," he wrote, "with affectionate greetings—this product of her pioneering resoluteness."

In May 1960, the FDA approved Enovid as a contraceptive device. By the end of 1961 some 408,000 American women were taking the Pill, by the end of 1962 the figure was 1,187,000, and by the end of 1963 it was 2.3 million and still rising. Of it, Clare Boothe Luce said, "Modern woman is at last free as a man is free, to dispose of her own body, to earn her living, to pursue the improvement of her mind, to try a successful career.''

The discovery made Searle a very rich company. To Chang's great regret, the Worcester Foundation never took any royalty. Nor, in the eyes of the Worcester people, was Searle generous in later years. Despite several representations on behalf of Pincus's family and of the Worcester people, Searle paid only three hundred dollars a month in benefits to his widow. When the Worcester people suggested repeatedly to Searle that the company might like to endow a chair at the Worcester Foundation in Pincus's honor, Searle not only declined but soon afterward donated $500,000 to Harvard to endow a chair in reproductive studies. It was the supreme indignity—rewarding the institution that had once denied Pincus tenure with a chair in his own specialty. To Pincus's colleagues in Worcester, it appeared that no good deed went unpunished. Nor were the Searle people very generous with Chang. Years after the Pill's development, Hudson Hoagland suggested that Searle (which was making millions) might give some financial aid to Chang, who was by the standards of science making very little. "Who the hell is M. C. Chang? We've never heard of him," a Searle executive asked. When that story was related to Chang, he quoted Confucius: "Do not get upset when people do not recognize you." "I hope," he added with a sardonic touch, "Chairman Mao will say the same."

Margaret Sanger's fears about a Catholic President turned out to be ill-founded. After a century of American Presidents who refused to deal with the issue of overpopulation, Kennedy expressed cautious approval of federal support for contraceptive research. In 1966, a year before Mrs. Sanger's death, Dwight Eisenhower and Harry Truman, neither of whom had been helpful to her while in office, became co-chairmen of Planned Parenthood's world-population committee.

FORTY-ONE

In 1955, in a quiet ceremony in Huntsville, Alabama, Wernher von Braun, at the age of forty-three, became an American citizen. This was not a particularly good time for von Braun and his German colleagues in the American space program at Huntsville. To a nation trying on the uncomfortable new role of international power, space seemed, if anything, a futuristic fantasy—and an expensive one at that. That was particularly true for the President and most of his chief advisers, men born in the previous century. But for von Braun, who believed the space age was already here (thanks in no small part to his own V-2 rockets, used by the Germans in World War Two), this was unusually frustrating. When he had first come to America he had even written a novel called *Mars Project,* a book based not on idle fancies but on real data. It envisioned a major national effort to make manned space trips a reality. He sent the

book off to a publisher, who replied that "it sounds too fantastic."
Eighteen other publishers turned it down. He could hardly believe no
one was interested.

Von Braun was probably at the moment the leading rocket
scientist in the world. His V-2 was the first successful ballistic missile,
and in the last year of the war, thirteen hundred of them had been
fired at London with mounting success. Had German technology
been on a slightly more accelerated schedule, Eisenhower mused
later, the V-2s might have threatened his capacity to land at Nor-
mandy and thereby altered the outcome of the war. At the end of
World War Two, von Braun and his team of German rocket scientists chose America as their future home as the Red Army pushed
toward Peenemünde, where they were headquartered. In January
1945, von Braun called his team together and told them, "Germany
has lost the war, but let us not forget that it was our team which first
succeeded in reaching outer space. We have never stopped believing
in satellite voyages to the Moon and interplanetary travel . . ." To
which of the victorious countries, he then asked, "should we entrust
our heritage?" That was an interesting choice of words—skills were
practical knowledge, whereas heritage was more like one's lifeblood.
They voted to stay together and to offer themselves to the Americans. The choice was relatively easy. "We despise the French; we are
mortally afraid of the Soviets; we do not believe the British can
afford us; so that leaves the Americans," one team member said later.
Richard Lewis, writing in *Appointment on the Moon,* noted of Dieter
Huzel, ("perhaps the most articulate of the émigrés") ". . . [he saw]
their role as Promethean bearers of a great technological skill for
mankind, forged in the fires of war, but of greater import as a means
of exploring space than as a weapon. In the chaos of Germany's
collapse, Huzel saw himself and his colleagues as men with a mission
to perpetuate the engineering science they had created. These men,
Huzel believes, tend to think of themselves as a group apart from the
Nazi war machine, with ambitions transcending its military and
political objectives."

The team slipped out of Peenemünde, burying most of their
important papers in a deserted mine, and with the aid of faked
papers, reached Bavaria and the American forces. Wernher's
brother, Magnus von Braun, who spoke relatively good English,
went out to hunt for an American soldier to whom they could
surrender. In time one was found, and Magnus announced to a
rather startled private: "My name is Magnus von Braun. My brother
invented the V-2. We want to surrender." When Wernher himself

appeared soon after, there was considerable doubt that he could actually be the father of the V-2. He was, said one American, "too young, too fat, too jovial." Then he began to talk. The American scientists were dazzled; his knowledge was so complete and he easily blended the practical with the visionary. Colonel John Keck, one of the debriefing officers, told reporters later, "This will make Buck Rogers seem as if he had lived in the Gay Nineties." Had anyone else spoken like this he would have seemed a dreamer, but when von Braun spoke listeners paid attention. "We were," said Keck, "impressed with their practical engineering minds and their distaste for the fantastic." So the deal was done, and the entire German team of over a hundred scientists came over. In addition, von Braun led his captors to several V-2s and gave the Americans important documents. The capture of the Germans was known as Operation Paperclip, and it was one of the great coups of the war, since the V-2 was not so much the last weapon of the old war as the first new weapon of the war that might come next. The Russians were furious. Stalin was a major promoter of the uses of science and technology, and he was well aware of the importance of Peenemünde. He had pushed his generals to the north rather than straight to Berlin.

When his troops reached the rocket camp, they found almost everything of value gone and Stalin was reportedly furious. "This is absolutely intolerable," he said, according to reliable defectors. "We defeated Nazi armies; we occupied Berlin and Peenemünde, but the Americans got the rocket engineers. What could be more revolting and more inexcusable? How and why was this allowed to happen?" In a way, the Red Army's race toward Peenemünde was symbolic: It was, without anyone knowing it, the beginning of the race for outer space, or what Winston Churchill once called "the wizard war."

Later, any number of American conservatives raged against the Soviet successes in Eastern Europe, but for all the territory swept up by the Red Army, the Americans, by getting the German scientists, had pulled off a major coup. In 1945, the Germans were far ahead of other nations in rocket developments, the Soviets were second, with a significant pool of talent, and the Americans, having diverted much of their scientific resources to developing nuclear weapons, were a poor third. But getting von Braun and his colleagues instantly made the Americans competitive. Rocketry was his life.

"For my confirmation," von Braun once noted, "I didn't get a watch and my first pair of long pants like most Lutheran boys. I got a telescope." His father was a large landowner and served in the Weimar government as minister of agriculture. Young Wernher was always fascinated by the stars and outer space. As a boy he tied six firework skyrockets to his child's wagon, lit them, and was delighted when the wagon went surging forth. "I was ecstatic. The wagon was totally out of control and trailing a comet's tail of fire, but my rockets were performing beyond my wildest dreams. Finally they burned themselves out with a magnificent thunderclap and the vehicle rolled to a halt. The police took me into custody very quickly," he noted. At prep school, he neglected his math courses until he was informed they were critical to the study of space. Soon he was doubling as a math teacher. In Berlin he enrolled at the Charlottenburg Institute of Technology and apprenticed at a local metal shop. At the shop he was ordered to make a perfect cube. He was furious. "Why waste time filing a chunk of iron?" But he submitted. The foreman measured it. His angles were off. Try again, he was told. So he did. His angles were still off. Again he tried; again his cube was imperfect. Finally, five weeks later, when his cube had shrunk from the size of a child's head to that of a walnut, the foreman said, "*Gut!*" It was an important lesson: Even dreamers have to perfect their practical skills.

At the age of eighteen, he and his friends experimented in an abandoned lot in Berlin, which they decided to call the Raketenflugplatz, or the Rocket Flight Field. Two years later, he was part of the embryonic German rocket team, under Dr. Hermann Oberth. Senior colleagues were already in awe of his extraordinary theoretical knowledge. Perhaps the Treaty of Versailles had limited German efforts in traditional weaponry, but it had said nothing about rockets and so the Germans began to undertake a major effort in this area. Von Braun soon became the leader of the team. In 1934, when it was decided a better place for testing than Berlin was needed, von Braun's mother suggested a little-known area on the Baltic coast called Peenemünde, where her father had often duck-hunted.

When the war began they were just finishing work on the V-1, a twenty-seven-foot-long subsonic rocket, which flew just low enough and slowly enough to be intercepted. At first Hitler did not seem particularly interested in their research. During his first visit in 1939, he looked around, listened to the briefings, and said nothing— to the scientists' bitter disappointment. Germany's stunning early successes in the war had seemed to eliminate the need for a secret weapon. Who needed a weapon of the future when the weapons of the present—the Panzer divisions and the Wehrmacht—were so effective. Still, von Braun and his team pushed ahead with the V-2. It was to have a range of about 160 miles and had to be small enough to be able to go through Germany's railroad tunnels. The first V-2, fired in July 1942, reached an altitude of one yard and blew up; the first successful launch was on October 3, 1942. It broke the sound barrier and reached an altitude of some 55 miles and a range of 120 miles. Walter Dornberger, the military commander of the rocket team, turned to von Braun and said: "Do you realize what we accomplished today? Today the space ship is born!" It was now merely a matter of more thrust from bigger payloads, and gaining greater reliability and accuracy. "Our main objective for a long time was to make it more dangerous to be in the target area than to be with the launch crew," von Braun once noted.

Then, just on the edge of success, the Peenemünde team received a message in March 1943, which seemed to doom its work. The Führer had had one of his psychic dreams, this one about the V-2. In his dream it had failed to reach London. Three months later, with continuing bad news from the eastern front, Hitler reversed himself. He granted an audience to Dornberger and von Braun, who made a brilliant presentation and showed dramatic film footage of their successes. Hitler was galvanized, and Dornberger later said he seemed almost to scold himself for not having been a believer earlier. "Europe and the world will be too small from now on to contain a war," he had said. "With such weapons humanity will be unable to endure it." He immediately began giving military orders, and the Peenemünde scientists were relieved of whatever illusions they may have had that they were creating vehicles for space travel. These were to be *weapons*. Hitler demanded that the payload be increased from one ton to ten tons. "What I want," he told Dornberg, "is annihilation." Dornberg answered, "When we started our development work we were not thinking of an all-annihilating effect. We—" Hitler interrupted him in a rage: "You! No, *you* didn't think of it. But *I* did!" One incident, though, convinced Dornberg of Hitler's military genius. Hitler asked how the V-2 would explode. Von Braun said that the explosive would have extra destructive power because it would hit the earth with such velocity. Hitler said he thought that the high speed would cause the V-2 to bury itself as it was exploding and thus throw up a great deal of earth. He suggested a supersensitive fuse that would explode on impact. Von Braun checked it out—to his surprise, Hitler was right.

The situation was not without a terrible irony as these brilliant men, working with one eye on the world of the future, were hounded by the very system they worked for. Von Braun was briefly arrested in 1944 by Himmler because he had been overheard saying that he was not really interested in weaponry but rather in space travel. Visionaries they might be, but they were working in Nazi Germany, and the rockets were manufactured at a nearby site by slave laborers, most of them from Russia. By some estimates, 150 of them a day died of malnutrition.

By the spring of 1944, they were producing three hundred V-2s a month (eventually, the figure would reach nine hundred). Production took place in underground facilities because RAF bombing strikes were so effective. On September 8, 1944, they launched their first V-2 (for Vengeance Weapon Two, by Goebbels's decree) against London. Forty-six feet long and five and a half feet in diameter, it weighed 28,000 pounds, most of which was fuel and a fuel tank. Its rocket engine had a thrust of 56,000 pounds, and it was launched vertically. It took about six minutes to hit London. It flew faster than a rifle bullet, and there was no defense against it, no possibility of interception. Because it flew faster than the speed of sound, it gave no warning until after it landed—the sound of it arrived after the rocket itself. Thus, the casualties were very high. One V-2, for example, landed at a market in London and killed a hundred people. According to Dornberger, some 3,745 rockets were fired between September 1944 and March 27, 1945, when Peenemünde closed down. Seventy-four percent landed within eighteen miles of the target, and 44 percent within six miles. They were surprisingly accurate, in retrospect, for this was still an experimental weapon. At the end of the war, von Braun and his team were working on both the A-9 and the A-10 rockets—"the America" rockets. The A-9 was, in effect, a jet airplane with wings that would glide for long periods above the atmosphere when its fuel was exhausted; the A-10 was to have 440,000 pounds of thrust and launch the A-9. These were the forerunners of intercontinental ballistic missiles. Launched from sites on the French coast, they were supposed to hit New York. The future was closing in even as the war was winding down.

After surrendering, von Braun and his people first ended up at the White Sands, New Mexico, testing grounds. Von Braun was, he liked to say later, not a POW but a prisoner of peace. The early days at White Sands were hardly easy ones. They were men between countries in terms of loyalty; Germany was gone, but they were not yet Americans. Actually, their real loyalty was not to any nation but to science, and their special vision was little understood by others. They were paid six dollars a day. They were not even allowed to send packages back to Germany. But by 1947 many of the families had arrived, and that year von Braun was allowed to go back to Germany to marry his eighteen-year-old first cousin.

Von Braun quickly found that Germany had been far ahead of the Americans in rocket development. The first American rocket they worked with was a WAC Corporal. It was much smaller than the V-2 and much slower. By 1950, the German team was transferred to the Army rocket center at Huntsville, Alabama. By this time it was clear that their new country would welcome them as citizens. At the same time, they continued to make steady progress. Von Braun dreamed of placing a satellite in space, but that demanded multiple-stage rockets—that is, rockets that launched other rockets to gain even higher altitude and greater speed. In 1949, he and his colleagues used a V-2 to boost a WAC to an altitude of 250 miles.

Von Braun was not merely a brilliant rocket scientist, but a kind of space poet who envisioned manned space flights to the moon and Mars. His most practical thoughts always seemed to others like dreams and fantasies. Years later, in July 1969, on the eve of the Apollo 11 launch of a manned trip to the moon, a news conference was held at which several NASA officials answered questions. Reporters repeatedly asked the officials what the true historic significance of the moon landing was. None of the officials had an answer except von Braun. For him the moon shot was one more major step in human evolution. It was comparable, he said, to the moment when life emerged from the sea and established itself on land.

He liked to tell friends of the excitement he had felt when he looked through his first telescope and saw the moon: "It filled me with a romantic urge. Interplanetary travel! Here was a task worth dedicating one's life to. Not just to stare through a telescope at the moon and the planets, but to soar through the heavens and actually explore the mysterious universe. I knew how Columbus had felt." Much later in his life, after a successful rocket launch, he walked away from the press center at Cape Canaveral and quoted Jules Verne to a friend, for it was Verne who had originally written in some detail about men flying to the moon: "Anything one man can imagine, other men can make real." His vision of what the moon would be like was very clear. Long before man landed there, he described to his biographer, Erik Bergaus, what it would be like: "Shadows and images in the strange nightly sunshine will seem haunted by a sense of loneliness . . ."

There was ambivalence among Americans about men like von Braun, once enemies who now were at the core of our rocket program. At Huntsville there were certain euphemisms with which the German scientists were described: They were called "first-generation Americans" or "former German scientists who are now American citizens." When people seemed to push the issue, General John

Medaris liked to emphasize that the Germans were here, "of their own volition." Nonetheless, in the earlier part of the fifties, some of the doubts were still there, and when a movie was made about von Braun's life, *I Aim at the Stars,* Mort Sahl, the comedian, added the line "But sometimes I hit London." Von Braun became in time not merely an American citizen but an enthusiastic American—a fan of the barbecue, a delighted deep-sea diver, a believer in the process of democracy—who added his voice to those advancing the cause of integration in the Huntsville, Alabama, schools.

Von Braun would talk about the period of 1945 through 1951 as a time when we lost six years and had no ballistic missile program to speak of. In 1956, he liked to note, we had gone to a crash ballistic missile. Only as the Russians started working on a missile did our program begin to move ahead. But it was no small irony, as Walter McDougall pointed out, that a team of scientists who had chosen America because of its limitless financial resources was almost from the start saddled with limitations that were primarily financial.

There was no delay in the Soviet missile program. At first, the Soviets had planned to base their nuclear strike force on bombers rather than rockets. But it became clear after the war that the U.S. had allies in Europe on whose territory they could base their bombers, but the Soviets had no such base in the Americas. So Stalin moved to develop missiles and Khrushchev continued the program after Stalin's death in 1953.

In theory at least, the Soviets were not far behind the Germans. They quickly picked up the second tier of German rocket scientists, nuts-and-bolts-men who had the capacity to reproduce the V-2 but lacked theoretical skills. Still the Russians thought space vitally important.

The Russians very soon had their own version of the V-2, though it did not, in the beginning, dramatically change their geopolitical situation. As Georgi Malenkov told Grigory Tokady, a rocket expert and one day a defector, ". . . the point is that the V-2 is good for 400 kilometers and no more. And after all, we have no intention of making war on Poland. Our vital need is for machines which can fly across oceans!" They were not about to waste time: By 1949 they had the T-1, with a range of about five hundred miles, and by 1952 they were working on the T-2. What they wanted was nothing less than an intercontinental ballistic missile.

If the Americans had von Braun, then the Russians had their own great rocket scientist: Sergei Korolev. Korolev was considered by other rocket experts a brilliant designer. He had been born in the

Ukraine, and was three years older than von Braun. He had eventually turned to designing, first as an airplane designer in the thirties, when the Soviets seemed to have little interest in space. Gradually, he moved toward missiles and shifted from winged rockets to pure ballistic missiles. He was a protégé of Mikhail Tukhachevsky, who was the leader in Soviet airplane and rocket design. Korolev was arrested in 1937 by Stalin, who was ambivalent about modern weaponry: He was in awe of it, and yet he feared the political ambitions of these unpredictable geniuses who were its architects. With that, Korolev vanished from view. But not from work. He was in a gulag, but a work gulag, a *sharashka.*

There he worked first on airplanes; only later was he transferred to another *sharashka,* where he could work on space. To a Westerner the anomaly of this—a man under a life sentence for treason working in a prison on the most secret scientific developments—is almost too much to comprehend. In the Soviet Union it was an accepted practice. Korolev was immensely valuable, but because he was so valuable, he was also dangerous. He consented to work because this way, at least, he got some rations, he was with his colleagues, and he was doing what he loved most of all. After the war Korolev, still technically a prisoner, was placed in charge of the shipment of what little remained in Peenemünde of the V-2 back to the Soviet Union. He supervised the interviews with the German rocket scientists the Americans had left behind. In 1953, after Stalin's death, he was allowed to join the Party, which he did in order to expedite his work.

If Korolev had to have a title, it would be "chief designer"; if he had to publish, it would be under the pseudonym of Sergeyev. If there were international conferences on space, he was never allowed to attend. By the time he was finally acknowledged as the towering figure of Soviet space, as James Oberg noted, in one of those endless ironies of Russian life, all achievements under Khrushchev were deleted from the history books. He was, not surprisingly, something of a cynical and pessimistic man. His motto, Oberg noted, was, "We will all vanish without a trace."

His vision had dazzled his political superiors. Khrushchev later wrote, "I don't want to exaggerate, but I'd say we gawked at what he showed us as if we were sheep seeing a new gate for the first time. When he showed us one of his rockets, we thought it looked like nothing but a cigar-shaped tube, and we didn't believe it would fly. Korolev took us on a tour of the launching pad and tried to explain how a rocket worked. We were like peasants in a marketplace . . ."

By the mid-fifties the Russians were far advanced on what was their basic rocket of the decade, the R-7. There was nothing very stylish about the R-7. It was, by the standards of rockets, short and fat. Because the Soviet metallurgists had had considerable difficulty developing a metal that could withstand the heat from a giant rocket engine, the R-7 was made up of clusters of smaller engines. There were twenty separate engines in the central cone and four great skirts, but they could bring together a total thrust of 1.1 million pounds. It would be able to carry a primitive atomic weapon of the period all the way to the United States. By 1955, the work toward completing the R-7 was going well enough that Soviet officials began to talk openly about launching an earth satellite during the International Geophysical Year, in 1957–58.

In America our rocket scientists were still working on what was effectively the back burner. It was indicative of how little weight missiles carried in the minds of the policymakers of the Truman administration that K. T. Keller, the president of Chrysler, was appointed Truman's special adviser on missiles; as Walter McDougall points out, he held the job for eleven months, never gave up his job at Chrysler, and never briefed the President on missiles. In the early budget struggles, the B-36 bomber won out over long-range-missile development, and money was poured into the strategic A-Command (SAC).

Years later, when Ike gave his farewell speech warning against the power of a military-industrial complex, he was much heralded; but the truth was that such views were always the bedrock of his philosophy. He was the second President who had to make difficult choices about complex and expensive weapons systems. He worried about the potential drain on the economy, and he believed that the Joint Chiefs cared little or nothing about the dangers of inflation. He spoke often in private about the danger of spending so much on weaponry and defense and in the process destroying the economy and thus weakening the country these weapons were going to protect. The federal budget, he liked to say, had risen from $4 billion a year in 1932 to $85.5 billion in 1952—with some 57 percent of that increase going to the Pentagon. "This country," he once noted, "can choke itself to death piling up expenditures just as surely as it can defeat itself by not spending enough for protection." Defense spending, he believed quite passionately, was dead weight; it was inflationary and subtracted from the nation's vitality rather than added to it.

The great American fear in the fifties was of Soviet intentions and capabilities. As Michael Beschloss pointed out, even the Moscow phone book was classified. Hitler's military build-up in the thirties had, because of the nature of armaments and of Germany's physical location, been self-evident, but the Soviet Union was something else. It was both secretive and vast; much of its territory had no possibility of being inspected; it was a veritable black hole for the new uncertain world power across the Atlantic that felt so threatened. We had made our great investment in SAC, the bomber attack fleet that was on constant alert, but the men around Eisenhower still feared a surprise Soviet attack.

Early photo-reconnaissance attempts to penetrate Soviet airspace with balloons were ineffective. The CIA became particularly worried about missile testing at Kapustin Yar, seventy-five miles east of Stalingrad, far out of the range of aerial surveillance. The need became obvious for some kind of new reconnaissance plane, one that would fly above Soviet air defenses. The photographic technology was already available; by the summer of 1955, the Air Force had the capacity to take a picture from 55,000 feet of Ike's golf ball on a putting green. The great American photographic genius Ed Land, who had invented the Polaroid camera, was absolutely sure the technology was there. In 1954 Philip Strong, a retired Marine general, went out to Burbank, California, to talk with America's most talented airplane designer, Kelly Johnson. "Kelly," he asked. "What would you do if all you were trying to do was get up as high as you could—get moderate speed but not great speed and just sit above their air defense?"

Johnson immediately responded to the challenge. "Jesus," he answered. "I've got just the thing for you—I'd take a Lockheed F-104. I'd give it wings like a tent. It's a cinch!" Johnson drew up plans that called for the plane to fly at an altitude of seventy thousand feet and have a range of some four thousand miles. James Killian, the president of MIT and a principal scientific adviser to the President, and Land went to see the President to convince him of the project's importance. The great question in Eisenhower's mind was whether the intelligence benefits of the flights outweighed the risks of violating Soviet airspace. Otherwise, Eisenhower was interested: Photo reconnaissance had been vital in World War Two, and he had been readily convinced of its tactical value. He was immensely frustrated by how Soviet secrecy fed anxiety in America, causing ever greater pressure on him to spend more and more on potentially useless weapons. To Killian's and Land's surprise, Ike gave tentative approval at the first meeting. His one restriction was that he did not want uniformed Air Force fliers violating Soviet airspace. That meant it would be the CIA's project.

That December Johnson flew to Washington for one more session, to go over cover stories and security. Richard Bissell, deputy director of the CIA, told Johnson that he did not care what the plane looked like as long as they could produce it quickly. That made things easier, for the Air Force traditionally cared about the cosmetic lines of its planes. What we want, said Bissell, is function. "Good," said Johnson. "That will save you a good deal of money. On the other hand I'm going to put my top force on it, and that's going to cost you money." So they bartered with each other, this man of the secret government and this brilliant designer, and in the end they struck a deal—$22 million for twenty planes, with Lockheed permitted to come back for more money if needed.

Each plane was built by hand at the Skunk Works, a secret area of the Lockheed grounds, named after the place in the comic strip "L'il Abner," where Kickapoo Joy Juice was brewed. This particular project was so secret that no janitors were cleared to enter the huge hangar with blacked-out windows where the planes were being built, and therefore the men in charge had to clean up after themselves and worked in constant litter. The code name was Aquatone, although the members of the team generally referred to it as Kelly's plane. Others called it simply The Angel.

Step by step, Johnson argued away the doubts of others. At such high altitudes might the pilot explode or pass out? Johnson said he would invent a pressurized suit to protect the pilot. Wouldn't the fuel evaporate quickly at that height? Johnson was confident a successful fuel could be created. Wouldn't the jet engines fail? Wait and see, he suggested. He was absolutely sure it could be done. The real problem was that the plane needed to stay in the air for perhaps ten hours at a time. This demanded immense amounts of fuel, which in turn created a huge burden of weight. It became, therefore, in the words of one of its early pilots, a young man named Francis Gary Powers, a hybrid, "a jet with the body of a glider." The final product was light, made of titanium and other lightweight metals. It could stay in the air for eleven hours, or 4,750 miles. The only thing ordinary about it was its name; fighters were designated by the letter *F*, bombers had the prefix *B;* but for reasons of secrecy this was called utility plane number two, or as it entered history, the U-2.

For plane aficionados it was a thing of beauty. Its lines were those of a jet, except they were wildly exaggerated; it was so low-slung that when it sat on the runway, its nose was at the height of a man. The fuselage was forty feet long, the wingspan eighty feet. In landing, the pilots had to be extremely careful, for it balanced more like a bicycle than a tricycle. In order to meet Washington's specifications, much had to be sacrificed, and in the case of the spy plane, as Francis Gary noted, "it was strength." "Each piece of structure," he wrote, "was a little thinner than a pilot would have liked. Where there was usually extra support, such as joints and junctures, in the U-2 there was none." It had, Powers said, "a beautiful symmetry all its own but [it was] not built to last." Some of the pilots talked at first about whether it was the world's first disposable plane, a sort of aeronautical Kleenex.

But it could fly at 70,000 feet (soon 80,000) and its cameras could capture the tiniest of objects on the ground some fourteen miles below. Land had created a camera that could swing from horizon to horizon and cover an arc of 750 miles. Most remarkable of all, Kelly Johnson and his people built the prototype from start to finish in only eighty-eight days. The pilots loved it instantly. Every day they were able to break the existing records for altitude: The only problem, Powers later noted, was that they could not boast about it.

Even Charlie Wilson, the great doubter of all things scientific and experimental, was an enthusiast. Generally, Wilson had no interest in the new science of weaponry. He was dubious about missiles and moon shots (he did not need to know if the moon was made of cheese, he liked to say) and he was not worried, as some of the science people around Eisenhower were, about Soviet missile developments. "You'll never convince me that the Russians are ten feet tall," he liked to say when anyone worried aloud about Russian missile progress. But Kelly Johnson took him to the training ground in Nevada and let him watch one of the planes in action. He was put on a radio phone with a pilot who had already been in the air for some eight hours and assured Wilson that he could stay aloft another hour and a half. With that, Wilson came aboard. As they decided to go from prototype to production, the cost of building some thirty planes was placed at $35 million—a bit bulky for the CIA's budget, Allen Dulles noted. Wilson volunteered to carry a significant part of the costs at Defense, though; money was elaborately laundered so there would be no financial tracks. When Johnson sent in his first two vouchers, the checks, for $1,256,000, were sent not to Lockheed but to Johnson personally at his Encino home.

The pilots had to be very good, but they were not to be flashy and colorful, like the great fighter jockeys of the past; rather they were men of endurance who worked in the shadows, the more anonymous the better. Gary Powers was typical of the pilots recruited for the program. He was not an ace, had not flown in Korea, and it took him more than two years to earn his officer's wings.

He was twenty-six when he was approached with an offer that would more than triple his salary as an Air Force first lieutenant. He was the son of an Appalachian miner who worked as a shoe repairman at night to make enough money to send his one son to a small religious college. Oliver Powers had made one vow: His son would never work in a mine. It was the son's idea to become a pilot instead of the doctor his father wanted him to be. He married Barbara Gay Moore when she was eighteen, the prettiest girl around Turner Air Force Base, in Albany, Georgia. A graduate of a local business college for girls, she was the daughter of the cashier at the PX.

Powers was not political or questioning, and he had no doubts about the mission as it was explained. But because of its secret nature, there was little he could tell his family about this exciting new assignment. Just before he went overseas, his father took him aside and said, "I've figured out what you're doing." "What do you mean?" Powers said. "I've told you what I'm doing." (There was a cover story about flying high-altitude weather reconnaissance.) "No, I've figured it out," his father said. "You're working for the FBI." Powers loved that his plane was his own, a single-seater. The hard part was the pressurization suit: "Once on," he noted, "it felt exactly like a too-tight tie over a badly shrunk collar." Because you couldn't go to the bathroom in it, the pilots could eat little food and drink no coffee while flying.

The suit was so heavy that it made them sweat heavily, and at the end of a long flight, they would wring the water out of their long johns. The job was, as much as anything else, about endurance. Because of the high altitude, before each flight they had to put on their suits and helmets and endure a two-hour denitrogenization process—in which they were given pure oxygen. It left the pilots with fierce headaches and earaches. The one tricky skill required was keeping the plane at just the right speed. At maximum altitude, if you went too slowly the plane stalled, and if you went too quickly, it began to buffet and become unmanageable. There was an automatic pilot, but it was considered unreliable.

In September 1956, Powers made his first flight, along the Soviet border, and by November of that year he was flying deep into Soviet territory. There was an ejector seat in the plane, but Powers, like the other pilots, was wary of it. It was, he wrote, like "sitting on a loaded shotgun." Not only were the pilots uncertain the device would work as designed, they did not entirely trust their sponsors; they suspected that the CIA might have designed it to blow them up so there would be no trace in case of a mishap. Though in fact it was not designed to blow them up, the pilots were well advised to be nervous. The last thing in the world the Agency wanted was that a U-2 pilot be shot down and then survive. Indeed, responding to questions from Eisenhower, Allen Dulles assured the President that a pilot could not survive a crash.

There had been some hope on the part of planners that the planes would fly above Soviet radar, but that proved wrong. From the beginning the Soviets were able to track the flights and they were furious both with the American violation of their airspace and at their own impotence, for they were powerless to shoot the planes down. On July 10, 1957, the Soviets made a formal protest, which contained a rather accurate description of what the U-2 had done and where it had gone. The State Department flatly denied it. John Foster Dulles himself wrote a letter saying that no *military* plane had violated Soviet space. He called his brother Allen and read it to him, and Allen Dulles told him, "Fine-perfect-good luck!" At the same time the Soviet officials could not go public with what they knew about the U-2 flights, for they could not admit to their own people that they were powerless in the face of such audacious American violations.

The photos from the first flights stunned Eisenhower. Not only could the U-2 take a clear photograph of a parking lot fourteen miles down, but you could even, he said, see "the lines marking the parking areas for individual cars." In terms of intelligence work, it was a breakthrough of gigantic proportion. The photos were better, fuller, and more accurate than anything they had ever seen before. "Photography," said Ray Cline, a senior CIA official, "became to the fifties what code breaking was to the forties." Now Ike could know what the Russians were up to in terms of bomber and missile construction. That ability would allow him to make informed choices about the American defense budget and not get caught up in a useless and unnecessary military buildup.

"I was able to get a look at every blade of grass in the Soviet Union," Allen Dulles boasted later, after it was all over. But the general public did not know it. The U-2 was a classic invention of the secret government and pointed up the problems of a two-tiered government in general. The intelligence provided by the U-2 was crucial information for the President as he formulated foreign policy, but he could never reveal it to the voters. Thus, at a moment when the U-2 was proving just how limited the Soviet military build up was, there was no public appreciation of it.

Indeed, one of the first things the U-2 proved was that there was no bomber gap, as some critics of the administration had claimed. There had been a nervousness since Russia's Aviation Day in 1955, when a squadron of Bison bombers had flown over the parade, followed by several other squadrons. The U-2 revealed that what the Soviets had almost surely done that day was flown the same few squadrons in repeated sorties. As for the missile gap, the U-2 showed that though the Soviets were working on their missiles, they had yet to launch an ICBM.

By the summer of 1956, von Braun was absolutely certain that the Soviets were planning to launch a satellite. Von Braun was completely confident that he and his colleagues could do it, too, if they could only get the go-ahead from Washington. But if von Braun dreamed of men in space, his nemesis, Charlie Wilson, dreamed of orderly figures and balanced budgets and of tidy weapons systems that he already understood. In early 1956 Wilson had arrived in Huntsville to look over the Army rocket program, and he had seemed a great deal less interested in that than in the old farmhouse near the base that officials had turned into a guesthouse. How much had this cost? Why had they painted these logs? (The logs, Major General John Medaris, the local commander, noted, were cedar logs and had not been painted.) Wilson clearly believed that Medaris and his rocket scientists were living the high life. From then on there was not, as Medaris hoped, greater interest in what von Braun and his team were doing, but merely more intense harassment by Army controllers. We had, Medaris believed quite rightly, the greatest space engineers and scientists in the world and we were doing almost nothing with them; to pay so little attention to the work of someone like von Braun was almost sinful.

For most of the decade, von Braun and his colleagues worked on the most important American rocket of the decade—the Redstone. It was not unlike the old V-2, only larger and more powerful—fifty-six feet long, and seventy inches in diameter. If it was more a hybrid than thoroughbred, that was a reflection that its architects were working with less money and fewer resources than they should have. Still, it was a rocket that von Braun and his people were proud of: It could, von Braun believed, readily launch the first of several of his dream projects—an earth satellite—by 1956. A report he prepared in 1954, entitled "A Minimum Satellite Vehicle," requested only $100,000 for the satellite program, pointing out, "It is only logical to assume that other countries could do the same. *It would be a blow to U.S. Prestige if we did not do it first*" (italics in the original).

Suddenly now, with the International Geophysical Year coming up, there was renewed interest in the missile program. The Americans planned to launch a satellite as part of it. Nor were they alone. The Soviets were beginning to talk ever more confidently about a satellite as well. For the race into space was now on. The Soviets, weak in other areas of modern weaponry, were working at a fever pitch and the Soviet leadership understood, as the more confident American leadership did not, the psychological nature of the race. Asked in 1954 whether he worried over whether the Russians might win the race to place a satellite in orbit, Charlie Wilson said, "I wouldn't care if they did."

But now Eisenhower understood the real value of getting a satellite up: photo reconnaissance. Predictably, the various branches of the military began to jockey for the honor of launching the satellite, even though there was no doubt that von Braun and his Army team were far ahead of everyone else. The Navy offered its Viking project—a generous description was that it was in the experimental stage. But for reasons that were absurd to the detached observer, a civilian team under the auspices of the Secretary of Defense chose the Navy. Thus did the United States pin its hopes, as historian Walter McDougall noted, "on a slim experimental first-stage rocket and three entirely new upper stages, expected to coax a grapefruit-sized satellite to orbital velocity before the end of 1958." "In retrospect," added McDougall, "the decision seems disastrous." Dr. Homer Stewart, the head of the committee and a physicist at Caltech, told von Braun immediately after the vote: "We have pulled a real boner." Von Braun was absolutely appalled by the decision.

The Army people protested bitterly, but to no avail. If anything, von Braun's superiors set out to hinder him. He launched his Jupiter C on September 20, 1956. It was to be a four-stage rocket, but the fourth stage, to von Braun's bitter disappointment, could not, under orders, be a live satellite. The Army, wary that von Braun might pull some sort of trick, made sure that the fourth stage was filled with sand. The launch was a stunning success. It reached a record altitude of 682 miles and a speed of 13,000 miles per hour, which probably would have been sufficient to hurl a satellite into space. The next morning von Braun confided, "We knew with a little bit of luck we could put a satellite in space. Unfortunately, no one asked us to do it."

At the same time the Navy program was running into serious problems, just as von Braun had suspected it would. It was no small thing, von Braun knew, to design a rocket from scratch. The Viking's guidance system kept gaining weight, despite the plans on the drawing board. Meanwhile, to anyone paying attention, there was growing confidence, indeed audaciousness, in the Soviet press. In May 1957 an announcement from the Soviet Academy of Science told Soviet citizens to prepare to track the satellite. A month later a trade publication gave ham radio operators detailed instructions on the course the satellite would take. On August 3, 1957, an R-7 was successfully launched. It did not carry a satellite, but the Soviets were clearly on the verge of a major success. On August 26, 1957, Khrushchev announced that "a super long-distance intercontinental multistage ballistic missile was launched a few days ago."

By the first week in October 1957, Walter Sullivan, *The New York Times* science reporter, had heard enough to go to the paper's Washington bureau and file a notice that he would write a story for the Saturday paper reporting that the Russians would launch a satellite at any moment. His story was never published, for it was overtaken by events. On the morning of October 4, the Soviets launched an intercontinental ballistic missile. By chance that evening, Sullivan attended a cocktail party at the Russian embassy in Washington for some fifty international scientists at the IGY conference. Sullivan was called to the phone and his office told him there was a wire-service report from Moscow that the Russians had placed a satellite in space. Sullivan whispered the news to American scientist Lloyd Berkner, who called for attention. "I am informed by *The New York Times* that a satellite is in orbit at an elevation of 900 kilometers. I wish to congratulate our Soviet colleagues on their achievement." Applause broke out in the room. The Soviet satellite was a relatively small aluminum alloy sphere that weighed 184 pounds and was 22.8 inches in diameter. It had two radio transmitters. The Russians called it *Sputnik,* which means "fellow traveler" in Russian.

No one in the Eisenhower administration, despite all the warnings, was prepared. Even worse, and this was almost surely generational, none of the senior men even saw at first what a psychological victory it was for the Soviets. Defense secretary Engine Charlie Wilson, who had an almost perfect instinct to say the wrong thing at the wrong time, called *Sputnik* "a useless hunk of iron." Sherman

Adams, Ike's closest personal assistant in the White House, said that America was not interested in getting caught up "in an outerspace basketball game." Clarence Randall, who was a White House adviser, called it "a silly bauble in the sky." Eisenhower himself was pounded with questions at his next press conference, on October 9. Merriman Smith began by asking, "Russia has launched an earth satellite. They also claim to have had a successful firing of an intercontinental ballistic missile, none of which this country has done. I ask you, sir, what are we going to do about it?" Eisenhower answered that there was no link between having *Sputnik* and an ICBM, although the Soviet success certainly showed that they could hurl an object a great distance. Moreover, he added, there had never been a race to get into space first. Nor did *Sputnik* prove that an ICBM could hit a target. But the questions kept coming. Finally, Hazel Markel of NBC asked, "Mr. President, in light of the great faith which the American people have in your military knowledge and leadership, are you saying that at this time with the Russian satellite whirling around the world, you are not more concerned nor overly concerned about our nation's security?" The President sought to calm such fears: "As far as the satellite is concerned, that does not raise my apprehensions, not one iota. I can see nothing at this moment, at this stage of development, that is significant in that development as far as security is concerned," he said. Thanks to the U-2 photographs, he had good reason for confidence; unfortunately, he could not share the evidence with the country.

But the younger men in the administration—Nixon, Cabot Lodge, Nelson Rockefeller—understood immediately the propaganda value of *Sputnik*. They knew that in the age of atomic weapons, any kind of scientific breakthrough on the part of the Soviets was seen as a threat. Percival Brundage, the director of the budget, went to a dinner party and said that *Sputnik* would be forgotten in six months. "Yes, dear," answered his dinner companion, the famed hostess Perle Mesta. "And in six months we may all be dead."

The success of *Sputnik* seemed to herald a kind of technological Pearl Harbor, which in fact was exactly what Edward Teller called it. A Democratic legislative aide wrote a paper for Lyndon Johnson showing him that this issue could take him to the White House. (He was wrong.) Some saw it as a rebuke to America's material self-indulgence. Johnson seized on a metaphor of Detroit and American affluence and complacency: "It is not very reassuring to be told that next year we will put a better satellite in the air. Perhaps it will even have chrome trim and automatic windshield wipers." Suddenly, it seemed as if America were undergoing a national crisis of confidence. Admiral Hyman Rickover criticized the American school system. A book called *Why Johnny Can't Read—and What You Can Do About It,* which had appeared two years earlier to little attention, suddenly became a smash best-seller. The president of Harvard, Nathan Pusey, was moved to declare that a greater percentage of the GNP should go to education.

It was a shattering moment. *Life* magazine printed an article called "Arguing the Case for Being Panicky." John Foster Dulles, defying logic and the facts, noted that the Soviets had had an advantage because of their capture of German scientists. *Sputnik* jokes abounded: A *Sputnik* cocktail was two parts vodka, one part sour grapes. One critic noted that as *Sputnik* went over the White House, it said, "Beep, beep, I like Ike, I like Ike."

The Soviets could not resist the temptation to gloat. Their leaders saw it as a victory over American materialism. At an international conference in Barcelona, Soviet space scientist Leonid Sedov told an American: "You Americans have a better standard of living than we have. But the American loves his car, his refrigerator, his house. He does not, as we Russians do, love his country." Khrushchev had a visceral sense of the impact of *Sputnik* on ordinary people, how terrifying and awesome it seemed. The Soviets, he boasted, could do this anytime. They would produce rockets like this by the dozens—"like sausages." When the Americans finally launched a satellite, he belittled it (although in scientific terms it was considerably more impressive than the Soviets'). The American satellites were small, like oranges, he said. The Americans would have to hurl many oranges into space to catch up with the Soviet people. Space became Khrushchev's newest propaganda weapon. In public he glorified not the scientists but the cosmonauts. They were his space children, "celestial brothers" of the Soviet people; he was their "space father."

The day *Sputnik* was launched, Neil McElroy, who was soon to replace Wilson as secretary of defense, was visiting Huntsville by chance with some of his top aides. They were touring the facilities when they heard the news. All von Braun's frustrations exploded: "We knew they were going to do it!" Then he added, "Vanguard will never make it. We have the hardware on the shelf. We can put a satellite up in sixty days." When McElroy left, von Braun, for the first time in months, seemed confident about the future of his program again. "They'll call me soon," he thought. "McElroy will give me the green light soon. He doesn't have any alternative." It took a month. On November 8, McElroy sent a telegram asking them to launch two satellites.

Soon there was *Sputnik II.* Launched on November 3, 1957, it weighed 1,120.29 pounds, some six times more than its predecessor, its orbit was even higher, and it carried a small dog, Laika. Clearly, the Soviets intended to put a man in space soon. It was another psychological triumph. But the worst was still to come. Jim Hagerty, Ike's press secretary, had announced right after *Sputnik* that the Navy team planned to put a satellite in orbit very soon. Hagerty's announcement stunned the Navy.

But the Navy team speeded up its schedule. Smarting from the Soviet success, the White House not only announced the launch but in effect showcased it as a major media event. On the day of the launch, there was talk of delaying because of high winds, but gradually they died down and the decision was made to go ahead. The countdown finished, and in the words of Kurt Stehling, a German engineer, "It seemed as if the gates of hell had opened up. Brilliant stiletto flames shot out from the side of the rocket near the engine. The vehicle agonizingly hesitated for a moment, quivered again, and in front of our unbelieving, shocked eyes, began to topple. It sank like a great flaming sword into scabbard down into the blast tube. It toppled slowly, breaking apart, hitting part of the test guard and ground with a tremendous roar that could be felt and heard even behind the two-foot concrete wall of the blockhouse and the six-inch bulletproof glass. For a moment or two there was complete disbelief. I could see it in the faces. I could feel it myself. This just couldn't be. . . . The fire died down and we saw America's supposed response to the 200-pound Soviet satellite—our four-pound grapefruit—lying amid the scattered glowing debris, still beeping away, unharmed."

"U.S. Calls It Kaputnik," chuckled the *London Daily Express.* "Oh, What a Flopnik!" headlined the *Daily Herald.* "Phut Goes U.S. Satellite," said the *Daily Mail.* It was a "Stayputnik," said another paper. Again the Soviets gloated. A prominent Soviet clown named Karandash (the Pencil) went into the arena with a small balloon. The balloon exploded. His assistant asked what it was. "That was *Sputnik,*" he said. The audience gasped. "The American *Sputnik,*" he added to great cheers.

So von Braun's team was left to recoup American prestige. Hopes were pinned on Missile #29. The date chosen for the launch was January 29, 1958. There was to be no premature publicity. The rocket was checked out at night so that newsmen would not catch on. The early part of the countdown went well, but the weather report was bad. They decided to delay the launch. Kurt Debus began to worry that the fuel in the rocket might start corroding the tanks. By January 31 he was pleading to launch.

Finally, everything seemed to come together. With some one hundred reporters in the grandstand, the launch took place at 10:-47:56 P.M. They knew immediately it was a good one. Everything seemed to work perfectly. At six minutes and fifty seconds into the flight, the final rocket, or kick stage, ignited and burned for six seconds and hurled the satellite into space. Von Braun was at the Pentagon with Army officials, including Wilbur Brucker, secretary of the Army, and William Pickering, the head of the Jet Propulsion Laboratory. The minutes seemed interminable as they waited for some hard confirmation of the orbit. No one wanted to call the President until it was a sure thing. The satellite was, by von Braun's calculations, supposed to pass the Pasadena tracking station at 12:41 Eastern time. At 12:40 they queried Pasadena. Had it heard anything? Nothing yet. At 12:43, the tension ever greater, they queried Pasadena again. Had it heard anything. "Negative," came back the answer. "Well, why the hell don't you hear anything?" asked Pickering. Brucker was nervous. "Wernher," he asked von Braun. "What happened?" Von Braun was sweating. Pickering, on the phone to Pasadena, yelled out, "They hear her, Wernher, they hear her." Von Braun looked at his watch. "She is eight minutes late," he said. "Interesting." Finally, Hagerty was allowed to call Eisenhower and tell him. "That's wonderful," he said. "I surely feel a lot better now." Then he paused and considered things. "Let's not make too great a hullabaloo about this," he added. America, after some significant and quite unnecessary humiliations, was finally in the space race.

FORTY-TWO

Television was turning out to be a magic machine for selling products, and the awareness of that was still dawning on Madison Avenue in the late 1950s. Yet the ad men had already discovered that television favored certain products and could sell them more readily: beer, cigarettes, various patent medicines and, above all, such big-ticket items as cars. No company spent more money on advertising or advertised its products better, as the country was riding the crest of that great economic wave, than GM.

Kensinger Jones, a young man in the advertising department of the Leo Burnett Company in Chicago, saw an ad in the industry journal *Advertising Age* around the middle of 1957—an unidentified company was looking for a television creative director to handle the world's largest account. Jones was immediately interested. He had worked at the Burnett company for some five years and had done well there, but he felt that it, like most advertising companies of the period, was still too print-oriented. As far as Jones could tell, it was a generational thing. He believed all the top people at all the top agencies had made their reputations by handling words—words were what they understood and responded to. Television made them uneasy. Some of them looked down on it; some of them feared it. Few of them seemed to realize the extent to which it had already changed their own industry. Even when they used it and thought they were using it well, Ken Jones thought, they didn't fully exploit its greatest strength: images. Instead, they did what they knew how to do best—employ words. As far as Jones was concerned, television was the dog and print was the tail, and the generation that dominated the ad agencies was letting the tail wag the dog. Leo Burnett himself seemed to realize he had to adapt to television, but he couldn't quite force himself to do it fully.

Jones especially liked the freedom offered in the early days of television commercials, when budgets were small and almost everything was done live. There were no rules and no one could tell you what you were not allowed to do. He had done one set of live commercials for a new pop-cap bottle for Pabst Blue Ribbon. It was seemingly simple: a flick of the thumb, and the cap was supposed to come flying off—except that it did not always work. Jones learned how to cut away quickly to something else—the continuation of the program, or another commercial—and then to come back when the cap was off. For the Green Giant vegetables, a major Burnett account, Jones helped create a huge puppet of the Jolly Green Giant. It was about two and a half feet tall, and he thought it was going to charm hundreds of thousands of young children. Jones was very pleased with himself and thought he had taken a giant step forward for the visual arts. But when the puppet Giant premiered, it was an absolute disaster. It lurched at the camera, like a Frankensteinian monster, frightening thousands of children. There were endless phone calls to the studio that day demanding that they get that awful thing off the air. Jones had learned a great deal in his experimental period, and he was confident he knew, as few others did, how to sell a product visually. In particular, he was pleased with a commercial he had done for Campbell's tomato juice in which he had used time-lapse photography to show the life of a tomato as it grew into one of the lucky vegetables chosen for the honor of being in Campbell's tomato juice.

Intrigued by the notice in *Ad Age,* Jones responded. The world's largest account had to be Chevy, he was certain. He was right: It was

Chevy, and it was handled by the Detroit firm of Campbell Ewald. He was called in for an interview, and the Ewald and General Motors people liked what they saw in him. He might be a television man, a relatively unpredictable breed as far as they were concerned, but he was a good son of the Midwest—born in St. Louis, educated at Washington University of St. Louis, and currently working in Chicago at Burnett, which fancied itself a bastion of Midwestern values in a profession dominated by Eastern and Californian elitism and snobbery. As such, he was not a man likely to look down on either cars or Detroit. Jones was thrilled when the job was offered to him; he liked the big budget—around $1 million. It was an amazing figure for the time; it meant that on a given commercial he could spend as much as $70,000 in production costs. In addition, Chevy's commitment to television advertising was imposing. Jones was soon in charge of spending some $90 million annually, and there were times when Chevy sponsored three major network shows—*My Three Sons* on ABC; *Route 66* on CBS; and *Bonanza* on NBC.

If Jones had thought people were a little slow to pick up on the uses of television at Burnett, that was no longer a problem at Chevy. In addition, he liked the openness and directness of the top professional people at Chevrolet, especially Ed Cole. Ed Cole, he thought, would not dream of telling him how to make a commercial. Instead, Cole's only marching orders were to make good commercials. Cole thought Chevy was making the best cars in its history, and he thought if the advertising men made commercials that were as good as his cars, the company would sell even more cars.

What Ken Jones wanted to do was use this new medium to tell stories visually and to minimize words. If there was to be storytelling, then let the camera do it. By coincidence, at almost the same time he went to Campbell Ewald, a friend of his named Bob Lawrence, who ran a small production company in New York, sent him some experimental films. They had been made independently by a cinematographer in Los Angeles named Gerry Schnitzer. When Ken Jones saw the films he was stunned: What Schnitzer had been doing on his own, with very little money, was exactly what he was looking for. Schnitzer's stories were short and arresting, and in some way they reflected the essence of American life. They were the work of an original and very gifted man. One of them showed a mailman making his rounds, coming upon a hopscotch board and, when he thought no one was looking, playing a secret game of hopscotch. In another, Schnitzer had waited by a drawbridge and caught the idle moments of people in their cars as the bridge was up and their lives were momentarily interrupted. In another film, he had quietly staked out a scene in Los Angeles where an older and obviously quite poor Mexican-American man was trying to sell a cocker spaniel puppy with a rope around its neck. A father, mother, and young daughter drove up and negotiated with the man, but they failed to make a deal and drove off. Then a little while later, obviously in response to the pleas of the child, the family came back and completed the deal. The simplicity of the scene was powerful.

Ken Jones saw those small stories and knew he had found his man—someone who could tell a story with a camera, used no narration, and had a vision of America that reminded Jones of Norman Rockwell's. He got in touch with Gerry Schnitzer immediately. Schnitzer had grown up in Brooklyn and gone to Dartmouth intending to be a writer, but had found much to his surprise that he liked using a camera better than a typewriter. He had written and directed some of the early *Bowery Boys* films and made some small films about the Canadian fishing and lumber industries for the Canadian Film Board. Eventually, he moved to California and continued making small, highly original films that contained no dialog. Commercial success had largely eluded him, in no small part because he had not actively sought it. Someone had used his films for children in remedial reading and writing classes. Here, children who were nominally loath to express themselves verbally, saw his films and were encouraged, perhaps by the lack of narration, to talk about what they had just seen. At the very least, that was a sign that he was touching an audience normally resistant to most traditional forms of communication. Schnitzer, in those days, was getting by on a very small amount of money, and no one on Madison Avenue seemed to have any interest in his work. Someone had sent him to meet Max Wylie, the creative director at one of the major New York firms, and Wylie, Schnitzer thought, had not only rejected his work but treated him with great contempt. In fact, Wylie had told Schnitzer he knew nothing about storytelling. "They're very pretty," Wylie had said, "but they're not really stories, are they? I mean, where are the words? Where is the story line? I'm afraid we can't sell tobacco with work like this." Then Schnitzer got a call from Ken Jones, who proposed they work together.

Schnitzer agreed, but he knew that he was going to be walking a very fine line between his art on one hand and commerce on the other. That meant he had to be very tight in his storytelling. There could be no ambiguities. The theme had to be very sharply focused, and there was to be no doubt when the commercial was over what the point of it was: to sell cars. Years later, he noted, though, that he and Jones were not selling cars but dreams.

The first commercial Schnitzer shot with Jones was for the 1958 Chevrolet. Jones deferred to Schnitzer's instinct for the right story. Schnitzer had thought about it. He wanted something that was basic to ordinary American life, something that touched every home and reflected a rite of passage to which Chevy could be connected. In the end he came up with a very simple idea. "How about a family at graduation time?" Schnitzer asked Jones. That was it, they agreed. So the commercial was shot at two minutes in length—then, and now, a lifetime as far as commercials were concerned.

It featured an unbelievably wholesome young blond teenager, a Tab Hunter lookalike, clearly soon to leave high school and go on to college and the right fraternity. It is prom night, and as the commercial begins, he is a little disorganized and running behind time. As he rushes out in his white dinner jacket, his family gathers at the door. They are immediately recognizable: a likeable, wise, and good-natured dad; a pleasant (but somewhat more severe) mom; and a younger sister, with the obvious look of a tomboy. There is a sense that they are sharing a secret, but it is a little hard to tell at first. This is all done deftly in mime, as Schnitzer wanted, with no sales pitch. The music in the background is the Chevy fight song of the period: "See the U.S.A. in Your Chevrolet," and it is played in a Les Paul/ Mary Ford style, to show that Chevy is hip. The boy leaves the house and heads to his jalopy, which is an American classic of the period, painted with folksy teenage mottos: ENTRANCE, it says on the front door, and GO ƨLOW on top, clearly an all-American car. As the boy heads toward his car, we see his eyes catch something else—another car parked in front of the house. We see his surprise. It is a brand-new Chevy convertible, with the top down. For the first time, the announcer speaks: "If it's happened once, it's happened a thousand times." The boy stops, looks at the new car, and then turns and looks back at the front door of his house, where the rest of his family is standing. The audience senses that there is a secret between Dad and Sis. Back and forth go the looks—boy to family, boy to new convertible. Finally, Dad smiles and reaches into his pocket for a set of keys. The boy rushes to get them, races to the convertible, and is about to drive off when he realizes he has forgotten something. The corsage is in the old jalopy. He gets the corsage and picks up his girlfriend, one well worthy of the car (the actress Shirley Knight, in one of her first roles). It is all clear: This is a great kid, a great family, a great car. Just to be sure, lest we may not have gotten it, the announcer says: "What a gal! What a night! What a car! The new Chevrolet!" When Jones and Schnitzer screened it for the first time, Jones knew he had a winner when the advertising manager of Chevy broke into tears and said, "It's perfect—it makes me think of my oldest son."

Among other things, the commercial signaled that a new, more affluent era was coming, even for teenagers. The age of the jalopy was over, it seemed to say, the age of tinkering and patching done with it. Dads from now on had better give their sons and daughters something worthwhile, *something brand-new,* when they graduated from high school. A new era was being announced and sold in a very new way.

The next major commercial the two men did together took place in the fall of 1958 and was known as the "Family Shopping Tour." It was very specifically designed to attack the almost un-American idea of not trading in a new car and instead trying to squeeze an additional year or two out of an old model. The economy had hit a soft patch that year; people were perhaps thinking of keeping their cars a little longer than in the past. The selling theme addressed this problem. It begins with a shot of a father and a son passing a Chevrolet window. Inside the showroom, a salesman is showing a 1959 station wagon to another family. The camera closes to a little girl hanging out the rear window of the new station wagon. She makes a face and sticks her tongue out at the boy, who is watching from the street. The salesman sees her and does a double-take, then smiles. The boy and the father keep looking at the station wagon. The camera picks up the byplay between the boy and the girl. Then the camera picks up the boy's mother (and the man's wife) carrying a load of groceries to an old car. She puts the groceries in the front seat and closes the door with considerable difficulty—she has to slam it three times before it catches. Then she casts a disapproving look at her husband's interest in the auto showroom. He makes things worse by pointing to the new Chevy wagon. She is not pleased. Clearly, they have had arguments about a new car before, and she has held the line against spending. Just then the door of the old car slips open and the groceries tumble out, including a bunch of oranges. The camera closes on one orange as it tumbles down the street, follows it, and by the time the orange finishes its roll, it has turned into the mother, father, and little boy, now inside the showroom, where the salesman is working on them. Mom gets into the station wagon and slams the door. It catches immediately. She smiles. The next shot is of the family on the road, all of them smiling heartily. The announcer says: "Fun to see. Fun to drive. Fun to buy.

The new Chevrolet." There were others to come—a driverless Chevy going through the streets of Paris as the style-conscious Parisians gape at it; a Chevy on the top of a mountain in southern Utah; and an airline pilot saying "My God, there's a car on that rock."

A few years later, after a string of remarkable successes, Jones and Schnitzer found that the Chevrolet management started to interfere, calling for more narration extolling the cars' virtues. Schnitzer thought it was because the corporate people "understood everything but the dreams." Some thirty years later, he pondered the reasons for the success of his early Chevy commercials and decided that it had to do with capturing the dreams and ambitions of ordinary families—*always,* he noted, *a family.*

As the cars were becoming more powerful all the time, the men running the company were becoming blander and the power of the financial men was growing. Ed Cole was becoming very much the exception. Central headquarters was growing ever more powerful at the expense of the divisions. For many GM people the critical moment came in 1958, when Frederic Donner became president. Donner's roots were in accounting but, unlike Harlow Curtice, who had also been an accountant, Donner was a man who gave off a sense of being interested only in numbers. When he traveled around the company, he was known to ask of the younger GM employees, "How much are we paying that young man?" His general reputation was for being shy and extremely private. He denied that: "I am not taciturn. I am not shy. I am not afraid of people and I don't even own a slide rule." His efforts at public relations, both inside and outside the company, were marginal: When Bob Dietch, the business editor of the Scripps-Howard chain asked for an interview with Donner as part of a series he was doing on the ten most influential businessmen in America, Donner at first refused. Dietch then said he would simply leave Donner off the list, and the latter changed his mind. The interview did not get off to a good start. "It's very nice of you to give me the time," Dietch said at the beginning. "Yes, I agree with that," said Donner, quite deadpan. "I think it's very nice of me too."

His ascent was a reflection of the changes at the company. At the daily meeting with the heads of the divisions, Fred Donner kept talking about the stock, about what the stock analysts in New York said about it. For Bunkie Knudsen, then the head of the Pontiac division, talk like this was downright sacrilegious. There had *never* been talk of the stock price at these meetings in the past. It was perfectly proper for the head of a company to talk about the need for profits, even the need to maximize profits, but to talk about driving the stock up and to talk about what Wall Street analysts thought of the company, he believed, was unthinkable. In the old days there had been a simple concept: The people in Detroit had to make good cars, and if they did, the people in New York would take care of the stock.

Donner's talk signaled something ominous to Knudsen: a profound change in the purpose of the corporation. It meant that profit, rather than the quality of the product, was now the objective of the corporation, and it meant, though few realized it at the time, that there would be an inevitable decline in the power of the engineering and manufacturing departments. It also signaled an even greater decline in the willingness of the corporation to experiment with new technology (each new development added costs to a car), and finally, it would lead to an unswerving drive to make the divisions as homogenous as possible, so that the same pins and screws and nuts and bolts and body shells could be used in each division. For a profound metamorphosis was taking place in America's largest and biggest industrial companies: the rise of financial experts over product men. It was a sure sign that these companies, unconsciously at least, believed that they were de facto monopolies and faced no real competitive challenges anymore. Rather, their only real concern was to maximize the profits that now seemed to be permanently theirs and to drive the stock up.

Bunkie Knudsen did not understand all of the ramifications of this, but he knew that something was terribly wrong. What begot greater performance on Wall Street did not necessarily mean greater performance in terms of autos; what was good for Wall Street was not, regrettably, always good for General Motors. When the meetings with Donner were over, Bunkie Knudsen could not go off and have lunch with any of his colleagues. Instead, he would go down to the Detroit Athletic Club and work out furiously to burn off his anger. Knudsen couldn't have seen it then, but the issue he was so upset about was nothing less than the entire purpose of American industry, whether it was to make the best product possible or whether it was merely to make the maximum profit possible each year. The two, it turned out, were not mutually compatible—not by a long shot. All of this placed the corporation in jeopardy.

The first shot across GM's bow was a small import whose makers rejected all the norms that were regarded as sacred in Detroit. It was smaller than most American cars—*much* smaller. It did not offer more power, more options, more luxury; it offered decidedly less. The "Bug," or "Beetle," as it was dubbed almost immediately, did not promise that next year's model would be hotter and sexier; in fact just the opposite was true—next year's model would be very much the same as this year's. This last was a basic repudiation of Mr. Sloan's philosophy, based as it was on the annual model change. In fact, the Volkswagen was so different from anything Detroit offered that it seemed to be immune to criticism. And there were advantages: It was cheap; it was reliable; it was fun; and because there were no model changes, repairmen always had an excellent inventory of parts and knew exactly what to do with them to fix the car should anything go wrong.

Volkswagen had placed a high priority on creating a strong service department and had sent its best mechanics to teach the American mechanics how to service a car whose problems were, given the nature of the car, quite simple. As such it got high marks from the start from customers for service, an area in which Detroit was just beginning to slip. Lack of spare parts had signaled the death knell for many other foreign imports. It was a no-frills approach; Volkswagen did not even do any serious advertising until 1959, because its executives in America believed in word-of-mouth advertising. Therefore, they felt that whatever extra money the car generated could be better spent on good service rather than on something as frivolous as advertising.

The Beetle was the dream of Ferdinand Porsche, the great German automotive genius who wanted to create a German version of the Model T, a car for ordinary workers. Porsche had been a great admirer of the first Henry Ford, and he had made a trip to America in 1937 to tour American factories. He was greatly impressed by the production lines and the confidence and life-styles of the workers. He had met with his hero Ford, and they spoke at great length of his desire to produce a comparable car in Germany. Did that bother Ford? he asked. No, answered the great industrialist. "If anyone can build a car better or cheaper than I can, that serves me right."

For a time before the war, Hitler had backed Porsche in his idea of a people's car—a "Volksauto" in German. But the car and its prospective buyers were overtaken by events, and the company never put the car into production. At the end of the war, no one knew quite what to do with the Volksauto plant; it was offered to various major auto companies, none of which was interested. In March 1948, it was offered to the Ford Company at a meeting attended by the young and inexperienced Henry Ford II, who had just taken over a nearly bankrupt company, and the actual head of the company, Ernie

Breech, then chairman of the board. Ford, who still deferred to Breech, asked his chairman what he thought of it. "Mr. Ford, I don't think what we're being offered here is worth a damn," Breech answered. With that the Wolfsburg plant was turned over to an exceptional man named Heinz Nordhoff, who not only rescued it but made it the premier symbol of Germany's industrial rebirth. His car, remarkably like Porsche's original design, was the perfect vehicle for a nation struggling to rebuild itself after a cataclysmic war. When Porsche eventually saw the production line, at that point producing 90,000 vehicles a year, he said, "Yes, Herr Nordhoff, that's how I always imagined it."

Nordhoff was a brilliant businessman. He knew immediately that he had to cut production time from 400 man-hours per car to 100, which he did, and he knew he needed better materials. He understood that the pride and commitment of his workers was of paramount importance, and he got rid of a sign in the parking lot that said BRITISH OFFICERS ONLY. What Nordoff needed was hard currency so that he could improve both his workplace and the quality of his cars. The only way to get it was to sell in the United States.

The Beetle's first venture to the land of the automotive giants was a good deal less than a complete success. Sensitive to postwar anti-German feelings, the company sent its first car to America in 1949 in the care of a Dutch salesman named Ben Pon. He had won the honor of bringing the Beetle to America by dint of his considerable success in selling it in Holland, where anti-German feeling was still very powerful. Pon brought one car to the States with him in January 1949 and ran into complete rejection. No American dealer would take him seriously. Pon did not get a lot of media attention and in the stories he did receive, the car tended to be referred to as Hitler's car. In the end he was forced to sell his one model to a dealer for $800 to cover his hotel bill. It was not, however, a permanent defeat. The next year, 1950, some 330 Volkswagens were sold in America. They seeped into the country, brought back by returning servicemen, who had picked them up in Europe. Gradually, a fragile dealer network was being created. But very quietly, relying as much as anything on word of mouth, the Beetle became a success. It happened because the car was everything it was said to be. By 1955 it was selling some 30,000 vehicles; by 1957, some 79,000.

Detroit from the start quite predictably treated the phenomenon of the Beetle with contempt. It was in the immortal words of Henry Ford II, "a little shit box." It lacked power, it lacked size, and it lacked style. It was two feet shorter than the smallest Chevy of its

time, and its 1300cc engine seemed an insult to the colossal engines
Detroit was producing. The car was not particularly comfortable
and the early models lacked even a gas gauge. It was a work of
minimalist but very sound engineering. Some of Detroit's engineers,
however, were impressed from the start, because it is in the nature of
engineers to be minimalists, to seek the most production for the least
amount of input. That most basic of engineering values had become
virtual heresy in Detroit after Kettering's high-octane gas had created the idea of power as an end in itself, accompanied by the waste
of power and fuel. In 1956, Arthur Railton, writing in *Popular Mechanics,* said of the VW: "The Volkswagen sells because it is, more
than anything else, an honest car. It doesn't pretend to be anything
it is not. Being an honest piece of machinery, it is one the owner can
be proud of. Wherever he looks, he sees honest design and workmanship. There are no places where parts don't fit, where paint is thin,
where the trim is shoddy. There are no body rattles, no water leaks.
Neither, of course, is there overstuff, false luxury either. There is
nothing about the car that is not sincere. One cannot imagine, for
instance, a Volkswagen with a fake air scoop or tail fins to make it
look like an airplane in flight."

To the degree that Detroit took the VW seriously, it was pleased
because it ended the pressure to build a small low-performance car,
which industry critics had been demanding since the end of the war.
Detroit, therefore, for a surprisingly long time, was happy to have
the VW at the low end of the line, costing only $1,280, to take care
of people it regarded as cranks—all those college professors, rocket
engineers, and architects who could afford to pay more but were
content to pay less. It was, after all, good basic transportation, the
perfect second car, particularly for Americans who took their self-
definition from something other than their cars. There was on the
part of Detroit's top people a certain amount of irritation with those
who could easily have afforded larger, more expensive cars and were
shirking their civic duty as Americans by buying the Beetle. "Gray
flannel non-conformists," one Detroit executive called them. Because it took up little space, it was easy to park in increasingly
crowded urban environments. That its owners represented a more
significant part of the market than their sheer numbers indicated,
that the people themselves were tastemakers, that by their education
and self-confidence they were making decisions more independently
than average American consumers, did not register quickly in Detroit. But when it did, Detroit sat up and took notice.

The growing success of the Volkswagen eventually convinced

General Motors that it would have to offer something competitive to protect the low end of the market. Somewhat reluctantly, GM gave the go-ahead on a small rear-end-engine car to the one person who truly hungered to do it: Ed Cole. By 1956, he was the general manager of Chevrolet, and what he envisioned was nothing less than a car that was totally new in its engineering and styling—in effect a faster, more high-powered, thoroughly Americanized Volkswagen. Almost as soon as he became general manager of Chevy, Cole set out to plan his small car. This time, however, unlike the earlier crash programs when he created the '55 Chevy, he did not have the full force of the corporation behind him. Quite the contrary. From the start Cole encountered the old wariness about doing a small car, particularly a new car that would have to be completely retooled. It soon became obvious that he was fighting a powerful corporate undertow of opposition. Some people in the company did not want to do small cars because they might not be successful, and some did not want to do them because they *might* be successful. To say that the company's more senior executives were ambivalent about the project is an understatement. At one point in 1958, Harlow Curtice visited the design room where Cole was preparing his model. He got inside the prototype Corvair and reportedly said, with some degree of irritation, "This is amazing—there's as much head room here as in a Buick." Then he paused and thought for a moment. "Take some of the headroom out. We can't have a little car like this with as much room as a big car." With that, Cole was more isolated within the ever more conservative corporation than he realized. Sure of his own vision, confident, indeed overly confident, of his strengths, he did not entirely understand his new marching orders. In reality, they went like this: We'll do your small car at GM, though it goes against our grain, but only on our terms. If there is a conflict between what you want and what we want, we, not you, will make the final decision. Energized by the excitement of a new challenge, Cole poured his energy into the Corvair. It would have a rear-engine drive and an air-cooled six-cylinder aluminum engine.

Three years in the essential design and creation, the Corvair debuted in the showrooms in September 1959. As far as Detroit executives were concerned, it was just in time, for the low end of the market had been consistently growing over the past decade and could no longer be ignored. In 1958, some 379,000 imported cars were sold in America; added to the growing sales of the little American Nash Rambler, the compacts now accounted for about 12 percent of the market. The Corvair had a chance, some automotive people thought, to be a superb small car. There was, on the part of its creator, a receptivity toward new ideas and new technology. But from the start it was always an orphaned car—the institution itself never really approved of it and the sales department at Chevy hated it. Arguments that Cole might have won when he was working on the '55 Chevy he now lost or had to compromise on, because he was fighting the culture of the company, and he could not prove that what he wanted was cost-effective. The Corvair's small size worked against it. Because it was a small car and not likely to make a large profit margin for the company, Harlow Curtice was able to set very strict limits on what it would cost. It had to sell for under $2,000, he said, which was Volkswagen's list price in 1959.

Cole's car, in comparison with the Volkswagen, was sporty—indeed, the name Corvair was meant to imply a kinship with the Corvette. It was 1,300 pounds lighter than the smaller Chevys of the time, but it was filled with compromises that bothered some of the engineers working on the program, and apparently bothered Cole, too. The tires were smaller than they should have been. The engine became a half-breed—part aluminum, part cast iron. Because of the size of the tires, the car had a tendency to swing out or, in the vernacular of auto engineers, to jack on corners, the rear tires losing traction if the driver did not have a particularly good feel for the car. A seasoned, experienced race driver soon realized that one of the keys to safe handling of the car was to keep the tire pressure at different levels for the front and rear tires, but few ordinary drivers paid attention to their tire pressure. Because its weight was differently aligned and the engine was in the rear, no one had much of a natural feel for driving it. The early tests reflected serious problems in handling. Cole's desire to add stability to the rear end through a stabilizing mechanism was lost in cost cutting. It was estimated that a better stabilizing system, such as a stabilizing bar, would have cost only about $14 or $15 more per car. Some of the Corvair engineers protested that the safety bar was necessary, but their protests were lost in the rush to get to market. There was, thought Cole's opposite number at Ford, Don Frey, who watched the birth of the Corvair and was aware of the fierce intramural struggle going on, a certain hubris to Ed Cole, and it showed here more than anywhere else. "We tested two of them," said Frey, who was generally an admirer of Cole's, "and we were appalled." Cole was so strong-willed that on occasion no one could stop him; this was one of the times he should have been stopped, Frey thought.

On sharp corners, particularly with neophyte drivers at the

wheel, the car had a tendency to flip at high speeds. Perhaps a race driver could handle the car, but what about ordinary Americans, many of them younger and anxious to go for higher speeds than the car was able to negotiate safely? What made this different was not that the Corvair was that much less safe than the Volkswagen, which was, if anything, less safe, a number of engineers thought. But there was less of a tendency on the part of its owners to drive the Beetle at high speed.

In addition, General Motors was about to come under a new and different kind of political and social scrutiny than in the past. By the time the stabilizing bar was added, in 1963, the number of lawsuits against Chevy on the Corvair was mounting and within a year would reach a hundred. Once the stabilizing bar was added and the tendency to swing out was eliminated, *Car and Driver* wrote a harsh epitaph for the early cost-conscious Corvair. It was, said the magazine, a bible of auto enthusiasts, "one of the nastiest-handling cars ever built. The tail gave little warning that it was about to let go, and when it did, it let go with a vengeance few drivers could deal with. The rear wheels would lose traction, tuck under and with the tail end jacked up in the air, the car would swing around like a 3-pound hammer on a 30-foot string. This is not to say that the car was unstable within the limits of everyday fair-weather driving—just that those limits were none too clearly posted, and once transgressed, you were in pretty hairy territory, indeed."

Among those following the flaws of the Corvair and the crippling accidents left in its wake was a young man named Ralph Nader. He had already set out on a lonely path as a kind of one-man consumer critic of Detroit and what he considered its lack of concern for the greater good of its consumers, including on the issue of safety. GM, in turn, would lash out at Nader and would be caught in the act. Humiliating Senate hearings would follow in which General Motors was forced to apologize for its arrogance. For the first time, the government began to pay attention to the auto industry and the impact of its decisions on the people of the nation. The legacy of the Corvair was that it connected the fifties to the sixties. At the same time, top executives at General Motors were convinced that their great mistake had not been in trying to do the car too cheaply, thereby making it a dangerous vehicle, but in bothering to produce a small car in the first place.

FORTY-THREE

The radio quiz shows had been, in retrospect, small
potatoes, with prizes to match. On *Take It Or Leave It,*
the ultimate challenge was the "$64 question"—a phrase
that even worked itself into the American vernacular by 1945. In the
new age of television, though, everything had to be bigger and better.
Americans were not going to sit home, glued to their television sets,
wondering whether some electronic stranger, who had briefly entered
their living rooms, was going to be able to double his winnings from
$32 to $64. In the postwar era that was pocket money.

Such was the dilemma facing Lou Cowan in early 1955. Cowan,
one of the most inventive figures in the early days of television,
needed a gimmick for a game show worthy of television, one so
compelling that millions of Americans would faithfully tune in. He
needed high drama, and what better way to achieve that than a *very*

large prize? Six hundred and forty dollars? Not so terribly exciting. Nor, for that matter, was $6,400. "But $64,000 gets into the realm of the almost impossible," he thought. Cowan liked the double-or-nothing format—so he envisioned a contestant who had answered a series of questions correctly and won the dizzying sum of $32,000. At that point it would be time to play double or nothing, for $64,000. With one answer to one question, an ordinary American could be wealthy beyond his or her wildest dreams.

The concept depended on the belief that seemingly unexceptional Americans did indeed have secret talents and secret knowledge. That appealed greatly to Cowan, who, with his Eastern European Jewish background, had a highly idealized view of his fellow citizens' potential to reach beyond the apparent limits life had dealt them. His was an idealistic, almost innocent belief in the ordinary people of the country. Cowan's wife, Polly, daughter of a successful Chicago businessman and a graduate of Sarah Lawrence College, most decidedly did not like the idea for the show. She thought it essentially a corruption of the real uses of learning—glorifying trivial memorization rather than true thought and analysis. She believed that the rewards for knowledge should not be huge amounts of cash, doled out in front of millions of cheering strangers, ultimately to benefit commercial hucksters; instead, it should be the joy of knowledge itself. She did not hesitate to make her feelings known to her husband and in a way the debate in the Cowan household reflected the schizophrenic nature of the program itself—a compelling mix of achievement, purity and, of course, avarice.

Polly's doubts did not deter her husband. With his generous and optimistic nature, he saw the show as emblematic of the American dream; it offered everyone not only a chance to become rich overnight but to win the esteem of his fellow citizens. It proved every American had the potential to be extraordinary. It reflected, one of his sons said years later, a "White Christmas" vision of America, in which the immediate descendants of the immigrants, caught up in their optimism about the new world and the nobility of the American experiment, romanticized America and saw it as they wanted it to be.

Cowan was an independent television packager, a familiar figure in the early days of television; he and others like him came up with ideas, found sponsors, and then sold the entire package to the then rather passive networks. He sold this idea to Revlon, which was so enthusiastic that Walter Craig, an executive of the advertising agency that worked for Revlon, locked the door at Cowan's initial presentation and said, "Nobody leaves this room until we have a signed contract."

The name of the program was *The $64,000 Question*. It aired for the first time from 10:00 to 10:30 P.M. in June 1955, on CBS. It was an immediate hit. Millions of people identified with the contestants—who were very much like neighbors. The program showed a CBS psychologist named Gerhart Wiebe who said, "We're all pretty much alike, and we're all smart." The show contained all kinds of dramatic touches attesting to its integrity. The questions sat all week in a locked vault at a bank, and when they finally arrived on the set, they were transported by an executive from Manufacturers Trust, who was accompanied by two armed guards. An IBM machine shuffled the questions on the set. Ed Murrow, the most distinguished American broadcaster of two generations, a man who had pioneered the socially conscious documentary and who was becoming increasingly skeptical about the future of prime-time television, watched the first broadcast and turned to his partner, Fred Friendly. "Any bets on how long we'll keep this time period now?" he asked. He was prophetic in his wariness.

Eight thousand dollars was the maximum a contestant could win on one show; then he or she had to come back next week. Suspense would start building. At the eight thousand-dollar level, the contestant had to enter an isolation booth, presumably so no one in the studio audience could whisper an answer. The speed with which the program enthralled the entire country was breathtaking. Its success surprised even Lou Cowan. The show offered hope of an overnight fortune, and it proved that ordinary people were not in fact necessarily ordinary. As such there was a powerful chord of populism to it. But more than anything else, it appealed to the viewers' sense of greed. Five weeks after its premiere, *The $64,000 Question* was the top-rated show on television. Studies showed that approximately 47.5 million people were watching. The sales of Revlon ("the greatest name in cosmetics") skyrocketed. Some Revlon products sold out overnight, and the show's master of ceremonies had to beg the public to be more patient until more Revlon Living Lipstick was available. The head of Hazel Bishop, a rival cosmetics company, subsequently blamed his company's disappointing year on the fact that "a new television program sponsored by your company's principal competitor captured the imagination of the public." It was the most primal lesson yet on the commercial power of television.

The contestants became the forerunners of Andy Warhol's idea of instant fame: people plucked out of total anonymity and beamed into the homes of millions of their fellow Americans. Between ten and twenty thousand people a week wrote letters, volunteering themselves or their friends to be contestants. After only a few appearances on the show, audiences began to regard the contestants as old and familiar friends. Perhaps, in retrospect, the most important thing illuminated by the show was how easily television conferred fame and established an image. Virtual strangers could become familiar to millions of their fellow citizens.

One of the first contestants, Redmond O'Hanlon, a New York City policeman, whose category was Shakespeare, reached the $16,000 plateau. At that point he decided to stop and, in his words, put "the conservatism of a father of five children" over "the egotism of the scholar." Soon Catherine Kreitzer, a fifty-four-year-old grandmother whose category was the Bible, reached $32,000. She was confident, Mrs. Kreitzer said, that she could win the full amount, but she stopped, quoting from the Bible: "Let your moderation be known unto all men." Perhaps the most engaging of all the early contestants was Gino Prato, a New York shoe repairman, whose category was opera. He easily reached the $32,000 plateau, whereupon his ninety-two-year-old father in Italy cabled him to stop at once. Prato, in time, became roving ambassador for a rubber-heel company, was given season tickets to the Metropolitan Opera, and went on to other television shows as well. If the producers faced a dilemma in the beginning, it was the hesitance of the top contestants to go for the ultimate question. Some of it was the fear of losing everything and some was the nation's then extremely harsh income tax schedules. As Kent Anderson pointed out in his book *Television Fraud,* a contestant who went for the whole thing was risking almost $20,000 in order to win only $12,000 more.

A Marine captain named Richard McCutcheon became the first contestant to go all the way. Bookies kept odds on whether or not he could get the right answer. His field was cooking, not military history. With an audience estimated at 55 million watching, on September 13, 1955, he became the first contestant to climb the television Mt. Everest. For $64,000 he was asked to name the five dishes and two wines from the menu served by King George VI of England for French president Albert Lebrun in 1939. He did: consommé quenelles, filet de truite saumonée, petits pois à la françaises, sauce maltaise, and corbeille. The wines were Château d'Yquem and Madera Sercial. The nation was ecstatic—it had a winner. "If you're symbolic of the Marine Corps, Dick," said Hal March, the emcee, "I don't see how we'll ever lose any battles."

Everyone involved seemed to profit from the show: Lou Cowan soon became president of CBS; the bank official who was in charge of the questions became a vice-president at Manufacturers Trust.

But no one profited more than Revlon. The impact of the show upon its revenues was a startling reflection of changes that were taking place every day in more subtle ways because of the ferocious commercial drive of television and its effect upon both consumers and industry.

Revlon, at the time, was the leading cosmetic company in the nation, but Coty, Max Factor, and Helena Rubinstein were relatively close behind in net sales. In 1953, for example Revlon had net sales of $28.4 million; Helena Rubinstein had $20.4 million; Coty had $19.6; Max Factor, $19 million; and Hazel Bishop, $9.9. All in all, it was a fairly evenly divided pie, and Revlon's sales increased on average about 15 percent annually in the years just before 1955. But sponsoring the quiz show changed all that. In the first six-month season, Revlon increased its sale from $33.6 million to $51.6—a stunning 54 percent increase. The stock jumped from 12 to 20. The following year saw sales increase to $85.7 million. By 1958 Revlon completely dominated its field. (Asked later by a staff member of a House subcommittee whether sponsoring *The $64,000 Question* had had anything to do with Revlon's amazing surge to the top, a somewhat disingenuous Martin Revson answered, "It helped. It helped.")

Not surprisingly, *The $64,000 Question* produced a Pavlovian response to its success. Suddenly the networks were flooded with imitations, all of them for big prize money. The people in Cowan's old organization came up with *The $64,000 Challenge*. Others produced *Tic Tac Dough, Twenty-One, The Big Moment, Beat the Jackpot*, and *The Big Board*. There was even talk of *Twenty Steps to a Million*.

By 1956, the appeal of these shows appeared to be limitless; then subtly, and soon not so subtly, there was the inevitable pressure that television especially seemed to inspire: to improve the show by manipulation, to *cast* it—that is, to ensure each contestant would find some special resonance with the millions of people watching at home. The process began naturally enough at first, with the preference to choose a contestant possessed of considerable charm over a contestant without it. Soon the producers, by pretesting, were able to tell where a candidate's strengths lay and what his weaknesses were, without the contestants themselves even knowing what was happening: Prato knew Italian opera but little about the German opera; McCutcheon knew French cuisine rather than Italian or British. "We wrote the questions into the matrices of their existence," Mert Koplin, one of the men who worked on *The $64,000 Question,* later said. As the pressure built for ratings, the manipulations grew more serious. Some guests would be put through dry runs only to find that when they appeared on the live shows, the questions were remarkably similar to the ones they had answered correctly in the rehearsal. (McCutcheon, it turned out, was deeply bothered by this and thought seriously of getting out; he was encouraged to remain a contestant by his family. Later he told Joe Stone, the prosecutor from the New York District Attorney's office, that he thought the shows were fraudulent and immoral, and he disagreed violently with the claim of the various producers that the rigging had hurt no one.)

The Revlon executives from the start were extremely outspoken about the guests on the two shows they sponsored, *The $64,000 Question* and *The $64,000 Challenge*. Starting in the fall of 1955, there was a weekly meeting in Martin Revson's (Charles Revson's brother) office, where he and his top advertising people critiqued the previous week's shows and contestants. Revson was not shy about telling what he wanted to happen and who he wanted to win. He posted a chart in the meeting room with the ratings on it; if the ratings were down, it was the fault of the contestants. Were the contestants too old? Too young? Were they attractive enough? The criticism was often brutal. (The Revsons apparently did not like a young psychologist named Joyce Brothers, who appeared as an expert on boxing. Thus the questions given her were exceptionally hard—they even asked her the names of referees—in the desire to get her off the show; their strategy had no effect: She became the second person to win $64,000.)

More and more, with so many different shows vying for public approval, the producers found it was the quality of the contestants themselves—and the degree to which the nation identified with them—that made the difference. When the Barry and Enright company, one of the big hitters in the world of game shows, introduced its new game in March 1956, called *Twenty-One,* loosely based on the card game of the same name, Dan Enright was confident it would be an immediate success. Two contestants would answer questions for points, without knowing how many points their opponent had. Enright thought it was a sure bet for unbearable dramatic excitement, especially since the audience would know more about the competition than the contestants themselves. He was dead wrong. The premiere was, he said later, a dismal failure, "just plain dull." The day after, Marty Rosenhouse, the sponsor, made an irate call to say he did not intend to own a turkey. "Do whatever you have to do," he told Enright, "and you know what I'm talking about." Those were the marching orders for Enright and his staff.

Fixing the show did not particularly bother Enright; the quiz shows had never been about intelligence or integrity as far as he was concerned; they were about drama and entertainment. "You cannot ask random questions of people and have a show," one game-show producer later said. "You simply have failure, failure, failure, and that does not make entertainment." That made it a predatory world, and Enright excelled in it. He was not, Dan Enright reflected years later, a very nice man in those days. He was totally compelled by work, wildly ambitious, and utterly self-involved. "I was determined to be successful no matter what it cost," he said, "and I was greedy, greedy, not for money, but for authority, power, prestige and respect." The end, he believed at the time, always justified the means. People were to be used; if you did not use them, he believed, they in turn would use you. Soon—with considerable fixing—*Twenty-One* became a huge success; at a relatively young age, Enright had already exceeded his own expectations, and he was wealthy and powerful. People coveted his attention and gave him respect. Thus he was able to rationalize everything he was doing.

From then on, *Twenty-One* became the prototype of the completely crooked show. Enright cast it as he might a musical comedy. He wanted not just winners and losers but heroes and villains. He tried for his first hero with a young writer named Richard Jackman, who appeared on the show on October 3, 1956. Before Jackman's appearance, Enright went over a vast number of questions with Jackman. At the end of the session, Enright told him, "You are in a position to destroy my career." Jackman had no idea what he was talking about, although he figured it out the next day, when the questions put before him were the very same questions used in the dry run. Jackman easily won $24,500, but then told Enright he wanted no part of being on a fixed program and withdrew. A worried Enright pleaded with him to continue, offering up all kinds of rationales. Finally, he got Jackman to accept a $15,000 check for his first appearance and convinced him to appear on one additional program, in order to bow out gracefully rather than just disappear mysteriously.

That left Enright with all that money to give out and no cast of characters. His first break had come a little earlier, when a young man named Herb Stempel wrote asking for a chance to be a candidate. Stempel had seen the debut of *Twenty-One* and had thought the questions rather simple. He had, he had always been told, a photographic memory. "The walking encyclopedia," one uncle called him. He had watched all the other shows and invariably got the right answers. "I have thousands of odd and obscure facts and many facets of general information at my fingertips," he wrote the producers. At the time, Stempel was an impoverished graduate student at City University, and his wife's moderately wealthy parents felt that their daughter had married beneath herself. Stempel was immediately invited to the offices of Barry and Enright, where he was given an exam consisting of 363 questions, of which he got 251 correct—the highest score anyone had gotten so far on the entrance exam. He was perfect for the show, except for one thing—he was short, stocky, and not particularly appealing on television.

He was, Enright decided, unlikeable. Because of that, Enright decided to exploit that and emphasize his unattractive side. Stempel had grown up in a poor section of the Bronx. His father, who had been a postal clerk, died when he was seven, and his mother suffered from high blood pressure and was on welfare from the time of her husband's death to when she died. There had seemed to Stempel an unfairness about his childhood from the start—other kids had fathers, he did not; other kids had some money, he did not. But his photographic memory was remarkable. For all the knowledge stored in his head, Enright thought, he was socially limited, and almost unable to sustain a conversation. To talk with him you had to ask a very specific question, and when you did, you got a specific answer and nothing more. "If you saw him," Enright said years later, "you had no choice but to root for him to lose."

A few days after the first meeting, Enright came by to see Stempel at the latter's home in Queens. Enright opened an attaché case and pulled out a bunch of cards similar to the ones used on *Twenty-One*. With that he began going over the questions in a dry run with Herb Stempel. Stempel got most of the answers right, and for the ones he didn't get, Enright supplied the answer. It was, Stempel began to realize, a rehearsal for *Twenty-One*. "How would you like to win $25,000?" Enright asked Stempel. "Who wouldn't," he answered. With that Enright had made him a co-conspirator, demolishing any leverage he might have if qualms arose in the future.

While he was at Stempel's Queens apartment Enright checked out his new contestant's wardrobe. Since he was to be portrayed as a penniless ex-GI working his way through school, he was to wear his worst clothes: an ill-fitting double-breasted blue suit that had belonged to Stempel's father-in-law. He also selected a blue shirt with a frayed collar to go with it. Enright made Stempel get a marine-style haircut, which made him look somewhat like a Nazi soldier, Enright thought, and thereby increased the audience's antipathy. Stempel was even told to wear a cheap watch, which, in Stempel's words, ticked like an alarm clock, the better to make a loud sound during the tense moments in the isolation booth. He was never to answer too quickly. He had to pause, to show some doubt and conflict, perhaps even stumble on an answer. Questions should look like cliffhangers. He was to carry a handkerchief and pat, not wipe, his brow. He was not to call Barry, the emcee, Jack on the air as everyone else did; rather he was to refer to him obsequiously as *Mr.* Barry.

Nor was he to deviate from his instructions. At one point, when he changed suits and wore a single-breasted one and got a better haircut, Enright warned him, "You're not paying attention to your lessons—you are not cooperating." Stempel realized the role he was to play was the nerd, the square, the human computer. It was a cruel thing to do, Enright reflected years later, to make a man who obviously had considerable emotional problems go before the American people in as unattractive an incarnation as possible.

If Stempel resented such treatment, it was still his one moment of glory. Suddenly, he was a hero on the CCNY campus. He could sense, as he walked across the campus, that other students were pointing him out and talking about him. Sitting one day in the cafeteria, he heard another student boast to a colleague, "Herb Stempel's in one of my classes." Another student, whom he had never met before, came up and told him that he and all his friends were all proud that Herb Stempel went to CCNY. There were covertly admiring glances from girls. It was heady stuff.

Good soldier that he was, Stempel was not a satisfactory winner for *Twenty-One.* His only real value was as a loser. The show needed a hero in a white hat—a handsome young gladiator to defeat him. In October the producers found him in the person of a young English instructor at Columbia University named Charles Van Doren. Al Freedman, Enright's deputy, met him at a cocktail party and was impressed by his intelligence and manner. "I think I've got the right person to beat Stempel with," Freedman told Enright, "someone very smart, who I think is going to come over very well on the show." Will he do it? Enright asked. "Yes," Freedman answered. "I think he'll do it, because his appearance will make erudition and education more popular."

Of all the people associated with the quiz-show scandals, the one who remains most indelibly burned on most people's memory is Charles Van Doren. He was the bearer of one of the most illustrious names in American intellectual life and he captivated the audience as no one else ever did. His manner—shy, gentle, somewhat self-deprecating, like a young, more intellectual Jimmy Stewart—was immensely attractive, for he was smart enough to win yet modest enough to seem just a little uneasy with his success. His father was the celebrated Columbia professor Mark Van Doren. His uncle Carl was just as famous a man of letters. He seemed to Freedman almost perfect for this particular show: He had a rare intellectual curiosity—apparently he was a speed reader and he read two or three books a day—and was informed on a broad range of subjects. Then, in addition to all else, there was the charm: Van Doren was someone whom the audience would see as an aristocrat, and yet there was nothing snobbish about him. He would appeal to ordinary people in every region of the country. Since it was a time when Stempel was, in the view of the producers, destroying the show, swallowing up more likable contestants, Van Doren's appeal was all the more attractive, and Freedman set out to get him on board.

That was not an easy process, though. A series of lunches followed, to seduce Van Doren, who remained largely unresponsive. Van Doren pointed out that he liked teaching very much, thank you; there was nothing else he coveted, and he was not interested in a career in television, not even as a lark. "It's not my world," he answered. "My world is academe and I like it very much." But the more he resisted, the more Freedman was impressed; his very reserve was tantalizing, and so Freedman continued to see him. One thing that both Enright and Freedman had mastered by this time was the art of discovering a potential contestant's vulnerability. Every man, they thought, had, if not his price, his special vanity, which was the weakness they could exploit. So Freedman, sensing that Van Doren's love of teaching was critical to turning him, began to emphasize how much he might help the world of education and the teachers of America by coming on board. Teachers all over the country would get a boost from his appearances; he would be able to show that teachers were role models, worthy of the respect of their fellow citizens. "You can be erudite and learned but show that you don't have to be an intellectual snob," Freedman said. At first Van Doren seemed rather amused by this transparent ploy.

Then it began to change. Van Doren asked Freedman what made him so sure that he, Van Doren, would actually win on the show. At that point Freedman gave him a brief but somewhat sanitized history of radio and television game shows, explaining that they were all controlled in some way, because the producers had to hold the interest of the audience as well as educate it. It was not a question of truth, or documentaries; rather, it was show business. Why, look at Eisenhower, he said. A book came out under his name, but it was most likely produced by a ghostwriter. Or a movie might show Gregory Peck parachuting behind the lines in Nazi Germany, but the person in the parachute was not Peck, but a double.

They kept in touch, and the seduction continued. "How much do you make as an instructor?" Freedman asked at one point. "About four thousand dollars a year," Van Doren answered. Freedman wondered aloud whether a young man could support a family on that salary. For the first time Van Doren asked how much money he might make as a contestant. Freedman explained that he might make as much as $50,000, or even $100,000. Van Doren asked Freedman how much the most recent contestant had won. Sixty thousand dollars, Freedman answered. Van Doren walked down some steps to leave, got to the bottom, and thought to himself, *Sixty thousand dollars! Sixty thousand dollars!* It took his breath away.

The next time they talked, Van Doren asked, "Who would have to know about it?" Freedman sensed that he had him. Just Enright and me, he answered. Freedman pledged to Van Doren that he would never turn him in. There were more talks; the seduction went on for several weeks. Finally, he agreed to go on; at first he asked to play it straight, but then it was explained to him that no one on *Twenty-One* played it straight.

It was a masterful stroke of casting: Van Doren turned out to be a superb performer. In contrast to the unattractive Stempel, he was, in Enright's phrase, the kind of young man "you'd love to have your daughter marry." He never seemed to lose his boyish innocence, which in fact he had lost from the start. At the height of his success, Van Doren seemed oddly immune to all the fuss. "Charlie," Freedman would say. "Do you know that somewhere between 25 and 30 million people watched you last night? Isn't that amazing?" Van Doren would simply shake his head: "It's hard for me to picture." Even more amazed than Charles was his father. Mark Van Doren wrote to his friend and former student Thomas Merton, the poet and Trappist monk, "About fifteen million people have fallen in love with him—and I don't use the word lightly."

Perhaps it was the contrast between Charles Van Doren's innate modesty and the hyped-up atmosphere of the quiz show, but there was no doubt about it—Charles Van Doren, not yet a Columbia Ph.D., merely a $4,000-a-year instructor, was one of television's first stars, and arguably its first intellectual star. Ironically, even his inner doubts worked for the show: The longer he stayed on the show, the more he hated what he was doing and the more he wanted to get off;

and some of that conflict must have shown through and made him an even more winning contestant.

The Van Dorens were an old American family, dating back to the eighteenth century. Because their name was Dutch and had the prefix Van, many assumed they were aristocrats; instead the family was one of hardworking salt-of-the-earth Midwesterners. Mark Van Doren's grandfather, William Henry Van Doren, had been a farmer, blacksmith, and preacher (and, noted Mark in his autobiography, "not much of a businessman"). But he stressed education and his son became a doctor and two of his grandsons, Carl and Mark, got Ph.D.s. As a young graduate student Carl wrote his mother of the hardships of student life: "Some days I grow a despicable coward and am nearly tempted to turn my back upon all the bright ideal to which I have been true now for nearly a third of my life, and drop my energies to a slighter task where there is a chance of wealth and ease after a time. I know I could be rich—but I don't care to be . . ."

Mark Van Doren was not only a professor—he had won a Pulitzer Prize in poetry and had written a distinguished biography of Hawthorne. His wife, Dorothy (and Charles's mother), was a former editor of *The Nation* and a novelist; his brother, Carl, won a Pulitzer Prize for biography in 1939, and Carl's wife, Irita, was book editor of *The Herald Tribune,* a position of considerable influence in those days. It was her affair with Wendell Willkie, during which she encouraged him to run for the Presidency, that inspired Howard Lindsay and Russell Crouse to write their hit musical *State of the Union.*

The Van Dorens were, in sum, a family that seemed to reflect the best of the liberal, humanist values of the era; Mark and Dorothy Van Doren had a town house in the Village and country house in northwestern Connecticut. If anything, Mark was the most blessed of them all, a successful and gifted poet and a truly beloved teacher, absolutely in command of his work, gentle, generous to, and tolerant of his students, even if their work was different from his (as in the case of Allen Ginsburg even before he emerged as an early Beat poet). One student later wrote that he had the gift of making "the difficult attainable through lightness." Another of his students, Alfred Kazin, later one of America's most distinguished critics, remembered the pleasure of Van Doren's lectures in a course on "the long poem." The sun would go down just as Van Doren was finishing the lecture, Kazin remembered, and then he would leave the campus and take the Seventh Avenue subway to his house in the Village, often accompanied by students, who used the subway ride to expand the classroom hour and who were often invited in for a drink or for tea.

Family friends included James Thurber (the Van Doren family cat was named Walter, after Thurber's character Walter Mitty), John Berryman ("Charlie, by the way," Mark Van Doren had written Berryman when his son was young, "values your letters if only for their stamps"), Joseph Wood Krutch, Franklin P. Adams, Jacques Barzun, Thomas Merton, Lionel Trilling, and Rex Stout.

The Van Dorens were not wealthy; money was always secondary to teaching and writing. As Mark Van Doren wrote Charles in the fall of 1952, in a letter filled with a father's pride that his son would soon be asked to teach English at Columbia at a salary of $3,600 a year: "Really Cha, I'm not advising you to say Yes. You would have to love it to do it at all, and the rewards, I don't need to tell you, are scandalously slight; they have always been for teachers, and they always will be. I have enjoyed it, even though I am quitting soon; but the enjoyment was the greater part of my pay . . ." (Indeed, one of the first things that Charles Van Doren did when he became successful on *Twenty-One* was to buy his parents a television set.)

Charles Van Doren reflected both the strengths and the weaknesses of so privileged and protected a background. He developed into an erudite classicist and gifted musician. But it was always there, the fact that he was a *Van Doren*. When he first went on the show, Jack Barry coyly asked him, "Just out of curiosity, Mr. Van Doren, are you in any way related to Mark Van Doren, up at Columbia University, the famous writer?" Van Doren: "Yes. I am. He is my father." Barry: "He is your father!" Van Doren: "Yes." Barry: "The name Van Doren is a very well known name. Are you related to any of the other well-known Van Dorens?" Van Doren: "Well, Dorothy Van Doren, the novelist and author of the recent 'The Country Wife' is my mother, and Carl Van Doren, the biographer of Benjamin Franklin, was my uncle." Barry: "Well, you have every reason in the world to be mighty proud of your name and your family, Van Doren . . ."

Coached by Freedman on how to answer, Charles Van Doren became very good at the theatrics of the show. He learned to stutter, to seem to grope toward answers he had already been given. He was good at the game, but not too good; the questions were answerable, his struggling implied, but they were not easy. (When Jack Barry, talking about the cast of *On The Waterfront,* asked him, among other things, for the name of the Best Supporting Actress, Van Doren had answered, "Uh well, the only woman I can remember in that picture was the one who played opposite Brando, but I would have thought that she would have got the Best Actress award. But if she's the only one I remember—let's see—she was that lovely frail

656 / DAVID HALBERSTAM

girl—Eva Saint—uh, Eva Marie Saint." Later, he noted, on the occasions when he had been given an answer, a curious pride made him go and look it up.

What Stempel, who hated him, and millions of others who were rooting for him could not understand about Van Doren was that coming from a family that accomplished was not without its burdens. What in life really belonged to Charles Van Doren independent of his family? Van Doren's life was not as enviable as it seemed. He was dealing with an age-old dilemma, made no easier by its familiarity—being the son of a famous and successful father and/or mother in the same profession. Charles had reluctantly decided to seek a career as an English professor. As a young man he had gone to Paris and tried to write a novel about patricide, although as he told Dick Goodwin, a House investigator, he had also asked for his father's help in editing it. There was a quality about his life that was oddly airless. As Van Doren himself said a few weeks after he finally came forward to admit that he had been part of the scam, "I've been acting a part, a role, not just the last few years—I've been acting a role for ten or fifteen years, maybe all my life. It's a role of thinking that I've done far more than I've done, accomplished more than I've accomplished, produced more than I've produced. It has in a way something to do with my family, I suppose. I don't mean just my father, there are other people in my family. But I've been running." Burdened and conflicted, uncertain about what was his and what was his family's, desperately needing successes and an identity of his own, Van Doren had been a perfect catch for someone like Enright. By going on the quiz shows, perhaps Charles Van Doren was seeking fame of his own; and for a brief time he became far more famous than his illustrious relatives; they were known only to a small elite; he was known to millions—his face was even on the cover of *Time*.

To Stempel, Van Doren was the enemy and the epitome of all the injustices he had suffered in terms of privilege and looks. "I felt here was a guy, Van Doren, that had a fancy name, Ivy League education, parents all his life, and I had just the opposite, the hard way up," he once told Enright. That Stempel, because of the deal he had made with the devil, would now have to give up his television celebrity, pretend that he was dumber than he was, and lose to someone he was sure he could beat was the unkindest cut of all.

When Enright first told Stempel it was his turn to lose, he angrily balked. The fame had proved to be addictive; he was in no hurry to give up his appearances on television. No, he said, he wouldn't do it. But Enright knew he was a street kid, and street kids kept their word. "Herbie, when this started, you gave me your word," Enright said. So Stempel agreed to take the fall, but he was bitter about it. He begged Enright to revoke the deal, to let him play Van Doren fair and square.

All of this was done under the sponsorship (but without the direct knowledge of) Pharmaceuticals Inc., a maker of patent medicines. So there was the bizarre spectacle of Jack Barry challenging these two intelligent young men with extremely serious questions and then switching back to his pitches for Geritol: "I guess I've asked thousands of questions at one time or another here on television. I haven't got enough used to it yet, but there is one simple question that I think almost everybody asks everybody else—I think you know the question—what's the weather gonna be like. . . . So, remember, if tired blood is your problem, especially in this rough weather after those colds or flu or sore throats or a virus, take either the good-tasting liquid Geritol or the handy Geritol tablets . . ." Pharmaceuticals Inc., like Revlon, reaped huge benefits from sponsoring the quiz shows; in the first year, its sales went from $10.4 million to $13.9.

The denouement for Herb Stempel came on the night of December 5, 1956. According to Enright's script, he was to lose by answering incorrectly a question the answer to which he knew perfectly well: which movie had won the Academy Award for Best Picture in 1955. The answer was *Marty,* and Stempel had seen the movie three times. He loved it because he could identify with its principal character, an unattractive but sensitive man who has as many feelings as someone who is handsome. That it was a movie he cared about made it all the harder. On the day just before he was to lose, he became so frustrated that he told a few of his friends that he was going to take a dive on the show. On the day of the program, NBC hyped the confrontation all day long: "Is Herb Stempel going to win over $111,000 on *Twenty-One* tonight?" an announcer would say over and over again as the day wore on. Stempel would talk back to the television set in his room: "No, he's not going to win over $111,000, he's going to take a dive."

Once the program began, he came perilously close to answering the *Marty* question correctly, breaking Enright's rules and just going for it. Years later he pondered how history might have been different: He would have won, he would not have proceeded to help blow the whistle on Enright, and Charles Van Doren would have lost and been able to go back gracefully to Columbia and to his real love, teaching. But he played by the rules, and Van Doren ended up riding a tiger. Van Doren, in time, became a national hero, with a record fifteen appearances on the show. He had greatly underestimated the power of television. Something that had begun as a lark turned into the young academic's nightmare. Hundreds of letters came in each day telling him how he represented America's hope for a more serious, cerebral future, particularly after the dark years of McCarthy had poisoned the minds of the American public about the value of education. Other universities offered him tenured professorships. There were offers to star in movies. NBC signed him to a three-year contract that included regular stints on the *Today* show, where he was to be the resident intellectual. His salary from the network was a staggering $50,000 a year. "I felt like a bullfighter in a bull ring with thousands and thousands of people cheering me on and all I wanted to do was get out of there," he later told Dick Goodwin. In the end his total winnings came to $129,000; but given the draconian taxes of the period, he actually took home only about $28,000. Stempel asked to challenge Van Doren one more time but was told that Van Doren would not take him on. Perhaps Vivienne Nearing, Van Doren's then opponent, might; when Stempel heard this, he understood immediately that in the forthcoming contest between Ms. Nearing and Van Doren, Van Doren was scripted to lose, so Stempel, nothing if not shrewd, took $5,000 of his savings and bet it two-to-one on Nearing.

Stempel won $10,000 but quickly squandered that and his prize money in a series of bad investments. His bitterness festered. He began to bug Enright, demanding a chance to play Van Doren ("that son of a bitch") in a clean, unfixed game. Enright became increasingly aware that Stempel was a live hand grenade. There was some talk about a place on another show. Stempel pledged to lose weight, " 'cause when I go on I want to look like a gentleman, not a little short, squat guy, like I looked on *Twenty-One*." At one point, Enright even secretly taped Stempel to show that the latter was blackmailing him and then skillfully cajoled him into signing a piece of paper that said there had been no fixing on *Twenty-One*. But none of this could stem Stempel's growing rage.

The one thing that neither Enright nor Freedman had counted on was the impact of all this on Stempel's psyche. It had all been traumatic, and they were now about to pay the price for what they had done. The key for fixing the show had been the ability to co-opt all the players; common sense decreed that those who had been part of the scam would keep quiet rather than hurt themselves. But Stempel was beyond the point of caring. What he wanted was revenge.

Stempel began to look for reporters who might write about the scandal. At first the press was wary of picking up the story because there was no way of corroborating it. Later Enright realized he had done an unspeakable thing: He had exploited a man who was emotionally vulnerable. Of all the things he had done during the quizshow rigging, that was the thing that, many years later, Enright was most ashamed of. He was not nearly as bothered by what he had done to Van Doren, who, he decided, was an intelligent adult with a fully workable moral compass and who knew exactly what he was doing.

In the district attorney's office there was a strong belief that the program had been rigged. But it was a hard case to break, for Enright and his deputy, Albert Freedman, had been careful fixers. The fixing had been done one-on-one, with no witnesses. Deniability was critical. In case a contestant changed his mind and wanted to talk, it was to be his word against that of a program executive; thus, charges of fraud against the program could be neutralized. There was to be as little overlapping as possible: Enright had fixed Stempel; Freedman had fixed Van Doren. They liked to co-opt the contestants even before they set foot on the show. That way they were less likely to turn on the men who had fixed them.

When the story of Stempel's charges finally broke in a New York newspaper, Enright received a call from an uncle. "Dan," his uncle said. "I hope this teaches you one thing." "What's that?" Enright asked. "Never bet on any animal that can talk," his uncle said. Enright soon discovered he had seriously underestimated the sheer power of the show. In his own mind he had done nothing that violated the moral code of the world of entertainment as he knew it. But the show had transcended mere entertainment: It had become the property of an entire nation. Enright had crossed over, without knowing it, into another sphere, with another set of ethics and standards. He was playing with this new instrument of television without knowing its true power.

Their phenomenal success, Freedman realized, had also stirred powerful resentment in other segments of the media. As evidence of the fixing began to surface, the ferocity with which the newspapers picked up the story stunned him. It was not covered as a minor scandal in the minor world of entertainment but as a threat to the republic—something on the order of the press coverage of Watergate, he later thought. He had greatly underestimated the dimensions of celebrity that the game shows conferred. The press, especially the city's more vulnerable newspapers, particularly those already suffering financially from television's ever more powerful reach—the *World Telegram,* the *Journal American,* and even the *Post*—feasted on the story as a means of showing that their prime competitor was not to be trusted.

It was a phenomenon of the fifties, Freedman thought. They were playing with this new instrument without knowing its real power: They had toyed with it as if it were merely an extension of radio, and they did not know that, in those days at least, it overwhelmed the people sitting at home watching and consumed those who went on the programs. A decade later, Freedman believed, the show might have been a success, but a much smaller one as the nation would have become far more immunized to the immediacy of television.

In 1957, Barry and Enright had sold the rights to the show to an eager NBC for $2 million. As the deal was being completed, Enright wondered whether they should tell the network that it was buying a rigged show. He called his agent, Sonny Werblin, an astute New York wheeler-dealer, and asked his advice. "Dan, have I ever asked you whether the show was rigged?" Werblin responded. No, Enright said. "And has NBC ever asked you whether the show was rigged?" Again Enright said no. "Well, the reason that none of us has asked," Werblin continued, summing up the morality of the networks on the issue in those days, "is because we don't want to know."

But Stempel refused to go away, and was becoming increasingly obsessive. In his own mind, he had carried the show, had made it what it was, and would get no long-term benefit. Enright had promised him a job when he'd agreed to take the fall, but—and it seemed typical to Stempel—he was now hedging on it. By contrast, Van Doren was being given a steady job at $50,000 a year from NBC. There was simply no justice, he felt. He kept calling reporters, trying to give his story to them, but libel laws were tougher then and there was no corroborating evidence.

Inevitably, the whole scam unraveled. A young woman who had been coached left her notebook in the outer office of one show. Another contestant saw the notebook, which contained many of the answers the woman was asked to give as a contestant, and complained. Others came forward. One contestant mailed a registered letter to himself in which he placed an exact description of the process and including the answers themselves—powerful evidence for the courts. Finally, the district attorney's office launched a broad investigation of the quiz shows. The evidence of rigging was overwhelming, but for reasons never quite clear, the judge in the case impounded all the evidence. With that, the quiz show scandal was passed to a congressional committee.

Gradually, the congressional investigation kept coming back to focus on Charles Van Doren, the young man who had charmed the entire nation. Van Doren steadfastly maintained his innocence and claimed that he had received no help. That meant he continued to lie to the prosecutors, to the New York grand jury investigating the quiz shows, to the media, to his employers, to his family, and to his own lawyer. In 1959 Richard N. Goodwin, a young investigator for the congressional committee looking into the quiz-show scandals, had to deal with Stempel, Van Doren, and the others. Goodwin's roots were not that different from Stempel's, but he empathized with Van Doren; if he, like Stempel, was Jewish and came from a rather simple background, then his innate talent as a member of the new generation of the meritocracy was already manifesting itself. He had gone to Tufts and then to Harvard Law School, where he had been first in his class and gained the ultimate accolade: He had been chosen as a Felix Frankfurter law clerk. Goodwin found Stempel's hatred of Van Doren distasteful; by contrast, Goodwin was charmed by Van Doren. Soon they became not hunter and hunted but almost pals, Dick and Charlie. Clearly, Van Doren was intrigued by Goodwin's exceptional intelligence, by the fact that in addition to being a brilliant young lawyer, he loved American literature; Goodwin in turn had never met anyone like Van Doren, so intelligent, so graceful, from an old family, utterly devoid of snobbishness. The evidence, Goodwin thought, overwhelmingly showed that Van Doren had to be part of a fix, but he *wanted* to believe Van Doren, and for a time Goodwin lacked the final piece of evidence to implicate him: Freedman, Van Doren's handler, had conveniently left the country for Mexico. Finally, under threat of the loss of his citizenship, he reluctantly returned.

When Goodwin had Freedman's testimony, he called Van Doren to let him know where the case stood, that the committee now had a lock on it. For the first time, Van Doren seemed to pause. The next time they met, there was a lawyer at Van Doren's side. Still, Van Doren protested his innocence. "Dick, someday I hope I'll be able to tell you why he [Freedman] is lying," Van Doren said. "Charlie, isn't it interesting that the only people not telling the truth are from the best families?" Goodwin answered, mentioning one other quiz contestant with an exceptional background. At this point Goodwin felt himself in a bind: He was absolutely sure Van Doren was lying, but he also saw no purpose in having the committee destroy him in public. It was, after all, not long after the McCarthy hearings and Goodwin still had vivid images of people whose lives had been ruined by their appearances before investigating committees. As far as Goodwin was concerned, the principal villains were the networks, which had averted their eyes from what was happening despite a number of warnings, the sponsors, who were the real beneficiaries, and the producers. Goodwin's lack of zeal in going after Van Doren did not please Stempel. There were endless phone calls from him: "Are you calling Van Doren [to go before the committee]? Are you calling Van Doren?" Stempel would ask. Finally, Goodwin asked, "Herb, why do you hate him so much?" "I don't hate him," Stempel protested. "Come on," Goodwin said. "You've been on my case since the beginning for one thing and one thing alone—to get him." At that point Stempel told of an incident in which he had gone over to shake Van Doren's hand at a charity benefit but Van Doren, according to Stempel, had turned away from him. That, thought Goodwin, sounded unlikely, because there was not a trace of snobbishness to Van Doren. But in some way he understood that even if it hadn't happened in reality, it had happened in Herb Stempel's mind.

Goodwin went to the committee members in closed session, said that he had more than enough information to show that the programs were rigged, but that he saw no need to destroy Van Doren in public before the committee. The committee members agreed, and the decision was made not to call him. With that, Goodwin told Van Doren, "Charlie, I know you're lying to me," he said. "Dick, I'm sorry you feel that way," Van Doren answered. The committee, Goodwin continued, had decided not to call him. But don't, he warned Van Doren, say anything publicly or do anything the committee might view as a challenge and which might force it to change its mind. With that, it seemed that Van Doren was home free. But then NBC told Van Doren that he had to send a telegram to the committee declaring his innocence or lose his job on the *Today* show. The obvious decision, Goodwin thought, was for Van Doren to tell NBC to stuff it and quit. Instead, pushed by his own pride, Van Doren took a fateful step and sent the telegram. It was a wildly self-destructive thing to do, Goodwin thought. Inevitably, he was subpoenaed. Goodwin, bothered by the coming confrontation, went to see his mentor, Justice Felix Frankfurter. Frankfurter had no personal connection with Van Doren and took a more objective view of what was happening: "A quiz-show investigation without Van

Doren," he said, "is like *Hamlet* without anyone playing Hamlet." Besides, Frankfurter added, Van Doren was not exactly innocent. He had been a willing participant. The fact that others in the scandal had done things worse did not exactly exonerate him.

On November 1, 1959, the night before Van Doren's appearance before the committee, Dick Goodwin invited him and his father to dinner. Goodwin remembered being touched by the mutual affection between the two and Mark Van Doren's self-evident relief that his son was going to be able to free himself of his terrible weight. The irony of all this—that the father and son who were so graceful and charming and who could, even in this most terrible hour, come to dinner and make a simple evening so rich with literate yet unpretentious conversation—did not escape Goodwin, who found himself torn by the entire experience.

The next day, a crush of journalists and photographers recorded Van Doren on the witness stand, beginning, "I would give almost anything I have to reverse the course of my life in the last three years. I cannot take back one word or action. The past does not change for anyone. But at least I can learn from the past. I have learned a lot in the last three weeks. I've learned a lot about life. I've learned a lot about myself, and about the responsibilities any man has to his fellow men. I've learned a lot about good and evil. They are not always what they appear to be. I was involved, deeply involved, in a deception. The fact that I, too, was very much deceived cannot keep me from being the principal victim of that deception, because I was its principal symbol. There may be a kind of justice in that . . ." Aware of Van Doren's great popularity, the committee members handled him gently and repeatedly praised him for his candor. Only Congressman Steve Derounian announced that he saw no particular point in praising someone of Van Doren's exceptional talents and intelligence for simply telling the truth. With that, the room suddenly exploded with applause, and Goodwin knew at that moment ordinary people would not so easily forgive Van Doren.

Stempel had taken a train to Washington, paying for the trip with his own money, to see Van Doren's appearance. In the crowded congressional hearing room, he wanted some kind of vindication. And although in the beginning his seat was far in the back, he had steadily edged forward so he could look in Van Doren's face: He wanted to see and hear the members of the Congress of the United States scolding this privileged young man for breaking faith with the

American people, but he was bitterly disappointed by what happened. "I felt terribly hurt by the way they praised him," he said years later. Afterward, Stempel grabbed Joseph Stone, the New York assistant DA who had done much of the early work on the case, and started to complain about the professors at CCNY who had turned down his proposal for a Ph.D. thesis. Even at what might have been a moment of triumph, it still seemed that he regarded himself a victim.

When it was over, a reporter asked Mark Van Doren if he was proud of his son and the old man said yes, he was. Are you proud of what he did on the quiz shows? another reporter asked, and Mark wavered for a moment and said no, he was not, but at least Charles could get back to what he ought to be doing—teaching. That was something, he added, that he was very good at. At that point one of the reporters told Mark Van Doren what he did not yet know: that the board of trustees at Columbia had voted that day to fire Charles Van Doren as an instructor. A friend noted that the decision must have been like an arrow through the heart of the old man.

Charles Van Doren wrote Dick Goodwin a poignant note the next day, thanking him for his kindnesses during the preceding few weeks. "The dinner was superb, the accommodations splendid, and the conversation even at times uncharged with passion and danger. What an extraordinary evening it was. I will of course never forget it. . . . Hunters," he continued, "used to say that the stag loved the hunter who killed it . . . thus the tears, which were the tears of gratitude and affection. Something like that *does* happen, I know. And Raskolnikov felt the same. Thus Gerry [his wife] and I do extend an invitation to you to come and wish you would come. There are a number of things I'd like to talk to you about—none of them having to do with quiz shows. I made the mistake of reading the papers. I should have taken your advice. I wish the next six months were already over. There have been many hard things. But I am trying to tell you that we will live and thrive, I think—I mean I know we will live and I think we will thrive—and that you must never, in any way, feel any regret for your part in this. Perhaps it is nonsense to say that, but I thought it might just be possible that you would. Charlie."

It was a traumatic moment for the country as well. Charles Van Doren had become the symbol of the best America had to offer. Some commentators wrote of the quiz shows as the end of American innocence. Starting with World War Two, they said, America had been on the right side: Its politicians and generals did not lie, and the

Americans had trusted what was written in their newspapers and, later, broadcast over the airwaves. That it all ended abruptly because one unusually attractive young man was caught up in something seedy and outside his control was dubious. But some saw the beginning of the disintegration of the moral tissue of America, in all of this. Certainly, many Americans who would have rejected a role in being part of a rigged quiz show if the price was $64 would have had to think a long time if the price was $125,000. John Steinbeck was so outraged that he wrote an angry letter to Adlai Stevenson that was reprinted in *The New Republic* and caused a considerable stir at the time. Under the title "Have We Gone Soft?" he raged, "If I wanted to destroy a nation I would give it too much and I would have it on its knees, miserable, greedy, and sick . . . on all levels, American society is rigged. . . . I am troubled by the cynical immorality of my country. It cannot survive on this basis."

The scandal illuminated some things about television in addition to its growing, addictive power: The first was the capacity of a virtual stranger, with the right manner, to project a kind of pseudo-intimacy and to become an old and trusted friend in a stunningly short time. That would have profound ramifications, as television increasingly became the prime instrument of politics. The other thing it showed, and this was to be perhaps its most powerful lesson, was that television *cast* everything it touched: politics, news shows, and sitcoms. The demands of entertainment and theater were at least as powerful as substance. Among the first to benefit from that new casting requirement was a young junior senator from Massachusetts, who, like Charles Van Doren, was young, attractive, upper-class, and diffident because he was cool on a medium that was hot. If Charles Van Doren was the major new star of television in the late fifties, then he was to be replaced by John Kennedy as the new decade started.

As for Charles Van Doren, he quickly dropped out of the public arena. He moved to Chicago with his young family and, drawing on a family connection with Mortimer Adler, the editor of the Great Books series, he worked for the Encyclopedia Britannica as an editor. His life in Chicago was largely private, and he was not often seen in that city's journalistic and literary circles. He and his wife, Geraldine Bernstein Van Doren, whom he had first met when she had a job answering the mail prompted by his early success on *Twenty-One,* reared two children there. He never wrote or spoke about the quiz-show events. When, on different occasions, journalists telephoned, suggesting that they were working on an article about that period and asked to speak with him, they were told that Mr. Van Doren was living a very happy life and did not need or want to get involved in their project. He was the editor of a number of important collections, including *The Great Treasury of Western Thought,* and *The Joy of Reading,* but his ability to promote the books, and thereby enhance both their sales and his own reputation, was limited by his wariness of going on television. He was aware that if he made a book tour, he was not likely to be asked about the history of Western thought, or about the relative influence of Plato, Aristotle, and St. Thomas Aquinas on our lives, but rather about Freedman, Enright, and Revson.

In the late 1980s, a distinguished television documentary maker named Julian Krainan was looking for a narrator-editor for a thirteen-part public television series on the history of philosophy. Krainan had read Van Doren's work, had loved *The Joy of Reading,* and was impressed by the powerful sweep of his intellect. Krainan, some fifteen years younger than Van Doren, had only the vaguest memory of the quiz-show scandals some thirty years after they had taken place. He contacted Van Doren, and gradually they began to agree on the outline of a public television series. They seemed to like each other and liked dealing with each other. Then Krainan's project hit a wall. The top people at PBS were wary about dealing with Van Doren until he himself dealt publicly with the quiz-show issue. At that point Krainan suggested doing a documentary on the quiz-show scandals. It would clear the air, lance the boil, and prepare the way for the multipart show on philosophy. Krainan also pointed out that Van Doren himself, on a number of occasions when the subject came up, always said that he had nothing to hide and nothing to apologize for.

Van Doren and Krainan went back and forth about doing a quiz-show documentary matter a number of times until one day Van Doren suddenly announced, "I'm going to do it. I should have done this a long time ago." But a few days later he called to say that he'd reconsidered. Krainan went ahead with his documentary, which was exceptionally well received and much praised for its fairness and sensitivity. Of the important players still living, only Charles Van Doren refused to participate.

FORTY-FOUR

The most indelible images of America that fall came from Little Rock, scenes captured by still photographers and, far more significantly, by movie cameramen working for network television news shows. The first and most jarring of these images was of angry mobs of white rednecks, pure hatred contorting their faces, as they assaulted the nine young black students who dared to integrate Little Rock Central High. The second and almost equally chilling image came a few weeks later, showing the same black children entering the same school under the protection of elite U.S. Army paratroopers. The anger and hatred that had been smoldering just beneath the surface in the South since the enactment of *Brown* v. *Board of Education* had finally exploded, and now because of television, the whole nation and soon the whole world could watch America at war with itself.

It was bound to happen sooner or later, but no one thought it would happen in Little Rock. Arkansas was a moderate state, as much a Southwestern state as it was truly Southern. Its medical and law schools had been integrated a decade earlier, without even a court order. Orval Faubus, the governor, was considered a moderate and there was no feverish quality to his voice when he spoke about issues of race. He seemed to lack the terrible hatred that infected so many Southern politicians. In 1955, when *Brown II* was handed down, Faubus had said: "It appears that the Court left some degree of decision in these matters to the Federal District courts. I believe this will guarantee against any sudden dislocation. . . . Our reliance must be upon the good will that exists between the races—the good will that has long made Arkansas a model for other Southern states in all matters affecting the relationship between the races."

In his successful 1956 campaign for reelection, Faubus barely mentioned the race issue, and the Little Rock plan for integration was so gradual that initially only nine black students were to attend a white school. The plan called for integrating at the high school level and working downward, one grade, one year at a time. Originally, Virgil Blossom, the school superintendent, wanted to do just the opposite—beginning at the lower levels and working upward, on the theory that younger children would have less learned prejudice. But he found that white parental fear in the lower grades was more intense: parents were less nervous about their teenagers than their first-graders.

Blossom wanted only the ablest and most mature black students. A list of eighty at the old Horace Mann School who were interested in transferring was drawn up. School officials quickly whittled the number down to thirty-two. That was easy: As Blossom explained to parents and children the pressures they would surely be subjected to, many dropped out. Blossom and his staff met with all thirty-two families—both parents and children. Some students were told they were not ready for either the social pressure or the school-work. A few good athletes were told they might be better off staying at Horace Man because at a white school they would have to face the possibility that other schools might cancel games as a result of their being on the teams. The list shrank to seventeen names, and then, as rumors and doubts continued, only nine. That pleased the white leadership. The entire process had been designed to minimize the emotional impact of integration on the whites. If the local black leadership was not entirely thrilled with the cautious approach, it had accepted it as law, for the Blossom plan clearly met the test of the Supreme Court and had been approved by the federal district court. Virgil Blossom was an affable man, whom Harry Ashmore, the executive editor of the liberal *Arkansas Gazette,* thought of as a "natural-born Rotarian." He was named Little Rock's man of the year in 1955, and both newspapers, the *Gazette* and the *Democrat*, as well as the city council and the chamber of commerce, backed his plan. Everybody in the local establishment seemed to be on board.

Harry Ashmore was the liberal working editor of the liberal *Arkansas Gazette,* one of the South's best newspapers and, as far as he was concerned, Little Rock reflected the gradual evolution taking place in much of the urban postwar South, with the ascendance of a more moderate generation of white leadership. These younger men, most of whom had fought in World War Two, and who had in some way been broadened by that experience, did not welcome integration, Ashmore thought. Most of them, in fact, probably preferred things the way they were. But unlike their parents, they were not violently opposed to integration. It was not as emotional an issue with them as it had once been. They were businessmen first and foremost, and they understood that the world had changed and that to fight to maintain white supremacy would be self-defeating—it was probably a lost cause. They accepted the idea of "social justice"— that is, a fairer legal and political deal for blacks—but they remained wary of what they considered "social equality"—which implied an integrated dance at a country club, for instance. That went against everything in their upbringing. At the heart of their position was a desire to do business as usual and an acceptance that when it came to the crunch, the presence of a white redneck mob in the street was a greater threat to tranquility and daily commerce than was the integration of a school system or other public facilities. Thus they accepted the law of the land because they saw it, in long-range business terms, as the path of least resistance.

A few days before the schools were to open, Benjamin Fine, the education editor of *The New York Times,* came to town to cover the event, and years later Ashmore was amused by Fine's initial purpose: to find out why Little Rock was handling so sensitive a matter with such exceptional ease. Fine visited Ashmore in his office, and the local editor predicted that there would be little more than routine verbal protests at the coming desegregation. In fact, just about everyone locally expected a rather peaceful transition. But Orval Faubus had started playing his cards ever closer to his vest, Ashmore noted. Still, the worst he expected was that Faubus would refuse to back the local police officials, thereby preserving his ties to the segregationists without overtly blocking the law of the land as mandated by the district court.

Little Rock authorities felt particularly comfortable with the Blossom plan because the nine black students were chosen not merely for their exceptional educational abilities but for their strength of character as well. They came from middle-class families, black middle-class to be sure, which meant smaller incomes than that of white middle-class families, but they all had a strong sense of home and family. Religion played an important part in most of their homes. Typical was Terrance Roberts, fifteen, the second of seven children. His father was a Navy veteran who worked as a dietician at the veterans' hospital in north Little Rock, and his mother ran a catering service out of their home. Though it was part of the white mythology that the NAACP in New York pushed unwilling parents to sacrifice their children to its subversive aims, the real drive to integrate usually came from the children themselves. The parents were nervous about a possible confrontation, but the children felt it was time to get on with integration. The *Brown* decision had been handed down three years previously, when they were twelve or thirteen, and with the idealism of the young, they trusted in their country and its laws. As Terrance Roberts told a reporter who asked him in the early days whether he was doing this at the urging of the NAACP, "Nobody urged me to go. The school board asked if I wanted to go. I thought if I got in, some of the other children would be able to go . . . and have more opportunities."

One thing few outsiders noticed was that the integration was scheduled for Little Rock Central, a school for working-class whites, while a new suburban high school, designed to serve the city's upper middle class, was not involved. The city establishment, which came from the world of upper-middle-class Little Rock, was, of course, absolutely unaware that there was a double standard here and accepted all too readily that its right to make the decisions on matters like this. They did not understand that others, less powerful, less successful, and less influential, would have to live with their decisions and might resent them. Daisy Bates, the head of the local NAACP, was aware of the class tensions that ran through the crisis, the rage on the part of the poor whites because they had to bear the burden of integration while the upper-class whites would be largely unaffected by it. At one point Mrs. Bates, referring to the deep class tensions that lay just beneath the surface in the white community, told one of the town leaders, "You may deserve Orval Faubus, but by God I don't!"

As the first day of school drew closer, Faubus's political position began to change. He was no longer Faubus, friend of moderates. He became evasive in dealing with school-board officials and other civic leaders. Those who thought they could count on him at least to remain neutral found that they either could not reach him or that if they did, he was ambivalent, in the opinion of some, or out and out slippery, in the opinion of others. "Governor, just what *are* you going to do in regard to the Little Rock integration plan?" Blossom asked him. Faubus paused and then answered: "When you tell me what the federals are going to do, I will tell you what I am going to do." Blossom thought that meant Faubus wanted the federal government to act decisively and thus remove any responsibility for integrating the schools from local officials, particularly from the governor. What was foremost in Orval Faubus's mind at that moment was not the education of the nine black children or the 2,000 white children whom they would join at Central High but rather his own political future in a state where, in the three years since *Brown,* race was beginning to dominate local political discourse. In Arkansas, the governor had to run for reelection every two years, and Arkansas voters were notoriously ungenerous about handing out third terms. Faubus was not a lawyer, he had no family wealth to fall back on, and he did not look forward to going back to being a rural postmaster. Other governors, their term of office over, could make a lateral move to a powerful Little Rock law firm and earn more than they ever had while in office. But that was not true of Faubus.

As the day for Little Rock's school integration approached, other politicians from the Deep South began applying pressure on Faubus to make him toe the line—to them he was the weak link in the chain of resistance. Mississippi senator James Eastland attacked him as being among the "weak-kneed politicians at the state capitols. . . . If the Southern states are picked off one by one under the damnable doctrine of gradualism I don't know if we can hold out or not." Faubus began to feel that he might, if he was not careful, become a politician who had obeyed the law only to find his political career ended overnight for his good deed. At the same time feelings were steadily becoming more raw, and Faubus could tell he was losing much of his room to maneuver. In the spring he had pushed a package of four segregationist bills through the Arkansas legislature. They had passed by votes of 81 to 1. That vote told him something. The governor knew the laws were pointless, that in a legal confrontation with the feds the state's powers were invalid, but he was beginning to respond to growing pressure around him and creating, if nothing else, a paper record. He was torn, as the deadline approached, between doing the right thing, and taking on the federal government to make himself a symbol of Southern white resistance.

Elsewhere in the Deep South segregationists were forming Citizens' Councils, local committees of white leaders pledged to stop integration. Regarding Faubus as something of a major liability, they decided to hold a major rally in Little Rock on August 22 and to bring in Marvin Griffin, the racist Georgia governor, and Roy Harris, the overall head of the Citizens' Councils, to speak at a ten-dollar-a-plate dinner. Faubus was not pleased by their visit; he knew they were trying to stoke the fires of racial resistance and to corner him. He complained about Griffin's visit to Virgil Blossom. "Why don't you telephone him and ask him to stay away?" Blossom suggested, somewhat innocently to the governor. "I'll think about it," Faubus answered. But Griffin and Harris came, stayed at the governor's mansion, and had breakfast with Faubus. From then on, Blossom noted, it became extremely difficult to reach Faubus.

Ironically, Faubus was not much of a racist. His roots were populist, but not racist populist. He was shrewd and earthy, from the Snopes school of politics, and was more intelligent and politically skilled than most of his critics suspected. His resentments were directed toward the upper class and business establishment of Little Rock, which he (rightly) suspected of looking down on him. His father, Sam Faubus, said later that Orval hated to be looked down on even as a little boy. There was, Harry Ashmore thought, something of a contradiction to Faubus's attitude toward the elite of Little Rock—he liked to put them on by pretending to be nothing but a good old country boy, as if he were still wearing his first store-bought suit, but when they believed him in that role, he resented it. He was, Ashmore liked to say, like an Airedale dog—a lot smarter than he looked. Later, after Little Rock had been torn apart by Faubus's decision to block integration, Ashmore noted that there had been plenty of earlier signs of which way he might go, since in the past whenever there had been any kind of crunch, Faubus had always followed his sense of what the preponderant feeling was among the poor whites, whom he knew so well and with whom he could so readily identify. His politics were the politics of class.

Faubus came from poor rural stock; he never even saw a black man until he was fully grown, when he went to Missouri to pick strawberries, his father later said. Sam Faubus was an old-fashioned, back-country radical who greatly admired Eugene Debs and was later appalled by his son's decision to block integration. (Sam Faubus was not a man to criticize his own flesh and blood openly, but he wrote a series of critical letters to the *Arkansas Gazette* under the pen name Jimmy Higgins.) Orval's childhood was poor: The water came from a nearby spring, the house was made of unfinished sawmill lumber, and the kitchen was completely unfinished. Orval graduated from grammar school in a one-room schoolhouse at the age of eighteen. He then became one of fifty people taking an exam for a third grade teacher's license, and he had gotten the highest marks. The certificate allowed him to teach school in Huntsville and attend high school at the same time. He got his high school diploma at the age of twenty-seven. By that time, he had been married for six years and he and his wife regularly spent their summers as migrant fruit-and-vegetable pickers. It was hard to find white people much poorer than they were and, Virgil Blossom noted, it was hard to find people that poor with so much ambition. In World War Two, he rose to the rank of major, came back, and bought a weekly paper in Huntsville; that brought him into the orbit of Sid McMath, the patrician liberal governor who was his first statewide sponsor and in whose cabinet he had served. (Later, McMath, appalled by the direction his protégé had taken, said, "I brought Orval down out of the hills and every night I pray for forgiveness.") He had helped McMath with the poor white vote, and he intended to run himself.

In 1954 Faubus ran for governor; he was so much the outsider in Little Rock that when he wrote his check for the $1,500 qualifying fee, it was not accepted until a friend who was a former state legislator endorsed it on the back. Because of his connection to McMath, he did reasonably well with blacks and upper-middle-class whites; as for poor rural whites, he was one of them. The one thing he remembered about that race was that it was one of the hottest summers in Arkansas history and all the other major candidates were traveling around in air-conditioned cars, but he made it, stop after stop, in the brutal heat, without any air-conditioning. He won even though, ironically enough, he had been red-baited for having briefly attended a small college with radical roots. As governor he appointed more blacks to state positions than any predecessor. Later, the liberal-moderate camp, including such men as Blossom, Ashmore, and Brooks Hays, the well-connected Little Rock congressman, cited the visit of Griffin and Harris as the turning point, the moment when Faubus looked at his political future, saw no middle ground, and made his choice.

Monday, September 2, fell on Labor Day; school was scheduled to start on Tuesday, September 3. By the beginning of the previous weekend, Faubus decided to call out the Arkansas National Guard—on the pretext of preventing violence, but in reality to block integration. Blossom found out about this only late on Monday night. According to Faubus, there were caravans of white racists heading for Central High. There would be bloodshed in the streets of Little Rock if the blacks tried to enter the school.

On the Sunday before school opening, Winthrop Rockefeller, the member of the famed Rockefeller family who had chosen to live in Arkansas, got wind of Faubus's plan to call out the National Guard and he rushed to the statehouse. There Rockefeller, the leader in trying to bring industry to a state desperately short of good jobs, pleaded with Faubus not to block integration. The governor told him he was too late: "I'm sorry but I'm already committed. I'm going to run for a third term, and if I don't do this, Jim Johnson and Bruce Bennett [the two leading Arkansas segregationists] will tear me to shreds."

What he did was very simple: He announced that he was unable to maintain the peace (thereby encouraging a mob to go into the streets), and then he placed the Arkansas National Guard on the side of the mob: Its orders, despite the specific mandate of the district court, were to keep the blacks out of the schools. The Guard encircled the school; meanwhile, the mob grew larger. The police force of the city was inadequate to deal with the mob, and the fire chief refused to permit the hoses of his fire wagons to be used against it. The black children were suddenly very much at risk. Daisy Bates, the leader of the local NAACP, asked black and white ministers to accompany them on Wednesday, September 4. She arranged for a police car to protect them. But as they approached the school, they were abused and threatened; when they finally reached the school, they were turned away by a National Guard captain, who said he was acting under the orders of Governor Faubus. What are your orders? someone asked one of the soldiers. "Keep the niggers out!" he answered. The confidence of the mob grew greater by the minute as it found that the law-enforcement forces were on its side. Sensing this, the ministers and children quickly retreated.

They were the lucky ones. One child, fifteen-year-old Elizabeth Eckford, had not gotten the message the night before about how they were to assemble together. Her father was a railroad-car maintenance worker who worked nights; her mother taught at a school for black children who were deaf or blind. The family did not have a phone. In the morning, an exhausted Daisy Bates completely forgot that she had not advised Elizabeth about the new arrangements. Elizabeth, like most of the other children involved in the early integration cases, had made the decision to go to Central very much on her own. Elizabeth wanted to be a lawyer, and she had heard that Central offered a speech course that might help her prepare for law school, while Horace Man did not. Her mother, Birdie Eckford, was unhappy about her choice, and when Elizabeth had suggested during the summer that they go to the school board office and get the requisite transfer forms for Central, Mrs. Eckford gently and vaguely agreed to do it some other time, hoping Elizabeth would forget about it. Two weeks later Elizabeth brought it up again. Again her mother tried to delay. Finally, near the end of August, Elizabeth demanded that her mother take her that very day to get the transfer. With that it was obtained. That first day of school she got up early and pressed her new black-and-white dress, one she had made herself to wear for her new experience in an integrated school. At breakfast the family television set was on and some commentator was talking about the size of the mob gathering in front of the school and wondering aloud whether the black children would show up. "Turn that TV off!" said Mrs. Eckford. Birdie was so nervous that Elizabeth tried to comfort her mother by saying that everything would be all right. Her father, she noted, was just as nervous, holding a cigar in one hand and a pipe in his mouth, neither of them lit. Before Elizabeth left, her mother called the family together and they all prayed.

Alone and unprotected, Elizabeth approached the school, and the crowd started to scream at her: "Here she comes! Here comes one of the niggers!" But she saw the National Guard troopers and was not scared, because she thought the soldiers would protect her. She tried to walk into the school, but a guard thrust his rifle at her and blocked her way. She walked a few feet further down to get by the guard but was blocked again by two other soldiers. Some white students were being let in at the same time, she noticed. Other soldiers moved toward her and raised their bayonets to make the barrier more complete. She was terrified now, blocked in her attempt to get to the school, aware that the mob was closing in behind her. Someone was yelling, "Lynch her! Lynch her!" Someone else yelled: "Go home, you bastard of a black bitch!" She tried to steady her legs as she turned away, the school now at her back. The mob pressed closer. "No nigger bitch is going to get in our school!" someone shouted. She was blocked in all directions. She looked down the street and saw a bench by a bus stop. If she could just make it to the

676 / DAVID HALBERSTAM

bench, she thought. When she finally got there, she felt she would collapse.

A man she had never known, Ben Fine, the education reporter for *The New York Times,* who was there to write his story on how Little Rock had stayed so calm, came over and put his arm around her and tried to comfort her. "Don't let them see you cry," he said. An elderly white woman (the wife of a white professor at a black college) came over and also offered her solace and tried to face the crowd down. The woman, despite the howls of the mob, managed to get Elizabeth on a bus and out of the combat zone.

Among those who had been there and caught all of it—the virulence of the white mob, its rage and madness mounting as it closed in, the lone young black girl who seemed to be bearing herself with amazing calm and dignity—was John Chancellor, a young reporter with NBC. He had watched Elizabeth Eckford's perilous journey with growing fear: one child, alone, entrapped by this mob. He was not sure she was going to make it out alive. He had wanted a story, a good story, but this was something beyond a good story, a potential tragedy so terrible that he had hoped it wasn't really happening. He was terribly frightened for her, frightened for himself, and frightened about what this told him about his country. He could not believe that someone had so carelessly allowed this child to come to school alone, with no escort. The mob gathered there in the street was uglier than anything he had ever seen before in his life. It was a mob of fellow Americans, people who under other conditions might be perfectly decent people, but there they were completely out of control. Chancellor wondered briefly where this young girl found her strength. It was almost as if he was praying: *Please, stop all of this; please, there's got to be a better way.* He watched in agony and captured it all for NBC.

Chancellor was a relatively junior reporter for NBC in the summer of 1957. He was thirty years old and based in Chicago. After working for the *Chicago Sun Times,* he had been hired by the local NBC station in Chicago in 1950, ostensibly as a news writer; but the real reason was that his superiors thought he could cover so-called street stories—fires and accidents. On the early *Camel News Caravan* with John Cameron Swayze, he would go out in the field with a cameraman and a sound man. He doubled as film editor, for the show's producer had asked him what he knew about editing film. Nothing at all, he answered. Well, buy a book, and read and find out about it, the producer had said, which Chancellor did. As a result he had become surprisingly expert in editing film, which in those days was 35mm and, in the vernacular of the trade, went through the gate at ninety feet a minute. He became in the process something of a film nut, and he came to understand, as few others of his generation did, the journalistic power of images. Years later he thought his tour as reporter-film editor taught him how to write for film, a process he might otherwise not have understood.

Most of the big-name journalists at the networks were still doing radio reporting when he had joined NBC. Some of the early television figures, such as John Cameron Swayze, the NBC anchorman ("Let's hopscotch the world for headlines," he would say every night), held their positions because they had been sufficiently low down in the radio pecking order that they had nothing to lose by going over to this new medium. Many others, like Chancellor, had roots in print and were learning television the hard way, since the rules were still being set every day as they worked.

On that Labor Day weekend in 1957, Chancellor had been poised to go to Nashville to report on school integration in the South, but his superior in New York, Reuven Frank, told him that according to the AP wire, Orval Faubus was going to call out the Arkansas National Guard to prevent court-ordered integration. That sounded like a bigger story than Nashville, so without stopping to pack, Chancellor raced to catch the last plane to Little Rock. He was relatively new to what was now becoming known as the Southern, or race, beat. His introduction to it had come back in 1955 with the Emmett Till case, still primarily a print story. But there had been a brief harbinger of the future the day after the acquittal of the two men accused of murdering Till. Chancellor happened to be in Memphis at the time and he was sent down to Sumner to do a radio report for *Monitor,* the lively NBC radio show of that period. Chancellor grabbed a primitive early-model tape recorder and drove over in the company of a man from the Jackson radio station. From the instant he arrived, Sumner had scared him: He had an eerie feeling that something terrible was going to happen as he walked up the street, interviewing blacks and whites alike on their opinion of the trial. Suddenly, a sixth sense told him that he was in trouble and he slowly turned to look behind him. There coming directly at him was a phalanx of eight or nine men in overalls and work shirts. Rage was etched in their faces. His car was ten feet away, and the Jackson radio man was in it, honking the horn. Chancellor was terrified, for he knew the men wanted to hurt him. For a split second he thought of running to the car, but the men were too close. He did the only thing he could think of. He took the microphone and pointed it at the first white man. "Okay," he said, "you can do what you want with me, but the whole world is going to hear about it and see it." The men stopped, he later speculated, because they had mistaken his tape recorder for a camera. It had been, he decided, like holding up a talisman to some primitive tribal chief, but it worked. With that, he walked to the car and drove away.

If print reporters and still photographers had been witnesses to their stories, then television correspondents, armed as they were with cameras and crews, were something more: They were not merely witnesses, but something more, a part of the story. Television reporters, far more than their print predecessors, contributed to the speeding up of social change in America. Little Rock became the prime example of that, the first all-out confrontation between the force of the law and the force of the mob, played out with television cameras whirring away in black and white for a nation that was by now largely wired.

Reuven Frank, the most powerful and cerebral figure in the NBC newsroom at the time, who more than anyone else created the standards of that network's journalism, understood immediately that the world of television was different. The cameramen he had inherited had a newsreel vision of shooting film—their ideal was two heads of state meeting and shaking hands. Frank wanted something different, something more subtle and more real. He believed if you were creative enough, you could create a mosaic of the country—its humanity, its diversity, and its tension points. He had a supple sense of the medium, and Chancellor remembered his own pleasure when Frank called to tell him after one report that his piece had "a lovely Mozartian unity to it." Frank emphasized constantly to his reporters that their role was to be, in some ways, minimal. Film was so powerful that a reporter was well advised to get out of the way and let the pictures do the talking. Certainly, that was true in Little Rock. The images were so forceful that they told their own truths and needed virtually no narration. It was hard for people watching at home not to take sides: There they were, sitting in their living rooms in front of their own television sets watching orderly black children behaving with great dignity, trying to obtain nothing more than a decent education, the most elemental of American birthrights, yet being assaulted by a vicious mob of poor whites. What was happening now in the country was politically potent: The legal power of the United States Supreme Court had now been cast in moral terms for the American conscience, and that was driven as much as anything else by the footage from the networks from Little Rock. The President, uneasy with the course of events, had failed to give any kind of moral leadership, and he had deliberately refused to define the issue in moral terms; now, almost unconsciously, the media was doing it instead, for the ugliness and the cruelty of it all, the white mob encouraged by a local governor tormenting young children, carried its own indictment. The nation watched, hypnotized, from its living rooms every night, what, in the words of television reporter Dan Schorr, was "a national evening seance." Every clip of film diminished the room to maneuver of each of the major players. With television every bit of action, Chancellor decided, seemed larger, more immediate; the action seemed to be moving at an ever faster rate.

On his arrival there, Chancellor thought, Little Rock had seemed a sleepy town, as yet unconnected to the ever greater bustle of modern American life. The pace of living seemed almost languid. Chancellor remembered a vivid symbol of the older America that still existed when he arrived. The bellboy who took him to his room at the old Sam Peck Hotel brought him a pitcher of iced water and then suggested that if he wanted any female companionship later in the evening, he need only call. One night, early in October, after the 101st had momentarily stabilized the situation, Chancellor had gone out to dinner with Harry Ashmore at Hank's Doghouse in North Little Rock. It happened to be the night that *Sputnik* went up, and the two of them had watched the news reports of this most remarkable achievement in the new space age. "Can you believe this?" Chancellor had said. "This means that men are really going to go to the moon." "Yes," said Ashmore. "And here we are in Little Rock fighting the Civil War again." It seemed to symbolize the time warp they were in.

At the beginning of the story, Chancellor could not broadcast live because there was still no AT&T equipment available. He had to race to the airport each afternoon for a chartered plane to take him to Oklahoma City, where he could do his broadcast live. The NBC show was on for fifteen minutes, which meant it contained twelve minutes of news. Network news was just coming of age. The previous fall, Swayze had been replaced by a new team of anchors: Chet Huntley, sturdy and steadfast, his reliability vouched for by his strong face, was electronically married to David Brinkley, mischievous and waspish, a perfect foil for the overpowering immediacy of television. It, along with the other two network shows, was creating a new electronic media grid binding the nation.

Chancellor now became their first star in the field. Every night NBC led with his story, in part, Chancellor suspected, because Reuven Frank understood what was happening—not only on the streets of Little Rock, but in the American psyche. It was perhaps the first time a television reporter rather than a print reporter had put his signature on so critical a running story. Chancellor not only worked hard but, to his credit, he never thought himself a star. An anchor-man, he liked to say years later, was someone who ran the last leg of a relay race; and some fifteen years later, when he did in fact become the anchorman of the *NBC Nightly News,* he took the additional title not of managing editor, but of principal reporter.

Little Rock made him famous, and the unique aspect to televi-sion fame was that his face became his byline. People came to associ-ate him with the story he was covering, and they began to feel they already knew him. Because of this, they were quicker to confide in him than in print reporters. Being a television reporter, he realized, meant instant access and instant connection, and in no small part because of his electronic fame, he soon obtained a secret mole inside the school. His mole, Chancellor discovered later, was a sixteen-year-old Little Rock boy named Ira Lipman, just starting his senior year. Ernest Green, one of the Little Rock nine, had been a locker-room attendant at the Jewish country club in Little Rock, where Lipman's parents had a membership. On a number of occasions Lipman had ended up driving Ernest Green home after work, and the two had struck up a friendship. Lipman thought Ernest Green pleasant and intelligent, with a rare gentleness about him. Their relationship had in his mind underlined the madness of segregation, the fact that the two of them could not have a normal friendship and that he had only managed to know him through a club where his parents were privi-leged members and Ernest Green was an attendant.

Lipman worked a few nights a week at the *Arkansas Gazette* and had once met another NBC reporter, Frank McGee. Now he decided to help Chancellor, because he felt he had a connection to NBC and also because he had seen Chancellor on television and thought him decent and fair-minded, a man who was trying to tell the truth about a difficult situation. He would gather information and then call Chancellor anonymously from a pay phone just outside the school. The first of his calls took place at the very beginning of the crisis. Chancellor did not have time to check out the information before he filed that day, but late that night, upon his return from Oklahoma City, he found the information to be accurate.

The next day Chancellor's youthful anonymous source called to chide him: "I'm very disappointed in you," he said. "I have all this terrific information and you didn't use it." Chancellor apologized, but promised to take the information more seriously in the future.

Not knowing his source's name, Chancellor comprehended in some way the background and the motivation of this young boy. Lipman always had to whisper lest another student discover what he was doing and tell someone. The boy was placing himself in great danger. But having this source gave Chancellor a terrific edge on the story, and he was able to move ahead of his print rivals.

Wallace Westfeldt, a reporter for the *Nashville Tennessean,* was amused by the spectacle of this reporter from the upstart institution of television news, who was gaining every day the grudging admiration of his older print colleagues. Westfeldt's own sources were excellent, since he had visited Little Rock several times before the crisis. Each night he would file his own story for the early edition of his paper and then sit in the Little Rock press club having a sandwich and a drink with the other reporters. As he ate, the *NBC Nightly News* would come on, and Chancellor would often have something that few, if any, of the print reporters had. Westfeldt could see them cursing under their breath, and when the news show was over, there would be a quiet exodus from the press club as reporters went to the phones to call their offices and update their own stories. Television, Westfeldt thought, was quickly catching up with print: If anything, in this story the new medium might have exceeded the old for the first time.

As Little Rock developed, the national media force focusing on civil rights crystallized. It had its own pecking order and rules. Johnny Popham, and soon his successor Claude Sitton, of the *Times* set the tone. There were also the legendary Homer Bigart, also of the *Times,* Bob Bird of the *Tribune,* Bob Baker of *The Washington Post,* and soon Karl Fleming of *Newsweek.* The older men in this brigade had often been war correspondents in World War Two and Korea, which helped—because the situation was not unlike a war on native soil; the younger men, by and large, were Southerners, because a Southern accent was considered helpful.

They were at risk all the time, for the mobs perceived them as liberals, Jews, and Communists. Several *Life* magazine reporters were beaten badly by the mob early in the crisis, and then the reporters were arrested by local officials for having been beaten up. The network people, because of their high visibility, the familiarity of their faces, and the obvious presence of their cameramen, were particularly vulnerable. Chancellor soon found that when he walked down the street, he would often be followed by cars full of segregationists, hate contorting their faces as they stared at him. At first he would panic. *Should I run?* he would ask himself, but he soon learned merely to keep walking. The locals became angrier and angrier—for television, in particular, was holding up a mirror of these people for the outside world to look at it, and the image in the mirror was not pretty. If you went to the sheriff's office to do an interview, Chancellor remembered, you gave your name and organization to the deputy, who would holler back so the entire office could hear, "Sheriff, there's some son of a bitch out here from the Nigger Broadcasting Company who says he wants to see you."

Because of the dangers, there were certain rules—a reporter never carried a notebook that he could not hide in a pocket. Popham's first rule of coverage was: Never take notes in front of the crowd. It was better to dress casual than sharp. A reporter never went out on a story alone. One did not argue with the segregationists or provoke them. Whatever moral abhorrence a reporter felt about the events taking place in front of him, it was to be kept bottled up. Ben Fine of the *Times,* an indoor man in the vernacular, had lost his cool when he comforted Elizabeth Eckford. He had started to argue with the mob and the *Times* had been forced to bring him back to New York.

Watching these journalists in Little Rock, as he had watched them almost two years earlier in Montgomery, Alabama, was a man named Will Campbell. A native of a tiny town called Liberty in south Mississippi, he had earned a bachelor's degree from Wake Forest and a master's from the Yale Divinity School: He was technically the Rev. Will Campbell, though for most of his life he never had a church. He liked to describe himself as "a Baptist preacher, but never on Sunday." The contradiction between his own liberalism and the conservatism of his church amused him, and he liked to say that he "was a Baptist preacher of the South, but not a Southern Baptist preacher." During the early days of the civil rights movement, he became an important but anonymous player. Sometimes his face would appear in the back of a photograph taken during some particular confrontation, but he would almost never be identified, just as his name would never appear in the news stories themselves, by agreement with the journalists for whom he had already become a valuable source. He was quoted hundreds of times in newspapers but never by name, instead, always as an anonymous reliable source, which he in fact was. He was a shrewd recorder and interpreter not only of the facts but of the intentions of the many different players involved, and he had important friends on all sides in these confrontations. His first job after school had been to serve as the chaplain at the University of Mississippi, but his liberal views on integration had almost immediately gotten him fired. Although violence had never been directed at him at Ole Miss, at one reception he had given, a turd had been discovered in the punch bowl. That had convinced him his days at Ole Miss were numbered. In 1956 he took a job as a kind of roving field agent for the National Council of Churches based in Nashville. Acting as a friend and adviser to those blacks threatened or in trouble, and connecting them to sympathetic people and agencies in the North, he was a ubiquitous figure, always on the move. The national reporters discovered he was able to move back and forth between different groups, bringing them information and making quiet, astute suggestions about what was likely to happen next.

Will Campbell, then thirty-three, understood as much as anyone the growing power of the media and what it meant to the Movement. Earlier in Montgomery, he had gained a sense of how it could define this story in moral terms. But one day early in the crisis at Little Rock, he had an epiphany about the importance of the media. He had been out in the streets watching the mob when a friend nudged him and pointed to a slim young man who seemed to be talking into the air. "That's John Chancellor of NBC," the friend noted. Campbell had never seen Chancellor in the flesh before, though he had heard of him. There seemed nothing remarkable about his appearance, nor did he seem to know anything more than Will Campbell himself about the violent situation playing itself out in front of them. But a few hours later, back in his hotel room, Campbell happened to turn on his television set and there was the very scene he had witnessed earlier in the day: Chancellor, shrunk now to about three inches on his screen, was calmly giving a summary of what was happening as the mob jostled and jeered behind him. The commentary, for most Americans, was chilling, and it struck Campbell in that instant that these modern journalists, both print and television, were the new prophets of our society. Moreover, they had, because of television, what the prophets of old had lacked—a mass audience to which they could transmit with stunning immediacy the events they witnessed. It was in their power, as it had been in the power of the prophets before them, the tent and brush-arbor revivalists, to define sin, and they were doing it not to a select few of the chosen but to the entire citizenry. They did not think of themselves as modern prophets and they did not think they were actually defining sin, but what they were doing, in Will Campbell's view, was just that, for there was no way that an ordinary citizen could watch these events through their eyes and words and pictures and not be offended and moved. What John Chancellor might as well have been doing, thought Campbell, was letting the film roll and repeating again and again, "This is a sin . . . this is a sin . . . this is a sin . . ."

Locally, Harry Ashmore had never had any doubt what he intended to do with his paper once Faubus drew the line, but he warned the paper's elderly owner, J. N. Heiskell, what the price of telling the truth and upholding the law would be. Heiskell brushed Ashmore's warnings aside. He had no desire to accommodate such demagoguery even if it meant losing subscribers and advertising (which, in a subsequent boycott of the *Gazette,* it did). "I'm an old man," Heiskell answered, "and I've lived too long to let people like that [Faubus] take over my city." Most editors at American newspapers of the era were not so brave. More often than not, they put their own survival first and tried not to offend local sensibilities. Often, in moments of crisis, their instinct would be to protect the community against its critics, to soften accounts of its failings and, above all, to blame outsiders. Harry Ashmore was having none of that. This was the moment, he was sure, when he would be judged with a finality.

Ashmore was fearless not only in how he covered the crisis in his own paper but also in opening up its resources to visiting reporters. That was true not only at the beginning of the crisis, when most of the Little Rock establishment supported the integration plan, but in the months to follow as well, as people (including, most notably, his competitors on the rival *Arkansas Democrat*) who once praised the plan began to falter and switch sides. Relatively early on, a top Justice Department official called Ashmore to get a reading on what was happening: "I'll give it to you in one sentence," he answered. "The police have been routed, the mob is in the streets and we're close to a reign of terror."

His paper became the general press headquarters. Visiting reporters would head over there every day, in effect to be briefed by Ashmore and his reporters on the day's events. Then, if they wanted to, they could go out for dinner with him as he talked on into the night, regaling them with stories of Arkansas politics. Orval Faubus might have been able momentarily to block the school integration, orchestrate the mob, and confuse the President of the United States as to his true aims, but he had met his match in Harry Ashmore. (Some thirty years later, at a conference at Fayetteville where panelists looked at the events of Little Rock in retrospect, Faubus began to sanitize his version of what had happened. His view by then, created to tidy up his place in history, was that through his actions he had only been trying to push President Eisenhower to act. Some one thousand people, almost all of them pro-integration, were attending the symposium, and one morning just before Faubus spoke, he and his old antagonist Ashmore had breakfast together. Faubus gave his version of what he was going to say, and Ashmore wished him well in getting away with it. "But remember, Orval," he said as the latter had gotten up from the table to give his speech. "This time I've got the mob on *my* side.")

Both the nation and the world watched with horror and fascination as Faubus steadily moved into the vacuum created by the Eisenhower administration. Largely unsympathetic to the idea of integration, the President had given little thought to the question of what might happen if the Southern states rebelled. Despite the constant rumblings about the possibility of serious Southern resistance, Eisenhower seemed ambivalent about the events unfolding so dramatically in the month after the *Brown* decision. Meanwhile, the job grew steadily more difficult, until in Little Rock the governor seemed to be openly defying the law of the land. A few men around Eisenhower, more committed to civil rights—Herbert Brownell, Richard Nixon, and Bill Rogers—thought that the President had underestimated Faubus from the start and that Faubus was aiming for a major constitutional confrontation for his own political gain.

Soon after the *Brown* decision, Attorney General Brownell, as the chief law enforcement officer of the country, had met with the attorneys general of the Southern states and spoken informally about what they could all do together to expedite the process of integration. He had asked for suggestions on how federal and state forces could make the transition as easy as possible. When he finished he was met by thunderous silence. Afterward one state attorney general took him aside and pointed out that each man in this room intended one day to become governor of his state. None therefore wanted to be seen as partners of the U.S. government in carrying out local integration. In fact, the state attorney general added, Brownell should expect significant opposition rather than assistance.

Ike was very much in conflict within himself over whether integration was right or wrong; his essential sympathies were with neither the nine children nor the mob in the street but primarily with his new and extremely wealthy and conservative Southern golfing and hunting friends, those old-fashioned Southern traditionalists who found integration objectionable. As such the President remained silent on the issue and continued to dally. This was alien and extremely uncomfortable territory for him. Conservative by nature, he saw even the smallest change in the existing racial order as radical and upsetting. In the brief period while he was president of Columbia University it had been decided (but not by him) to give Ralph Bunche an honorary degree. Bunche was then at the peak of his career at the UN, and possibly the most honored and least controversial black man in the country. But Ike was uneasy with the choice, because it meant Bunche and his wife would have to join the other recipients for drinks and dinner. It wasn't that Ike was against Bunche receiving the degree, he confided, but he wondered if *the other* recipients would object to socializing with the Bunches. To his considerable surprise, the evening went off smoothly and several of the other recipients went out of their way to seek out the Bunches. The man to whom Eisenhower told this story, his friend Cy Sulzberger, was quite shocked; it showed, he thought, not only how biased Ike was about black people but how little he understood his own bias. Now, in the midst of a major constitutional crisis, to aides who suggested that he speak in favor of integration on the basis of moral and religious principles if nothing else, he answered somewhat disingenuously that he did not believe you could force people to change what was in their hearts. To those who suggested he meet with black leaders to talk about the nation's growing racial tensions and the threat of increased white Southern resistance, he answered, in a particularly telling moment, that if he did, he would have to meet as well with the leaders of the Ku Klux Klan.

Eisenhower did finally meet with Faubus in Newport, Rhode Island, much against Brownell's wishes. The attorney general warned the President repeatedly that the governor was thinking only of his reelection campaign. Faubus at first played Eisenhower extremely well: He had come not to exploit the issue, he claimed, but as an anguished moderate who wished only for a little more time. Ike, it seemed, was amenable to that: a little more time to do something that he himself could not readily understand. He began to speak of a compromise solution. Faubus later wrote that Eisenhower turned to Brownell in one of their sessions and asked, "Herb, can't you go down there [to Little Rock] and ask the Court to postpone this thing for a few days?" Brownell answered, "No, we can't do that. It isn't possible. It isn't legally possible. It can't be done." Brownell explained that the case was in the jurisdiction of the courts. Ike still seemed uncertain. Faubus noted: "I got the impression at the time that he was attempting to recall just what he was supposed to say to me, as if he were trying to remember instructions on a subject on which he was not completely assured in his own mind." Eisenhower, with no moderate solution available, finally turned up the heat and believed that he had gotten Faubus to agree to back down. But then as soon as Faubus returned to Little Rock, he reneged on his promise. When asked if he hadn't backed off his promise made at Newport, he answered, "Just because I said it doesn't make it so."

That did it as far as the President was concerned. "Well, you were right, Herb," he angrily told Brownell. "He did just what you said he'd do—he double-crossed me." If Eisenhower did not entirely comprehend the moral issue at stake, or for that matter the legal one, he certainly understood a personal challenge. A man who had been a five-star general did not look kindly on frontal challenges by junior officers. After vacillating for so long, he came down hard, seeing the issue not as a question of integration so much as one of insurrection. He sent in troops of the 101st Airborne to protect the nine children and he federalized the Arkansas National Guard. For the first time since Reconstruction days, federal troops were sent into the South to preserve order. Little Rock, Dean Acheson wrote Harry Truman at the time, terrified him, "a weak President who fiddled along ineffectually until a personal affront drives him to unexpectedly drastic action. A Little Rock with Moscow and the SAC in the place of the paratroopers could blow us all apart."

More than thirty years later, John Chancellor could still talk about the day the 101st Airborne came to Little Rock as if it had happened yesterday: The soldiers marched into the area and set up their perimeter. Their faces were immobile and, unlike the Guardsmen's, betrayed no politics, just duty. As they marched in, the clear, sharp sound of their boots clacking on the street was a reminder of their professionalism. Chancellor had never thought much about the Constitution before; if anything, he had somehow taken it for granted. But he realized that day that he was watching the Constitution in action. There was something majestic about the scene: it was a moment at once thrilling and somehow frightening as well.

With the arrival of the 101st, the nation yet again witnessed a stunning spectacle on television: armed soldiers of one of the most honored divisions in the United States Army escorting young black children where once there had been a mob. When the segregationists in the street protested, the paratroopers turned out to be very different from the National Guard soldiers who had so recently been their pals. The men of the 101st fixed their bayonets and placed them right at the throats of the protestors, quickly moving them out of the school area. That first morning, an Army officer came to Daisy

Bates's house, where the children had gathered, and saluted her. "Mrs. Bates," he said. "We're ready for the children. We will return them to your home at three-thirty." It was, said Minniejean Brown, one of the nine, an exhilarating moment. "For the first time in my life I felt like an American citizen," she later told Mrs. Bates.

For the moment, the law of the nation had been upheld against the will of the mob and the whims of a segregationist politician. The black children were escorted to and from school every day by the soldiers. Little Rock seemed to calm down. Faubus screamed about the encroachment of states' rights by the federal government and bemoaned the fact that Arkansas was occupied territory. Why, he himself, he said, had helped rescue the 101st when it was pinned down at Bastogne during the Battle of the Bulge (which was untrue—by the time his outfit had arrived, the 101st had already stopped the last German drive).

After a few weeks, with the situation seemingly under control, the government pulled out the 101st and put the federalized Arkansas National Guard in charge. With that, the situation began to deteriorate. The mob was no longer a problem, but inside the school there was a systematic and extremely well organized assault upon the nine children by high-school-age segregationists. They not only harassed the black children but, more effectively, any white child who was courteous or friendly to them.

It was a calculated campaign (organized, school officials suspected, right out of the governor's mansion). The school bullies, behaving like youthful Klansmen, knew they had behind them the full power of the state government and the increasingly defiant Arkansas population. That meant the job of protecting the nine fell on a handful of teachers and administrators in the school. The nine students were in for a very hard and ugly year. There was a relentless assault upon them—kicking, tripping, hitting them from behind, harassing them with verbal epithets as they walked down the hall, pouring hot soup on them in the cafeteria. Their lockers were broken into regularly, their books stolen. The school administrators knew exactly who the ringleaders were but found them boastfully proud. One girl told Elizabeth Huckaby, the vice-principal, that she was entirely within her rights. All she had done, the girl said, was to use the word *nigger*. It was as if her rights included harassing others for racial reasons.

How, in retrospect, the nine children stood all of this is amazing, but they did, showing remarkable inner strength and character, again and again turning the other cheek. On many occasions they seemed ready to break, and one or two would show up in Ms. Huckaby's office in tears, exhausted by the cruelty and on the verge of quitting. It was the job of Ms. Huckaby and others to plead with them to keep going and to remind them that if they faltered, it would merely be harder on the next group, because the segregationists would be bolder with success. Only one of the nine did not finish the first year: Minniejean Brown. Perhaps the most enthusiastic and emotional of the nine, she seemed to be the one least able to turn away from the harassment. Soon, the segregationists realized that she was the weak link and turned their full force on her. Minniejean on occasion fought back. Tormented in the cafeteria one day by her enemies, she dumped a soup bowl on the head of a student and was suspended. She tried desperately to control herself but in time responded once too often and was expelled. Immediately, cards were printed up that said, ONE DOWN. EIGHT TO GO.

Some of the black children's parents wanted them to pull out at various times during the year, fearing the price was simply too high. But Daisy Bates was strong: She reminded the children again and again that they were doing this not for themselves but for others, some as yet unborn. They were now, like it or not, leaders in a moral struggle. That year Ernest Green graduated, and twenty years later, he was perhaps the most successful member of the graduating class: As an assistant secretary of labor in the cabinet of Jimmy Carter, he was the featured speaker at the twentieth reunion of his classmates.

In a way, everyone seemed to have gotten something out of Little Rock. The civil rights leaders learned how to challenge the forces of segregation in front of the modern media, most notably television cameras. The networks, new and unsure of their role, had found a running story composed of almost nothing but images, which would not only prove compelling to viewers but which would legitimize its early reporters for their courage and decency (just as the broadcasts of Ed Murrow and his CBS colleagues had been legitimized radio during World War Two). In the months after the quiz-show scandals rocked the networks, there was a calculated attempt to address the resulting loss of prestige by giving the news shows ever greater freedom to cover such important events as Little Rock. Not just the news shows but the networks themselves were suddenly in the business of building respectability. John Chancellor in time would go on to one of the most distinguished careers in American journalism and public life, as anchor of the *Today* show, as head of the Voice of America and, finally, as anchorman of the NBC news.

No one, of course, gained more than Orval Faubus. He portrayed himself as the victim of massive federal intervention, the lonely man who believed in states' rights and the will of his own people. No longer could any good (white) citizen of Arkansas be for segregation and against Faubus. A third term, which had seemed unlikely before Little Rock, was guaranteed. With two moderate candidates running against him in 1958, he beat their combined total of votes by more than two to one. A fourth term followed. And a fifth term. And finally a sixth. On occasion there was talk of retirement, but he had, wrote the *Arkansas Gazette,* ridden off into more sunsets than Tom Mix. His decision to block integration set the stage for a generation of Southern politicians, most notably George Wallace, who had learned from Little Rock how to manipulate the anger within the South, how to divide a state by class and race, and how to make the enemy seem to be the media. The moderate position had been badly undermined at Little Rock, and an era of confrontation was to follow, Harry Ashmore wrote prophetically in *Life* in 1958.

A year after Little Rock, Daisy Bates suggested that she come to the White House with the nine children. It would be a wonderful thing, she suggested, for the children, who had endured so much hatred and violence, to be received by the President of the United States. The idea terrified Eisenhower's White House staff. In truth, it was a hard thing to say no to. Sherman Adams, the White House chief of staff and the boss of Frederick Morrow, the one black man on Ike's staff, shrewdly put the ball in Morrow's court. Adams asked Morrow: Was Mrs. Bates's request a wise one? No, said Morrow, because it was not a question of whether the President sympathized with the nine children. Rather, if he met with them, it would so enrage Southern leaders that it would diminish his role as a leader on such issues in the future. In addition, he added, the meeting would only subject the students "to more abuse than ever before, and certainly the President does not want to be a party to this kind of affair." "You are absolutely correct," Adams told Morrow. "That was my thinking on the meeting." Adams had one more move left. Would Morrow please call Mrs. Bates to tell her? It was, Morrow noted, a call he dreaded making, but he knew the rules and he knew what he was there to do. He was a team player, so he did it. He suggested that if she and the children came to Washington, he would set up a specially conducted tour of the White House.

No aspect of the crisis, particularly the role played by Orval Faubus, escaped the notice of Martin Luther King, Jr. He was nothing if not political, and he understood the emerging politics of protest brilliantly. King knew from his experience in Montgomery, where television news was making its earliest inroads, that what he was doing was no longer merely local, that because of television, for the first time the nation was convening each evening around 6 or 7 P.M.

King and his people were conducting the most perilous undertaking imaginable, for they knew that the more skillfully they provoked their enemies, the more dramatic the footage they would reap, and also the more likely they were to capture the moral high ground. King was appealing to the national electorate at the expense of the regional power structure, which he considered hostile anyway. He needed some measure of white backlash, and he needed, among other things, proper villains. He wanted ordinary white people to sit in their homes and watch blacks acting with great dignity while Southern officials, moved by the need to preserve a system he hated, assaulted them. As such he was the dramatist of a national morality play: The blacks were in white hats; the whites, much to their surprise, would find themselves in the black hats. A play required good casting and Martin King soon learned to pick not just his venues carefully, but also his villains.

Montgomery, for all its successes, had lacked villains. Certainly, the local officials in Montgomery had mistreated the black protesters, but there was no one brutal figure who had come to symbolize the evils of segregation and who could be counted on, when provoked, to play into the hands of the Movement. But Orval Faubus was a different matter, a man who made ordinary Americans recoil. As the Movement grew, King was offered various cities as platforms for his protests, but he was always careful to select those with the ugliest and crudest segregationists—such men as Bull Connor, in Birmingham, and Sheriff Jim Clark, in Selma. In the past, segregation had been enforced more subtly, often through economic threats. Blacks would lose their jobs if they signed petitions asking schools to desegregate, for example. Racial prejudice had been like a giant beast that never came out in the daytime; now King and others like him were exposing it to bright light, fresh air, and the eye of the television camera and the beast was dying.

The timing of King's protest was critical: 1955 and 1956 marked the years when the networks were just becoming networks in the true sense, thanks in large part to the network news shows. Along with John Kennedy, King was one of the first people who understood how to provide action for film, how, in effect, to script the story for the executive producers (so that the executive producers thought they were scripting it themselves). It was an ongoing tour de force for

King: a great story, great action, constant confrontation, great film, plenty of moral and spiritual tension. There was a hypnotic effect in watching it all unfold; King treated the television reporters assigned to him well. He never wanted a confrontation that the network newsmen could not capture on film and feed to New York, nor did he, if at all possible, want the action too late in the day that it missed the deadlines of the network news shows. So it was that the Movement began and so it was that television amplified and speeded up the process of political and social change in America.

One of the most powerful currents taking place and changing in American life in this decade—taking place even as few recognized it—was the increasing impact and importance of black culture on daily American life. This was particularly true in the fifties in two areas critically important to young Americans: music and sports. In popular music the influence of black culture was profound, much to the irritation of a generation of parents of white teenagers. While Elvis was the first white country artist to use the beat, he was merely part of a larger revolution in which not only were many of the features of black music being used by white musicians, but black musicians were increasingly accepted by white audiences as well. Chuck Berry, Little Richard, Sam Cooke, Ike Turner, and Fats Domino were now integrated into the white hit-charts. The other evolution, equally important, was taking place in sports, and it had a significant impact on the society. With the coming of television, professional sports, particularly football and basketball, had a far greater national impact than they had ever had before. What had once happened before relatively small crowds now happened simultaneously in millions of American homes; in effect, it was going from the periphery to the very center of the culture.

In terms of the coming of technology and the coming of the gifted black athletes, a dual revolution was sweeping across the country: in the quality of athletic ability of those able to play, and in the number of people now able to watch. Professional football, which, in comparison with professional baseball, had been virtually a minor sport before the arrival of television, now flowered under the sympathetic eye of the camera, its importance growing even as the nation was being wired city by city and house by house for television. Suddenly, professional football had become a new super sport, the first true rival to Major League baseball for the nation's affection.

In baseball, the coming of Jackie Robinson had been quickly

followed by the coming of several other magnificent black players—
Willie Mays, Monte Irvin, Ernie Banks, and Henry Aaron. From the
start, because Brooklyn had signed the first black players, the other
National League teams had been forced to go to the same extraordinary talent pile, while the American League, holding on to the prejudices of the past, lagged far behind in its acquisition of great black
players. NL, the traditional newspaper abbreviation for the National
League, the black players liked to joke, now had come to stand for
Negro League. Willie Mays seemed to be the model for the new
supremely gifted black athlete, making plays that had never been
made before, playing gracefully and aggressively, with an exuberant
style all his own. As much as anything, he showed that the new-age
black athlete had both power and speed: In 1955 he had hit fifty-one
home runs and stolen twenty-four bases. A new kind of athlete was
being showcased, a player who, in contrast to most white superstars
of the past, was both powerful *and* fast. Sociologists, physiologists,
and historians might soon debate the reasons for this—why black
athletes seemed so much faster and athletically more gifted than
white athletes of seemingly comparable size—but the changes
wrought in all of America's national sports were dramatic. And the
black athletes themselves laughed about the difference, saying of a
particular black player who had neither speed nor leaping ability that
he had the white man's disease, which meant that he could not jump
very high or that he was not very fast.

Clearly, a social revolution wrought by great athletes was taking
place, and it was in many ways outstripping the revolution engineered by the Supreme Court of the United States and by Martin
Luther King, Jr., in the streets of the nation's Southern cities. If the
face of America, at its highest business, legal, and financial level, was
still almost exclusively white, then the soul of America, as manifested
in its music and its sports, was changing quickly. In sport after sport,
blacks became the dominating figures, first in baseball, and then in
professional football in 1957, when Jim Brown, the great running
back, was drafted by Cleveland after playing at Syracuse. Brown, so
superior an athlete that he was also considered the greatest lacrosse
player of his era, had had professional offers in baseball and basketball as well as football, but it was in football that he made his
reputation. As a pro player he was not unlike Mays in that he
combined both speed and power. In the past, great running backs
either were swift and ran to the outside or were big and powerful and
ran inside, but Jim Brown was something new, he almost alone could
do both.

But it was in basketball that the revolution most quickly took place and was most quickly completed. Basketball soon became the professional sport with the highest percentage of black players; yet as recently as 1947, John Gunther had written that although blacks could play college football in the Big Ten, they could not compete in basketball. "This is an indoor sport and taboos are strong (though not so strong as in the South) against any contact between half-clad, perspiring bodies, even on the floor of a gym," he had noted.

The basketball revolution began in 1956, when Arnold (Red) Auerbach, the coach of the Boston Celtics, made a complicated deal at draft time in order to get the rights to a young man who had starred at the University of San Francisco. The young man was named William F. Russell, Jr. Russell was part of the great black migration to the North and the West; he was born in Louisiana but had gone to California as a boy. His father was a proud man who had ended up working in a small trucking business in California. (Later, in 1965, when Bill Russell, by far the most valuable player in professional basketball, signed a contract for $100,001 a year, that extra dollar being there to put him ahead of Wilt Chamberlain, his great rival, he had suggested that his father never work again. "Of course I'm going to work," said Charlie Russell. "I've given that place eighteen good years out of my life. Now I'll give them a couple of bad years.")

Before the signing of Russell, Auerbach already had the reputation as the smartest coach in the league. Now his reputation, because of this particular trade, was going to grow considerably in the years to come. No mind that Russell had been the key player on the University of San Francisco teams that had won two national championships and had lost only one college game in which he played. Though Russell's defensive skills were something of a given, some professional scouts worried because he was not a good shooter. Certainly, few experts thought Russell's play would completely transform the game. He was six feet nine and a half inches which was tall (although others were taller), and he was quick, but quickness was not yet considered as important as heft and muscle, and doubts remained about his professional ability—and particularly about his strength, since he was to play regularly against men not only as tall as he, but twenty-five pounds heavier. Auerbach had been asking around the college ranks whether Russell had the guts to play in the rough and physical pro game.

At that time the Celtics, in an eight-team league, were good, but not quite good enough: They had good shooters and a supremely gifted ball handler and passer in Bob Cousy, but they were not champions and they lacked a dominating big man. At the end of the '55–'56 season Auerbach had promised his frustrated players that he would somehow manage to get them a big man in the draft. That he did. He drafted Russell, whose ability to dominate the college game was so complete that by the end of the 1955 season, the NCAA had put into effect what was called "the Russell rule," which widened the foul lanes from six to twelve feet in a flawed attempt to limit his dominance as an inside scorer and rebounder.

On draft day Rochester, which had the first chance at Russell, passed and took Sihugo Green, in large part because Russell was so good that he had other options, such as playing for the all-black road-storming Harlem Globetrotters. Russell was said to want a salary of $25,000, an unheard-of sum in those days. The Globetrotters had announced that they would pay him $50,000, but in fact their offer was about a third of that. Worse, Abe Saperstein, the famed owner of the Globetrotters, had enraged Russell by meeting with Russell and his college coach and negotiating with the coach as if Russell were not there. The racial overtones of the meeting were rich, the implicit sense that Russell was a boy, indeed a colored boy, who could not make a business decision himself; when the meeting was over there was no chance of Russell playing with the Globetrotters. It had been unlikely in the first place that someone with Russell's overwhelming pride would choose to play with a team of barnstorming black athletes who portrayed themselves as basketball buffoons, rather than to test himself against the best white professional talent in the country.

The next pick in the draft belonged to St. Louis. It was at this moment that Red Auerbach made his trade. He gave up a talented and popular player, center Ed Macauley—who averaged about twenty points a game but was spindly and was not exactly a power player and who wore down during the regular season—plus the draft rights to another potentially gifted player, Cliff Hagan, for the rights to Russell. Russell signed for $22,500. (Six thousand dollars was going to be held out because he joined the Celtics late, after leading the American team to an Olympic victory in Melbourne, but Walter Brown, the Celtics' owner, decided that was unfair and held out only three thousand, in effect splitting the difference with Russell.)

With that trade, Auerbach went from being very smart to being a genius. He told Russell to concentrate on rebounding and not to worry about scoring. "We'll count rebounds as baskets for you," he told him. In Russell's first year, the Celtics won the NBA championship, and Russell became not merely the best player in the league, but he began his tour as the most dominating team athlete of modern American sports. His first game came on December 22, in the Boston Garden against the St. Louis Hawks, on national television. Bob Cousy remembered it vividly: Even though Russell was new, there was an immediate sense on the part of his teammates that the future had arrived and that the game had changed because of him; he not only rebounded as Auerbach had promised, but he brought a different dimension to defense. There had never been anything like him before, Cousy thought at the time—the quickness, the superb timing, a big man playing with the agility and speed of a small man.

The Celtics were suddenly a brand-new team. (In his first game Russell had played only sixteen minutes but had gotten twenty-one rebounds.) A few days later, in a game in New York that was part of a doubleheader, he held Neil Johnston of the Warriors, then the game's third leading scorer, without a field goal for the first forty-two minutes. Russell also gathered in eighteen rebounds; the next night in another game against the Warriors, he took down *thirty-four* rebounds in twenty minutes of play, blocked a number of shots, and led the Celtic fast break. The new age had arrived. Even Auerbach, as shrewd as he was, Cousy thought, did not realize how much he was getting when he drafted Russell.

When Russell had been measured in college, the tape never indicated what a superlative athlete he was. He played a good deal taller than his height indicated. Even in college he had been surprised at the things he could do that other players could not. He had found that when he went up for a rebound, he was different from other players—not only did he seem to go higher (on one occasion in college he found he was looking down at the basket, which meant he was jumping at least forty-eight inches off the ground), but he seemed to hang in the air longer; the other players returned to the ground while he stayed in the air. In later years this would be known as hang time. Russell was both extremely agile and extremely powerful. Not only was he a superb jumper, he had exceptional timing; indeed, his hand-to-eye coordination and the timing of his jumps reflected a rare athletic skill. His intelligence matched his athletic ability; he seemed, he later noted, to be able to anticipate what the player he was guarding was going to do next. With him, playing defense in basketball became as much of an art as hitting was to a great baseball player like Ted Williams or Stan Musial. Among other things, Russell was left-handed, which meant that his more athletic hand was keyed to the shooting hand of most players he defended against. He was supremely intelligent, a master not only at psyching teammates but intimidating his opponents, and he was one of the proudest men ever to play any sport.

He played for the Celtics, but Boston was never his home. He was acutely aware of the city's prejudices, that the Celtics, though champions, rarely sold out at home. He responded to the schizophrenia of the white sports fan who covets autographs but, at least in Russell's opinion, does not covet black neighbors, by refusing to sign autographs. He had once, as a collegian, been invited to a conference at the White House, but then had driven the segregated highway back to his original home in Louisiana, where on stops along the road he had been treated as "just another black boy, just so much dirt, with no rights, with no element of human courtesy or decency shown to me or mine." He had decided before he even turned pro that he would always be polite with fans, that he would speak only when spoken to, but that he would not be a caricature of a black---a dancing, joking buffoon.

His gifted teammate Bob Cousy, who was the best passer of his era, was always intrigued by the contradictions in Russell. Russell played the game brilliantly, but he did not even particularly seem to like the game. He was a notoriously poor practice player, perhaps the most indifferent one on the team. But he played with a special fury in the real games, as though this sport was the only outlet, Cousy thought, for all the racial anger stored up within him. *This,* the intensity of his play seemed to say, was his answer to prejudice and discrimination and to existing myths about things that blacks could not do but that whites could do. He was a great big-game player, although it was said that he was so tense before a game that he inevitably had to go to the locker room and throw up just before the tipoff. In those days the Celtics' archrivals were the St. Louis Hawks, and in St. Louis, then a Southern city, the crowd seemed to him to be the most racist in the league, the epithets the most vile; it was a place where even the coffee shops denied him service. He played particularly well in St. Louis.

In the past, the dominating big players had been white, usually strong but slow. When they blocked a shot, it was generally because the offensive player had taken a poor shot. Russell was something completely new, the forerunner of a different player in a different game, the big man who got down court faster than the other team's small men. He blocked shots that had never been blocked before. Players on other teams not only had to correct the arc of their shots but change the very nature of their offense when they played against him. When opponents brought the ball up the court, they always looked to see where Russell was. He averaged more than twenty rebounds a game, and his rebounding was so formidable that it unlocked the Boston offense, leading to the Celtics' fast break and what were often easy baskets. He changed, in the most elemental sense, the very tempo of the game. In the past a team had brought the ball up rather leisurely, passed it around, and a shot was taken. When that happened, the roles of the two teams changed, the offensive team going on defense, and vice versa, but they changed comparatively slowly—the offensive team had a few extra seconds to pull itself together, get back down court, and set up on defense, while the offensive team had somewhat leisurely taken a few seconds to rearrange itself and then take the ball up the court for offense. With Russell the tempo of the game seemed to have no break; now it was continuous, offense flowing into defense instantaneously. It was now a game for the swift and the agile. In Russell's first ten years in Boston, the Celtics won the championship nine times, including one stretch of eight championships in a row. In his thirteen seasons there, the Celtics won the title eleven times.

FORTY-FIVE

L ate in his presidency, Dwight Eisenhower came under increasing scrutiny personally. *Sputnik* was only the first of several psychological setbacks for America, the impact of which neither the President nor the men around him fully comprehended. Soon after, in November 1957, the Gaither report leaked out. It was prepared by the Security Resources Panel of the Science Advisory committee of the Office of Defense Mobilization and was officially titled "Deterrence and Survival in the Nuclear Age." It took its nickname from committee chairman Rowan Gaither and was a chilling piece of work. Based on information available to most laymen (and certainly with no knowledge of the Soviet weaknesses as sighted by the U-2), it implied that we were slipping in our nuclear capacity while the Soviets were becoming stronger all the time. The evidence, it reported, "clearly indicates an increasing threat which may become critical in 1959 or early 1960." The Russians seemed to be ahead of us in all aspects of defense and weapons technology, and even worse, their GNP was said to be growing at a faster rate than ours (a particularly preposterous idea, given the crude nature of Soviet industry). Clearly, the barbarians were not merely at the gate, they were able to fly over it with missiles and nuclear warheads. The Gaither committee recommended $25 billion for the building of bomb shelters all over the country and another $19 billion on increased budgeting for weaponry. William C. Foster, the head of Olin Mathieson Chemical Corporation, who was on the committee, said, "I felt as though I were spending ten hours a day staring straight into hell." Eisenhower was now in the embarrassing position of having appointed a blue-chip panel whose conclusions he would have to reject or at least ignore. This, after *Sputnik* and Little Rock, seemed to confirm the view of an administration of older men no longer in touch, unaware of how quickly the world was changing. Herblock, the talented and influential *Washington Post* cartoonist, was drawing Eisenhower as a slightly addled, goofy, ineffectual figure, confused by what he was doing and why he was doing it.

In a sense, the U-2 helped stabilize the relationship between the two superpowers. But because the information it provided could not be introduced into the democratic system, Eisenhower was oddly paralyzed. What he knew, ordinary citizens could not know. At one point, frustrated by all the pressure coming at him on the domestic front to intensify the arms race, Eisenhower said with some irritation, "I can't understand the United States being quite as panicky as they are."

Nevertheless, in the last three years of the Eisenhower administration, a debate began over an alleged missile gap, which did not, in fact, exist. In a way it was not without its own justice: The Republicans had won in the past in no small part because they had blamed the Democrats for losing countries to Communism; in the early part of the Cold War, the Republicans had exagerrated the natural anxieties of the Cold War. The result was that not only had the Democrats vowed never to be accused of being soft on Communism again, they were determined to find an issue that showed they were, if anything, even more vigilant and tougher. McCarthy's attacks guaranteed that the national debate would shift ever more to the right. With *Sputnik* and the so-called missile gap, the Democrats, though careful not to attack the President frontally, managed to make it seem as if his best days were behind him.

He had nothing to offer but himself and his word in defense of his policies. He had no proof. That lay locked in the CIA's vaults. But there was no guarantee, beloved and trusted as he was, that his word alone was good enough now. Part of this was the erosion caused by his health. His personal signature had always been his physical vigor, his ruddiness and vitality, but like Truman before him, he had found the brutal rigors of the American presidency in the postwar era to be a killing job. Truman, with his plowboy constitution and simple life-style, had withstood the physical erosion remarkably well, but Eisenhower was not as lucky. In September 1955, Eisenhower had suffered his first heart attack; less than a year later, he was struck with ileitis. He underwent a stomach operation, even though there was considerable nervousness among his doctors about subjecting a man who had so recently suffered a heart attack to so serious an operation. Then, in November 1957, he suffered a mild stroke. The exhausting quality of the job was taking its toll. The doctors told him to avoid "irritation, frustration, anxiety, fear, and above all anger." "Just what do you think the presidency *is*?" he asked.

In fact, he had never entirely wanted the job, nor for that matter did he like it very much after he got it. Cy Sulzberger, an old friend from Paris days, visiting him some twenty months into his administration, was surprised to find him "uneasy, irascible, crotchety, and not quite sure of himself. I felt sorry for him." He was surrounded by politicians, whom he tended to describe as sons of bitches, who came to see him when they needed help getting reelected but who in no way supported his program. The longer he stayed in office, the more disillusioned he became. After one meeting with congressional leaders late in his presidency, he turned to an aide and said, "I don't know why anyone should be a member of the Republican party." He would talk often of the time when his term was up and he would be a free man again. When Everett Dirksen and Charlie Halleck spoke wistfully about the fact that it was a shame that he could not run again because of the Twenty-Second Amendment, he quickly disabused them of any desire he might have for a third term. Nor, he added, did he think anyone should be President after he was seventy. The job was taking its toll.

As the *Sputnik*-defense spending crisis deepened, his behavior seemed passive compared to the almost primal energy of Nikita Khrushchev. Khrushchev was something new for Americans to contemplate. Stalin had been a completely foreboding figure, the paranoiac as ultimate dictator, inflicting his dark vision on all those unlucky enough to fall under the rule of the Soviet empire. Khrushchev was quite different—ferocious, volatile, shrewd, vengeful, very much the angry peasant. If Stalin had represented the worst of Soviet Communism, then Khrushchev to many Americans was even more threatening, for he seemed to reflect the peasant vigor of this new state. Was America finally attaining a broad affluence only to find that the comforts of middle-class existence had weakened it? Crude, unpredictable, occasionally violent, Khrushchev seemed to be the embodiment of the sheer animal force of the Soviet Union, its raw power and, perhaps Americans many feared, its irresistible will.

There was something chilly about Khrushchev, pounding his shoe and threatening to bury capitalism, at the UN. Contrasting his own poverty with the affluent backgrounds of those Western figures he dealt with, he seemed to imply their good manners were a weakness. "You all went to great schools, to famous universities—to Harvard, Oxford, the Sorbonne," he once boasted to Western diplomats. "I never had any proper schooling. I went about barefoot and in rags. When you were in the nursery, I was herding cows for two kopeks. . . . And yet here we are, and I can run rings around you all. . . . Tell me, gentlemen, why?"

Many Americans worried that the very material success of America in the postwar years—all those cars, kitchen amenities, and other luxuries—had made us soft and vulnerable to the Soviet Union, where people were tougher and more willing to sacrifice for their nation. Was there strength and truth in poverty? Styles Bridges, a conservative Republican senator, seemed to talk in this vein when he said that Americans had to be less concerned with "the height of the tail fin in the new car and be much more prepared to shed blood, sweat and tears, if this country and the free world are to survive."

Part of Eisenhower's problems, as he entered the last phase of his presidency, was that he could never bring himself to lobby the most important members of the press on his own behalf, or even on behalf of his policies. Because of network-television news shows, the national press corps was growing ever more influential as a force—if not in policymaking, then certainly in the way policy was seen by the general public. Yet in his relations with the press, Eisenhower still saw himself as the general and the press as obedient privates and corporals who liked him personally, shared his vision of the war and, given the circumstances of the national effort, all but saluted him. Therefore he thought he had not needed to get into the pit and explain. All he had to do was give his version. A challenge to his policy from people who, in his opinion, did not have a tenth of his experience and training, who were outsiders and had never made a hard decision, would quickly ignite his anger. He had entered the presidency feeling that way and not having needed the press corps during his election run when their bosses, like Paley, Sarnoff, Whitney, and Sulzberger, had practically begged him to come in.

As President, he assumed the press would be properly respectful. A press corps that did otherwise was, to him, untrustworthy and quite possibly dishonest. It was not that he had not had opportunities to bring the press in. When he took office, various columnists volunteered to be insiders, to report what the administration was doing but could not say. The first and perhaps most brazen of these offers came from Joseph Alsop, who dropped by early in the administration to talk with Robert Cutler, Ike's national security secretary. Cutler was an old Boston friend, a fellow member of the Porcellian Club at Harvard. Alsop pointed out the many Republican connections in his own family and suggested he could serve the administration with his column by publishing certain administration perceptions and thoughts without attribution. "Such a person, trusted by a President, could provide an anonymous channel to help shape public opinion," Alsop said. But Cutler told Alsop to get his information like any other reporter—by attending press conferences and talking with Jim Hagerty. The administration, Cutler said, was not interested in deals. Alsop was not pleased: This was clearly beneath him. Cutler clearly did not understand the new hierarchy of Washington journalism.

This was fairly typical. Ike barely knew the names of the men and women who covered the White House every day. He knew the names of only the most senior reporters who reported on him. He did not read the major papers, and when he did, it made him angry. To his mind, *The New York Times* was "the most untrustworthy paper in the world." He gave little access to its top people. Once the President asked Cy Sulzberger what Arthur Krock, the paper's conservative columnist, was doing lately. Writing his column three times a week, Sulzberger said. "Is that so?" said the President. Then Ike noted that he liked Krock, which came as a surprise to Sulzberger, who knew that Krock had been trying in vain to see the President for more than a year. The President continued: He also liked one other columnist, though he often had trouble with his name: "And you know who another good reporter is—that's that little fellow—what's his name?—that little fellow who works for—" Sulzberger asked if the President meant Roscoe Drummond. "Yes," said the President. "Roscoe, that's the fellow I meant."

Eisenhower disliked Walter Lippmann, the great sage of the era, and thought him usually wrong. He hated Ed Murrow: "I can't stand that gangster [Ed] Murrow. I can't stand looking at him. I have no use for him. He always looks like a gangster with a cigarette hanging out of his mouth." But it was Joe Alsop, who became, to his mind, the lowest of the low as the columnist began to establish himself as the foremost journalistic critic of Eisenhower's defense policies.

If there ever was a time and an issue when Eisenhower needed journalistic support, particularly from influential columnists, it was over his defense policies in the last three years of his administration. If ever there was an angry critic of them, it was Alsop. He was snobbish, vain, talented, hardworking, egocentric, and well connected to the powerful people in Washington, either through clubs, family connections, or the capacity to intimidate them by using his column as a lever. Close to hard-line Democrats like Acheson, Alsop soon became unusually influential in creating the impression that Eisenhower was somewhat confused, an ill-informed figure who was out of touch with reality and whose defense policies were putting American security in jeopardy. As he wrote his friend Isaiah Berlin in April 1958: "One prays—how odd it seems!—for the course of nature to transfer the burden to Nixon (who exactly resembles an heir to a very rich family . . . now utterly distraught because Papa has grown a little senile and spends his family fortune out the window— really he is like that). I lunched with him the other day and he all but asked me how it was possible to argue with a ramolli papa without getting disinherited yourself!"

Eisenhower's last three years as President saw him virtually alone on this issue, standing up to a powerful array of critics in insisting that America had more than enough defense, that there was no missile gap, and that the nation's security was not in jeopardy. Allied against him were such powerful and influential Democrats as Lyndon Johnson, Stuart Symington, and Jack Kennedy, who were busy positioning themselves for a shot at the presidency. With this issue they could show that not only were they *not* soft on Communism, but they actually wanted to strengthen America. They had their allies in the government, most notably in the Air Force, which always wanted more bombers and more missiles. The Democrats and the liberal-centrist columnists were in touch with influential military sources, who were not privy to the U-2 intelligence and who were absolutely sure that the Soviets were moving ahead of us. "At the Pentagon they shudder when they speak of the Gap, which means the years 1960, 1961, 1962 and 1963," the Alsops wrote typically in that period. "They shudder because in those years the American government will flaccidly permit the Kremlin to open an almost unchallenged superiority in the nuclear striking power that was once our superiority." At the moment, voices like those of the Alsops had a certain power; the tensions of the Cold War and the success of *Sputnik* had frightened many in the political center.

The truth was that as Eisenhower entered the final years of his presidency, his primary objective was to establish his legacy, which he saw as limiting the arms race. He knew from the U-2 photos that the Soviets were not a threat, so it seemed logical to get a test-ban treaty of some sort. In 1959 he said with some melancholy, "We haven't made a chip in the granite in seven years." His closest advisers urged him to let Symington and other Democratic critics see some of the photos taken by the U-2. That would end much of the criticism. But Eisenhower would not budge. He thought there was no way to keep the flights secret if the opposition leadership was let in. So the flights continued in secret. A spy satellite that would fly over the entire world would not be ready, it appeared, until some time in 1961.

His critics and his enemies became bolder. The Air Force generals were the worst, he believed. They seemed to be teaming up with the munitions people—he used the old-fashioned phrase from World War One to describe the booming new defense industry—to push for endless redundant military systems. "I'm getting awfully sick of the lobbies by munitions," he told the Republican leaders. Indeed, he sensed their primary motivation was greed: "You begin to see this thing isn't wholly the defense of this country, but only more money for some who are already fatcats."

When in the wake of *Sputnik* members of his own cabinet pushed for a dramatic increase in defense and space spending, he revealed his irritation. "Look," he had said. "I'd like to know what's on the other side of the moon, but I won't pay to find out this year." It was taking all his will to keep the military and the defense contractors from escalating the arms race. Even when he did increase defense spending substantially, he told his aide Andrew Goodpaster that two thirds of the increase was for public opinion. "God help the nation when it has a President who doesn't know as much about the military as I do," he would say.

It is our contradictions that make us interesting. Eisenhower, the famed general, wanted more to be a man of peace than a man of war. Jingoism in other men had always made him uneasy. When he heard the news of the success of the atomic bomb on Hiroshima, though it meant a quick end to the war in the Pacific, he was left with a feeling of severe depression, caused by the arrival of a new and terrifying chapter in man's capacity to destroy man. Mary Bancroft, Allen Dulles's acute lady friend, even thought that Ike's hatred of war was a weakness, not unlike, she said, a prostitute who values her chastity. He was a curious combination of qualities: part shrewd and conniving, and alternately innocent, naive, and trusting. He was the most political of generals, and yet he thought politicking on the part of others unseemly. He was a man who knew that his greatest asset, as a leader not just in the United States but throughout the world, was that the entire world seemed to trust him and believe in him, but he sharply increased the use of clandestine operations to overthrow governments that he disliked in underdeveloped countries. He had hoped, after the war, for a rapprochement with the Russians, but his anti-Communism seemed to harden during much of his administration. He could barely restrain his contempt toward Adlai Stevenson when he raised the issue of limiting nuclear testing in 1956, and yet in the final years of his administration he hungered, more than anything, for some form of accord with the Russians on limiting nuclear testing and perhaps even on limiting the production of nuclear weapons.

By 1958 he had begun to reduce the number of U-2 flights. He had always been uneasy with them. He knew they were provocative, and he himself would point out that nothing would move the United States more quickly to war than the knowledge that the Soviets were overflying us and taking pictures. In 1959 he became even more cautious. He was beginning to build new links to Khrushchev, and he did not want them jeopardized by the U-2 flights. There was a constant tug-of-war between him and Allen Dulles and Richard Bissell, who was in charge of the flights; the CIA always seemed to want one more flight, one more picture, or a new flight pattern just a little deeper into Soviet airspace. Soon there was a byplay, Bissell and Dulles asking for more flights, and Ike trying to hold the line and giving them fewer than they wanted and more than he wanted.

What the President did not know was that the U-2 pilots themselves were becoming more nervous. There was evidence by the fall of 1958 that the Soviets were not only tracking them with radar but firing SAMs (surface-to-air missiles) that were coming, as Powers put it, uncomfortably close. The U-2 pilots, Powers noted later, knew that the Soviets were having problems with their guidance systems, but by 1960 new SAM-2 missiles were being installed throughout the country. They had a far greater range than their predecessors, and the CIA estimated that they could hit a target seventy thousand feet high. At the same time the planes themselves were becoming heavier as more equipment was being added.

Powers was fast becoming the most senior pilot in the group: His personal life was something of a ruin; he and his wife spoke often of divorce. There was no brilliant Air Force career waiting; it was as if he had found his niche in this demanding but boring job, which above all else required endurance. He seemed so ordinary that it was hard to think of him as a spy. As James Donovan, one of the intelligence men who handled him later, said, he was just the kind of man the CIA would want. "Powers was a man, who, for adequate pay, would do it (fly a virtual glider over the Soviet Union) and as he passed over Minsk, would calmly reach for a salami sandwich." The world of the White House, of course, and the world of the U-2 pilots did not intersect. Dwight Eisenhower might have his doubts about the continued viability of the flights, and Francis Gary Powers, his doubts, but they did not share them. In 1959 a new engine arrived, stronger and able to fly at higher altitudes, but there was an increasing edginess among the pilots.

In 1959 Eisenhower invited Khrushchev to visit America, thinking that it would be for two or three days, but somehow in the confusion Khrushchev accepted for ten days. Someone asked the President what he wanted the Soviet leader to see, and the response was Eisenhower at his best: Levittown, he said. It was a town "universally and exclusively inhabited by workmen." (This was not an entirely accurate statement.) He wanted the premier to fly in a chopper with him and see the District. In addition, he wanted Khrushchev to go to Abilene, "the little town where I was born," and see for himself "the story of how hard I worked until I was twenty-one, when I went to West Point." The President noted that when Nixon had debated Khrushchev in Moscow, the Soviet leader had said that Americans knew nothing of hard work. Well, said the President, "*I* can show him the evidence that *I* did and I would like for him to see it." But most of all, he added, "I want him to see a happy people. I want him to see a free people, doing exactly as they choose, within the limits that they must not transgress the rights of others."

When Khrushchev finally came, it was a circus; every journalist in America turned out, for Americans had never seen a Soviet dictator in the flesh before, and this was no ordinary Soviet dictator—for Khrushchev always provided, if nothing else, good theater. Eisenhower and Khrushchev got on fairly well, although there was a sense that the boisterous Khrushchev was a bit much for the restrained Eisenhower. In private meetings, they minimized the differences between the countries. How was it, Khrushchev asked, that a general, a man whose entire mission in life had been waging war, was so committed to finding the peace? There might have been some moments of exhilaration during the last war, but "now war has become nothing more than a struggle for survival," the President answered. He was not afraid to say that he was afraid of nuclear war, and everyone else should be.

On the whole the trip went well. Khrushchev invited Eisenhower not just to come to Russia himself but to bring along his whole family. Ike, in one of his better moods, said, "I'll bring along the whole family. You'll have more Eisenhowers than you know what to do with." For Eisenhower, this was everything he had hoped for: He would visit Moscow and bring back a limited test ban treaty; personally, he would end the worst of the Cold War. This was why he had become President. In the summer of 1960 he would attend a summit meeting with the French, British, and Russians in Paris and from there fly on to Moscow. A process of peace might truly begin and this, surely, would be the triumph of his presidency.

The less frequently the U-2 pilots flew, the more difficult each flight became. There were indications that the program was losing some of its secrecy. A model-airplane magazine published an article about the plane in March 1958, complete with drawings. It was also said that the official paper of the Soviet air force had reported on the flights and called the plane "the black lady of espionage." An American mole working in Soviet intelligence reported that the Soviets had a great deal of intelligence on the U-2, something that apparently surprised both Dulles and Bissell. In addition, in the summer of 1958 Hanson Baldwin, the military writer for *The New York Times,* spotted one of the U-2s on the tarmac while he was in West Germany and understood immediately what the plane's purpose was. He lunched with Robert Amory, one of Allen Dulles's top people, and said he was going to do a story—after all, he had seen it without violating security. "*Jesus, Hanson, no!*" Amory said. It would undermine America's most important intelligence program. They argued for a time and in the end Allen Dulles talked to Arthur Hayes Sulzberger, the *Times* publisher, who decided to hold the story. But, as Sulzberger told Dulles, the story had been set in type—in case someone like Drew Pearson got it, too. Gradually, the top people in Washington journalist circles, like Arthur Krock and Scotty Reston and Chal Roberts, of *The Washington Post,* found out about the U-2 but did not write it up. As Michael Beschloss noted, knowing about the U-2 became something of a status symbol on the Washington dinner-party circuit.

In Washington, in late April 1960, Eisenhower was preparing for the summit and wanted no more flights. "If one of these aircraft were lost when we were engaged in apparently sincere deliberations, it could be put on display in Moscow and ruin my effectiveness," he said to one aide. But Dulles and Bissell pleaded for one last flight, claiming it was unusually important: They wanted one more good look at the Soviet missile installation at Tyuratam. Again Eisenhower, accustomed over the years to listening to his subordinates, went against his better judgment and relented.

At the U-2 base in Turkey, Powers, by this time the only remaining member of the original group, was assigned the flight. For the first time, a U-2 would fly all the way across the Soviet Union. The flight would begin in Peshawar, Pakistan, and would end nine hours and 3,800 miles later in Bodo, Norway.

In the language of the pilots, the flights had been getting dicier and dicier all the time; this flight took these anxieties a step further. The pilots had always had unanswered questions about what to do in case they were shot down. Was there anyone they could contact? Powers had asked one of the briefing officers. No, he was told. How much should he tell? he asked. "You may as well tell them everything because they're going to get it out of you anyway," he was told.

The flight was delayed several times because of weather and was finally set for the last day of April. Powers slept poorly. He was not pleased with the plane he had been assigned; it was, he thought, a lemon—plagued by malfunctions. He carried his regular identification—a violation of the rules and a sign that the pilots were becoming complacent—and a new piece of equipment: a silver dollar with a pin. In case of capture by the Soviets, the pilots were to stick the pin in a groove, from which would seep out a sticky brown substance. Injecting yourself with the substance would make it appear that you had died from eating bad shrimp. The pilots had agreed among themselves they would not use the pin even if worst came to worst.

Fully dressed in his sealed flight suit, Powers climbed into the plane that morning at 5:20 A.M. and waited for the final clearance to come from the White House. It was clear to him by this point that Washington was approving each flight. As he sweated, a friend outside took off his shirt and held it over the cockpit in order to shield him from the sun. Finally, at 6:26 he was allowed to take off. He soon picked up the trail of a Russian jet. It was traveling at supersonic speed toward him. But he remained confident; Soviet planes still flew far below him. Unfortunately, he soon began to have problems with his own plane. When he put it on automatic pilot it began to malfunction, so he flew it manually. For a moment he considered aborting the mission, but then decided to go ahead. He was flying toward Sverdlovsk (formerly known as Ekaterinburg) for what would be the first U-2 trip over that city when he heard a dull thump. The aircraft pitched forward. A tremendous orange flash hit the cockpit and lit the sky around him. *My God,* he thought to himself. *I've had it now.* Later, Powers decided (and Kelly Johnson agreed) that what had happened to him was a near miss, which tore the fragile plane apart but spared his life.

He struggled with the plane, fearing the ejection seat. The plane was completely out of control, spinning wildly and hurtling toward the ground. He was sure that both wings had been severed. He finally managed to get out of the plane: For a time he fell rapidly through the air, an exhilarating feeling, even better, he thought, than floating in a swimming pool. Finally, he got his parachute open. When he landed, he was quickly picked up by a local farmer and turned over to the KGB.

In Washington on the afternoon of May 1, Dwight Eisenhower was notified by Andrew Goodpaster that a U-2 was missing and had apparently been shot down. They both lamented the death of the brave young pilot. The one thing Allen Dulles had promised Dwight Eisenhower was that if the Russians shot down a plane, the pilot would not live. It was a question Eisenhower had raised on several occasions. Dulles would always answer that it was unlikely the Soviets could shoot one down, and if they did, the pilots would blow up the planes before taking their own lives. That they would *never* capture a live pilot was the great given, thought John Eisenhower, the President's son, who was serving as his aide at the time and going over the U-2 requests. There was no reason to think that even though a U-2 was missing a major crisis was in the works. With the amount of fuel Powers had on board the plane, Andy Goodpaster, the President's closest aide, said, "there is not a chance of his being alive." In the White House, aides started working on a cover story.

At first Powers was sure the Soviets were going to execute him. But then he was moved from Sverdlovsk to Moscow, and he began to believe for the first time that he might be permitted to live and that the Soviets might use him in the propaganda war. Perhaps Khrushchev, he thought, might take him to the upcoming summit and present Powers to Eisenhower was something which belonged to him.

Years later Chip Bohlen, one of the top American Kremlinologists, said that Khrushchev took the U-2 as a personal insult; it was a personal embarrassment, because he had promised his colleagues in the Politburo that Eisenhower could be trusted. (Khrushchev himself later said that the U-2 affair was the beginning of the end for him in terms of his ability to hold power.) Khrushchev decided to bait a trap for the Americans. On May 5, he announced that the Russians had shot down a spy plane. He seemed, however, to be allowing some room to maneuver for the President, who could say that he had not known what the CIA was doing. Unfortunately, Eisenhower was already under severe criticism for not being the master of his own house. Khrushchev did not let on that the pilot was alive. In Washington the administration came up with a cover story about a weather plane that had flown off course, and thereby walked right into the baited trap. Eisenhower was confident that Khrushchev had no proof. At best there had been a quick flash on the radar, and perhaps some wreckage.

On May 7, six days after Powers had been shot down, Khrushchev announced to the Supreme Soviet that he had the wreckage of the plane and the live pilot and, of course, the film. "The whole world knows that Allen Dulles is no great weatherman," he said. He mentioned the gold rings and gold watches that Powers, like other U-2 pilots, carried with him in case he needed to barter with the local people. "Perhaps he was supposed to fly still higher, to Mars, and seduce the Martian ladies!" He showed some of the photos taken by the plane. "Here—*look at this*! Here are the airfields—*here*! Fighters in position on the ground. Two little white strips. *Here they are!* . . ."

For the next day American officials squirmed and pointed fingers at each other, trying to decide what the next cover story would be and who would take the fall. Some suggested the commander of the base in Turkey be relieved. Others thought that Allen Dulles should resign for the good of his country, thus protecting the President and perhaps saving the summit. Eisenhower, however, was not a man who liked scapegoats. (When his son, John, told him he should get rid of Allen Dulles because Dulles had misled him on the issue of whether a pilot could survive, the President was very angry. "I am *not* going to shift the blame to my underlings!" he had said.) Gradually, the truth began to seep out. The President was responsible for flights like this, came a statement.

But whatever victory Khrushchev had scored overseas, he was sure he was the loser at home, the man who had preached trust but who, on the eve of so important a meeting as the summit, had been betrayed by the Americans. He now felt isolated, vulnerable to the hard-liners, who hated his efforts to deal with the West.

The Americans took a terrible beating in the propaganda game; the only question now was whether the summit could be saved. Eisenhower told reporters he still intended to go to Paris but that he would not be able to go to Moscow. Allen Dulles was allowed to meet with a group of eighteen select congressional leaders, and he and an aide showed some of the U-2 photos as a means of justifying them. What pleasure there was in knowing that the Soviet threat was overrated vanished in shards of shattered diplomacy.

The Paris summit was a disaster. Khrushchev chose to thunder his way through it. He shouted so loudly that de Gaulle, the host, tried to quiet him by saying, "The acoustics in this room are excellent. We can all hear the chairman." Eisenhower, listening to himself and his country being berated by the angry First Secretary, wrote a note to Christian Herter, who had replaced the ailing Foster Dulles as secretary of state: "I'm going to take up smoking again," he observed mordantly. Khrushchev told de Gaulle that he could not understand why Eisenhower had admitted his involvement with the U-2. To him it was not a sign of American candor but of contempt for himself personally and for Russia as a nation.

For Eisenhower there would be no trip to Moscow, no sightseeing with the Khrushchevs, no warm toasts, and no test-ban treaty. That which he had wanted most desperately—a genuine beginning of peace—had been shot down along with Powers. His administration would end, he said somewhat bitterly, much as it had begun—without any real progress. "I had longed," he said just before he died, "to give the United States and the world a lasting peace. I was able only to contribute to a stalemate." Yet Eisenhower may have underestimated the most important achievement of of his Administration—the fact that the worst did not happen. In the years of his Presidency both superpowers developed the hydrogen bomb along with intercontinental delivery systems. Yet his own essential decency, and the respect his own nation held for him, allowed him to soften the most terrible furies of that time and permit a relatively safe passage through those years.

Some thought the failure was Powers's. What had happened to great patriots like Nathan Hale? wondered the liberal educator Robert Hutchins. Hanson Baldwin was shocked that Powers had not committed suicide. Was Powers yet another reflection of a too affluent America gone soft? William Faulkner thought the Russians might release him immediately as a reflection of their contempt for what America had become. The Russians at least were not about to execute him. They sentenced him to ten years.

FORTY-SIX

The American clandestine campaign against Fidel Castro began so tentatively that the people who were its authors did not even realize they were taking a fateful step. By the late 1950s those who posed legal and moral questions about clandestine operations were considered naive. The success of the coup in Guatemala was a precedent for covert action elsewhere in the region, and American policy had apparently been established: essential indifference to the needs of the people living there in favor of the interests of the large American companies in the region, most notably United Fruit. Given the increased feelings of nationalism in much of the area because of advances in modern communications, it was not a happy situation.

The CIA agents who had engineered the Guatemalan coup were now considered to be experts, though in general their knowledge of the region was marginal, few spoke Spanish, and they tended to seek

out only far right-wing military men as agents. In Cuba the government of Fulgencio Batista had to come apart in the latter part of the
fifties. Few countries were headed by so greedy or cruel a dictator as
Batista. His base of popular support was surprisingly small, and
Cuba boasted, by Latin American standards, an increasingly sophisticated urban middle class. That power was slipping from Batista's
hands and that his armed forces were corrupt and of dubious loyalty
were not exactly secrets either in Havana or in Washington.

The Cuba of the fifties was an ugly and decadent place, a play-
land for rich Americans who wanted to escape the puritanical atmosphere of their home country, where they could gamble legally
and buy whatever they wanted in terms of sexual gratification. It
was a place of gambling, drinking, sex shows, prostitution. One
mulatto star of the sex shows was known by the Americans as
Superman, because of the heroic size of his penis, which was a
tourist attraction of sorts, a must-see for many Americans on their
Havana vacations. Superman would pretend to have sex with a
number of women onstage every night. He did not particularly like
his job, but he made $25 a night for it, which was for him a great
deal more money than he could make working in the cane fields for
United Fruit.

The gambling casinos were run by the American mob, and a
healthy percentage of the profits went to Batista himself. Nothing
worked without bribes and kickbacks. The key players in the regime—the secret police, the top military, and the bagmen who were
responsible for the deliveries of money back and forth to the casinos—were handsomely rewarded with large cash bonuses, given out
personally by the dictator each month in unmarked brown en-
velopes. This method implied that the dictator could, if he so chose,
withhold the bribe the following month if things did not go to his
liking. It was all surprisingly well organized. Batista's control of the
Cuban political and military process, wrote John Dorschner and
Roberto Fabricio, "resembled the organization of a large criminal
mob more than it did a traditional government."

A regimental commander had to pay Batista $15,000 a month
in kickback money from the gambling houses in his area. That alone
gave Batista more than $1 million a year. But the main casinos in
Havana were the heart of the action. They were controlled by the
American mobster Meyer Lansky, and the dictator's take was a neat
$1.28 million a month. It was always paid on Monday at noon.
Someone from Lansky's operation would slip into the presidential
palace with a briefcase full of money. From there a portion of the

money would percolate down through the Batista system—to the secret police and the torturers, of course.

Batista had ruled Cuba, directly or indirectly, legally or illegally, for much of the preceding two decades. He had risen to power through the army, taking over in a coup while still a sergeant in 1940. Shrewd and tough, he skillfully exploited Cuba's potential for corruption. Taking a brief sabbatical after his first tour of office, he returned at the beginning of the fifties, shed his first wife, and married a young, ambitious woman who coveted social acceptance from Havana's snobbish aristocracy. Since Batista was the son of a cane cutter and a mulatto, that was not a realistic aspiration. He was blackballed at the elegant Havana Yacht Club—the vote against him was said to be one of the rare free elections in Cuba.

He proceeded to extract his revenge by accumulating fabulous wealth—including cattle ranches, sugar plantations, and his own airline. He and his wife were world-class shoppers and clotheshorses. He loved to eat and turned it into something of an art form; during endless meals, he would periodically go off to vomit so that he could eat more. He loved to play cards with his pals, and rich though he was, even here he cheated, using waiters to tip him off about his opponents' cards. He delighted in his control of the political apparatus, and he started each day by meeting with a trusted aide from the secret police, who brought him up to date on gossip gathered from wiretaps. "The novel," the briefing was called and it was the dictator's favorite moment of each day. A man like that has enemies and Batista went everywhere surrounded by teams of bodyguards, equipped with machine guns.

The key to his survival, of course, was the support of the United States, which in the past had committed itself to him unwaveringly: It was a policy set in part by hoods like Lansky, in conjunction with the more respectable businessmen from United Fruit, who were getting what they wanted out of Batista's Cuba. But by 1957 his power had declined. There was a growing debate within the State Department about Batista's effectiveness as an agent of American policy. The top people in the Latin American division of the State Department thought that Batista's reign was already in its twilight, and that the United States should separate itself from supporting him so uncritically. The U.S., they thought, should work quickly to help create an alternative government, one far more liberal and democratic, which could keep up with the increasing demands for social change in the country. If we did not, the choice of Batista's successor might well be outside our control. Worse, there was the likelihood that this violent, oppressive regime on the right might well create its mirror image, a brutal regime of the left.

Yet Batista had one important American supporter: Earl E. T. Smith, a wealthy contributor to Eisenhower's campaign and the American ambassador to Cuba. Smith liked to say that he was the second most powerful man and occasionally the most powerful man in Cuba, and he managed to sabotage the attempts of moderates in Havana, including church leaders, to find some kind of moderate successor to Batista.

Smith's policy was perfect for Batista, because the two got on so well. Smith was very conservative. The only Cubans he talked to were wealthy, right-wing ones. Of the U.S. he would say, "I have lived in two eras, One when the country was run by the classes, and now when it is run by the masses. Something in between is probably best but I'll be honest. I enjoyed it more when it was run by the classes." Almost his entire embassy dissented from his view that Batista (or a Batista proxy) was a valid instrument of American policy, but Smith silenced them by refusing to sign off on their reporting. When it was clear that Batista was on his way out, Smith still continued to sabotage the attempts of moderate leaders in Cuba to bring some kind of moderate coalition government to power. Years later, Wayne Smith, a young political officer at the time, wrote of Earl Smith that he had come to see Batista as "a bulwark against Communism. In fact Batista was exactly the opposite; it was Batista who brought about the conditions that opened the door to radical solutions."

Yet time had already passed Batista by. He ruled by force, had no popularity among the peasants, and his army was commanded by men who held their ranks for political reasons. The brutality of his regime offended almost everyone. In an age of modern communications, his attempts at manipulation were pathetically transparent. Even as Batista's government was collapsing in 1958 and Fidel Castro was gathering his forces for the final military strike, Batista was sending out press releases on his forces' alleged victories to journalists whom he bought and sold—but Castro was using his own rebel radio to reach the Cuban masses. In Havana, given the nature of the regime, almost nothing the government said was believed, while almost everything that came from Castro's radio had credibility, born of the fact that he was challenging a tyrant.

William Wieland, the State Department's director for Caribbean and Mexican affairs, was the leader of those officials anxious to get rid of Batista and replace him with someone more centrist. Wieland wanted Batista out in no small part because he feared the coming of someone like Castro. In 1958 he had told colleagues at a State Department meeting that if "Batista was bad medicine for everyone, Castro would be worse."

Such fears were justified: If there was a growing disgust with Batista and his police brutality in Havana, then up in the hills of the interior, a guerrilla force was growing, pledged not only to bring Batista down but to install a revolutionary government in his place. Thirty years after he had come to power, Fidel Castro would appear to many in the West merely as an anachronism, a surviving Stalinist, a man who had sported his beard, fatigues, and Marxist rhetoric for too long. But when he first came to power, he possessed the mystique of the brave young rebel who risked his life to bring down a hated dictator and who seemed to promise a more enlightened, freer Cuba. He had gained immensely from the sheer cruelty of the Batista regime.

By the time he came down from the mountains, his myth was greater than his actual military power. Ironically, in contrast to Batista, Castro was the child of privilege, the son of a successful planter who leased large land holdings from United Fruit and sold his cane back to it. Fidel was sent to Jesuit schools and to the University of Havana law school, but from the start he had been a rebel. As a student he was part of a plot against Trujillo, the Dominican dictator, and after Batista retook power in Cuba in 1952 by means of a coup, it was the young Castro who led a group of rebels against a regimental garrison headquarters on July 26, 1953. Most of his men were captured then, and some sixty-nine were tortured and murdered either in prison or in hospitals. That brutality shocked many Cubans, and church leaders intervened with Batista, demanding that if any more rebels were caught, they be tried. That probably saved Castro, who was captured about a week after the attack.

Castro had a natural instinct for the dramatic, and he represented himself at his trial. Thus allowed to cross-examine state witnesses, he used the trial as a means of highlighting Batista's brutality and corruption. He read voraciously while in prison, and wrote a pamphlet, "History Will Absolve Me," which outlined the historical and legal case for overthrowing tyrants. After close to two years he was released in a general amnesty. By this time he had become a national figure and, as far as Batista was concerned, a marked man. In December 1956, he led a small band of followers to Oriente province, where he hoped to start a guerrilla movement. Instead he was ambushed by government forces. About sixty of his men were killed or taken prisoner, and only about twenty made it into the rugged mountains.

As Castro hid with two of his colleagues that first night after the ambush, he talked about the revolution he intended to lead and of how he would defeat Batista. Even though he was staring total annihilation right in the face that night, he was not given to doubting himself. Clearly, he saw himself as a man of destiny. He was a true believer in himself and his cause, and so in time were his men. As he and a handful of men moved into the rugged terrain of the interior on those first days, he asked a peasant. "Are we already in the Sierra Maestra?" The peasant said that they were. "Then the revolution has triumphed," Castro said. In Havana the Batista forces put out an announcement that Fidel Castro was dead. It was picked up and sent all over the world by the United Press, an act for which Castro never forgave the agency.

In the beginning his forces were tiny, but he received a major break when a *New York Times* journalist and editorial writer, Herbert Matthews, appeared at his camp only two months after Castro arrived. Matthews was something of a romantic, in the view of his *Times* colleague Tad Szulc. His liberal politics had been profoundly shaped during the time he covered the Spanish Civil War. He had hated the idea of Franco's victory. Matthews was instantly taken with Castro, whom he viewed as a brave, attractive young nationalist fighting against the dark forces of despotism. For Matthews Cuba was a replay of Spain, Szulc believed. He was fifty-seven when he met Castro, easily old enough to be Castro's father, and he seemed to feel almost paternal toward the younger Cuban rebel.

Castro did a masterful job of making his small unit seem much larger. He kept Matthews in camp and dispatched different men to what were supposed to be other camps; guerrillas, supposedly from different rebel headquarters, reported in to Castro in front of Matthews. It was, wrote Tad Szulc, quite literally guerrilla theater. Matthews stayed for a few days and then filed his reports to the *Times*. "Fidel Castro, the rebel leader of Cuba's youth, is alive and fighting hard and successfully in the rugged, almost impenetrable vastness of the Sierra Maestra," he began. He portrayed Batista's forces as frustrated by Castro's charismatic force. "The personality of the man is overpowering. It was easy to see that his men adored him and also to see why he has caught the imagination of the youth of Cuba all over the island. Here was an educated, dedicated fanatic, a man of ideals, of courage and of remarkable qualities of leadership." When Matthews' stories were printed they had immense impact, not least by proving that Castro was alive, not dead as Batista had claimed.

In the making of the legend of Fidel Castro, the Matthews

stories played a crucial role. There was something exceptionally romantic about the young leader leaving his privileged life and going into the mountains with a few men and vowing never to return until he could walk into Havana with his revolution. It was a timeless myth, part Robin Hood, part Mao, and given the excesses of Batista, it found wide acceptance. Fidel Castro might have been hundreds of miles away in the distant mountains, but with those articles, in the minds of millions of Cubans, he *lived*.

From his mountain base, he waged a guerrilla campaign similar to the Chinese Communists' under Mao and the Vietminh's in Vietnam. They attacked only when their strength was superior, then slipped quickly back into the mountains. The purpose of every engagement was to capture more weapons, not to kill. They lived simply, largely off the soil. The officers ate after the men and they ate the same rations. They treated the peasants well and never stole from them. They treated captured soldiers generously as well, often converting them. The life was hard, which was fine with Castro—he wanted hard men of conviction and purpose, not summer soldiers.

Slowly, his band grew in size. In March 1958, after some sixteen months, he opened a second front in the northern section of Oriente. His forces, compared to those of Batista, were still small, but their deeds were greatly magnified by rumors. In the spring of 1958 Batista opened a major offensive against him. Some ten thousand men were used to drive Castro's men into a tiny defensive perimeter, but at that critical point the Batista troops pushed no further.

From then on there was a complicated dynamic at work: Castro was becoming stronger, and Batista was becoming weaker, and it was clear that American policymakers were becoming increasingly uneasy. The Americans no longer had confidence in Batista, but they had no one with whom to replace him. It was getting very late, and with the passage of time, not only was Castro's reputation growing more powerful, but his claim to succeed Batista was seen as more and more legitimate in the eyes of most Cubans. There was still considerable talk at the higher levels of the State Department's Latin American affairs section of a third force—nationalist, liberal, tainted neither by Batistaism nor Castroism. The problem with the third force, here as in other countries, most notably Vietnam, was that the Americans could not readily invent one at the last minute. The role of leader had to be *earned* and the only person earning the title, the respect, and the love of his fellow Cubans was Fidel Castro.

In November 1958, Castro began to take his men down from the hills. If he was not entirely ready for the final strike, he was nonetheless aware that Batista was near collapse and he was wary that the Americans might take his prize and give it to someone else. At the time he began his final assault on Havana, Castro probably had several thousand men, while Batista had 40,000 soldiers and an additional 30,000 police officers. But as Castro moved forward it became more and more of a rout. Real battles were relatively rare. Instead, there were more and more instances when the Batista forces simply surrendered en masse. The Batista regime at the end was like "a walking corpse," in the words of one observer. Castro's growing victory march, his ever easier road to Havana, came as much from the old order collapsing of its own weight as it did from his exceptional military leadership of the rebels. It was a government literally rotting away.

In Havana Earl Smith had wanted to continue to support Batista, but in December he was told to tell Batista to leave the country. In the final hours of the Batista regime, there was a desperate attempt to have Colonel Ramon Barquin take over the government as an anti-Castro leader. But if he had once been something of a hero, who had tried to lead a coup against Batista, he had been taken out of play by the failure of his movement and his years in Batista's prison. What might have worked twenty months earlier was now a useless footnote to the fast-moving stream of history. No one knew this better than Barquin. "What can I do?" he asked a friend in the CIA. "All they left me with is shit."

The Americans had ended up with no one whose deeds spoke for themselves and whose charisma might match that of Castro. The third-force policy had produced nothing of consequence. The Americans were, wrote Wayne Smith, "like a bridge player who had held his aces too long until they were trumped."

On January 8, 1959, Castro entered Havana as a victorious conqueror. Rarely had anyone present seen a celebration quite like it. Like Moses parting the Red Sea, one journalist said. Havana, as he entered, was still filled with armed Batista loyalists. Some of Castro's soldiers wanted to precede him as he walked through the streets, for the city was still dangerous, but Castro would have none of it. Like MacArthur landing in Tokyo in August 1945 and walking around unarmed, he understood the power of the symbolic gesture, as few around him did. The people, he had said, would protect the revolutionaries. He would walk ahead of this massive parade and he would do it unarmed. "I will prove that I know the people," he said. Of the joy that ran throughout the country there was no doubt, and of his immense broad-based popularity there was no doubt; and also of the dilemma for American policymakers there was also no doubt.

How far left was Castro? Was he a Communist? And what should American policy be now? These were the critical questions for the Eisenhower administration. There was little in the way of definitive proof that Castro was actually a Communist. In the beginning, at least, there was the strong possibility he was a nationalist with no larger allegiance to any doctrine. In fact, there was a Communist party in Cuba, which had joined with Castro only relatively late in his struggle. His success had been largely indigenous. The weapons he used were primarily captured from Batista's troops. Asked by Washington whether Castro was a Communist or not, the embassy put together a very careful report that said he had no links to the Communist party; nor, for that matter, did he have much sympathy for it. But there was much about him that gave cause for concern. Wayne Smith's analysis noted at the time, for ". . . he seemed to have gargantuan ambitions, authoritarian tendencies, and not much in the way of an ideology of his own. He was also fiercely nationalistic." Given the history of relations of the two countries, "he did not hold the U.S. in high regard. One could imagine him turning to the Communists. All depended on what he thought would best advance his interests—and Cuba's as he interpreted them." The CIA largely concurred with this analysis. As late as November 1959, the deputy director of the CIA told a Senate committee, "We believe that Castro is not a member of the Communist Party and does not consider himself to be a Communist."

On his first trip to the United States in April 1959, at the invitation of the American Society of Newspaper Editors, an invitation that greatly irritated Dwight Eisenhower, Castro was on his best behavior and generally said all the right things. He was against dictatorships. He was for a free press, which he said was the first enemy of a dictatorship. His nominally conservative hosts gave him a standing ovation. He laid a wreath at the Lincoln Memorial. He told the Senate Foreign Relations Committee he would not expropriate United States property. The one person he did not charm was Vice-President Nixon, who met with him for three and a half hours as Eisenhower's proxy. Shrewd and analytical, Nixon knew in this instance that his own career was very much at stake—he had attacked the Democrats for losing China, and after all, now here was Cuba only ninety miles away with an unknown radical as its leader.

In some ways Nixon was impressed with Castro. He found him intelligent and forceful. He could well understand his appeal in Cuba, but he was bothered by Castro's answers on why he did not hold elections (the Cuban people, Castro answered, did not want them) and why he was executing some of his opponents without fair trials (the Cuban people did not want them to be given trials). In a long memo to the President and Secretary of State Christian Herter, who had replaced Foster Dulles, Nixon wrote, "Castro is either incredibly naive about Communism or is under Communist discipline." He had reason to worry, for Castro was soon to be his responsibility.

Nixon himself was fast approaching a critical moment in his career: his run for the presidency in 1960. After serving as Vice-President for almost seven years, he was seething with frustration and resentments. The vice-presidency is a job largely without portfolio in the best of circumstances, and these were hardly the best of circumstances, for he raged at his treatment by Ike. By 1958 Nixon was caught in a political bind, one partly of his own making. He needed to upgrade his image to that of someone worthy of the presidency. He had to redo himself and make a move to the center, without changing so completely that the Republican right would turn on him. Yet at the same time improvements in communications technology were making it more difficult to tailor speeches for specific audiences without there being a record. Some of his speeches in the Rocky Mountain states during the 1956 campaign had caused considerable controversy, but the local papers had not done a particularly serious job of covering them.

In 1958 *The New York Times* sent Russell Baker, then a young reporter, to cover him with a tape recorder. At the first stop, when Baker had pushed the recorder up so that it could catch Nixon at a press conference, Nixon had seen the machine, had understood the game immediately, and had answered Baker's first question with a diatribe against his paper. It was clearly going to be harder than ever to be a hydra-headed candidate in American politics. Which Nixon would he choose to be as he entered his presidential run—the combative anti-Communist Nixon of the earlier, harsher campaigns, or the new Nixon, more centrist, less partisan, acceptable to the entire country? During the 1960 campaign Ken Galbraith asked Kennedy if he was tired from the brutal daily campaign routine. No, he was not tired, Kennedy answered, but he felt sure that Nixon was and he felt sorry for him. Why? Galbraith asked. "Because I know who I am and I don't have to worry about adapting and changing. All I have to do at each stop is be myself. But Nixon doesn't know who he is, and so each time he makes a speech he has to decide which Nixon he is, and that will be exhausting."

Escaping the past and moving from one constituency to another was not easy, even for someone as politically nimble as Richard Nixon. In an off-record interview with David Astor, the British publisher, Nixon addressed the ugliness of the 1950 campaign against Helen Gahagan Douglas: "I'm sorry about that episode. I was a very young man." When a version of the interview came out in *The New Republic,* Nixon angrily denied the statement and claimed that he had nothing to apologize for.

He was still wary of being accused of being soft on Communism. The one thing, he wrote in a memo to his speechwriters in July 1959, that they should never put in his speeches was an endorsement of the idea of peaceful coexistence. "This is the Acheson line in the State Department and I will not put it out!!!!!! Cushman [his Marine aide and NSC liaison, Major Bob Cushman], tell all of them—it is never to be used again . . . or whoever does it will be shipped [out] on the next plane."

In the summer of 1959, he had scored a coup in his so-called "kitchen debate" with Khrushchev. Nixon had gone to Moscow as the head of a large delegation to open a trade fair. Ambassador Llewellyn Thompson warned Nixon on arrival that the Russians were primed for a fight because of their anger over the Captive Day resolution, which Washington annually issued and to which no one, of course, paid virtually any attention except the Soviets. When Nixon went to the Kremlin for his first meeting with the Soviet leader, Khrushchev observed that Senator McCarthy might be dead but apparently his spirit lived on. Nixon tried to change the subject, but Khrushchev pushed on, earthy as ever: "People should not go to the toilet where they eat. This resolution stinks. It stinks like fresh horse shit, and nothing smells worse than that!" Nixon, remembering that the Russian leader had been a pig farmer, said there was one thing that smelled worse "and that is pig shit." With that Khrushchev smiled and agreed to change the subject.

But the tone had been set. From then on it seemed a mutual boasting competition. Whatever America did, the Russians did better. As the two men toured a model American house, which was a part of the exhibition, Nixon claimed that though the Soviet Union might be ahead in rocket power, America was ahead in middle-class housing. But the house was not good enough for the Soviet first secretary: The Russians would build better housing than the West, he boasted, housing that would last for several generations.

When Nixon tried to talk about the new consumer devices that made life easier in these houses, Khrushchev scorned them. Some of them, he said, were probably out of order. Others were worthless. "Don't you have a machine that puts food into the mouth and pushes it down?" he asked sardonically. "You do all the talking and you do not let anyone else talk," Nixon finally complained. "I want to make one point. We don't think this fair will astound the Russian people, but it will interest them. . . . To us, diversity, the right to choose, the fact that we have a thousand different builders, that's the spice of life. We don't want to have a decision made at the top by one government official saying that we will have one kind of house. That's the difference."

But Khrushchev was not Nixon's problem as 1959 became 1960 and the campaign for the presidency began. The problem was Castro. If Nixon and the Republican party were vulnerable on any one issue, it was Cuba. Vietnam had been a close call, but the President had shrewdly managed to put the blame on our allies. But Cuba was a wild card. Castro had come to power, our influence with him was minimal, and yet the President did not seem very interested in Cuba; his mind was elsewhere. He, unlike Richard Nixon, did not have to run for the presidency in 1960. Whatever else Dwight Eisenhower thought about Cuba, it had nothing to do with his political future.

A new ambassador, Phillip Bonsal, a highly professional career officer, had replaced Earl Smith, and Bonsal had made it clear that he wanted to create some kind of dialogue with Castro. But it was increasingly apparent by the fall of 1959 that Castro was on a course to the left: Both his words and actions were increasingly upsetting to American authorities. In October 1959 Huber Matos, one of the top men in the revolution, criticized the rising influence of the Communists in Castro's inner circle; Matos was immediately arrested and sentenced to twenty years in prison. By November 1959, almost all of Castro's moderate ministers were gone, replaced by men either from the Communist party or sympathetic to it. In November a Soviet trade delegation arrived and was given the red-carpet treatment, and in February 1960, Anastas Mikoyan visited Cuba, to an unusually warm welcome. More and more, Castro seemed to be on a deliberate collision course with Washington.

Castro continued his brutal executions of former Batista sympathizers, and his rhetoric was increasingly hostile to the United States. Perhaps both sides carried too much baggage from the past to be friends now. When a French ship that was unloading munitions exploded, Castro angrily blamed the United States, though there was no evidence of American involvement, nor did any show up later. Wayne Smith, a man not averse to criticizing American policy, felt that the explosion was probably caused by carelessness. But the incident seemed to mark the point of no return. Castro started buying petroleum products from the Soviet Union, and when Soviet tankers arrived, the three local refineries—two of them American, one British—refused to refine the crude. With that, Castro nationalized the refineries. By the end of the summer he had nationalized a large amount of American property. The Americans, in retaliation, ended the Castro sugar quota, refusing to buy the remaining 700,000 tons of it.

On his second visit to the United States, Castro was not so amiable a guest. He arrived for the United Nations General Assembly in September 1960 and stayed at the Hotel Theresa in Harlem—in itself a major political statement. He dined with Khrushchev at the Soviet mission in New York. With such moves Castro was thinking not of his place in Cuba but of his place in the world. Even the sympathetic Herbert Matthews, Wayne Smith noted, had written about Fidel's "Messiah complex." "Fidel," Matthews had written, "has all along felt himself to be a crusader if not a saviour." For a man like this, Cuba was too small a stage. He wanted to be a major figure on the international stage, and to do that he had to be free of the United States.

To Tad Szulc, the distinguished *New York Times* reporter who covered Castro for years and later wrote a major biography of him, that explanation made the most sense. Castro, Szulc believed, was a man of instinct and circumstances as much as he was of ideology. He was shrewd, emotional, extremely talented, and overwhelmingly ambitious. Given Castro's view of himself, given his desire to be a worldwide revolutionary figure, it was inevitable, Szulc thought, that he would go the way he did. It was not by chance that he kept the fatigues and the beard long after he had left the Sierra Maestra. His decision was, thought Szulc, not at all very ideological, but rather very pragmatic—indeed instinctive. Therefore the question for American policymakers was not whether or not the Eisenhower administration had played him incorrectly in those important early months, for there was simply no right way to play him. He was going in a very different direction because it was the way he wanted to go. He could not be a major revolutionary figure of world-wide status and yet be an ally of the leading capitalist power.

Nevertheless, America was largely without a policy toward Cuba. As the unthinkable happened—a radical, left-wing, quite possibly Marxist, government had taken power—the American response was almost automatic. On January 18, 1960, the CIA division responsible for the Western Hemisphere held its first meeting on Castro and Cuba. As the regulars assembled, everyone's spirits were high. Many of them were veterans of the successful coup against Arbenz six years earlier and looked forward to a repeat success. When Jake Engler (a professional pseudonym), one of the men in charge, called David Atlee Phillips, who had run the radio station during the Arbenz coup, he gave Phillips three guesses what they were going to deal with. The answer was easy: "Cuba. Cuba. And Cuba," Phillips said. When Phillips was reunited with Howard Hunt, who had been one of the high-level operatives in the Guatemalan coup, Hunt was excited. "Welcome aboard, Chico," he said. They were all so confident; it was, they thought, like a reunion; Guatemala had been a piece of cake, and Cuba now would be a bigger one. The operating group proceeded enthusiastically, ignoring all intelligence estimates from the embassy and from the CIA, which portrayed Castro as remarkably invulnerable to guerrilla insurrection. Rather, they showed a far more sophisticated and developed country than Guatemala, and also that Castro was a truly formidable figure, in no way a target comparable to Arbenz. If he was losing some popularity through his increasingly brutal tactics of suppressing all domestic political opposition, then he compensated by developing his own secret police.

Wayne Smith vacationed in Miami in the summer of 1960 and found the city rife with surprisingly detailed accounts of a new clandestine operation which was obviously intended to topple Castro. "We're going to take care of Castro just like we took care of Arbenz," one man, obviously a CIA agent, told Smith. "It was easy then and it'll be easy now." The smugness of the CIA men stunned Smith and others. There was one CIA agent who liked to move around the Miami exile community telling Cuban exiles that he carried the revolution with him in his checkbook.

The planning for the anti-Castro operation was all done in a rush. The driving force was Richard Bissell, who had been so successful in the development of the U-2. Though Bissell was inexperienced in running an operation like this, he was a fierce taskmaster and pushed things through ruthlessly. Time was of the essence. Cuban pilots were said to be learning to fly MiGs in the Soviet Union, and any operation needing air cover would lose its advantage when they returned. Pressure was also being applied by Richard Nixon, who much more so than Eisenhower supported the operation. Eisenhower remained ambivalent about Cuba. He did not like Castro and he was irritated by what Castro was doing, but his second tour was almost done. His warnings to the CIA people were not unlike those he had made in the past; if it was to be done, he wanted it to succeed. It was all or nothing for him. But he clearly had his doubts. At one meeting in March 1960, Eisenhower said Cuba might be "another black hole of Calcutta."

Nixon, though, did not want Castro's Cuba to be an issue in the 1960 campaign. "How are the boys doing at the Institute?" Nixon would ask his liaison with the NSC, Robert Cushman referring to the CIA's operation in Cuba. It was clear, Cushman thought, that Nixon wanted the operation to take place before the election. Predictably, things did not develop smoothly. The ablest top-level CIA officer, Dick Helms, who was involved in something of a power struggle with Bissell at the time, wanted no part of it. Throughout the Agency, the word was out that Helms was staying away from the Cuba thing—a signal to many other of the Agency's more senior people to stay away as well. Helms, as Peter Wyden noted in his book on the Bay of Pigs, was known to have "a nose for incipient failures."

There were four parts to the operation: the creation of what was called a responsible government in exile, a powerful propaganda effort, a covert intelligence operation inside Cuba, and, most important, the training of a paramilitary Cuban force in exile. On March 17, 1960, Eisenhower gave his official approval to go ahead on the paramilitary unit. The plan called for training twenty-five Cuban exiles, who would in turn train other exiles to overthrow Castro. From then on, what happened was a striking case of an ill-conceived, ill-advised policy being carried forward by its own institutional momentum. Many people thought the plan was foolish and ill-conceived, but no one wanted to take responsibility for stopping it; finally, it became impossible to stop.

In mid-August, 1960, Ike approved a budget of $13 million for the covert operation. But still things lagged behind schedule. The presidential election was heating up. Bissell was confident that Nixon would approve the final plan. Of Kennedy he was not so sure. Nixon, thought his aide Robert Cushman, was getting very restless. There was constant pressure from him to find out how things were going. The truth was, Cushman thought, they were not going that well. Early operations in which agents were dropped into Cuba backfired, and the agents were easily picked up. It was decided that the operation needed to be bigger, with a fifty-kilowatt radio station, a rebel air force based in Nicaragua, and a full-scale landing in Cuba of more than one thousand men. It was now not so much a covert operation as an invasion. Eisenhower was still ambivalent. "Where's

728 / DAVID HALBERSTAM

our government in exile?" he kept asking Allen Dulles. In the late fall, he showed his skepticism yet again at a meeting with Dulles and Bissell. "I'm going along with you boys, but I want to be sure the damned thing works."

Soon it became clear there would not be time to launch the operation while Eisenhower was still President. And with that perhaps the last chance to kill the operation had died. For it would have been easy for Eisenhower, an experienced military man with solid anti-Communist credentials, to call off his own program; it was not so easy for a young Democratic President, vulnerable to accusations of a lack of experience and of being insufficiently anti-Communist, to stop a program that was so far advanced.

So the plan moved forward and continued to grow. Soon it was six hundred men instead of four hundred; then it was seven hundred fifty, and then over one thousand. Then it became less a covert guerrilla force and more a full-scale landing from the sea, supported by a small hired air force. That was one of the most difficult maneuvers of all in military terms. The more men were needed, the less secrecy there would be and the more the operation would depend on increased airpower. In fact the operation had become something of an open secret by the fall of 1960. Castro had agents everywhere, and even if he had not, the size of the force, the swagger of its members as they boasted of what they would do, had guaranteed that Castro would know many of the details.

That meant that Richard Nixon's worst nightmare about the 1960 campaign had come true. The Cuban dilemma had not been settled, Castro was sticking his finger in America's eye from his safe haven ninety miles away, and the formation of an exile expeditionary force lagged well behind schedule. The Democrats, as he had suspected, were about to nominate John Kennedy, who would make a formidable opponent.

Kennedy was young, attractive, contemporary, skilled as few politicians of his generation were at using television. He also represented the resurgence of the Democrats as hard-liners. Accused of being soft on Communism in the past, they were now determined to show that if anything, they were tougher foes of Communism than the Republicans. They did this somewhat deftly: They did not actually accuse the Republicans of being soft on Communism; instead, they claimed that the country had lost its edge during the Eisenhower years. America had become self-satisfied and lazy, and the world was leaving America behind, particularly in the race for friends in the third world. They spoke of a missile gap (which did not exist) and again and again of Castro's Cuba.

John Kennedy was a cool and very controlled young man, privileged, well educated, but in some ways very much the son of his Irish-immigrant father. If the passions and rage of Joe Kennedy had been obvious, those of his son were not: He appeared not as an angry immigrant but, thanks to the tailoring of Harvard, as reserved and aristocratic—the first Irish Brahmin. Be more Irish than Harvard, the poet Robert Frost would ask of him at his inauguration a year later. The Kennedy signature was a kind of rugged masculinity, a physical and emotional toughness. Kennedy men did not cry, and they did not make themselves vulnerable on issues of anti-Communism. "Isn't he marvelous!" an excited Joe Alsop had said to a colleague after watching Kennedy's announcement for the presidency. "A Stevenson with balls."

Because he was as good at listening as speaking, he soon recognized that the country's anxieties over the Cold War now had more to do with Castro than with Khrushchev. All he had to do was mention, as he did frequently, that Cuba was only ninety miles away, eight minutes by jet, and the audience would explode in anger and frustration. Typically, in a speech on October 15, in Johnstown, Pennsylvania, he said: "Mr. Nixon hasn't mentioned Cuba very prominently in this campaign. He talks about standing firm in Berlin, standing firm in the Far East, standing up to Khrushchev, but he never mentions standing firm in Cuba—and if you can't stand up to Castro, how can you be expected to stand up to Khrushchev?" So ironically, Kennedy attacked Nixon for the administration's softness on Castro, but Nixon, privy to the CIA's preparation of the clandestine operation, could not respond.

If television played a role in previous presidential elections, this was the first in which it became the dominating force. In past elections, Kennedy might have been denied the nomination because the party bosses (most of them, ironically, Catholic) were against him, fearing an anti-Catholic backlash. But Kennedy used the primaries to prove he could win predominantly Protestant strongholds, and the key to that was his skillful use of television.

Kennedy had been a natural on television—from the start the camera had liked him. He was attractive, he did not posture, and he was cool by instinct: Television was a cool medium—the more overheated a candidate, the less well he did on it. Kennedy's gestures and his speaking voice seemed natural—perhaps it was a reaction to the old-fashioned blarney of his Irish-American grandfather, who had campaigned by singing Irish songs. John Kennedy did not like politicians who gave florid speeches; he greatly preferred understatement. His own speeches were full of humor, irony, and self-depreciation, and that helped him in what was to be the defining moment of the 1960 campaign—the first presidential debate.

By contrast, television was a problem for Nixon. Not only were his physical gestures awkward, but his speaking tone was self-conscious and artificial. What often came through was a sense of insincerity. To Eisenhower's secretary, Anne Whitman, "The Vice-President sometimes seems like a man who is acting like a nice man rather than being one." That was a critical distinction, particularly for a man entering the television age, because if there was one thing the piercing eye of the television camera was able to convey to people, it was what was authentic and what was artificial.

The first debate changed the nature of politics in America, and it also crowned the importance of television politically and culturally. From then on, American politics became a world of television and television advisers; the party machinery was soon to be in sharp decline as the big-city political bosses no longer had a monopoly on the ability to assemble large crowds—television offered much larger ones. Until that night in Chicago, Kennedy had been the upstart, a little-known junior senator who had hardly bothered to take the Senate seriously. Nixon, on the other hand, had been Vice-President for eight years; he was experienced, had visited endless foreign countries and met with all the leaders of the world. He also fancied himself a not inconsiderable debater, and he was confident he would do well against Kennedy.

Kennedy, who viewed Nixon with a cool snobbishness, arrived in Chicago early. He had spent much of the previous week in California, and he was tanned and glowing with good health. Knowing that this was the most important moment in the campaign, he had minimized his campaign schedule and spent much of his time in his hotel resting. He also practiced with his staff members, who posed likely questions and likely Nixon answers.

Nixon, by contrast, arrived in terrible shape. He had been ill earlier in the campaign with an infected knee, and he had never entirely recovered. Others on his staff tried to tell him to rest and prepare himself, but no one could tell him anything. Old and once trusted advisers had been cut off. Frustrated by Eisenhower's treatment of him for the last seven and a half years, Nixon had become megalomaniacal in 1960 as far as his veteran staff was concerned, determined to be his own campaign manager as well as candidate. Ted Rogers, his top television adviser, found that Nixon would not even talk with him about planning for the coming debates. Rogers kept calling the Nixon campaign plane to see how the candidate was doing and how he looked, and the answer always come back that he was doing well and looked fine.

At one point Rogers flew out to Kansas City to talk with Nixon about the debate but had not been able even to see him. Have you got him drinking milkshakes? Rogers asked the staff on the plane, and was assured that the candidate looked just fine. The first debate was set for Monday, September 26. Nixon, ill and exhausted, flew out late on Sunday night and went on a motorcade through Chicago, stopping for rallies in five wards and getting to bed very late. Then on Monday, even though he was clearly exhausted, he made another major campaign appearance in front of a labor union. His staff prepared possible questions and answers for him, but he was in no mood to look at their work. Late Monday afternoon, Rogers was permitted a brief meeting. He was stunned by how badly Nixon looked. His face was gray and ashen, and his aides had not even bothered to buy him new shirts—so his shirt hung loosely around his neck like that of a dying man. The only thing he wanted to know from Rogers was how long it would take to get from his hotel to the studio.

At the studio, both candidates turned down the makeup offered by the station. It was gamesmanship: Each man feared that if he used any makeup, then the next day there would be newspaper stories about it, or, even worse, a photo. But Kennedy had a good tan and his aide Bill Wilson did a slight touch-up with commercial makeup bought at a drugstore two blocks away. Because of his dark beard, Nixon used something called Shavestick. The CBS professionals were as shocked by Nixon's appearance as Ted Rogers had been. Don Hewitt, the producer (later to be the executive producer of *60 Minutes*), was sure that a disaster was in the making and that CBS would later be blamed for Nixon's cosmetic failures (which in fact happened).

Nixon was extremely sensitive to heat, and he sweated profusely when the television lights were on (years later, as President, he gave fireside chats from the White House with the air-conditioning turned up to the maximum so that he would not sweat). He had started out in the debates by looking ghastly, gray and exhausted. Then while some 80 million of his fellow Americans watched, it got worse. He began to sweat. Soon there were rivers of sweat on his gray face, and the Shavestick washed down his face. In the control room Rogers and Wilson were sitting with Hewitt, who, Rogers decided, was the most powerful man in the country at that moment because he controlled the camera. Earlier, during the negotiations, both sides had agreed on the number of reaction shots that could be used—that is, how many times the camera would focus on one candidate while the other candidate was speaking. At first Wilson had called for more reaction shots of his man, Kennedy, and Rogers had called for more reaction shots of his man. But soon they had switched sides: Watching Nixon in a kind of cosmetic meltdown, Wilson called for more shots of *Nixon* and Rogers called for more of *Kennedy*—anything to get that relentlessly cruel camera off Nixon's gray face as it dissolved into a river of sweat. "That night," Russell Baker wrote thirty years later, "image replaced the printed word as the natural language of politics."

Nixon had been warned by others that he must not attack too harshly, that otherwise he would seem like the Nixon of old; even Eisenhower had told him that he must not be too glib. That had stung, for it was nothing less than a rebuke, the President's way of saying that he thought Nixon was, in fact, too glib (what stung even more was learning that Ike did not even bother to watch the debate). When it was all over, Nixon thought he had won. Kennedy knew otherwise, particularly when the door to WBBM opened and there was Dick Daley, the boss of the Chicago Democratic machine, who had so far shunned Kennedy in Chicago. Now he was eager to congratulate him, eager to come aboard. The next day Kennedy drew huge crowds wherever he went, and the people seemed to feel a personal relationship with the candidate. For Nixon the news was a great deal worse. The parents of Rose Woods, his longtime secretary, called from Ohio to ask if there was anything wrong with him. Even Hannah Nixon called Rose to inquire about her son's health.

Later, Ted Rogers mused that eight years of Nixon's experience as Vice-President had been wiped out in one evening. Rogers wondered how Nixon could have been so careless about so vital a moment in the campaign, and later he decided that it was the sum of everything that had gone before: anger over his treatment by Eisenhower as Vice-President; his subsequent determination to make all the important decisions in this campaign himself and to listen to none of his old advisers; and finally, his belief that because of the Checkers speech, he was an expert on television. Unfortunately, anyone who understood television could have warned him that Kennedy was a formidable foe in front of a television camera.

.   . .

The debate between these two young men, each born in this century, each young enough to be Dwight Eisenhower's son, seemed to underscore how quickly the society had changed in so short a time. It showed not only how powerful the electronic medium had become, but also how much it was already speeding the pace of life in America. Not everyone was pleased by the change wrought in American politics by television. Dean Acheson was not moved by either candidate as he watched the debate and it had made him feel older. To him both candidates appeared to be cold, mechanistic figures who had, with the aid of pollsters and advertising executives, figured out, down to the last decimal point, what stand to take on every issue. "Do you get a funny sort of sense that, so far at least, there are no human candidates in this campaign?" he wrote Harry Truman. "They seem improbable, skillful technicians. Both are surrounded by clever people who dash off smart memoranda, but it is not all pulled together on either side, by or into a man. The ideas are too contrived. . . . These two . . . bore the hell out of me."

AUTHOR
INTERVIEWS
FOR *THE FIFTIES*

Ralph Abernathy, Tom Adams, Naohiro Amaya, Michael Arlen, Harry Ashmore, Russell Baker, James Bassett, Laura Pincus Bernard, Hans Bethe, Stanley Booth, Herbert Brownell, Will Campbell, M.C. Chang, John Chancellor, David Cole, Bob Cousy, Geoff Cowan, Keith Crain, Robert Cumberford, Mike Dann, David E. Davis, Anthony De Lorenzo, Sophie Pincus Dutton, Jock Elliot, Dan Enright, Jerry Evans, Jules Feiffer, Estelle Ferkauf, Eugene Ferkauf, David Fine, Karl Fleming, Al Freedman, Don Frey, Betty Friedan, Betty Furness, Frank Gibney, Paul Gillian, Herman Goldstine, Dick Goodman, Dick Goodwin, Katharine Graham, Harold Green, Wayne Greenhaw, Sidney Gruson, Oscar Hechter, Thomas Hine, Mahlon Hoagland, Sandra Holland, Townsend Hoopes, Robert Ingram, Evelyn Pincus Isaacson, Joe Isaacson, Ray Jenkins, W. Thomas Johnson, Kensinger Jones, Chuck Jordan, Ward Just, Stanley Katz, Alfred Kazin, Murray Kempton, Bunkie Knudsen, Florence Knudsen, Julian Krainan, A.J. Langguth, William Levitt, Ira Lipman, Susan McBride, David McCall, Frank McCullough, Dick McDonald, Jay Milner, Frederic Morrow, Stan Mott, Leona Nevler, Stan Parker, Knox Phillips, Sam Phillips, John Alexis Pincus, Michael Pincus, Earl Pollock, Johnny Popham, Bill Porter, G.E. Powell, Waddy Pratt, Joel Raphaelson, Richard Rhodes, David Riesman, Matthew Ridgway, Kermit Roosevelt, Sr., Al Rothenberg, Harrison Salisbury, Gerald Schnitzer, Don Schwarz, Sheldon Segal, Joel Selvin, Robert

Serber, Don Silber, Claude Sitton, Reggie Smith, Dick Starmann, Herb Stempel, Tad Szulc, Henry Turley, Fred Turner, Sander Vanocur, Bill Walton, Tom Watson, Jr., Thomas Weinberg, Victor Weisskopf, Wallace Westfeldt, Marina von Neumann Whitman, Jerome Wiesner, Kemmons Wilson, Sloan Wilson, Bill Winter, Andy Young

Additional Author Interviews

Roger Ailes, Louis Cowan, Helen Gahagan Douglas, Albert Gore, Leonard Hall, Averell Harriman, Don Hewitt, Larry L. King, Murrey Marder, Earl Mazo, Mollie Parnis, Rosser Reeves, James Reston, Ted Rogers, Pierre Salinger, David Schoenbrun, Dan Schorr, C.L. Sulzberger, Bill Wilson

BIBLIOGRAPHY

Abernathy, Ralph. *And the Walls Came Tumbling Down*. New York: Harper Perennial, 1989.

Acheson, Dean. *Present at the Creation: My Years in the State Department*. New York: Norton, 1969.

Adams, Sherman. *First-Hand Report*. New York: Harper and Row, 1961.

Alabama Oral History Project: Interview with Virginia Durr, *Memoir Vol. II*, November 24, 1976.

Allen, Fred. *Treadmill to Oblivion*. Boston: Little, Brown and Co., 1954.

Alsop, Joseph W. *I've Seen the Best of It: The Memoirs of Joseph W. Alsop*. New York: W.W. Norton & Co.

Alsop, Joseph and Stewart Alsop. *We Accuse!: The Story of the Miscarriage of American Justice in the Case of J. Robert Oppenheimer*. New York: Simon and Schuster, 1954.

Alvarez, Luis W. Alvarez: *Adventures of a Physicist*. New York: Basic Books, 1987.

Ambrose, Stephen. *Eisenhower, Vol. 2: The President*. New York: Simon & Schuster, 1984.

Ambrose, Stephen. *Nixon: The Education of a Politician, 1913–1962*. New York: Simon & Schuster, 1987.

Anderson, Kent. *The History and Implications of the Quiz Show Scandals*. Westport: Greenwood, 1978.

Andrews, Bart. *The I Love Lucy Book.* New York: Doubleday & Co., 1985.

Appelbaum, Irwyn. *The World According to Beaver.* New York: Bantam Books, Inc., 1984.

Appleman, Roy. *South to the Naktong, North to the Yalu. June–November, 1950.* Washington D.C.,: Office of the Chief of Military History, Department of the Army, 1961.

Ashmore, Harry. *Hearts and Minds: The Anatomy of Racism from Roosevelt to Reagan.* New York: McGraw Hill, 1982.

Aspery, William. *John von Neumann and the Origins of Modern Computing.* Cambridge, Massachusetts: Massachusetts Institute of Technology Press, 1990.

"Attack on the Conscience," *Time.* Vol LXIX: February 18, 1957.

Barmash, Isadore. *More than They Bargained for: The Rise and Fall of Korvettes.* New York: Labhar-Friedman Books, 1981.

Barnouw, Erik. *A History of Broadcasting, Vol II: The Golden Web.* New York: Oxford University Press, 1968.

Barnouw, Erik. *A History of Broadcasting, Vol. III: The Image Empire.* New York: Oxford University Press, 1970.

Bates, Daisy. *The Long Shadow of Little Rock.* Fayetteville: The University of Arkansas Press, 1962.

Bayley, Edwin. *Joe McCarthy and the Press.* Madison, Wisonsin: University of Wisconsin Press, 1981.

Bayley, Stephen. *Harley Earl and the Dream Machine.* New York: Knopf, 1983.

Berg, Stacey Michelle. Undergraduate thesis, Harvard University.

Berghaus, Erik. *Reaching for the Stars.* New York: Doubleday, 1960.

Bernays, Edward. *Biography of an Idea: Memoirs of Public Relations Council Edward L. Bernays.* New York: Simon & Schuster, 1965.

Bernstein, Jeremy. *Hans Berthe: Prophet of Energy.* New York: Basic Books, 1980.

Beschloss, Michael. *The Crisis Years: Kennedy and Khrushchev, 1960–1963.* New York: HarperCollins, 1991.

Beschloss, Michael. *Mayday: Eisenhower, Khrushchev, and the U-2 Affair.* New York: Harper and Row, 1986.

Blair, Clay. *Ridgway's Paratroopers.* New York: Doubleday & Co., 1985.

Blair, Clay. *The Forgotten War: America in Korea, 1950–1953.* New York: New York Times Books, 1987.

Blossom, Virgil. *It Happened Here.* New York: Harper and Row, 1959.

Blumberg, Stanley and Gwinn Owens. *Energy and Conflict: The Life of Edward Teller.* New York: Putnam, 1976.

Booth, Stanley. *Rythym Oil.* New York: Pantheon, 1992. note: stet spelling

Bradley, Omar with Clay Blair. *A General's Life.* New York: Simon & Schuster, 1983.

Branch, Taylor. *Parting the Waters: America in the King Years, 1954–1963.* New York: Simon & Schuster, 1988.

Brochu, Jim. *Lucy in the Afternoon: An Intimate Biography of Lucille Ball.* New York: William Morrow & Co., 1990.

Bundy, McGeorge. *Danger and Survival: Choices About the Bomb in the First Fifty Years.* New York: Random House, 1988.

Cal Fullerton Archives: Interviews with Jane Milhous Beeson, Elizabeth Cloes, Guy Dixon, Douglas Ferguson, Saragrace Frampton, Olive Mashburn, Oscar Mashburn, Charles Milhous, Dorothy Milhous, Lucile Parson, Hubert Perry, Paul Ryan, Ralph Shook, Paul Smith, Madeline Thomas, Lura Walfrop, Samuel Warner, Merel West, Marcia Elliot Wray, and Merton Wray.

Carey, Gary. *Marlon Brando: The Only Contender.* New York: St. Martin's Press, 1985.

Cassady, Carolyn. *Off the Road: My Years with Cassady, Kerouac, and Ginsberg.* New York: Morrow, 1990.

Caute, David. *The Great Fear: The Anti-Communist Purge Under Truman and Eisenhower.* New York: Simon & Schuster, 1978.

Chambers, Whittaker. *Witness.* New York: Random House, 1952.

Christenson, Cornelia V. *Kinsey: A Biography*. Bloomington: Indiana University Press, 1971.

City vs. Charlotte Colvin. Transcript from the circuit court of Juvenile Court and Court of Domestic Relations, Montgomery County, Alabama, March 18, 1955.

Clarke, Arthur, ed. *The Coming of the Space Age*. New York: Meredith Press, 1967.

Coffey, Thomas M. *Iron Eagle: The Turbulent Life of General Curtis LeMay*. New York: Crown Publishing Group, 1987.

Cohen, Marcia. *The Sisterhood: The True Story Behind the Women's Movement*. New York: Simon & Schuster, 1988.

Collins, Joseph Lawton. *War in Peacetime: The History and Lessons of Korea*. Boston: Houghton Mifflin, 1969.

Cooke, Alistair. *A Generation on Trial*. New York: Knopf, 1982.

Costello, William. *The Facts About Nixon*. New York: Viking Press, 1960.

Cotten, Lee. *The Elvis Catalog*. New York: Charlton Associates, 1987.

Coughlin, Robert. "Dr. Edward Teller's Magnificent Obsession." *Life*, No. 37, September 6, 1954.

Cray, Ed. *Chrome Colossus: General Motors and its Times*. New York: McGraw Hill, 1980.

Cray, Ed. *General of the Army: George C. Marshall*. New York: W.W. Norton, 1990.

Currie, Majorie Dent, ed. *Current Biography Yearbook*. New York: H.W. Wilson Co., 1949.

Currie, Majorie Dent, ed. *Current Biography: Who's News and Why-1953*. New York: H. W. Wilson Co., 1954.

Currie, Majorie Dent, ed. *Current Biography Yearbook*. New York: H.W. Wilson Co., 1956.

Dalton, David. *James Dean: The Mutant King*. New York: St. Martin's Press, 1974.

Davidson, Sarah. "Dr. Rock's Magic Pill." *Esquire*, December, 1983.

Davis, K. Charles. *Two-Bit Culture: The Paperbacking of America*. Boston: Houghton Mifflin Co., 1984.

Davis, Nuell Pharr. *Lawrence and Oppenheimer; The Da Capo Series in Science*. New York: Da Capo Press, 1986.

Dean, William with William Worden. *General Dean's Story*. New York: Viking, 1954.

Diamond, Edwin and Stephan Bates. *The Spot: The Rise of Political Advertising on Television*. Cambridge: MIT Press, 1988.

Diggins, John Partrick. *The Proud Decades*. New York: Norton, 1988.

Donovan, Robert J. *Conflict and Crisis: The Presidency of Harry S. Truman, 1945–1948*. New York: Norton, 1972.

Donovan, Robert J. *Tumultuous Years: The Presidency of Harry S. Truman, 1949–1953*. New York: Norton, 1982.

Dornberger, Walter. *V-2*. New York: Viking, 1952.

Dorschner, John and Robert Fabricio. *The Winds of December*. New York: Coward, McCann and Geoghegan, 1980.

Dulles, Eleanor L. *Eleanor Lansing Dulles: Chances of a Lifetime: A Memoir*. New York: Prentice Hall, 1980.

Dundy, Elaine. *Elvis and Gladys*. New York: Macmillan, 1988.

Dunleavy, Steve. *Elvis: What Happened*. New York: Ballantine, 1982.

Edwards, Anne. *Vivien Leigh*. New York: Simon & Schuster, 1977.

Eisenhower, Dwight D. *Mandate for Change*. New York: Doubleday, 1963.

Escot, Colin and Martin Hawkins. *Sun Records: The Brief History of a Legendary Record Label*. New York: Quick Fox, 1975.

Fall, Bernard. *Hell in a Very Small Place: The Siege of Dien Bien Phu*. Philadelphia: J. B. Lippincott Co., 1967.

Farre, Robert, ed. *The Diaries of James C. Hagerty*. Bloomington, Indiana: Indiana University Press, 1983.

Faubus, Orval. *Down from the Hills*, Vol I. Little Rock: Pioneer Press, 1980.

FBI Documents on J. Robert Oppenheimer, May 27, 1952– Albuquerque Office.

Fehrenbach, T.R. *This Kind of War: A Study in Unpreparedness.* New York: Macmillan, 1954.

Fenton, John. *In Your Opinion.* Boston: Little, Brown, 1960.

Ferrell, Robert H., ed. *Dear Bess: The Letters from Harry to Bess Truman, 1910–1959.* New York: Norton, 1983.

Ferrell, Robert H., ed. *Off the Record: The Private Papers of Harry S. Truman.* New York: Harper & Row, 1980.

Fiore, Carlo. *Bud: The Brando I Knew.* New York: Delacorte Press, 1974.

Fox, Stephen. *The Mirror Makers.* New York: Morrow, 1984.

Friendly, Fred. *Due to Circumstances Beyond Our Control.* New York: Random House, 1967.

Gans, Herbert J. *The Levittowners: Ways of Life and Politics in a New Suburban Community.* New York: Pantheon, 1967.

Garrow, David. *Bearing the Cross.* New York: William Morrow & Co., 1986.

Geller, Larry and Joel Specter with Patricia Romanowski. *"If I Can Dream": Elvis's Own Story.* New York: Simon & Schuster, 1989.

Gifford, Barry and Lawrence Lee. *Jack's Book.* New York: St. Martin's Press, 1978.

Goldman, Albert. *Elvis.* New York: McGraw-Hill, 1981.

Goldman, Eric. *The Crucial Decade: America 1945–1955.* New York: Knopf, 1956.

Goodchild, Peter. *J. Robert Oppenheimer: Scatterer of Worlds.* Boston: Houghton Mifflin, 1981.

Goodwin, Richard N. *Remembering America: A Voice from the Sixties.* Boston: Little, Brown & Co., 1988.

Gorman, Joseph Bruce. *Kefauver.* New York: Oxford University Press, 1971.

Goulden, Joseph. *The Best Years: 1945–1950.* New York: Atheneum, 1976.

Goulden, Joseph C. *Korea: The Untold Story.* New York: Times Books, 1982.

Gray, Madeline. Margaret Sanger: *A Biography of the Champion of Birth Control.* New York: R. Malek, 1979.

Green, Harold P. "The Oppenheimer Case: A Study into the Abuse of Law." *The Bulletin of the Atomic Scientist,* September, 1977.

Greenshaw, Wayne. *Alabama on My Mind.* Boulder: Sycamore Press, 1987.

Grossman, James K. *Black Southerners and the Great Migration.* Chicago: University of Chicago Press, 1989.

Guiles, Fred L. *Legend: The Life and Death of Marilyn Monroe.* Toronto: Madison Press Books, 1985.

Guiles, Fred L. *Norma Jean: The Life of Marilyn Monroe.* New York: Paragon House, 1993.

Gunther, John. *Inside USA.* New York: Harper, 1947.

Guralnick, Peter. *Feel Like Going Home.* New York: Perennial Library, 1989.

Hagerty, James C. *The Diary of James C. Hagerty: Eisenhower in Mid Course.* Bloomington: Indiana University Press, 1983.

Haining, Peter, ed. *Elvis in Private.* New York: St. Martin's Press, 1987.

Halberstam, David. *The Reckoning.* New York: Morrow, 1986.

Halberstam, David. *The Powers that Be.* New York: Knopf, 1979.

Harris, Warren G. *Lucy & Desi.* New York: Doubleday & Co., 1990.

Hastings, Max. *The Korean War.* New York: Simon & Schuster, 1987.

Hearings of the Subcommittee of the Committee on Interstate and Foreign Commerce, Eighty-Sixth Congress, II, Vol. 51.

Hendrik, George. *The Selected Letters of Mark Van Doren.* Baton Rouge: LSU Press, 1987.

Hewlett, Richard and Francis Duncan. *Atomic Shield: A History of the U.S. Atomic Energy Commission.* University Park: Pennsylvania State University Press, 1969.

Higham, Charles. *Brando: The Unauthorized Biography.* New York: New American Library, 1987.

Hine, Thomas. *Populuxe.* New York: Knopf, 1986.

Hiss, Tony. *Laughing Last: Alger Hiss.* Boston: Houghton Mifflin Co., 1977.

Holmes, John Clellon. *Go.* New York: Thunder's Mouth Press, 1988.

Hopkins, Jerry. *Elvis: The Final Years.* New York: Berkley, 1983.

Hoopes, Townsend. *The Devil and John Foster Dulles.* Boston: Little, Brown and Co., 1973.

Hoover, J. Edgar. *Masters of Deceit: The Story of Communism in America and How to Fight It.* New York: Henry Holt, 1958.

Horowitz, Irving L. *C. Wright Mills: An American Utopian.* New York: The Free Press, 1983.

Huckaby, Elizabeth. *Crisis at Central High: Little Rock 1957–1958.* Baton Rouge: LSU Press, 1980.

Hughes, John Emmet. *The Ordeal of Power.* New York: Atheneum, 1963.

Huie Letters at Ohio State University.

Hunt, Howard. *Give Us This Day.* New Rochelle: Arlington House, 1971.

Immerman, Richard. *The CIA in Guatamala: The Foreign Policy of Intervention.* Austin: University of Texas Press.

Institutional VFM Interview

Jackson, Kenneth T. *Crabgrass Frontier: The Suburbanization of the United States.* New York: Oxford University Press, 1985.

James, Clayton D. *The Years of MacArthur: Triumph and Disaster, 1945–1964,* Vol. III. Boston: Houghton Mifflin, 1985.

Johnson, Haynes. *The Bay of Pigs.* New York: Norton, 1964.

Kazan, Elia. *A Life.* New York: Knopf, 1988.

Keats, John. *The Crack in the Picture Window.* Boston: Houghton Mifflin, 1957.

Kempton, Murray. *Part of Our Time.* New York: Delta Books, 1955.

Kennan, Erland A. and Edmund H. Harvey. *Mission to the Moon.* New York: Morrow, 1969.

Kennedy, David. *Birth Control in America.* New Haven: Yale University Press, 1970.

Kerouac, Jack. *On the Road.* New York: NAL/Dutton, 1958.

King, Martin Luther, Sr. and Clayton Riley. *Daddy King: The Autobiography of Martin Luther King, Sr.* New York: William Morrow & Co., 1980.

Kluger, Richard. *Simple Justice: The History of Brown vs. the Board of Education & Black America's Struggle for Equality.* New York: Alfred A. Knopf, 1975.

Knox, Donald with additional text by Alfred Coppel. *The Korean War: An Oral History- Pusan to Chosin.* San Diego, California: Harcourt Brace Jovanovich, 1985.

Kroc, Ray with Robert Anderson. *Grinding It Out: The Making of McDonald's.* Chicago: Contemporary Books, 1977.

Lamm, Michael. *Chevrolet 1955: Creating the Original.* Stockton, CA: Lamm-Morada Inc., 1991.

Lamont, Lansing. *Day of Trinity.* New York: Atheneum, 1965.

Lapp, Ralph. *The Voyage of the Lucky Dragon.* New York: Harper and Row, 1958.

Larrabee, Eric. "Six Thousand Houses That Levitt Built." *Harper's,* No. 1971: September, 1948.

Lewis, Richard. *Appointment on the Moon.* New York: Viking, 1968.

Lilienthal, David. *The Journals of David Lilienthal: The Atomic Energy Years, 1945– 1950,* Vol. 2. New York: Harper and Row, 1964–1983.

Love, John. *McDonald's: Behind the Arches.* New York: Bantam, 1986.

Lurie, Leonard. *The Running of Richard Nixon.* New York: Coward, McCann, and Geoghegan, 1972.

Lyon, Peter. *Eisenhower: Portrait of a Hero.* New York: Little, Brown, 1974.

Maharidge, Dale and Michael Williamson. *And Their Children Came After Them.* New York: Pantheon, 1990.

Mailer, Norman. *Marilyn.* New York: Warner Books, 1975.

McCann, Graham. *Marilyn Monroe: The Body in the Library*. New Brunswick: Rutgers University Press, 1988.

McCullough, David. *Truman*. New York: Simon & Schuster, 1992.

The McDonald's Museum, Oak Park, CA; Tapes and letters.

McDougall, Walter A. *The Heavens and the Earth*. New York: Basic Books, 1985.

McKeever, Porter. *Adlai Stevenson: His Life and Legacy*. New York: William Morrow, 1989.

McLellan, David and Dean Acheson, eds. *Among Friends: The Personal Letters of Dean Acheson*. New York: Dodd Mead, 1980.

Manchester, William. *The Glory and the Dream: A Narrative History of America 1932– 1972*. Boston: Little, Brown and Co., 1973.

Manchester, William Raymond. *American Caesar: Douglas MacArthur*. Boston: Little, Brown, 1978.

Marshall, S.L.A. *The River and the Gauntlet*. New York: William and Co., 1953.

Martin, John Bartlow. *Adlai Stevenson of Illinois: The Life of Adlai Stevenson*. New York: Doubleday, 1976.

Mathews, Herbert L. *A World in Revolution*. New York: Scribners, 1971.

Mayer, Martin. *Madison Avenue, USA*. New York: Harper and Bros., 1954.

Mazo, Earl. *Nixon: A Political and Personal Portrait*. New York: Harper and Bros., 1959.

Medaris, John B. *Countdown for Decision*. New York: G.P. Putnam's Sons, 1960.

Meehan, Diana. *Ladies of the Evening: Women Characters of Prime-Time Television*. Metchuen, NJ: Scarecrow Press, 1983.

"Meeting of Minds," *Time*. Vol LXXII: September 15, 1958.

Michelmore, Peter. *The Swift Years: The Robert Oppenheimer Story*. New York: Dodd, Mead, and Co., 1969.

Miles, Barry. *Ginsberg: A Biography*. New York: Simon & Schuster, 1989.

Miller, Arthur. *Timebends: A Life*. New York: Grove Press, 1987.

Miller, Merle. *Plain Speaking*. New York: G.P. Putnam's Sons, 1974.

"Mr. Little Ol' Rust," *Fortune*. Vol XLVI: December, 1952.

The Montgomery Advertiser, July 10, 1954.

Morella, Joe and Edward Z. Epstein. *Forever Lucy: The Life of Lucille Ball*. New York: Carol Publishing Group, 1986.

Morgan, Ted. *Literary Outlaw*. New York: Henry Holt, 1988.

Moritz, Michael. *Going for Broke: The Chrysler Story*. Garden City, New York: Doubleday, 1981.

Morris, Roger. *Richard Milhous Nixon*. New York: Henry Holt, 1989.

Morris, Roger. *Richard Nixon: The Rise of an American Politician*. New York: Henry Holt, 1990.

Mosley, Leonard. *Dulles: A Biography of Eleanor, Allen, and John Foster Dulles and their Family Network*. New York: Dial Press, 1978.

Moss, Norman. *Men Who Play God: The Story of the H-bomb and How the World Came to Live With It*. New York: Harper and Row, 1968.

"Most House for the Money," *Fortune*. Vol. XLVI: October, 1952.

Museum of Radio and Television Broadcasting; Tapes.

Nader, Ralph. *Unsafe at Any Speed*. New York: Grossman, 1965.

Nelson, N. Walter Henry. *Small Wonder: The Amazing Story of Volkswagen*. New York: Little, Brown & Co., 1967.

The New York Times, Vol. VIII: April 8, 1934, 6:4

Nicosia, Gerald. *Memory Babe: A Critical Biography of Jack Kerouac*. Fred Jordan, ed. New York: Grove Press, 1983.

Nixon, Julie. *Pat Nixon: The Untold Story*. New York: Simon & Schuster, 1986.

Norton-Taylor, Duncan. "The Controversial Mr. Strauss." *Fortune*. Vol. L: January, 1955.

Oates, Stephen B. *Let the Trumpet Sound: The Life of Martin Luther King, Jr.,* New York: Harper & Row, 1982.

O'Reilly, Kenneth. *Hoover and the Un-Americans: The FBI, HUAC, and the Red Menace.* Philadelphia: Temple University Press, 1983.

Oshinsky, David. *A Conspiracy So Immense.* New York: Free Press, 1983.

Ottley, Roi. *The Lonely Warrior: The Life and Times of Robert S. Abbot.* Chicago: Henry Regnery, 1955.

Packard, Vance Oakely Packard. *The Hidden Persuaders.* New York: Pocket Books, 1981.

Parry, Albert. *Russia's Rockets and Missiles.* New York: Doubleday, 1960.

Patterson, James T. *Mr. Republican.* Boston: Houghton Mifflin, 1972.

Pauly, Phillip. *Controlling Life: Jacques Loeb and the Engineering Ideal in Biology.* New York: Oxford University Press, 1987.

Pepitone, Lena and William Stadiem. *Marilyn Monroe Confidential.* New York: Simon & Schuster, 1979.

Phillips, David Atlee. *The Night Watch.* New York: Atheneum, 1972.

Pomeroy, Wardell B. *Dr. Kinsey and the Institute for Sex Research.* New York: Harper and Row, 1972.

Potter, David. *People of Plenty.* Chicago: University of Chicago Press, 1954.

Powers, Francis Gary with Curt Gentry. *Operation Overflight.* New York: Holt Rinehart and Winston, 1970.

Powers, Richard. *G-Men: Hoover's FBI in American Popular Culture.* Carbondale: Southern Illinois University Press, 1983.

Powers, Richard. *Secrecy and Power: The Life of J. Edgar Hoover.* New York: Free Press, 1987.

Prados, John. *The Sky Would Fall.* New York: Dial Press, 1983.

Prados, John. *The Soviet Estimate.* New York: Dial Press, 1982.

Presley, Dee and Billy, Rich, and David Stanley with Martin Torgoff. *We Love You Tender.* New York: Delacorte Publishing, 1980.

Press, Howard. *C. Wright Mills.* Boston: Twayne Publishers, 1978.

Pringle, Peter and James Spigelman. *The Nuclear Barons.* New York: Holt, Rinehart, and Winston, 1981.

Quain, Kevin, ed. *The Elvis Reader.* New York: St. Martin's Press, 1992.

Raines, Howell. *My Soul is Rested: Movement Days in the Deep South Remembered.* New York: Putnam Publishing Group, 1977.

Ratcliff, J. D., "No Father to Guide Them," *Colliers.* March 20, 1937.

Reed, James. *From Private Vice to Public Virtue.* New York: Basic Books, 1978.

Rhodes, Richard. *The Making of the Atomic Bomb.* New York: Simon & Schuster, 1986.

Ridgway, Matthew. *The Korean War.* New York: Doubleday & Co., 1967.

Roosevelt, Kermit. *Countercoup: The Struggle for the Control of Iran.* New York: McGraw Hill, 1979.

Rosenbaum, Ron. "The House that Levitt Built." *Esquire,* No. 100, December, 1983.

Rothe, Anna and Evelyn Lohr, eds. *Current Biography: Who's News and Why, 1952.* New York: H. W. Wilson Co., 1953.

Rovere, Richard. "What Course for the Powerful Mr. Taft?" *The New York Times Magazine,* March 22, 1953.

Roy, Jules. *The Battle of Dien Bien Phu.* London: Faber, 1965.

Rubin, Barry. *Paved With Good Intention: The American Experience and Iran.* New York: Oxford University Press, 1980.

Russell, Bill. *Go Up for Glory.* New York: Berkley Publishing, 1980.

Ryan, Mary P. *Womanhood in America: From Colonial Times to the Present.* Danbury, CT: Franklin Watts, Inc., 1975.

Sakharov, Andrei, trans. Richard Lourie. *Memoirs.* New York: Knopf, 1990.

Salisbury, Harison. *Without Fear of Favor: The New York Times and Our Times.* New York: Times Books, 1980.

Schlesinger, Stephen and Stephen Kinzer. *Bitter Fruit: The Untold Story of the American Coup in Guatamala.* New York: Doubleday, 1982.

Schwartz, Bernard and Stephan Lesher. *Inside the Warren Court, 1953–1969.* New York: Doubleday & Co., 1983.

Schwartz, Bernard. *Super Chief: Earl Warren and His Supreme Court, A Judicial Biography.* New York: New York University Press, 1983.

Selvin, Joel. *Ricky Nelson: Idol for a Generation.* Chicago: Contemporary Books, 1990.

Selznick, Irene Mayer. *A Private View.* New York: Knopf, 1983.

Serrin, William. *The Company and the Union: The Civilized Relationship of the General Motors Corporations and the United Automobile Workers.* New York: Knopf, 1973.

Sheehan, Robert. "How Harland Curtice Earns his $750,000." *Fortune,* No. 53, February, 1956.

Shepley, James and Clay Blair. *Hydrogen Bomb: The Men, The Menace, The Mechanism.* Westport, CT: Greenwood Publishing Group, 1971.

Shickel, Richard. *Brando: A Life in Our Times.* New York: Atheneum, 1991.

Simon, James F. *The Antagonists: Hugo Black, Felix Frankfurter, and Civil Liberties in Modern America.* New York: Simon & Schuster, 1989.

Smith, Alice Kimball and Carles Weiner, eds. *J. Robert Oppenheimer: Letters and Recollections.* Cambridge, Mass.: Harvard University Press, 1980.

Smith, Richard Norton. *Thomas Dewey and His Times.* New York: Simon & Schuster, 1982.

Smith, Wayne. *The Closest of Enemies.* New York: Norton, 1987.

Sochen, June. *Movers & Shakers: American Women Thinkers and Activists, 1900–1970.* New York: Times Books, 1974.

Stern, Philip M. *The Oppenheimer Case: Security on Trial.* with the collaboration of Harold P. Green, special commentary by Lloyd K. Garrison. New York: Harper & Row, 1969.

Stone, Joseph and Tim Yohn. Prime Time and Misdemeanors. New Brunswick: Rutgers University Press, 1992.

Strauss, Lewis. *Men and Decisions.* Garden City, N.Y.: Doubleday, 1962.

Street, James H. *The New Evolution in Cotton Economy.* Chapel Hill: University of North Carolina Press, 1957.

Sullivan, William C. *The Bureau: My Thirty Years in Hoover's FBI.* New York: Norton, 1979.

Sulzberger, C.L. *The Last of the Giants.* Boston: Macmillan, 1970.

Sulzberger, C.L. *A Long Row of Candles: Memoirs and Diaries 1934–1954.* New York: Macmillan, 1969.

Summers, Anthony. *Goddess: The Secret Lives of Marilyn Monroe.* New York: NAL/ Dutton, 1986.

Szasz, Verenc Morton. *The Day the Sun Rose Twice: The Story of the Trinity Site Nuclear Explosion, July 16, 1945.* Albequerque: Univeristy of New Mexico Press, 1984.

Szulc, Tad. *Fidel: A Critical Portrait.* New York: Morrow, 1986.

Talese, Gay. *Thy Neighbor's Wife.* New York: Doubleday & Co., 1980.

Taylor, Robert. *Fred Allen: His Life and Wit.* Boston: Little, Brown and Co., 1989.

Theoharis, Athan G. and John Stuart Cox. *The Boss: J. Edgar Hoover and the Great American Inquisition.* Philadelphia: Temple University Press, 1988.

Theoharis, Athan G. *The Yalta Myths: An Issue in U.S. Politics, 1945–1955.* Columbia, Mo.: University of Missouri Press, 1970.

Thomas, Evan and Walter Issacson. *The Wise Men: Six Friends and the World they Made.* New York: Simon & Schuster, 1988.

Tilman, Rick. *C. Wright Mills: A Native Radical and His American Intellectual Roots.* University Park: Penn State University Press, 1984.

Truman, Margaret. *Harry S. Truman.* New York: William Morrow and Co., 1973.

Ulam, S.M. *Adventures of a Mathematician.* New York: Scribner's, 1976.

Van Doren, Mark. *The Autobiography of Mark Van Doren.* New York: Harcourt, Brace, Jovanovich, 1958.

Vaughan, Paul. *The Pill on Trial.* New York: Coward-McCann Inc., 1970.

Vineberg, Steven. *Method Actors.* New York: Schirmer Books, 1991.

Wakefield, Dan. *New York in the Fifties.* New York: Houghton Mifflin, Seymour, Lawrence, 1992.

Ward, Ed and Geoffrey Stokes and Ken Tucker. *Rock of Ages:* The Rolling Stone *History of Rock & Roll.* New York: Simon & Schuster, 1986.

Warren, Earl. *The Memoirs of Earl Warren.* New York: Doubleday & Co., 1977.

Watson, Thomas H. and Peter Petre. *Father, Son and Co.* New York: Bantam, 1990.

Weaver, John D. *Earl Warren: The Man, The Court, The Law.* Boston: Little, Brown, Inc., 1967.

Weinstein, Allen. *Perjury: The Hiss-Chambers Case.* New York: Knopf, 1978.

Wertheim, Arthur. *The Rise and Fall of Milton Berle in American History, American Television.* New York: Times Books, 1978.

Weyr, Thomas. *Reaching for Paradise: The Playboy Vision of America.* New York: Times Books, 1978.

White, G. Edward. *Earl Warren: A Public Life.* New York: Oxford University Press, 1987.

Whitfield, Stephen. *A Death in the Delta.* New York: Free Press, 1988.

"Who's a Liar," *Life.* Vol. 30, No. 14: April 2, 1951.

Wickware, Francis Still. "Report on Kinsey." *Life,* August 2, 1948.

Wilford, John Noble. "Wernher von Braun, Rocket Pioneer Dies," *The New York Times.* Vol. CXXVI: June 18, 1977.

Williams, Edwina Dakin as told to Lucy Freedman. *Remember me to Tom.* New York: G. P. Putnam's Sons, 1963.

Williams, Robert Chadwell. *Klaus Fuchs, Atom Spy.* Cambridge, Massachusetts: Harvard University Press, 1987.

Williams, Tennessee. *Memoirs.* Garden City, New York: Doubleday and Co., 1975.

Wilson, Sloan. *The Man in the Gray Flannel Suit.* New York: Simon & Schuster, 1955.

Windham, Donald. *Lost Friendships.* New York: William Morrow and Co., 1983.

Wise, David and Tom Ross. *The Invisible Government.* New York: Bantam, 1964.

Wise, David and Tomas B. *The U-2 Affair.* New York: Random House, 1962.

Wyden, Peter. *Bay of Pigs.* New York: Simon & Schuster, 1979.

Ydigoras, Miguel Fuentes. *My War with Communism.* Englewood Cliffs, NJ: Prentice Hall, 1963.

Yeakey, Lamont. *The Montgomery Bus Boycott, 1955–1956.* Unpublished Phd. thesis, Columbia University.

Yergin, Daniel. *Shattered Peace.* New York: Penguin, 1990.

Yergin, Daniel. *The Prize: The Epic Quest for Oil, Money and Power.* New York: Simon & Schuster, 1991.

York, Herbert F. *The Advisors: Oppenheimer, Teller and the Superbomb.* Stanford, Ca.: Stanford University Press, 1989.

NOTES

CHAPTER ONE

p. 4 ALL MIDDLE CLASS CITIZENS OF: Smith, *Thomas Dewey and His Times,* p. 554.

5 TOM DEWEY HAS NO REAL: Patterson, *Mr. Republican,* p. 269.

6 THE BAREFOOT BOY FROM WALL: Smith, p. 306.

6 THE CHOCOLATE SOLDIER: Smith, p. 487.

6 IF YOU READ THE *CHICAGO:* Smith, p. 35.

6 COLD—COLD AS A FEBRUARY: Smith, p. 299.

6 HE STRUTS SITTING DOWN: Patterson, p. 547.

7 THOSE CONGRESSIONAL BUMS: Smith, p. 513.

7 CAMPAIGNING FOR THE PRESIDENTIAL NOMINATION: Smith, p. 529.

7 SMILE, GOVERNOR: Smith, p. 26.

7 HE HAD FORBIDDEN ONE OF: Smith, p. 471.

7 YOU CAN'T SHOOT AN IDEA: Smith, p. 487.

7 GOING AROUND LOOKING UNDER BEDS: Smith, p. 507.

8 HIS FACE WAS SO SMALL: Interview with Herbert Brownell.

8 HIS PLATFORM, SAID SAMUEL ROSENMAN: Smith, p. 504.

8 TO THESE HISTORIC FOUR SENTENCES: Patterson, p. 425.

9 INTO THE WRONG WAR: Caute, *The Great Fear: The Anti-Communist Purge Under Truman and Eisenhower*, p.41.

10 COMMUNISM AND REPUBLICANISM: Caute, p. 26.

10 PARTY LABELS DON'T MEAN ANYTHING: Morris, *Richard Nixon: The Rise of an American Politician*, p. 745.

10 WHEN I TOOK UP MY: Chambers, *Witness*, p. 741.

10 WHO GOES OUT EVERY MORNING: Patterson, p. 477.

10 I WATCH HIS SMART-ALECK: Thomas and Isaacson, *The Wise Men: Six Friends and the World They Made*, p. 547.

11 SHAVE IT OFF: Caute, pp. 42–43.

11 MY MOTHER'S ENTHUSIASM FOR THE: McLellan and Acheson, *Among Friends: The Personal Letters of Dean Acheson*, p. 2.

11 WAS NOT A MODERN, CENTRALIZED: McLellan, p. 189.

12 IF YOU AND ALGER ARE: Weinstein, *Perjury: The Hiss Chambers Case*, p. 10.

12 DON'T WORRY LITTLE ONE: Weinstein, p. 8.

12 AN AMERICAN GENTLEMAN, ONE OF: Cooke, *A Generation on Trial*, pp. 107–8.

13 LET'S WASH OUR HANDS OF: Cooke, p. 15.

13 NIXON HAD HIS HAT SET: Cooke, pp. 16–17.

13 I AM AN OUTCAST: Chambers, pp. 148–49.

13 THERE WAS NO ONE WHO: Interview with Murray Kempton.

15 AS 1949 WENT ON: Goldman, *The Crucial Decade*, p. 104.

15 THERE WAS A STRONG DESIRE: Cooke, p. 9.

16 EACH GOT THE OTHER WRONG: Interview with Murray Kempton.

16 THAT, ACCORDING TO ONE OF: Hiss, *Laughing Last*, p. 132.

16 HE RECKLESSLY LUMPS SOCIALISTS, PROGRESSIVES: Weinstein, p. 519.

17 WE KNEW THAT AT YALTA: Theoharis, *The Yalta Myths*, p. 93.

17 IT SEEMS THAT THE ONLY: Theoharis, pp. 78–79.

17 I DO NOT INTEND TO: Goldman, p. 134.

18 CHRIST'S WORDS SETTING FORTH COMPASSION: Goldman, p. 134.

18 HAD HE, MUSED SCOTTY RESTON: McLellan, p. 221.

18 A TREMENDOUS AND UNNECESSARY GIFT: Goldman, pp. 134–35.

18 ONE MUST BE TRUE TO: McLellan, p. 227.

18 WE HAVE GOT TO UNDERSTAND: Goldman, p. 125.

19 WE ARE FACED WITH EXACTLY: Yergin, p. 350.

CHAPTER TWO

21 THE GREAT WHITE JAIL: Truman, *Harry S Truman*, p. 260.

21 TWO-DOLLAR WORDS: Truman, p. 26.

21 HAD BREAKFAST IN THE COFFEE SHOP: Ferrell, *Dear Bess: the Letters from Harry to Bess Truman 1910–1959*, p. 468.

22 HIS UNUSUALLY BAD EYESIGHT: McCullough, *Truman*, p. 41.

22 THANKS TO THE RIGHT LIFE: Ferrell, p. 478.

22 THREE THINGS RUIN A MAN: McCullough, p. 181.

23 BRIGHT GRAYNESS: McCullough, p. 333.

23 A MAN OF IMMENSE DETERMINATION: Truman, p. 268.

23 STRAIGHTFORWARD, DECISIVE, SIMPLE, ENTIRELY HONEST: McCullough, p. 351.

23 HE MUSED ABOUT HOW MANY: Donovan, *Tumultuous Years*, p. 155.

24 SHORTLY AFTER TRUMAN'S INAUGURATION AS: Truman, p. 415.

24 IF IT EXPLODES—AS I: Blumberg and Owens, *Energy and Conflict: The Life of Edward Teller*, p. 149.

24 NOW I KNOW WHAT HAPPENED: Moss, *Men Who Play God: The Story of the H-Bomb and How the World Came to Live with It*, p. 34.

25 THE ARMY THOUGHT THE SOVIETS: Blair and Shepley, *The Hydrogen Bomb: The Men, the Menace, the Mechanism*, p. 13.

25 THAT THE RUSSIANS COULD NOT: Rhodes, *The Making of the Atomic Bomb*, p. 760.
25 WHEN HE FIRST MET HEAD: Davis, *Lawrence and Oppenheimer*, p. 260.
26 ARE YOU SURE?: Moss, p. 24.
26 HE THEN SPECULATED THAT CAPTURED: Lilienthal, *The Journals of David Lilienthal*, p. 571.
26 I'M NOT CONVINCED THAT RUSSIA: Moss, p. 25.
26 WHAT WE'D FEARED EVER SINCE: Lilienthal, p. 570.
26 THIS IS NOW A DIFFERENT: Donovan, p. 99.
26 RUSSIA HAS SHOWN HER TEETH: Donovan, p. 103.
26 STAY STRONG AND HOLD ON: Davis, p. 294.
26 THE ERA WHEN WE MIGHT: Pringle and Spigelman, *The Nuclear Barons*, p. 88.
27 INDEED AMERICA'S DEMOBILIZATION: Donovan, *Conflict and Crisis: The Presidency of Harry S Truman, 1945–1948*, p.127.
27 AROUND A TABLE WAS A: Collins, *War in Peacetime: The History and Lessons of Korea*, p. 39.
28 UNKNOWN TO TRUMAN AT THE: Lamont, *Day of Trinity*, p. 261.
28 A SCIENTIST CANNOT HOLD BACK: Lamont, p. 261.
29 IN THE LAST MILLISECOND: Szasz, *The Day the Sun Rose Twice: The Story of the Trinity Nuclear Explosion, July 16, 1945*, p. 89.
29 NOW WE'RE ALL SONS: Lamont, p. 242.; Szasz, p. 90.
29 OPPENHEIMER HIMSELF WENT BACK: Oppenheimer, *Letters and Recollections*, p. 297.
29 WHEN JAMES CONANT RETURNED: Szasz, p. 203.
29 YOU WILL BELIEVE THAT THIS: Oppenheimer, p. 297.
29 GIVEN THE FACT THAT IN: Rhodes, p. 563.
29 THE MORE WE WORKED: Rhodes, pp. 416–17
30 BETTER BE A SLAVE UNDER: Blumberg and Owens, p. 121.
30 AN IMMENSE GULF BETWEEN THE: Bundy, *Danger and Survival: Choices About the Bomb in the First Fifty Years*, p. 198.
30 THE BOMB, WHOSE GLARE ILLUMINATED: Alsop, Joseph and Stewart, *We Accuse*, p. 6.
31 I. I. RABI, THE NOBEL LAUREATE: Davis, p. 185.
31 THERE, JOHNNY VON NEUMANN: Alvarez, *Alvarez: Adventures of a Physicist*, p. 130.
31 A SPIRIT OF ATHENS: Davis, p. 186.
31 WHEN ANYONE MENTIONS LABORATORY DIRECTORS: Davis, p. 182.
32 HE WAS SO MUCH SMARTER: Interview with Victor Weisskopf.
32 YOU DON'T UNDERSTAND ENOUGH ABOUT: Interview with Victor Weisskopf.
32 ASK ME A QUESTION IN LATIN: Blumberg and Owens, p. 76.
32 I WAS AN UNCTUOUS, REPULSIVELY: Pringle and Spigelman, p. 114.
32 YEARS LATER, DESPITE HIS IMMENSE: Oppenheimer, pp. 61 and 300.
32 THERE WAS A TERRIBLE SADNESS: Interview with Victor Weisskopf.
33 TROUBLE IS THAT OPPIE IS: Michelmore, *The Swift Years: The Robert Oppenheimer Story*, p. 20.
33 I GOT OUT OF THERE: Blair and Shepley, pp. 32–33; and Michelmore, p. 23.
33 THERE'S A HUGE DIFFERENCE BETWEEN: Davis, p. 51.
33 WHY I CHOSE THAT NAME: Oppenheimer, p. 290.
34 IF THE RADIANCE OF A: Lamont, p. 297.
34 THE DAY AFTER THE NAGASAKI: Davis, p. 251.
34 IF YOU ASK: Rhodes, p. 758.
34 LET THE SECOND TEAM TAKE: Davis, p. 251.
34 HE REALLY IS A TRAGIC: Lilienthal, p. 69.
35 MOST IMPORTANT MILITARY RESOURCE: Rhodes, p. 751.
35 ON WHICH HE DREW LITTLE: Acheson, *Present at the Creation: My Years in the State Department*, p. 153.
35 MISTER PRESIDENT, I HAVE BLOOD: Donovan, p. 155.
36 THE GREATEST EVENT IN THE: Pringle and Spigelman, p. 93.

36 TOTAL POWER IN THE HANDS: Pringle and Spigelman, p. 93.
36 WOULD PUSH THE ADMINISTRATION: Donovan, vol. 2, p. 152.
36 WHAT SHALL WE DO: Rhodes, p. 767.
36 I'M NOT WORRYING ABOUT THE: Rhodes, p. 768.
37 FAILING TO GET OPPENHEIMER: Bernstein, *Hans Bethe: Prophet of Energy*, p. 94.
37 EDWARD, I'VE BEEN THINKING IT: Moss, p. 53.
37 I HAVE EXPLAINED THIS TO: Bernstein, p. 94.
38 SO MUCH SO THAT LESLIE: Goodchild, *J. Robert Oppenheimer: Shatterer of Worlds*, p. 93.
38 TRUMAN TOLD LILIENTHAL THAT STRAUSS: Lilienthal, p. 89.
38 BUT IN 1917, WHEN HE: Strauss, *Men and Decisions*, p. 6.
38 WHEN DO YOU WANT TO: Strauss, p. 8.
39 HE HAS MORE ELBOWS THAN: Norton-Taylor, "The Controversial Mr. Strauss," *Fortune*, January 1955.
39 ALL PLIABILITY: Alsop and Alsop, p. 19.
39 VERY SMART AND VERY VAIN: Donovan, p. 150.
39 FAR LESS IMPORTANT THAN ELECTRONIC: Stern, *The Oppenheimer Case: Security on Trial*, p. 130; and Davis, pp. 289–90.
39 IT SEEMS TO ME THAT: Blumberg and Owens, p. 202.
40 ON THE OTHER HAND: Donovan, p. 152.
41 ELFRIEDE SEGRE WOULD WATCH HIM: Lamont, p. 78.
41 STANISLAW ULAM, THE BRILLIANT MATHEMATICIAN: Williams, *Klaus Fuchs: Atom Spy*, pp. 40 and 76.
42 WHAT CONCERNS ME IS REALLY NOT: Oppenheimer, pp. 89–90.
43 OVER MY DEAD BODY: Stern, p. 138.
43 THERE ARE GRADES OF MORALITY: Lilienthal, p. 581.
43 MAKES ME FEEL I WAS: Lilienthal, p. 581.
43 ONLY PSYCHOLOGICAL: Davis, p. 312.
43 AS LONG AS YOU PEOPLE: York, *The Advisors: Oppenheimer, Teller, and the Superbomb*, p. 65.
44 ENOUGH EVIL HAD BEEN BROUGHT: Bundy, p. 216.
44 I DON'T BLITZ EASILY: Lilienthal, p. 594.
44 WE KEEP SAYING: Lilienthal, p. 577.
45 I DON'T THINK SO: Williams, p. 2.
45 ON JANUARY 27, 1950, AN: Williams, p. 116.
46 HE DID NOT, THE PRESIDENT: Williams, p. 116.
46 CAN THE RUSSIANS DO IT: Lilienthal, Vol. 2, pp. 632–33.
46 THE ROOF FELL IN TODAY: Lilienthal, p. 634.
46 SENATOR BRIEN MCMAHON, LEWIS STRAUSS: Blumberg and Owens, p. 213.
46 IT WAS ALWAYS MY INTENTION: Williams, p. 134.
47 YES SIR, I'LL TELL THEM: Sakharov, *Memoirs*, p. 160.
47 THE SOVIET GOVERNMENT: Sakharov, p. 99.

CHAPTER THREE

50 IN THE MIDDLE OF A SPEECH: Bayley, *Joe McCarthy and the Press*, pp. 17–18.
51 "HOWARD SHIPLEY," MCCARTHY WROTE: Bayley, p. 29; author interview with Frank McCullough.
53 WHEN SOME CRITICISM OF MCCARTHY'S ATTACKS: Bayley, p. 14.
54 IN ONE OF HIS FIRST SPEECHES: Patterson, *Mr. Republican*, p. 444.
54 HE WAS, SAID HIS OLD FRIEND: Oshinsky, *A Conspiracy So Immense*, p. 503.
54 THEN HE ROARED WITH LAUGHTER: Bayley, p. 73.
54 "HE WAS," SAID SENATOR PAUL DOUGLAS: Oshinsky, p. 15.
55 HE GOES FORTH TO BATTLE: Oshinsky, p. 397
55 "I WASN'T OFF PAGE ONE: Oshinsky, p. 118

55 SO THE REPORTERS SAT THERE: Bayley, p. 130.
55 "JOE COULDN'T FIND A COMMUNIST: Bayley, p. 68
56 HE NEVER HAS ANY PLANS.": Bayley, p. 151.
56 TYDINGS, USING A SUBCOMMITTEE: Caute, *The Great Fear*, p. 36.
56 "HOW STUPID CAN YOU GET?": Beschloss, *Mayday*, p. 83.
57 "IF THE NEW DEAL IS STILL IN CONTROL: Oshinsky, p. 50.
57 WHERRY OF NEBRASKA, FAMOUS FOR: Oshinsky, p. 36.
57 AND WHELKER OF IDAHO, WHO FANCIED: Oshinsky, p. 133.
57 HE REFERRED TO PEOPLE IN THE STATE DEPARTMENT: Patterson, p. 443.
58 IT PORTRAYED TAFT AS THE SPOILED CHILD: Patterson, pp. 458–59.
58 HE SHOULD "KEEP TALKING AND IF ONE CASE: Patterson, p. 455.
59 BUT, AS ROVERE LATER WROTE: Rovere, "What Course for the Powerful Mr. Taft?", p. 9.
59 WHEN SPILLANE'S FIRST BOOK, *I, THE JURY: Life,* June 23, 1952.
59 HE WAS THE AVENGER: Kenneth Davis, *Two Bit Culture,* p. 181.
60 TERRY SOUTHERN NOTED: *Esquire,* July 1963.
60 VICTOR WEYBRIGHT, THE CHIEF EDITOR: *Fortune,* September 1963.
61 THE EVIL OF THE COMMUNISTS: Davis, p. 182.
61 JAMES SANDOE OF THE *HERALD TRIBUNE: Life,* June 23, 1952.
61 "NO, ANYBODY CAN BE A WINNER: *Esquire,* July 1963.

CHAPTER FOUR

62 "IF THE BEST MINDS HAD SET OUT: Goulden, *Korea: The Untold Story of the War,* p. 3.
62 "A SOUR LITTLE WAR,": Thomas and Isaacson, *The Wise Men,* p. 507.
63 THEY WERE, HE SAID, "THE SAME BREED: Blair, *The Forgotten War: America in Korea, 1950–1953,* p. 38.
64 "I AM NOT SUFFICIENTLY FAMILIAR: Blair, p. 39.
64 "REGARDING AMERICAN POLICY," HE ADDED: Hastings, *The Korean War,* p. 39.
64 "ITS POLITICAL LIFE IN THE COMING PERIOD": Blair, p. 41.
65 DEIGNING TO COME TO SEOUL: Blair, p. 44.
66 "DEAN REALLY BLEW IT: Author interview with Averell Harriman.
66 "[THE CHINESE PEOPLE] HAD NOT OVERTHROWN: Acheson, *Present at the Creation,* pp. 355–56.
67 TO OMAR BRADLEY, IT COULD: Bradley, *A General's Life,* p. 474.
67 THE TRUMAN DEFENSE BUDGET, CABELL PHILLIPS: Manchester, *American Caesar,* p. 550.
67 AS ACHESON ONCE NOTED, THE FOREIGN POLICY: Thomas and Isaacson, p. 338.
68 AS CHIANG COLLAPSED OF HIS OWN WEIGHT: Hastings, p. 43.
69 TRUMAN, REFLECTING THE FEARS OF MANY: Thomas and Isaacson, p. 544.
69 WHEN LT. GEN. MATTHEW RIDGWAY SAW THE FIRST: Ridgway, *The Korean War,* p. 192.
69 "WE ARE GOING TO FIGHT,": Blair, p. 67.
69 "BY GOD I AM NOT GOING TO: Blair, p. 67.
69 WE HAD TO DRAW THE LINE SOMEWHERE: Bradley, p. 535.
70 EVENTS WERE TAKING OVER: Bradley, p. 539.
70 ACCORDING TO GENERAL WILLIAM DEAN: Dean, *General Dean's Story,* p. 29.
70 "THEY HAD NOT ENLISTED,": Fehrenbach, *This Kind of War,* p. 148.
71 ONLY AS THEY BOARDED THE PLANES: Knox, *The Korean War,* p. 33.
71 WHEN WORD OF THE NORTH KOREAN: Knox, p. 6.
71 MOST OF ITS TRAINING HAD: Knox, p. 10.
71 ONE OF ITS OFFICERS WROTE LATER: Blair, p. 93.
71 ONE COLONEL IN THE 34TH INFANTRY: Fehrenbach, p. 109.
72 THE KOREANS CHEERED THEM AS THEY: Knox, P. 17.
72 NO THOUGHT OF RETREAT OR DISASTER: Blair, P. 98.
73 "THOSE ARE T-34 TANKS, SIR: Knox, p. 19.

74 INSTEAD OF A MOTLEY HORDE: Blair, p. 102.
75 BY JULY 10, JUST SIX DAYS: Blair, p. 101.
75 ONE DAY AFTER ARRIVAL IN-COUNTRY: Appleman, *South to Naktong*, p. 214–15.
76 WHEN ONE BATTALION COMMANDER, MORGAN: Blair, p. 214.
76 "WE ARE FIGHTING A BATTLE: Appleman, pp. 207–8.
77 MACARTHUR WAS SUPREMELY CONFIDENT: Blair, p. 188.

CHAPTER FIVE

79 FROM THEIR YEARS TOGETHER IN THE PHILIPPINES: Blair, *The Forgotten War: America in Korea, 1950–1953*, pp. 78–79
79 EISENHOWER THOUGHT A YOUNGER COMMANDER: Blair, pp. 78–79
79 "ARTHUR MACARTHUR," ONE OF HIS AIDES: Manchester, *American Caesar*, p. 30.
79 ON THE DAY OF HIS FINAL EXAM: Manchester, p. 47.
80 "YOU MUST GROW UP TO BE: Manchester, p. 41.
80 "I AM DEEPLY ANXIOUS: Manchester, p. 93.
80 "CONSIDERING THE FINE WORK: Manchester, p. 93.
80 SHE WROTE PERSHING: Manchester, p. 134.
80 WHEN HER SON BECAME CHIEF: Manchester, p. 144.
81 A DISTINGUISHED PORTRAIT PAINTER: Manchester, p. 111.
81 "NOT ONLY HAVE I MET HIM: Manchester, p. 166.
81 IN THEM THE CODE WORD: Manchester, p. 184.
82 ONLY MEDIOCRE COMMANDERS TRIED: Manchester, p. 369.
82 ROOSEVELT, WHO HAD ALWAYS RECOGNIZED: Manchester, pp. 357–58.
83 IT WILL BE LIKE AN ELECTRIC FAN: Hastings, *The Korean War*, p. 100.
83 "MAKE UP A LIST OF AMPHIBIOUS: Manchester, p. 574.
84 "I CAN ALMOST HEAR THE TICKING: Blair, p. 232.
84 REAR ADMIRAL JAMES DOYLE, WHOSE JOB: Manchester, p. 576.
84 THE NEXT DAY SHERMAN WAS AS NERVOUS: Blair, pp. 232–33.
84 "THE SORCERER OF INCHON: Thomas and Isaacson, *The Wise Men*, p. 537.
84 FROM THEN ON, MATT RIDGWAY: Ridgway, *The Korean War*, p. 44.
85 "PSYCHOLOGICALLY, IT WAS ALMOST: Blair, p. 237.
85 "AND WHAT TO DO WITH MR. PRIMA DONNA: Margaret Truman, *Harry S Truman*, p. 260.
86 "IF HE'D BEEN A LIEUTENANT: Miller, *Plain Speaking*, p. 294.
86 YEARS LATER, JOE COLLINS: J. Lawton Collins, *War in Peacetime*, p. 215.

CHAPTER SIX

87 "PLEASE DON'T TALK TO ME: Blumberg and Owens, *Energy and Conflict*, p. 21.
87 "WHEN HE WAS SIX: Blumberg and Owens, p. 3.
88 ANOTHER TEACHER ADDRESSED HIS: Blumberg and Owens, p. 23.
89 WE, MEN LIKE WEISSKOPF AND I: author interview with Hans Bethe.
90 STAN ULAM LATER WOULD REMEMBER: Ulam, *Adventures of a Mathematician*, p. 164.
90 "THAT I WAS NAMED TO HEAD: Bernstein, *Hans Bethe*, p. 81.
90 "ONE MIGHT SAY," BETHE COOLY NOTED: Bernstein, p. 81.
90 AS TELLER'S POSITION ON THE H-BOMB: interviews with Bethe and Weisskopf.
91 "HE WAS," SAID ENRICO FERMI: Blumberg and Owens, p. 185.
91 A FEW MONTHS LATER, A LIBRARIAN: interview with Serber.
91 INCREASINGLY HE BECAME FRIENDLY: interviews with Bethe and Weisskopf.
92 AND YET NONE KNEW BETTER: Stern, *The Oppenheimer Case*, p. 160.
92 SOMEWHAT TO HIS SURPRISE, SAKHAROV: interview with Jerome Weisner.
93 BECAUSE AN ELECTRON WEIGHED: Watson, *Father, Son, and Co.* p. 189.
93 "BECAUSE WE ARE SHARING: Watson, p. 135.
94 BECAUSE OF THIS OBSESSION: Aspery, *John von Neumann and the Origins of Modern Computing*, p. iv.

94 "IT ALL CAME SO EASILY FOR HIM: interview with Herman Goldstine.

95 WEYL INDEED SOLVED IT: interview with Herman Goldstine.

95 VON NEUMANN TURNED TO HERMAN: interview with Herman Goldstine.

95 IT WAS, ULAM THOUGHT: Ulam, p. 207.

96 EGALITARIAN SOCIETIES LIKE AMERICA: interview with Goldstine.

96 IT WAS IN DANGER: Watson, pp. 189–90.

97 OPPENHEIMER JOINED THEM: Ulam, p. 217.

97 THAT HELPED CONVINCE ULAM: Ulam, pp. 223–24.

97 ALL TELLER COULD SAY: interview with Bethe.

98 YET TO HIS SCIENTIFIC PEERS: interview with Bethe.

98 EARLIER GAC SKEPTICISM ABOUT: Rhodes, p. 772.

98 HIS EGOCENTRISM BECAME SOMETHING: Ulam, p. 212.

98 IT WEIGHED SOME SIXTY-FIVE TONS: Farre, ed., *The Diaries of James C. Hagerty*, p. 6.

99 AT THE TIME HE USED TO JOKE: Blumberg and Owens, p.290.

99 AS THE NEEDLE ON THE SEISMOGRAPH: Rhodes, p. 777.

99 TELLER SAID THAT HE: Rhodes, p. 296.

CHAPTER SEVEN

102 BUT THEIR WEAKNESSES WERE NOTED: Fehrenbach, *This Kind of War*, p. 300.

103 LATER HE CAME TO REFER TO THEM: Hastings, *The Korean War*, pp. 142–43.

104 "AFTER ALL," HE SAID: Hastings, p. 130.

104 "BY THAT TIME I COULD FEEL THE HAIR: Blair, *The Forgotten War: America in Korea, 1950–1953*, p. 371.

104 ONE NCO THOUGHT THE SITE: Knox, *The Korean War*, pp. 434–38.

104 SOME 600 MEN IN THE REGIMENT: Ridgway, *The Korean War*, p. 58.

105 DURING WORLD WAR TWO MACARTHUR: Acheson, *Present at the Creation*, p. 424.

105 JACK CHILES, ALMOND'S G-3: Blair, p. 377.

106 THEY HAD STRUCK WITH GREAT SUCCESS, Acheson, p. 466.

106 BUT, HE NOTED, "WE SAT AROUND: Thomas and Isaacson, *The Wise Men*, p. 537.

107 "IF SUCCESSFUL, THIS SHOULD FOR ALL: Blair, pp. 534–35.

107 AS CLAY BLAIR NOTED, IT TIPPED: Blair, pp. 534–35.

107 INSTEAD HE PLUNGED NORTHWARD: Ridgway, p. 86.

107 MACARTHUR, JOE COLLINS WROTE: Collins, *War in Peacetime*, p. 142.

108 "WE'RE STILL ATTACKING AND WE'RE: Blair, p. 462.

108 THE MOMENT ALMOND FLEW AWAY: Blair, p. 463.

108 "MY FRIEND, I'M SORRY: Marshall, *The River and the Gauntlet*, pp. 318–20.

109 VANDENBERG GAVE HIM A LONG LOOK: Ridgway, p. 62.

109 "THIS WAS," ACHESON LATER NOTED: Acheson, p. 475.

110 THEN MACARTHUR TOLD HIM: Ridgway, p. 83.

110 "HE WAS," NOTED A WEST POINT: Blair, *Ridgway's Paratroopers*, p. 6.

111 I'D SAY, "MATT, GET THE HELL: Blair, *Ridgway's Paratroopers*, p. 111.

111 THE MEN SEEMED TO GO ABOUT: Ridgway, p. 86.

111 "WE COULD GET OFF INTO: Ridgway, p. 89.

111 WHAT HE WANTED TO CREATE: Ridgway, p. 90.

111 "THE STRENGTH AND MEANS WE HAVE: Blair, *The Forgotten War: America in Korea, 1950–1953*, p. 159.

112 "MICHAELIS," HE ASKED, "WHAT: Blair, *The Forgotten War: America in Korea, 1950–1953*, p. 605.

112 ANOTHER HIGH OFFICER SAID: Blair, *The Forgotten War: America in Korea, 1950–1953*, p. 634.

112 "RIDGWAY ALONE," SAID COLLINS: Collins, p. 255.

112 AS OMAR BRADLEY, NOT A MAN: Bradley, *A General's Life*, p. 608.

112 YEARS LATER NOTING THAT AMERICA: Hastings, p. 188.

113 IN 1954 MACARTHUR TOLD JIM LUCAS: Ridgway, p. 159.

754 / NOTES

113 BY THIS TIME THE TOP BRITISH: Hastings, p. 200.
113 IN ORDER TO DO THIS HE WAS: Bradley, p. 616.
114 "I'VE COME TO THE CONCLUSION: Truman, *Off the Record,* pp 210–11.
114 HE KNEW THIS, HE SAID: Blair, *The Forgotten War: America in Korea, 1950–1953,* p. 801.
115 TRUMAN, TYPICALLY WAS BLUNTER: James, *The Years of MacArthur, Triumph and Disaster,* p. 616.

CHAPTER EIGHT

116 SHE SITS BESTRIDE THE WORLD: Goulden, *The Best Years: 1945–1950,* p. 426.
117 HE OWNED A CAR AND A HOUSE: Yergin, *The Prize: The Epic Quest for Oil, Money, and Power,* p. 541.
117 HAD MARX WITNESSED THE INDUSTRIAL EXPLOSION: Author interview with Naohiro Amaya.
118 IN 1949, COAL ACCOUNTED FOR TWO THIRDS: Yergin, p. 546.
118 LIKE MANY RETURNING VETERANS: Author interview with William Levitt.
118 WE AT GENERAL MOTORS: Cray, *Chrome Colossus: General Motors and Its Times,* p. 7.
119 THE TREATY OF DETROIT: Serrin, *The Company and the Union: The Civilized Relationship of the General Motors Corporation and the United Automobile Workers,* p. 170.
120 PEOPLE DON'T WANT THE KIND OF CAR: Cray, p. 348.
120 TYPICALLY, WHEN TWO BROTHERS: Author interview with Dick McDonald.
121 IMPRACTICAL TOYS: Serrin, p. 94.
122 I BELIEVE IT IS REASONABLE: Serrin, p. 91.
122 THE GROWTH OF CORPORATE ENTERPRISE: Cray, p. 278.
122 A BUYER COULD CHOOSE A CAR: Halberstam, *The Reckoning,* p. 96.
122 WE HAD NO STAKE: Bayley, *Harley Earl and the Dream Machine,* p. 29.
122 AFTER WORLD WAR TWO: Moritz, *Going for Broke: The Chrysler Story,* p. 52.
123 WERE BROUGHT ABOUT BY A DELIBERATE: Bayley, pp. 16–17.
123 THE TROUBLE WITH SMALL MODELS: Bayley, p. 38.
123 I'M HERE WITH HARLOW: Author's group interview with GM designers: Chuck Jordan, Bill Porter, Stan Parker, Paul Cillian, and Don Schwarz.
124 MY SENSE OF PROPORTION TELLS ME: Hine, *Populuxe,* p. 95.
124 AT THE LOWER HEIGHT: Author's group interview.
124 THE WORLD STANDS ASIDE: Author's goup interview.
124 THE COST TO THE COMPANY: Author interview with Robert Cumberford.
124 NO SON OF MINE: Author interview with Robert Cumberford.
125 EVEN HIS SHOES LOOKED: Author's group interview.
125 WELL THE NEXT TIME: Author's group interview.
125 IF IT HAD NOT, HE: Author's group interview.
126 HOW CAN YOU COMPLAIN: Author's group interview.
126 AT FORD HE WAS KNOWN: Author interview with Don Frey.
126 IS IT RESPONSIBLE TO CAMOUFLAGE: Hine, p. 93.
127 THE 1957 FORD WAS GREAT: Hine, p. 99.
127 GENERAL MOTORS IS IN BUSINESS: Author interview with Robert Cumberford.
127 LISTEN, I'D PUT SMOKE STACKS: Author interview with Stan Mott.
127 IT GAVE THEM [THE CUSTOMERS]: Hine, p. 83.
127 DYNAMIC OBSOLESCENCE: Hine, p. 85.
128 I AM A WRENCH AND PLIERS MAN: Halberstam, p. 322.
128 WHEN MOTHER NATURE FORMED PETROLEUM: Halberstam, p. 323.
128 FOUNDED BY WOODBRIDGE FERRIS: Author interview with Anthony De Lorenzo.
129 HE COULD SEE BEYOND THE FIGURES: Author interview with Anthony De Lorenzo.
129 HARLEY, WHAT DO YOU DRIVE: Author interview with Anthony De Lorenzo.
129 YOU NEVER STAND STILL: Cray, p. 354.

129 THE LAST PERSON TO REALLY RUN: Cray, p. 380.
130 YOU KNOW WHAT THE BOSS: Sheehan, "How Harland Curtice Earns His $750,000," *Fortune*, February 1956, p. 135.
130 FIFTY PERCENT, HELL: Author interview with Bunkie Knudson.
130 A ROUGH ESTIMATE: Cray, p. 362.
130 AN AVERAGE OF 4.5 MILLION: Cray, p. 362.

CHAPTER NINE

131 $5,000, WHICH WAS THEN: Fenton, *In Your Opinion*, p. 25.
131 RIGHT AFTER THE WAR: Goulden, *The Best Years: 1945–1950*, p. 426.
132 GRADUATE CARPENTERS: Author interview with William Levitt.
132 LEVITTOWN HOUSES WERE SOCIAL CREATIONS: Jackson, *Crabgrass Frontier: The Suburbanization of the United States*, p. 236.
132 NO MAN WHO OWNS HIS: Larrabee, "Six Thousand Houses That Levitt Built," *Harpers*, September 1948, p. 84.
133 THE NAVY PROVIDED HIM: Author interview with William Levitt.
133 JUST BEG, BORROW, OR STEAL: Author interview with William Levitt.
134 THE REAL ESTATE BOYS: Jackson, p. 233.
134 IN 1944 THERE HAD BEEN ONLY: Jackson, p. 233.
134 WE BELIEVE THAT THE MARKET: Larrabee, p. 87.
134 THE ORIGINAL NAME WAS SOMETHING: Author interview with William Levitt.
136 THE SAME MAN DOES THE SAME THING: "The Most House for the Money," *Fortune*, October 1952, p. 152.
137 EIGHTEEN HOUSES COMPLETED: Author interview with William Levitt.
138 A RETIRED MARX BROTHER: Larrabee, p. 79.
138 MY FATHER ALWAYS TAUGHT ME: Larrabee, p. 83.
138 THE JOB OF THE UNION: Author interview with William Levitt.
138 IF ONLY IN THREE-CENT STAMPS: Larrabee, p. 83.
139 FOR LITERALLY NOTHING DOWN: Keats, *The Crack in the Picture Window*, p. 7.
140 A MULTITUDE OF UNIFORM, UNIDENTIFIABLE: Jackson, p. 244.
140 ABOUT THE HORROR OF BEING: Rosenbaum, "The House that Levitt Built," *Esquire*, December 1983, p. 380.
140 NOW LEWIS MUMFORD CAN'T CRITICIZE: Gans, *The Levittowners: Ways of Life and Politics in a New Suburban Community*, p. 9.
141 I THINK BY NOW WE'VE SHOWN: Rosenbaum, p. 386.
141 THE NEGROES IN AMERICA: Currie, *Current Biography Yearbook* (1956), p. 375.
141 IN THE THIRD LEVITTOWN: Gans, p. 9.
142 BY 1955 LEVITT-TYPE SUBDIVISIONS: Jackson, p. 233.

CHAPTER TEN

Major sources: author interviews with Eugene and Isabelle Ferkauf and *More Than They Bargained For: The Rise and Fall of E.J. Korvetts* by Isadore Barmash.

CHAPTER ELEVEN

155 WE WERE BOTH PUSHING LIGHTS: Author interview with Dick McDonald.
156 PAT, I THINK YOU'VE OUTLIVED: Author interview with Dick McDonald.
156 WE WEREN'T GOING TO SELL: Author interview with Dick McDonald.
156 I CAN'T GIVE YOU THE FULL: Author interview with Dick McDonald.
156 MY GOD, THE CARHOPS WERE SLOW: Love, *McDonald's: Behind the Arches*, p. 14.
157 THE MORE WE HAMMERED AWAY: Love, p. 14.
158 POSING AS A FREE-LANCE WRITER: Author interview with Dick McDonald.
158 OUR WHOLE CONCEPT WAS BASED: Love, p. 14.
158 IN THIS, THEY WERE GREATLY: Love, p. 17.

159 IN 1952 THEY WERE ON: Love, p. 20.
159 I HAVE NEVER SEEN ANYTHING: Love, p. 25.
160 WHAT THE HELL FOR: Love, p. 22.
160 WE ARE GOING TO BE: Love, p. 23.
161 ON THE DAY OF THE SENIOR: Kroc with Anderson, *Grinding It Out: The Making of McDonalds,* p. 39.
161 YOU COULD MIX CONCRETE: Kroc, p. 6.
161 IN 1939 HE STARTED HIS OWN: Love, p. 34.
162 HE IMMEDIATELY LIKED WHAT HE: Kroc, p. 6.
161 MR. MULTIMIXER: Kroc, p. 8.
162 SOMETIME LATE IN THE NIGHT: Author interview with Fred Turner.
163 HAVE YOU FOUND A FRANCHISING: Love, p. 40.
163 IT WAS PRACTICALLY LIFE OR DEATH: Love, p. 47.
163 THESE WERE THE FORERUNNER: Author interview with Fred Turner.
164 THE PEOPLE WHO WOULD EAT: Author interview with Waddy Pratt.
164 I'VE MADE UP MY MIND THAT: Author interview with Waddy Pratt.
164 THAT DEMANDED A CONDIMENT STATION: Love, p. 142.
165 WE HAVE FOUND OUT, AS YOU HAVE: Love, p. 31.
165 EVERY NIGHT YOU'D SEE HIM: Love, p. 71.
166 HE GAVE HIS TOP PEOPLE: Author interview with Fred Turner and Dick Starmann.
166 THAT SOB BETTER BE GOOD: Love, p. 91.
166 MY NAME'S RAY KROC, AND I'M: Author interview with Waddy Pratt.
166 I GUESS YOU WISH YOU: Author interview with Dick Starmann.
167 FROM THE START HIS RESTAURANT: Love, p. 73.
167 NOTHING IN THE WORLD CAN: From tapes at the McDonald's Museum in Oak Park.
167 TO THE DAY HE DIED: Author interview with Turner and Starmann.
167 KROC WENT BALLISTIC AND DEMANDED: Author interview with Dick Starmann.
168 RAY, WHAT IN GOD'S NAME: Author interview with Waddy Pratt.
168 WHEN BEEF, STEAKS, AND CHOPS: Letter written December 17, 1969; in the McDonald's Museum.
168 RAY, YOU'VE GOT TO BE CRAZY: Love, p. 73.
169 HE TREATED HIS SUPPLIERS WELL: Love, pp. 129–30.
170 I PUT THE HAMBURGER ON: Love, p. 211.
170 RIDICULOUS TO CALL THIS: Institutional VFM interview.
170 IF THEY WERE DROWNING: The McDonald's Museum.
170 CONSIDER, FOR EXAMPLE, THE HAMBURGER BUN: Kroc, p. 92.
171 TOWARD THE END OF HIS LIFE: Author interview with Dick Starmann.
171 ART, I'M NOT NORMALLY A VINDICTIVE MAN: Love, p. 201.

CHAPTER TWELVE

Major sources: "Kemmons Wilson," *Time* magazine, June 12, 1972; "Kemmons Wilson and Holiday Inn," by Ed Weathers, *Memphis* magazine, September 1985. Author interviews with friends and family.

CHAPTER THIRTEEN

180 A DEVICE THAT PERMITS PEOPLE: Taylor, *Fred Allen: His Life and Wit,* p. 284.
181 TELEVISION WAS ALREADY CONDUCTING ITSELF: Allen, *Treadmill to Oblivion,* p. 238.
181 SOUNDED LIKE A MAN WITH FALSE TEETH: Taylor, p. 3.
181 WHY DON'T YOU LOOK UP: Taylor, p. 284.
181 HE'S AFRAID GOD MIGHT RECOGNIZE HIM: Taylor, p. 250.
182 SITUATED ON THE SHORES: Allen, p. 80.
182 YOU WOULDN'T DARE TALK TO ME: Taylor, p. 239.
182 EVEN WITHOUT THE COMING OF TELEVISION: Allen, p. 238.
183 A MEDIUM THAT DEMANDS ENTERTAINMENT: Allen, p. 239.

183 REDUCED TO ESSENTIALS A QUIZ SHOW: Allen, p. 106.
183 FOR ME MORE INTERESTING THAN LINDBERGH'S: Taylor, p. 289.
183 WHEN TELEVISION BELATEDLY FOUND ITS WAY: Allen, p. 239.
184 IT IS THE STORY OF A RADIO SHOW: Taylor, p. 353.
184 IN 1950 THERE WERE 108 DIFFERENT SERIES: Barnouw, *A History of Broadcasting: The Golden Web*, Vol. 2, p. 285.
185 IN NEW YORK CITY, FIFTY-FIVE THEATERS CLOSED: Barnouw, p. 286.
186 YOU TAKE A KID AT THE AGE OF FIVE: Berle, *Milton Berle: Current Biography* (1949), p. 69.
186 ACCORDING TO VARIETY, OF THE: Wertheim, *The Rise and Fall of Milton Berle in American History, American Television*, p. 72.
187 PEOPLE WHO CALLED HIM AT HOME: Wertheim, p. 74.

CHAPTER FOURTEEN

188 PART OF HIS SUCCESS WITH ORDINARY PEOPLE: Author interview with Albert Gore.
189 I'VE MET MILLIONS OF SELF-MADE: Halberstam, *The Powers that Be*, p. 226.
189 WELL, ESTES, YOU'RE A CONGRESSMAN: Gorman, *Kefauver*, p. 6.
189 SHAME ON YOU, ESTES KEFAUVER: Gorman, p. 7.
189 WE ARE ANXIOUS TO GET EVERYTHING: Gorman, p. 46.
189 PET COON FOR THE SOVIETS: Gorman, pp. 48–49.
190 DON'T YOU WANT TO BE VICE-PRESIDENT: Author interview with Katharine Graham.
191 BY SOME ESTIMATES ONLY 1.5 PERCENT: Gorman, p. 91.
192 SOME 70 PERCENT OF NEW YORK: Manchester, *The Glory and the Dream: A Narrative History of America, 1932–1972*, p. 600.
192 THE WEEK OF MARCH 12, 1951: "Who's a Liar," *Life*, April 2, 1951, pp. 19–25.
194 HE COULD NOT ATTEND THE AWARDS: Gorman, p. 102.

CHAPTER FIFTEEN

Major sources: Andrews, *The I Love Lucy Book;* Brochu, *Lucy in the Afternoon;* Diggins, *The Proud Decades;* Fox, *The Mirror Makers;* Harris, *Lucy & Desi;* Morella and Epstein, *Forever Lucy.*

CHAPTER SIXTEEN

203 "IF THEY DO NOT," HE SAID: James, *The Years of MacArthur*, p. 610.
203 THE SENATE HEARINGS THAT FOLLOWED: Collins, *War in Peacetime*, p. 290.
204 AS WILLIAM MANCHESTER WROTE, MACARTHUR'S: Manchester, *American Caesar*, p. 628.
204 MACARTHUR STILL, ON OCCASION: Manchester, p. 182.
205 BUT ON THE PRO SIDE, HE WROTE: Patterson, *Mr. Republican*, p. 505.
205 IT WAS A CARTOON OF A DINOSAUR: Patterson, p. 561.
205 BUT EVEN AS A PARTISAN FIGURE: Patterson, p. 440.
205 ROOTED AS IT WAS IN THE MIDWEST: Patterson, p. 519.
206 HE FINISHED FIRST IN HIS CLASS: Patterson, p. 30.
206 HAVE I MENTIONED ANYTHING: Patterson, p. 43.
207 "MODERN WAR," HE SAID, OPPOSING: Patterson, p. 243.
207 IN 1946–47 *FORTUNE*: Smith, *Thomas Dewey and His Times*, p. 442.
208 ON ANOTHER OCCASION HE WAS: Patterson, p. 215.
208 WHY ARE ALL THESE PEOPLE COMPLAINING: Patterson, p. 214.
209 WHEN HE WAS FINISHED, MACARTHUR PATTED: Alsop, *I've Seen the Best of It*, p. 338.
209 IN 1948, IMMEDIATELY FOLLOWING HIS DEFEAT: Smith, p. 554.
209 HE TOLD HIS FRIEND BILL ROBINSON: Beschloss, *Mayday*, p. 293.
209 ". . . NOW AS ALWAYS AN OPPORTUNIST: Sulzberger, *A Long Row of Candles*, vol. 1, p. 685.
209 "A VERY STUPID MAN: Sulzberger, p. 702.

209 IN MAY 1951 EISENHOWER WROTE: Lyon, *Eisenhower*, pp. 428–29.
209 AS HE WAS BEING PULLED INTO: Sulzberger, p. 752.
210 A REPRESENTATIVE FROM *MCCALL'S:* Lyon, p. 430.
210 AS THE POLITICAL PRESSURE GREW: Sulzberger, p. 754.
210 "DON'T CALL ME," EISENHOWER SAID: Sulzberger, p. 715.
211 IN FACT HE RESEMBLED NO ONE: interview with Jock Elliott.
212 AT ONE POINT, JOHN WAYNE: Smith, p. 591.
212 "I LIKE IKE," SAID EISENHOWER'S: Patterson, p. 519.
212 TAFT WAS AMUSED AND REPLIED: Patterson, p. 571.
212 BACK CAME THE MESSAGE: Patterson, p. 558.
213 AFTERWARD HE SHOOK NIXON'S: Smith, p. 394.
213 FROM THEN ON NIXON BECAME: Morris, *Richard Milhous Nixon*, p. 684.
213 HE WAS, IN THE WORDS OF DEWEY'S: Smith, p. 591.
213 "I THOUGHT THE CONVENTION HAD TO: Smith, p. 596.
213 "WHAT ABOUT NIXON: Smith, p. 596.
213 HENRY CABOT LODGE, IKE'S OFFICIAL: Morris, p. 733.
219 "WHY DON'T YOU GRAB THIS FELLOW: Martin, *Adlai Stevenson of Illinois*, p. 269.
219 "AM FORTY-SEVEN TODAY—STILL: McKeever, *Adlai Stevenson*, p. 104.
219 "NEVER WENT TO OXFORD: Martin, p. 278.
220 WHEN ARVEY CAME BY, STEVENSON: Martin, p. 279.
220 FOR A TIME STEVENSON HEDGED: McKeever, p. 113.
220 WHEN ARVEY READ STEVENSON'S: McKeever, p. 114.
220 DURING ONE FIGHT LEWIS HAD: McKeever, p. 26.
220 GEORGE BALL, ONE OF THE BRIGHT: Martin, p. 380.
221 FOR MUCH OF HIS ADULT CAREER: McKeever, p. 70–71.
221 WHEN DREW PEARSON WROTE THAT: McKeever, p. 166.
222 "HE COULDN'T UNDERSTAND IT: McKeever, p. 179.
222 "WHAT ARE YOU TRYING TO TELL: McKeever, p. 180.
223 "I THINK WE HAVE TO LEAVE: McKeever, p. 185.
223 HE NEVER HAD TO DO IT: McKeever, p. 37.

CHAPTER SEVENTEEN

224 DUFFY DECIDED THAT THEY HAD TO RECAST IKE: Author interview with Jock Elliot.
225 MY SECRET SELF: Fox, *The Mirror Makers*, pp. 189, 191.
226 WELL, FIRST I'VE GOT TO GET: Mayer, *Madison Avenue, USA*, pp. 35–36.
226 WERE THE MOST HATED COMMERCIALS: Fox, p. 188.
226 NOT BAD FOR SOMETHING WRITTEN: Diamond and Bates, *The Spot*, p. 40.
226 IF WE EVER GET OUT OF PACKAGED: Mayer, p. 55.
226 WHEN HIS FRIENDS COMPLAINED: Author interview with David McCall.
226 WITHOUT SUBTLETY, AND WITHOUT CONCERN: Fox, p. 193.
227 THE MOST UNCONFUSED MIND: Mayer, p. 49.
227 THIS NEW MEDIUM OF TELEVISION WAS: Author interview with Rosser Reeves.
227 THE PRINCE OF HARD SELL: Fox, p. 192.
227 ON OCCASION IT WOULD BE KNOWN: Fox, p. 189.
227 THE UNCHECKABLE CLAIM: Mayer, p. 50.
227 I HAD SOME OIL INTERESTS: Diamond and Bates, p. 53.
228 THE QUICKEST, MOST EFFECTIVE AND CHEAPEST: Diamond and Bates, p. 54.
229 YOU LOSE PENETRATION: Mayer, p. 296.
229 EISENHOWER, MAN OF PEACE: Author interview with Rosser Reeves.
229 YOU GET THE AUDIENCE BUILT UP: Diamond and Bates, p. 54.
229 YOU TEND TO LOWER YOUR HEAD: Author interview with David Schoenbrun.
230 HE'S NOT GOING TO SAY IT: Author interview with Rosser Reeves.
230 TO THINK THAT AN OLD SOLDIER: Author interview with Rosser Reeves; and Mayer, p. 297.

230 REAL PEOPLE IN THEIR OWN CLOTHES: Diamond and Bates, p. 57.

231 NO, NOT IF WE HAVE A SOUND: Diamond and Bates, pp. 599–600.

231 ROSSER, I HOPE FOR YOUR SAKE: Author interview with David Ogilvy.

231 IT WAS PIONEER WORK: Author interview with Rosser Reeves.

231 FACED WITH THIS DILEMMA: Fox, p. 310.

231 EISENHOWER HITS THE SPOT: Halberstam, *The Powers That Be,* p. 236.

232 REEVES REMEMBERED CLEVELAND: Author interview with Rosser Reeves.

232 AN UNINFORMED ELECTORATE CAN LEAD: Mayer, p. 303.

232 THIS IS THE WORST THING: Author interview with Louis Cowan.

232 TO BOTH REPUBLICANS AND DEMOCRATS: Halberstam, p. 229.

233 LOU, OLD BOY, WE: Author interview with Louis Cowan.

233 TONIGHT I WANT TO TALK: Museum of Radio and Television Broadcasting.

233 THE NEW G.I. BILL INTELLECTUALS: Author interview with Michael Arlen.

233 HE'S TOO ACCOMPLISHED AN ORATOR: Barnouw, *The Golden Web,* p. 298.

235 IN HIS ALMOST PAINFUL HONESTY: McKeever, *Adlai Stevenson: His Life and Legacy,* p. 249.

235 SURE, ALL THE EGGHEADS: Goldman, *The Crucial Decade: America 1945–1955,* p. 222.

235 I FIND MYSELF CONSTANTLY BLACKMAILED: McKeever, p. 252.

236 BUT, I DON'T HAVE TO WIN: McKeever, p. 213.

236 WHEN AN AMERICAN SAYS: Goldman, p. 221.

236 THE MEN WHO HUNT COMMUNISTS: Martin, *Adlai Stevenson of Illinois: The Life of Adlai Stevenson,* p. 658.

237 THEY ARE SO POOR THEY: Morris, *Richard Milhous Nixon: The Rise of an American Politician,* p. 757.

237 OUR THINKING WAS THAT: Morris, p. 760.

237 TELL THEM ABOUT THE $16,000: Morris, p. 772.

238 OF WHAT AVAIL IS IT: Lyon, *Eisenhower, Portrait of a Hero,* p. 456.

238 THE LITTLE BOY CAUGHT WITH JAM: Morris, p. 791.

239 GENERAL, I NEVER THOUGHT SOMEONE: Author interview with Ted Rogers.

239 SHERM, IF YOU WANT TO KNOW: Mazo, *Nixon: A Political and Personal Portrait,* p. 125.

240 YOU'LL KNOW. YOU'LL JUST KNOW: Author interview with Ted Rogers.

240 WHY DO WE HAVE TO TELL PEOPLE: Morris, p. 831.

241 WALKING OFF THE SET INTO: Author interview with Ted Rogers.

241 WELL, ARTHUR, YOU SURELY GOT: Mazo, p. 132.

241 BEN, TONIGHT WILL MAKE HISTORY: Lyon, p. 461.

241 HE MAY ASPIRE TO THE GRACE: Morris, p. 856.

242 A DISTURBING EXPERIENCE: Morris, p. 854.

242 THERE WAS JUST ONE THING: Morris, p. 854.

242 FUCK 'EM; WE DON'T NEED: Author interview with Ted Rogers.

CHAPTER EIGHTEEN

243 STEADY MONTY, YOU CAN'T SPEAK: Bradley and Blair, *A General's Life,* p. 330.

250 NO, MARDER SPECULATED, HIS BEAT: Author interview with Murrey Marder.

250 JOE, YOU'RE A REAL SOB: Oshinsky, *A Conspiracy So Immense,* p. 132.

250 A PIMPLE ON THE PATH OF PROGRESS: Hagerty, *The Diary of James C. Hagerty: Eisenhower in Mid-Course,* p. 27.

251 I KNOW THAT CHARGES OF DISLOYALTY: Oshinsky, p. 236.

251 NOT JUST HIS DEMOCRATIC OPPONENTS: Cray, *General of the Army: George C. Marshall,* p. 369.

251 IT TURNED MY STOMACH: Bradley and Blair, p. 656.

251 HYPOCRITICALLY CALLING INTO QUESTION: Bradley and Blair, p. 655.

251 HE TOLD HIS GODDAUGHTER: Cray, p. 728.

251 BUT EISENHOWER'S HATRED OF MCCARTHY: Adams, *First Hand Report*, p. 148.
251 HE DON'T TAKE SHOVIN'!: Adams, p. 15.
252 I KNOW ONE FELLOW I'D: Oshinsky, p. 359.
252 I WILL NOT GET IN THE GUTTER: Adams, p. 135.
252 COULDN'T YOU TELL THEM: Oshinsky, p. 287.
252 ON THE MORNING OF THEIR APPEARANCE: Oshinsky, p. 287.
252 SO FAR AS I'M CONCERNED: Oshinsky, p. 290.
252 KISS MY ASS, VAN: Oshinsky, p. 504.

CHAPTER NINETEEN

255 HER LADYSHIP IS FUCKING BORED: Edwards, *Vivien Leigh*, p. 178.
257 THIS CHARACTER HAS NEVER HAD: Williams, T. *Memoirs*, p. 136.
258 HOW DID YOU LIKE YOU'SELF: Williams, E., *Remember Me to Tom*, p. 148.
258 SOMEWHERE DEEP IN MY NERVES: Williams, T., p. 17.
259 I WAS NOT A YOUNG MAN: Williams, T., p. 52.
259 AUNT ELLA AND AUNT BELLE: Williams, T., p. 117.
260 HE DID IT EVERY MORNING: Kazan, *A Life*, p. 261.
260 HE PUT WRITING BEFORE KNOWING: Windham, *Lost Friendships*, p. 113.
261 WHY ME? WHY ME?: Selznick, *A Private View*, p. 295.
262 I AM SURE YOU MUST HAVE: Kazan, p. 329.
263 I COME FROM A FAMILY: Kazan, pp. 190–191.
263 IT'S FINE, LEAVE IT. Kazan, p. 19.
264 WHY YOU NOT LEARNING SOMETHING: Kazan, p. 40.
264 HEY, GEORGE, YOU GOT A DEAD ONE: Kazan, p. 70.
264 HOW CONFIDENT THEY WERE: Kazan, p. 40.
264 FOUR YEARS OVER IN MASSACHUSETTS: Kazan, p. 49.
265 VERY HIGH CLASS: Kazan, p. 91.
265 TELL US WHAT YOU WANT: Kazan, p. 57.
266 ALL THEY WANT IS A STAGEHAND: Kazan, p. 100.
267 WELL, WHAT IS IT: Higham, *Brando: The Unauthorized Biography*, p. 76.
267 HE WAS ABOUT THE BEST-LOOKING: Williams, p. 131.
268 I HATE ULTIMATUMS: Fiore, *The Brando I Knew*, p. 60.
269 THIS PUPPY THING WILL BE: Carey, *Marlon Brando: The Only Contender*, p. 13.
270 I TAUGHT HIM NOTHING: Higham, p. 38; and Carey, p. 15.

CHAPTER TWENTY

273 "GOD," HE NOTED, "WHAT A: Christenson, *Kinsey,* pp. 117–18.
273 "AS YOU MAY KNOW WE ARE: Pomeroy, *Dr. Kinsey and the Institute for Sex Research,* p. 191.
274 "YEARS AGO MY BANKER: Pomeroy, p. 50.
274 HE ONCE TOLD A COLLEAGUE, WARDELL: Pomeroy, p. 8.
274 AFTER HIS DEATH WARDELL POMEROY: Pomeroy, p. 472.
274 "NOW, BRUCE," KINSEY SAID: Pomeroy, p. 29.
274 TO ONE YOUNG MAN WHO APPLIED: Pomeroy, p. 71.
275 AS A BOY HE COLLECTED STAMPS: Pomeroy, p. 16.
275 HE WROTE HIS FIRST BOOK: Christenson, p. 29.
275 EARLE MARCH, A SAN FRANCISCO: Pomeroy, p. 166.
276 CLARA KINSEY WAS KNOWN ON: Wickware, "Report on Kinsey," p. 98.
276 WHEN HE BEGAN HIS STUDIES: Pomeroy, pp. 72–73.
276 BY 1939 HE WROTE TO A: Christenson, p. 107.
277 THOSE WHO THOUGHT HE WOULD DO: Christenson, p. 113.
277 THE WAR MADE THINGS HARDER: Christenson, p. 114.
279 HIS CRITICS WERE, HE NOTED: Pomeroy, p. 284.

279 "AND THEN THERE ARE SOME: Pomeroy, p. 147.
280 KINSEY TURNED HIM DOWN: Pomeroy, p. 346.
280 THEN THE FIRESTORM BEGAN: Pomeroy, p. 364.
280 THE WORST THING ABOUT THE REPORT: Christenson, p. 162.
280 AGAIN KINSEY WAS DISHEARTENED: Pomeroy, p. 160.
281 LATER IN ANOTHER LETTER TO RUSK: Christenson, p. 190.
281 "DAMN THAT RUSK: Pomeroy, p. 16.
281 ANDERSON PLEADED WITH HIM: Christenson, p. 193.
281 "IT IS A SHAME," HE NOTED: Christenson, p. 199.

CHAPTER TWENTY-ONE

283 IT WAS SHE WHO INTRODUCED US: Gray, *Margaret Sanger: A Biography of the Champion of Birth Control*, pp. 58–59.
284 I AM ANARCHIST, TRUE, BUT: Gray, p. 74.
284 OH, JULIET, THERE NEVER WAS: Gray, p. 159.
284 LOOK THE WHOLE WORLD IN THE FACE: Kennedy, *Birth Control in America*, p. 1.
286 IT WAS NO LONGER MY LONE FIGHT: Reed, *From Private Vice to Public Virtue*, p. 112.
286 IF YOU LIKE MY RELIGION: Gray, p. 158.
286 IT IRKS MY VERY SOUL: Reed, p. 112.
287 RICH AS CROESUS: Vaughan, *The Pill on Trial*, p. 25.
287 HE WAS RATHER SHOCKED: Gray, p. 438.
288 YOU HAVE THE POWER TO CHANGE: Author interview with Oscar Hechter.
288 BUT THIS IS JUST A CRUISING: Author interviews with Laura Pincus Bernard, John Alexis Pincus, and Oscar Hechter.
288 A CONTENTED JEWISH PEASANTRY: Pauly, *Controlling Life: Jacques Loeb and the Engineering Ideal in Biology*, p. 185.
289 SCARED PEOPLE, CREATING VISIONS: Reed, p. 321.
289 RABBITS BORN IN GLASS: *The New York Times* (April 8, 1934), VIII 6:4.
289 PICTURED PINCUS AS A SINISTER: Reed, p. 321.
289 MAN'S VALUE WOULD SHRINK: Ratcliff, *Colliers*, March 20, 1937, p. 73.
292 PINCUS WAS VERY GENTLE: Author interview with John Pincus.
292 LIZUSKA, EVERYTHING IS POSSIBLE: Vaughn, p. 6.
293 GOODY, HOW DID YOU GET: Author interview with Oscar Hechter.

CHAPTER TWENTY-TWO

296 IF THERE WAS ONE FIGURE WHO: Nicosia, *Memory Babe*, p. 475.
296 "WELL, WELL!" CARR SAID: Miles, *Ginsberg*, p. 36.
296 HE HAD TO BE A GENIUS: Morgan, *Literary Outlaw*, p. 102–3
296 GINSBERG WROTE IN HIS JOURNAL: Morgan, p. 89.
297 DETERMINED TO BE A WRITER: Gifford and Lee, *Jack's Book*, p. 34.
297 KEROUAC'S FIRST IMPRESSION: Miles, p. 44
297 GINSBERG WROTE HIS OLDER: Miles, p. 39.
297 BURROUGHES, GINSBERG AND KEROUAC: Gifford and Lee, p. 38.
298 THE DEAN LOOKED AT HIM: Miles, p. 60
298 THESE YOUNG REBELS DID NOT: Morgan, p. 96.
298 THE ASPIRED TO BECOME: Gifford and Lee, p. 39.
299 "THESE JERKS," BURROUGHES ONCE: Morgan, pp. 139–40.
299 "WHERE IS YOUR FORMER, FINE: Miles, p. 59.
300 SHARING THE SUBWAY CAR WITH: Holmes, *GO*, pp. 140–41
300 IN *GO* HOLMES DESCRIBED: Holmes, p. 36.
301 THE FIRST WORDS THAT NEAL CASSADY: Cassady, *Off the Road*, p. 2.
301 MARIJUANA, THEN KNOWN AS TEA: Holmes, p. 141.
301 AS BARRY GIFFORD AND LAWRENCE: Gifford and Lee, p. 170.

301 LATER, THE DEFINITION WAS REINVENTED: Morgan, p. 154.
301 MALCOLM COWLEY, THE DISTINGUISHED: Gifford and Lee, p. 187.
302 THAT, GREGORY CORSO LIKED TO: Gifford and Lee, pp. 180–81.
302 HOLMES NOTED THAT DOWN DEEP: Gifford and Lee, p. 129.
302 KEROUAC DESCRIBED HIM IN: Kerouac, *On the Road,* p. 5.
303 WHAT HE EXEMPLIFIED, TED MORGAN: Morgan, p. 159.
303 "WHEN NEAL CAME TO TOWN: Gifford and Lee, p. 127.
303 KEROUAC SEEMED A MAN: Gifford and Lee, p. 129.
304 ON THIS POINT HOLMES HELD: Holmes, pp. xx–xxi.
304 HE WROTE IT, HIS FRIEND JOHN: Gifford and Lee, p. 156.
304 IT WAS, IN HOLMES'S WORDS: Gifford and Lee, p. 157.
304 THE PROBLEM, HE ADDED: Cassady, p. 187.
305 GIL MILSTEIN, A TALENTED: Gifford and Lee, p. 170.
305 IT WAS TIME, HE DECIDED: Miles, p. 135.
305 HE WROTE KEROUAC, "I AM: Miles, p. 185.
305 THE RESULT WAS POETRY AS IF: Miles, p. 188.
306 FERLINGHETTI AGREED TO PUBLISH: Miles, p. 193.
306 "IT HAD," TED MORGAN LATER: Morgan, p. 256.
306 "THIS POEM WILL MAKE YOU FAMOUS: Miles, p. 196.
306 FERLINGHETTI SENT GINSBERG A CABLE: Morgan, p. 257.
306 *ON THE ROAD* OFFERED A NEW VISION: Kerouac, p. 3.
306 WHAT KEROUAC DID, TED MORGAN: Morgan, p. 288.
307 QUITE THE CONTRARY: "THE FIRST: Miles, p. 232.

CHAPTER TWENTY-THREE

311 ALL THEY TALKED ABOUT WAS: Adams, *First Hand Report,* p. 20.
312 I HAVE TO NOMINATE THAT DIRTY: Morris, *Richard Milhous Nixon: The Rise of an American Politician,* p. 734.
313 A LITTLE MAN IN A BIG HURRY: Morris, p. 739.
313 PLAYS BOTH SIDES AGAINST THE MIDDLE: Morris, p. 447.
313 THE COMMIES DON'T LIKE IT: Morris, p. 564.
314 HIS TELEVISION ADVISER IN HIS SUCCESSFUL: Personal interview with Roger Ailes.
314 THOUGH THE FAMILY LIVED ON A FARM: Ambrose, *Nixon,* p. 20.
315 AS NIXON'S COUSIN JESSAMYN WEST: Morris, p. 25.
315 HE WAS NOT A QUAKER: Interviews with Paul Smith, Guy Dixon, Douglas Ferguson, Hubert Perry, Merton Wray, Paul Ryan, Merel West, Olive and Oscar Mashburn, Dorothy Milhous, Charles Milhous, Jane Milhous Beeson, Ralph Shook, Lucile Parson, Samuel Warner, Madeline Thomas, Elizabeth Cloes, Marcia Elliot Wray, Saragrace Frampton, and Laura Walfrop from the archives of the Cal Fullerton Library.
315 THE HARDEST PIECE OF SOIL: Cal Fullerton Library.
315 HE NEVER MADE A PENNY: Cal Fullerton Library.
316 I AM NOT GOING TO WEAR: Cal Fullerton Library.
316 WHEN THE OIL BOOM STRUCK: Lurie, *The Running of Richard Nixon,* p. 22.
316 HE ALWAYS CARRIED SUCH A WEIGHT: Morris, p. 61.
316 THERE WAS, SHE THOUGHT TOO: Lurie, p. 22.
317 ONE WHO HAS KNOWN RICHARD: Morris, p. 848.
317 NOR FOR THAT MATTER WAS BEWLEY: Cal Fullerton Library.
318 SHE DID HER PART NICELY: Ambrose, p. 99.
318 WHEN SHE PRETENDED NOT TO BE: Nixon, *Pat Nixon: The Untold Story,* p. 58.
318 YES—I KNOW I'M CRAZY: Nixon, p. 58.
318 IT IS OUR JOB TO GO FORTH: Nixon, p. 68.
318 THEIR WEDDING RING COST $324.75: Nixon, p. 68.
319 TOO MANY RESTRICTIONS ETC.: Nixon, p. 82.

319 WHETHER IT'S THE LOBBY: Nixon, p. 83.
319 I AM WRITING YOU THIS SHORT: Morris, p. 271.
320 NIXON LIFE STORY LIKE FILM: Morris, p. 606.
321 I THINK: WILL IT PACK: Nixon, p. 187.
322 YOU CANNOT BE TIRED, YOU: Ambrose, p. 96.
322 I DETEST TEMPER; I DETEST SCENES: Nixon, p. 21.
324 THE MANAGER OF OUR DEPARTMENT: Nixon, pp. 47–48.
325 NIXON HAD THE MOST HATEFUL FACE: Author interview with Larry King.
325 IT WAS, ROGERS LATER DECIDED: Author interview with Ted Rogers.
325 HE WAS MOST COMFORTABLE: Author interview with Helen Gahagan Douglas.
325 I GUESS I CAN MAKE IT: Nixon, p. 115.
325 I DON'T THINK I CAN: Nixon, p. 122.
326 IN PUBLIC, HE WOULD ALWAYS PRAISE: Author interview with James Bassett.
326 OUR HEARTS WERE BREAKING: Nixon, p. 424.
327 JIM BASSETT, WHO WORKED WITH NIXON: Author interview with James Bassett.
327 HE'S NEVER LIKED ME: Author interview with Len Hall.
327 NO, NO, DEAR DON'T DO THAT: Author interview with Mollie Parnis.
331 HOW COULD THAT BE: Ambrose, p. 801.

CHAPTER TWENTY-FOUR

329 INDEED OPPENHEIMER LATER JOKED: Stern, *The Oppenheimer Case*, p. 206.
330 HE EVEN APOLOGIZED LIGHTLY: Stern, p. 111.
330 THEY SHOULD LEAVE THIS TO OPPIE: interview with Victor Weisskopf.
331 "HE WAS," WEISSKOPF SAID DRILY: interview with Weisskopf.
331 "THE DIFFERENCE WITH ME: interview with Hans Bethe.
331 "SOME PEOPLE PROFESS GUILT: Ulam, *Adventures of a Mathematician*, p. 224.
331 "OUR PLANE SEEMED TO STAND: Blair and Shepley, *The Hydrogen Bomb*, p. 63.
332 AT THE TIME, HERBERT MARKS: Stern, *The Oppenheimer Case*, p. 206.
333 "HARRY," GREEN SAID: interview with Harold Green.
335 OPPENHEIMER, IN THE WORDS OF THE AEC: Green, "The Oppenheimer Case."
333 STRAUSS BROOKED NO DISSENT: Joseph and Stewart Alsop, *We Accuse*, p. 19.
334 YET WHAT WAS TAKING PLACE: interview with Green.
336 HIS JOB WAS SOON DISSOLVED: Sullivan, *The Bureau*, p. 108.
336 HIS LUNCH RARELY VARIED: Powers, *Secrecy and Power*, p. 314.
336 IN TRUTH, HE OFTEN BET: Sullivan, p. 87.
336 HOOVER WOULD STAY IN: Powers, p. 314.
336 HE ENSHRINED THE AMERICAN: Hoover, *Masters of Deceit*, p. 16.
337 AS TWENTIETH-CENTURY STANDARDS: Powers, pp. 3–4.
338 THEREAFTER THE ANTEROOM: Powers, *G-Men*, p. 114.
338 BUT HOOVER FOUGHT OFF: Powers, *G-Men*, p. 115.
338 "NO ORGANIZATION THAT I KNOW: Theoharis and Cox, *The Boss*, pp. 160–61.
338 WHEN WILLIAM SULLIVAN JOINED: Sullivan, p. 33.
339 WHEN HOOVER WAS ASKED IN LATER: Sullivan, p. 37.
339 "ANYTIME I NEED: Sullivan, p. 38.
339 FROM THAT MOMENT ON, WROTE: Sullivan, p. 38.
340 "WE GAVE MCCARTHY EVERYTHING: O'Reilly, *Hoover and the Un-Americans*, p. 337.
340 WHEN A REPORTER FROM THE: Powers, *Secrecy and Power*, p. 321.
340 THE HOUSE SUBCOMMITTEE ON THE: O'Reilly, p. 325.
341 IN THE FALL OF 1952: Stern, p. 195.
342 IN THE COPY TO HOOVER: Blumberg and Owens, *Energy and Conflict*, p. 304.
342 EISENHOWER ORDERED THAT A "BLANK": Stern, p. 221
343 "JACK, I'M SORRY": Michelmore, p. 206.
344 HE SAT THAT FIRST DAY: Stern, p. 232.
344 "WHAT YOU SHOULD SAY: interview with Weisskopf.

344 HE DID NOT, HE WROTE: Stern, p. 233.
345 "THE SUN'S RISING IN: Moss, *Men Who Play God*, p. 8.
346 "SOME KIND OF WHITE SAND: Lapp, *The Voyage of the Lucky Dragon*, p. 34.
346 "THE INDIVIDUALS WERE UNEXPECTEDLY: Lapp, p. 53.
346 "YOU LOOK LIKE A NEGRO: Lapp, p. 56.
346 "FROM THIS DAY ON, UNHAPPINESS: Lapp, p. 87.
346 ONE OF THE SEAMEN TOLD: Moss, p. 90.
347 AT ONE POINT HE CRIED: Lapp, p. 169.
347 "IF I WERE THE REDS: Hagerty, *The Diary of James C. Hagerty*, p. 42.
*347 ON APRIL 2, 1954: Hagerty, p. 40.
348 LUIS ALVAREZ, ANOTHER OPPENHEIMER: Alvarez, *Alvarez*, p. 180.
348 "SOMEHOW," WEISSKOPF WROTE: Stern, p. 255
349 ASKED WHY HE HAD TOLD: Stern, p. 280.
349 "THERE HADN'T BEEN A PROCEEDING: Stern, p. 305.
349 HE WAS SORRY TO HEAR ABOUT: Stern, p. 335.
349 AFTER BEING RECRUITED BY STRAUSS: FBI documents on J. Robert Oppenheimer, May 27, 1952, Albuquerque office to director.
350 WHEN ROBB ASKED TELLER: Blumberg and Owens, p. 361.
350 THIS WAS THE CRITICAL: Blumberg and Owens, pp. 362–63.
350 FINALLY CAME THE DENOUEMENT: Coughlin, "Dr. Teller's Magnificent Obsession," p. 74.
350 OPPENHEIMER, IN A POLITE VOICE: Coughlin, p. 74.
351 WHEN OPPENHEIMER HAD BEEN ASKED: Stern, p. 380.
351 *YOU DOUBLE-DEALING, LYING:* interview with Green.
351 HE DID IT, GREEN NOTED: interview with Green.
351 EISENHOWER BECAME NERVOUS: Hagerty, p. 43.
351 LATER, AFTER THE REVIEW BOARD: Hagerty, p. 61.
352 OPPENHEIMER SMILED AND ANSWERED: Stern, p. 451.
352 "THE LOS ALAMOS LABORATORY: Davis, *Lawrence and Oppenheimer*, p. 316.
352 WHILE A ROOM FULL OF PROMINENT: Stern, p. 447.
353 FRIENDS HEARD THEIR YOUNG DAUGHTER: Stern, p. 378.
355 IT WAS ONE OF THE MOST COMPLETE: Coffey, *Iron Eagle*, p. 165.
355 NOT EVERYONE IN THE AIR FORCE: Coffey, p. 246.
355 LEMAY ANSWERED, "IT DOESN'T: Coffey, p. 272.
356 HE BELIEVED, RIGHT UP UNTIL: Coffey, p. 331,
356 "SOME OF US," HE WOULD ADD: Coffey, pp. 331–2.
356 HE THOUGHT ARMY BASE SECURITY: Coffey, p. 311.
356 "THIS AFTERNOON," HE TOLD THEM: Shepley and Blair, *The Hydrogen Bomb*, p. 192.

CHAPTER TWENTY-FIVE

359 A WORD FROM ONE [BROTHER]: Schlesinger and Kinzer, *Bitter Fruit: The Untold Story of the American Coup in Guatemala*, p. 108.
360 THE GENERAL MANAGER OF THE WAR: Candee, *Current Biography: Who's News and Why—1953*, p. 580.
360 GODDAMNIT, LET'S HAVE IT OUT: Lyon, *Eisenhower: Portrait of the Hero*, p. 328.
360 I LOVE THAT MAN: Lyon, p. 367.
360 COLD FISHY EYE: Mosley, *Dulles: A Biography of Eleanor, Allen, and John Foster Dulles and their Family Network*, p. 283.
360 HE WAS A SMALL MAN: Roosevelt, *Countercoup: The Struggle for Control of Iran*, p. 4.
360 ROOSEVELT, IF YOU CAN'T KEEP: Roosevelt, p. 4.
361 SO THIS IS HOW WE GET: Roosevelt, p. 8.
361 AS I LISTENED TO HIM: Rubin: *Paved with Good Intentions: The American Experience and Iran*, p. 74.

361 INARTICULATE AS USUAL BUT ENTHUSIASTIC: Roosevelt, p. 18.
361 WE SHOULD PROCEED: Roosevelt, p. 17.
361 THAT'S THAT THEN: Roosevelt, p. 18.
362 THE LAST PERSON YOU'D EXPECT: Mosley, p. 326.
362 ONE PERCENT OF THE POPULATION: Rubin, p. 22.
362 BY CONTRAST, THE AMERICAN EMBASSY: Rubin, p. 54.
362 IN 1950, THE BRITISH GOVERNMENT: Lyon, p. 488.
363 YOU DO NOT KNOW HOW CRAFTY: Rubin, p. 66.
363 DON'T YOU REALIZE THAT RETURNING: Rubin, p. 68.
363 TO EMBODY IRAN PERSONALLY, ITS: Rubin, p. 59.
364 BUT BEING CALLED ON SO OBVIOUS A PLOY: Acheson, *Present at the Creation: My Years at the State Department,* p. 504.
364 ESSENTIALLY A RICH REACTIONARY: Acheson, p. 504.
364 PULL UP YOUR SOCKS: Roosevelt, p. 115.
365 IT WAS A GREAT ADVENTURE: Roosevelt, p. 138.
365 HE WAS BARELY LITERATE: Roosevelt, pp. 138–40.
366 THE OLD BUGGER: Roosevelt, p. 163.
366 ROOSEVELT ALSO BROUGHT WITH HIM: Rubin, p. 82.
366 I WISH YOUR IMPERIAL MAJESTY: Roosevelt, p. 168.
367 HAPPY TO REPORT: Roosevelt, pp. 190–91.
367 AS A SOUVENIR OF OUR RECENT ADVENTURE: Roosevelt, p. 201.
367 THE SHAH IS A NEW MAN: Lyon, p. 552.
367 WELL I CAN SAY THAT THE STATEMENT: Wise and Ross, *The Invisible Government,* p. 113.
367 YOUNG MAN, IF I HAD BEEN: Roosevelt, p. 207.
367 OUR AGENT THERE, A MEMBER: Lyon, p. 552.

CHAPTER TWENTY-SIX

369 HIS EYES . . . GLEAMING: Roosevelt, *Countercoup: The Struggle for the Control of Iran,* p. 4.
370 BUT ROOSEVELT FIGURED THAT: Author interview with Kermit Roosevelt.
372 IF THAT COLONEL OF YOURS: Beschloss, *Mayday: Eisenhower, Khruschev, and the U-2 Affair,* p. 126.
372 YOU DON'T KNOW WHAT YOU'RE: Schlesinger and Kinser, *Bitter Fruit: The Untold Story of the American Coup in Guatemala,* p. 146.
372 I'LL TELL THE TRUTH TO DICK RUSSELL: Beschloss, p. 129.
372 FOR UNFRIENDLY COUNTRIES: Beschloss, p. 126.
372 ALLEN, CAN'T I EVER MENTION A NAME: Beschloss, p. 128.
372 ALAS, NO, BUT I WISH: Mosley, *Dulles: A Biography of Eleanor, Allen, and John Foster Dulles and Their Family Network,* p. 125.
373 HE REFUELED HIMSELF ON PARTIES: Mosley, p. 282.
373 HIS AFFAIRS WERE SO NOTORIOUS: Mosley, p. 125.
373 DELICIOUS SENSE OF SIN: Dulles, *John Foster Dulles,* p. 2.
373 I CAN MAKE AN EDUCATED GUESS: Mosley, p. 282.
373 SMITH APPARENTLY THOUGHT DULLES TOO: Mosley, p. 294.
375 AS IN THE PAST, HE RESERVED: Schlesinger and Kinzer, p. 108.
375 THAT GOOD INDIAN LOOK ABOUT HIM: Hunt, *Give Us This Day,* p. 117.
375 I WANT YOU ALL TO BE DAMN: Lyon, *Eisenhower: Portrait of the Hero,* p. 611.
376 IT ALSO CONTROLLED EITHER DIRECTLY: Schlesinger and Kinzer, p. 12.
376 BY 1950, THE COMPANY REPORTED: Immerman, *The CIA in Guatemala: The Foreign Policy of Intervention,* p. 73.
376 WILD AND DANGEROUS BEAST: Immerman, p. 32.
376 SO! YOU TOO ARE A COMMUNIST: Ydigoras, *My War with Communism,* p. 26.
377 THEN IT'S TRUE: Ydigoras, p. 36.

377 POLITICAL REVOLUTION WAS NO PROBLEM: Bernays, *Biography of an Idea: Memoirs of a Public Relations Council,* pp. 757–58.

377 HIS IDEALISM COINCIDED WITH THE: Immerman, p. 46.

377 THE BANANA MAGNATES, CO-NATIONALS: Schlesinger and Kinzer, p. 47.

378 JUST GIVE ME THE ARMS: Mathews, *A World in Revolution,* 262.

379 A STAR-SPANGLED-BANNER GUY: Schlesinger and Kinzer, p. 55.

379 THE GOVERNMENT WILL FALL IN: Sulzberger, *The Last of the Giants,* p. 826.

379 SEEMED MUCH MORE CIA. THAN STATE: Sulzberger, p. 826.

379 AGRARIAN REFORM HAD BEEN INSTITUTED: Immerman, p. 138.

380 WE ARE MAKING OUR FOURTH OF JULY: Immerman, p. 141.

380 IF ARBENZ IS NOT A COMMUNIST: Schlesinger and Kinzer, p. 139.

380 ALLEN DULLES HAD ANOTHER AGENT: Immerman, p. 155.

380 WELL BOYS, TOMORROW AT THIS: Schlesinger and Kinzer, p. 13.

380 IN FACT, THE NEWS WAS SO PUBLIC: Immerman, p. 3.

381 MEXICO CITY WAS NOT AN ONEROUS: Author interview with Sidney Gruson.

381 YOU'RE CRAZY, YOU KNOW YOU: Author interview with Sidney Gruson.

382 TURNER, WE CAN DO THIS: Author interview with Sidney Gruson.

382 SYDNEY, WE WANT YOU TO STAY: Author interview with Sidney Gruson.

383 A MAJOR GENERAL, A NO-NONSENSE: Salisbury, *Without Fear or Favor: The New York Times and Its Times,* p. 477.

383 HE BEGAN TO PRESS THE HEAD: Salisbury, pp. 479–82.

384 MR. PRESIDENT, WHEN I SAW HENRY: Eisenhower, *Mandate for Change,* pp. 424–26.

384 THINKING OF THE TERRIBLE LOSSES: Phillips, *The Night Watch,* p. 50.

385 PEOPLE WERE COMPLAINING THAT: Immerman, p. 141.

385 AND THAT IF HE HAD BROUGHT: Schlesinger and Kinzer, p. 195.

385 COLONEL, YOU'RE JUST NOT CONVENIENT: Schlesinger and Kinzer, pp. 206–7.

385 IT WOULD BE BETTER IN: Schlesinger and Kinzer, pp. 207–208.

386 HE WOULD, HE SAID, MAKE EVERYTHING: Immerman, p. 181.

386 THERE WAS NOTHING CONCLUSIVE: Immerman, p. 186.

386 BECAUSE OF MY RESPECT FOR: Salisbury, p. 481.

386 A MAN HAVING HIS [GRUSON'S]: Salisbury, p. 482.

386 MY JUDGEMENT, FORMED ON THE BASIS: Salisbury, p. 482.

386 CYRUS SULZBERGER, WHO BELIEVED GRUSON: Author interview with Cyrus Sulzberger.

CHAPTER TWENTY-SEVEN

388 AS REINHOLD NEIBHUR: Hoopes, *The Devil and John Foster Dulles,* p. 37.

389 YES, SAID DULLES, AND HE: Hoopes, p. 74.

389 THERE WERE REPORTS THAT AT THE LAST: Hoopes, p. 137–38.

389 HE COMPLAINED TO CLOSE AIDES: Hoopes, p. 129.

389 STILL HE HONORED EISENHOWER: Adams, *First-Hand Report,* p. 89.

390 EISENHOWER, ON THE OTHER HAND: Hoopes, p. 200–201.

390 "MR. DULLES MAKES A SPEECH: Hoopes, p. 149.

391 THE WRITER CAME AWAY: Hughes, *The Ordeal of Power,* p. 70.

391 AT THAT POINT CRONKITE NOTED: Hoopes, p. 132.

391 ALEXANDER CADOGEN, AN ASSISTANT: Dulles, *John Foster Dulles,* pp. 119–20.

391 IKE LATER SAID HE ANSWERED: Prados, *The Sky Would Fall,* p. 26.

392 THE ITALIANS OF COURSE WERE: Mosley, *Dulles,* p. 329.

392 WHEN JOHN FOSTER WAS FIVE, HIS MOTHER: Hoopes, p. 11.

392 SEEING HIS YOUNGER SISTER CRYING: Mosley, p. 19.

393 YEARS LATER, WHEN SHE WAS ASKED: Mosley, p. 30.

393 "IT MADE THEM BOSSY: Dulles, p. 81.

393 "HE KNEW," HIS SISTER LATER: Dulles, p. 80.

394 HE REMAINED "A MAN OF WATERTOWN: Dulles, p. 91.

395 HUMPHREY SEEMED TO SPEAK: Hoopes, p. 196.
396 SOON THERE WERE A VARIETY: Hoopes, p. 200.
398 USING THE KIND OF WORDS: Fall, *Hell in a Very Small Place*, p. 28.
398 IN 1946 GENERAL JACQUES PHILIPPE LECLERC: Halberstam, *Ho*, p. 84.
399 NAVARRE WAS NOT ENTHUSIASTIC: Roy, *The Battle of Dien Bien Phu*, p. 7.
399 EVEN MORE OMINOUS WAS A WARNING: Roy, pp. 8–9.
399 "IN THAT CASE THEY ARE DONE: Roy, pp. 8–9.
399 THE WARNING FROM SALAN: Roy, p. 68.
399 "NOT ONE SOU: Prados, p. 96.
399 GEORGE HUMPHREY, THE SECRETARY: Prados, pp. 27–28.
400 THEY HAD THE MOST PRIMITIVE: Roy, pp. 72–73.
400 WHEN GIAP'S NAME WAS: Roy, p. xix.
400 SPEAKING OF THE FRENCH ARROGANCE: Roy, p. xix.
400 THE NAME DIEN BIEN PHU: Prados, p. 3.
401 IN NOVEMBER 1953, RESPONDING: Fall, pp. 35–36.
401 AS BERNARD FALL, THE HISTORIAN: Fall, p. 49.
401 YEARS LATER, MAJOR MARCEL: Fall, p. 5.
402 WHEN NAVARRE HIMSELF VISITED: Fall, p. 103.
402 ONCE AGAIN THEY HAD MADE: Roy, p. 52.
402 THEY COULD CARRY UP TO: Roy, p. 105.
402 IT WAS NOTHING OF THE SORT: Roy, p. 131.
402 HE SHRUGGED HIS SHOULDERS: Roy, p. 174.
403 "I AM COMPLETELY DISHONORED: Fall, p. 156.
403 "LET'S HAVE NO ILLUSIONS: Roy, p. 179.
403 "FIRST WE SEND THEM PLANES: Prados, p. 49.
404 "YOU COULD TAKE ALL DAY TO DROP: Prados, p. 92.
404 "THE DAMN REPUBLICANS: Halberstam, *The Best and the Brightest*, p. 139.
405 BUT THE FRENCH DEMURRED: Fall, p. 307.
405 "I HAVE SPENT MORE TIME: Prados, p. 96.
405 AT ONE POINT IN EARLY APRIL: Prados, p. 105.
405 A FEW DAYS LATER, AT A PRESS: Prados, p. 115.
406 RIDGWAY SAW AIRPOWER: interview with Ridgway.
406 WHEN HE BRIEFED EISENHOWER: interview with Ridgway.
407 AS THE IDEA OF INTERVENTION: Fall, p. 309.
407 THAT NIGHT ALL FRENCH: Fall, pp. 415–16.
408 IN APRIL THAT YEAR THE *TIMES*: Prados, p. 89.
408 "WE HAVE A CLEAN BASE: Hughes, p. 208.
408 IT WAS, HE NOTED, "A MODERN: Hoopes, p. 310.
409 "YOU HAVE TO TAKE CHANCES: Hoopes, p. 310.
409 HEARING LATER OF DULLES'S BOASTS: Fall, p. 459.

CHAPTER TWENTY-EIGHT

411 FRANKFURTER REFERRED TO BLACK: Schwartz, *Super Chief*, p. 81.
411 HIS CLOSE FRIEND, JUDGE LEARNED HAND: Schwartz and Lesher, *Inside the Warren Court*, p. 130.
411 HE SAID OF BLACK: Schwartz and Lesher, p. 52.
411 OF A BLACK OPINION: Schwartz and Lesher, p. 52.
411 BLACK, WHO WAS AWARE: Schwartz and Lesher, p. 53.
411 IN A LETTER TO HAND: Schwartz and Lesher, p. 53.
411 DOUGLAS RETURNED THE SENTIMENTS: Schwartz and Lesher, p. 53.
411 ONCE AFTER HEARING AN UNUSUALLY LONG: Schwartz and Lesher, p. 24.
412 "THIS MAN," PHILIP ELMAN: Schwartz, p. 73.
412 THEY WERE, HE THOUGHT: Simon, *The Antagonists*, p. 200.
413 THE DISPARITY WAS EVEN: Kluger, *Simple Justice*, p. 257.

413 IF THE PACE WITH WHICH: Kluger, p. 217.
413 SO, HE NOTED, HE HAD "WRAPPED: Kluger, p. 224.
414 "THE FOURTEENTH AMENDMENT: Kluger, p. 222.
414 "JUSTICE BROWN, IN SHORT: Kluger, p. 80.
414 IN A PASSIONATE DISSENT: Kluger, p. 82.
415 HE ADDED: "THE WHITE: Kluger, p. 82.
415 WHEN THE COURT MET: Schwartz and Lesher, p. 23.
415 "WE CAN'T CLOSE OUR EYES: Schwartz and Lesher, p. 23.
415 "THIS IS THE FIRST INDICATION: Kluger, p. 656.
415 SPECULATION BEGAN TO CENTER: Schwartz, p. 17.
416 THE POVERTY OF HIS FATHER'S LIFE: Warren, *The Memoirs of Earl Warren,* p. 16.
416 THAT THEY HAD NOT YET RISEN UP: Weaver, *Warren,* p. 105.
416 IN JUNE OF 1943, WARREN: Kluger, p. 662.
417 LATER HE EXPRESSED CONSIDERABLE: White, *Earl Warren,* p. 77.
417 THAT A RECORD OTHERWISE: interview with A.J. Langguth.
417 HIS CRITICS THOUGHT HIM: White, p. 180.
417 FROM THEN ON, HE INCLUDED: Warren, p. 161.
417 WHEN HIS LAW CLERKS TWITTED: Schwartz and Lesher, p. 143.
417 "WARREN'S GREAT STRENGTH: Schwartz and Lesher, p. 33.
417 EDGAR PATTERSON, HIS DRIVER: Schwartz, p. 97.
417 JOHN GUNTHER, ONE OF THE VERY BEST: Gunther, *Inside U.S.A.,* p. 18.
418 HIS LAW CLERK, EARL POLLOCK: Kluger, p. 695.
418 WARREN, HUGO BLACK WROTE: Simon, p. 222.
419 "EARL WARREN," ANTHONY LEWIS: Kluger, p. 667.
419 PREVIOUS CASES, HE LATER TOLD: Kluger, p. 678.
419 THE LAW, HE SAID: Kluger, p. 679.
419 WARREN WANTED A MINIMUM: Kluger, p. 679.
419 JUSTICE TOM CLARK HAD: Kluger, p. 706.
420 "THESE ARE NOT BAD PEOPLE: Schwartz and Lesher, p. 87.
420 WHEN FRANKFURTER CIRCULATED: Kluger, p. 37.
421 THE MIXING OF THE RACES: Kluger, p. 60.
422 FINALLY THE CHIEF JUSTICE MADE: Kluger, p. 698.
422 "THERE ARE MANY CONSIDERATIONS: Schwartz and Lesher, p. 87.
422 JACKSON'S CLERK, BARRETT: Kluger, p. 697.
The major source for the remainder of this chapter is an author interview with Frederic Morrow.

CHAPTER TWENTY-NINE

430 HIS MOTHER, MAME BRADLEY, WORKED: Whitfield, *A Death in the Delta,* p. 15.
431 THE AVERAGE WHITE ADULT HAD: Whitfield, pp. 23–24.
431 A CROSSROADS MARILYN MONROE: Whitfield, p. 110.
433 WE'VE GOT TO HAVE OUR MILAMS: From the Huie letters at Ohio State.
433 THE WHITES OWN ALL THE PROPERTY: Huie letters.
434 I AM CAPABLE OF DRINKING: Huie letters.
434 WHAT ELSE COULD WE DO: Huie letters.
435 HAVE YOU EVER SENT A LOVED SON: Whitfield, p. 23.
437 I'VE GOT ALL THESE REPORTERS: Whitfield, p. 23.
438 A DELTA SHERIFF COULD OFFICIALLY: Whitfield, p. 27.
438 MORNIN' NIGGERS: Author interview with Jay Milner and Murray Kempton.
438 CLARENCE, AS FORMER GOVERNOR BILL: Author interview with Bill Winter.
439 HE HAD THREE PLANES FOR CROP: Whitfield, pp. 29–30.
439 THIS NIGGER SAID THERE'S: Whitfield, p. 37.
439 WASN'T IT JUST LIKE THAT: Whitfield, pp. 31–32.
440 WHEN A CLARKSDALE RADIO STATION: Whitfield, p. 37.

440 THE MOST HE NEEDED WAS: Whitfield, p. 37.
440 YOUR ANCESTORS WILL TURN OVER: Whitfield, p. 34.
440 WELL, I HOPE THE CHICAGO NIGGERS: Whitfield, p. 34.
440 IT WOULD HAVE BEEN A QUICKER DECISION: Whitfield, p. 34.

CHAPTER THIRTY

441 JOURNALISTS, AS THE NOTED: Author conversation with James B. Reston.
442 IN THE LATE 19TH: Grossman, *Black Southerners and the Great Migration,* p. 13.
443 THEY COULD GET THE WRINKLE: Ottley, *The Lonely Warrior: The Life and Times of Robert S. Abbot,* p. 159.
443 WHY THE MINIMUM WAGE IN THE PACKING: Grossman, p. 15.
443 INSTEAD, IN HIS PAGES, A BLACK: Ottley, p. 110.
443 A COLORED MAN CAUGHT WITH: Ottley, p. 110.
444 IT WAS ESTIMATED THAT TWO THIRDS: Grossman, p. 75.
444 A RELIGIOUS PILGRIMAGE: Ottley, p. 163.
444 COME NORTH WHERE THERE IS MORE: Ottley, p. 161.
444 WITH TREMBLING AND FEAR: Grossman, p. 110.
445 IT WAS, HE CONFIDED TO HIS BROTHER: Maharidge and Williamson, *And Their Children Came After Them,* p. 40.
445 AT AN EARLY AGE HE: "Mr. Little Ol' Rust," *Fortune,* December 1952.
446 I KNEW I HAD HOLD OF SOMETHING: "Mr. Little Ol' Rust," *Fortune.*
446 GOOD HEAVENS, RUST, YOU CAN'T: Rust, "The Origin and Development of the Cotton Picker," Monograph.
447 WHEN THE RUST MACHINE FIRST: "Mr. Little Ol' Rust," *Fortune.*
447 THE MISSING LINK IN THE MECHANICAL: "Mr. Little Ol' Rust," *Fortune.*
447 I SINCERELY HOPE THAT YOU: Maharidge and Williamson, pp. 42–43.
447 E. H. CRUMP, THE POLITICAL BOSS: Street, *The New Evolution in Cotton Economy,* p. 125.
447 IF IT DOES MY WORK: Maharidge and Williamson, p. 42.
448 THERE WAS A LONG TIME: Author interview with G. E. Powell.
448 WHEN IN 1949, IT FINALLY: Maharidge and Williamson, p. 105.
449 A GOOD PICKER CAN AVERAGE: Goulden, *The Best Years,* p. 128.
449 EVERYONE WAS ENTHUSIASTIC: Author interview with Powell.
453 SOME ESTIMATED THAT BY 1955: Street, p. 170.
453 IN 1952 THE NATIONAL COTTON COUNCIL: "Mr. Little Ol' Rust," *Fortune.*
454 SO ESPY'S TELEVISION PEOPLE SHOT: Author interview with Bill Winter.

CHAPTER THIRTY-ONE

The section on Elvis Presley is based on a number of books, including biographies by Albert Goldman; Elaine Dundy; Steve Dunleavy; Dee Presley, Rich Stanley, and David Stanley; Stanley Booth; Kevin Quain; Larry Geller and Joel Spector; Peter Haining; Jerry Hopkins; Lee Cotten; Peter Guralnick; Colin Escot and Martin Hawkins; and Geoffrey Stokes, Ed Ward and Ken Tucker, as well as interviews with Sam Phillips of Sun Records and a number of other Elvisologists. In addition I spent four years as a reporter on the *Nashville Tennessean* covering, among other things, the music beat. That allowed me, through the courtesy of my friend, Chet Atkins, who ran the RCA studio, to watch sessions of Elvis recording during those early days in Nashville. I also knew Colonel Tom Parker quite well in those days, and much to my surprise he kept his promise to let me be the one reporter allowed on Elvis's train when the singer returned from the Army.

Section on James Dean:
479 IN A BOOK THAT WAS IN NO SMALL PART: Schickel, *Brando,* p. 1.
479 DEAN "WAS SO ADORING: Kazan, *A Life,* p. 538.

770 / NOTES

479 ON OCCASION DEAN SIGNED: Dalton, *James Dean, The Mutant King,* p. 159
479 DEAN WAS, WROTE STEVEN VINEBERG: Vineberg, p. 187.
480 DICK SCHICKEL NOTED THE ADVANTAGES: Schickel, p. 11.
480 DEAN ANSWERED THAT IT CAME: Dalton, p. 248.
481 HIS TALENT, ESPECIALLY HIS ABILITY: Dalton, p. 92.
482 "THEY'RE LIKE FIGHTERS: Dalton, p. 153.
482 "HE WAS SHOWING OFF: Kazan, p. 534.
482 "THERE WAS NO POINT IN TRYING: Dalton, p. 162.
482 THEN, PLAYING ALONG WITH: Dalton, p. 154.
482 THE TECHNICIANS WORKING ON THE SET: Kazan, p. 535.
483 THAT DELIGHTED KAZAN: Kazan, p. 535.
483 "MUST I ALWAYS BE MISERABLE: Dalton, p. 159.
483 THAT PLEASED KAZAN: Kazan, p. 537.
483 "HE'D SHOW ME THE GODDAMN: Dalton, p. 194.
484 ON THE SET OF *GIANT:* Dalton, p. 238.
484 DEAN IS, ONCE AGAIN: Dalton, p. 238.
484 IN TRUTH HE WAS NOT FOND: Kazan, pp. 538–39.
485 SUDDENLY *ALIENATION* WAS A WORD: Schickel, p. 6

CHAPTER THIRTY-TWO

486 BY ROUGH ESTIMATES, 49.3 MILLION: Cray, *Chrome Colossus* p. 362.
487 ZORA ARKUS-DUNTOV, A TOP GM DESIGNER: interview with David. E. Davis.
488 INSTEAD HE TURNED TO HIS AIDE: interview with Al Rothenberg.
489 AS THEY WERE HEADING BACK: interview with Tony de Lorenzo.
490 HEADING THE CORPORATION AFTER HEADING: interview with Tom Adams.
490 IN ADDITION THE STYLING OF THE CAR: Cray, p. 363.
493 COLE'S MOTTO, A FRIEND NOTED: Lamm, *Chevrolet 1955,* p. 6.
493 HE SCOURED THE COMPANY: Lamm, p. 10.
493 ALMOST EVERYTHING ABOUT THE 1955: Lamm, p. 6.
493 IT WAS, CLARE MACKICHAN: Lamm, p. 30
493 "HELL, I WOULDN'T WANT TO MAKE: Lamm, p. 29.
494 "IT SURE AS HELL IS: interview with David Cole.
494 "HE WANTED THE AVERAGE GUY: Lamm, p. 39.
494 OR AS HARLEY EARL SAID TO HARLOW: Lamm, p. 29.
494 THAT WAS WHAT THE PUBLIC WANTED: interview with Al Rothenberg.

CHAPTER THIRTY-THREE

495 IN THE HOME IT WAS TO BE: Hine, *Populux,* p. 15.
495 POPPY CANNON, A FOOD WRITER: Hine, p. 24. The material on Betty Furness comes from an author interview with her.
500 [WE] DISCOVERED, SAID ROSSER: Diamond and Bates, *The Spot,* p. 40.
500 THE SPEED WITH WHICH TELEVISION'S: Fox, *The Mirror Makers,* p. 210.
500 "SHOW THE PRODUCT," SAID BEN: Fox, p. 211.
500 MANY ADVERTISERS DID THAT: Fox, p. 211.
500 IT WAS, ROSSER REEVES SAID: Diamond and Bates, p. 40.
500 THE ADVERTISING FIRMS THAT ADAPTED: Fox, pp. 175, 210.
501 "WHY DON'T YOU BE ONE OF THOSE: Fox, p. 208.
501 "ADVERTISING," HE WROTE, "NOW COMPARES: Potter, *People of Plenty,* p. 167.
501 STUDIES COMPARING THE HEALTH: Fox, p. 209.
501 "I SOLD MY INTEREST: Mayer, *Madison Avenue, USA,* p. 11.
502 BUT IN THE NEW AGE OF TELEVISION: interview with David McCall.
502 A KIND OF MISGUIDED ETHIC: interviews with Don Frey, Tom Adams, and Campbell Ewald.

503 "OUR SOD-BUSTING DELIVERY: Fox, pp. 222–23, 225.
503 HIS CHILDREN BARELY SAW: Fox, p. 224.
504 OF THE ORIGINAL ADS: interview with David McCall.
504 THE ADS BEGAN TO TALK ABOUT: Packard, *The Hidden Persuaders*, p. 21.
504 THERE WAS A NEW WESTERN SONG: Packard, p. 21.
505 "CAPITALISM IS DEAD: Packard, p. 21.
505 WINTHROP ALDRICH, THEN THE HEAD: interview with David McCall.
505 ERNEST DICHTER, ONE OF THE FIRST: Packard, p. 57.
506 THIS WAS, HE BELIEVED: Packard, p. 58.

CHAPTER THIRTY-FOUR

The main sources for this chapter are author interviews with friends of Ricky Nelson, Joel Selvin's *Ricky Nelson: Idol for a Generation*, *The World According to Beaver* by Irving Applebaum, and *Ladies of the Evening: Woman Characters in Prime Time* by Diana Meehan.

CHAPTER THIRTY-FIVE

521 "WITHOUT TALKING ABOUT IT MUCH: Wilson, *The Man in the Gray Flannel Suit*, p. 3.
521 "FEW PEOPLE CONSIDERED GREENTREE: Wilson, p. 109.
522 WHEN THE NEIGHBORS GATHERED: Wilson, p. 109.
522 TRY FOR $15,000, ONE OF HIS: Wilson, p. 4.
522 THEN SHE SIGHS: Wilson, p. 6.
522 "WHEN YOU COME RIGHT DOWN: Wilson, p. 7.
522 HE COULD ALSO HAVE WRITTEN: Wilson, p. 8. The biographical material on Sloan Wilson is based on material from an interview with Wilson by the author.
526 "I HAVE NEVER KNOWN," HE: Press, *C. Wright Mills*, p. 13.
526 MILLS'S WORK WAS IMPORTANT: interview with Stanley Katz.
527 WHEN IT WAS HIS TURN TO RESPOND: Tilman, *C. Wright Mills*, p. 8.
528 ALIENATION CAME NATURALLY TO HIM: Press, p. 13.
528 HIS PARENTS FORCED HIM TO SING: Horowitz, *C. Wright Mills*, p. 6.
528 HE ONCE TOLD KURT WOLFF: Horowitz, p. 84.
528 AFTER AN UNHAPPY START: Wakefield, *New York in the Fifties*, p. 256.
529 CLARENCE AYRES, A PROFESSOR: Tilman, p. 6.
529 IN THIS LETTER WRITTEN: Tilman, p. 7.
529 IN MADISON, HE SEEMED TO MAKE: Horowitz, p. 47.
529 MILLS, HE SAID, WAS "AN EXCELLENT: Horowitz, p. 72.
530 IN MADISON HE MARRIED: Horowitz, p. 6.
530 HE TOLD MILLS TO "STICK: Horowitz, p. 58.
530 HE WAS TAKING POLITICS: Horowitz, p. 62.
530 HIS ATTITUDE AS IRVING: Horowitz, p. 66.
531 "ORGANIZE THE WORKERS: Press, p. 50.
531 THE LIBERALISM OF THE SOCIETY: Horowitz, p. 70.
531 "I WROTE MY WAY OUT OF THERE: Wakefield, p. 35.
531 "MILLS," WROTE HOROWITZ, "WAS CAUGHT: Horowitz, p. 83.
531 HE WOULD LATER SAY OF *WHITE COLLAR:* Wakefield, p. 35.
532 "WE WERE BOTH CONGENITAL: Horowitz, p. 77.
532 THEY BOTH HAD, HE NOTED: Horowitz, p. 77.
532 HE WAS, THOUGHT WAKEFIELD: Wakefield, p. 33.
533 AS HOROWITZ NOTED, IT HIT ON: Horowitz, p. 244.
533 RIESEMAN THOUGHT THERE WAS: interview with Rieseman.
533 THERE MIGHT BE, HOFSTADER: Horowitz, p. 251.
534 BELL'S CRITICISM STUNG: Tilman, p. 203.

534 AMERICA, HE THOUGHT, WAS: Tilman, p. 12.
535 HE CONTINUED TO SMOKE AND DRINK: Horowitz, p. 6.
535 "MILLS," AS IRVING HOROWITZ: Horowitz, p. 283.

CHAPTER THIRTY-SIX

539 SHE TOLD HIM TO GO RIGHT: Garrow, *Bearing the Cross*, p. 12.
540 BUT IF SHE HAD NOT PLANNED: Garrow, p. 12.
541 ONCE VIRGINIA DURR HAD TURNED: Yeakey, *The Montgomery, Alabama Bus Boycotts, 1955–1956*, p. 275.
541 AS THE BUS DRIVER CONTINUED TO SHOUT: Oates: *Let the Trumpet Sound: The Life of Martin Luther King, Jr.*, p. 8.
541 DID THEY BEAT YOU: Yeakey, p. 255.
542 OH, THE WHITE FOLKS WILL KILL YOU: Durr, *Memoir, Vol. II,* (Nov. 24, 1976); and Yeakey, p. 275.
542 IF YOU THINK YOU CAN GET: Yeakey, p. 275.
543 WELL, I'LL TELL YOU ONE: Raines, *My Soul is Rested*, p. 44.
543 EVEN GOD CAN'T FREE PEOPLE WHO: Abernathy, *And the Walls Came Tumbling Down,* p. 17.
544 ATTEMPTS ON THE PART OF BLACK: Yeakey, p. 97.
544 THERE IS GOING TO BE A SECOND DAY: *The Montgomery Advertiser,* July 10, 1954, pp. 1A–5A; and Yeakey, p. 90.
545 SHE INSISTED SHE WAS COLORED: from transcript of *City vs. Claudette Colvin* in the circuit court of Juvenile Court and Court of Domestic Relations, Montgomery County, Alabama (March 18, 1955); and Yeakey, p. 235.
547 NOW, LET US SAY THAT WE: King, "Speech at Holt Church"; cited in Yeakey, p. 668.
547 FIVE YEARS BEFORE THE BUS BOYCOTT: Yeakey, p. 17.
549 I'LL KILL YOU, KILL YOU: King, Sr., *Daddy King*, p. 47.
549 A MAN'S ANGER GETS THE BEST OF HIM: King, Sr., p. 47.
549 NOW, KING, YOU KNOW GOD DOESN'T LOVE: King, Sr., p. 14.
549 WHY, REVEREND KING, YOU MUST BE FIXIN': King, Sr., p. 22.
550 YOU'RE JUST NOT COLLEGE MATERIAL: King, Sr., p. 75.
550 APPARENTLY, YOU CAN START CLASSES: King, Sr., p. 77.
551 HE WAS THE MOST PECULIAR CHILD: Oates, p. 8.
553 THE SHACKLES OF FUNDAMENTALISM WERE: Oates, p. 19.
553 YOU WILL NOT BE MARRYING ANY ORDINARY: Oates, p. 45.
553 AT FIRST BAPTIST, THEY DON'T MIND THE PREACHER TALKING: Abernathy, pp. 118–119.
553 KEEP MARTIN LUTHER KING IN THE BACKGROUND: Oates, p. 48.
554 JOHNSON WAS AMUSED WHEN, IN THE MIDDLE: Author interview with W. Thomas Johnson.
554 I DON'T WANT TO LOOK LIKE AN UNDERTAKER: "Attack on the Conscience," *Time* February 18, 1957, p. 19.
554 THEY PREACHED THE GOSPEL: Abernathy, p. 114.
555 COMES THE FIRST RAINY DAY: Oates, p. 75.
555 THE NEGROES ARE LAUGHING: Yeakey, p. 487.
555 SHOOTIN' MARBLES, FOR EXAMPLE: Yeakey, p. 397.
557 AN ALMOST PERFECT CROSS BETWEEN: Author interview with Karl Fleming.
557 HE SPOKE MORE AND MORE SCATHINGLY: Author interviews with Robert Ingram, Ray Jenkins, Wallace Westfeldt, Karl Fleming, Wayne Greenhaw, Claude Sitton, Tom Johnson, and Harry Ashmore.
557 WE LOVE OUR CITY HERE: Greenhaw, *Alabama on My Mind*, p. 60.
557 THE KINDEST THING THAT COULD BE SAID: Author interviews.
559 AND YOU NEVER KNOW WHAT COLOR: Author interview with Wallace Westfeldt.
560 I WOULDN'T TRADE MY SOUTHERN BIRTHRIGHT: *Time,* February 18, 1957, p. 19.
560 I HAVE THE FEELING: Oates, p. 95.

560 MARTIN LUTHER, STAND UP FOR: Oates, pp. 88–89.
560 VISION IN THE KITCHEN: Branch, *Parting the Waters,* p. 202.
561 THEY GON' TO KILL MY BOY: Oates, p. 93.
561 I HAVE BEGUN THE STRUGGLE: Oates, p. 93.
562 GET ME MY CHICKEN GUN: Author interviews with Wayne Greenhaw and Ray Jenkins.

CHAPTER THIRTY-SEVEN

Major sources for the section on Marilyn Monroe are *Timebends* by Arthur Miller; *Marilyn: A Biography* by Norman Mailer; *Marilyn Monroe: The Body in the Library* by Graham McCann; *Norma Jean: The Life of Marilyn Monroe* and *Legend: The Life and Death of Marilyn Monroe* by Fred Lawrence Guiles; *Goddess: The Secret Lives of Marilyn Monroe* by Anthony Summers; and *Marilyn Monroe Confidential* by Lena Pepitone with William Stadiem. The major sources for the section on Hugh Hefner and *Playboy* are *Thy Neighbor's Wife* by Gay Talese and Thomas Weyr's *Reaching for Paradise: The Playboy Vision of America.*

CHAPTER THIRTY-EIGHT

577 "BECAUSE YOU WOULDN'T HAVE LET: Davis, *Two-Bit Culture* p. 257.
577 "BUT IF YOU GO BENEATH: Toth, *Inside Peyton Place,* p. 1.
579 AS KENNETH DAVIS NOTED IN HIS BOOK: Davis, p. 259.
579 "FOR PERHAPS THE FIRST TIME IN POPULAR: Davis, p. 255.
581 "HOW COULD YOU BE SO STUPID: Toth, p. 49.
581 "I AM TRAPPED: Toth p. 60.
583 "I KNOW THIS IS A BIG BOOK: Toth, p. 94
583 BY CONTRAST MESSNER LOOKED: Toth, p. 94.
583 LATER SHE DECIDED THAT WHAT: interview with Leona Nevler.
584 INTERESTINGLY ENOUGH, A CRITIC: Toth, p. 145.
584 THE PEOPLE IN NEW YORK: interview with Nevler.
584 "THIS BOOK BUSINESS: Toth, p. 151.
585 YEARS LATER GEORGE METALIOUS: Toth, p. 178.
584 ALMOST AS SOON AS THE INTERVIEW: Toth, p. 163.
585 "OUR MOTHER HAD TO BE TOLD: Toth, p. 225.

CHAPTER THIRTY-NINE

587 A POLL OF BOTH MEN AND WOMEN: Ryan, *Womanhood in America,* p. 188.
587 AT THE BEGINNING OF THE NEW DEAL: Sochen, *Movers and Shakers,* p. 162.
587 THE *LADIES HOME JOURNAL* EVEN PUT: Ryan, p. 188.
588 IN JUST TWO YEARS SOME TWO MILLION: Ryan, p. 190.
590 "WHEN JIM COMES HOME," SAID: Hine, *Populux,* p. 55.
590 "THE TWO BIG STEPS: Hine, p. 31.
The material on Betty Friedan comes from an interview with the author, *It Changed My Life* and *The Feminine Mystique,* both by Ms. Friedan, and *The Sisterhood* by Marcia Cohen.

CHAPTER FORTY

601 HE BEGAN TO FIT SOME OF HIS: Davidson, "Dr. Rock's Magic Pill," p. 100.
601 "DEAR MADAM," HE WROTE BACK: unpublished manuscript by Mahlon Hoagland.
602 "HE [PINCUS] WAS A LITTLE SCARY: Vaughan, *The Pill on Trial,* p. 32.
602 "THEY DID IT," THE YOUNG HOAGLAND: interview with Mahlon Hoagland.
603 "AFTER ALL, IF YOU COULD PATENT: Vaughan, p. 21.
604 "THE R.C. CHURCH," SHE WROTE: Gray, *Margaret Sanger,* p. 435.

604 BY DOING SO HE WAS ABLE TO "LIBERATE: Pauly, *Controlling Life,* p. 194.
604 HE WOULD TELL HIS AUDIENCES: Pauly, p. 194.
604 "TO MARGARET SANGER," HE WROTE: Kennedy, *Birth Control in America,* p. vii.
604 OF IT CLARE BOOTH LUCE: Davidson, p. 108.
605 WHEN THE STORY WAS RELAYED TO CHANG: interview with M. C. Chang and Mahlon Hoagland.

CHAPTER FORTY-ONE

607 WE DESPISE THE FRENCH: McDougall, *The Heavens and the Earth,* p. 44.
607 THESE MEN, HUZEL BELIEVES, TEND: Lewis, *Appointment on the Moon,* p. 24.
607 MY NAME IS MAGNUS VON BRAUN: McDougall, p. 44.
608 TOO YOUNG, TOO FAT, TOO JOVIAL: Rothe and Lohr, *Current Biography: Who's News and Why 1952,* p. 608.
608 THIS WILL MAKE BUCK ROGERS: McDougall, p. 44.
608 WE WERE IMPRESSED WITH THEIR: McDougall, p. 70.
608 THIS IS ABSOLUTELY INTOLERABLE: McDougall, p. 44.
608 FOR MY CONFIRMATION: Noble, "Wernher von Braun, Rocket Pioneer Dies," *The New York Times,* June 18, 1977, p. 24.
609 I WAS ECSTATIC: Berghaus, *Reaching for the Stars,* p. 40.
610 DO YOU REALIZE WHAT WE: Clarke, *The Coming of Space,* p. 49.
610 OUR MAIN OBJECTIVE FOR A LONG TIME: Medaris, *Countdown for Decision,* p. 38.
610 WITH SUCH WEAPONS, HUMANITY: Medaris, p. 38.
610 WHAT I WANT IS ANNIHILATION: Dornberger, *V-2,* p. 103.
610 VON BRAUN CHECKED IT OUT: Berghaus, p. 78.
612 SHADOWS AND IMAGES IN THE STRANGE: Berghaus, p. 29.
612 FORMER GERMAN SCIENTISTS WHO: Medaris, p. 117.
613 BUT IT WAS NO SMALL IRONY, AS: McDougall, p. 99.
613 THEY QUICKLY PICKED UP THE SECOND TIER: Parry, *Russia's Rockets and Missiles,* p. 115.
613 THE POINT IS THAT THE V-2: McDougall, p. 53.
614 I DON'T WANT TO EXAGGERATE: McDougall, p. 59.
615 HE HELD THE JOB FOR ELEVEN MONTHS: McDougall, p. 105.
615 THIS COUNTRY, HE ONCE NOTED: McDougall, p. 126.
616 BY THE SUMMER OF 1955, THE AIR FORCE: Wise and Ross, *The U-2 Affair,* p. 46.
617 A JET WITH THE BODY: Powers and Gentry, *Operation Overflight,* p. 22.
618 YOU'LL NEVER CONVINCE ME: Wise and Ross, p. 43.
619 I'VE FIGURED OUT WHAT YOU'RE DOING: Powers and Gentry, p. 39.
619 ONCE ON, IT FELT LIKE: Powers and Gentry, p. 22.
619 SITTING ON A LOADED SHOT GUN: Powers and Gentry, p. 62.
622 I WOULDN'T CARE IF THEY DID: Manchester, *The Glory and the Dream,* p. 787.
622 IT IS ONLY LOGICAL TO ASSUME: McDougall, p. 119.
623 A USELESS HUNK OF IRON: Kennan and Harvey, *Mission to the Moon,* p. 62.
624 A SILLY BAUBLE IN THE SKY: Parry, p. 190.
624 AS FAR AS THE SATELLITE IS CONCERNED: Ambrose, *Eisenhower the President,* pp. 429–30.
624 YES, DEAR, AND IN SIX MONTHS: Lewis, p. 55.
625 A BOOK CALLED: Manchester, p. 793.
625 ONE CRITIC NOTED THAT AS: Parry, p. 190.
625 YOU AMERICANS HAVE A BETTER: Manchester, p. 793.
625 CELESTIAL BROTHERS: McDougall, p. 286.
625 THEY'LL CALL ME SOON: Berghaus, p. 327.
626 IT SEEMED AS IF THE GATES OF HELL: Clarke, p. 19.
626 PHUT GOES U.S. SATELLITE: Lewis, p. 58.
626 THAT WAS SPUTNIK: Parry, p. 191.

627 THEY HEAR HER, WERNHER, THEY: Berghaus, p. 321.
627 SHE IS EIGHT MINUTES LATE: Lewis, p. 67.
627 LET'S NOT MAKE TOO GREAT: McDougall, p. 168.

CHAPTER FORTY-TWO

The material for the section on advertising and General Motors is based on interviews with Kennsinger Jones, Gerald Schnitzer, Al Rothenberg, and Barney Knudsen. Sources used for the section on the Volkswagen and the Corvair are *Small Wonder: The Amazing Story of Volkswagen* by Walter Henry Nelson, *Unsafe at Any Speed* by Ralph Nader, and author interviews with David E. Davis, Don Frey, and several General Motors executives.

CHAPTER FORTY-THREE

643 BUT $64,000 GETS INTO THE REALM: Anderson, *Television Fraud: The History and the Implications of the Quiz Show Scandals*, p. 6.
643 SHE DID NOT HESITATE TO MAKE: Author interview with Geoff Cowan.
643 IT PROVED EVERY AMERICAN HAD: Author interview with Geoff Cowan.
643 NOBODY LEAVES THIS ROOM: Barnouw, *The History of Broadcasting: The Image Empire*, p. 56.
644 WE'RE ALL PRETTY MUCH ALIKE: Anderson, p. 39.
644 ANY BETS ON HOW LONG: Friendly, *Due to Circumstances Beyond Our Control*, p. 77.
644 A NEW TELEVISION PROGRAM SPONSORED: Barnouw, p. 58.
645 THE CONSERVATISM OF A FATHER: Anderson, p. 9.
645 LET YOUR MODERATION BE KNOWN: Anderson, p. 9.
645 IF YOU'RE SYMBOLIC OF THE MARINE CORPS: Anderson, p. 20.
646 IT HELPED. IT HELPED: *Hearings of the Subcommittee of the Committee on Interstate and Foreign Commerce, Eighty-sixth Congress, II*, Vol. 51, p. 811.
646 WE WROTE THE QUESTIONS INTO: Author interview with Russell Baker.
647 LATER HE TOLD JOE STONE: Stone and Yohn, *Prime Time and Misdemeanors*, pp. 206–7.
647 DO WHATEVER YOU HAVE TO DO: Author interview with Dan Enright.
648 YOU CANNOT ASK RANDOM QUESTIONS: Stone and Yohn, p. 119.
648 THUS HE WAS ABLE TO RATIONALIZE: Author interview with Enright.
648 THE WALKING ENCYCLOPEDIA: Author interview with Herb Stempel.
649 IF YOU SAW HIM: Author interview with Enright.
649 ENRIGHT MADE STEMPEL GET: Author interview with Enright.
649 STEMPEL WAS EVEN TOLD TO WEAR: *Hearings*, p. 26.
650 YOU'RE NOT PAYING ATTENTION: *Hearings*, p. 29.
650 IT WAS A CRUEL THING TO DO: Author interview with Enright.
650 I THINK I'VE GOT THE RIGHT: Author interview with Enright.
651 YOU COULD BE ERUDITE AND LEARNED: Author interview with Al Freedman.
652 IT TOOK HIS BREATH AWAY: Author interview with Dick Goodman.
653 CHARLIE, DID YOU KNOW THAT: Author interview with Al Freedman.
653 NOT MUCH OF A BUSINESSMAN: Van Doren, *The Autobiography of Mark Van Doren*, p. 16.
653 THE DIFFICULT ATTAINABLE THROUGH: Van Doren, p. 275.
653 THE SUN WOULD GO DOWN JUST AS: Author interview with Alfred Kazin.
654 VALUES YOUR LETTERS IF ONLY: Hendrick, *The Selected Letters of Mark Van Doren*, p. 136.
654 REALLY, CHA, I'M NOT: Hendrick, p. 136.
655 I FELT HERE WAS A GUY: "Meeting of Minds," *Time*, September 15, 1958.
657 I FELT LIKE A BULLFIGHTER: Author interview with Dick Goodwin.
657 'CAUSE WHEN I GO ON: "Meeting of Minds," *Time*.

658 HE WAS NOT NEARLY AS BOTHERED: Author interview with Enright.
658 DAN, I HOPE THIS TEACHES YOU: Author interview with Enright.
659 DAN, HAVE I EVER ASKED YOU: Author interview with Enright.
660 DICK, SOME DAY I HOPE: Author interview with Goodwin.
662 A QUIZ SHOW INVESTIGATION WITHOUT: Author interview with Goodwin.
663 THE DINNER WAS SUPERB: Goodwin, *Remembering America*, pp. 57–58.
664 IF I WANTED TO DESTROY: Stone and Yohn, p. 251.
665 OF THE IMPORTANT PLAYERS STILL: Author interview with Julian Krainan.

CHAPTER FORTY-FOUR

668 NATURAL-BORN ROTARIAN: Author interview with Harry Ashmore.
668 AT THE HEART OF THEIR: Author interview with Ashmore.
668 TO FIND OUT WHY: Author interview with Ashmore.
668 IN FACT, JUST ABOUT: Huckaby, *Crisis at Central High: Little Rock 1957–1958*, p. ix.
669 NOBODY URGED ME TO GO: Blossom, *It Happened Here*, p. 82.
669 YOU MAY DESERVE ORVAL FAUBUS: Ashmore, *Hearts and Minds: The Anatomy of Racism from Roosevelt to Reagan*, p. 253.
670 GOVERNOR, JUST WHAT *ARE* YOU GOING: Blossom, p. 53.
670 IF THE SOUTHERN STATES ARE PICKED: Blossom, p. 30.
671 WHY DON'T TELEPHONE HIM: Blossom, p. 54.
671 HIS FATHER, SAM FAUBUS, SAID: Ashmore, p. 261.
671 HE WAS, ASHMORE LIKED TO SAY: Author interview with Ashmore.
671 LATER AFTER LITTLE ROCK HAD: Ashmore, p. 253.
671 FAUBUS NEVER EVEN SAW A BLACK: Ashmore, p. 260.
672 IT WAS HARD TO FIND WHITE: Blossom, pp. 50–51.
672 I BROUGHT ORVAL DOWN FROM: Ashmore, p. 255.
672 IN 1954 FAUBUS RAN FOR GOVERNOR: Faubus, *Down from the Hills*, p. 16.
673 I'M SORRY, BUT I'M ALREADY: Ashmore, p. 259.
673 KEEP THE NIGGERS OUT: Blossom, p. 84.
675 HE WAS TERRIBLY FRIGHTENED FOR HER: Author interview with John Chancellor.
677 YOU CAN DO WHAT YOU WANT: Author interview with Chancellor.
677 A LOVELY MOZARTIAN UNITY: Author interview with Chancellor.
678 A NATIONAL EVENING SEANCE: Author interview with Daniel Schorr.
678 WITH TELEVISION EVERY BIT OF ACTION: Author interview with Chancellor.
678 CAN YOU BELIEVE THIS: Author interview with Chancellor.
680 LIPMAN ALWAYS HAD TO WHISPER: Author interview with Chancellor.
680 WESTFELDT COULD SEE THEM CURSING: Author interview with Wallace Westfeldt.
680 AT FIRST HE WOULD PANIC: Author interview with Chancellor.
681 SHERIFF, THERE'S SOME SON: Author interview with Chancellor.
681 A BAPTIST PREACHER BUT NEVER: Author interview with Will Campbell.
683 THIS IS A SIN: Author interview with Campbell.
683 I'M AN OLD MAN: Ashmore, p. 258.
683 I'LL GIVE IT TO YOU IN ONE: Bates, *Long Shadow of Little Rock*, p. 93.
684 BUT REMEMBER ORVAL: Author interview with Ashmore.
684 IN FACT, THE STATE ATTORNEY GENERAL: Author interview with Herbert Brownell.
685 THE MAN TO WHOM EISENHOWER: Sulzberger, *A Long Row of Candles: Memoirs and Diaries*, p. 649.
685 THE ATTORNEY GENERAL WARNED THE PRESIDENT: Author interview with Brownell.
685 HERB, CAN'T YOU GO DOWN THERE: Faubus, p. 257.
685 IT WAS ONLY WHEN BROWNELL: Author interview with Brownell.
685 I GOT THE IMPRESSION THAT: Faubus, p. 255.
686 JUST BECAUSE I SAID IT: Ashmore, p. 269.
686 WELL, YOU WERE RIGHT, HERB: Author interview with Brownell.
686 A WEAK PRESIDENT WHO FIDDLED: McLellan and Acheson, *Among Friends: The Personal Letters of Dean Acheson*, p. 132.

687 FOR THE FIRST TIME IN MY LIFE: Bates, p. 104.

687 ALL SHE HAD DONE: Huckaby, p. 77.

692 NL, THE TRADITIONAL NEWSPAPER ABBREVIATION: Author interview with Reggie Smith.

693 THIS IS AN INDOOR SPORT AND TABOOS: Gunther, *Inside America*, p. 285.

693 OF COURSE I'M GOING TO WORK: Russell, *Go Up for Glory*, p. 17.

694 AT THE END OF THE '55: Author interview with Bob Cousy and Bill Walton.

694 $6000 WAS GOING TO BE HELD OUT: Stout, "Scientist in Sneakers", *Boston* magazine, February 1989.

694 WE'LL COUNT REBOUNDS AS BASKETS: Russell, p. 123.

695 THERE HAD NEVER BEEN ANYTHING: Author interview with Cousy.

696 JUST ANOTHER BLACK BOY: Russell, p.37.

696 *THIS*, THE INTENSITY OF HIS PLAY: Author interview with Cousy.

CHAPTER FORTY-FIVE

699 I FELT AS THOUGH I WERE: Lyon, *Eisenhower: Portrait of a Hero*, pp. 756–57.

699 I CAN'T UNDERSTAND THE UNITED: Ambrose, *Nixon*, p. 434.

700 JUST WHAT DO YOU THINK: Beschloss, *Mayday*, p. 113.

700 UNEASY, IRASCIBLE, CROTCHETY: Sulzberger, *The Last of the Giants*, p. 103.

700 HE WAS SURROUNDED BY POLITICIANS: Sulzberger, *Giants*, p. 102.

700 I DON'T KNOW WHY ANYONE: Ambrose, p. 596.

701 YOU ALL WENT TO GREAT SCHOOLS: Beschloss, *The Crisis Years: Kennedy and Khrushchev, 1960–1963*, p. 34.

701 THE HEIGHT OF THE TAIL FIN: Beschloss, *Crisis*, p. 149.

702 SUCH A PERSON, TRUSTED BY: Beschloss, *Mayday*, p. 94.

702 TO HIS MIND, *THE NEW YORK TIMES*: Beschloss, *Mayday*, p. 2.

702 ROSCOE, THAT'S THE FELLOW: Sulzberger, *A Long Row of Candles: Memoirs and Diaries*, p. 922.

702 I CAN'T STAND THAT GANGSTER: Sulzberger, *Giants*, p. 579.

703 ONE PRAYS—HOW ODD IT: Beschloss, *Mayday*, p. 153.

704 WE HAVEN'T MADE A CHIP: Beschloss, *Mayday*, p. 7.

704 YOU BEGIN TO SEE THIS THING: Ambrose, p. 516.

704 LOOK, I'D LIKE TO KNOW WHAT'S: Ambrose, p. 433.

704 EVEN WHEN HE DID INCREASE: Ambrose, p. 433.

704 GOD HELP THE NATION WHEN: Beschloss, *Mayday*, p. 209.

704 WHEN HE HEARD THE NEWS: Beschloss, *Mayday*, p. 7.

706 POWERS WAS A MAN, WHO: Beschloss, *Mayday*, p. 350.

706 I CAN SHOW HIM THE EVIDENCE: Ambrose, p. 536.

707 HE WAS NOT AFRAID TO SAY: Beschloss, *Mayday*, p. 209.

707 I'LL BRING ALONG THE WHOLE: Beschloss, *Mayday*, p. 213.

707 THE BLACK LADY OF ESPIONAGE: Powers, *Operation Overflight*, p. 67.

707 AS MICHAEL BESCHLOSS NOTED, KNOWING: Beschloss, *Mayday*, p. 234.

708 IF ONE OF THESE AIRCRAFT: Beschloss, *Mayday*, p. 233.

708 YOU MAY AS WELL TELL THEM: Powers, p. 71.

708 INJECTING YOURSELF WITH THE SUBSTANCE: Powers, p. 69.

709 THAT THEY WOULD *NEVER* CAPTURE: Beschloss, *Mayday*, p. 8.

709 THERE IS NOT A CHANCE OF HIS: Beschloss, *Mayday*, p. 37.

709 PERHAPS KHRUSCHEV, HE THOUGHT, MIGHT: Powers, p. x.

710 YEARS LATER, CHIP BOHLEN, ONE: Beschloss, *Mayday*, p. 239.

710 THE WHOLE WORLD KNOWS THAT ALLEN: Beschloss, *Mayday*, pp. 59–60.

710 I AM NOT GOING TO SHIFT: Beschloss, *Mayday*, p. 271.

711 I'M GOING TO TAKE UP SMOKING: Beschloss, *Mayday*, p. 284.

711 I HAD LONGED TO GIVE THE UNITED STATES: Beschloss, *Mayday*, p. 388.

CHAPTER FORTY-SIX

713 SUPERMAN WOULD PRETEND TO HAVE SEX: Dorschner and Fabricio, *The Winds of December*, p. 21.

713 RESEMBLED THE ORGANIZATION OF A LARGE: Dorschner and Fabricio, p. 65.

714 SINCE BATISTA WAS THE SON OF A CANE: Dorschner and Fabricio, p. 63.

714 HE LOVED TO EAT: Dorschner and Fabricio, p. 65.

714 A MAN LIKE THAT HAS ENEMIES: Dorschner and Fabricio, p. 67.

715 SMITH LIKED TO SAY THAT HE: Dorschner and Fabricio, pp. 48–49.

715 I HAVE LIVED TWO ERAS: Dorschner and Fabricio, pp. 48–49.

716 BATISTA WAS BAD MEDICINE: Smith, *The Closest of Enemies*, p. 36.

716 IRONICALLY, IN CONTRAST TO BATISTA: Szulc, *Fidel: A Critical Portrait*, p. 105.

716 HISTORY WILL ABSOLVE ME: Szulc, p. 297.

717 ARE WE ALREADY IN THE SIERRA: Dorschner and Fabricio, p. 34.

717 THE PERSONALITY OF THE MAN: Szulc, p. 413.

719 THE BATISTA REGIME AT THE END: Smith, p. 38.

719 WHAT CAN I DO: Dorschner and Fabricio, p. 461.

719 THE AMERICANS WERE, WROTE WAYNE SMITH: Smith, p. 36.

719 LIKE MOSES PARTING THE RED SEA: Dorschner and Fabricio, p. 492.

720 FOR HE SEEMED TO HAVE: Smith, pp. 15–16.

720 WE BELIEVE THAT CASTRO: Johnson, *The Bay of Pigs*, p. 25.

721 CASTRO IS EITHER INCREDIBLY NAIVE: Wyden, *Bay of Pigs*, pp. 28–29.

721 AT THE FIRST STOP WHEN BAKER: Author interview with Russell Baker.

721 BECAUSE I KNOW WHO I AM: Halberstam, *The Best and the Brightest*, p. 98.

722 I'M SORRY ABOUT THAT EPISODE: Ambrose, *Nixon: The Education of a Politician 1913–1962*, p. 220.

722 THIS IS THE ACHESON LINE: Ambrose, p. 520.

722 IT STINKS LIKE FRESH HORSE: Ambrose, pp. 522–23.

723 YOU DO ALL THE TALKING: Ambrose, p. 524.

723 WAYNE SMITH, A MAN NOT: Smith, p. 49.

724 FIDEL HAS ALL ALONG FELT HIMSELF TO BE: Smith, p. 49.

724 HE COULD NOT BE A MAJOR: Author interview with Earl Mazo.

725 CUBA. CUBA. AND CUBA: Wyden, pp. 21–22.

725 WELCOME ABOARD CHICO: Wyden, pp. 21–22.

725 THERE WAS ONE CIA OFFICER: Wyden, p. 31.

726 IT WAS CLEAR, CUSHMAN THOUGHT: Wyden, p. 29.

726 HELMS, AS PETER WYDEN NOTED IN: Wyden, p. 48.

726 THE PLAN CALLED FOR TRAINING: Wyden, p. 25.

727 I'M GOING ALONG WITH YOU: Wyden, p. 68.

728 ISN'T IT MARVELOUS: Author interview with Mazo.

728 MR. NIXON HASN'T MENTIONED CUBA: Kennedy, *Speeches of John F. Kennedy: Presidential Campaign of 1960*, p. 607.

729 THE VICE-PRESIDENT SOMETIMES SEEMS: Ambrose, p. 601.

731 EVEN HANNAH NIXON CALLED ROSE: Ambrose, p. 575.

731 UNFORTUNATELY, ANYONE WHO UNDERSTOOD: Author interviews with James Bassett, Ted Rogers, Bill Wilson, Pierre Salinger, Don Hewitt, and Leonard Hall.

732 DO YOU GET A FUNNY SORT OF SENSE: McLellan and Acheson, *Among Friends: The Personal Letters of Dean Acheson*, p. 193.

INDEX

"How Dulles Averted War" (Shepley), 408
"Howl" (Ginsberg), 306–7
Howling Wolf, 468
Huckaby, Elizabeth, 687–88
Hucksters, The (Wakeman), 500–501
Hudson, Richard, 558
Hughes, Emmet John, 390–91, 408
Huie, William Bradford, 433, 434, 435, 440
Hulton, Graham, 214
Humphrey, George, 395, 399
Huncke, Herbert, 301
Hunt, E. Howard, 359, 372, 375, 725
Huntley, Chet, 678
Huzel, Dieter, 607
hydrogen bomb, 28–48, 87, 330, 332,
341–42, 343
  Air Force and, 37–38
  computer technology and, 92–93
  debate over, 28–30
  development of, 42–47
  Lucky Dragon incident and, 344–48
  Oppenheimer and, 30–40, 42–43
  politics and, 36, 39–40
  Soviet Union and, 47, 99–100
  Teller and, 34–37, 43–44, 46, 91
  tests of, 97–99
  Truman's decision on, 36, 42, 44, 45–46

I, The Jury (Spillane), 59–60
I Aim at the Stars, 613
I Love Lucy, 197–201, 239, 503
"I'm All Right, Mama," 458
Immerman, Richard, 377
"I'm Walkin'," 517
Indochina War, 358, 397–99, 403–9
Inside Peyton Place (Toth), 579–80
Institute for Sex Research of Indiana
  University, 278
Invasion of the Body Snatchers, The, 140
Iran, 359
  CIA coup in, 360–68, 370
Irvin, Monte, 692
Irwin, James, 603
"I Say He's a Wonderful Guy" (Pat
  Nixon), 321
Isbell, Marion, 178–79
isolationism, isolationists, 6, 9, 56, 67, 310,
370, 371
  McCormick and, 214–18
  1952 election and, 204, 205, 209
  Taft and, 207

Jackman, Richard, 648
Jack's Book (Gifford and Lee), 301
Jackson, Kenneth, 135, 142
Jackson, Robert, 410, 411, 412, 418, 420,
421, 422
Jackson (Miss.) *Daily News,* 447
Japan, 17, 27, 28, 62, 63, 64, 82, 346, 347,
355, 371

Jenner, William, 17, 54, 57, 251, 252, 341
Jewish Farmer, 288
JOHNNIAC, 97
Johns, Vernon, 543, 553
Johnson, Kelly, 616, 617, 618, 709
Johnson, Louis, 45
Johnson, Lyndon B., 53, 404, 406, 624,
703
Johnson, Tom, 554
Johnson, Wallace, 177
Johnston, Neil, 695
Joint Chiefs of Staff, 17, 44–45, 67, 69–70,
83–84, 103, 109, 395, 396, 399, 615
Joint Committee on Atomic Energy, 36,
331, 342
Jones, Curtis, 430, 431, 432, 435
Jones, Kensinger, 628–34
Jones, Margo, 267
Jordan, Will, 474
Joy of Reading, The (Van Doren), 665
Jurist, Edward, 648
Justice Department, U.S., 118, 129, 337,
544

Kael, Pauline, 483
Kammerer, Dave, 298
Kazan, Elia, 255–57, 260, 262–66, 267,
270–71, 479, 480, 482–85
Kazan, Molly Day Thacher, 260, 265, 266
Kazin, Alfred, 653
Keats, John, 134, 139
Keck, John, 608
Kefauver, Estes, 188–94, 222, 223
Keiser, Laurence "Dutch," 108
Kelley, Tom, 566, 569, 570
Kempton, Murray, 13, 15, 16, 437
Kennan, George, 15, 18, 64, 84, 330, 349
Kennedy, John F., 92, 314, 604, 605, 664,
690, 703, 721, 726, 727, 728–31
Kern, Nathan, 452
Kerouac, Jack, 296, 297, 298–305, 306, 307
Kerr, Deborah, 501
Kerr, Robert S., 203
Kessel, Barney, 518
Kessie, Jack, 573
Kettering, Charles, 119–20, 127–28, 638
Keyes, Evelyn, 564
Keynes, John Maynard, 394
Khrushchev, Nikita, 66, 613, 614, 623,
625, 700–701, 705, 724, 728
  "kitchen debate" and, 722–23
  U.S. visit of, 706–7
  U-2 affair and, 709–11
Killian, James, 616
Kim Il Sung, 65–66
King, B. B., 468, 469
King, Coretta Scott, 552, 553, 554
King, Martin Luther, Jr., 543, 692
  background of, 548–54
  boycott and, 546–47, 556–57, 559–62

AUTHOR'S NOTE

I am a child of the fifties. I graduated from high school in 1951, from college in 1955, and my values were shaped in that era. I wanted to write a book which would not only explore what happened in the fifties, a more interesting and complicated decade than most people imagine, but in addition, to show why the sixties took place—because so many of the forces which exploded in the sixties had begun to come together in the fifties, as the pace of life in America quickened. In large part this book reflects my desire as a grown man to go back and look at things that happened when I was much younger. I was a reporter in the South in the early days of the civil rights struggle; I went to Mississippi in 1955 immediately after graduation specifically because the Supreme Court had ruled on the Brown case the year before, and I thought therefore the Deep South was the best place to apprentice as a journalist. I was a reporter in

West Point, Mississippi, when the Emmett Till trial took place in Sumner that summer. As I became aware of the vast press corps which was arriving in Tallahatchie County to cover the case, I knew instinctively that something important was taking place. I got an assignment from the old *Reporter* magazine to do a piece on the trial, and I faithfully read the various papers of the different reporters covering it. On my days off, I went over to watch them at work there. (I also managed to stay as far from Clarence Strider as I could—I still remember his threatening figure.) But when I sat down to write at the time, I was not able to pull off the piece I wanted, and it fizzled. Some thirty-eight years later I have taken what I sensed but could not articulate then, and tried to make it a part of this book. That is true of other experiences from those days as well. I have a clear memory, from countless visits to the bus stations in Nashville, Memphis, and Jackson, Mississippi, of large families of blacks headed North with all of their belongings. Clearly a great migration was then taking place, and I saw it, yet did not see it. This event of great historic importance went right by me until I finally understood its meaning some twelve years later when Andy Young talked to me about it one day while I was reporting on Martin King. Later, when I was a reporter in Nashville, I was assigned to cover the country music beat. That led to a friendship with Chet Atkins, the distinguished guitarist, who was also in charge of RCA's studios, and who would, on occasion, discreetly let me sit in when the young Elvis was recording there. Yet only later would I become fully aware of the importance of the new music as a sign of the political, economic, and social empowerment of the younger generation.

A book as long as demanding as this requires the help of many colleagues and I would like to thank among others my editor Douglas Stumpf, his assistants Leslie Chang, Erik Palma, and Jared Stamm. I am also grateful to Carsten Fries, Veronica Windholz, and Patty O'Connell at Random House, Fernando Villagra, Amanda Earle, Danny Franklin, Martin Garbus, Bob Solomon, Gary Schwartz, Ken Starr and Philip Roome, the staff of the New York Society Library where I spent long and happy hours, Pat Martin at the Worcester Foundation, Geoffrey Smith at the archives at Ohio State, who helped me look at Bill Huie's papers, Vicky Lem McDonald at the Museum of Broadcasting, and Keith Roachford in Senator Bill Bradley's office for helping me with the transcript of the Quiz Show hearings.

ABOUT THE AUTHOR

DAVID HALBERSTAM is the author of eleven previous books, including his highly praised trilogy on power in America, *The Best and the Brightest, The Powers That Be,* and *The Reckoning.* His book, *Summer of '49,* was a number one *New York Times* hardcover bestseller. David Halberstam's latest book is *October 1964,* an electrifying look at the historic Yankees–Cardinals World Series. He has won every major journalistic award, including the Pulitzer Prize. He lives in New York City.

Pulitzer Prize–winning author
DAVID HALBERSTAM
Published by Ballantine Books.
Available in your local bookstore.

Or call 1-800-733-3000 to order by phone and
use your major credit card.
Or use this coupon to order by mail.